ENCYCLOPEDIA OF
EUROPEAN SOCIAL HISTORY

EDITORIAL BOARD

ENCYCLOPEDIA OF
EUROPEAN SOCIAL HISTORY

FROM 1350 TO 2000

VOLUME 3

Peter N. Stearns

Editor in Chief

Charles Scribner's Sons

an imprint of the Gale Group

Detroit • New York • San Francisco • London • Boston • Woodbridge, CT

1 3 5 7 9 11 13 15 17 19   20 18 16 14 12 10 8 6 4 2

Printed in United States of America

Library of Congress Cataloging-in-Publication Data
Encyclopedia of European social history from 1350 to 2000 / Peter N. Stearns, editor-in-chief.
      p.   cm.
      Includes bibliographical references and index.
      ISBN 0-684-80582-0 (set : alk. paper) — ISBN 0-684-80577-4 (vol. 1)—ISBN
   0-684-80578-2 (vol. 2) — ISBN 0-684-80579-0 (vol. 3) — ISBN 0-684-80580-4 (vol. 4)
   — ISBN 0-684-80581-2 (vol. 5) — ISBN 0-684-80645-2 (vol. 6)
      1. Europe—Social conditions—Encyclopedias.   2. Europe—Social life and
   customs—Encyclopedias.   3. Social history—Encyclopedias.   I. Stearns, Peter N.
   HN373 .E63 2000
   306′.094′03—dc21
                                                                        00-046376

CONTENTS OF THIS VOLUME

CONTENTS OF OTHER VOLUMES

VOLUME 6

ALPHABETICAL TABLE OF CONTENTS

COMMON ABBREVIATIONS USED IN THIS WORK

A.D.   *Anno Domini,* in the year of the Lord

AESC   *Annales: Économies, Sociétés, Civilisations*

ASSR   Autonomous Soviet Socialist Republic

b.   born

B.C.   before Christ

B.C.E.   before the common era (= B.C.)

c.   *circa,* about, approximately

C.E.   common era (= A.D.)

cf.   *confer,* compare

chap.   chapter

CP   Communist Party

d.   died

diss.   dissertation

ed.   editor (pl., eds.), edition

e.g.   *exempli gratia,* for example

et al.   *et alii,* and others

etc.   *et cetera,* and so forth

EU   European Union

f.   and following (pl., ff.)

fl.   *floruit,* flourished

GDP   gross domestic product

GDR   German Democratic Republic (East Germany)

GNP   gross national product

HRE   Holy Roman Empire, Holy Roman Emperor

ibid.   *ibididem,* in the same place (as the one immediately preceding)

i.e.   *id est,* that is

IMF   International Monetary Fund

MS.   manuscript (pl. MSS.)

n.   note

n.d.   no date

no.   number (pl., nos.)

n.p.   no place

n.s.   new series

N.S.   new style, according to the Gregorian calendar

OECD   Organization for Economic Cooperation and Development

O.S.   old style, according to the Julian calendar

p.   page (pl., pp.)

pt.   part

rev.   revised

S.   *san, sanctus, santo,* male saint

ser.   series

SP   Socialist Party

SS.   saints

SSR   Soviet Socialist Republic

Sta.   *sancta, santa,* female saint

supp.   supplement

USSR   Union of Soviet Socialist Republics

vol.   volume

WTO   World Trade Organization

?   uncertain, possibly, perhaps

ENCYCLOPEDIA OF
EUROPEAN SOCIAL HISTORY

Section 10

SOCIAL STRUCTURE

SECTION 10: SOCIAL STRUCTURE

SOCIAL CLASS

Charles Tilly

Social class has attracted a great deal of attention, not to mention bitter dispute, from social historians. Social class refers to categorical differences among clusters of persons when material inequality constitutes *(a)* the categorical boundaries or *(b)* a likely cause of differences among bounded categories. Social class by no means exhausts human inequality. People have often organized large material inequalities around gender, age, race, ethnicity, religion, and locality, none of which qualify ipso facto as class. People also vary individually with respect to strength, size, health, volatility, and a number of other traits that affect the quality of their lives. Social class may shape or interact with these other forms of inequality, but it remains analytically distinct from them. If the idea of social class has deeply informed the study of social history, it has also generated profound disagreement among specialists in the field. As they disagree about class, analysts actually struggle over the salience, durability, impact, and categorical clustering of inequality in human life.

As they should, historians generally exclude a wide variety of human inequalities (for example, by gender, height, or religion) from social class. Beyond that minimum agreement, however, they range from considering class differences as fundamental in social life at one extreme, to denying the very existence of social classes at the other. Anyone who uses class terms to describe unequal positions or social relations makes a further theoretical commitment. Class terminology implies that the positions or relations in question cluster into categories having some degree of internal coherence and some connection with each other. Precisely the extent, nature, origins, and consequences of such coherence and connection remain controversial and the objects of extensive historical investigation.

HISTORY OF CLASS TERMINOLOGY AND CLASS ANALYSIS

Contending ideas of class circulated long before social history formed as a distinctive discipline. The Latin word *classis* referred to a vertical division of the Roman population according to property and entered English with that meaning during the sixteenth century. Over the next century the English word "class" applied increasingly to categories of the population; but "development of class in its modern social sense, with relatively fixed names for particular classes (lower class, middle class, upper class, working class and so on) belongs essentially to the period between 1770 and 1840, which is also the period of the Industrial Revolution and its decisive reorganization of society" (Williams, 1976, p. 51). By that time writers as diverse as James Madison, Hannah More, and James Mill freely used class terms to describe the world they saw around them. In the 1840s, when Karl Marx and Friedrich Engels began treating social classes as fundamental divisions under capitalism, they incorporated common usage into their innovative theory.

So doing, however, Marx and Engels opened an enduring split between self-consciously materialist analysts of social processes and others who generally recognized differences among social classes but rejected marxist explanations of those differences. In the Marx-Engels account, material relations within every mode of production generated their own class divisions. As Marx later put the general point:

> It is always the direct relationship of the owners of the conditions of production to the direct producers—a relation always naturally corresponding to a definite stage in the development of the methods of labour and thereby its social productivity—which reveals the innermost secret, the hidden basis of the entire social structure, and with it the political form of the relation of sovereignty and dependence, in short, the corresponding specific form of the state. (Marx, 1972, p. 791)

Accordingly marxists have commonly analyzed history in terms of distinct modes of production: primitive communism, feudalism, capitalism, and more (Marx, 1964). Each mode, in this analysis, centers on a characteristically different opposition of classes. Marx devoted the great bulk of his attention to capitalism. Although capitalism harbored multiple classes, he argued, its central processes of exploitation generated increasing division between capitalists, who owned the means of industrial production, and wage workers or proletarians, whose effort fructified those means. That divided material infrastructure, furthermore, shaped the basic institutions of social life, including government, education, and kinship. So ran the strict marxist view.

COMPETING NOTIONS OF CLASS

Since Marx's day social historians have repeatedly polarized for and against this relational and production-based conception of social class. Some dispute its exact application to particular historical settings, some forward alternative conceptions of class, and some deny the very applicability of class categories to the situations they study. A characteristic (if slightly disingenuous) statement comes from the great student of France's Old Regime hierarchies, Roland Mousnier:

> Despite beginning with the conviction that social classes were indeed what Marxists mean by that term, that classes had started to exist when societies emerged from so-called primitive communism, and that class struggle was if not the whole of history at least one of its most important elements, my research with my students on societies and institutions brought us to quite different conclusions. We are now persuaded the Marxist conception of social class only applies to certain kinds of societies and has been improperly extrapolated. If we want a general term for the great variety of social hierarchies, we will do better to use the expression *social stratum,* which designates a universal concept, a family. (Mousnier, 1976, p. 5)

As elements of a social stratum, Mousnier names:

- distinctive part in the social division of labor
- distinctive way of carrying out that effort
- disposition of effort by members of at least one other stratum
- mentality and style of life
- means of existence resulting from its social role

For location within a system of production, Mousnier thus substitutes function in society at large. His conception has several powerful consequences. It displaces the origins of inequality from relations of production to societal function; considers societies to consist of two or more unequal strata, differentiated vertically, in virtual isolation from each other; and excludes the lowest social level (who dispose of no one else's effort) from designation as a distinct stratum. Mousnier goes on to argue that Old Regime France was a society of orders (honor-differentiated strata), not of classes, and that French classes formed

only with nineteenth-century industrialization. He explains that change not as a direct consequence of alterations in productive relations but as an effect of shifting values: "social classes are a type of strata existing in societies where value judgments place the production of material goods and the creation of wealth at the top of the scale of social functions, in a market economy where capitalist relations of production prevail" (Mousnier, 1976, p. 7). Mousnier distinguishes five "scales" of stratification, legal, social status, economic, power, and ideological, whose relative prominence varies from society to society and age to age (Mousnier, 1973, pp. 15–18). Thus, in the widespread view represented by Mousnier, different societies value different attributes and rank people accordingly (compare with Barber, 1957). Class therefore represents no more than a special case of a general phenomenon.

Despite its concessions to other principles of differentiation, the Mousnier-style analysis clearly presents class as a particular variety of position, individual or collective, in a hierarchy of prestige, wealth, or power. Standard marxist views just as clearly differ. They identify class as collective location within a system of production. They stress inequality but deny hierarchy in the sense of orderly (and especially consented) precedence. Over the long run these two positions have contended for dominance within social history, yet other social historians have dissented from the two majority positions. Some (e.g., Parkin, 1979) have emphasized shared relations to consumption markets, while others (e.g., Stedman Jones, 1983) have based their conceptions of class on shared consciousness or culture. Later we shall return to these alternative views, as well as to denials that class exists at all.

Before World War II, most western European social historians used class terms loosely and descriptively, attributing distinctive characteristics to upper classes, middle classes, workers, peasants, and other categories but considering problems of class formation, class consciousness, and class distinction peripheral to their enterprise. In economic and political history, however, questions of class then loomed larger. There the causes and consequences of poverty, the origins of capitalism, and the changing power of landholders, merchants, and manufacturers became sites of acute controversy. Within each controversy at least one party attributed significance to changing class relations. In Great Britain, for example, left-leaning historians, such as R. H. Tawney, Sidney Webb, and Beatrice Webb, placed class firmly on the historical agenda. Soviet historians and non-Soviet marxists also organized much of their analyses around class cate-

COMPETING CONCEPTIONS OF SOCIAL CLASS

1. Hierarchical position. A social class is a rank or stratum defined by recognized and effective differences in prestige, wealth, or power. For example, lords, merchants, and serfs are seen as public actors rather than legal categories. This implies vertical divisions crossing large populations and resting on widespread agreement, however grudging, and promotes social history of changing rank orders, their public representations, and their implications for styles of life.

2. Market connection. A social class is a population segment defined by distinctive relation to land, labor, and commodity markets. For example, gentry, farmers, merchants, artisans, and tenants are seen as owners, producers, and especially consumers. This implies extensive but differentiated markets with significant impacts on the well-being of their participants and promotes social history of material culture, property, and consumption.

3. Consciousness and culture. A social class is a set of people who regard each other as social equals or share a distinctive body of understandings, representations, and practices. For example, the aristocracy contrasts with the bourgeoisie as a community and style of life. This implies well-defined boundaries, extensive connections, and mutual recognition within boundaries and promotes social history of changing understandings, representations, and practices.

4. Location in production. A social class designates occupants of a large but distinctive position within a system of material production. For example, capitalists versus proletarians are defined by control of capital versus dependence on the sale of labor power. This implies broad categorical divisions across whole systems of production and the significant impact of productive position on overall welfare. It promotes social history linking politics and social life to the changing organization of production and investigating shifts in forms and degrees of inequality.

5. Chimera. In a particular setting or in general, social class is an illusion or at best a mistaken description of inequalities better characterized in other ways. For example, "middle class" is viewed as a broad idea about the population majority in contemporary industrial countries. This implies fragmentation of differences in material inequality and promotes social history of ideas about identity and inequality as well as investigation of nonclass bases of inequality.

gories. But it took the populist social history of the 1950s and thereafter to make social class an inescapable preoccupation.

Marxist and materialist historians outside the Soviet Union—for instance, Jürgen Kuczynski, Eric Hobsbawm, and Georges Lefebvre—led the way. They highlighted social class from two different angles: as a general framework for historical analysis and as an object of intense empirical study. The general framework featured the rise, fall, transformation, and conflict of different classes, with marxist ideas of social development its leading impetus. Social historians, however, spent relatively little effort on general theories. They concentrated especially on the empirical study of social classes, more often working classes than any others.

A kind of populism swept over the field: enthusiasm for writing social history from the bottom up, for recovering and broadcasting the authentic vox populi. Populism became even more prevalent as it coupled with the campus mobilizations of the 1960s. Many students then moved into history with the hope of giving voice to the powerless and of identifying historical precedents for current struggles. Some took up analyses of popular political mobilization and rebellion, others reconstruction of workers' daily lives, still others detailed investigation of social inequality and mobility. For a while it looked as though social history and sociology would form an indissoluble alliance. Sociology beckoned as the only social science discipline prepared to take class seriously.

Dynamic Interaction. In Ford Madox Brown's idealized juxtaposition of social classes, *Work* (1852–1865), navvies (ditchdiggers) dig a sewer in Hamstead, north of London, near Brown's home. Their work blocks the way of a wealthy couple on horseback. At left a poor flowerseller precedes women of the middle classes, one of whom distributes a temperance tract. In the foreground, a poor girl in an ill-fitting dress watches after her younger siblings. At right two intellectuals, the historian Thomas Carlyle (wearing the hat) and the Christian social theorist F. D. Maurice, observe the scene. BIRMINGHAM MUSEUMS AND ART GALLERY, BIRMINGHAM, U.K./BRIDGEMAN ART LIBRARY

Then E. P. Thompson almost single-handedly changed the field's direction. No doubt a number of social historians had already become uneasy about the formalism, structural reductionism, and methodological conventionality of the sociology they saw invading their enterprise. They were already ripe for a more literary, ethnographic, and interpretive account of social life, especially one that offered a larger place to consciousness than most sociologists allowed. Still, in 1963 Thompson roared onto the terrain like an invading army. Descending from the heights of literary criticism and biography, he daringly attacked on two fronts, machine-gunning mechanistic marxism even as he cannonaded conservative condescension. At least for England from the 1780s to the 1830s, he swept the field, persuading a wide range of readers that something he called the "making" of a working class occurred through a sustained series of struggles and

convincing the rest that they now had a new, seductive leftist thesis to combat.

Thompson scored his fellow marxists for structural reductionism—for assuming that one can read out people's motives and states of consciousness from their location within relations of production. The formation of class consciousness, he countered, is an arduous, contingent, struggle-ridden process whose vagaries historians must retrace in detail. Class, he objected, does not spring directly from economic position but emerges from dynamic interaction with other people. Class is a relation, not an attribute. Class consciousness, he further claimed, draws crucial parts of its content from available political understandings—in the case of eighteenth-century English plebeians, notably beliefs in the rights of freeborn Englishmen and in the priority of the moral economy over political economy. Thus he drew marxist class analysis toward a much more phenomenological, ethnographic, cultural, and idea-oriented approach than the one previously employed by most of its practitioners.

A fierce, witty polemicist, Thompson directed equal scorn toward liberal and conservative analysts of working-class experience. He attacked two recurrent errors: (1) reduction of workers' actions to ill-considered impulses generated by sudden hardship or rapid social displacement and (2) assumption that the working classes lacked sophisticated understandings of politics and economics and therefore responded gullibly to the exhortations of demagogues. To rebut these views he poured ample ingenuity and energy into uncovering popular ideas concerning rights and obligations; tracing connections among participants in such activities as machine breaking; and matching the slogans, symbols, avenging actions, testimonies, and demands of working-class activists with doctrines in the literary record.

With a literary historian's panache, Thompson mustered an extraordinary range of evidence for his thesis, drawing connections between political philosophy and popular culture, enormously broadening conceptions of relevant texts, and giving popular utterances and crowd actions a literary standing they had rarely achieved before. His victorious vision of class formation in England inspired numerous historians of other Western countries to search for parallel constructions in their own territories and periods, so much so that the phrase "making of the working class" acquired the immortality of a cliché.

Thompson never quite escaped the shadow of teleology. The idea of working class formation—of "making"—easily attaches to the teleological notion that every mode of production assigns a destiny to each of its constitutive classes (Katznelson and Zolberg, 1986). The big historical questions thus become how and to what degree each class actually fulfills its destiny. By stressing consciousness, Thompson forwarded the idea that class formation depends critically on the developing mutual awareness of people who already occupy a distinctive location within the system of production. Indeed Thompson's *The Making of the English Working Class* (1963) stops in 1832, by which time, in his account, popular struggles during the 1790s had prepared working-class consciousness, postwar conflict had sharpened it, worker mobilization around reform had accelerated it, and the exclusion of most workers from benefits of the 1832 Reform Act had embittered it. But the full denouement still lay ahead, presumably in Chartism and its aftermath.

So great a challenge could not go unanswered. Sociologically inclined critics (e.g., Calhoun, 1981)

objected that Thompson misread the organizational bases of popular collective action, while critics who were speeding toward discourse and consciousness even faster than Thompson himself had (e.g., Jones, 1983) rejected Thompson's concessions to structural determinism. Still others (e.g., Anna Clark, 1995; Frader and Rose, 1996) complained that Thompson had produced an excessively masculine account of class formation, quite neglecting the crucial place of women and gender relations in the process. Since Thompson, historical studies of class have frequently formed their battle lines along epistemological and ontological divides: explanation versus interpretation, realism versus idealism, practical action versus consciousness, sociology versus anthropology.

The works of Patrick Joyce and James Vernon on nineteenth-century Britain are representative. Both sought refuge from marxist realism in linguistic analysis, Joyce fretfully and Vernon with shrill bravado. Each proposed his own interpretation of English popular culture and its creeds as an alternative to the Thompsonian history of class formation. In the baker's dozen of essays that fill his *Visions of the People* (1991), Joyce explored a wide variety of materials recording popular discourse, popular literature, slogans, demands, theater, dialect, and much more, asking to what extent their uses set workers off from other people and to what degree they conveyed direct awareness of class difference as formative experience and source of grievances. Joyce concentrated on Lancashire and the North between 1848 and 1914, eventually concluding with great unease that something like widely shared class consciousness began to emerge not in Thompson's 1790s but toward World War I.

Vernon's *Politics and the People* (1993), for its part, took on all of England from 1815 to 1867 but used as recurrent points of reference close studies of public politics in Boston, Lewes, South Devon, Tower Hamlets, and Oldham. Although his announced period overlapped the one examined by Thompson, Vernon did not aim his empirical investigation at Thompson's account of political action between 1815 and 1832. Instead he looked chiefly at post-Reform politics to document his claim that for ordinary English people the public sphere, far from opening to democratic participation, actually narrowed dramatically between 1832 and 1867.

Despite avoiding direct confrontation with Thompson's treatment of 1780 to 1832, Joyce and Vernon both sought self-consciously to displace Thompsonian analysis of class formation. They did so by means of three maneuvers: denial that economic experience shapes class consciousness; insistence on the variety of economic and social experience; and embedding of all meaningful experience in language. In so doing each made two further moves he did not quite recognize and therefore did not bother to defend. The first was to adopt radical individualism, an assumption that the only significant historical events or causes consist of mental states and their alterations. The second was to doubt the intersubjective verifiability of statements about social life. Together the two moves brought them close to solipsism, the doctrine denying the possibility of any knowledge beyond that of the knower's own individual experience.

Vernon and Joyce thereby avoided questions of agency: who does what to whom and with what effects. Their occultation of agency separates them from conventional historical narrative, in which limited numbers of well-defined, motivated actors, situated in specific times and places, express their ideas and impulses in visible actions that produce discernible consequences. Those consequences typically are the objects of explanation. Conventional narrative entails not only claims to reasonably reliable knowledge of actors, motives, ideas, impulses, actions, and consequences but also (a) postulation of actors and action as more or less self-contained and (b) imputation of cause and effect within the narrative sequence. Solipsism makes most of these elements difficult, and denial of agency renders them impossible.

Vernon and Joyce also ruled out alternative modes of social-scientific analysis, which require less access to other people's consciousness as well as allowing actors, actions, and environment to interact continuously but demand strong conceptions of causal connection (Bunge, 1996; Hedström and Swedberg, 1998). Either solipsism or denial of agency suffices to command rejection of these forms of social analysis. In short the Joyce-Vernon philosophical position obliterates any possibility of historical explanation. It also undermines any grounds they might propose for accepting the validity of their interpretations in preference to Thompson's or anyone else's. At this point social history reaches an impasse (Joyce, 1995). Yet the rich, sensitive deployment of textual analysis in the Joyce and Vernon studies underlines the strong desirability of uncovering firmer philosophical ground. The challenge is to incorporate the explanation of texts, discourse, and changing consciousness into the ongoing work of social history.

SOCIAL-HISTORICAL INVESTIGATIONS OF CLASS

Despite many dud grenades hurled across the lines in both directions, fortunately debate did not much de-

ter historians' concrete investigations of social class. Hobsbawm, for example, continued to turn out major historical syntheses pivoting on broadly marxist class analyses. In collaboration with social scientists, drawn from many disciplines besides sociology, social historians have actually advanced the program of explanation (see Mohr and Franzosi, 1997; Monkkonen, 1994; Morawska and Spohn, 1994). Two developments look particularly promising: (1) systematic study of class-relevant language and texts in the context of their production, transmission, and political deployment and (2) introduction of network models and metaphors into the analysis of class relations. Both, as it happens, draw some of their inspiration from Thompson, the first from Thompson's broad treatment of texts and the second from Thompson's insistence on class as a social relation rather than an individual attribute.

An excellent example of linguistic analysis in political context comes from Marc Steinberg's treatment of dialogue among workers, employers, and public authorities in Britain's Spitalfields, Ashton-Stalybridge, and elsewhere during the early nineteenth century. Steinberg showed how available forms of discourse channeled interaction among the parties to struggle but also changed as a consequence of that interaction, indeed in the very course of struggle. Responding more or less directly to the work of Joyce, Vernon, and other linguistically sensitive historians, Steinberg concluded:

> I have argued that despite recent critiques from the linguistic turn, theories of historical class formation and of political process and resource mobilization provide essential windows on fundamental processes that have been and continue to be part of great transformations in the modern world. I have also maintained, however, that the critics raise compelling issues concerning the centrality of discourse in class formation and collective action. Although rejecting the linguistic turn's alternatives, I have proposed revising Thompson's perspective on class and the political process/resource-mobilization model of contentious action with discourse as a critical intervening process. Rather than choose between material and discursive analyses, we need to conjoin the explanatory powers that each perspective offers. (Steinberg, 1999, p. 229)

Such inquiries promise to narrow the epistemological and ontological fissures that have riven studies of class.

The network approach to social relations receives prominent attention in Don Kalb's study of class transformations in North Brabant, Netherlands, between 1850 and 1950. Both the dispersed shoemaking industry and the large-scale manufacturing of the Philips Corporation attracted Kalb's relentless curiosity as he combined material from collective biography, administrative records, governmental correspondence, and interviews of survivors. Kalb characterized his approach as anthropological:

> My case studies of class formation in subregions of industrializing Brabant tend to illustrate that an anthropological interest in popular culture, discourse, and everyday life can, and indeed should, be wedded to social power and social process. This is so not only because power, change, and inequality are central aspects of social life that ought not be missed by any serious analyst of human affairs (that is, unless he or she accepts political irrelevance), but more importantly because class-oriented analysis can reveal crucial ambiguities, contradictions, divisions, limits, obstacles, and dynamics of culture that cannot be uncovered in other ways. In short, by consciously elaborating an approach based on a materialist idea of class with the intention to study social power and social process, I claim a more penetrating methodology for explaining and understanding culture. (Kalb, 1997, p. 2)

This historical anthropology of class rests not only on examination of utterances and representations but also on reconstruction of the dynamic social relations that constitute class. Both the linguistic and the network versions of recent class analysis retain an emphasis on relations of production but make unprecedented efforts to integrate dialogue, daily practice, and social ties as more than straightforward expressions of productive organization.

DEFINING SOCIAL CLASS

What then is social class? As the foregoing discussion suggests, social historians have generally adopted one of five answers to the question.

1. Social class consists of position, individual or collective, in a hierarchy of prestige, wealth, or power or is a special case of such hierarchical differentiation.
2. Social class describes a connection, individual or collective, to markets that produces significant differences in quality of life.
3. Social class resides in mutual consciousness or shared culture among sets of persons who collectively regard themselves, however justly or unjustly, as superior or inferior to others.
4. Social class is or depends on collective location within a system of production.
5. Social class is an illusion or at best a mistaken description of inequalities better characterized in other ways, for example, as variable individual competence, ethnic culture, or occupational specialization.

Except for the last, these competing views do not entirely exclude each other. But they imply different priorities. Marxist social historians have, for example,

sometimes combined the first four in the argument that collective location within a system of production determines both hierarchical position and relation to consumption markets while shaping mutual consciousness and culture. Thus arguing, marxists give priority to production. Other social historians assign priority to hierarchical location, consumption markets, or consciousness. In line with the first or the fifth alternative, still others deny the validity of class as description or explanation of social behavior for particular situations or even for history in general. Inequalities, even hierarchies, may exist, doubters declare, but they do not constitute social classes. When social historians do speak of social class, however, they generally stress one of the first four competing conceptions. Hierarchical and productivist ideas (alternatives one and four) have predominated in social history over the long run, but the other three positions have all competed at times.

What is at stake in this competition? Social historians who treat class as *hierarchical position* often take vertical division as part of a natural order given by custom, historical accretion, prevailing values, or social function. Relations among classes therefore play little or no part in their explanations of class differences. Changes in class structure, according to such a view, result from long-term, incremental alterations in values, mentalities, population composition, or societal type. In functional versions of the argument, agrarian societies simply require one type of hierarchy, industrial societies another.

Social historians who emphasize *connections to markets* as bases of class distinctions generally consider classes to be recent social creations. Their existence depends on the commodification of capital, land, goods, and services. This commodification can create distinct classes when two conditions converge: (1) segmented access to markets and (2) variable property rights according to the kinds of goods in question or the status of their possessors.

Emphasizing relations to labor and commodity markets, Max Weber made a famous statement of this view:

> Those who have no property but who offer services are differentiated just as much according to their kinds of services as according to the way in which they make use of these services, in a continuous or discontinuous relation to a recipient. But always this is the generic connotation of the concept of class: that the kind of chance in the *market* is the decisive moment which presents a common condition for the individual's fate. Class situation is, in this sense, ultimately market situation. The effect of naked possession *per se,* which among cattle breeders gives the non-owning slave or serf into the power of the cattle owner, is only a fore-runner of real "class" formation. (Weber, 1968, vol. 2, p. 928)

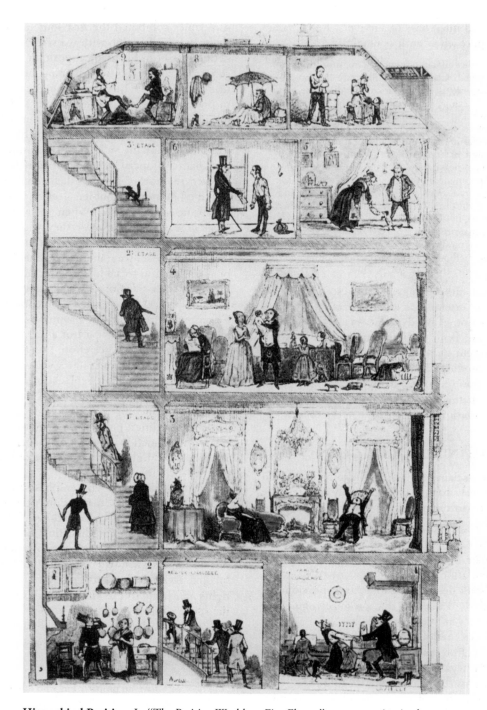

Hierarchical Position. In "The Parisian World on Five Floors," servants maintain the household below stairs on the ground floor, the wealthy live on the first floor, a comfortable young family occupies the second floor, the lower classes feed their cat and put off their creditors on the third floor, while servants, artists, and the poor live in the attic. Drawing by Lavielle, c. 1850. PRIVATE COLLECTION

Weber explicitly distinguished class divisions from status group and party divisions, which he regarded as more crucial where labor and commodity markets were ill developed. Other historians have added markets for land to Weber's labor and commodity markets. In such a perspective class and class conflict become salient under certain special conditions, notably the predominance of land, labor, and commodity markets, but classes do not exist everywhere, need not form regular hierarchies, and often coexist with cross-cutting divisions by status and party.

To focus class analysis on *mutual consciousness and shared culture* articulates well the widespread idea that social categories matter only to the extent that people recognize and participate in them. The idea appeals to an odd assortment of social historians. They include not only methodological individualists (who regard rationally deliberated choices as prime historical motors), but also phenomenologists (who regard individual consciousness as the seat and source of human action) and theorists of mentalities (who regard society-wide shifts of shared understandings as driving forces in history). In any of these lines of thought, classes only exist if, when, and because many people come to conceive of them as existing. Consequently, for them processes of class formation and transformation operate chiefly within the cognitive sphere.

Social class as *collective location within a system of production* introduces relations among members of different categories much more explicitly into class analysis. The view has two contrasting versions, one aligned approximately with classical and neoclassical economics, the other identified broadly with marxism. The economistic version considers that markets link holders of different sorts of capital, including human capital, and apportion rewards among them according to the current value of their capital to productive processes. Although Adam Smith argued explicitly that organizational and power differentials affected what different classes (for example, merchants and landless laborers) could gain from market relations, within those limits he laid down the doctrine of returns proportionate to productive contributions. Smith's successors have portrayed production as built around freely contracted bargains among holders of different varieties and quantities of capital. Classes therefore correspond to divisions with respect to capital. Following this understanding, extensive historical research has gone into changes in living standards and in material inequality. Increasing inequality in income, wealth, and welfare becomes the evidence of increasing class differentiation (Kaelble, 1983).

Marxists counter neoclassical explanations of class differences with an interpretation of productive

relations, not as freely contracted bargains but as exercises of coercion among inherently unequal parties. The organization of production, in this view, lays the bases of class divisions; those divisions arise from unequal interaction among categories of participants in productive processes and generally involve struggle. For either the economistic or the marxist view, then, change in the organization of production generates change in class structure.

Finally, some claim that social class is a *chimera*. In fact the rejection of class analysis for particular situations or for history in general arises from several rather different groups of social historians. Antimarxists (including former marxists) sometimes take the fully revolutionary proletariat of Marx's *Communist Manifesto* (1848) as their standard for existence of a class, then set out to prove that workers' consciousness or behavior fell short of the standard. Joyce and Vernon undertook just such proofs. (This form of argument provides an ironic counterpoint to the frequent marxist practice of explaining workers' failure to act collectively against their exploiters by the absence of conditions for class-conscious action sketched in the *Manifesto*.) Market enthusiasts sometimes argue that competition among unequally competent individuals produces differential rewards but nothing like social classes. Students of race, ethnicity, gender, religion, and other forms of categorical inequality often claim that what other historians see as class differences actually result from discrimination in these other arenas.

The choice among conceptions of class does not merely concern the words historians apply to the same phenomena. It involves profoundly different understandings of how history works. Competing views of fundamental social processes are at stake. Advocates of hierarchical models, for example, commit to the existence of an overarching social system or culture that generates, sustains, and transforms the relevant hierarchies. Interpreters of class as grounded in production relations, however, inevitably attribute coherence and power to material production. Such contrasting worldviews have implications far outside the workings of class.

COMPETING DEFINITIONS OF CLASS AND SOCIAL HISTORICAL ANALYSIS

To appreciate those implications, it is helpful to examine a trio of historical phenomena whose explanation depends in part on social class. In these cases the choice of one class conception or another should make a difference to the explanation itself. Beginning with obvious cases, the examination then moves to increasingly subtle manifestations of social class: first the development of capitalism, then popular political contention, finally demographic change.

Development of capitalism.

All accounts of capitalist development recognize changing configurations of work and capital. They differ greatly, however, in the significance attributed to social classes. Views of class as hierarchical position generally treat class formation as a significant by-product, but not a significant cause, of capitalist development. Causes lie elsewhere: in a society's inevitable differentiation, in alterations of collective mentalities, or perhaps in the diffusion of new technologies. Market-connection accounts of class leave somewhat more space for class formation as a cause of capitalist development, since changes in the character of merchants and of consumers both affect the organization and extent of markets. Nevertheless, market-connection models generally portray their major relations with class formation the other way around: however it occurs, expansion of labor and commodity markets differentiates participants into distinct categories—social classes—disposing of contrasting bundles of goods, services, work opportunities, and life chances.

To argue that social class resides in mutual consciousness or shared culture does not necessarily rule out origins of class consciousness or class culture in hierarchy or market position. Yet it does predispose its advocates to favor ideological and cultural explanations of capitalism as well. (In fact Weber stressed the influence of a Protestant ethic on the development of European capitalism while laying out one of the most coherent market-connection conceptions of class.) Such explanations abound; they often pivot on the assertion that western European culture predisposed its beneficiaries to competitive enterprise, an assertion that typically gives great weight to capitalist entrepreneurs in the creation of capitalism as a whole.

Analysis of class as collective location within a system of production likewise typically gives great weight to capitalist entrepreneurs but in relation, often in struggle, with other social classes. In such analyses class relations constitute major elements of any productive system, class interactions alter production, and class structure responds sensitively to shifts in the logic of production. Historians who regard class as a chimera are predisposed to explain the development of capitalism in terms of autonomous, impersonal forces, such as science, technology, the market, or changing mentalities. Thus different conceptions of social class imply distinct approaches to explanations of capitalist development.

Popular political contention.

Popular political contention means ordinary people collectively making claims bearing on other people's interests when some government is either the object of those claims or a significant third party to them. Popular political contention includes collective retribution for moral offenders, intervillage fights, invasions of enclosed fields, deliberate disruptions of public ceremonies, market conflicts, strikes, and rebellions, but it also includes the demonstrations, public meetings, petition drives, and electoral campaigns that nineteenth-century Europeans eventually lumped together as social movements (Tilly and Tilly, 1981). Popular political contention does not involve social classes by definition. Indeed nonclass categories, such as religion, gender, ethnicity, and locality, have often figured in European contention. Nevertheless, differing conceptions of class have significant implications for the description and explanation of popular political contention.

Strong marxist views of class imply one of two positions. Either (1) all popular contention rests at bottom on class interests and class conflict, in which case apparent nonclass action stems from false consciousness or indirect effects of class formation; or (2) in the long run class interests and class conflict supersede other forms of division, hence other bases of contention. In the first position, excavating nationalism or religious conflict with sufficient care will eventually expose its foundation in class structure. In the second position, a variety of solidarities, interests, and conflicts arise in the short run, but, within any given mode of production, class polarization eventually prevails. Indeed that polarization eventually produces a crisis in which popular contention propels transition from one mode of production to another.

A competing version of social class as collective location within a system of production depends on non-marxist economics. If, as this second version implies, classes form around market-mediated divisions with respect to capital, popular political contention may still have a class basis. But two rather different scenarios apply. One is the case of a class having shared interests in the production of some collective good, such as protection of its kind of capital from predation or erosion, redistribution of returns from capital, or monopoly control of some market. In this case standard collective action problems arise.

A second scenario, however, involves collective reactions to consequences of occupying a common economic location, as when a labor market segment shrinks (handloom weavers are a famous European example), crucial commodities suddenly become more expensive (bread prices are a famous European example), or a productive resource disappears (enclosures of common lands are a famous European example). In contrast to the first scenario, economic analysts commonly regard the contention involved in such cases as irrational, since it resists the inexorable long-run logic of the market and of returns to capital. Nevertheless, both scenarios call up economistic accounts of class action that differ significantly from marxist accounts.

Obviously conceptions of social class as hierarchy, as market connection, as shared culture, or as illusion point to still other characterizations of popular political contention. Social theorists in the styles of Gaetano Mosca and Vilfredo Pareto have, for example, repeatedly spun out hierarchical theories of class in which political struggles emerge chiefly from efforts of subordinates to displace currently ruling classes. Shared-culture theorists of class, in contrast, typically take several steps beyond Thompson by making political tradition, altered consciousness, and response to evocative symbols central to popular action (see Herzog, 1998; Hunt, 1984; Sewell, 1980). Clearly, competing conceptions of social class lead analysts of popular political contention in significantly different directions.

Demographic change. Each approach to class has distinctive implications for the study of basic demographic processes, especially categorical differences in birth, death, marriage, sickness, mobility, and growth or decline (for a general introduction to the literature, see Willigan and Lynch, 1982). Demographers commonly think in terms of populations and imagine that categories are little more than convenient identifiers for subpopulations likely to have more homogeneous experiences than the population as a whole (Desrosières, 1998). The relevant categories then include age, sex, religion, ethnicity, and nationality, but they also include representations of class, such as income, occupation, or estimated social standing.

Social historians who study population processes more often take the categories seriously. They do so on either or both of two grounds: that the sheer existence of known unequal categories is a social fact with consequences for social behavior, including demographic behavior; and that the categories actually represent inequalities in social ties, culture, and quality of life more or less accurately.

Still, our competing answers to the question "What is social class?" lead to different expectations concerning categorical differences and their explanations. Class as hierarchical position lends itself readily to the expectation of continuous differences in behavior as a function of proximity to elite values and resources. Explanations of such differences may well involve varieties of upbringing and education, but they also can emphasize social connections or access to resources and opportunities. Discontinuous distributions and well-marked boundaries—for example, in types of illness or in contraceptive behavior—then suggest discontinuous distributions of upbringing, connections, resources, and opportunities.

If social classes consist of population segments defined by distinctive relations to land, labor, and commodity markets, continuous distributions appear less likely as causes or effects of inequality. Segmented labor markets, for example, bundle interpersonal connections, identities, mobility opportunities, and a wide variety of resources (Tilly, 1998, chapter 5). Observing such effects, analysts can plausibly explain categorical differences in mortality and age at marriage by delineating clustered and market-driven differences in exposure to risks and opportunities.

Consciousness and culture? If a social class is a set of people who regard each other as social equals and share a distinctive body of understandings, representations, and practices, certainly their sharing should affect their demographic behavior and change. In fact two different kinds classes of effects should occur, the first resulting from the existence of a boundary around equals and the second resulting from shared culture. The boundary presumably limits sexual relations, marriage, kinship, mutual aid, and information flows, all of which affect birth, death, marriage, sickness, mobility, and growth or decline. The shared culture presumably includes such demographically crucial matters as contraception, abortion, child care, diet, health care, migration, and sexual practices. These are not mere speculations; many students of population change have bet heavily on class differences in consciousness and culture for their explanations (e.g., Gillis, Tilly, and Levine, 1992; Poppel, 1992).

However, about as many have adopted conceptions of class as depending chiefly on location in production. Once again a distinction arises between advocates of neoclassical and marxist approaches to the problem. For neoclassically inclined analysts, class effects on demographic change occur through the formation of similar conditions for individual decision making that affects fertility, mortality, mobility, and other demographic processes (see Goldstone, 1986; Wrigley, 1987). Although marxist reasoning sometimes overlaps with neoclassical explanation in this regard, marxists in general assign more importance to social relations at production sites. In the best social history, to be sure, those production sites include households and neighborhoods as well as shops and factories (see Hanagan, 1989; Levine, 1984, 1987).

Some students of demographic change, however, declare class a chimera. A case in point is Simon Szreter's study of fertility change in Great Britain from 1860 to 1940. Szreter organized interpretation of his voluminous data around an attack on the (common) idea of nationwide fertility differentials and declines corresponding to class differences and responding to diffusion of ideas and knowledge downward through the class hierarchy. He argued instead *(a)* that rising costs of raising children moved couples toward increasingly effective prevention of conception by means of sexual abstinence and coitus interruptus, *(b)* that this happened not class by class but according to small-scale variations among occupations and localities, and *(c)* that changing gender relations mattered far more than any effects one could reasonably attribute to class. Szreter summed up his findings:

> The evidence presented here suggests that falling fertility among this part of the nation was far from a process graded by neat and identifiable, nationally applicable status or social class patterns. It was the relatively massive, and highly localised variations between communities, especially in the degree to which their labour markets were sexually segregated and divided, which may well largely account for occupational fertility differentials during this period of falling fertilities. This was something which was integrally linked to the history of local industrial relations and work practices in each of these places. (Szreter, 1996, p. 364)

Szreter rejected class interpretations in the name of local and occupational particularism. In that respect he joined the sort of attack on Thompsonian class analysis mounted by Joyce and Vernon.

Examination of ideas about capitalism's development, popular collective action, and demographic change establishes that competing conceptions of class do not matter for themselves alone. They lead to different explanations of major social phenomena. The same sort of demonstration applies to historical studies of welfare, of migration, of family structure, of electoral politics, or of revolution. The conclusion would be the same: social historians contend about social class because the experiences those words point to are fundamental and because competing conceptions of social class entail conflicts about the very nature of social processes.

The debate need not remain, however, a battle of philosophical premises. Social historians are a skeptical, practical, empirical lot. The synthesis among production-based, relational, and discursive approaches to social class promises to give them superior guidance in actually explaining the processes of change and conflict they so painstakingly document.

See also **Marxism and Radical History** *(volume 1);* **Capitalism and Commercialization; The Industrial Revolutions** *(volume 2);* **Collective Action** *(volume 3); and other articles in this section.*

BIBLIOGRAPHY

Aminzade, Ronald. *Ballots and Barricades: Class Formation and Republican Politics in France, 1830–1871.* Princeton, N.J., 1993.

Barber, Bernard. *Social Stratification: A Comparative Analysis of Structure and Process.* New York, 1957.

Bearman, Peter S., and Glenn Deane. "The Structure of Opportunity: Middle-Class Mobility in England, 1548–1689." *American Journal of Sociology* 98 (1992): 30–66.

Belchem, John. *Industrialization and the Working Class: The English Experience, 1750–1900.* Aldershot, U.K., 1990.

Bottomore, T. B. *Classes in Modern Society.* New York, 1966.

Bunge, Mario. *Finding Philosophy in Social Science.* New Haven, Conn., 1996.

Calhoun, Craig. *The Question of Class Struggle: Social Foundations of Popular Radicalism during the Industrial Revolution.* Chicago, 1981.

Clark, Anna. *The Struggle for the Breeches: Gender and the Making of the British Working Class.* Berkeley, Calif., 1995.

Clark, Samuel. *State and Status: The Rise of the State and Aristocratic Power in Western Europe.* Montreal, 1995.

Desrosières, Alain. *The Politics of Large Numbers: A History of Statistical Reasoning.* Translated by Camille Naish. Cambridge, Mass., 1998.

Engelstein, Laura. *Moscow, 1905: Working-Class Organization and Political Conflict.* Stanford, Calif., 1982.

Esping-Andersen, Gøsta, ed. *Changing Classes: Stratification and Mobility in Post-Industrial Societies.* Newbury Park, Calif., 1993.

Frader, Laura L., and Sonya O. Rose, eds. *Gender and Class in Modern Europe.* Ithaca, N.Y., 1996.

Geremek, Bronislaw. *Poverty: A History.* Translated by Agnieszka Kolakowska. Oxford, 1994.

Gillis, John R., Louise A. Tilly, and David Levine, eds. *The European Experience of Declining Fertility, 1850–1970: The Quiet Revolution.* Cambridge, Mass., 1992.

Goldstone, Jack A. "The Demographic Revolution in England: A Re-Examination." *Population Studies* 49 (1986): 5–33.

Grusky, David B., ed. *Social Stratification: Class, Race, and Gender in Sociological Perspective.* Boulder, Colo., 1994.

Grusky, David B., and Jesper B. Sørensen. "Can Class Analysis Be Salvaged?" *American Journal of Sociology* 103 (1998): 1187–1234.

Hanagan, Michael P. *Nascent Proletarians: Class Formation in Post-Revolutionary France.* Oxford, 1989.

Hanagan, Michael P. "New Perspectives on Class Formation: Culture, Reproduction, and Agency." *Social Science History* 18 (1994): 77–94.

Hedström, Peter, and Richard Swedberg, eds. *Social Mechanisms: An Analytical Approach to Social Theory.* Cambridge, U.K., 1998.

Herzog, Don. *Poisoning the Minds of the Lower Orders.* Princeton, N.J., 1998.

Hobsbawm, E. J. *The Age of Capital, 1848–1875.* London, 1975.

Hobsbawm, E. J. *The Age of Extremes: A History of the World, 1914–1991.* New York, 1994.

Hobsbawm, E. J. "Class Consciousness in History." In *Aspects of History and Class Consciousness.* Edited by István Mészaros. London, 1971. Pages 5–21.

Hobsbawm, E. J. *Labouring Men.* London, 1964.

Hunt, Lynn. *Politics, Culture, and Class in the French Revolution.* Berkeley, Calif., 1984.

Jones, Gareth Stedman. *Languages of Class: Studies in English Working Class History, 1832–1982.* Cambridge, U.K., 1983.

Joseph, Antoine. "The Solidarity of Skilled Workers: Creating a Logic of Particularism." *Journal of Historical Sociology* 6 (1993): 288–310.

Joyce, Patrick. "The End of Social History?" *Social History* 20 (1995): 73–92.

Joyce, Patrick. *Visions of the People: Industrial England and the Question of Class, 1848–1914.* Cambridge, U.K., and New York, 1991.

Jütte, Robert. *Poverty and Deviance in Early Modern Europe.* Cambridge, U.K., 1994.

Kaelble, Hartmut. *Industrialisierung und soziale Ungleichheit: Europa im 19. Jahrhundert: Eine Bilanz.* (Industrialization and social inequity in nineteenth-century Europe.) Göttingen, Germany, 1983.

Kalb, Don. *Expanding Class: Power and Everyday Politics in Industrial Communities, the Netherlands, 1850–1950.* Durham, N.C., 1997.

Katznelson, Ira, and Aristide R. Zolberg, eds. *Working-Class Formation: Nineteenth-Century Patterns in Western Europe and the United States.* Princeton, N.J., 1986.

Korpi, Walter. *The Democratic Class Struggle.* London, 1983.

Kriedte, Peter. *Peasants, Landlords, and Merchant Capitalists: Europe and the World Economy, 1500–1800.* Cambridge, U.K., 1983.

Kuczynski, Jürgen. *The Rise of the Working Class.* Translated by C. T. A. Ray. New York, 1967.

Lachmann, Richard, and Julia Adams. "Absolutism's Antinomies: Class Formation, State Fiscal Structures, and the Origins of the French Revolution." *Political Power and Social Theory* 7 (1988): 135–175.

Lefebvre, Georges. *The Coming of the French Revolution, 1789.* Translated by R. R. Palmer. Princeton, N.J., 1947.

Levine, David. *Reproducing Families.* Cambridge, U.K., 1987.

Levine, David, ed. *Proletarianization and Family History.* Orlando, Fla., 1984.

Linder, Marc. *Labor Statistics and Class Struggle.* New York, 1994.

Lis, Catharina. *Social Change and the Labouring Poor: Antwerp, 1770–1860.* New Haven, Conn., 1986.

Marx, Karl. *Capital.* Vol. 3. London, 1972. First published in 1894.

Marx, Karl. *Pre-Capitalist Economic Formations.* Edited by Eric Hobsbawm. Translated by Jack Cohen. London, 1964.

McNall, Scott G., Rhonda F. Levine, and Rick Fantasia, eds. *Bringing Class Back In.* Boulder, Colo., 1991.

Merriman, John M. ed. *Consciousness and Class Experience in Nineteenth-Century Europe.* New York, 1979.

Mohr, John W., and Roberto Franzosi, eds. "Special Double Issue on New Directions in Formalization and Historical Analysis." *Theory and Society* 28, nos. 2 and 3 (1997).

Monkkonen, Eric H., ed. *Engaging the Past: The Uses of History across the Social Sciences.* Durham, N.C., 1994.

Morawska, Ewa, and Willfried Spohn. " 'Cultural Pluralism' in Historical Sociology: Recent Theoretical Directions." In *The Sociology of Culture: Emerging Theoretical Perspectives.* Edited by Diana Crane. Oxford, 1994. Pages 45–90.

Mörner, Magnus, and Thommy Svensson, eds. *Classes, Strata, and Elites: Essays on Social Stratification in Nordic and Third World History.* Gothenburg, Sweden, 1988.

Morris, R. J. *Class and Class Consciousness in the Industrial Revolution, 1780–1850.* London, 1979.

Mosca, Gaetano. *The Ruling Class (Elementi di scienza politica).* Edited by Arthur Livingston. Translated by Hannah D. Kahn. New York, 1939.

Mousnier, Roland. *Recherches sur la stratification sociale à Paris aux XVIIe et XVIIIe siècles.* Paris, 1976.

Mousnier, Roland. *Social Hierarchies, 1450 to the Present.* Edited by Margaret Clarke. Translated by Peter Evans. New York, 1973.

Osberg, Lars, ed. *Economic Inequality and Poverty: International Perspectives.* Armonk, N.Y., 1991.

Pareto, Vilfredo. *The Mind and Society: A Treatise on General Sociology.* Edited by Arthur Livingston. Translated by Andrew Bongiorno and Arthur Livingston. 4 vols. New York, 1963. English version first published in 1935.

Parkin, Frank. *Marxism and Class Theory: A Bourgeois Critique.* New York, 1979.

Poppel, Frans van. *Trouwen in Nederland: Een historisch-demografische studie van de 19e en vroeg-20e eeuw.* Wageningen, Netherlands, 1992.

Roy, William. "Class Conflict and Social Change in Historical Perspective." *Annual Review of Sociology* 10 (1984): 483–506.

Sen, Amartya. *Inequality Reexamined.* Cambridge, Mass., 1992.

Sewell, William H., Jr. *Work and Revolution in France: The Language of Labor from the Old Regime to 1848.* New York, 1980.

Steinberg, Marc W. *Fighting Words: Working-Class Formation, Collective Action, and Discourse in Early Nineteenth-Century England.* Ithaca, N.Y., 1999.

Steinmetz, George. "Reflections on the Role of Social Narratives in Working-Class Formation: Narrative Theory in the Social Sciences." *Social Science History* 16 (1993): 489–516.

Szreter, Simon. *Fertility, Class, and Gender in Britain, 1860–1940.* Cambridge, U.K., 1996.

Tawney, R. H. *The Acquisitive Society.* New York, 1948. First published in 1920.

Thompson, E. P. *The Making of the English Working Class.* London, 1963.

Tilly, Charles. *Durable Inequality.* Berkeley, Calif., 1998.

Tilly, Charles. "Proletarianization and Rural Collective Action in East Anglia and Elsewhere, 1500–1900." *Peasant Studies* 10 (1982): 5–34.

Tilly, Chris, and Charles Tilly. *Capitalist Work and Labor Markets.* Boulder, Colo., 1998.

Tilly, Louise A., and Charles Tilly, eds. *Class Conflict and Collective Action.* Beverly Hills, Calif., 1981.

Vernon, James. *Politics and the People: A Study in English Political Culture, c. 1815–1867.* Cambridge, U.K., 1993.

Webb, Sidney, and Beatrice Webb. *The History of Trade Unionism.* London, 1920.

Weber, Max. *Economy and Society: An Outline of Interpretive Sociology.* Edited by Guenther Roth and Claus Wittich. Translated by Ephraim Fischoff et al. 3 vols. New York, 1968.

Williams, Raymond. *Keywords: A Vocabulary of Culture and Society.* New York, 1976.

Willigan, J. Dennis, and Katherine A. Lynch. *Sources and Methods of Historical Demography.* New York, 1982.

Wirtschafter, Elise Kimerling. *Social Identity in Imperial Russia.* DeKalb, Ill., 1997.

Wright, Erik Olin. *Class Counts: Comparative Studies in Class Analysis.* Cambridge, U.K., 1997.

Wrigley, E. A. *People, Cities, and Wealth: The Transformation of Traditional Society.* Oxford, 1987.

SOCIAL MOBILITY

Hartmut Kaelble

A standard theme of social history, social mobility was one of the topics that inspired modern social history's beginnings in the 1960s and the 1970s in Europe and the United States. Historians approached the topic for various reasons. One of their central motivations was to determine the equality of social opportunities in certain periods and contexts—that is, whether modern industrial or service societies helped or hindered chances of upward mobility for men as well as for women. In an era when the industrial and then the tertiary societies were becoming predominant in the United States and Europe, and historians turned to certain central topics, including increasing openness or reinforced exclusiveness of modern elites; the rising or declining chances of social ascent for descendants from the lower classes or from immigrants or ethnic groups; and the broadening or reduced access to channels of social ascent such as education, business enterprises, public bureaucracies, family networks, politics, sports, and entertainment. Moreover, social mobility was frequently discussed by historians in a comparative perspective. European and American historians explored both the myth of the unique chances for social ascent in America and the myth of unrestricted social mobility in communist countries. They also started to investigate societies outside the Western world.

DEFINITIONS AND METHODS

What do historians mean by social mobility? For the most part their investigations center on the social mobility of individuals rather than the grading up or down of entire social groups or classes. Thus the heading of social mobility does not cover the decline of the European aristocracy or of the urban artisanal elite; the ascent of the middle class, or of various professions, or of ethnic groups and groups of immigrants; or the decline or ascent of women. Although the study of social mobility takes these changes in social hierarchies into account, they are usually not its main theme.

Moreover, the study of social mobility does not focus on the geographical mobility of individuals, as the term might suggest, but rather on mobility within social structures and hierarchies. To be sure, a good many studies of social mobility do treat immigration and geographical mobility as a factor in social mobility; local studies especially treat the mobile as a group of historical individuals who are difficult to trace, hence creating severe methodological difficulties. The theme of transience has been particularly important in eighteenth- and nineteenth-century United States and European history. Wider studies of immigration have also tested causes (in terms of threatened downward mobility) and results (in terms of comparing mobility results for different immigrant groups) where geographic migration was involved.

Another defining feature of the study of social mobility is its concentration on occupational mobility. In investigations of intragenerational mobility, historians trace the mobility of individuals among different occupational positions or their persistence in the same occupation throughout their lives. In investigations of intergenerational mobility, historians compare the occupations of an individual with that of his or her father, mother, and ancestors at specific points in their lives. Occupation is usually seen as the crucial indicator of the situation of an individual in a historical society. To be sure, historians are fully aware of the limitations of this concept of occupational mobility. They are highly sensitive to the fact that the occupational activity of an individual in history, more often than today, might comprise a simultaneous plurality of occupations or include professions that are still in the making and thus without a clear position in the society of that time. In addition, a change in education, religious affiliation, or social networks might be as important as the change in occupation. Finally, historians are fully aware that, the farther back into history a study goes, the less reliable and distinct does occupation as an indicator of the social position of an individual become.

With occupation as the key indicator of social hierarchies, social mobility studies seek a highly differentiated body of knowledge about societies in the past. They explore variations in income, properties, educational training, prestige, and social networks among occupations by means of linking various historical sources; individuals can be traced through marriage license files, tax files, census materials, last wills, records of churches and public administrations, and autobiographical sources. The competence of historians in linking various sources has shown a marked improvement.

The study of social mobility has been criticized for various methodological reasons. Many historians argue that the sources normally used provide only a crude idea of the historical reality; they consider data on only two or three points of time in a whole life and on only one occupation insufficient and unsatisfying. In addition, by focusing on occupations the study of social mobility excludes large parts of the population. This is especially true for women, whose historical mobility until the first half of the twentieth century mainly involved marriage rather than occupational activity. It is also true in a more fundamental way for societies in which large parts of the population did not yet have distinct and single professions. This type of mobility study therefore has less to say about peasant societies or early modern urban societies than about modern industrial societies. Moreover, critics object that the quantitative study of social mobility concentrated too heavily on quantifiable aspects of objective circumstances and neglected entirely the subjective dimension of experiences, motivations, and mentalities. Defining status is a cultural matter, and occupations change in status over time. This variability requires sensitivity in mobility assessments.

These criticisms spurred some new trends in the methods of historical research on social mobility, with the result that the study of social mobility has achieved a higher level of sophistication. Individual careers are explored in micro studies of as many details as possible, with attention to autobiographical materials that often cannot be analyzed quantitatively. Studies of a few individual cases in which source materials are rich are given priority over quantitative studies of all members of a local society. This type of micro study is rarely limited to social mobility but covers a large variety of social aspects. In addition, studies of social mobility in which occupation is not predominant are becoming more important. Thus the study of the social mobility of women has begun, though only very few studies on gender differentials exist. It has become clear that the results are highly interesting, showing that the history of the social mobility of women is clearly different from that of men. Some studies also try to include subjective matters and trace the impact

of mentalities and experiences on social mobility. Furthermore, the number of international and interregional comparative studies of the history of social mobility has increased somewhat, using the rich results of about thirty years of historical research in this field.

INTERDISCIPLINARY COOPERATION

Social mobility is one of the major fields of social history in which research comes not only from historians but also from scholars of other disciplines. This is especially true for three crucial aspects of the history of social mobility: Political scientists have sponsored important investigations using the historical perspective in exploring the recruitment of the elites, particularly the political and administrative elites. Educationists and sociologists have participated in the historical research on educational opportunities in schools and in higher education. The most important contribution comes from sociologists in the investigation of the overall trends of social mobility during the twentieth century.

In the early years of the social mobility field, historians were strongly encouraged by the work of major historical sociologists such as Pitirim Sorokin, Seymour M. Lipset, Reinhart Bendix, and D. V. Glass, who had published studies of the history of social mobility. In this interdisciplinary cooperation, quantification became an important bridge between historians and sociologists. Later, a sort of division of labor emerged between the two fields. Sociologists usually explore social mobility on the level of entire countries by means of cohort analysis, which is based on actual surveys and traces differences between older and younger age cohorts, assuming that these differences represent historical changes in social mobility. They sometimes use separate, often more detailed surveys for different age groups and compare their life stories, going on to write international comparisons of historical trends of social mobility. Sociologists also developed highly sophisticated statistical indicators for measuring trends and international differences. By contrast, historians usually explore social mobility on the local or regional level, using the variety of sources discussed above. Some historians claim to be able to study social mobility for entire regions or even countries from the early modern period onward on the basis of these sources. In selecting different types of cities and villages and in comparing local studies on a transregional and transnational level, historians also can investigate general tendencies of social mobility. Historians mostly use simpler quantitative methods of analysis that are less difficult to understand than the indicators used by sociologists. As the links between these two disciplines are disappointingly weak, the reader is obliged to consult the sociological as well as the historical literature.

MAIN QUESTIONS

Four major questions have especially attracted the attention of historians of social mobility: Did industrialization and modernization produce an increase, decrease, or no change in social mobility? Did social mobility advance in the United States and in communist societies, especially as compared to Western European societies? How were opportunities for social mobility different for each gender? What was the discourse of contemporaries on social mobility?

Social mobility in modern society. The increase in social mobility in the nineteenth and twentieth centuries means different things to different authors in the field. Greater mobility, in the context of industrialization and modernization, can signify a more meritocratic recruitment, especially for the few most prestigious, most powerful, and best-paid positions. That mobility may occur between occupations; it may be upward as well as downward; it may apply to job mobility within the same social class. Increased social mobility may encompass the chances of both genders and of minorities. Sometimes it refers specifically to a clear increase in the opportunities of the lower classes as compared to the opportunities of the upper and middle classes, rather than greater mobility across the board.

The advocates of the view that social mobility has undergone a general increase often point specifically to the rising number of upwardly mobile persons since industrialization. They argue that various major social changes led to greater social mobility and social ascent. The general decline of the fertility rate during the late nineteenth and early twentieth centuries made it possible for parents not only to invest more in the individual help and education of their children but also to promote their own professional careers. The rapid expansion of secondary and higher education, especially since the end of the nineteenth century, enlarged enormously the chances for better training. The rapid increase of geographic mobility since the second half of the nineteenth century led to a widening of the labor market and to a greater variety of new chances. Among the active population, the fundamental shift from the predominance of agrarian work up to the nineteenth and early twentieth centuries to the predominance of service work, especially since the

1970s, generated substantial social mobility between occupations. The distinct increase in the sheer number of occupations in all modern societies since the industrial revolution also must have led to more social mobility. The general change in mentalities; the weakening of the emotional identification with specific professions, social milieus, and local milieus; and the rising readiness for job mobility and for lifelong training further enlarged the number of socially mobile persons. The rise of the welfare state, the mitigation of individual life crises, and the guarantee of individual social security clearly improved the chances for further training and for the purposeful use of occupational chances. Government policies aimed at enhancing educational and occupational opportunities for lower classes, for women, for ethnic and religious minorities, and for immigrants also have had an impact on social mobility. The list of factors attesting to an increase in social mobility in the nineteenth and twentieth centuries is substantial.

Yet there are those who see social mobility as having remained stable or even declined. They are a heterogeneous group, with arguments stemming from very different ideas of social developments. It is sometimes argued that nineteenth- and early-twentieth-century industrialization led not only to a rising number and a fundamental change of occupations but also to a class society in which the major social classes—the middle class, the lower middle class, the working class, the peasants, and in some societies also the aristocracy—tended to reinforce the demarcation lines between classes and hence to reduce rather than enlarge the number of mobile persons. Other advocates of the skeptical view argue that the fundamental upheaval of modern societies during industrialization led to a unique volatility in social mobility, both upward and downward, and that modern societies thereafter became more closed: the generation of pioneers in business ended, most occupational careers became more formalized and more dependent on higher education, modern bureaucracies emerged, and mentalities adapted to the modern, highly regulated job markets.

Other scholars argue for the stability of social mobility rates in a different and much more narrow sense: they argue that long-term changes in social mobility from the industrial revolution until the present were mostly structural; that is, they depended almost exclusively on the redefinition of the active population rather than on the reduction of social, cultural, and political barriers. In this view social mobility remained stable if one excepts the changes simply induced by alternations in occupational structure; peasants, for example, became workers, which constituted a real change, but not necessarily a case of upward mobility. Still other scholars posit a stable inequality of educational and occupational chances for the lower classes, women, and minorities in comparison with those for the middle and upper class, the male population, or the ethnic majority.

Out of this long debate has grown, since the beginning of quantitative studies of social mobility after World War II, a large number of historical studies of social mobility. Their wide range of results can be distilled to three main points: First, only in very rare cases was a clear decline in social mobility rates found. Most studies show either stable or increasing rates of social mobility, depending upon the type of community and country and the generation and period under investigation. However, there is no overwhelming overall evidence for either the stability or increase of social mobility rates. Second, changes of overall social mobility rates do in fact depend to a large degree on changes in occupational and educational structure. Thus one can say that modern societies became more mobile to a large degree because education expanded so much and because occupational change became so frequent and normal. Finally, much evidence indicates that the increase of educational and social mobility of the lower classes and women did not impair the educational and occupational chances of the middle and upper classes and men. Except for the eastern European countries in some specific periods, social mobility was usually not a zero-sum game.

Social mobility in the United States and the communist bloc.

The question of advanced social mobility in the United States dates at least from the early nineteenth century, when the French historian Alexis de Tocqueville argued that American society offered more chances for upward social mobility than did Europe. For a long time the subject was approached from a moral perspective, concerning the advantages and disadvantages of a mobile society. After World War II some social scientists attacked the notion that American society was in fact more mobile, the American sociologist Seymour M. Lipset being the most prominent. He argued that industrialization and social modernization everywhere led to the same basic increase in social mobility; overall international figures on rates of social mobility and of social ascent after World War II did not show any American superiority in those terms. Lipset's attack on what was a myth of long standing provoked a debate among academics and intellectuals. American influence in the world had reached its peak, and the model of the American way of life in general was undergoing intense debate both

in America and in Europe. Skepticism about the American superiority in social mobility was voiced by Simone de Beauvoir, the French intellectual, who wrote in *L'Amérique au jour le jour* (1948) after travel in the United States that "there is almost no hope any more for the lower class to move up into this [upper] class." Other social scientists as well as writers defended the notion of advanced American social mobility. Ralf Dahrendorf, the German sociologist, argued in his book *Die angewandte Aufklärung: Gesellschaft und Soziologie in Amerika* that "much direct evidence exists that [the United States] offers the opportunity of social ascent also to those who would have been stopped in Europe by the rigid social hierarchies."

Evidence in three areas was put forward to prove that America was a leader in social mobility. Detailed empirical studies by sociologists demonstrated that lead in some crucial aspects, especially mobility in the professions. American higher education was more extensive and offered greater access to the professions than did the European counterpart. Hence the social ascent from the lower classes into the professions that are based on higher education was clearly more frequent than in Europe. In addition, comparative historical studies on late-nineteenth- and early-twentieth-century American and European cities showed that in a special sense a modest American lead existed during that period: unskilled workers in fact moved up into white-collar positions in American cities somewhat more frequently than in European cities. Finally, historians demonstrated that the important difference between American and European societies could be found in the idea of social mobility rather than in the actual rates of mobility. Americans continuously believed that their country offered more opportunities than the rigid European societies.

Studies in the late twentieth century tended to argue that American society no longer leads Europe in general social mobility. To be sure, international comparisons show that strong and persistent differences in social mobility between cities and countries existed and still exist. Hence it is difficult to accept the assertion of a worldwide convergence of social mobility through industrialization and modernization. However, probably because of the fundamental social changes in Europe since World War II, there is no clear evidence for a general American lead in social mobility against the whole of Europe.

Neither as provocative nor as persistent, nevertheless the subject of social opportunities in communist countries, especially in the USSR during the 1920s and 1930s and in the Eastern European nations in the late 1940s and 1950s, attracted its share of social mobility studies. During these periods rates of upward social mobility into the higher ranks of the social hierarchy were substantial compared to rates in Western European societies. This was true partly because higher education expanded rapidly; partly because the communist abolition of the business and landowning elites and the seizure of power by the Communist Party opened up top positions for social ascent in industry and agriculture, politics and administrations; and partly because employment structure changed rapidly during rapid industrialization. However, the rise of social opportunities in communist countries was, if it existed at all, largely limited to the period of the initial upheaval. Most comparative studies of the 1970s and 1980s show that rates of social mobility were not distinctly higher in the eastern part of Europe compared to the western part. This change occurred for several reasons: the communist political and administrative elite became exclusive and gentrified; in several communist countries the expansion of higher education slowed down, and hence the student ratio in Eastern Europe in general fell below the ratio in Western Europe; and social change slowed down.

Gender contrasts in social mobility. Except for a few studies, the history of gender contrasts in social mobility is largely unexplored. But gender contrasts undoubtedly will add important new aspects to the general debate about long-term trends in social mobility. The existing studies point to four conclusions. First, in a more radical sense than in the study of male mobility, female mobility raises the question of whether social mobility should in fact be centered around occupational mobility or whether other factors such as marriage and unpaid or partially paid work in emerging professions are to be taken into account much more than they have been so far. In the end, marriage might turn out to be an important channel of upward or downward mobility for men as well in past societies. Second, female mobility raises the question of greater downward mobility during the transition to modern society, when female activity outside the family sphere increased. A study of female social mobility in twentieth-century Berlin demonstrates that a large number of active women became intergenerationally déclassé during the early parts of the century. Further studies are required to corroborate the results. Third, the study of the social mobility of women demonstrates much more clearly than the study of the social mobility of men the effects of economic crises and fundamental transitions on social mobility. Opportunities for women seem to have depended strongly on economic prosperity, on long-term social stability. In periods of economic crisis and rapid transitions

such as the upheaval of 1989–1991, women more than men belonged to the losers. Here again the study of female mobility might draw the attention of historians to a more general aspect of mobility that was not sufficiently investigated. Finally, the social mobility of women also demonstrates that definite changes in social opportunities can be achieved only in the long term. Even though important channels of upward social mobility such as education offered equal chances to women, this did not lead to a parallel improvement of occupational chances for women. It is highly doubtful that the explanation for this gap can be found simply in the study of institutions and context factors. Historical studies of the experience of social mobility and the perception of social mobility will become more important than they have been so far.

The discourse on social mobility. The historical study of social mobility has begun to be conducted in the light of another field of inquiry, the history of identities and the debate about modernity. Unlike the aspect of social opportunities, this aspect of the subject is relatively unexplored. One approach to it is by way of the history of European identity. In the decades before World War I, Europeans became aware of the rise of the superior American economy and the more liberal American society. European self-understanding was no longer based on an implicit feeling of superiority over all other societies; rather, it was tinged with a growing uneasiness about modernity. Tocqueville was a very early example of this worried European self-understanding. More advanced social opportunities in America came to symbolize modernity and, therefore, relative European backwardness. Such opportunities were welcomed by the more liberal Europeans and described as a horrifying social scenario without any fixed hierarchies by the more conservative.

This debate gradually changed when Europe entered the period of a fundamental crisis of self-understanding between World War I and roughly the 1960s. The idea of open social opportunities gradually was shared by all Europeans. However, some Europeans still saw Europe as a backward society with lower social opportunities than the United States. Other Europeans argued that one of the last aspects of European superiority was the greater room for individuality allowed by European society compared to the conformity of American society. These Europeans, among them Simone de Beauvoir, thus saw Europe as the society with more opportunities for the individual. When the historical study of social mobility began, this initial debate was still going on. After the 1970s or so European self-understanding changed again, overcoming the period of fundamental identity crisis.

Social ascent became less important as an element of European self-understanding and as a theme of the debate over modernity.

THE DECLINE OF THE TOPIC AND ITS FUTURE

During the 1980s and 1990s social mobility was much less frequently investigated by historians. The major trend of social history was directed to other themes, other fundamental questions, and other methods. A variety of factors contributed to this declining interest in social mobility.

First, the initial wave of studies of social mobility appeared to be repetitive, and the subject seemed to have lost its former innovative power. After the completion of the first twenty or thirty local studies of social mobility during the nineteenth and twentieth centuries in the United States and Europe, historians failed to develop a convincing strategy showing which type of community in which country and period promised to open new insights. Historians did not rush to investigate the seventh industrial or fourth port city in the sixth industrializing country. In addition, the more sophisticated the methods and the use of sources became, the more time-consuming and expensive the individual study of social mobility grew to be. This rising standard of the study of social mobility was only partially compensated by the technical progress of personal computers. One can say that the quality standard for social mobility studies by historians rose dramatically, while the chance to present additional new arguments declined. At the same time, the gap between the quantitative methods employed by historians and sociologists widened, and thus the study of social mobility by sociologists was less encouraging for historians. Moreover, some of the questions that inspired the historical study of social mobility—the more open American society, the effects of industrialization and modernization—were asked much less frequently. These questions lost their former urgency once it was widely accepted that social mobility rates were about the same in most societies and that an upward trend in social mobility in the nineteenth and twentieth centuries in industrializing and modernizing countries could not be proved. Finally, the thematic trends in historical research made social mobility seem less modern a theme. The quantitative and social scientific profile of the historical study of social mobility made it less attractive among the mainstream thematic trends of historical research, which led toward a return to political history, toward a cultural history inspired by anthropological questions unconnected with social mobility, or toward a social history dealing primarily with discourses, mentalities, and microworlds.

To be sure, it would be misleading to say that historians abandoned social mobility as a theme. Quite the opposite, the study of discourses, mentalities, values, and microworlds often treated the social mobility of individuals and rendered it a normal topic of the historian. But the label of social mobility no longer appeared on the title pages of books, chapters, or articles.

The future of the study of social mobility is that of a normal theme among many others in history rather than a top theme in an expanding branch of history, as in the 1960s and 1970s. In this more modest but realistic sense, one can expect and hope for four sorts of studies on neglected aspects of social mobility. The first is the so far neglected study of social mobility beyond Western Europe and the United States, leading to international comparisons in a geographic dimension including Eastern European, Asian, African, and Latin American cases. The questions of social opportunities in advanced and developing societies and of the particularities of Europe will then be answered in a much more comprehensive way than they have been so far. Gender contrasts is the second aspect deserving of future study. Our knowledge of the social mobility of women, in contrast to that of men, is still very limited. The subject should be pursued through case studies of contrasting countries, various activities of women, and contrasting general conditions such as prosperity and economic depression, peace and war, stability and transitions. A third future theme involves specific factors of social mobility such as religion, types of family, immigration, unemployment and poverty, background in terms of social milieu, and social upheavals and transitions. Historians will probably explore these contexts of social mobility in case studies of a certain number of individuals rather than in quantitative studies of entire communities, thus attending to the subjective experience of social mobility. Finally, the history of social mobility debates, as delineated here, is itself deserving of further study.

See also **The Industrial Revolutions** *(volume 2);* **Gender and Work; History of the Family** *(volume 4);* **Schools and Schooling; Higher Education** *(volume 5); and other articles in this section.*

BIBLIOGRAPHY

Berghoff, Hartmut. *Englische Unternehmer, 1870–1914: Eine Kollektivbiographie führender Wirtschaftsbürger in Birmingham, Bristol, und Manchester.* Göttingen, Germany, 1991.

Boyle, Susan C. *Social Mobility in the United States: Historiography and Methods.* New York, 1989.

Cassis, Youssef, ed. *Business Elites.* Aldershot, U.K., 1994.

Charle, Christophe. *Les élites de la République: 1880–1900.* Paris, 1987.

Dahrendorf, Ralf. *Die angewandte Aufklärung: Gesellschaft und Soziologie in Amerika.* Frankfurt am Main, Germany, 1968.

Dijk, Henk van. "Regional Differences in Social Mobility Patterns in the Netherlands between 1830 and 1940." *Journal of Social History* 17 (1984): 435–452.

Erickson, Robert, and John Goldthorpe. *The Constant Flux: A Study of Class Mobility in Industrial Societies.* Oxford, 1992.

Fitzpatrick, Sheila. *Education and Social Mobility in the Soviet Union, 1921–1934.* Cambridge, U.K., 1979.

Goldthorpe, John H. *Social Mobility and Class Structure in Modern Britain.* Oxford, 1980.

Grusky, David B., and Robert M. Hauser. "Comparative Social Mobility Revisited: Models of Convergence and Divergence in Sixteen Countries." *American Sociological Review* 49 (1984): 19–38.

Haller, Max, ed. *Class Structure in Europe: New Findings from East-West Comparisons of Social Structure and Mobility.* Armonk, N.Y., 1990.

Handl, Johann. "Occupational Chances and Occupational Opportunities of Women: A Sociohistorical Analysis." *Journal of Social History* 17 (1984): 463–488.

Kaelble, Hartmut. *Social Mobility in the 19th and 20th Centuries: Europe and America in Comparative Perspective.* Leamington Spa, U.K., and Dover, N.H., 1985.

König, Wolfgang, and Walter Müller. "Educational Systems and Labour Markets as Determinants of Worklife Mobility in France and West Germany: A Comparison of Men's Career Mobility, 1965–1970." *European Sociological Review* 2 (1986).

Kurz, Karin, and Walter Müller. "Class Mobility in the Industrial World." *Annual Review of Sociology* 13 (1987): 417–442.

Lequin, Yves, et al. *L'usine et le bureau: Itinéraires sociaux et professionnels dans l'entreprise XIXe et XXe siècles.* Lyon, France, 1990.

Lipset, Seymour Martin, and Reinhard Bendix. *Social Mobility in Industrial Society.* Berkeley, Calif., 1959.

Lundgreen, Peter, Margret Kraul, and Karl Ditt. *Bildungschancen und soziale Mobilität in der städtischen Gesellschaft des 19. Jahrhunderts.* Göttingen, Germany, 1988.

Mayer, Karl Ulrich, Bogdan W. Mach, and Michal Pohoski. "Job Changes in the Federal Republic of Germany and Poland: A Longitudinal Assessment of the Impact of Welfare-Capitalist and State-Socialist Labour-Market Segmentation." *European Sociological Review* 10 (May 1994): 1–28.

Miles, Andrew. *Social Mobility in Nineteenth- and Early-Twentieth-Century England.* Houndsmills, U.K., and New York, 1999.

Payne, Geoff, and Pamela Abbott, eds. *The Social Mobility of Women: Beyond Male Mobility Models.* London, 1990.

Ramsøy, Natalie Rogoff. *Recent Trends in Occupational Mobility.* Glencoe, Ill., 1953.

Sewell, William H., Jr. *Structure and Mobility: The Men and Women of Marseille, 1820–1870.* Cambridge, U.K., 1985.

Sorokin, Pitirim. A. *Social and Cultural Mobility.* Glencoe, Ill., 1959.

Vincent, David, and Andrew Miles, eds. *Building European Society: Occupational Change and Social Mobility in Europe, 1840–1940.* Manchester, U.K., 1993.

THE ARISTOCRACY AND GENTRY

Jonathan Dewald

Implicitly if not always explicitly, privileged groups—aristocrats and gentry—have long been central to historians' understanding of European social history. In part their importance reflects the extraordinary influence that these groups exercised on society as a whole through the eighteenth century and to a lesser degree thereafter. In England the high aristocracy, numbering about two hundred families, held about one-fourth of the kingdom's land; in seventeenth-century Bohemia, an even smaller nobility held two-thirds of the land. Political and social influence matched this economic hold, so that in some regions aristocrats and gentry enjoyed a near monopoly on high positions in the church, army, and administration. To a significant extent, these intertwining forms of domination (and the ideological justifications that accompanied them) defined Europe's social order before the French Revolution, and thus helped define the revolution itself: revolutionary leaders labeled as "aristocrats" even their non-noble enemies, because they hoped that their new society would be one without aristocrats, without even the concept of aristocracy. For similar reasons, aristocrats and gentry also have considerable importance in the history of Europe since 1815, although their social importance declined in the nineteenth and twentieth centuries. They pose the question of modernization, for they had to manage the transition to an increasingly democratic and industrial social order, in which claims to privilege had lost much of their ideological and practical relevance. How they accomplished this transition, and with what effects on the society around them, has important implications for understanding the larger processes of change in European society.

The present essay deals mainly with the years through 1789, when aristocrats and gentry dominated European society most completely. The final section examines how the age of revolutions affected these groups and how they coped with the new world of the nineteenth and twentieth centuries.

IDEALS, DEFINITIONS, RANKINGS

The ancient world had bequeathed to early modern Europe (notably via Aristotle's *Politics*) a political and personal definition of "aristocracy" as the rule of the best men. Family background and wealth were understood to contribute to fitness for this public role, but did not necessarily define it; leading families might have unworthy descendants, and social newcomers might have the abilities needed for political excellence. This understanding of social status stood in some tension with a second that had developed during the early Middle Ages and that divided society into three orders: clerics who prayed, nobles who defended and governed, and commoners who met society's economic needs. This view presented the aristocrat as principally a warrior, and it increasingly associated social status with birth. Its fullest elaboration came in the eighteenth century, when Henri de Boulainvilliers, comte de Saint-Saire, described the French aristocracy of his day as direct descendants of fifth-century Frankish warriors and argued that they continued to display the qualities of those remote ancestors.

By Boulainvilliers's time, though, a third vision of the aristocrat had come to dominate most people's thoughts, that of the "gentleman," the "honnête homme," who had the education and self-control needed for constructive social interaction. This vision had developed first in the courts of sixteenth-century Europe and received early discussion in Baldassare Castiglione's *The Courtier* (1528). It did not require military or governmental position, though it was compatible with their exercise, nor was it coterminous with good birth, since it rested so heavily on personal attainments. Castiglione even asked whether the ideal courtier needed noble birth at all, though he ultimately answered in the affirmative. Although theoretically undermining distinctions of birth, the ideal of the gentleman ultimately strengthened them, since it treated ideals of aristocratic behavior as ethical universals, desirable in all men and women but best realized by those born into high society and enjoying the leisure for self-improvement.

All three traditions circulated widely in old regime Europe, their divergences producing significant instability in ideas about the social order, for each valorized different qualities and implied different standards of behavior. But most contemporaries agreed on some basic definitions and assumptions. They distinguished first between upper and lower nobilities, the former enjoying great wealth and political influence, the latter having only local authority, and in some instances not much more wealth than their peasant neighbors. In some regions political events embodied this division. In Austria and England political assemblies included special chambers for the lords, setting them apart from the mass of other nobles, as well as from the commoners. In France on the other hand such distinctions were vaguer; a peerage and other high titles existed, but received little institutional reinforcement. Monarchs tended to sharpen these status distinctions by granting more elaborate titles to leading families in their realms, often to secure political loyalty but sometimes for mere cash. In Spain, Charles V created the order of grandees in 1520, marking off the highest nobility from the rest, and its numbers increased tenfold over the next two centuries; the Austrian Order of Lords increased fivefold between 1415 and 1818; in Carinthia there was a ninefold increase between 1596 and 1726. Historians have described these creations as an "inflation of honors," which tended to devalue respect for titles by creating so many of them; expressions of disrespect can be found in contemporary commentaries.

Definitions of these "mere gentry" varied widely from one European country to another. In France all were designated as "noble," and they enjoyed most of the privileges of even the wealthiest lords. In the Holy Roman Empire distinctions tended to be clearer. There an intermediate level of knights stood between the mere gentry and the lords, and in many regions they were sufficiently organized to enforce for themselves some special privileges. In England only the peers (numbering about fifty in the early sixteenth century and about two hundred in the eighteenth) held formal titles of nobility, while the great majority of landowners formed a very loosely defined gentry, without any legal distinctions. In most of continental Europe, the balance between these two groups shifted decisively over the early modern period, partly because of the inflation of honors, which elaborately confirmed the loftier families' superiority to the mere gentry, and partly because of economic changes. Mere gentry

Mere Gentry in the Nineteenth Century. *The Squire and the Gamekeeper, or The Demurrer,* painting (c. 1860) attributed to James Lobley (1829–1888). PRIVATE COLLECTION/THE BRIDGEMAN ART LIBRARY

were often unable to meet the obligations of high status, and the economically successful among them tended to be absorbed into the higher aristocracy. In fifteenth-century Austria there had been four families of knights for every family of lords; four centuries later there were twice as many lords as knights. In England, by contrast, the gentry seem to have kept pace, beneficiaries of their society's growing wealth and widening social opportunities.

COUNTER IDEALS: THE TRADITION OF SOCIAL CRITICISM

Already in the Middle Ages aristocrats' determination to view themselves as society's leaders encountered ideological opposition from a variety of groups, and complaints continued throughout the early modern period. In several countries the fourteenth century witnessed outright violence against aristocrats and their properties. The leaders of the French Jacquerie (1358) explained their movement as a response to the aristocracy's failure to fulfill its basic function, that of protecting the rest of society. In the fifteenth century a successful rebellion of Catalonian peasants was accompanied by widespread denunciations of lords' greed and improprieties, and in the early six-teenth century a series of German peasant move-ments questioned the need for any form of aristocracy. Seventeenth-century Castilian nobles too complained of the enmity shown by the commoners around them. Peasants were not alone in this truculence. In the early sixteenth century, leading humanist writers like Eras-mus, Thomas More, and Sebastian Brant mocked aristocrats' pretensions and questioned the value of their social contributions, especially their contribu-tions as warriors. When Enlightenment writers took up these themes in the eighteenth century, they thus expanded on longstanding views, but they gave these old ideas new coherence and force. They systemati-cally judged aristocratic privilege against the criterion of social utility, suggesting that traditional aristocratic behavior represented a serious drain on society's pro-ductive resources. These ideas circulated widely in the eighteenth century and affected the decisions of ad-ministrators in several countries.

THE GEOGRAPHY OF
SOCIAL DISTINCTION

Important common traits marked Europe's experience of aristocratic society, partly because aristocrats them-selves moved frequently across national lines. Their education often involved travel, and often so did their careers, with both soldiers and administrators moving across national boundaries, especially among the small states of central Europe and within the vast Habsburg orbit. When they moved, such men found essentially familiar social arrangements, for ideologies and cus-toms displayed important similarities. At its upper levels, aristocratic society was European as well as national.

But there were also important differences be-tween regions, giving the aristocracies themselves dis-tinctive characteristics and different relations with the rest of society. A first distinction separated eastern from western Europe and centered on differences in local powers. East of the Elbe River, in central Ger-many, these might be very great. Aristocratic estate owners enjoyed extensive rights to demand labor from the peasants around them and to control their mar-riages and movements. In western Europe, estate own-ers had far less power, and even as a title serfdom survived in few regions, entailing only some economic disadvantages. A second division separated northern from Mediterranean Europe. Near the Mediterranean, aristocrats had lived in cities since the Middle Ages and saw little essential difference between themselves and other wealthy city dwellers. This was especially

true in Italy, but even in Spain, which took nobility very seriously, the title "honored citizen" expressed the near-noble stature enjoyed by the wealthiest city dwellers. In northern Europe, in contrast, aristocrats tended to live in the countryside and visited the cities rather reluctantly. They saw little common ground be-tween themselves and urban merchants, and tended to resist the latters' efforts to attain higher status.

The most important difference had to do with the number of aristocrats themselves. Early modern Europe was divided between regions where even the mere gentry were rare and regions where they were much more common. The latter included Poland and Hungary, along Europe's eastern frontier, and Castile in the west, all regions that had been battlefields of European expansion. Expansionist war against ethnic enemies had been one cause of frequent ennoble-ment, tempting peasants and city dwellers to take up military careers. In all three countries nobles easily counted for 10 percent of the total population before the eighteenth century, and in some districts densities might be higher still: in some Castilian towns the proportion could reach one-third. In the longer-Christianized core of Europe, there were many fewer such possibilities, and nobles were much less numer-ous, at most 2 percent of the population of sixteenth-century France, and closer to 1 percent by 1700; around 1 percent in most regions of Germany and Bohemia; 1 percent in the Kingdom of Naples; 0.4 percent in early-sixteenth-century Holland.

Some of these differences tended to diminish over the early modern period, especially during the eighteenth century. Nobles became better educated and more familiar with other national cultures. Ger-man nobles who had the resources were expected to tour Europe as part of their education, and many Brit-ish nobles did the same. Northern nobles became more urbanized, and the profusion of nobles in Spain, Poland, and Hungary diminished; in late-eighteenth-century Spain, nobles represented 4.6 percent of total population. Yet change was not all in the direction of greater homogeneity, for nobles found themselves more closely tied to their national cultures in the eighteenth century, simply because those cultures had acquired more force and coherence. Many eighteenth-century governments also controlled their leading subjects' movements and loyalties more closely than had been the case before 1700. Prussia represented the extreme case, with its nobles forbidden even to leave the king-dom without the king's approval and never allowed to seek employment in other kings' armies. The loose cosmopolitanism of earlier centuries survived best in the Habsburg lands, which continued to attract the ambitious from throughout Europe. Only sixteen of the 157 field marshals in the eighteenth-century Habsburg army came from its own territories; thirty-nine came from outside the German-language region altogether.

PRIVILEGE

According to much early modern social theory, aristocrats and gentry enjoyed special rights because of the special functions they performed, and notably because of their military service: French nobles spoke of paying a "tax of blood" on the battlefield, which exempted them from paying the cash levies demanded of others. In fact, however, privileges tended to reflect the political bargains that governments had struck with these their most powerful subjects. In this practice France represented the extreme case. In 1439 the Crown asserted its monopoly over direct taxation but in implicit exchange exempted nobles and other privileged groups from these impositions. Thus the geography and history of privilege tended to vary with the strength of the government rather than with the extent of aristocratic services. In England, where royal government had become strong very early, all subjects paid taxes, and only the peerage enjoyed some judicial privileges. In Spain, France, most of the Holy Roman Empire and Germany, nobles enjoyed freedom from most taxes, while in Brandenburg-Prussia the nobles consented to some taxation in exchange for other kinds of advantage, such as a near monopoly on official positions, tax-free grain exports, and a monopoly on beer brewing. In most of these regions nobles also had some legal advantages in managing their properties. Feudal law in France allowed them to avoid dividing property among their heirs, thus helping preserve family fortunes over the generations. In Spain the government allowed noble families to establish entails that performed this function even more effectively, protecting property from both division by inheritance and the indebtedness of individual owners.

These circumstances meant that many forms of privilege tended to diminish over the last century of the old regime, as governments became more assertive and effective. Louis XIV set an example in 1695 when, desperate for funds to pay his armies, his government introduced the capitation, a direct tax that the nobles were to pay like everyone else. Initially assessed according to social standing, the capitation soon became simply a tax on revenue, and in the eighteenth century it was assessed with some fairness. Wealthier nobles now paid a substantial tax, though they remained exempt from many other taxes. In 1731 the duke of Savoy completely abolished nobles' fiscal exemptions

in his realm, and the Habsburgs did the same in 1771. This scarcely meant the end of all aristocratic privileges, and some new ones emerged in these very years. In 1751 France established a military academy exclusively for nobles, and in 1781 ruled that only members of old noble families could hold military commissions. But nobles in these countries had a strong and justified sense that their special place within society was under attack.

SOCIAL MOBILITY

In principle noble families symbolized social stability, the continued dominance of old family lines. Yet the nature of aristocratic society itself created some need for social mobility because old families regularly failed to produced heirs. In fact they had a strong interest in limiting the number of their children so as to create as few inheritance divisions as possible and thus maintain familial dignity in the next generation. Family limitation became especially common in the eighteenth century as methods of birth control became more widely known and as religious inhibitions on their use diminished. In addition, by the eighteenth century large numbers of nobles remained unmarried: an astounding 50 percent of the children of the upper nobility in the Catholic Westphalia region of Germany and 25 percent of the peerage in Protestant England. This lack of reproduction, together with early modern diseases, against which nobles enjoyed no special protection, and the added danger that their sons might die in battle, meant that many noble families died out. One historian of France has estimated that in each generation about 20 percent of families disappeared, and roughly comparable rates have been established for other European countries.

If the order was to maintain its numbers, a substantial flow of new families had to replace those that disappeared, and this was everywhere the case. A variety of mechanisms governed this mobility, some of them formal, some informal and even illegal. Sovereigns could grant titles of nobility, and some official positions brought nobility to anyone who held them; the Roman legal tradition even accorded the status to anyone who had an advanced degree in the law. Until about 1600, however, most new entrants to the nobility simply assumed the status, their only justification being military service or ownership of a fief, both of which their contemporaries normally associated with high status. Control over the process was mainly local and depended on the readiness of other nobles to accept newcomers' claims. In Germany, for instance, local colleges of knights refused to accept any new families whose credentials they doubted, and such families would have difficulty finding noble marriage partners for their children. Cathedral chapters had similar ideas and rejected candidates whose ancestry was uncertain.

After 1600, however, the state increasingly intervened in processes of social mobility, from motives that were both practical and ideological. Contemporaries viewed the determination of social status as an aspect of sovereignty, part of what marked a state as free from interference by higher authorities and fully in control of its own population. Thus disputes over ennoblement offered useful symbolic ground for the German principalities to demonstrate their independence from the Holy Roman Empire by raising new families to high status without the emperor's approval. Conversely, the kings of France insisted that only they, and not high nobles within the realm or battlefield commanders, could give out titles. In much the same way, the practical realities of ennoblement also produced ambiguous effects, encouraging some princes to be generous in granting titles, others to be restrictive. Already in the 1540s the French king was openly selling titles of nobility for cash; but such grants meant enlarging the numbers of the tax-exempt and (in the thinking of late-seventeenth-century administrators) of the economically unproductive. As a result, government policy might oscillate wildly during the sixteenth and early seventeenth centuries, with rulers shifting between open and restrictive policies as their immediate financial needs dictated. Even their personal convictions might play an important role. In England, Elizabeth I was reluctant to grant high titles, whereas her successor James I enjoyed granting large numbers of them and even created a new formal category within the British gentry.

On balance, though, the state's increasing hold over the process of ennoblement restricted new entries to the nobility. Indeed, restriction became an explicit goal of seventeenth-century economic improvers, who worried that social advancement diminished the number of society's producers while increasing the number of idle consumers. Pamphleteers in Spain and royal administrators in France both expressed this concern, and in 1666 the French government took concrete steps to address it. Louis XIV's mercantilist minister Jean-Baptiste Colbert launched a series of investigations of noble titles, with fines and public embarrassment for those who had "usurped" a title. Providing documentary proof of noble status became a more common experience throughout Europe in these years. Some schools, many religious institutions, a growing number of legal positions, and most groups of military officers all asked candidates for proof of their status before admission. The era of casual usurpation

was over, and the result in most regions was a visible decline in numbers of nobles; families continued to die out, probably at greater rates than in earlier centuries, but there were fewer replacements for them. In eighteenth-century France and Spain, nobles represented about half the share of population they had represented in 1600. Only in Britain did numbers actually increase in these years, apparently a reflection of British wealth and of the loose processes of social mobility that continued to prevail there. In much of continental Europe, in contrast, the eighteenth-century nobility formed a very small group: well under 1 percent of total population in much of Germany, about 1 percent in France, a mere 0.3 percent in Bohemia. Ordinary people could spend much of their lives without encountering them.

ECONOMIC SITUATIONS

The wealth and financial prospects of nobles, though varying enormously, everywhere reflected a fundamental ideological imperative: they were to be a ruling class, devoting their energies to public matters and warfare. Their views of themselves restricted the kinds of work that they could undertake and raised ethical questions about many economic activities. Pursuing money could only interfere with that imperative, drawing their attention from public to private matters and causing disrespect among those lower in society. In France and Spain formal rules of derogation required that any nobles working with their hands or engaging in most kinds of commerce lose their status and the privileges that went with it.

Such rules were never followed absolutely, and they left large zones for calculation and innovation. Certainly there was no prohibition on the careful pursuit of economic interests. Fifteenth-century nobles had unsophisticated but reasonably effective accounting techniques, and they moved quickly when they thought they were being cheated. Nor did they confine themselves to collecting rents on landed estates. Geographic accident offered some of them commercial possibilities, and they took full advantage. In the sixteenth century, as Louis Sicking has shown, the high-born lords of Vere operated something like a merchant marine on their island estate off the Netherlands coast. Prussian nobles took advantage of their easy access to the Baltic and dominated the grain trade in their region, using their tax advantages to drive out their commoner competition. In Seville sixteenth-century nobles took a leading role in trans-Atlantic commerce; in Genoa nobles involved themselves in banking; even in France, which perhaps took derogation more seriously

Tenant Paying Rent. Frontispiece to *Boke of Surveying* by Anthony Fitzherbert, 1523. NORTH WIND PICTURE ARCHIVE

than other countries, seventeenth-century nobles loaned money to the Crown, employing middle-class front men for this profitable enterprise, and a few financed overseas ventures. Above all there was England, whose aristocracy had never felt much inhibition about commercial activity and whose gentry already in the fifteenth century moved easily in and out of London commerce.

If ideology permitted the nobles a range of economic options, most nonetheless confined themselves to a limited set of these, focusing on their estates and viewing the market economy with suspicion. Hence the seriousness of governmental efforts in the later seventeenth and eighteenth centuries to change thinking on the matter of nobility and money. Officials like Colbert, worried by the French economy's failure to match its Dutch and British competitors, sought to propagate a far wider conception of economic activity, one that celebrated commerce and encouraged even those of high status to undertake it. Eighteenth-century writers took up these themes in France, Spain, and the German states. Governments now sought to end the concept of derogation and actively encouraged the development of a "commercial nobility," the term used by one such advocate. By the end of the century, such ideas apparently had a significant impact on nobles' thinking. Many more now spoke glowingly of the importance of commerce, and more now participated in it.

Until that point, land remained by far the most important form of aristocratic wealth, the group's main source of income and the focal point for most of its economic calculations. Given the geographic variety of Europe itself, landowning might vary widely from one region to another. Already in the sixteenth century some English estates included coal mines, a natural adjunct to control of land itself. In Germany late medieval estates derived very significant income from fish-farming in ponds created for the purpose, and both German and Bohemian estates produced substantial amounts of beer. The region around Bordeaux in southwestern France included large tracts of vineyard, much of it in the control of noble estate owners. More important than this variety, however, were the basic patterns that gave estates a common look across much of Europe. In the fifteenth century most estates consisted of more than acreage; in fact the direct control of land might play a subordinate role in the estate economy. Instead, owners depended chiefly on the rents (usually fixed since the high Middle Ages) that they collected from peasants within their estates' territories and on the powers they exercised. This bundle of rights and powers defined the estate as a lordship rather than a mere property, and nobles viewed their status as closely associated with lordship itself. In feudal theory medieval warriors had been granted lordships as recompense for military service, and both theory and practice gave many lords real powers over their tenants. Most conferred on their owners the right to judge minor property disputes, and a minority had the right of high justice, which allowed them to try capital crimes.

If the structure of lordship was fundamentally similar across Europe, so also were the threats that lordship faced in the fifteenth and sixteenth centuries. The plagues and warfare of the late Middle Ages made it difficult to find tenants and sharply reduced demand for agricultural goods; both rents and estate values declined as a result. After the damage had been made good, governmental currency manipulations and a rapidly growing money supply after 1500 sharply reduced the value of fixed rents. Governments also tended increasingly to intervene in judicial matters, making judicial rights a source of expense and harassment.

By the mid-sixteenth century, lordship was in severe difficulties in many regions, and in England it had largely disappeared. Nobles thus had to find new ways to manage their lands, and enough did so that lordship itself and the nobles who depended on it survived into the late eighteenth century. They reoriented their estates to focus on the direct control of land and other resources rather than on permanently fixed rents. Mainly this meant acquiring land from the peasantries, who had controlled most of it in the late Middle Ages, and across Europe a vast wave of peasant expropriation, usually by outright purchase, less often through legal manipulations, marked the sixteenth and seventeenth centuries. Nobles had other important opportunities to acquire land during these years. As lords, they could claim exclusive control over the woodlands and pastures of their estates, and in England and Prussia they had the right to expel long-settled tenants and reorganize their farms into much larger domains. In regions that became Protestant, the mid-sixteenth century made church lands available for nobles to purchase, and even Catholic France sold off some church land between 1563 and 1586. Aristocratic and gentry acquisitions from these combined sources went farthest in England, northern Germany, and eastern Europe, somewhat less far in France and Italy. Everywhere, though, the process placed nobles in an excellent position to benefit from the economic changes of the seventeenth and eighteenth centuries. With population growing throughout Europe, farm and forest products enjoyed vigorous markets in these years, and better commercial networks improved nobles' ability to profit from these opportunities. Estate owners along the Baltic Sea thus became the principal suppliers of the fast-growing cities of the Low Countries, which needed to import most of their grain.

This economic reorientation, from the collection of feudal rents to domain management, left nobles to face the problem of labor organization. Given their reluctance to involve themselves directly in economic activity, and their absolute refusal to work with their hands, they needed to assemble the labor and managers that would make their newly constructed domains profitable. East of the Elbe River, in central and eastern Germany, Bohemia, Denmark, and Poland, nobles found an essentially political solution to this need by demanding several days' work from each farm within their lordships, a move made possible by the relative weakness of governments in the region, at least until the eighteenth century. To the west landowners had no such ability to use constrained labor, and most of them turned instead to tenant farmers, who would manage the land on short-term leases and take on the problems of organizing production and marketing produce. The rise of a new class of villagers, the tenant farmers, thus accompanied the peasantry's loss of its properties. In northern Europe these farmers tended to be wealthy and powerful figures, the principal employers within their own villages and allied to similarly powerful figures in the villages nearby. In southern France and Italy, the tenant was a less impressive figure. There sharecropping predominated,

and tenants depended on landowners to supply the capital for running their farms. In turn, the owners received a much larger share of the harvest—at least one-half, often more—than in the north.

Whatever the labor system, and no matter how much power it seemed to accord them, aristocratic landowners always had to confront villagers' resistance to their wishes. Occasionally such resistance might take the form of mass violence, as in the German Peasants' War of 1524–1526, or the Breton revolts of the Red Bonnets in 1675, both of them directed against the excesses of seigneurial power. Although these rebellions were put down savagely, they had the lasting effect of moderating landlords' demands. In the long run, however, much more significant were the smaller acts of resistance that the economic system itself accorded villagers. Even the servile labor system of eastern Europe offered such possibilities, as the most rigorous oversight could not turn serfs into enthusiastic workers; some accommodation with their interests was needed if they were to work effectively. In the west the tenant farmer held a much more powerful position against the landowner. He (and occasionally she, as many widows took over their husbands' farms) had capital and skills that could not be easily replaced, and few nobles were eager to take on the high-risk trade in agricultural commodities. Village communities also turned readily to lawsuits against lords and landowners.

Such inevitable negotiations with those who did the actual work of farming were a first limit on nobles' economic circumstances. The pressures of an increasingly consumer-oriented society were another. During the seventeenth and eighteenth centuries, a widening array of goods appeared in European markets, new architectural and artistic styles, as well as more purely material items like foods, clothing, carriages, and furniture. Even some early modern moralists stressed the propriety of nobles' spending lavishly, because expenditure demonstrated the solidity of their place atop the social order and rendered visible the differentiations on which that order rested; the less serious-minded mocked those who fell behind the fashions. Probably the seventeenth century was the most difficult period in this regard. Urbanization and the expansion of courts brought nobles into greater contact with one another and made divergences from fashion more conspicuous. It was during these years that the out-of-touch country gentleman became a stock element in French and British comedies. Another literary theme came equally to the fore, that of the nobleman who had spent his way into bankruptcy. The lure of consumption was probably the leading economic problem nobles faced.

Relations among different levels within the nobility began to change as well, for the need to keep up with the fashions raised questions about the status of poor nobles who could not afford these new levels of expenditure. Poor nobles had always been numerous, if only because inheritance patterns in many regions favored one son and left his brothers and sisters with inadequate funds. These men and women were not entirely without resources; they survived as dependents and servants of the great, and the rapidly expanding armies of the latter part of the seventeenth century offered many of them military careers. Indeed, their fate became something of a public preoccupation in the later seventeenth and the eighteenth centuries, and wealthy patrons founded special schools that would prepare young noblewomen for marriage and young noblemen for military careers. But these supports could not sustain the mass of poor nobles, and the difficulties of maintaining their status in an age of conspicuous consumption forced many out of the nobility after 1650.

DEALING WITH THE STATE

Their view of themselves as governors and warriors made nobles especially sensitive to their relations with state power, and in most regions state institutions accommodated themselves to this sensitivity. Feudal traditions encouraged princes, however grandiose their ambitions, to consult with their leading subjects, assembled in formal deliberative bodies. Nobles had at least one chamber to themselves in these parliamentary bodies; and both the political chaos of the late Middle Ages and the difficult decisions required by the Reformation forced even the most autocratic princes to listen carefully to these political voices. After the sixteenth century, however, this need diminished, and with it princely concern for political consultation. The French government failed to convene its Estates General after its last session in 1614, despite frequent consultations during the previous century. In much of Germany the chronology was similar: parliamentary assemblies had met regularly over the sixteenth century and had maintained their right to approve new taxes, but after the mid-seventeenth century princes levied taxes without consent, and assemblies met much less often.

The decline of political consultation caused important political tension in the early modern period, for nobles took seriously their longstanding claim to guide their princes. Angry at their apparent exclusion from princely decisions, nobles entered readily into plotting and occasionally into outright rebellion. Most

European states had to contend with some form of aristocratic rebellion over the early modern period, culminating in the wave of rebellions of the 1640s, the years of the English Civil War, Portugal's liberation from Spain, the Fronde in France, and rebellions in Catalonia, Naples, Palermo, and elsewhere. Governments won out in most of these contests, for by this point no private army could hold out against trained royal troops. But the examples of Catalonia and England demonstrated that governments could not take victory for granted, and that aristocratic malcontents had to be closely watched.

Traditionally, historians have understood the decline of political consultation in terms of a larger triumph of absolute monarchy, the process by which princes disciplined their nobles, taught them the futility of violence, and reduced them to a more or less prosperous servitude, with few real political functions. Later interpretations, however, stressed collaboration between kings and their most powerful subjects and suggested that, over the seventeenth and eighteenth centuries, nobles in fact exchanged one political role for another, more effective one. Parliamentary mechanisms for political consultation weakened, but nobles' share of administrative and military positions actually grew, allowing them substantial influence on the government policies they now executed. There were more military positions in these years of frequent warfare and growing armies, though nobles responded variously to these opportunities: in seventeenth-century Bavaria and the Paris basin, for instance, relatively few nobles fought, whereas in Prussia and Brittany the military was both a cultural ideal and an important economic resource.

Civil positions were also available, as governments needed many more judges, tax collectors, and local governors. In the sixteenth century these civil servants came from varied social levels, mixing some gentlemen and some men of very humble backgrounds within a middle-class majority. By the seventeenth century, however, most European civil services were becoming more exclusive and less tolerant of lowborn outsiders. Acutely aware of the powers they exercised and the wealth their positions conferred, upper-level civil servants tended to form themselves into dynasties, passing their offices on to their sons, and increasingly claiming nobility on the basis of their offices. The process went farthest in France, where a distinctive "nobility of the robe" (so named for the robes that French judges were to wear at all times) acquired official recognition in the mid-seventeenth century, but some version of this rise in social status could be seen in many countries. The results varied substantially from one region to another. In Spain and France

Courtiers at Versailles. Masquarade at Versailles, c. 1720. Nineteenth-century lithograph. THE ART ARCHIVE

a fusion of official and military nobilities had taken place by this time, with frequent intermarriages and considerable readiness of old noble families to prepare their sons for official careers. In most of Germany, on the other hand, official nobles failed to obtain complete acceptance by older families, despite receiving ennoblement from the princes they served.

Finally, nobles had almost exclusive control over the courts of early modern Europe, and in the seventeenth and eighteenth centuries these institutions played a crucial role in setting public policy. Like armies and civil services, courts grew over the period, partly as a reflection of the growing power of kings themselves. Kings wanted to make their courts attractive to their leading subjects and offered a range of frivolous, increasingly elaborate pleasures. But the real business of the courts was serious, for in them both policies and careers were shaped. Kings sought advice from their courtiers, and anyone who hoped to play a leading military or political role had to make his voice heard at court. Nobles who came to court had to conform to standards of self-control and of elegance in behavior and speech, and they had to show proper respect for those more powerful than themselves who enjoyed particular closeness to the king; but these demands did not imply passivity or domestication. Nobles indeed gave up their traditions of rebellion after about 1660, but the change reflected their successful collaboration with princes rather than a loss of political vigor.

All these new forms of political engagement required new levels of education, and rising educational standards applied to even the wealthiest and the high-est born. Those hoping for careers in administration or the judiciary needed long training in Latin literature and Roman law, certified by university degrees. At court formal education counted for less, and indeed courtiers often made fun of the judges' ponderous Latin learning. Yet educational demands applied to courtiers as well, for they needed to speak gracefully and to display a command of the culture around them; the ideal courtier of the late seventeenth century was a writer as well, whose letters and verse might circulate widely. Even military service required some education. Seventeenth- and eighteenth-century armies required much more disciplined training than their medieval predecessors, and it was now expected that commanders know enough mathematics to use firearms effectively. Greek and Roman military theorists also acquired a new relevance because seventeenth-century tactics accorded such importance to infantry formations. Nobles had very practical reasons for educating themselves, and a series of new institutions met their educational needs. Some attended the universities, but in the seventeenth century Jesuit colleges (and their imitators) adapted much better to their expectations, teaching not only languages and literature but also mathematics, science, and social skills like public speaking and dancing. They intended to form young men capable of effective social leadership, exactly what nobles wanted. It was a sign of the new educational standards that in the 1630s Louis, prince of Condé—heir to a great fortune, destined for a military career, and a close relative of the French king— was sent to the Jesuits for his education.

THE AGE OF REVOLUTIONS

Nobles confronted severe and unexpected challenges in the late eighteenth and nineteenth centuries that brought an end to many forms of social dominance they had previously enjoyed. The French Revolution in 1789 was only the most dramatic of a long series of changes, ending many formal social distinctions and some forms of aristocratic property as well. Feudal rents disappeared altogether, along with the offices whose possession had been an important item in many nobles' portfolios. New law codes required equal inheritance divisions, making it harder for dynasties to sustain their position over the generations. Perhaps most important, the Revolution ended any illusions nobles might have had as to their hold on the rest of society. They had witnessed or imagined rebellion in previous centuries, but few had envisioned an attack on their very existence as a social category; nineteenth-century nobles could never escape this consciousness, and it led them to panicky exaggerations of even small social challenges. Nor were these experiences (and the fears they stimulated) limited to France. Before 1789, indeed, the main assaults on aristocratic power and privilege had occurred in the domains of the Habsburg emperor Joseph II. He had ended nobles' tax privileges and limited landowners' powers over serfs. The French example gave much greater urgency to such reforms, for princes hoped that reform might forestall violence and allow effective competition with the French enemy. In other regions the French imposed their social models directly, ending privileges, titles, and feudal powers wherever their armies conquered.

Other challenges were less dramatic but in the long run even more threatening. The nineteenth century was a difficult time for landowners in all categories because the rules of international competition so rapidly changed. Grain from Russia and the Americas now appeared on European markets, and constantly improving modes of transportation intensified competition even within Europe. Tariff protection like the English corn laws came under pressure, and other groups in society were becoming richer and less patient with aristocratic guidance. Industrialization and banking rapidly created new fortunes, and new wealth was visible even among working farmers, who in many regions could be seen buying land and educating their children in social graces. Even if their own economic circumstances remained prosperous, aristocrats knew they were losing ground relative to others in their society.

The nineteenth century ended the aristocracies' domination of Europe's politics and their preeminence within its economy. Yet until late in the century, this collection of changes hurt the aristocracies less than was once believed. Historians have shown that most aristocratic families survived the French Revolution with their properties intact, enabling a return to social and political prominence after 1815. Throughout Europe many actually profited from nineteenth-century industrial development, investing in enterprises and sitting on corporate boards; in any case the new industrialists were often eager to ally both politically and personally with old families. Rapid urbanization made some of their lands much more valuable, and some were also able to introduce agricultural improvements. Despite the democratic currents of the age, they also managed to hold on to political power with surprising efficacy. Through the mid-nineteenth century, electoral systems tended to favor landowners, as did supposedly meritocratic systems of recruitment to the expanding civil services, which rested partly on the social skills and classical learning that the old ruling groups had long commanded. Even courts retained some significance, giving members of old families significant

Monarch and Lords. Queen Elizabeth II addresses the House of Lords, London, 24 November 1998. ©AFP/ CORBIS

influence over policies in France, Germany, and Italy and career advantages as well. Aristocrats even benefited from the new technologies of the late nineteenth and early twentieth centuries, dominating the newly founded automobile clubs of England and France and playing a prominent role in early aviation.

Only at the very end of the nineteenth century did traditional elites lose their central place in European life, and then the sources of crisis were mainly political rather than economic or social. An anti-aristocratic government came to power in England, and its taxes on inheritance undermined what had been the aristocracies' greatest strength, their ability to accumulate wealth generation after generation. World War I destroyed the monarchies and courts of central Europe and discredited aristocratic political influence. For many families the war was an economic disaster as well, destroying savings and rendering many investments worthless. It has been plausibly argued that 1918 rather than 1789 marked the end of aristocratic society in Europe. And there were still political maneuvers: many German aristocrats used support for conservative politicians to win favorable tariff policies for their agricultural goods in the 1920s and into the Nazi era. Even at the beginning of the twenty-first century, numerous aristocratic families survive, the 1980s and 1990s having brought them significant economic advantages. Their lands and houses, even their bric-a-brac, have increased enormously in value. Despite generations of republican criticism, they remain culturally self-confident, and the society around them has become more respectful of their values. Aristocratic society has disappeared from Europe, in the sense that aristocracies no longer place their imprint on other social groups or determine the values of society as a whole. The aristocracies themselves remain, demonstrating yet again their own capacity for survival and the tenacious power of social inequality itself.

See also **Estates and Country Houses; Land Tenure; Peasant and Farming Villages; Serfdom: Eastern Europe; Serfdom: Western Europe** (*volume 2*); **Revolutions** (*in this volume*); **Gestures; Inheritance; Manners** (*volume 4*); *and other articles in this section.*

BIBLIOGRAPHY

Surveys and Comparisons

Adamson, John, ed. *The Princely Courts of Europe, 1500–1750.* London, 1999.

Clark, Samuel. *State and Status: The Rise of the State and Aristocratic Power in Western Europe.* Montreal, 1995.

Dewald, Jonathan. *The European Nobility, 1400–1800.* Cambridge, U.K., 1996.

Elias, Norbert. *The Court Society.* Translated by Edmund Jephcott. Oxford, 1983.

Hale, John Rigby. *War and Society in Renaissance Europe, 1450–1620.* Baltimore, 1985.

Jones, Michael. *Gentry and Nobility in Late Medieval Europe.* New York, 1986.

National Studies of the Early Modern Period

Astarita, Tommaso. *The Continuity of Feudal Power: The Caracciolo di Brienza in Spanish Naples.* Cambridge, U.K., and New York, 1992.

Beik, William. *Absolutism and Society in Seventeenth-Century France: State Power and Provincial Aristocracy in Languedoc.* Cambridge, U.K., and New York, 1985.

Dewald, Jonathan. *Pont-St-Pierre, 1398–1789: Lordship, Community, and Capitalism in Early Modern France.* Berkeley, Calif., 1987.

Dominguez Ortiz, Antonio. *Las classes privilegiadas en la España del antiguo régimen.* Madrid, 1973.

Endres, Rudolf. *Adel in der frühen Neuzeit.* Munich, 1993.

Elliott, John Huxtable. *Spain and Its World, 1500–1700: Selected Essays.* New Haven, Conn., 1989.

Forster, Robert. *The House of Saulx-Tavanes: Versailles and Burgundy, 1700–1830.* Baltimore, 1971.

Hagen, William. "How Mighty the Junkers? Peasant Rents and Seigneurial Profits in Sixteenth-Century Brandenburg." *Past and Present* 108 (1985): 80–116.

Nassiet, Michel. *Noblesse et pauvreté: La petite noblesse en Bretagne, XVe–XVIIIe siècle.* Brittany, 1997.

Nicolas, Jean. *La Savoie au 18e siècle: Noblesse et bourgeoisie.* 2 vols. Paris, 1977–1978.

Nierop, Henk F. K. van. *The Nobility of Holland: From Knights to Regents, 1500–1650.* Translated by Maarten Ultee. Cambridge, U.K., and New York, 1993. Translation of *Van riddes tot regenten.*

Sicking, Louis. *Zeemacht en onmacht: Maritieme politik in de Nederlanden, 1488–1558.* Amsterdam, 1998.

Stone, Lawrence. *The Crisis of the Aristocracy, 1558–1641.* Oxford, 1965.

Stone, Lawrence, and Jeanne C. Fawtier Stone. *An Open Elite? England, 1540–1880.* Oxford and New York, 1984.

The Nineteenth and Twentieth Centuries

Cannadine, David. *The Decline and Fall of the British Aristocracy.* New Haven, Conn., 1990.

Higonnet, Patrice. *Class, Ideology, and the Rights of Nobles during the French Revolution.* Oxford and New York, 1981.

Lieven, Dominic. *The Aristocracy in Europe, 1815–1914.* New York, 1992.

Mayer, Arno. *The Persistence of the Old Regime: Europe to the Great War.* New York, 1981.

THE MIDDLE CLASSES

Margaret R. Hunt

"The middle class" is a term widely applied in the nineteenth and twentieth centuries to people who occupy the middle position between those who have to labor continually in order to survive, and those who hold ancestral "blood rights" to monopolize political power, economic resources, and social privilege. Historically this "middle class" has displayed great regional variability and much internal complexity and been highly sensitive to fluctuating business cycles. Impossible to pin down precisely, the status of being "middle class" is often assumed to inhere most authentically in commercial people (manufacturers, retailers, wholesalers, merchants), though it is frequently applied to more diverse groupings, which might include civil servants, "upper" white-collar salary earners, professionals, teachers and other intellectuals, *rentiers* (those who live on income from investments), and even (it has been argued) *apparatchiks* (bureaucrats). Common usage by social historians differentiates between the periods before and after industrialization—a phenomenon that occurred at different times in different European nations. For the period before industrialization there is a tendency to favor terms like "bourgeoisie," "burgher class," or "the middling sort." After industrialization there seems to be a preference for "middle class" or "middle classes."

Because of this imprecision, some historians have called for eliminating the term entirely on the grounds that it is too vague and, due to its central role in marxist polemic, too overdetermined to be really useful. Thus an influential group of historians has also argued that any and all attempts to categorize people, even very loosely, according to their economic role or market position constitutes rank reductionism.

Beyond definitional issues, few people are neutral on the subject of the middle class. And it would be difficult to find a group that has been subjected either to so much hostility or so much praise. Blamed for everything from colonialism to environmental degradation, from sexual repression to twelve-tone music, from facism to urban blight, the middle classes are also routinely viewed as people without whom no nation can rise to distinction: the bulwark of the law, the engine of economic development, and the bedrock of morality and family values.

BEFORE INDUSTRIALIZATION: THE "RISING" AND "FALLING" MIDDLE CLASSES

The germ of the "middle class" is generally thought to be medieval town or city dwellers, often members of crafts guilds, grain or livestock merchants, notaries, moneylenders, and the like. These individuals ("bourgeois," "burghers," or "citizens") could be found most often in those places blessed with a relative abundance of towns, most notably in the late medieval and early Renaissance period, the Italian peninsula, Flanders, or along the north coast of Germany. It seems likely that some of these groups' practices and traditions derived from those of medieval traders, many of them of Middle Eastern origin. Nonetheless, the Italians, particularly, invented a number of practices and procedures, most notably bookkeeping, international banking, and moneylending, as well as a close attendance on the law courts, that were to exert a great influence on later generations. These burghers were also often deeply committed to local civic or guild prerogatives, which they sometimes had to work hard to protect from the depredations of local lords.

The fifteenth, sixteenth, and seventeenth centuries saw a very significant growth in some parts of Europe in the number and size of cities; an increase in the power, complexity, and military belligerence of many early modern monarchies and nation states; the breakup of the old Catholic consensus; a significant intensification of extra-European long-distance trade as a result of the "discovery" of the New World and of new trade routes to the East; and the passing of economic dominance from the Mediterranean states to northwestern Europe. None of these developments was a distinctly "bourgeois" phenomenon. Nonethe-

DID THE BOURGEOISIE RISE?

"The bourgeoisie, historically, has played a most revolutionary part," wrote Karl Marx and Friedrich Engels in *The Communist Manifesto* of 1848. In one pugnacious phrase they set the terms of the debate for generations of social historians to come. Who was (and is) the bourgeoisie? Is it the same as the "middle class"? Has it ever been as unified a group as Marx and Engels seem to imply? What roles has it *in fact* played in revolutionary times? How much responsibility does it bear for the less dramatic, but in their way "revolutionary" transformations that have created the world we now inhabit, and were those transformation inevitable? Does bunching disparate individuals and collectivities together into so-called "classes" obscure more than it illuminates?

Not surprisingly, historians seeking answers to these questions have lavished a good deal of attention upon the great western European political revolutions of the seventeenth, eighteenth, and nineteenth centuries. Christopher Hill's *English Revolution, 1640* (1940) argued that the parliamentary side was powerfully aided and abetted by urban merchants and bankers and capitalist estate owners, and that the revolution had the effect of making England "safe" for capitalism. Marx himself unequivocally called the French Revolution of 1789 "the French bourgeois revolution" (Marx, *Capital*, 1984, Vol. I, p. 92), and several generations of French historians, perhaps most prominently Albert Soboul, have labored to expose the lineaments of the historic defeat of feudalism that it is said to have represented. Similar claims have been made for the long, if intermittent, Dutch war of independence against Spain in the sixteenth and seventeenth centuries, the American Revolution of 1776, the (failed) 1848 revolutions, various nationalist revolutions against Ottoman rule, and both the abortive Russian Revolution of 1905 and the first phase of the Revolution of 1917.

Other historians (Alfred Cobban, François Furet, Colin Lucas, for France; J. H. Hexter, Hugh Trevor-Roper, Conrad Russell for England; and many others) have strenuously combatted the notion that any or all of these revolutions represent "bourgeois revolutions." Critics of the "bourgeois revolution" thesis argue that most of these revolutions were actually initiated by members of the nobility, and that they often look more like an "aristocratic reaction" than they do a revolution against feudalism. They note that in none of these revolutions can one find "bourgeois" groups lining up on only one side of the conflict. Moreover, the ideals of most revolutionaries seem far removed from the mundane concerns of bankers, merchants, or industrialists, and have often had the effect of retarding economic growth rather than promoting it. Sometimes it is nobles who espouse "progressive" social and economic policies. These critics have significantly undermined reductionist identifications of class status or "material conditions" more generally with the urge to revolution and indeed with "ideology" more generally.

However, a less desireable tendency of much of their work has been to detach social and economic issues entirely from the process of historical change and to imply that politics and ideology float entirely free of social and economic conditions. Their revolutions often look like chance occurrences within a bland world of consensus, or the outcome of thousands upon thousands of atomized acts of individual frustration.

Later historians undertook a variety of efforts to reinsert social and economic data into a more ideologically nuanced and causally complex picture of the great and small European revolutions. Christopher Hill's writings from the 1980s, far more than did the *English Revolution, 1640,* acknowledge the political heterogeneity of men of trade, and emphasize the long-term results of the revolution, many of them "unintended," rather than any unconscious, much less purposeful desire to establish a more capitalist society. Lynn Hunt's *Politics, Culture, and Class in the French Revolution* (1984) replaces the narrow question of the relationship of ideology to "class" with an emphasis on region, occupation, and "insider" versus "outsider" status. She points out, contrary to Marx's opinion, that there was nothing inexorable about the way the revolution unfolded and that it did little either for the health of commerce or to restore political stability. However, she also shows that, after a slow start, "new men," notably professionals, and to some extent merchants and manufacturers, played a very significant role in revolutionary, as well as counterrevolutionary politics, creating, as well as seizing, the opportunities presented by the new political culture of the 1790s. She concludes that "while revolutionary politics cannot be deduced from the social identity of revolutionaries, . . . neither can it be divorced from it . . ." (Hunt, 1984, p. 13). Her account thus cautiously adopts part of the marxist schema, while rejecting historical determinism and insisting that occupation is only one among many variables that influence political ideology and political participation.

Historians of the middle class have, in the 1980s and 1990s, been as much if not more concerned with the differences that divide this class than with the commonalities that occasionally and inconsistently unite them. Few have been able to locate a single, unified middle class. Rather this is a group or groups riven not only by differences of relative market positioning, but also by gender, religion, race, nationality, and age. As a result, some historians have sought to replace the old notion of a single middle class with two or more classes. Thus R. S. Neale argues for both a "middling class" and a "middle class." Among social historians of Germany it is common to differentiate between the middle and upper bourgeoisie, the *Bürgertum,* and a lower-middle class, the *Kleinbürgertum* or *Mittelstand.* The *Bürgertum* is often further differentiated into the *Bildungsbürgertum* (professionals, academics, intellectuals, some salaried government officials) and the *Wirtschaftsbürgertum* (entrepreneurs, capitalists, managers, *rentiers*). To these debates may be added the large and growing literature on the lower middle class in numerous countries, which often focuses on the way its members pursue divergent political paths from other middle-class groupings.

If the bourgeois revolutionary looks less resolute, less class conscious, and indeed less like a single class than it used to, the notion of a bourgeois revolution has experienced something of a comeback, though in substantially altered form. A particularly influential position is that of David Blackbourn and Geoff Eley, as articulated in a number of books and articles focusing upon German history in the nineteenth and early twentieth centuries. They argue that, while it is true that the revolutions of 1848 were, in most places, an abject failure in terms of winning the middle class any significant political power, nonetheless Wilhelmine Germany experienced what they call a "silent Bourgeois revolution." There, in Blackbourn's words,

> an economically progressive bureaucracy served almost as a kind of surrogate bourgeoisie, leveling the ground on which the capitalist order would stand, as well as undertaking some of the preliminary construction work on its own account. Secularization removed property from the "dead hand" of the church; the peasantry was emancipated and a free market in land confirmed; guild restrictions were pruned away; and internal tariffs to freedom of trade were removed." (Blackbourn and Eley, *The Peculiarities of German History,* 1984, pp. 176–77).

Blackbourn goes on to point out that after unification, the Wilhelmine government established technical schools and other incentives to innovation, founded a national bank, improved communication and transportation, and reformed commercial law and practice. While the state was clearly key, capitalists were hardly supine in this period. They oversaw the emergence of the public limited company and developed a variety of ways of mobilizing capital and facilitating exchange. Older industries, particularly heavy industry, recorded considerable gains, while a variety of new manufacturers came into being. At the same time modern conceptions of the rule of law gained widespread acceptance and middle-class people flocked to clubs, societies, and philanthropic associations.

If Blackbourn's view of Germany's development is more positive than we are accustomed to, his conception of modernity is more complex than simply "the rise of the bourgeoisie." As he shows, enthusiasm for and commitment to the notion of progress was diffused very widely across society, involving the state, working-class groups, aristocrats, and capitalists. And those who opposed it were similarly diverse, including more traditional small-scale capitalists (small producers) and sectors of the working class, peasantry, and nobility.

If one reconfigures one's vision to see the late nineteenth century (as Blackbourn and Eley seem to be urging us to do) in terms of an embrace of and confrontation with modernity rather than "the rise of the bourgeoisie" it becomes clear why so many middle-class people were deeply ambivalent about and alienated from both capitalism and modernity more generally. Undoubtedly one of the more interesting features of the middle class, particularly in the modern period, has been its enthusiasm for self-criticism, as well as the number of self-proclaimed "class exiles" it has managed to generate. Karl Marx and Friedrich Engels (1820–1895), the son of a lawyer and the son of a factory owner, respectively, were only two among many. While some among the alienated middle class actually came from declining groups (we need to remember that many middle-class people were downwardly mobile in the nineteenth and early twentieth century), it seems likely that many of them were simply articulating a more widespread and less class-specific anxiety about the pace and unpredictability of modernization—an anxiety to which almost anyone might be prone, but which intellectuals were far more likely to articulate.

Be that as it may, much scholarly work on the middle class(es) written since World War II has focused

(continued on next page)

DID THE BOURGEOISIE RISE? (continued)

on their putative psychic insecurity and the way in whichthey were perpetually "creating" themselves as individuals, families, and classes. This problem has especially appealed to scholars on the left, who have contributed an important body of work tracing the establishment of a normatively "middle-class" culture. Thus, to mention just one among many, Eric Hobsbawm has pointed out the way that the English middle class not only favored particular types of sport (tennis, golf) over others marked as lower class (for example, football) but, in his words, "made amateurism, i.e. leisure both to pursue sports and to achieve high standards at them, the test of 'true' sportsmen" (Hobsbawm, "The Example of the English Middle Class," p. 141).

The problem of how the middle class made itself has been taken up with especial enthusiasm by later scholars influenced by postmodernism, who, while they have perhaps been insufficiently critical of the term "middle class" itself (presumably because the group's fuzzy boundaries and mutability lend themselves so well to the sorts of analysis they prefer), have nonetheless added many new nuances to our picture of the middle class(es). They have also made it harder either to make inflated claims about middle-class hegemony or to engage in what Lynn Hunt calls "a mechanistic deduction of politics from social structure" (Hunt, *Politics, Culture, and Class,* 1984, p. 11).

Particularly important interventions have been made with respect to questions of gender. The output of books and articles on women and gender has been huge, touching on topics as diverse as mistress-servant relations, fashion, shopping and consumerism, marriage and divorce, philanthropy, and the women's rights movements. They paint a complicated picture of a middle class riven by gender insecurity and conflict, but one in which women fulfilled a wide variety of "class" functions, from patrolling racial and other status boundaries to supplying significant amounts of capital and invisible, unpaid labor.

Race has also emerged as a key factor in the formation of a European middle class. In a book entitled *Race and the Education of Desire* (1995), Ann Stoler argues that in both Britain and the Netherlands "[the] cultivation and unique sexuality [of the bourgeois body] was nourished by a wider Colonial world of Manichaean distinctions: by Irish, 'Mediterranean,' Jewish, and non-European Others who provided the referential contrast for it" (Stoler, 1995, p. 136). For Stoler, too, the middle class is a nervous and unstable entity, which, far from "rising" in any definitive way, is forever trying to create itself at other groups' expense.

In the late twentieth century, at least in western Europe, many commentators argue that the middle classes, have become so fragmented and atomized as to be largely unintelligible. The disruptions of World Wars I and II; the triumph of consumption over production; the rise of mass culture (especially radio, television, and advertising) at the expense of more localized and class-specific cultures; the centrality of forms of identity based upon race, religion, party, and affinities other than social class, and the taxonomic challenges posed by such developments as the sharp growth of a white-collar "salariat"; the expansion of the service sector; and the migration of many manufacturing jobs to underdeveloped countries, have, they argue, made the nineteenth-century language of class and class cultures obsolete. It must be said though that the end of the cold war and the apparent world wide defeat of communism has revived the claim that what we saw in the late twentieth century was the ultimate victory of the entrepreneurial middle class and the installation of a new universalism of pure individual self-interest free of traditional impediments, such as national borders. It may be that the term "middle class" is a sort of semantic fossil that no longer bears any relationship to actual social formations. However, the fact that it remains indispensable in common usage may be a signal that history and historians have not seen the last of this hard-to-define, never-quite-rising, yet strangely persistent body.

---

less, all had a significant impact on trade and consumption and hence the growth of an urban "middling sort."

The new cities, with their complex provisioning needs, offered numerous opportunities for trade and commerce, while at the same time providing the locus for a wide range of civic and cultural activities.

The new states provided an unending supply of jobs suitable to lowborn but literate men, while its wars helped bring into being a whole new class of army contractors and middlemen. In these years men (and occasionally women) of commerce learned how to work closely, and generally unobtrusively, with city, provincial, and even national governments in a symbiotic relationship that was, more often than not, to both sides' advantage. Not surprisingly, some of the richest commercial families consolidated their wealth as well as their social position by moving up into the nobility, either by marriage alliances or by outright buying of titles, though the percentage of middling people who actually succeeded in doing this was probably small.

Few social historians any longer view the Protestant Reformation as a stealth move by capitalists—or even a development that necessarily favored them. Max Weber's famous claim in the *Protestant Ethic and the Spirit of Capitalism* (1904–1905) that Calvinism, in particular, "taught" its adherents how to be better entrepreneurs, and hence was more positively correlated with business success than Catholicism, has fallen before copious evidence about the entrepreneurial zeal of Catholics. Historians now argue that both the Protestant and Catholic Reformations offered an expanded role in culture and politics for literate non-elites and urban people in general. There also seems to be a guarded consensus among historians that the period saw an increased valuation of work and of secular activities for their own sake, as expressed in the new attention to natural (as opposed to supernatural) explanatory frameworks characteristic of the so-called "scientific revolution," and later the eighteenth-century Enlightenment.

At the same time, religious differences (between Catholics and Protestants, Jews and Gentiles, or even, in those parts of Europe under the domination of the Ottoman Empire, Muslims and others) cut a deep cleavage through groupings that one might, based on material considerations alone, have expected to make common cause. This was to be an enduring theme: while economic issues clearly play a role in group identity, they very seldom tell the whole story, and they are often "trumped"—or, quite simply, they disintegrate—before other allegiances.

The intensification of both long-distance and "domestic" trade ruined many bourgeois people while drawing others into the new trade nexus: many of the early shareholders in overseas adventures were members of the nobility, a high-living group that has seldom been averse to making money, particularly if it did not have to get its hands dirty. However, as with most entrepreneurial activity in the early modern period (with the partial but important exceptions of mineral extraction and, in some parts of Europe, some capitalist agriculture), the people who actually did the hands-on managerial work of banking, short- and long-distance trade, manufacturing, and getting the grain to market—those who took on the real risk—tended to be people of bourgeois stock.

Long-distance trade in particular, due both to the high profits that can come from it and its extreme volatility, came in some sense to define the upper reaches of the entrepreneurial classes, men who became veritable merchant princes (and were sometimes ennobled for their pains), but who manifested a certain lack of permanence that was characteristic of their class. These were families who could stand on the pinnacle of worldly success only to fall with a suddenness that seemed to call all human projects into question. In not a few countries these nerve-wracking roles fell disproportionately to "outsiders" of one sort or another: Huguenots or dissenters in England; Jews (particularly the Sephardim) in Holland; Armenians, Jews, and ethnic Greeks in the Ottoman Empire; ethnic Germans in Bohemia; various nonnationals in the Russian Empire. Often these groups were excluded from more traditional occupations or labored under various civil disabilities. Those who could, took advantage of far-flung kinship networks and the presumed solidarity of co-religionists to ensure accountability in a time of slow communication and few safeguards against cheating or peculation.

The prolonged depression that afflicted southern and central Europe from the 1580s on signals one of the fundamental realities of middling life, one that militates powerfully against the vision of these people as a unified whole. At the heart of entrepreneurial endeavor is, and has been, competition—between families, between nations, between regions, between old and new industries. Moreover, this competition is played out within a universe that is highly unpredictable. Economic trends then and now are far easier to discern in retrospect than they are while they are happening. Regions that, in one century or even one generation, are at the heart of a bustling trade, can go into full decline in the next as a result of war, a change of government, trade restrictions, epidemic disease, a succession of bad harvests, or simply a change of taste. A once-vibrant center of commerce that formerly supported large-scale trade in a range of commodities can turn into a depopulated backwater that supports little but barter and a few desultory livestock sales. Centers turn into peripheries, and peripheries become the centers of new economic systems. The European middle classes, like their investments, were constantly rising and falling.

Seventeen-century Holland: a "bourgeois" society. By the mid-seventeenth century the particular alignment of center and periphery that has in some if not all respects survived in Europe to this day was already evident. Undoubtedly, the most significant marker of this was the phenomenal success of the

Dutch Merchant. A senior merchant of the Dutch East India Company, presumably Jacob Mathieusen, and his wife, survey the fleet at Batavia (now Jakarta, Indonesia). Painting by Aelbert Cuyp (1620–1691). ©RIJKSMUSEUM-STITCHTING, AMSTERDAM

United Provinces of the Netherlands. Auspiciously located athwart the main land, river, and sea routes linking east and central Europe, the British Isles, France, and the Mediterranean states, with well-developed connections to the East Indies via the Dutch East India Company and the West Indies via the Dutch West India Company, the Netherlands were well situated to monopolize a gigantic proportion of seventeenth-century waterborne commerce. As a result of their successful war of independence against Spain, the United Provinces also possessed a republican polity, and a laudable, if at times somewhat fractured, patriotic spirit. In a century almost everywhere characterized by economic depression and a declining or stagnant population, the Netherlands stood out as the exception. In so doing it came to represent both for contemporaries, and for many modern-day historians, the quintessential early modern bourgeois (or, to use the Dutch term, *burgerlijk*) society.

Some of the Dutch provinces boasted local nobilities, but they played a far smaller cultural role and had less political power than in many European nations. Instead, power lay in the hands of civic elites, most of whom had risen via mercantile wealth, and who tended to have strong links to Calvinism. They oversaw a unique culture that came, in its own time, to be the talk of Europe. Contemporaries struggled to define just what made the Netherlands so unusual. By reconstructing what they saw, we can get a sense of how complex the problem of the "middle class" is. By

the seventeenth century there was already a well-developed association between middling urban dwellers (generally traders or masters) and traits like a strong belief in the power of work, compulsive thriftiness, an exaggerated attention to time, high rates of literacy and numeracy, and a certain lack of both imagination and martial virtues. Contemporary efforts to explain the "Dutch miracle" by reference to such characteristics can be seen in printed tracts, plays, and other cultural productions of the time in a number of European languages. These characterizations seem to have derived from empirical observation of at least some businesspeople (though adherence to these precepts must have been extremely variable) puzzled efforts to try to figure out why some prospered when others failed, a tendency (to which modern historians are not immune) to identify prescription too closely with actual behavior, and a desire to cut an overweening group (that is, the Dutch) down to size.

These stereotypes have a very long history in relation to "the middle classes." And their sheer ubiquity suggests that they need to be taken seriously at the level of discourse, if less often at the level of behavior. However, as the United Provinces show, they are far too reductionist to stand on their own as a credible description of people's behavior across the board. Thus, as Simon Schama explains in *The Embarrassment of Riches: An Interpretation of Dutch Culture in the Golden Age* (1987), the good burghers of Amsterdam, Rotterdam, and like cities were hardly exemplars of Max Weber's "worldly asceticism"; instead they boasted sumptuous houses (many of which can still be seen gracing the Keizersgracht and Herengracht Canals in Amsterdam), and cultivated a taste for serious eating, drinking, and tobacco consumption. Amsterdam shoppers could find whole streets and districts devoted to bookselling, nautical goods, spices, haberdashery, house furnishings, textiles, flowers, and even pets, those decorative little parasites that were just then becoming de rigueur in respectable homes. They could also tour a well-developed red-light district, roughly coterminous with its present-day location. Seventeenth-century Hollanders' commitment to work was just as likely to manifest itself in elaborate civic rituals, or, in the case of women, in the less-than-profitable activity (in monetary terms) of housecleaning as it was in the mundane activity of making money. While the Dutch certainly preferred peace to war, they could hardly be described as lacking in martial vigor, not only fighting off Spanish imperial domination in the Eighty Years' War (1568–1648), but repeatedly going to war with other European nations in defense of their trade.

And whatever else might have been imputed to the Dutch in the seventeenth century, a lack of imagination was not one of them. Visitors marveled at the way the Dutch East India Company built its own bevy of artificial islands in the midst of the harbor, Amsterdamers' ingenious methods for lifting huge ships over sandbars, the number and variety of the city's philanthropic and correctional institutions, the Dutch distaste for persecuting people on grounds of religion (though they made an exception for Catholics), their penchant for covering their walls with pictures from everyday life, and last, but by no means least, their remarkable ability to wrest huge tracts of land from the sea and turn them into lush farmland.

"Middling culture" in post-revolutionary England. In the seventeenth century Holland's main competitor (and emulator) was England. England's mid-century revolution, as well as the Glorious Revolution of 1688 were, in the first instance, conceived by political elites, not by bourgeois elements, but the period of upheaval gave rise to a number of changes that profoundly affected the climate of commerce and the lives of middling people. A series of bloody wars waged against the Dutch by both parliamentary and royalist regimes significantly reduced that nation's control over waterways and key export commodities, and by the late seventeenth century this had resulted in a significant increase in the British volume of trade. A fairly high degree of religious toleration was instituted under Oliver Cromwell (1599–1658), carried

through into the Restoration, and then enshrined permanently in the revolution settlement of 1689. England, unlike Holland, possessed a genuine aristocracy and gentry, which wielded real power in the cities and towns, in the rural areas, and in Parliament.

This fact has led historians to ask whether the middling sort in England really differed in cultural terms from their social superiors. The upper echelons of the middling sort undeniably "aped" the gentry to some degree; however, most middling people could not afford to live like the gentry, nor could they contemplate intermarrying with them. These people's lives, as is true of commercial people everywhere in the early modern period, were characterized by a great deal of insecurity and by a close engagement with trade and industry—something one seldom finds among the gentry. At the same time, one characteristic that the middling shared with their betters, but that differentiated them from many of their inferiors, was that by this time the vast majority of urban middling people, both male and female, knew how to read and write. One sign of this, a very advantageous one from the point of view of social historians, is that it became something of a fashion among middling groups beginning in the late seventeenth century to pen diaries and autobiographies. As a result we have extremely revealing diaries from a wide range of middling city dwellers.

This historical trove makes it possible to develope a few generalizations about "middling culture" (it seemed to be much concerned—at least rhetorically—with keeping good accounts; it was quite pious, though not necessarily more than other groups we know something about; it was much concerned about time-management issues), but it also shows how difficult it is to generalize about middling individuals. Thus, some middling diarists were more concerned about the state of their souls than the condition of their businesses, while others seldom went to church. Some were disgusted by aristocratic pretension, and others hobnobbed with them, and so on. Perhaps one of the few things that drew together the middling sort was an acute consciousness of risk: unlike their superiors there was no cushion between them and the vagaries of the market.

Economic differentiation and the middle classes in the eighteenth century. By the end of the seventeenth century, and still more so as the eighteenth century unfolded, a considerable amount of economic differentiation was making itself felt in Europe. It was by no means the case that all of the Northwest was prosperous. Ireland was already manifesting the results of British policies aimed at eliminating it as potential competition in the realm of finished goods. Large parts of Scandinavia were too cold to produce much in the way of agricultural exports. On the other hand, there were zones of very considerable economic strength even in otherwise underdeveloped or stagnant economies. For example, Catalonia, in northern Spain, developed a robust, urbanized economy. Istanbul and other Ottoman port towns, despite having largely lost the spice trade to Holland, still supported a very considerable carrying trade around the Black Sea and the eastern Mediterranean. Parts of the Balkans, notably Bulgaria, would soon develop a fairly significant textile industry, fueled both by the Ottoman army's need for uniforms, and by a growing demand from central Europe and the Middle East. Nations lucky enough to possess large mineral and ore deposits—for example, Sweden and Russia—hastened to exploit them. But many parts of Europe remained or became economically marginal or "trapped" in underdevelopment as the North Atlantic economies' respective stars rose.

Although at the time it was standard to blame what was sometimes referred to as "the productive classes" for the state of affairs (contemporaries often bemoaned the small size of their local middle class or complained about their addiction to luxury and idleness), that is only part of the story. Commercial people did, in certain times and places, move away from trade and hole up in "safe" investments, such as country houses (this is what seems to have happened in the Venetian republic in the seventeenth century). But those traders who could afford it have always done this, particularly when market exposure was very high, the climate of trade unfavorable, or the nature of commerce undergoing alteration. The case of Venice is, in that sense, instructive, for there were many external factors influencing the health of the economy. As Jan De Vries succinctly puts it in *Economy of Europe in an Age of Crisis, 1600–1750:*

> Beginning in 1602 a rapid succession of new problems overwhelmed [the Venetian republic]. The spice trade was lost for good to the Dutch and English who had now begun their penetration of the Indian Ocean; the textile industry suffered from high costs and withered away in the following half-century; the city's position as an international center of book publishing became untenable because of the rejuvenated Catholic Church; the Thirty Years' War deprived Venice of her most important market while the debasement of the Turkish currency sharply increased the cost of cotton and silk up to the Venetians.
>
> In an economy like this one it would have taken a very great innovatory capacity indeed—multiplied many times over—for the economy to sustain itself at anything like the levels of the previous century. And it is very likely that even that would not have worked. In

such an environment, commercial people make choices, and typically they choose safety rather then risk. (De Vries, 1976, p. 26)

It is also undeniably the case that some regions actively discouraged commercial endeavor, and hence the growth of a self-sufficient urban middling class, and in some cases any urban centers at all. In Spain the social hierarchy was top-heavy with nobles, who disdained commerce, and members of the clergy, whose profits, at least in theory, were measured in souls rather than in *réals;* economic policy-making through the second half of the sixteenth and seventeenth centuries was famously obtuse. Grazing policies led to soil deterioration. Rivers were allowed to silt up. The crown decided to expel Jews and Muslims—both relatively industrious minorities. The bloated ranks of the clergy, in particular, must have attracted many a promising youth who, in the Netherlands, would have turned to commerce; the purchase of noble status, which in Spain was particularly difficult to combine with commerce, must have claimed many more.

In the case of the Ottoman Empire, merchant and banking activity tended to be left to ethnic minorities, while Muslims monopolized official state and military positions. Different confessional groupings often lived segregated lives, under largely distinct legal systems; each *millet,* as these communities were called, was overseen by a small, self-perpetuating group generally heavily dominated by the clergy. Though some *millets* were open to outside influence (the Greek and Jewish communities in particular tended to cultivate connections to western Europe, particularly from the eighteenth century on), the system encouraged insularity, inflexibility, and a lack of integration between the imperial bureaucracy and the main economic actors, as well as between different sectors of the economy—since particular ethnic groups tended to monopolize each trade, manufacture, commercial, or financial sector. These problems were exacerbated by the devastating wars of the eighteenth century, followed in the late eighteenth and nineteenth centuries by the social upheavals and political repression that accompanied the various struggles for independence against Ottoman rule.

For its part, eastern Europe carried on a booming but lopsided trade with the northwestern European powers. By the seventeenth century a significant portion of western and southern Europe's food needs were supplied by importing—generally on Dutch ships—grain grown in the gigantic estates of eastern Europe. The turn to monoculture for export and the progressive "enserfment" of much of the peasantry made for an immobile, impoverished labor force and

Means of Production. Ironworks at Königshütte, Silesia, c. 1835. MARY EVANS PICTURE LIBRARY

a small, often absentee landowner class. This caused a marked decline in consumer demand and the result was that towns in the area east of the river Elbe declined in number, population, and degree of economic diversification. Middlemen—the tiny nascent middle class—tended to be west central Europeans (especially ethnic Germans), Huguenots, or Jews, but the latter particularly were often subjected to popular and state violence, exclusion from certain trades and professions, special taxes, and confinement to ghettos or delimited territories, such as the Pale of Settlement. Eastern Europe, in economic terms, entered into a relation of economic dependency with western Europe.

INDUSTRIALIZATION AND BEYOND

The role of the middle classes in industrialization. Economic historians disagree as to whether the technological and productive breakthroughs (of which factory production was only one part), which began in England in the second half of the eighteenth century, warrant the term "industrial revolution." But even those who do accept the term agree that this was an extremely protracted revolution, whose social effects on the owners of capital, workers, and consumers came slowly and in very unpredictable and diverse ways. Most social historians date the onset of a full-blown middle-class in England from the period approximately 1780 to 1820 and use the term "middle class" loosely for those who owned the means of production (factories), displayed patterns of consumption "typical" of middle class people, or had middle- or upper-level managerial or professional positions.

Predictably, there has been much debate about the extent to which industrialization, and indeed, the whole process of modernization of which industrialization was only one part, was "bourgeois"-driven. Certainly in the case of England, members of the nobility invested in infrastructure improvements, such as canals and later railroads, just as they had purchased shares in slave-trading voyages. In some other parts of Europe economic development had a very *dirigiste* character, planned and controlled by the state. State interventions in the economy were already habitual in Russia and the Ottoman Empire by the eighteenth century, and most European states, in both the west and east, engaged in practices designed to nurture national industries and penalize foreign competition, and indeed continue to do so into the twenty-first century. European modernization did not happen in a laissez-faire universe.

However, despite the involvement of political elites (whether by outright government intervention or via noble investments), it seems fair to say that the vast majority of people who oversaw the processes of modernization and who benefited most directly from them were middle class. These men and women invested their capital in (and shouldered the risks of) the new factories, came up with the technical innovations that transformed production, managed the ever-expanding networks by which new commodities were spread across Europe, brought in raw materials from the colonies (sometimes, as in India, after taking steps to stamp out indigenous manufacturing), and learned to exploit the labor of much poorer Europeans (many of them recently arrived from the rural areas) more efficiently.

As the numbers of the middle class grew, they formed a key group of consumers. Though the middle-class people were not the only audience for the new commodities (urban working-class demand, at least in countries that supported such groups, was also significant, and so was that of older elites), they adopted lifestyles that allowed them to showcase new fashions, new styles of architecture, and new patterns of leisure behavior. At the same time, patterns of behavior and consumption associated with the more developed parts of western and central Europe began to be imitated in other parts of Europe. This process was, however, very uneven. Thus, in the less integrated areas of the Balkans, eighteenth- and early-nineteenth-century mercantile elites still tended to emulate the style and tastes of Turkish elites. It was only in the early- to mid-nineteenth century that they began to imitate central European (particularly Viennese) middle-class tastes, and display in their homes such items as chairs, glassware, and candlesticks of Czech and Saxon manufacture. Similar patterns could be found throughout the more far-flung, inaccessible, economically underdeveloped regions of Europe, while the nineteenth-century discovery and valorization of regional difference also exerted a countervailing influence on the forces of cultural homogenization.

Politics and the middle classes in the nineteenth century.
The late eighteenth and nineteenth centuries saw a number of profound changes in the political and social landscape. The French Revolution was not a bourgeois revolution in the sense that Karl Marx (1818–1883) imagined, but it did clear away some of the tangled system of privilege that characterized the ancien régime. In England, the so-called Great Reform Bill of 1832 had more warrant to be called "middle class," at least in terms of impact, though it is notable that it had to be voted in by an electorate of gentlemen and aristocrats. It doubled the number of men entitled to vote from perhaps one in ten to one in five, but ensured through a property qualification that men of the laboring classes and

probably large sections of the lower middle classes would continue to be excluded.

By the first half of the nineteenth century, many European nations supported growing intelligentsias. Especially in central and eastern Europe and within the Ottoman Empire, these were often partially (though never slavishly) Western oriented: many of their members had been educated abroad; they were disdainful of traditional elites (and especially of the entrenched power of the clergy and ruling dynasties) and anxious to modernize. This tendency overlapped with a series of newly militant nationalist movements, most of them organized and led by students, intellectuals, and professionals, though often in the face of widespread hostility, not least by other sectors of the middle class, (in some cases their own older relatives). These movements, often more cultural than political, displayed many common features. Thus, in a number of the Balkan lands, by the early nineteenth century movements had arisen that stressed national education, tended to adopt romantic conceptions of the national spirit, and were much given (in good bourgeois style) to gathering together in clubs, cultural organizations, and subversive societies. This movement of the young tended to be highly critical of older, traditional elites and often the clergy (thus, in Bulgaria many nationalists objected strenuously not just to the Ottoman establishment but to what they viewed as the excessive power of the Greek Orthodox Church). Similar nationalist movements made up of young, generally middle-class people, were active throughout the first half of the nineteenth century and often beyond in many of the old imperial regimes of Europe.

In the face of this sort of pressure many of the most tradition-bound governments made concessions that, in the long run, favored the growth of a middle class, such as, in the case of the Austro-Hungarian and Russian Empires, freeing the serfs and partially reforming the law courts. Some governments took steps to open their bureaucracies to new men; the Ottomans, in their dwindling empire, began permitting non-Muslims to hold government office. Governments everywhere became more efficient, and many took up issues of public health and education—long popular among middle-class people. Some (largely western) European nations had by this time extended suffrage far enough down the social scale to cover virtually all middle-class men.

However, it would be wrong to view these signs of change as a "rise of the bourgeoisie" in any simple sense; rather we should probably see them as complicated, and in some countries rather tense attempts at co-existence. Traditional elites, often aristocrats by blood, continued to wield huge amounts of political

Intellectuals. Breakfast at the home of the English poet Samuel Rogers in the 1810s included the dramatist Richard Brinsley Sheridan, the poets Thomas Moore, William Wordsworth, Robert Southey, Samuel Taylor Coleridge, and Lord Byron, the actor John Philip Kemble, the sculptor John Flaxman, the Scottish writer James Mackintosh, the statesman Henry Petty-Fitzmaurice Lansdowne, the clergyman and essayist Sydney Smith, the American writer Washington Irving, and the Scottish jurist and critic Francis Jeffrey. ART ARCHIVE, LONDON

power and cultural prestige well into the twentieth century in many European countries, and they were often quite reluctant to share either commodity. Sometimes they looked down even on the richest industrialists. And middle-class groupings were themselves highly differentiated in terms of income, rank, and prestige, though not so differentiated that they could not at times pull together with lightning speed in the face of challenges by newly militant working-class groups.

Middle classes and separate spheres. By the mid-nineteenth century, a middle-class culture with some at least partially distinctive characteristcs had been established in western Europe, and there were numerous other middle-class enclaves throughout Europe, some of which emulated what they conceived to be the lifestyle of western Europeans; others of which charted their own course. But what was this lifestyle? A key criterion often used to distinguish "middle-class culture" was the existence of the privatized family, with-

drawn from the boisterous street or village culture of earlier days, and supporting women who, ideally, did not work for pay. In the case of England, an important marker of this has been said to be the tendency for manufacturing families to move their homes away from their factories or place of work. The equivalent in the case of city dwellers was to move to the suburbs then springing up around most major towns. There is no doubt that this did come to be the pattern in a number of places and among some occupations and income groups. However, even in England, professionals were much more likely to combine home and workplace, as were small retailers. And in many other parts of Europe, middle-class people, particularly the urban lower-middle class, seems to have had neither the money nor the inclination to withdraw from traditional patterns of local sociability. To this day, particularly in southern European towns, but also in the smaller urban centers of northern and central Europe one can see patterns of visiting, public ritual, charitable activity, and public sociability (for example, public drinking) that belie the claim that the middle-class family has withdrawn from the public sphere.

Later historians, moreover, tended to reject the theory of "separate spheres," which long held such a prominent place in women's history. Critics argue that "separate spheres" was always more of an ideological construct than a representation of reality, and that the more injudicious uses of this theory have had the effect of diverting attention from the important ways in which the sphere of women and the family supported and intersected with the sphere of work and politics. Recent research suggests that middle-class women's capital and their unpaid labor in and outside the home was crucial to the maintenance of their class. Women and men often pursued common class or group aims, and they shared broadly similar belief systems. While some middle-class Englishmen were seeking to apply scientific management techniques to factory work, some middle-class women were seeking to rationalize the labor of charity-school children so as to make "social welfare" turn a profit. And no sooner had some middle-class women left paid employment than others began agitating for the vote, seeking to break into male professional monopolies, such as medicine, and trying to turn women's philanthropic activities into paid employment opportunities for themselves and other middle-class women. If there ever was a "golden age" of separate spheres, it was short-lived, at least in the English case.

Middle class associational life.

The nineteenth-century middle class is often associated in people's minds with ostentatious religious faith, and much has been made, especially in Protestant countries, of middle-class attraction to evangelical and pietistic movements. Religion, for many groups, became a vehicle to greater personal discipline; a bulwark of family patriarchy; the seedbed for other kinds of cultural, philanthropic, and reform organization; and the basis from which to criticize—as well as to convert—traditional elites and the poor. There is no doubt that the nineteenth century saw a number of movements for spiritual renewal within a variety of denominations (Catholics, Jews, and others).

However, it does also seem to be the case that, in a large number of European countries, piety came to be more and more the province of women, either because more women than men continued to see religion as a source of strength, or because secular and anticlerical (and, in the case of Jews, assimilationist) tendencies seemed less disturbing when confined to men. Whatever the reasons for it, this newly secular mood contributed to the burgeoning of more rationalist and scientific approaches to a variety of "modern" problems, including town planning, public health, education, communications, transportation, the organization of factory work (for example, the adoption of the assembly line and of scientific management techniques), and more efficient methods of mobilizing capital.

Societies and clubs became a central feature of middle-class existence in the nineteenth century, though the roots of this went back quite a bit further in many countries, and they were never uniquely middle class. Both men and women entered into these societies, which many commentators have viewed both as a crucial stepping-stone to full participation in civil society and as an indication of the expansion of civil society as a site of independent community life. The scale and range of these groups was very wide. They included freemasonic and other semisecret fraternal associations, literary societies, chambers of commerce, societies for suppressing criminals, drama groups, prayer groups, missionary societies, and both temperance and philanthropic enterprises.

By the late nineteenth century and earlier in some places, middle-class people were also involved in a dizzying range of political clubs and societies. Some of these were broadly "liberal," perhaps the posture we associate most readily with the middle-class; however, middle-class people also flocked to confessional parties that were often—if not always—deeply conservative and respectful of traditional elites and to nationalist parties that were frequently both nativist and racist. Moreover, a not insubstantial number of them turned to radical or even revolutionary groups endorsing positions as diverse as anarchism, communism, bohemianism, and free love. It should also be noted that the nineteenth century also saw a very significant growth in working-class clubs and political organizations, and, in not a few areas, societies that sought to appeal to both middle-class and working-class groups, either by appealing to common confessional or national loyalties, or by taking up common moral concerns, such as temperance or prostitution. A great many largely middle-class organizations also actively sought out aristocratic patronage.

As all this suggests, there no distinctively middle-class politics in the nineteenth (or for that matter the twentieth) century. Affiliations varied according to town, the sector of the middle class from which one came, religion, nationality, and individual preference, among other factors. That having been said, there probably is a case to be made that a less ideological middle-class politics were to be found at the local level. Again, it is not to be expected that middle-class people have always agreed, or ever will. However, there is a tremendous amount of evidence that middle-class people were heavily involved, throughout Europe, in efforts to bolster local culture and commerce. This might involve gaining concessions from city governments in favor of assembly halls or other meeting places, lobbying for covered markets, better roads, new bridges, or better public health precautions, banning the running of livestock from the center of town, and attempting, with municipal assistance, to suppress popular customs that were deemed destructive of property. In eastern Europe, in particular, middle-class groups often lobbied for tax or trade concessions, or protection. This was particularly a problem for Jews who, whether rich, middle-class, or poor, were often the object of violent attacks or attempts—both legal and extra-legal—to limit their mobility, confine them to a narrow group of occupations, or extort money from them. Civic improvement with its close links to community policing and—in the case of some minority groups, community defense—was never the monopoly of middle-class people, but it was something they made peculiarly their own.

Middle-class education and its impact.

Education has long been closely linked to middle-class status. Middling town dwellers were already highly literate even in the late sixteenth century in many parts of Europe. The eighteenth and nineteenth centuries also saw a significant increase in middle-class women's literacy. Historically, middling or middle-class education had tended to have a more functionalist thrust than the education their betters received. There tended to be a good deal of emphasis on skills, such as bookkeeping (often for both boys and girls), and the preferred foreign languages were more likely to be commercial languages, such as French and German (or, sometimes in the Ottoman Empire, Arabic), rather than Latin and Greek. Literacy, as well as accounting skills, were routinely required of clerks and middle-class apprentices in the nineteenth century. Other skills that middle-class parents and teachers sought to inculcate into the children under their care might include better use of one's time, careful oversight of expenditures, a good writing hand, close attention to detail, and sexual restraint. None of these was unique to middle-class people, yet one does get the impression that middle-class parents and teachers went to unusual lengths to teach their children these various "prudential values." This tendency was perhaps attributable to the strains and insecurities that characterize this stratum of the population in most European countries, as well as to perceived need, in some places, to combat the continued appeal of aristocratic patterns of leisure and conspicuous consumption.

One very significant result of the high level of education accorded to women was the emergence of several middle-class women's occupations dependent either upon literacy or on a fairly high degree of education. The eighteenth century saw the establishing of purpose-built schools for girls, often, at least in western Europe, owned and directed by middle-class women entrepreneurs. In some countries such schools were run by aristocratic women and designed for aristocratic girls. In the eighteenth century, and even more in the nineteenth, significant numbers of women began penning novels and other literary productions for a living. Women journalists, newspaper impresarios, political controversialists, and feminists (such as Mary Wollstonecraft Godwin [1759–1797] in England, Olympe de Gouges [1748–1793] in France, or Eleanora de Fonseca Pimentel [1752–1799] in Naples) began to emerge, though the fact that Wollstonecraft died in childbirth, Gouges under the guillotine, and Fonseca Pimentel at the hands of a Neapolitan anti-Jacobin mob suggests something of the obstacles in the way of radical women. By the end of the nineteenth century there were women physicians in a number of European countries, virtually all of them of middle-class stock, and middle-class women also began to make inroads into government service (particularly within the emerging welfare or health sector), teaching, and even—in a few countries and in a very small way—the military officer corps. By the first decade of the twentieth century, there were small or large women's rights movements in almost all the European nations—in not a few cases several separate movements, broken down (as in the Czech lands) by ethnicity and religion, or, in Germany and some other places, by class and religion. Middle-class women's exuberant entry into the world of paid work and politics in country after country further undermines the claim that "separate spheres," if they ever existed in the full sense of the term, were as fundamental a feature of middle-class culture as has sometimes been claimed.

Middle-class morality and sexual behavior.

Sexual restraint had long been a central part of middle-class people's self-definition, though up through at least the seventeenth century, it had to compete in some countries with claims about the out-of-control sexuality of citizens' wives. Typically, in the early modern period, this ideal was linked to a vision of well-ordered, pious patriarchal households, in which women, children, and servants deferred happily to the authority of the male head; both women and men respected their marriage vows; and no woman went to the altar pregnant. Even a brief perusal of contemporary court

Portrait of a Family. Anonymous portrait of the family of Wilhelm Friedrich Erich, Hamburg, Germany, 1828. BILDARCHIV PREUSSISCHER KULTURBESITZ, BERLIN

records, middling people's own writings, or parish records confirms that middle-class people were not appreciably more likely than any other group to adhere to these admonitions in practice, and this may partially explain why they were so commonly accused of hypocrisy with respect to sexual morality.

A potentially greater problem for social historians is the great diversity across Europe in terms of the way institutions like the household, or marriage were defined. Thus, in some parts of Europe a middle-class family, particularly within what is sometimes called the rural bourgeoisie might include three or even four generations (historical demographers call this the stem family), while in other parts of Europe it might look more "nuclear," along what is sometimes thought of as the northwestern European model. Similarly, in some parts of Europe and in some classes, both men and women tended to marry in their mid-to late twenties with only a slight gap in ages, while in others they did so at younger ages; or women might marry substantially older or younger men. In some areas, and within some classes or religious groups, middling or middle-class marriage alliances came, at some point in the early modern period, to derive from the individualistic choice of the bride and groom. In other areas, classes, or religions, they continued, in some cases into the twentieth century, to be arranged by intermediaries. Because so many of the assumptions about what constitutes middle-class family culture have been based on the model of northwestern Europe, and specifically England, many questions remain about the ways other middle-class groups organized sexuality and family life.

One pattern that seems to have been widespread after the early twentieth century, though again this occurred at greatly varying speeds, was the early resort by middle-class families to the use of birth control. This occurred in part because of the greater likelihood of children surviving to adulthood, something that presumably was easier to achieve in the relatively clean, well-fed homes of the middle-class than in the squalid and starved habitations of the poor. Many commentators also attribute this phenomenon to a desire to invest greater educational resources in a smaller number of children, and in some countries it was bolstered by advocates of sex reform, and by feminists—as well as, in the post–World War II period, by some national governments. Again, we need to know more about how this trend spread historically, and how it conflicted and intersected with different religions, occupations, regions, and classes.

By the eighteenth or, some have argued, the nineteenth century, a well-developed discourse had arisen to the effect that middle-class people were the most moral, the most industrious, the most ingenious, and the most orderly of citizens. They were superior both to their feckless, idle, and self-indulgent superiors, and their crime-disposed, dirty, and riot-prone social inferiors. Against this there also developed a strong strain of criticism that identified the middle classes with greed, philistinism, narrowness, and hypocrisy. Karl Marx's *Capital* probably induced relatively few people to adopt dialectical materialism *in toto* (though the notion of the rise of the middle class did become an ineradicable part of most people's conception of the West). But it did revive certain older notions of middle-class philistinism and greed and present them in a new, modernized form. This posture of self-doubt became, over the course of the nineteenth century, very common among middle-class people themselves. Dynamic groups often excel at self-criticism (a tried-and-true form of narcissism), and the middle classes have always made time for self-examination.

At the dawn of the twentieth century one of the most interesting new developments in this vein came via the theories of Sigmund Freud (1856–1939). Psychoanalysis, based largely on clinical studies of middle-class Viennese girls, promised a whole series of new insights into sexuality, gender, unconscious drives, and the process of modernization. And it turned a spotlight on the whole problem of bourgeois hypocrisy, newly universalized and partially valorized as "sexual repression." In the 1930s members of the Frankfurt school, first in Frankfurt and then in exile in the United States, developed a series of syntheses of Freudian, Marxian, and Weberian thought that helped carry this strain of critical middle-class self-reflection into the twentieth century, emphasizing, among other things, a critique of enlightenment rationalism and technologism, and a new interest in the imprisoning (and occasionally liberating) possibilities of culture and consumerism.

The middle classes in the modern era: a balance sheet.

As we have seen, though the nineteenth-century middle classes at times displayed certain common characteristics, many factors militated against their developing a common consciousness. The middle classes were constantly fragmenting. Middle-class Protestants disliked the Catholics and winked at or participated in the persecution of Jews, while middle-class Jews were often riven by disagreements over assimilation and regional identity. Groups defined as "foreign" (for instance, Sudetenland Germans in Czechoslovakia) often saw themselves having little in common with countrymen of their same class. Middle-class women and middle-class men were, in many places, divided over women's education, the entry of women into the professions, religion, and sexuality.

More than anything else it was this divided character that was bequeathed to the twentieth century.

Looking back from the vantage point of the beginning of the twenty-first century, we can see that the project of making the world safe for business has had mixed success in the twentieth century. If it ever had been a distinctively middle-class project, if there really had been a middle-class ascendancy as complete as some people assert, and if trade had been the only things on most people's minds, neither World War I nor World War II—both of which did untold damage to trade and infrastructure, as well as causing the deaths of millions of people—would have happened as they did. Clearly the turn to socialism in Russia after 1917 and of large parts of east central and Eastern Europe after 1945 did little for private enterprise. It did much, however, to build up an extensive class of *apparatchiks,* many of them thoroughly imbued with recognizably bourgeois tastes and managerial ideals, committed to ideals of universal education and better public health, and much occupied with infrastructural development.

Still, the world is undoubtedly safer for some middle-class people and their investments than it once was. In the twentieth century, and especially in the post-1945 period, generations of incremental improvements in commercial law, insurance, management efficiency, worker-management relations, education, infrastructure, communications, and medicine, largely overseen by middle-class people and offering an opportunity for many more to attain that status, have given rise to an unprecedented degree of prosperity over large parts of Europe. Even the former Soviet bloc has not been immune to these changes. There has been an unprecedented unlocking of consumer demand, unlike anything seen in previous centuries.

However, one result of this has been to render the term "middle-class" even more problematic than before. The vast majority of the population of many European countries would now be considered middle class if one went by levels of consumption alone. Universal education, democracy, welfare states, and relatively cheap goods have revolutionized the ways people live and think. Aristocracies and monarchies have largely disappeared; where they do survive they enjoy largely ritual functions. To a far greater degree than was true in previous centuries, there is now a common mass culture in which most people participate (or in which they aspire to participate).

At the same time, modernization has led to increasing inequalities in income, while the need for cheap labor during the postwar economic boom (exacerbated by the fact that rising expectations had persuaded many Europeans to refuse the dirtiest, least

Consumerism in the Former Soviet Bloc. Vaci Utica, a shopping street in Budapest, 1995. BARRY LEWIS/©CORBIS

prestigious, and least remunerative jobs) led to a major influx of people from the former colonies and less prosperous parts of Europe, such as Greece and Turkey, into the more dynamic economies to the north and west. Some of these immigrants have raised several generations in their adopted countries and have themselves succeeded in achieving a level of success that might be called "middle class." Key players in the new global economy, the more prosperous parts of Europe now benefit hugely from cheap goods manufactured in less-developed regions, while an "investing class" supports global free-trade initiatives, multinational mergers, and expansive advertising campaigns that decimate local industries and already fragile middle-class groupings in formerly protectionist Third World economies. Of course, in some fundamental sense, this is not new.

Social historians often call for the abolition of the term "middle class," but it seems to have a life of its own. The many contemporary projects intended to overcome the heritage of socialism in east central and eastern Europe routinely decry the absence of an entrepreneurial middle class. Few discussions of economic development in the Third World can do without a plea for policies designed to build up or offer support to the "middle class"; with the advent of globalization these voices have grown shriller but, if anything, louder. Western European politicians routinely seek to appeal to "middle-class" groups. Social critics still blame them implicitly for much that is wrong with society, though there is a trend toward pointing the finger more precisely at "multinational corporations," "polluters of the environment," "the World Bank and the IMF," "The European Union," "NATO," or the "energy-wasting First World" rather than the old "middle class." Already claims are being made to the effect that Europeans (along with North Americans and a few others) now constitute a new kind of aristocracy, that, in the way of the old aristocracies, monopolizes the world's resources, interferes disproportionately in its politics, and seeks to define its culture, all by virtue of "blood rights" based upon race, geography, and history. It remains to be seen to what extent the passing of the critical torch to developing nations and their own intelligentsias will result in entirely new conceptions of individuals and collectivities, and to what extent it will end up recapitulating the old antinomies in a new context.

See also **The Industrial Revolution** *(volume 2);* **Urbanization** *(volume 2);* **Suburbs and New Towns** *(volume 2);* **Nationalism** *(volume 2);* **Gender and Work** *(volume 4);* **Gender and Education** *(volume 4);* **History of the Family** *(volume 4);* **Sexual Behavior and Sexual Morality** *(volume 4);* **Psychiatry and Psychology** *(volume 4);* **Middle-Class Work** *(volume 4);* **Schools and Schooling** *(volume 5); and other articles in this section.*

BIBLIOGRAPHY

Blackbourn, David, and Geoff Eley. *The Peculiarities of German History: Bourgeois Society and Politics in Nineteenth-Century Germany.* Oxford and New York, 1984.

Davidoff, Leonore, and Catherine Hall. *Family Fortunes: Men and Women of the English Middle Class, 1780–1850.* Chicago, 1987.

De Vries, Jan. *Economy of Europe in an Age of Crisis: 1600–1750.* Cambridge, U.K., 1976.

Frader, Laura L., and Sonya O. Rose, eds. *Gender and Class in Modern Europe.* Ithaca, N.Y., 1996.

Green, S. J. D. "In Search of Bourgeois Civilization: Institutions and Ideals in 19th Century Britain." *Northern History* 28 (1992): 228–247.

Hunt, Lynn, Avery. *Politics, Culture, and Class in the French Revolution.* Berkeley and Los Angeles, 1984.

Hunt, Margaret R. *The Middling Sort: Commerce, Gender, and the Family in England, 1680–1780.* Berkeley and Los Angeles, 1996.

Hurd, Madeleine. "Education, Morality, and the Politics of Class in Hamburg and Stockholm, 1870–1914." *Journal of Contemporary History* 31, no. 4 (1996): 619–650.

Jones, Robert. "Jacob Sievers, Enlightened Reform, and the Development of a 'Third Estate' in Russia." *The Russian Review* 36 (October 1977): 424–437.

Kocka, Jürgen, and Allen Mitchell, eds. *Bourgeois Society in Nineteenth-Century Europe.* Oxford, 1993.

Mantran, Robert. "Foreign Merchants and the Minorities in Istanbul During the Sixteenth and Seventeenth Centuries." In *Christians and Jews in the Ottoman Empire: The Functioning of a Plural Society.* Edited by Benjamin Braude and Bernard Lewis. New York and London, 1982.

Marx, Karl. *Capital: A Critique of Political Economy.* New York, 1984. Original published in 1867.

Marx, Karl, and Friedrich Engels. "The Communist Manifesto." In *Basic Writings on Politics and Philosophy.* Edited by Lewis S. Feuer. Garden City, N.Y., 1959. Pages 1–41. Originally published in 1848.

Mayer, Arno. "The Lower Middle Classes as Historical Problem." *Journal of Modern History* 47, (Sept. 1975): 409–436.

Meininger, Thomas A. "Teachers and Schoolboards in the Late Bulgarian Renaissance." In *Bulgaria Past and Present: Studies in History, Literature, Economics, Music, Sociology, Folklore, and Linguistics.* Edited by Thomas Butler. Columbus, Oh., 1976.

Schama, Simon. *The Embarrassment of Riches: An Interpretation of Dutch Culture in the Golden Age.* New York, 1987.

Stoler, Ann Laura. *Race and the Education of Desire: Foucault's History of Sexuality and the Colonial Order of Things.* Durham, N.C., 1995.

Todorov, Nikolai. "The City in the Bulgarian Lands from the Fifteenth to the Nineteenth Century." In *Bulgaria Past and Present: Studies in History, Literature, Economics, Music, Sociology, Folklore, and Linguistics.* Edited by Thomas Butler. Columbus, Oh., 1976.

PROFESSIONALS AND PROFESSIONALIZATION

James C. Albisetti

The word "profession" in English and its equivalents in the Romance languages originally had a religious connotation, as in "profession of faith." Its second major meaning was occupation or job, what someone does to earn a living, as in the distinction between an amateur and a professional athlete. In the Germanic languages, words such as *Beruf* in German and *beroep* in Dutch had similar connotations, combining notions of a religious calling or vocation with a more mundane sense of occupation. Thus all who worked had a profession.

Yet ever since the later Middle Ages, European languages and societies have also distinguished certain professions—especially the clergy, lawyers, and physicians—as distinct from the rest. Such "liberal" professions did not involve production or trade, as manual occupations did. Most of their practitioners obtained advanced education in the liberal arts and in their specialties at universities, although in the case of the English common law, training took place at the Inns of Court, sometimes called the third university in England alongside Oxford and Cambridge.

Throughout the early modern era, from the sixteenth through the eighteenth centuries, professionals played important but far from leading roles in societies dominated by monarchs and hereditary aristocracies. As will be shown, their authority and autonomy were circumscribed in many ways. English cartoons depicting lawyers as devils and the sharp ridicule that writers such as Molière and Voltaire directed at physicians, and in the latter's case at clergy as well, suggest both the visibility and the limited respect that they enjoyed. From this perspective, the nineteenth and early twentieth centuries emerge as the great age of professionalization, when physicians and lawyers gained significantly in prestige and power, and other groups—engineers, architects, dentists, teachers, accountants, nurses—began to fight for similar positions in society.

The main era of professionalization thus coincided with the transition from an estate-based to a class-based society, where merit and achievement displaced birth as the major pathway to status and influence. Yet the professions occupied an ambiguous place in the classic examinations of the rise of the middle classes in this era. Adam Smith considered them to do "unproductive labor," and Karl Marx's definition of classes according to their relationship to the means of production also left professionals in an uncertain position. Many professionals themselves, with a devotion to avowedly unpractical classical education and a frequently expressed disdain for "materialism," did not identify themselves closely with merchants and industrialists. Such distinctions have led many German scholars to divide the middle class into two groups, the educated and the economic bourgeoisie (*Bildungs- und Wirtschaftsbürgertum*).

Modern scholarly attention to the professions as a whole began with sociologists rather than historians; the most influential work has probably been that of Magali Sarfatti Larson. Sociologists tended to build their models and theories of the professions primarily on the experience of lawyers and physicians in England and the United States. A composite picture drawn from such works would suggest that a profession is a full-time occupation that brings high status and a comfortable if not magnificent income. It is based on formal training in a field of specialized knowledge that is confirmed by some type of certification. The professional provides services to clients, not products to customers, and earns fees or even honoraria rather than wages or a salary. Members of a profession follow a code of professional ethics, policed by associations of professionals rather than the state or some other outside body. Larson herself suggested that such professional associations also try to constitute and control the market for their members' services, especially in limiting competition from uncertified practitioners.

Occupations striving to achieve such professional status thus pursue collective rather than individual mobility in what has been called a "professionalization project." Such projects often involve the aspiration to reach, or not to fall behind, the condition of another profession (or of the same one in another country), as several examples from Germany in the late nineteenth century illustrate. In 1878 architects in the civil service opposed the admission of graduates of nonclassical secondary schools to their ranks because they would be at a disadvantage vis-à-vis classically trained civil servants with law degrees. For many years the German Physicians' Association resisted admission of young men with Latin but not Greek, and of women, to the study of medicine because such a step would lower their prestige compared to lawyers. Secondary-school teachers fought for many years, and ultimately obtained in 1909, equal pay with judges in the civil service who had university training of equivalent length. A Protestant Pastors' Association in the Prussian state church, founded in 1892, sought pay scales equal to those of secondary teachers for the same reason.

Larson's analysis contains elements of both the benevolent and the conspiratorial interpretations of professionalization that exist throughout the scholarly literature. On the one hand, the process appears as the victory of expertise, honesty, or even disinterested service over incompetence, fraud, and quackery. On the other, it involves the establishment of monopoly, exclusion of nonprofessionals, and limitation of choice for the public. Whether a regulation such as the establishment in 1858 of a Medical Register of all medical practitioners in England did more to protect the public from incompetents or to protect those on the Register from competition is an open question. Given the frequency with which professional associations tried to limit numbers through increased educational requirements, in the long run monopoly and expertise may well have worked together.

Historians and sociologists have offered various criticisms of this functionalist model of professions. One is that it treats the professional as defined by his—rarely her—work, to the exclusion of concerns of religion, ethnicity, gender, age, or region. It also views members of professions primarily as united in common aims rather than as competing with each other for clients or divided between elites and ordinary practitioners. It ignores ethnic and religious divisions within a profession, an issue of great significance in central and eastern Europe, where, for example, the creation of a Czech-language university in Prague in 1883 alongside the venerable German one reflected divisions in the professions and the population at large. In Hungary as of 1910, 49 percent of doctors, 45 percent of lawyers, and 39 percent of engineers were Jewish, a situation that tended more to divide than to unite the professions.

Another broad criticism of the functionalist model is its too narrow focus on the individual physician or lawyer in practice for himself. Not only does this focus exclude from consideration the clergy and military, which generally operate in hierarchical organizations separate from the market, but from the perspective of all of continental Europe it seriously underplays the role of the state in the certification, regulation, and even employment of professionals. Among the most striking examples are the creation of a new legal profession in Russia by decree in 1864 and the establishment of almost all the professions after 1878 in the newly independent Bulgaria, a country that had no university for the first ten years of its existence. Some German scholars have suggested the term "professionalization from above" to distinguish this process from the "projects" of existing occupational groups. Others, accepting the Anglo-American view of the free professional, have even argued that German academic *Berufen* in which large numbers of practitioners were state employees should not be considered as professions; they often speak of a process of *Berufskonstruktion* rather than professionalization. An inclusive view of learned professions needs to take into account their relations not only with clients but also with the state and with the universities, the transmitters and discoverers of the knowledge on which professional expertise relies.

THE EARLY MODERN PERIOD

In this era, the Christian clergy in Europe possessed some characteristics of a modern profession, even though in many countries it remained a separate "estate." Priests and pastors, at least in theory, possessed special knowledge and some form of certification; they performed services such as baptism, marriage, and distribution of communion that others could not. The Protestant Reformation, of course, fragmented the clergy, though many regions retained a high level of religious homogeneity. The Lutheran doctrine of the priesthood of all believers, along with translations of the Bible into vernacular languages, reduced to a degree the special expertise of pastors. The rise of dissident sects and even itinerant preachers also undermined the clergy's monopoly.

The hierarchical structure of the established churches, whether Catholic, Orthodox, or Protestant, meant that the individual priest or pastor had a very different relation to colleagues than does a member of a modern professional association. The extent to which prominent positions (or sinecures), especially in the Catholic Church, remained in the hands of younger sons of royal or noble families suggests how small a role academic merit played. The dependence for appointments on patrons, or in the case of dissenting

Lawyers. Lawyer with a client, watercolor by Honoré Daumier (1808–1879). NATIONAL MUSEUM OF WALES, CARDIFF

sects on the congregations themselves, meant clergymen had little self-regulating autonomy. As late as 1835, private individuals controlled appointments to 48 percent of the livings in the Church of England, bishops 12 percent, the Crown 9 percent, and various institutions, especially the colleges of Oxford and Cambridge, the remaining 31 percent.

Lawyers in early modern Europe had more characteristics of a modern profession, although they certainly did not have a monopoly of legal business or the administration of justice. The extreme case was Russia, where until 1864 there were no formal requirements for judges, court clerks, prosecutors, or attorneys, although the state did employ officials with legal training. Farther west, in many areas nobles administered justice on their own estates, royal servants without legal training controlled some courts, and churches ran others.

Most of Europe witnessed the development of a two- or three-tiered system of legal practitioners in the early modern era. Holders of law degrees, or in England those barristers admitted to the "bar" by the Inns of Court, established a monopoly over verbal pleading in court and some forms of legal advice. On the Continent these lawyers were known by such terms as *avocat, abogado, avvocato, Advokat,* or *Anwalt.* Below them in prestige was a second group, trained primarily through apprenticeship rather than formal schooling, men who were experts in procedure and expedited—or deliberately delayed—the progress of cases through the courts. The *procureur, procurador, procuratore,* or *Prokurator* was more often an officer of the court than the representative of a client, in contrast to the English solicitor, who also trained through apprenticeship. The *solicitador* also existed in Spain,

although with no formal requirements. By the late eighteenth century, Prussia and much of Switzerland had moved toward a single type of attorney, abandoning these distinct levels.

Lenard Berlanstein's study of lawyers in the region of Toulouse during the eighteenth century suggests the high level of self-recruitment in the legal profession, as well as the social distinctions between its levels. Thirty-one percent of *avocats* were sons of *avocats,* and a similar percentage of *procureurs* were sons of *procureurs.* Whereas no son of an *avocat* had entered the lower branch, about 11 percent of *avocats* were upwardly mobile sons of *procureurs.*

Notaries or scriveners also performed significant amounts of legal business, especially creation and verification of documents in societies with low rates of literacy. They also trained by apprenticeship. The Company of Scriveners in London claimed a monopoly over conveyancing, or legal transfer of property, from the early 1600s until the mid-1700s, when solicitors, newly organized as the Society of Gentlemen Practisers, succeeded in breaking the guild's monopoly, an early example of a professionalization project aimed at enlarging the market for attorneys' services.

Physicians in early modern Europe enjoyed less of a monopoly than did lawyers, confronting as they did a wide variety of barber-surgeons, herbalists, midwives, and other purveyors of cures, at least some of whom could claim as much therapeutic success as physicians. Medicine functioned more like a trade than did law, which helps to explain why many fewer nobles undertook its study than obtained at least some legal training. For many physicians, the practice of medicine was not a full-time occupation, if only because it did not provide a comfortable income. Those fortunate enough to serve a monarch or wealthy noble ended up in a client-patron relationship far removed from the ideal of the autonomous professional.

As in the legal profession, medicine had several types of practitioners. Physicians, usually with a university degree, dealt primarily with internal diseases; they alone were supposed to prescribe medicine. Surgeons, who generally learned through apprenticeship, treated external wounds and infections and might set broken bones, thus engaging in manual work that physicians avoided. In rural areas, such surgeons were often the only medical practitioners available. Apothecaries dispensed, but were not supposed to prescribe, medicine. In England these three different groups developed as the Royal College of Physicians, the Company (later College) of Surgeons, and the Society of Apothecaries. Yet by the early nineteenth century such divisions were breaking down; what became the British Medical Association had its origins in a movement of "general practitioners" who possessed multiple qualifications.

During the eighteenth century, Dutch and Scottish universities were leading centers of innovative medical education. Between 1750 and 1800 Scottish medical schools graduated about twenty-six hundred physicians, ten times the production of Oxford and Cambridge. On the Continent, advances in practical medicine also emerged from institutions established to train army surgeons, such as the Joseph Akademie founded in Vienna in the 1780s and the Pepinière established in Berlin a decade later.

The "profession of arms" in this era was a profession only in a loose sense. Most officer corps were dominated by, and some were restricted to, aristocrats and upper gentry. In England, officers' commissions could be purchased as late as 1870. Although all officers underwent special training, formal educational requirements developed most consistently in the less prestigious engineering and artillery branches. When England opened an artillery school at Woolwich in 1741, it was the last major power to do so.

By the late eighteenth century, lawyers, physicians, and clergymen certainly enjoyed a reasonable amount of prestige on the basis of their specialized training and their social functions. Yet in societies that were still predominantly agricultural and where members of the nobility still dominated politics and patronage, they had neither the status nor the autonomy that many of their successors in the nineteenth and twentieth centuries would seek, and that some would obtain.

THE MODERN ERA

In the modern era, political upheavals often provided the opportunity or the necessity to restructure the professions. Most drastic was the dismantling of the legal and medical professions in 1791 by the revolutionary French government, hostile as it was to special social privileges and to symbols of the Old Regime. In the course of the nineteenth century, the unifications of Italy and Germany, the Compromise of 1867 that resulted in the Austro-Hungarian Dual Monarchy, the great reforms in Russia after the Crimean War, and even the new Swiss constitution of 1874 brought important changes to the professions. That so many of these changes occurred during the great age of laissez-faire liberalism, when guild restrictions and legal discrimination on the basis of religion disappeared from much of Europe, led to intriguing conflicts between defenders of freedom of occupation and professionals interested in control over the market for their services.

In the first decade of the nineteenth century, Napoleon recreated professions of certified lawyers and physicians in France. The reform of the legal profession established orders of *avocats* who controlled the admission of degree holders to practice through a system of apprenticeship and the swearing of an oath. They also enforced professional ethics, but the orders had no control over the number of students graduating from the legal faculties. The new system again included a second tier of attorneys, now known as *avoués,* who, though still tied to particular courts, came to represent clients more like the English solicitors. With some modifications, this system also had lasting influence in areas that had been parts of Napoleon's French empire, including the later independent Belgium, German territory west of the Rhine River, and northern Italy.

When Russia created a legal profession separate from the state service in 1864, it adopted a mixture of Western models. It took from Prussia the single-tier or fused profession, from France and England the idea of councils of the bar to regulate the profession, especially apprenticeship after the degree. For many years, however, such councils existed in only a few major cities. Shortages of trained lawyers also led to establishment of other classes of attorneys with lesser qualifications and fewer privileges. Quotas limiting the number of Jews admitted to the bar, introduced by Alexander III, forced many Jewish attorneys to remain in the lower categories, whatever their qualifications.

The Austrian and Hungarian halves of the Dual Monarchy adopted new regulations for the legal profession in 1868 and 1874, respectively. Both lifted restrictions on the number of attorneys admitted to practice and provided for creation of lawyers' chambers. Whereas the Hungarian regulations imitated the French system of having the chambers control admission to practice, Austria retained state examinations as the crucial determinant. In imperial Germany, new regulations introduced in 1878 brought the single-tier profession to all of the country and also established lawyers' chambers with disciplinary powers. Yet the German lawyers' chambers did not have control over entrance to the profession, and graduates intending to enter private practice still did the large majority of their apprenticeship in the civil service.

The Swiss constitution of 1874 allowed the individual cantons to decide whether to require a proof of competence for professionals. Shortly thereafter, several cantons abolished the "lawyers' monopoly" over pleading in court, in the case of Zurich allowing anyone with full citizenship rights to do so. Court decisions in the case of Emilie Kempin-Spyri later clarified that a woman, even with a law degree, did not possess such rights and could not plead. A referendum in the canton of Zurich in 1898 reversed both decisions, re-creating a closed bar and granting women access to it. In the late nineteenth century only Sweden had as open a bar as did these Swiss cantons.

When Napoleon reestablished certification for physicians in 1803, he did so without creating any corporate body like the orders of lawyers; university degrees sufficed for admission to practice. Nineteenth-century France also possessed lower-level medical practitioners known as *officiers de santé*, or officers of health, in essence replacements for the Old Regime's surgeons. Other countries also continued to have similar less thoroughly trained medical personnel. Prussia, however, eliminated its schools for such surgeons around 1850; Austria followed suit by 1871, closing even the Joseph Akademie. France eliminated the officers of health in 1892. That their Russian equivalents, known as the *feldsher*, continued to exist until after the Bolshevik Revolution of 1917 suggests the continuing shortage of trained physicians in rural Russia.

Perhaps the most controversial regulation of the medical profession was that enacted in 1869 by the North German Confederation and extended to the southern German states after unification in 1871. This regulation took place in the context of a new Commercial Code (*Gewerbe Ordnung*), and thus treated medicine as a trade. The new rules did establish a uniform four-year university course for prospective physicians and freed practitioners from an earlier requirement that they had to treat all patients who came to them. Yet in accord with the Commercial Code's general support for freedom of occupation, it allowed anyone to practice the "healing arts," within some limits, as long as he or she did not claim to be a certified physician. Many physicians would later consider their inclusion under the code as humiliating and its regulations an invitation to quackery.

Physicians' chambers with some disciplinary powers were established in Prussia in 1887, Austria in 1891, and Italy in 1910. These bodies did not control entry into the profession, however, as some lawyers' chambers did. Corporate groups of English physicians, even after the creation of a General Medical Council in 1858, had more control over entry than did most of their continental colleagues.

The percentage of physicians in private practice tended to decrease as one moved from west to east. Even in England, some were employed by Poor Law Unions to treat the destitute. Many Italian cities employed physicians for similar purposes; in 1876, Hun-gary mandated that towns hire physicians for the poor. A significant number of doctors in Russia worked for the local government boards, or *zemstva*. In Bulgaria as of 1910 only 20 percent of physicians were in private practice.

The development of health and disability insurance for workers, beginning in Germany in the 1880s, had mixed consequences for the professional position of physicians. It brought them more patients as workers had to visit them for verification of claims, but it also subordinated them to insurance boards that were often dominated by workers. The issue of whether insurance boards could dictate which physicians their patients had to use even led to very "unprofessional" behavior by German physicians—a series of strikes in several cities in the 1900s.

As mentioned above, the nineteenth century witnessed drives for professional status by several new occupations. A common feature was a transition from on-the-job training or apprenticeship to formal academic culture, what in the history of engineering has been called a shift from "shop culture" to "school culture." Such academic training seldom took place in the established universities; when it did, as sometimes happened with dentistry and pharmacy, entrance requirements could be lower and the course of study shorter than for traditional fields. More typical was the experience in Sweden, which founded outside its universities new technical colleges, schools of business, an agricultural college, and institutes for forestry, veterinary science, social work, and dentistry. The establishment of a chair in engineering at Cambridge University in 1875 was an unusual step; even there, no engineering laboratory existed until 1894.

Engineering and teaching can illustrate some of the issues involved in professionalization of the less traditional occupations. In the eighteenth century some monarchs had created corps of royal servants trained in technical fields, such as the graduates of the French École des Ponts et Chaussées (school for bridges and roads) founded in 1747 and those of a school of mines opened in 1783. In this area the French Revolution did not break with the traditions of the Old Regime; in 1795, it added the École Polytechnique, which in the course of the nineteenth century became more prestigious than the medical or legal faculties in France. Yet even this elite institution provided a striking example of the sense of inferiority associated with "practical" studies when in the 1850s it began to award extra points on its notoriously competitive entrance examination to boys who had obtained the *baccalauréat*, or classical secondary diploma, that was a requirement for lawyers, physicians, and secondary teachers.

Apart from elite groups like the *Polytechniciens,* engineers often struggled to establish a clear professional identity and a controlled field of activity. An engineer could be an entrepreneur or an employee; and whatever his training, it was often difficult to say what an engineer did that an architect, builder, or skilled mechanic could not do. England saw the creation of a Society of Civil Engineers as early as 1771 and even a royal charter for an Institute of Civil Engineers in 1828; yet the first examinations to certify engineers did not take place until 1898. In Italy, only with the creation of a national register of engineers in 1922 were some official functions as inspectors reserved to those so recognized. Licensing of engineers came to Hungary in 1923.

In the field of education, teachers in boys' secondary schools gained general recognition as professionals in the nineteenth century, even though most were salaried employees, often of the state. Graduation from a university became the normal preparation, to which many countries added some form of pedagogical training and/or practice teaching. England, where secondary education enjoyed the greatest autonomy from the state, was an exception; headmasters of private schools resisted the notion that their teachers (or they themselves) needed attestation of pedagogical competence.

Elementary teachers often organized earlier and more comprehensively than did those in secondary education, yet their professionalization projects usually fell short of the desired success. Lacking university education and often from distinctly lower socioeconomic backgrounds than other nineteenth-century professionals, elementary teachers could not claim the income or prestige of the learned professions. Their work with children replicated what all parents did, thus did not appear to be based on any special skills, a perception reinforced by the high rate of turnover among them. Both a result and a cause of the continuing low status of elementary teachers was that many of them were women or even teenaged girls.

WOMEN AND THE PROFESSIONS

Throughout most of modern European history the liberal professions have been male preserves. In medicine the advance of professional monopoly in the nineteenth century involved the exclusion of women from some areas, especially assistance at childbirth. The development of obstetrics and gynecology tended to bring the physician rather than the midwife to the aid of women in labor.

Sociologists often speak of the "typing" of certain occupations as "women's work" and of the "tip-ping" of an occupation in that direction once women reach a certain percentage of those working in a field. Among the less prestigious professions in modern European history, nursing is an example of the former phenomenon, elementary school teaching of the latter. Nursing proved particularly difficult to professionalize, for several reasons. Well into the nineteenth century most nursing was little more than custodial work performed by women of the lower classes. An alternative model developed as members of Catholic orders or Protestant deaconesses devoted themselves to care of the sick, but this made nursing appear as a charitable activity more than a skilled profession. The example of Florence Nightingale and the development of the Red Cross from the 1860s helped make nursing a more respectable occupation with formal training. A British Nurses' Association formed in 1888 to push for a professional register like that existing for physicians, an idea opposed by Nightingale. Legislation authorizing such a register did not pass until 1919, with the register itself being created in 1925.

Women had served as teachers throughout the early modern period, though most often in family settings or small, private "dame schools" that taught young children. From the late sixteenth century Catholic teaching orders such as the Ursulines ran both boarding and day schools for girls. Beginning in the early nineteenth century, formal training and certification of young women to teach in the burgeoning public elementary schools spread across Europe. The rate and degree of feminization of the teaching profession, however, were far from uniform. Around 1900, the proportion of elementary school teachers who were women varied from about 20 percent in Germany to nearly 75 percent in both England and Russia. Such women had less professional autonomy than did their male colleagues, being subjected at various times to marriage bans and often paid noticeably less for the same work. That many women teachers left after a few years to get married reinforced the idea that elementary teaching was not a professional career.

Secondary schooling in Europe remained overwhelmingly single-sex until the 1960s and 1970s, except in the Soviet Union and its satellites. Women secondary teachers long remained restricted to teaching girls. Yet even in this area, practices varied widely. Men had virtually disappeared from girls' secondary schools in England by the 1890s, and in France few men taught on a full-time basis in such schools. In Austria and Russia at that time, however, girls' schools tended to employ women only in the lower grades or in language, music, and sewing classes.

The struggles of women to gain access to the medical profession have been well documented by

Women in Medicine. Examination of Elizabeth Garrett Anderson, an American candidate for a medical degree from the Faculty of Medicine, Paris, 1865. COURTESY OF THE NEW YORK ACADEMY OF MEDICINE LIBRARY

Thomas Bonner. Broad interest in the admission of women to medical study and practice emerged in much of Europe during the 1860s, when the "woman question" became a hotly debated topic. The University of Zurich, founded only in 1834, gave the first modern medical degree to a woman, the Russian Nadezhda Suslova, in 1867. By the turn of the century women had gained access to practice across the continent. In England and Russia, medical training took place mostly in single-sex environments, but elsewhere women gained admission to existing universities.

Supporters of women physicians often argued that they were needed to protect the modesty of female patients, and many of the pioneers specialized in obstetrics and pediatrics. In the struggle for admission of women to the legal profession, however, arguments about a special need for female lawyers or about special female talents for the law played a much smaller role. That demands for access to the bar rested so squarely on doctrines of equal rights may well have contributed to the fact that in every European country admission of women to the legal profession trailed their admission to medicine. Success came in some areas—the Scandinavian countries, the Netherlands, France, and some Swiss cantons—around the turn of the century. In most of the rest of Europe, women gained access to the bar in the years after World War I. Two holdouts were Hungary and Bulgaria, which did not allow female attorneys until after World War II.

DEPROFESSIONALIZATION

Professionals can lose as well as gain status, income, control of the market, and autonomy. Over the last two centuries, the process of professionalization has undergone a variety of reversals. The decline of the clergy from its position as first estate of the realm to a profession ignored, if still granted respect, by large segments of the population is the most obvious long-term example. The abolition of the legal and medical professions during the French Revolution was a much more radical, if less enduring, eradication of professional status and privilege. The lay competition for doctors allowed under the German Commercial Code of 1869 and that for lawyers in the canton of Zurich under the Swiss constitution of 1874 serve as examples of loss of control of the market for services. Oversupplies of new entrants to the professions, whether caused by booming university enrollments or, as in Hungary after 1919, by the migration of professionals from lost territories, have devalued credentials for many. Legislation mandating the admission of women to the legal profession, which proved necessary everywhere but the Netherlands, amounted to a partial loss of control over entrance by the bar associations and lawyers' chambers.

Authoritarian governments in the nineteenth century often made it difficult or impossible for trained professionals to form associations. In the twentieth century, dictatorships have overturned status hierarchies and undermined or abolished professional autonomy in many ways. Perhaps the most insidious occurred in the first months of the Third Reich, when the Nazi regime issued decrees aimed at "restoration" of, and prevention of overcrowding in, the civil service. Under the guise of restoring prestige and limiting competition, the Nazi state expelled communists, socialists, Jews, and women from positions in the civil service, professions, and universities. Although such measures may have been in line with the professionalization project of German nationalist male professionals, these decrees also obliterated any notion of professional autonomy as it had been conceived in the nineteenth century.

In the late twentieth century, two less blatant processes eroded older ideas of the professions in other ways. One is the decline, especially in medicine and law, of the individual practitioner who for many formed the model of the professional. Members of large law or engineering firms, or physicians in group practice, continue to have advanced training and certification, but they have often become employees as much as autonomous professionals. The second process has been the proliferation of academic credentials in an age of mass higher education, which has led to more and more occupations claiming professional status, not all of which can enjoy significant prestige. Important as well has been the devaluation of the concept of a professional itself. When a German hotel advertises the availability of a "state-certified masseur" and German automobile manufacturers show "professional drivers" on their test tracks, it appears that the twenty-first century may see a return to the earlier meaning of the word as any occupation.

See also **Civil Society; Bureaucracy** *(volume 2);* **Medical Practioners and Medicine; Middle-Class Work** *(volume 4);* **Higher Education; Teachers** *(volume 5); and other articles in this section.*

BIBLIOGRAPHY

Abel, Richard L., and Philip S. C. Lewis, eds. *Lawyers in Society.* 3 vols. Berkeley, Calif., Los Angeles, and London, 1988–1989.

Albisetti, James C. "The Feminization of Teaching in the Nineteenth Century: A Comparative Perspective." *History of Education* 22 (1993): 253–264.

Albisetti, James C. "*Portia ante Portas:* Women and the Legal Profession in Europe, ca. 1870–1925." *Journal of Social History* 33 (2000): 825–857.

Balzer, Harvey, ed. *Russia's Missing Middle Class: The Professions in Russian History.* Armonk, New York, and London, 1996.

Berlanstein, Lenard R. *The Barristers of Toulouse in the Eighteenth Century.* Baltimore, 1975.

Bonner, Thomas Neville. *Becoming a Physician: Medical Education in Britain, France, Germany, and the United States, 1750–1945.* New York and Oxford, 1995.

Bonner, Thomas Neville. *To the Ends of the Earth: Women's Search for Education in Medicine.* Cambridge, Mass., 1992.

Burrage, Michael and Rolf Torstendahl, eds. *Professions in Theory and History: Rethinking the Study of the Professions.* London, 1990.

Corfield, Penelope J. *Power and the Professions in Britain, 1700–1850.* London and New York, 1995.

Frieden, Nancy Mandelker. *Russian Physicians in an Era of Reform and Revolution, 1856–1905.* Princeton, N.J., 1981.

Geison, Gerald L., ed. *Professions and the French State, 1700–1900.* Philadelphia, 1984.

Jarausch, Konrad H. *The Unfree Professions: German Lawyers, Teachers, and Engineers, 1900–1950.* New York and Oxford, 1990.

Jarausch, Konrad H., and Geoffrey Cocks, eds. *German Professions, 1800–1950.* New York and Oxford, 1990.

Kagan, Richard L. *Lawsuits and Litigants in Castile, 1500–1700.* Chapel Hill, N.C., 1981.

Kovacs, Maria M. *Liberal Professions and Illiberal Politics: Hungary from the Habsburgs to the Holocaust.* New York, 1994.

Larson, Magali Sarfatti. *The Rise of Professionalism: A Sociological Analysis.* Berkeley, Calif., 1977.

Malatesta, Maria, ed. *Society and the Professions in Italy, 1860–1914.* Translated by Adrian Belton. Cambridge, U.K., 1995.

McClelland, Charles E. *The German Experience of Professionalization: Modern Learned Professions and Their Organizations from the Early Nineteenth Century to the Hitler Era.* Cambridge, U.K., 1991.

McClelland, Charles, Stephan Merl, and Hannes Siegrist, eds. *Professionen in modernen Osteuropa/Professions in Modern Eastern Europe.* Berlin, 1995.

Perkin, Harold. *The Rise of Professional Society: England since 1880.* London and New York, 1989.

Prest, Wilfred R., ed. *Lawyers in Early Modern Europe and America.* New York, 1981.

Prest, Wilfred R., ed. *The Professions in Early Modern England.* London, 1987.

Siegrist, Hannes. *Advokat, Bürger, und Staat: Sozialgeschichte der Rechtsanwälte in Deutschland, Italien, und der Schweiz (18.–20. Jh).* 2 vols. Frankfurt am Main, 1996.

Witz, Anne. *Professions and Patriarchy.* London and New York, 1992.

STUDENTS

Keith Vernon

Students occupy a curious social position. They are in a transitory phase and do not quite make up a socioeconomic, gender, or age group. They are an elite drawn predominantly from privileged sectors of society and destined for positions of authority, yet they are frequently poor, have few responsibilities, and are constantly associated with disorder. Until the late twentieth century students constituted only a tiny minority of national populations but carried enormous political, social, economic, and cultural significance. Inevitably the term has been applied variously at different times, and it has been argued that the student as an identifiable and self-conscious social role only acquired currency during the early nineteenth century. Here the term will be used to refer broadly to people attending a university or comparable institution of higher learning. Three aspects of students as a social group will be considered: First, the question of the size and composition of the student population; second, the nature of and parameters affecting student life and experience; and finally, the problem of student movements that have on occasion threatened the social and political order.

THE STUDENT POPULATION

The dimensions of the student population at any particular time are not easy to determine. Records are frequently incomplete, and definitions vary. Enrollment is one thing, attendance at classes another, and completing a degree something else altogether. Nevertheless, it is important to try to gain some idea of how large the student body has been and of its social composition. Three phases can be identified, the first two of which have received serious historical attention. Expansion, beginning in the mid–sixteenth century, faded to a stagnant period in the eighteenth century; sustained growth occurred from the early nineteenth century to the mid-twentieth century; and a rapid increase followed World War II. The numbers given below, however, are approximate and indicate scale

only. Students have generally come from a limited if broadening range of social backgrounds, but student status has not been simply a function of wealth.

The view of university history as a medieval golden age succeeded by early modern decline was challenged by Lawrence Stone, who argued that England experienced an educational revolution from the mid-sixteenth century to the 1630s. A number of new colleges were established, and the student populations at Oxford, Cambridge, and the Inns of Court increased to represent some 2.5 percent of men aged sixteen to twenty, participation rates that were not equaled until the twentieth century. Studies of other European universities revealed similar patterns of institutional development and student expansion, although with different timings. Student numbers in Castile peaked in the 1590s with even higher participation rates, whereas in the Dutch Republic the rise started only in the early seventeenth century or, at the University of Coimbra, in the late seventeenth century. Some Italian universities displayed similar trends, but others did not. The revolution seems to have left Prague University untouched.

The English educational revolution derived predominantly from an influx of young gentlemen who sought places in the expanding and secularizing state bureaucracies or who wanted the educational skills to secure their positions in volatile situations. In Castile changing forms of state patronage put a premium on degrees, which fueled the growth in universities. Other investigations suggested that liberally cultivating, humanistic education did have a role, but the concentration on law degrees confirmed the importance of secular knowledge useful to the state. The participation of the aristocracy in other European universities may not have been quite as significant as in England or Castile, but the social and cultural tone of many universities undermined the medieval image of the poor scholar.

Universities and their student populations declined, however, as war and religious controversy made study more hazardous and new colleges, especially

Aristocratic Finishing School. The West Room and Dome Room of the Old University Library, Cambridge, England. Drawing (1800) by Thomas Rowlandson (1756–1827). FITZWILLIAM MUSEUM, UNIVERSITY OF CAMBRIDGE, U.K./THE BRIDGEMAN ART LIBRARY

those run by the Jesuits, cornered a large slice of the market. An oversupply of graduates made traditional forms of place seeking more attractive. Educationally, the continued scholasticism of the universities failed to accommodate the new experimental sciences. By the eighteenth century universities had become just one of several forms of aristocratic finishing, where a fairly undemanding smattering of education was added to traditional gentlemanly accomplishments. Toward the end of the century, however, resurgent nation-states once again recognized the value of a ruling cadre drawn from a wider base but undergoing uniform acculturation through a more rigorous university education.

The transformation of the university during the nineteenth century brought about fundamental changes in the size and composition of the student population. Across Europe national university systems were reformed and expanded. Existing universities grew and embraced a wider range of functions. More universities were founded, and novel institutions slowly achieved recognition at the university level. Altogether the student population grew fitfully but on a steadily upward curve, while new entrants turned the aristocratic university into a middle-class institution. Fritz Ringer, in *Education and Society in Modern Europe* (1979), led the way in analyzing these changes. Fairly detailed studies are available for several European countries. While the problems of quantification are multiplied when comparing different countries, a consideration of Germany, France, and Russia can indicate some of the trends and complexities.

In the German states student enrollments grew from just under 12,000 in the mid-1830s to almost 16,500 in 1875, to nearly 34,000 in 1900, and to 55,500 in 1911. Technical institutes, which acquired close to university status by the end of the century, added almost 5,500 students to the totals in 1875; 10,400 in 1900; and over 11,000 in 1911. The French faculties and *grandes écoles* (institutions of specialized higher learning) saw their populations rise from just over 11,000 in 1876 to 42,000 in 1914. These numbers suggest comparable participation rates for universities, though higher for Germany if the technical institutes are added, but still tiny fractions of the population—a rise from less than 0.5 per 1,000 people aged 20 to 24 to 1 per 1,000 in the last quarter of the century. During the volatile period of university development in Russia, from the 1860s to 1900, numbers and participation rates remained much lower than in France and Germany but nevertheless showed noticeable increases. In 1836 Russian university students numbered only 2,000, which rose to 5,000 by 1859 and to about 8,000 by 1880. Some 7,000 attended specialized institutes. Rapid expansion in the early twentieth century produced enrollments totaling some 130,000 by 1914.

The development and reform of university systems was closely connected to the expansion of state administrations and the rising demand for professionals in more prosperous industrial and commercial nations. In France the centralized Napoleonic university was geared toward providing experts for the postrevolutionary state. In the wake of Napoleonic devastation in central Europe, the Humboldtian ideal of the university as a means of national regeneration laid the foundations of the modern German university. At the same time rising prosperity brought the possibility of university education within the reach of a wider sector of the population. Concerns about overproduction of graduates, professional overcrowding, and academic proletarianization, however, were widespread. Attempts to control numbers were most overt in Russia, where the autocracy initially expanded the university system in the early nineteenth century but suppressed it in the 1860s and 1880s. In Germany state officials discouraged young men from entering a university in the stagnant mid-century. Later in the century connections to the state strengthened, which meant many civil service posts required a university degree. Student numbers rose rapidly as industrial prosperity allowed more people to consider the opportunities university educations afforded. It is perhaps surprising that French participation rates kept pace with those in Germany given that France experienced little overall population increase and its levels of industrialization were much lower. Entrance was extended to applicants from nonclassical schools, and the service sector for urban populations offered opportunities for graduates.

Being a student was the privilege of a small minority, yet the social spectrum from which students were recruited widened throughout the nineteenth century to make universities predominantly middle class. Technical institutes recruited even more from the middle classes, and where teacher training was considered a part of higher education, as it came to be in Britain, the working class began to be represented. Access, however, was not simply a function of wealth. Different countries, different institutions, and even different faculties reveal idiosyncratic patterns. Even more caveats are made when addressing questions of social background, but the available evidence is interesting.

A striking feature of German students was the prevalence of those with learned professional backgrounds. Approximately 50 percent had educated or professional but not necessarily wealthy fathers, although the proportion declined to 30 percent by the 1880s. Those coming from the commercial and industrial sectors increased their share to about 30 percent of the total. In France the expense of secondary education reserved higher education for the affluent,

but the number of students from petty bourgeois backgrounds grew. Different *grandes écoles,* however, attracted different clienteles. The École Polytechnique during the Second Empire drew almost 70 percent of its students from upper bourgeois families, 19 percent from the liberal professions, and only 11 percent from trades backgrounds. The École Centrale had higher proportions from the lower bourgeois levels, while the École Normale replicated the German pattern in attracting more students from the educated classes. Among the faculties law was the elite, even though medical fees were higher. It was easier to set up a medical practice, whereas law required more patronage connections. Russian universities were dominated by the nobility, which comprised over 65 percent of students in 1865 and remained a significant 35 percent as late as 1914. Middle-class elements increased their share from 3 percent to 11 percent over this period, and the petty bourgeois increased from 5 percent to 23 percent. The peasantry had a presence of between 5 percent and 10 percent, but these students were from families of some substance.

Variations around the theme were repeated across Europe during the nineteenth century. Oxford and Cambridge had aristocratic overtones until the mid-nineteenth century and remained wealthy preserves thereafter. The new civic universities, however, drew more from the local middle classes. The Scottish universities had a reputation for inclusiveness, generating a powerful mythology of the humble "lad o' pairts" bringing his barrel of oatmeal and herrings to sustain him through a term's study in the city. Swedish universities were familiar with students from modest and peasant farming backgrounds, although Uppsala had a more aristocratic clientele than did Lund. Universities in southern and eastern Europe remained much fewer and more like the aristocratic finishing schools of the eighteenth century. Through the late nineteenth century Germanic reforms were initiated, and some countries attempted to create a wider student cadre through scholarships, often to foreign universities. The Serbian government enabled small numbers to study at Vienna or in Germany.

Wealthy aristocrats pursued university educations primarily for cultural refinement, although younger sons still needed to find careers. Humboldtian ideals revived the faculties of philosophy. But universities were dominated by the professional faculties, and the new entrants to the universities sought secure and remunerative employment. How far, though, could becoming a student lead to social mobility? Professional self-recruitment was a significant element, and university education might be a calculated and sacrificial investment by the educated classes to maintain their social status. Newly rich industrialists might seek social and cultural elevation for their sons by preparing them for the professions. The principal form of social mobility, however, was probably that of marginal middle-class people striving for greater security through advancement into the professions or, more likely, civil service.

The most momentous change to the composition of the student population came with the admittance of women into the previously male preserve of the university. Education formed a central issue of the predominantly middle-class women's campaigns of the 1860s as a means both to intellectual self-realization and economic independence. In the face of considerable prejudice, women were initially permitted only as auditors on the approval of individual professors. In the 1870s women were cautiously granted entry and slowly grew to be a noticeable if minor presence. A common first step was in medical education, where traditional arguments allowed that women should be treated by other women. Even when women were admitted, however, it was rarely on the same terms as men, and areas of the curriculum, notably theology and law, remained closed for some time. Attempts to steer women into feminized courses were not successful, and women opted primarily for medicine or philosophical subjects that could lead to teaching or literary work.

Formal admission, however, was not the whole problem. No particular legal obstacles prevented women from entering a university in France, but the lack of female secondary education imposed an effective block. The universities received the first applications in the mid-1860s, but by 1882 only nineteen women had graduated. During the first decade of the twentieth century female representation grew from 3 percent to 9 percent of French university students. A royal decree in 1873 allowed women into the University of Lund, but only fifteen enrolled during the 1880s. There, too, numbers increased noticeably in the early twentieth century. Greater hostility in Germany meant women were only officially allowed into universities in Baden in 1901 and Prussia in 1908, although over 4,000 women represented 7 percent of German students by 1914. In England the civic universities quietly admitted women in the 1870s, while Cambridge and Oxford conceded women informal entry but remained vehemently opposed to women graduating until well into the twentieth century. The Russian women's movement won temporary access to university teaching in the late 1850s and the 1870s. From the late 1890s, however, higher courses for women expanded dramatically, with over 5,000 in 1905; 28,000 in 1912; and around 34,000 by 1914.

Oxford Undergraduates. Undergraduates on their way to class, Oxford, November 1938. HULTON GETTY PICTURE LIBRARY

This almost equaled the 35,000 men in universities, although men dominated the special institutes. Higher courses were officially recognized as equivalent to a university education in 1911.

During the first decades of the twentieth century women helped maintain the steady expansion of student numbers. As in other areas of life, they proved more than capable of replacing the men who relinquished the university during World War I. Technological warfare also reemphasised the importance of highly trained experts in industrialized economic and military situations. In democratic countries university systems were consolidated, expanded further, or reformed. The totalitarian regimes of the 1930s, however, introduced a different kind of university planning and control. The Soviet Union pioneered serious attempts to introduce the working classes into traditionally noble universities. Initially the country established preparatory courses for workers, but more forceful proletarianization increased working-class representation from about 25 percent of students in 1928 to 58 percent in 1932. The proportion of women also increased from 28 percent in 1927 to 43 percent a decade later. Overall numbers rose spectacularly during the planning years. Total enrollment stood at

176,000 in 1928 and climbed to 508,000 at the end of five years, then slowed to reach 619,000 on the eve of World War II. By contrast, the Nazi regime brought stagnation to the universities, and women's participation particularly declined as restrictions forced them back into the home.

The most dramatic increase of the student population occurred during the second half of the twentieth century, which witnessed a transformation from a still primarily elitist conception of the university toward mass higher education. World War II further emphasized the importance of experts, especially technologists, while affluence and state subsidies brought university education within the reach of a wider range of the population. Student numbers climbed rapidly after the war, then rose exponentially during the 1960s in almost every European country. In Greece numbers rose from 28,302 in 1961 to 53,305 just four years later. In the Netherlands the total of 40,000 students in 1960 jumped to over 100,000 in 1970. Some 17,000 students participated in Swedish university-level education in 1950; 37,000 by 1960; but 125,000 in 1970. Participation rates by 1975 reached over 10 percent of those 20 to 24 years old in many countries and 15 percent to over 20 percent in some. The glaring exception was in Britain, where universities remained essentially elitist. Higher education did expand there in the postwar period, but participation rates climbed slowly to under 9 percent of the age group. Graduation rates, however, were similar to those of other European countries.

Women's representation in Western Europe increased from an average of 25 percent of the student population in the mid-1950s to 30 percent in the 1960s and some 38 percent in 1975. Rates in Eastern Europe were 5 percent to 10 percent higher for each date. Working-class participation, however, remained well below the working-class presence in the population generally. Only the imposed egalitarianism of eastern bloc countries approached representative working-class inclusion, although even there working-class students took a disproportionate number of evening, part-time, and correspondance courses. Three-fifths of Polish students in the 1960s still came from white-collar backgrounds.

In the economic uncertainty of the mid-1970s, the belief that ever-increasing student numbers were necessarily a benefit for either economy or society evaporated. The optimistic assumptions of postwar planners were undermined, and growth rates slowed appreciably. In Hungary, Czechoslovakia, and Poland student numbers actually declined. Exceptions included Italy and Spain, where university reforms led to large-scale expansion. Economic and political in-

stability combined with frequent educational reform affected national patterns of student recruitment in innumerable, specific ways. Through the 1990s, however, general trends returned to noticeable expansion. European Organization for Economic Cooperation and Development (OECD) countries registered increases in enrollment of between 25 percent and 50 percent with extremes of stasis in the Netherlands and over 150 percent increase in Portugal. Even in Britain rapid expansion during the 1990s saw participation rates approach European averages. Concerns for the importance of the knowledge economy once again put a premium on higher education. Women took most advantage of the new opportunities, almost reaching equal representation, and the need to widen participation again became an important issue. Working classes continued in marked underrepresentation among students, but for large sectors of the population higher education approached a common experience.

STUDENT LIFE

Experiences of student life are as varied as students themselves and their particular situations. A poor scholar in a small college is likely to have a different kind of experience from a wealthy young man at a large city university, which will be quite unlike that of a middle-class woman attending a provincial institution. Nevertheless, certain underlying structures shape student life in similar ways. A student's primary occupation is in principle to study. Yet academic work has never constituted the only aspect of student existence, and patterns of study and recreation organized daily life. As university courses became more organized and matriculation required a lengthy period of preparatory schooling, students became more like each other, and variations of experience were less extreme. A fundamental distinction in university structure also had important ramifications for the boundaries of student life. Collegiate-style universities regulated their students strictly. Free universities undertook tuition only, and although not without regulation, their students were at greater liberty to arrange their own affairs.

Early modern universities defined few educational requirements for entrance. Students enrolled when they were ready or were sent and embarked on a course of study with few set parameters besides periodic examinations if they wanted to graduate. The student's academic day routinely was scheduled around a series of lectures, private study sessions, and exercises. Teaching centered on the didactic professorial lecture, although the slow or ambitious might have

Academic Work. Students in an art class, Poland, c. 1900. SCHULLER COLLECTION/©CORBIS

supplementary private lessons. Lectures commonly involved repetition from set texts, and exercises were their subsequent regurgitation. College scholars had further supervised study, while free students were left to their own devices at the end of lessons. The timetable continued until the student felt ready to perform the formal oral disputations required for a degree. These were supposed to be rigorous examinations of several hours duration, but indications are that through the period they often degenerated into sham debates. A large proportion of students, however, did not and never intended to graduate.

The increased influence of the aristocracy in universities had important implications for the character of student life. Wealthier students demanded better facilities and cultivated more genteel lifestyles, which further pushed up costs. Italian-style court dress, including, disturbingly, wearing a rapier, replaced the scholar's gown, but the more barbaric customs associated with academic and fraternal rituals also were slightly refined. University authorities feared that attempts by poor students to emulate their betters would be ruinous. In the colleges they might eke out an existence from scholarships or serving their wealthier fellows, but outside they had to negotiate what terms they could from innkeepers and landladies. The common distractions of drinking, gambling, and womanizing could lead to debt, disorder, and discipline from university or town authorities. Students enjoyed various freedoms from normal civic legislation, and riotousness was a frequent problem, especially when highly strung aristocrats with swords were involved. Collegiate institutions became increasingly popular options in attempts to supervise behavior more closely.

While the mendicant scholars of medieval tradition were fast disappearing, students were also becoming more sedentary. Academic peregrination was an important feature of early universities, and a good deal of mobility survived in the sixteenth century. With universities still not numerous, students could travel long distances, often across borders. Students might study at one place but graduate at another or move to study with famous professors. Tolerant universities in northern Italy and the Netherlands attracted Protestant students from central Europe. The wars that racked Europe in the sixteenth and seventeenth centuries, however, made travel more hazardous, and religious conflicts made authorities more suspicious of foreign students. In the seventeenth century universities increasingly divided along confessional lines and drew more from national or regional pools.

During the scholastic torpor of the eighteenth century, wealthy students acquired a smattering of education to complete their genteel training. Little serious study was undertaken, and few degrees were completed. The nineteenth-century reforms that reemphasised learning and knowledge infused the ideal of the student with greater seriousness of purpose. Universities increasingly recruited from preparatory schools, which confirmed the age of entry at late teenage and made matriculation more of an obstacle. Exercises became more common and rigorous, with written examinations replacing oral disputations. Degree courses were shortened to three to five years, and graduation rates rose as degrees offered more secure routes into professional or administrative careers.

The German principles of *Lehrfreiheit* and *Lernfreiheit* (freedom to teach and freedom to learn) gave enormous scope to both professors and students. Seminars and laboratory classes were profound innovations in university teaching, although they could have contradictory implications. At best students could perambulate to different universities to study with acknowledged experts. All too often, however, such opportunities were reserved for the newly emerging postgraduate student, while the rising numbers of undergraduates were taught by overworked junior staff. Among the dominant professional faculties dictatorial lectures remained common to ensure conformity to external requirements. *Lehrfreiheit* also affirmed the right of students to be free from tutelary restrictions, and as more national university systems followed the German model, the collegiate tradition declined again. Although very different in organization, the French university, too, did not see its role as supervising students' lives. The principal exception was in England, where the collegiate system retained a powerful influence. As Oxford and Cambridge colleges were reformed academically from their former, seminary-like existences, the collegiate system was preserved vigorously as central to university education. Even the civic universities, though much closer to the German academic style, still fostered a pastoral concern for student welfare.

Despite the increasingly academic ethos that prevailed throughout the nineteenth century, life beyond the classroom remained fundamental to the student experience. Students always gathered for conviviality, more freely so in the unsupervised free university, where the inn could be literally a home away from home. Societies, clubs, and fraternities were also inevitable, combined by region, social or cultural proclivity, or elitist exclusiveness. Forms of student sociability coalesed around several stereotypes, most spectacularly the German dueling corps. These corps were bound by chivalric codes of honor exercised in ritualistic or seriously harmful sword fighting. Although often on the edge of legality, the German corps were tolerated. French student organizations were so effectively proscribed that communal activity failed to develop during the nineteenth century, and sociability took on bourgeois norms, revolving around café society. By contrast, English universities actively fostered the corporate spirit, especially through team games. The cult of athleticism that swept the English universities in the late nineteenth century began to affect German universities by the end of the century and even extracted some French students from the cafés.

Unsurprisingly women's experiences at universities were somewhat different from their male counterparts'. Women frequently faced hostility, and numbers until the early twentieth century were so few that isolation could be a problem. Many female pioneers were somewhat older than the average student, and significant numbers attended foreign universities. Women students generally, however, tended to go to the nearest university and to live at home, where traditional constraints applied. Where women were in residence, behavior was closely supervised, and women were careful to avoid attracting the faintest scandal. Even so the opportunity to study was commonly a deeply significant life experience. Women formed their own social organizations, which expanded with growing numbers. As the novelty wore off, grudging acceptance among men ultimately gave way to more cordial relations. Observers noted that as the gentleman's club atmosphere was dismantled, male students' conduct improved, but women pioneers sometimes were disappointed by their successors' lack of missionary zeal.

Mass higher education in the twentieth century had profound implications for the nature of student life and the quality of the experience. Being a member of a university community of twenty thousand people presented a different prospect from being one of a few hundred. The diversification of the student population helped broaden student culture and began to break down some of the stereotypes. Many students shouldered adult responsibilities of work, marriages, and families, which could supersede identification as a student. Older students returning to education undermined the notion of a traditional university age group. Correspondance or evening classes, as in the Russian and Polish universities or the British Open University, were essentially an addition to ordinary working life. More institutions allowed students to stay at home, which affected the nature of student communities. Going away from home remained a distinctive feature of English student culture, but in other respects British exceptionalism declined as the university system moved toward mass participation. European universities in turn developed halls of residence and student organizations.

More people had the opportunity to attend a university, but the experiences of mass higher education were often unhappy. While enrollments exploded, facilities frequently did not keep pace, and extra numbers of students were squeezed into an essentially nineteenth-century pattern. Class sizes expanded beyond the capacities of both tutors and physical spaces. Adherence to misplaced ideals of academic autonomy allowed professors to retreat into private research, divorced from the everyday lives of undergraduates, while the junior lecturing staff struggled to cope with the increased numbers of students. Library resources failed to keep pace, as did work spaces and halls of residence. Dissatisfaction with university life was inevitable, leading to high dropout rates, increasingly politicized student movements, and ultimately outbreaks of frustrated violence.

STUDENT MOVEMENTS

Students and disorderliness have long been associated and within limits largely indulged. Disputes between town and gown could cause headaches for civic and university authorities, but students could also pose more serious political threats to the state. While the vast majority of students were readily acculturated to societal norms, concentrations of intelligent and enthusiastic youth free from adult responsibilities could be breeding grounds of radical ideas and movements. For the most part student organizations were founded for purely sociable purposes, but they could develop wider political directions. These were mostly syndicalist, to pursue student interests qua students. Authorities' fears, however, were also regularly vindicated when student movements participated in revolutionary activities. Interest in student movements was heightened by the demonstrations of the 1960s, attracting sociological and psychological as well as historical interpretations.

The early modern university continued the medieval tradition of students forming into nations based on their places of origin. Along with ease of language and custom or mutual support and protection in potentially hostile environments, nations offered some home comforts in a strange place. For similar reasons host states sometimes regarded university nations with equal suspicion. The early modern student, however, stood as an apprentice in the community of scholars, a lowly but integral part of the university establishment who was perhaps less likely to want to overthrow it. A self-aware student consciousness that emerged from the romantic ethos and revolutionary movements of the early nineteenth century meant students identified more with their peer groups and formed organizations to pursue their own specific interests.

For the most part student organizations were concerned with everyday matters of student welfare. They formed credit and welfare unions to help with finances and accommodations or arranged social events. By the end of the nineteenth century corporate student unions had formed in most universities primarily to help with welfare and social issues but in some countries also to provide a means of communicating student views to the university authorities. National bodies made up of individual university unions organized in the twentieth century, but attempts to coordinate them into an international movement in the interwar period had little success. Internationalist ideals in the postwar period were similarly undermined as divisions reappeared along cold war lines. Student organizations became increasingly politicized in the postwar period. Syndicalist student trade unionism recast students as intellectual workers and demanded the rights of labor organizations, but student movements also acquired a wider political platform.

Nineteenth-century authorities tried to avoid politicization of student organizations. Political student movements arose first in France and Germany, where idealistic students regarded themselves as leaders of the revolutionary tide. In France the restoration government successfully contained them, but in Germany the nationalistic *Burschenschaften* (youth associations) garnered sympathy from others who wanted to see a united Germany. When some students resorted to assassination, the movement was pushed underground, but it reemerged in the revolutionary outbreaks of 1830 and 1848. The Russian student movement engaged in a sixty-year campaign against the autocratic state that spawned serious confrontations in the early and late 1860s and the early 1880s and a strike in 1899 involving some 13,000 students that shut the universities for over a year. In 1905 students held mass revolutionary rallies at St. Petersburg University. Nationalistic student movements operated in Poland and the Balkans by the late nineteenth century.

Interpretations of these movements has spanned the historical and sociological spectrum. Particularly interesting is the question of generational conflict. Lewis Feuer in *The Conflict of Generations* (1969) argued that student movements include a revolt against the perceived failures of their fathers' generation. The interpretation is difficult to establish historically, and student movements rarely had wider generational support, requiring the addition of more prosaic cultural and socioeconomic factors. In Germany in the 1830s

Student Boycott. Students picket at the entrance of the London School of Economics, March 1967. HULTON GETTY PICTURE LIBRARY

and 1840s universities experienced professional over-crowding, which eased in mid-century with the onset of industrialization, in time with the rise and fall of student disturbances. Russian students in the late 1850s reform period saw themselves as the leaders of national regeneration and opposition to state autocracy, and this ideology was reinforced in subsequent cohorts as the established student culture.

In the late 1960s universities around the world were rocked by outbursts of student protest. Virtually every Western European country was affected, most significantly France, where demonstrations in 1968 led to a general strike and an election. Violence continued in Italy into the 1970s but was much more muted in Britain and the Netherlands. Unrest in Western countries combined specific student grievances with global political concerns. Conditions for students had declined with the rapid movement to mass higher education. Classes were crowded, professors were distant, and facilities were overburdened, while the graduate job market was increasingly competitive. Students brought up in the permissive 1960s chafed against seemingly authoritarian regulations and restrictions. In a pattern that recapitulated nineteenth-century conflict, a protest about student

matters that met with overt force commonly triggered much larger and more violent demonstrations combined with wider economic, environmental, or political concerns, to which some commentators have added generational angst. Several countries responded by revising their university systems to allow greater rights and freedoms for students, including representation on governing bodies.

Eastern Europe also experienced outbreaks of unrest, noticeably Czechoslovakia. In Spain student protests carried major political implications. To many in these countries the grievances of Western students appeared trivial. For them universities and student bodies offered rare platforms for political opposition to authoritarian regimes, which could be viciously suppressed, as in Hungary. In general campuses calmed down in the late twentieth century, but at the beginning of the new millennium students around the world, including in parts of Europe such as the Balkans, continued to lead the opposition to repressive or one-party states. The combination of intelligence, energy, and idealism that is the hallmark of students provided a fundamentally important wellspring of change in the modern period. The outcomes can never be entirely controlled.

See also **Student Movements** *(in this volume);* **Gender and Education** *(volume 4);* **Higher Education** *(volume 5); and other articles in this section.*

BIBLIOGRAPHY

The early modern scholar

Chartier, Roger, and Jacques Revel. "Université et société dans L'Europe moderne: Positions des problèmes." *Revue d'Histoire Moderne et Contemporaine* 25 (1978): 353–374. Issues and preliminary findings arising from the Dominique Julia, Roger Chartier, and Jacques Revel project.

Julia, Dominque, and Jacques Revel, eds. *Les universités européenes du XVIe au XVIIIe siècle: Histoire sociale des populations étudiantes.* Vol. 2: *France.* Paris, 1989. Companion volume to the following but focused on France.

Julia, Dominique, Jacques Revel, and Roger Chartier, eds. *Les universités européenes du XVIe au XVIIIe siècle: Histoire sociale des populations étudiantes.* Vol. 1: *Bohême, Espagne, États italiens, Pays germaniques, Pologne, Provinces-Unies.* Paris, 1986. Wide-ranging investigation of Stone's educational revolution thesis in European universities.

Kagan, Richard L. *Students and Society in Early Modern Spain.* Baltimore, 1974. Extension of the educational revolution thesis to Spain.

Ridder-Symoens, Hilde de, ed. *A History of the University in Europe.* 2 vols. Cambridge, U.K., 1996. Very useful survey; volume 1 deals with medieval universities, and volume 2 concerns early modern universities.

Stone, Lawrence. "The Educational Revolution in England, 1560–1640." *Past and Present* 28 (1964): 41–80. Seminal study of students in early modern England.

Stone, Lawrence, ed. *The University in Society.* 2 vols. Princeton, N.J., 1974. Diverse collections.

The nineteenth-century student

Albisetti, James C. *Schooling German Girls and Women: Secondary and Higher Education in the Nineteenth Century.* Princeton, N.J., 1988. Study of the importance of German women's campaigns against particular hostility.

Dyhouse, Carol. *No Distinction of Sex? Women in British Universities, 1870–1939.* London, 1995.

Jarausch, Konrad H. *Students, Society, and Politics in Imperial Germany: The Rise of Academic Illiberalism.* Princeton, N.J., 1982.

Jarausch, Konrad H., ed. *The Transformation of Higher Learning, 1860–1930: Expansion, Diversification, Social Opening, and Professionalization in England, Germany, Russia, and the United States.* Chicago, 1983. Important work in the systematization literature of comparative studies of the development of modern educational systems.

Johanson, Christine. *Women's Struggle for Higher Education in Russia, 1855–1900.* Kingston, Canada, 1987. Women's campaigns' engagement with Russian autocracy to achieve higher education.

McClelland, Charles E. *State, Society, and University in Germany, 1700–1914.* Cambridge, U.K., 1980. Key study of the relationships among state, society, and university reform.

Ringer, Fritz K. *Education and Society in Modern Europe.* Bloomington, Ind., 1979. Large, pathbreaking study of educational institutions and their student populations.

Weisz, George. *The Emergence of Modern Universities in France, 1863–1914.* Princeton, N.J., 1983.

Student numbers and mass higher education

Altbach, Philip G., ed. *International Higher Education: An Encyclopedia.* London and New York, 1991. A wide-ranging survey that includes thematic essays and national analyses.

Flora, Peter, et al. *State, Economy, and Society in Western Europe 1815–1975: A Data Handbook in Two Volumes.* Vol. 1: *The Growth of Mass Democracies and Welfare States.* Chicago and London, 1983.

Mitchell, B. R. *European Historical Statistics, 1750–1975.* 2d revised ed. London, 1981.

OECD. *Education at a Glance 2000.* Paris, 2000.

Student movements

Feuer, Lewis S. *The Conflict of Generations: The Character and Significance of Student Movements.* New York and London, 1969. Study of student movements across the globe in the nineteenth and twentieth centuries using psychological and sociological analyses of generational conflict, written in the wake of the Berkeley protests and on the eve of the demonstrations in Europe.

"Generations in Conflict." *Journal of Contemporary History* 5, special issue (1970): 3–190. Diverse collection of essays on students, youth movements, and protests in many European countries, written in the aftermath of 1968.

ARTISTS

Alexander Varias

Artists have occupied a unique position in European civilizations. As conveyors of the perceived truths, ideals, and values of their societies, they stand among the elites yet rarely attain positions of political or economic power. They either hold people in awe with their skill and genius or gain contempt through eccentrically expressed visions conveyed in oral poetry, written script, stone, metal, pigments, or music.

THE RENAISSANCE

In the ancient and medieval worlds, artistic creation was attached to civic and religious architecture, whether in a temple, an assembly hall, a cathedral, or a stock exchange. Even so prominent a contributor to Italian Renaissance art as Giotto created his greatest works for churches, like the Arena Chapel in Padua or the Church of St. Francis in Assisi. During the medieval era, artists were also customarily regarded as craftspeople in terms of their social status. The situation changed during the late Middle Ages and the Renaissance, especially in Florence, when artists emerged as individuals uniquely expressing visions of genius and creating works that could stand apart from architectural structures. While medieval artists' names are obscure, the names of Renaissance artists are familiar. To account for this change, Jacob Burckhardt, the prominent nineteenth-century historian who originated the concept of the Italian Renaissance, underscored the central importance of individual fame to Quattrocento and Cinquecento Italy (fifteenth- and sixteenth-century Italy). Artists perceived themselves as great individuals, and they were encouraged by public adulation to do so. Giorgio Vasari, the originator of art history, went so far as to refer to Michelangelo as "divine" (Goldwater and Treves, 1945, p. 98). A survey of names associated with the Italian Renaissance seems to confirm such a shift in status: Giotto, Masaccio, Sandro Botticelli, Donatello, Leon Battista Alberti, and Leonardo da Vinci to name but a few.

At the same time the perception of aesthetic works and the nature of artistic genius, ambition, and freedom experienced transformations. Artists viewed freedom as a necessary condition for the execution of their greatest works. While Renaissance art broke from medieval traditions in emphasizing bodily bulk, three-dimensionality, and a general sense of realism, particular artists diverged in style. Masaccio emphasized massive bodies and projected shadows in a setting dominated by perspective, as seen in his great frescoes in the Brancacci Chapel of Santa Maria del Carmine in Florence. Andrea Mantegna and Domenico Ghirlandajo followed the rules of perspective while using color and composition in individual, recognizable manners. Filippo Brunelleschi formalized the preconceptions behind the new approach to painting in a scientific theory describing the visual perception of objects placed in varying degrees of distance from an imaginary observer. His theory became the strict rule for three-dimensional realism to which painters had to adhere for at least the next four centuries.

Botticelli and Fra Filippo Lippi gave their works a harder edge in the *cruda e seca* (dry) style with pronounced lines as described by Vasari. Vasari seemed fonder of Leonardo's use of subtle shadows and toning to create a smoky ambience summed up as chiaroscuro (light-dark).

Yet Renaissance artists participated in a common reverence for antiquity and nature. Erwin Panofsky explained the differences between the Italian Renaissance and earlier, minor "renascences" through the expanded historical consciousness of the fifteenth century, which caused contemporaries to view antiquity as a lost world whose pagan gods were no longer threatening to Christianity. Along with this came a newfound reverence for nature. Leonardo deemed painting "the sole imitator of all the visible works of nature" (Goldwater and Treves, 1945, p. 48), and Vasari, of a similar mentality, believed that "design cannot have a good origin if it has not come from continual practice in copying natural objects" (Goldwater and Treves, 1945, p. 95).

PERSPECTIVE

As artists sought to induce a picture-window effect of three-dimensionality during the Renaissance, they concentrated painterly methods on the development of perspective. The technique consisted of utilizing a series of diagonal lines, as part of the side angles of an object or scene, to draw the viewer into an imagined distance. It was as if the observer were seated before a window and looking through it.

Perspective was developed through a series of innovations. Thirteenth- and fourteenth-century Italian artists like Giotto, Cimabue, and Duccio concentrated on the side angles of thrones on which the Madonna with child was seated—a scene inherited from Byzantine panels, but now imbued with more three-dimensional realism. Nevertheless, the perspective was limited and so offered a dissonant scale. During the fifteenth century, artists in Florence especially made additional strides in enhancing the sensation of "proper" perspective. Masaccio, Andrea Mantegna, and others clarified vision within the framework of one-point perspective in which people, objects, and landscapes were depicted in a visual space leading to a single vanishing point in the distance. Masaccio's canvases also revealed an understanding that objects closer to the viewer were seen with greater clarity while those in the distance seemed vaguer in outline. Rendering atmospheric effects by means of shadows and other gimmicks thus complemented the effect.

Leon Battista Alberti, the great Renaissance architect, summarized the principles of perspective in his treatise, *Della pittura* (1436; On painting). The development of modern art during the late nineteenth and twentieth centuries involved the dismantling of perspective in favor of more abstract painterly concerns.

Artists' expanded sense of freedom collided with a counterdependence on wealthy and prestigious individuals who alone could commission their works. It was obvious, after all, that artists needed monetary and other forms of support to create their works. In the process they encountered the enhanced fame and power of great families in Florence like the Medicis, the Strozzis, and others who patronized artists. In fact artistic patronage in Florence, Siena, Rome, Venice, and other centers became a new claim to fame for bankers, merchants, and politicians already pushing themselves onto the public stage of recognition. So much dependence upon powerful patrons could only conflict with artists' growing sense of absolute creative freedom.

The influence and power of patrons was so pronounced that Renaissance artists often had to paint subjects dictated to them by their patrons. In one instance, in 1457 Fra Filippo Lippi painted a work according to the careful instructions of Giovanni di Cosimo de' Medici, who wanted to give the painting to King Alfonso V of Naples (Baxandall, 1988, p. 3). One of the most famous Renaissance works, *La Primavera* (c. 1478) by Botticelli, concerned a Neoplatonic theme emphasized by the famous thinker Marsilio Ficino and was intended to instruct allegorically and pictorially Lorenzo de' Medici's second cousin in the philosophy and art of *humanitas* (Gombrich, 1978).

Subjects attached to Christianity, Christian saints, and biblical stories were still as dominant as they had been during the Middle Ages. Yet Renaissance art also included mythological scenes derived from ancient literature, portraits of prominent social figures, historical scenes, and still lifes.

Changes in the physical locations of works of art also underlined contemporary values revolving around artistic purpose. Previously sculpture or painting was attached directly to architectural edifices or common objects like vases. Phidias's great sculptured frieze was part of the Parthenon of Athens. Gislebertus's sculpture depicted Last Judgment scenes on the tympanum over the central entrance of the French Romanesque cathedral in Autun. The stained glass windows of Chartres Cathedral presented scenes from the Old and New Testaments in Gothic form. Such works, designed for public display, were civic and religious in nature and evoked town pride. How different it was for individuals to commission artistic works for display in a Renaissance villa or palazzo, where they could amuse visitors or provide educational lessons to members of the patronizing family. In addition, small objects can be moved, be sold, be purchased, be stolen, be expropriated, or disappear under historical circumstances. While sculptural friezes and remnants of temples have been moved to museums, such as the sculptures from Pergamum that were transferred to Berlin, generally the more miniature the scale of the work, the easier its displacement—a reality conducive to the later creation of museums.

Eventually other figures besides heads of powerful commercial and financial families offered patronage. Pope Julius II commissioned key works by Michelangelo in the Sistine Chapel and Raphael Sanzio in the papal rooms within the Vatican. Artists north of the Alps during the fifteenth century benefited from monarchical patronage. For instance, Jan van Eyck was supported by John of Holland, count of Holland, between 1422 and 1425 and Philip the Good, duke of Burgundy, from 1425 to 1441.

THE AGE OF THE BAROQUE

Heinrich Wölfflin, in *Principles of Art History* (1932), viewed the history of the early modern artistic period as corresponding to classical Renaissance art and Baroque art. Wölfflin distinguished the two by the closed style of the former and the open, loose form of the latter. Scholars adopted this schema, which became a traditional heritage that students scrutinized in their professional devotion. Wölfflin neglected the Mannerist movement of Italian painters, who radically rejected Renaissance stability, calm, and studied realism and developed a predilection for eccentric composition, bizarre body positions, and frenzied emotional states. Parmigianino, Bronzino, and Il Rosso were among Mannerist artists whose eccentricity defied the popular taste for standard Renaissance formulas and styles.

During the Counter-Reformation the prominent sculptor Gian Bernini produced Baroque works with dramatic swirling, twisting forms. Attracting the patronage of the papacy, Bernini and his school of sculptors were commissioned to create statues for the interior and the outside colonnade of the new St. Peter's.

The royal and aristocratic figures in France backed works by Leonardo da Vinci and others. Indeed, political leaders established a tie between state and religious power and monumental art. Marie de Médicis continued this trend when she hired Peter Paul Rubens to decorate a prominent room in the palace that eventually became the Louvre museum in Paris. At its most dramatic, art embellished the royal persona of the Sun King, Louis XIV, and his new residence at Versailles, the most famous of Baroque palaces.

The seventeenth-century Baroque Age produced the sculptural and architectural forms in Versailles, the landscape of Le Nôtre gardens at Versailles, and the immense scale of sculptural decoration in St. Peter's, the most grandiose forms of state and church patronage. In this obvious equation between art and power in European society, art was specifically intended to overwhelm observers with the majesty of the patron who made it possible.

Rubens and Bernini were conscious of their dependence upon powerful political figures and were proud of the social status they achieved through con-

nections with the world of the elite. Nevertheless, patronage and commissions did not always work out satisfactorily, as in the case of Caravaggio. The artist's unusual angles, theatrical lighting, and intense naturalism made his patrons uncomfortable, though he intended for his works like *The Supper at Emmaus* (c. 1598) and *Entombment* (1603–1604) to support the Catholic Church's positions and dogmas during the turbulent era of the Counter-Reformation. It did not help that Caravaggio also was accused of murder and led a socially scandalous life.

A number of artists of the time carried out their works in less public circumstances, forcibly or voluntarily pursuing independent artistic paths. The context of Protestant culture in Holland made such a disjuncture with the past especially stark, affecting artists' social connections. Among the artists in this situation were Frans Hals, Jan Vermeer, Judith Leyster, Rembrandt, and Jacob van Ruisdael, who continued the technique of capturing light that emanated from a single source. Following Caravaggio's lead, Hals, Vermeer, and Leyster represented the trail of an external light source illuminating an interior. While Hals and Leyster developed a more impressionistic style, Vermeer painted with a detailed, near-photographic quality. In his later works Rembrandt embued his subjects with an aura-like light projecting outward from the body, unlike an external spotlight. Rembrandt's light envelops his subjects mysteriously and mystically. In Dutch genre painting of landscapes, still lifes, and scenes of gathered town burghers, everyday subjects became popular. Historians scrutinize works like Rembrandt's *The Nightwatch* (1642), Vermeer's *Young Woman with Water Jug* (c. 1660), and Ruisdael's landscapes with an eye to the cultural and social transformations in historical material life.

These artists' creative efforts did not reap the support and security patrons gave to other artists, but they were at more liberty to portray accurately the Dutch society in which they lived. Leyster's career as a painter reflects how rarely women were able to pursue artistic endeavors in European civilization. A student of Hals, Leyster married another contemporary artist, Jan Miense Moenaer. While she did not paint much in the last several decades of her life, her early still lifes and portraits achieved some renown, and Leyster was considered a precocious outsider to the world of art. With few exceptions, such as Hildegard von Bingen, artistic callings were restricted to men, and women who desired to paint, sculpt, design buildings, compose music, or write faced many obstacles. Leyster and the Renaissance writer Christine de Pisan paved the way for women's eventual aesthetic expression.

State Power and Monumental Art. *The Felicity of the Regency of Marie de Médicis* by Peter Paul Rubens. The painting is one of twenty-four paintings in the Medici Cycle, depicting events in the life of Marie, widow of Henry IV of France and mother of Louis XIII, that Rubens (1577–1640) produced between 1622 and 1625. MUSÉE DU LOUVRE, PARIS/GIRAUDON/ART RESOURCE, NY

Aristocratic Lifestyle. *The Swing,* painting by Jean-Honoré Fragonard (1732–1806). WALLACE COLLECTION, LONDON/ALINARI/ART RESOURCE, NY

ENLIGHTENMENT AND REVOLUTION

During the eighteenth century, transformations in the position and status of artists unfolded in a dual manner. In the Age of Enlightenment artists both sought support from patrons and authorities and assumed a growing role as social critics of the latter. Philosophes revealed how intellectuals could foster important relationships with monarchs and yet be outspoken socially. For example, Voltaire established a close connection with Frederick the Great of Prussia but remained an outcast in France for criticizing the Old Regime on the Continent. That course was also evi-

dent among painters, sculptors, poets, and musicians, including Mozart and Antonio Salieri, who both sought support from the Habsburgs of Vienna.

France under Louis XV was highlighted not only by the Enlightenment but by Rococo art, as in the works of Jean-Antoine Watteau, François Boucher, and Jean-Honoré Fragonard. While the Rococo style has been mocked as frivolous and overly ornamental, surpassing the Baroque in swirling designs and fleshiness by exponents of ten, its artists also conveyed many social observations. Boucher's works depict the apparently ultrasexualized atmosphere of Louis XV's inner circle, as in the scandalously erotic

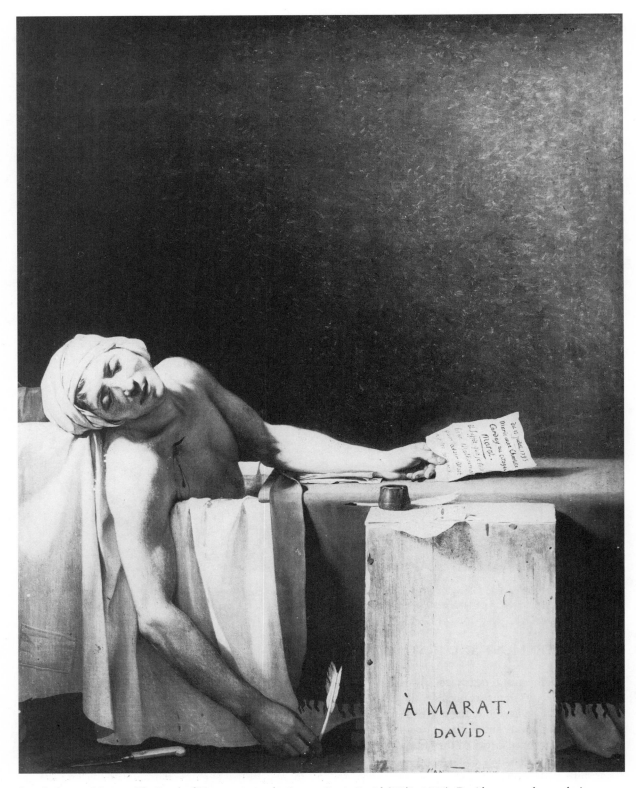

Revolutionary Martyr. *The Death of Marat,* painting by Jacques-Louis David (1748–1825). David portrays the revolutionary journalist after being stabbed to death by Charlotte Corday on 13 July 1793. [For an image of Marat's newssheet, *L'Ami du Peuple,* stained with his blood, see the article "Journalism" in volume 5.] MUSÉE D'ART ANCIEN, BRUSSELS/GIRAUDON/ART RESOURCE, NY

images of Mme. de Pompadour and Mlle. Murphy, and a world of hedonistic and epicurean pleasures matching the range of colors in the rainbow. Fragonard's *The Swing* (c. 1768) is a toned down but still vigorous portrayal of the aristocratic lifestyle of the era. Watteau's works express more elegiac and wistful visions of society with both critical representations of contemporary upper-class mores and reflections of popular life. Watteau's *The Embarkation for Cythera* (1717) and *Gilles, the Jester* (c. 1718) in particular provide social perspective through the decorative Rococo lens.

The eighteenth century also witnessed the dominance of Salons as the state-sponsored, official exhibition centers of paintings for the popular audience. Salons were artists' only means of reaching that audience and offered the possibility of bypassing patrons. The philosophe Denis Diderot, who wrote criticisms of works exhibited in eighteenth-century Salons, particularly praised the moralistic works of Jean-Baptiste Greuze and, seemingly sounding an alarming note, vigorously defended artistic independence.

Diderot may have been looking into the future. The last two decades of the eighteenth century were a critical point at which painting and political statement converged, in other words the period when the French Revolution was in the making. Jacques-Louis David's artistic career most reflected this convergence. His work developed from subtle, insinuating critiques of the ancien régime, as in *The Oath of the Horatii* (1784), to open statements of propaganda extolling the political events of the day. In several instances David resorted to outright heroic idolization of revolutionary figures, as in *The Death of Marat* (1793). David's works reflect the emergence of Neoclassicism as an artistic, painterly style. Architecturally Neoclassicism updated and synthesized ancient Greek and Roman forms, such as columns, pediments, entablatures, arches, and domes. Perhaps the most famous Neoclassical structures are the Panthéon in Paris and Thomas Jefferson's villa "Monticello," both of which seem to sum up the contemporary belief in reason and clarity.

In painting Neoclassicism rejected both the Baroque and the Rococo and adopted tighter brush strokes and a more formal, often austere style. Ancient life, particularly that of the Romans, was a common subject for Neoclassical artists, who selected key moments of ancient history or mythology as subjects to provide moral commentaries on contemporary mores and authority. Thus David's *The Oath of the Horatii* extolls Roman republican virtues, while his *Lictors Bringing Brutus the Bodies of His Sons* (1789) praises the assassins of caesars. As an enthusiastic participant in the French Revolution, David viewed

> the arts in the light of all those factors by which they should help to spread the progress of the human spirit, and to propagate and transmit to posterity the striking examples of the efforts of a tremendous people who, guided by reason and philosophy, are bringing back to earth the reign of liberty, equality, and law. (Goldwater and Treves, 1945, p. 205)

In the light of Robespierre's Reign of Terror, the commitment of French revolutionary leaders to the rule of law may be questioned. David's career, however, seems an artistic chronicle of the Revolution. He depicted many key events of the upheaval, such as the Tennis Court Oath of 1789, ritual death by guillotine, and the deaths of key revolutionaries like Marat. David's greatest painting presents Marat as a martyr, murdered in his bath by a political foe, Charlotte Corday, a letter from whom remains in Marat's hand. A strong line dividing light from shadow adds a theatrical effect to the scene. Surviving the dictatorships by Robespierre and Napoleon Bonaparte, David proved as adept at transforming his image as Talleyrand and adapted politically from one regime to another. Not surprisingly David depicted Napoleon as an emperor crowned in glory, which contravened his depiction of the heroic, tragic Brutus, who would have placed the achievements of Bonaparte alongside those of Julius Caesar.

ROMANTICISM

During the same era artists used their work openly to attack acts of political oppression. Francisco Goya explicitly and graphically portrayed the acts of murder and injustice committed by Napoleon's troops during the French occupation of Spain. Goya's monumental *Third of May* captures the gesture of a local villager about to be gunned down by troops. He adopted the Romantic style, rejecting the more calculated and restrained Neoclassical style he considered no longer appropriate to the age. The increased tone of passion and the strong color and brushwork accompanied a marked intensification of the artist's unique individualism. Goya's individualism was especially heightened in macabre works of his "black period," like *The Pilgrims* and *Saturn Devouring His Children* (1821–1823), depicting morbid and violent scenes caught in a ghostly atmosphere of fear, mystery, and gloom.

The work of Théodore Géricault exhibits a similar Romantic trend. His *Raft of the Medusa* (1819) represents survivors of a shipwreck stretched out or standing, desperately adrift on a fragile raft, facing a threatening sea and sky. Several among them wave to a distant ship, the outline of which can barely be made out on the horizon. This scene, based on a historical episode, presents Romantic drama at its highest. Géricault in his short career also created paintings of the insane and in his collective work captured the general Romantic reverence of the awesome, the sublime, and the grotesque. At various levels those characteristics describe paintings of Goya, Caspar Friedrich, and Eugène Delacroix and the music of Beethoven and Hector Berlioz. In another vein J. M. W. Turner used intense color schemes and loosely applied brushstrokes to convey a Romantic reverence for the sea that influenced the Impressionists.

The career of Jean-Auguste-Dominique Ingres seemingly indicates a return to art blessed by the academy. In fact, Ingres's works are filled with eroticism and Romantic expressions of individuality. The tendency for artists to pursue their craft beyond the confines of the Salons and through defiance of conventional expectations was still in motion, as evidenced by Gustave Courbet, who provoked unprecedented outrage and contempt from critics. Alexandre Dumas the younger wrote a notorious diatribe:

> From what fabulous crossing of a slug with a peacock, from what genital antitheses, from what sebaceous oozing can have been generated . . . this thing called M. Gustave Courbet? . . . With the help of what manure, as a result of what mixture of wine, beer, corrosive mucus and flatulant oedema can have grown this sonorous and hairy pumpkin, this aesthetic belly, this imbecilic and impotent incarnation of the Self? (Clark, 1973, p. 23)

Courbet's works departed from the subject matter and style of Romanticism. Although his individualism reflected the "Romantic rebellion," he was among the first painters to create in the Realist manner and to focus on subjects considered neither important nor attractive. This inclination had a disruptive effect on the public, and Meyer Schapiro noted (in *Modern Art*) Courbet's revolutionary role in connecting avant-garde aesthetics with political concerns.

Courbet's rustic, peasant manner was at odds with bourgeois ideas of correct behavior. Although he did not rival Gérard de Nerval's eccentric behavior traits, such as walking a pet lobster on a leash, Courbet exhibited an unpolished Rousseau-like manner that widened the divide between new artists and the bourgeois public. This divide was most emphasized by the Bohemians, who cultivated a lifestyle and a manner of expression intended to bewilder the bourgeoisie. The eventual Bohemian slogan, *épater les bourgeoisie* (scorn the bourgeoisie), inspired followers throughout the nineteenth and much of the twentieth century. In Paris Bohemians congregated in select areas, at first

AVANT-GARDE

The changes from romanticism to realism to impressionism and on to other movements in modern art involved not only revolutionary styles and subject matter. Enmeshed within the entire processs that originated in France was a stark confrontation between the artists and the art audience. Official exhibition galleries and salons became the center for a clash revolving around visual expecations.

By and large, the audience was made up of the bourgeoisie, which carried to the gallery demands for heroic and official subjects executed through proper finish and idealized and realistic at the same time. Rebellious artists like Gustave Courbet and Édouard Monet and those who came after them insisted on less accepted subjects and styles that did not fit the conventional formula. The response to their work from audiences and critics was often scathingly hostile. Yet they persisted. The ensuing battle of tastes and temperaments reflected their adamancy, and the term "avant-garde" denotes the near military devotion they brought both to their work and to their confrontation with hostile critics.

As painting became abstract and further removed from familiar patterns, the contrast between artisitic trends satisfying to the larger public world and the ambitions of the avant-garde grew ever more pronounced until familiarity and the market transformed the situation by the early twentieth century. Neverthelesss, countless instances of bafflement and anger expressed toward an unusual work or art continue to be found. Frequently, such art is assumed to be "avant-garde"—an interpretation that underlines how much of modern art has assumed the presence of an artistic elite consciously marching to the intrinsic demands of the work of art, which they feel alone in being able to formulate.

centered around the Latin Quarter and during the last two decades of the century around the newly incorporated district of Montmartre, known also as "La Butte" (the Hill). By the end of the nineteenth century the two centers of Bohemian activity were distinguished as polar opposites. Latin Quarter Bohemians were considered more intellectual, a trait perhaps derived from the presence in that district of the Sorbonne. Montmartre's Bohemians were, in contrast,

In the Salon. *Four O'Clock in the Salon,* closing time for the annual official painting exhibition in the Grande Galérie of the Louvre. Painting (1847) by François-Auguste Biard (1798–1882). Musée du Louvre/Erich Lessing/Art Resource, NY

more outrageous in behavior and were associated with new sexual mores, exotic dance and music, and the supernatural. (See Varias, 1996, pp. 20–40, for further discussion of the contrasting ambience of Parisian Bohemian quarters.) At all times they invited and received contempt from the middle class and prided themselves on their great social distance from official Paris. Ironically, Bohemians tended to be from the middle class or bourgeoisie, and their individualistic revolt perhaps is explained by family conflicts.

MANET AND THE IMPRESSIONISTS

Courbet's defiance of academic, historical standards inspired upcoming artists to adopt similar individualistic stands and to paint as they wished. Patricia

Mainardi studied the decline of the Salon and in *The End of the Salon* (1993) connected that reality to other social and economic problems. During the Second Empire of Napoleon III and the first decades of the Third Republic, Édouard Manet and the Impressionists set about obviating the authoritative position of the Salons. They chose subjects from contemporary French society and used the style and colors they deemed most appropriate to that world. Causing as much outrage and offense as did Courbet's *The Burial at Ornans* (1850), Manet's *Le déjeuner sur l'herbe* (1863) and *Olympia* (1863) were considered sexually provocative, banal, and harsh all at the same time. Manet's male subjects frequently were dandies with top hats, black coats, and cravats. The center of Parisian aesthetic life immortalized in the poetry and criticism of Charles Baudelaire, these men frolicked around the streets of Paris as *flâneurs* (drifters). The ethos of dandies included a deliberate flaunting of the self and an obliviousness to public moral standards. For Baudelaire and other dandies, the use of hashish was part and parcel of a growing rebellion among aesthetes aiming to transcend life's mundane concerns. Eventually a conservative reaction became just as commonplace after the disillusionment of the 1848 Revolution.

While Manet's use of flat forms and colors received critical, caustic rebukes, the casual attitudes toward prostitution and sexuality suggested by *Olympia* and *Le déjeuner sur l'herbe* especially conflicted with the posture of moral uprightness assumed by bourgeois men yet belied by their conduct. Manet's later works, such as *A Bar at the Folies-Bergère* (1882), depict the new cafés and cabarets of the boulevards in the Paris rebuilt by Napoleon III, his planner Baron Georges-Eugène Haussmann, and their architects. In the new city interaction among the various social classes increased, and moral standards relaxed, which to conservatives suggested decadence or what the sociologist Émile Durkheim later called "anomie" (social instability).

Manet's relation to the Impressionists is ambiguous. He was a fellow artistic rebel and influence but not a coexhibitor. In fact the Impressionists wished to continue and surpass Manet's stylistic revolution. For the most part the Impressionists' work was refused exhibit space at the Salons, so they formed a *Salon des Refusés* (Exhibition of the refused). Camille Pissarro, Alfred Sisley, Claude Monet, Pierre-Auguste Renoir, and Mary Cassatt captured the true character of color as affected by light at different times of the day. As they followed what they considered a scientific pursuit, the artists, scornfully called "Impressionists" by hostile critics, applied loose and broad brushstrokes, forcing audiences to decipher a scene by stepping back from the canvas. Impressionist works represent purely natural settings, as in Monet's *Impression, Sunrise* (1872), from which the artists obtained their name, and Pissarro's *View of Pontoise* (1868), and scenes of leisure and social life, as in Renoir's *Le moulin de la Galette* (1876) and Monet's *Argenteuil Basin* (1872). These canvases center on brightly illuminated scenes and show the reflection and cascade of colors caused by sunlight on fog-enveloped riverbanks or on snow-covered villages. Cassatt's domestic scenes of mothers with infants also employ the Impressionist method. Cassatt's work and that of Berthe Morisot are important examples of women's contributions to artistic movements. In addition, Camille Claudel, the unhappy mistress and student of Auguste Rodin, is counted among the most creative and innovative nineteenth-century sculptors. As they defied the public's taste for familiar "uplifting," "idealized," and "finished" works, these artists created an artistic avant-garde that identified itself by its dedication to "higher" aesthetic standards.

Along with the striking style, the social settings and situations depicted in Impressionist works also stand out. Impressionists delighted in the gaiety and color in gatherings of people at leisure. Broad vistas of street life provided momentary glimpses of crowds. Impressionism focused on transitory views of the fragile natural world, whose never-repeating forms depend on the season, the time, the day, and the weather. Yet the concern for the momentary also centered around views of the social world. During the later part of his career, Pissarro sat behind windows in rooms several floors above street level, viewing the diverse patterns of people meandering through the streets and boulevards of Paris or the marketplace in Rouen. His excitement in painting such a scene was evident in a letter he wrote to his son Lucien from Rouen on 26 February 1896:

> I have effects of fog and mist, of rain, of the setting sun and of grey weather, motifs of bridges seen from every angle, quays with boats; but what interests me especially is a motif of the iron bridge in the wet, with much traffic, carriages, pedestrians, workers on the quays, boats, smoke, mist in the distance, the whole scene fraught with animation and life. . . . Just conceive for yourself: the whole of old Rouen seen from above the roofs, with the Cathedral, St. Ouen's Church, and the fantastic roofs, really amazing turrets. . . . It is extraordinary. (Varias, 1996, p. 157)

Pissarro wrote letters to a variety of acquaintances, including his children, fellow artists, and political subversives, in which he expressed his artistic sentiments. The artist was born on St. Thomas in the Virgin Islands, descended from Jewish Portuguese parents. While at the heart of the Impressionist revolt in painting, he was also deeply involved in the French anarchist movement during the last two decades of the nineteenth century. His commitment derived from early sympathies with the grievances of the downtrodden, whose plight he had witnessed during his first stay in Paris in 1847, the year before the outbreak of a revolution. Pissarro's political and social consciousness grew during the years, especially after the cataclysmic Paris Commune of 1871.

POLITICAL ENGAGEMENT

Other political movements had certainly elicited artistic engagement. French revolutionary sentiments

Domestic Scene of Mother and Infant. *Mother and Child on a Green Background,* also called *Motherhood,* painting (1897) by the American artist Mary Cassatt (1845–1926). MUSÉE D'ORSAY, PARIS/GIRAUDON/ART RESOURCE, NY

strongly attracted David. Goya angrily gave visual expression to his sense of outrage at the injustices inflicted by Napoleon's troops on the Spanish people. Delacroix depicted events during the Greek War of Independence in his devotion to universal justice and ideals. Nationalism and socialism also attracted artists' contributions. Nevertheless, anarchism uniquely enticed artists' enthusiastic involvement in its vocal defense of complete individual freedom. When Mikhail Bakunin and other libertarians broke with Karl Marx at the meeting of the International Workingmen's As-

sociation held in London in 1864, they complained about the Marxists' exclusive concern for the industrial proletariat and their addiction to state power. In contrast, anarchists were determined to destroy the state forever. Anarchism appealed to political rebels, who distrusted the state, but it also drew many artists, who vowed to further the Romantic goal of individual creativity and to reject all attempts to confine expression within certain preordained paths.

Anarchism particularly appealed to Pissarro in that, unlike Marxism, it held a positive role for peasants and artisans. Painters such as Pissarro, who depicted rural landscape scenes and admired peasants as a natural part of that charming world, found inspiration in peasants. It was, therefore, natural for Pissarro and other artists to portray scenes deemed proper to anarchist ideology, that is, social injustice, revolt, and rural settings. At times they stressed those subjects on canvas; at other times they gave their services to anarchist journals and newspapers in an attempt to reach a wider audience among the discontented masses.

An idealistic formula for freedom and justice, anarchism was also a movement driven by a variety of goals, including a vague sense of a larger communal purpose in which free individuals played key parts. Anarchist leaders envisioned artistic images as politically useful efforts to communicate the movement's ideas and aims to the people. As such messages were considered more successful when they were simple and direct, the line between free expression and propagandistic dictates grew thin. Pissarro found himself at the center of a conflict pitting politically engaged avant-garde artists dedicated to unhindered art against editors and other leaders desiring certain themes conveyed in particular styles. In the clash between political concerns and aesthetic ends, anarchist leaders viewed art as a major propaganda vehicle on the same footing with pamphlets and meetings.

This struggle was difficult for Pissarro, who seemed equally committed to both art and the anarchistic social ideal. While he wished to contribute to the spread of anarchism, he balked at calls from anarchists like Peter Kropotkin for subjects stressing work, revolt, and social justice. Anarchist leaders generally pushed artists toward a style that was accessible to the masses, generally realistic, and uncomplicated by the standards of the avant-garde. Pissarro believed that artists were in danger of losing their separate status if they were absorbed into the surrounding society and viewed simply as other workers. He wrote, "Let us be artists first" (Varias, 1996, p. 135). Lucien Pissarro wrote, "Every . . . work of art is social . . . because he who has produced it makes fellow men share the most passionate and purest emotion which he has felt before the sights of nature" (Varias, 1996, p. 136). Paul Signac, another anarchist and painter, viewed his own political activism as an expression of his individual character but not a mandate for painting in a particular manner.

By the 1880s Pissarro, Signac, and Georges Seurat created Neoimpressionist or Pointillist works, which continued experiments in color and light but reduced the size of brushstrokes to tiny points of paint. At that time Paul Gauguin and Vincent van Gogh expressed inner states of feeling and psychic sensations using intense colors and unconventional compositions. Paul Cézanne, while maintaining the use of Impressionist color schemes, tightened his brushstrokes to create compact geometric planes. Cézanne achieved an unnatural appearance that seemed to defy the law of gravity and the truths of perspective that had stood behind Western painting since the Renaissance. These artists, although challenging the conventional perceptions of nature, believed that they expressed nature's deepest levels of reality and furthered the avant-garde's alienation from official and popular taste.

During the first years of the twentieth century, Pablo Picasso and Georges Braque, gaining impetus from Cézanne's canvases, depicted still lifes in the fragmented, multiperspective style known as Cubism. Roger Shattuck in *The Banquet Years* (1968) related Cubism to the cultural forms of the twentieth century in its emphasis on abrupt juxtaposition. In Cubist works the avant-garde artists followed their own artistic inclinations rather than the seemingly iron laws of nature. Henri Matisse's Fauvist works, which unleashed color and line in even more striking ways, followed suit. A newly invigorated interest in the primitive also was seen both in Picasso's and Matisse's works and the later sculpture of Amadeo Modigliani, who became known more for his colorful, highly stylized erotic paintings of nude women in a long Italian tradition of painterly focus.

Artists felt that their modernistic works were more in keeping with the true character of nature. Nevertheless, any suggestion that they were breaking from the conventional sense of reality and bewildering the art audience would have been met with a shrug of the shoulders. Artists had embarked on their own subjective course and were attempting to reach positions that most people could not comprehend. The public would just have to catch up to them. Other movements took shape, such as Expressionism in Germany and Austria, influenced by the pathbreaking works of van Gogh and the color of Matisse. In Austria *jugendstil* (young style) attracted the new generation of artists, including Oskar Kokoschka, and a clash of values and tastes was unleashed. By 1912 the new styles crossed the Atlantic and were displayed in the Armory Show in New York City that made Alfred Stieglitz and Georgia O'Keeffe American avant-garde personalities. In all cases the aesthetic revolution seemingly was promoted by youth, isolated individuals, an enclosed avant-garde, and Bohemians, who were to some degree or another combined in an unstable unit but who always challenged familiar notions of reality.

The Card Players. Painting by Paul Cézanne (1839–1906). Musée d'Orsay, Paris/Art Resource, NY

WORLD WAR I AND AFTER

Europeans experienced World War I between 1914 and 1918, and a series of revolutionary movements erupted in Russia and eastern and central Europe toward the war's conclusion. As Bolshevism became established in Russia and related Socialist movements nearly succeeded in Germany, the questions asked during the anarchist-artist convergence in *fin de siècle* (end of the century) France resurfaced, albeit in a different vein. These questions again revolved around the link between art and politics.

In 1917 the outbreak of the revolution in Russia brought initial euphoria, even among anarchists. During the early 1920s a number of artists converged on Russia and attempted to create avant-garde movements rooted in the novel ideals and aspirations of the revolution. While French and German influences abounded, a particularly Russian movement, Constructivism, emerged under the influence of Vladimir Tatlin, whose enormous metallic, abstract tower statue was never completed. Constructivists aspired to merge the abstract principles of the avant-garde with the technology of the machine age. Even such an apparently revolutionary movement proved too much for

the Bolshevik elite, which viewed social realist art as more readily able to communicate simple, concrete messages to the masses. By the end of the decade avant-garde artists were exiting the Soviet Union in search of aesthetic freedom in western Europe or the United States. The filmmaker Sergey Eisenstein, himself director of the pro-Bolshevik films *Potemkin* (1925) and *October* (1928), found the climate under Joseph Stalin inhospitable.

In other areas of Europe the convergence of artistic goals with political and social goals was equally evident. Before the war and the Fascist takeover of power, the Italian Futurists Umberto Boccioni, Filippo Marinetti, and Giacomo Balla created canvases that positively conveyed the dynamism of cars, airplanes, city streets, and the general excitement of the machine age. The human body itself was portrayed as a machine in motion, as in Boccioni's metallic statue *Dynamism of a Soccer Player in Motion* (1913). The Futurist style was influenced by Cubism, parallel efforts by Marcel Duchamp, and the bright, vibrant colors of Fauvism and Expressionism. Futurists heightened their revolutionary position by glorifying war, revolution, and even the destruction of museums where traditional works of art were displayed. On the latter point they shared a position with the Dadaists. However, the Dadaists rejected traditional culture out of a hatred for a civilization that had caused such universal destruction during World War I. Duchamp's own Dadaist inclinations led him to offer a urinal as a piece of sculpture and two renderings of the *Mona Lisa*, one with a mustache called *LHOOQ* (1919) and the other without a mustache called *Rasée*. In both instances he relished the chance to mock the public's reverential view of art. While Dadaists tended to be indifferent to politics, Futurists found Benito Mussolini's Fascist regime conveniently willing to employ their aesthetic devices in reshaping Italian society.

Expressionism and other abstract currents circulated throughout Weimar Germany both before and after the war. From the war years on Käthe Kollwitz combined modernism with a needed dose of humanism and compassion in works that depicted the horrors and pathos of war. Her work emphasized a pacifistic message that she continued to convey throughout her life, even as she experienced the trauma of the Second World War.

Weimar artists, notably the painters Ernst Kirchner and Emil Nolde, also used bright colors and simplified forms to suggest emotional states of exhilaration or disturbance. Wassily Kandinsky, reaching the logical conclusion of this development, painted works of complete abstraction, sprawling fields of color entitled as such. In sculpture Ernst Barlach paralleled those simple compositions, although the Romanian sculptor Constantin Brancusi led the progress toward abstraction.

The practical arts were also affected by the desire for change. The German Bauhaus school widened the divide between the avant-garde and public expectations regarding artistic form and visual appearance. In this case, however, the conflict revolved around the question of whether the shapes and materials of the industrial world were appropriate for high artistic status. In his Bauhaus school Walter Gropius envisioned a revolution in architecture, furniture, and interior design that would utilize the lines and materials of industry. As did Futurists, Dadaists, and Surrealists, he advocated the elimination of traditional materials. Influenced by tastes in the United States, Gropius designed buildings from which all ornaments were removed and in which the exterior and interior reflected each other, promoting the birth of the glass skyscraper supported by steel girders. Mies van der Rohe later encapsulated the esteem for streamlined design in art deco, modern architecture, and other areas of design when he said, "Less is more." Functionalist aesthetics conflicted with the popular preference for traditional design, which was considered more cozy and warm, and the Nazis sought to gain political capital by portraying the Bauhaus as "un-German."

After he seized power in Germany, Adolf Hitler, in dealing with the avant-garde, followed Stalin's precedent rather than Mussolini's. While Futurist art was acceptable to Fascist goals, Nazis regarded Expressionism and other modern art movements with suspicion and labeled them "anti-Aryan." Hitler, a frustrated artist, regarded monumental Neoclassicism as the appropriate form for Nazi architecture, sculpture, and painting and decided artists were to use a pseudo-Greek style to convey heroic masculinity. In the process Expressionism was largely suppressed. In the late 1930s Hitler and Joseph Goebbels championed an exhibition of Expressionist art, entitled "degenerate art," as a warning to Germans.

Cinema, however, was both acceptable and convenient to Nazi propaganda aims of mobilizing mass enthusiasm. Posters, radio addresses, and mass rallies using the latest available technology were all important to Nazi ends. Most notably, the films of Leni Riefenstahl successfully linked Nazism with a vision of dynamism and the promised future. In *Triumph of the Will* (1936) and *Olympia* (1938), depicting the Nürnberg rally of 1934 and the 1936 Berlin Olympics respectively, Riefenstahl promoted a Nazi modernistic vision similar to that of Italian Futurists but with the benefit of the editing and montage of film. Of course such works reinforced Nazi power and thus war, racism, and extermination. Riefenstahl later claimed that she only worked for Hitler and did not support his goals.

Avant-garde experiments in art continued through the 1930s. Surrealism, already evident in the works of Giorgio De Chirico during the 1920s, evoked paradoxical images defying ordinary explanations but hinting at the underlying symbolic, dreamlike states of the subconscious described contrastingly by Sigmund Freud and Carl Jung. Salvador Dalí and Joan Miró of Spain and René Magritte of Belgium were in the forefront of Surrealism. Dali particularly lived in the eccentric way that the public had come to expect of Bohemians.

Avant-garde concepts and political concerns connected closely in Picasso's massive mural, *Guernica* (1939), which dramatically portrays the bombing of a Basque town during the Spanish Civil War. The savagery of the war and the sinister nature of the political infighting among forces resisting the invasion of Francisco Franco's troops were also described by George Orwell, among others. Picasso's painting is a graphic, close-up view of air bombardment's effects on life, yet his abstract modern art conveys the anon-

Italian Surrealism. *The Uncertainty of the Poet,* painting by Giorgio de Chirico (1888–1978).
TATE GALLERY, LONDON/ART RESOURCE, NY

ymous horror of the twentieth century. The style in use, after all, was largely Cubist.

At the end of the Second World War the central artistic scene shifted from Europe to New York, where Arshile Gorky and Willem de Kooning participated in the movement known as Abstract Expressionism. This current was most famously epitomized by Jackson Pollock's drip paintings that originated in mythological scenes and ended in the complete immersion of the subject in abstraction. The European artistic world thereafter contended with the arrival of American art as California and other areas emerged as centers of creativity. Nevertheless, important European figures, including German artists such as Joseph Beuys and Anselm Kiefer, retained key positions. Kiefer's desolate, barren landscapes are haunting works of art.

In the midst of the war, however, Europeans took the lead in cinema and bypassed Hollywood. In France, Marcel Carné clandestinely created *Children of Paradise* (1945) during the Nazi occupation. Italian Neorealism originated in a collaboration between Roberto Rossellini and Federico Fellini. In *Open City* (1945) and *Paisan* (1946) they used a semidocumentary format to characterize the desolation and poverty of Italian life during the closing days of the war. As the term "Neorealist" implies, the filmmakers' aim was to capture the ordinary world of people by avoiding the entertainment-oriented methods of Hollywood directors and focusing on nonglamorous subjects. During the next several decades Fellini, a former comic-strip artist, widened the scope of his films by stretching the sense of realism to include psychic states and fantasy. In doing so he in-

Italian Neorealism. Giulietta Masina and Anthony Quinn in Federico Fellini's film *La strada* (1954). KOBAL COLLECTION

vited the criticism of purists, who objected to his departure from strict realism. Nevertheless, he vividly portrayed Italian society as it was transformed from the poverty-laden world of *La Strada* (The Road) (1954) to the ultramaterialistic jet-set world of Rome's Via Veneto in *La Dolce Vita* (The Sweet Life) (1960), where the scavenging paparazzi reporters roamed in fierce pursuit of vapid celebrities. Neorealism also influenced French directors like Jean-Luc Godard and François Truffaut, who rendered the surrounding world in novel cinematic forms.

Western European art after the Renaissance was created out of the several impulses that shook artists. The desire to represent reality and yet transform it in the process was certainly a central motivation, albeit that the perception of reality could change relative to the time. Both Renaissance and Cubist art were justified in such terms. Additionally, European artists pursued individualism, which encouraged them to take chances, experiment with techniques, and break with rules. Restlessness and change became a part of the development of art, and succeeding artistic movements nearly fit a pattern, although one that could have taken a different direction if circumstances had been altered. Patterns are usually imposed by outside observers. It is tempting to suggest a direct relationship between artistic culture and social change, yet that bond is questionable because many ongoing aesthetic concerns are exclusive to artists. The complexities within art history are vast because the creative personality itself is a myriad of labyrinths evading central definition.

See also other articles in this section.

BIBLIOGRAPHY

Baxandall, Michael. *Painting and Experience in Fifteenth Century Italy.* New York, 1988.

Blunt, Anthony. *Art and Architecture in France, 1500–1700.* New York, 1988.

Clark, T. J. *Image of the Artist.* London, 1973.

Goldwater, Robert, and Marco Treves, eds. *Artists on Art, from the XIV to the XX Century.* New York, 1945.

Gombrich, E. H. *Symbolic Images.* Oxford, U.K., 1978.

Haskell, Francis. *History and Its Images: Art and the Interpretation of the Past.* New Haven, Conn., 1993.

Haskell, Francis. *Patrons and Painters: A Study in the Relations between Italian Art and Society in the Age of the Baroque.* New Haven, Conn., 1980.

Hauser, Arnold. *The Social History of Art.* New York, 1951.

Herbert, Eugenia W. *The Artist and Social Reform.* New Haven, Conn., 1961.

Herbert, Robert L. *Impressionism: Art, Leisure, and Parisian Society.* New Haven, Conn., 1988.

Hughes, Robert. *The Shock of the New.* New York, 1981.

Mainardi, Patricia. *The End of the Salon: Art and the State in the Early Third Republic.* Cambridge, U.K., 1993.

Nochlin, Linda. *Realism.* Harmondsworth, U.K., 1971.

Panofsky, Erwin. *Renaissance and Renascences in Western Art.* New York, 1969.

Panofsky, Erwin. *Studies in Iconology: Humanistic Themes in the Art of the Renaissance.* New York, 1962.

Rosenberg, Jakob, Seymour Slive, and E. H. ter Kuile. *Dutch Art and Architecture, 1600 to 1800.* Baltimore, 1966.

Rosenblum, Robert. *Transformations in Late Eighteenth Century Art.* Princeton, N.J., 1967.

Schama, Simon. *The Embarrassment of Riches.* New York, 1987.

Schapiro, Meyer. *Modern Art: Nineteenth and Twentieth Centuries.* New York, 1978.

Schapiro, Meyer. *Theory and Philosophy of Art: Style, Artist, and Society.* New York, 1994.

Schorske, Carl E. *Fin-de-Siècle Vienna.* New York, 1979.

Shattuck, Roger. *The Banquet Years: The Origins of the Avant-garde in France, 1885 to World War I.* New York, 1968.

Varias, Alexander. *Paris and the Anarchists: Aesthetes and Subversives during the Fin de Siècle.* New York, 1996.

Vasari, Giorgio. *Lives of the Most Eminent Painters, Sculptors, and Architects.* Translated by Gaston du C. de Vere. New York, 1976.

Willett, John. *Art and Politics in the Weimar Period: The New Sobriety, 1917–1933.* New York, 1978.

Wölfflin, Heinrich. *Principles of Art History: The Problem of the Development of Style in Later Art.* Translated by M. D. Hottinger. New York, 1932.

THE MILITARY

Michael S. Neiberg

The military has been relatively neglected by social historians. Military history, for its part, has been written from either an operational or a top-down model that leaves little room for issues of interest to social historians. But the military has played far too important a role in European social history to be so marginalized. Studying the military has value beyond a general attempt to "bring the state back in" to social history. As reflections of the societies they serve, militaries can provide great insight into larger societal patterns. This essay will outline the basic roles and social implications of military institutions in Europe from the end of feudalism to the late twentieth century in four periods: the age of monarchy; the age of nationalism; the world wars; and the postwar period.

DEFINITIONS

Military institutions, by definition, have a monopoly on the legitimate use of organized violence as a means for realizing the state's political, social, and economic objectives. With that definition in mind, one must understand that no monolithic "military" exists, even within one state. Navies and armies, for example, have traditionally differed in their social composition, political outlook, and place within society. In most European states, the relationship between the two (after the creation of air forces, three) main branches of service has usually been unequal. In England, for example, the navy has always been dominant whereas in Russia and Germany the army has been dominant.

Because they are bureaucratic and hierarchical, militaries often look and act like other large public institutions. Nevertheless they differ in their relationship to the management of violence. Militaries, unlike many similar institutions, must accept the potential for high levels of fatalities as a routine part of their mission. Whereas police and fire departments, for example, experience death as an abnormality or an accident, militaries must accept it as a normal consequence of performing their primary function. They differ as well in the centrality they have to modern

European nation-states. Military institutions, charged as they are with defense and power projection, are often able to make greater demands on the state than any of their counterparts. Because they are tied to national interest, they are able to demand more from citizens than most other national institutions. This was particularly true after the state became powerful enough to compel military service from young men. After the nineteenth-century introduction of conscription, the military became a unifying institution in many European states.

In times of war, militaries often extend control into areas normally under civilian purview. In peacetime as well, the size and power of militaries can become a threat to the very societies they are designed to serve. Because they possess a monopoly on large-scale violence and have access to advanced weapons technology, they have the power to threaten other national institutions if not kept in check. As a result, European states have developed elaborate systems to maintain control of their armed forces. The patterns that emerge from these systems are generally known as "civil-military relations," although no single "civilian" or "military" viewpoint exists within a given state.

Relationships between civilian and military spheres operate on several levels. On the highest level, civilian and military elites can differ in terms of their value systems, their social background, or their views on contemporary political issues. On a more general level a military "mentality" can emerge that separates the armed services culturally and socially from civilian society. Without controls to prevent the gap from growing too large, militaries can become disconnected from civilian society and lose the support of the people. Thus, maintaining good civil-military relations is vital to the health of a stable political system.

Samuel Huntington identified two models of civil-military relations: "subjective" control and "objective" control. Although his model has been criticized, its general outline (with a few modifications to suit our present purposes) remains a valid starting point for discussions of civil-military relations. In the subjective model, formal constitutional and societal checks exist to limit the power and influence of military systems. These include the right of the citizenry to keep and bear arms, the creation of civilian ministries to oversee military services, and the control of military funding by parliaments or other legislative bodies. In most representative systems, the fear of one political party using the military against another is often as large or larger than fears of an outright military coup. European militaries have traditionally played a less direct role in politics than, say, their Latin American counterparts. The European fear, then, is that the creation of large armies could upset internal order by providing a political opponent with a formidable weapon. Subjective controls can also include competing and countervailing hierarchies like secret police (the Nazi Gestapo) or parallel chains of command (the Soviet commissar system). Of course, if used improperly, these controls can help a dictator stay in power by increasing his control over the military, as some historians argue Adolf Hitler did in the 1930s. They can also impair the military's performance.

The objective model of control involves imbuing a military with a professional value system that acts as its own check. Huntington argued that this model produced smoother civil-military relations than the subjective model. An objective system, he contended, builds on the military's own emphasis on ethical and behavioral codes. These codes stretch back as far as the chivalric codes that guided warrior conduct in the Middle Ages. Their ideal product is a nonpartisan and nonpolitical military that sees meddling in civilian affairs as antithetical to its own mission. Objectively controlled militaries are thus kept strong enough to serve the state's interest, but pose no threat to the state itself. By creating this kind of professional military, however, a society runs the risk of creating a military that exists as a "society apart," with values and beliefs that differ significantly from civilian counterparts. By the late twentieth century subjective and objective systems coexisted in most developed states.

States have another option for reducing the threat posed by militaries: they can keep them intentionally small and inept. In the 1930s, for example, France invested large sums of money into a chain of defenses on the German border known as the Maginot Line. The decision to build the line emanated from France's experiences in World War I, but Alistair Horne and others have argued that it also provided a way for Third Republic politicians to satisfy the voters' desires for security against Germany without creating a politically unreliable army garrisoned in the nation's interior. Third Republic politicians often saw

greater dangers from their countrymen in other parties than they did from foreigners. Creating a powerful army that could end up in the hands of political opponents after the next election was therefore politically unpalatable. With both subjective and objective controls failing, French politicians chose to keep the army on the frontiers both as a check on Germany and as a defense against its own army intervening in French internal affairs. The Soviet Union chose a similar (though much bloodier) strategy when it removed thousands of officers in the purge trials of the 1930s. Joseph Stalin preferred political reliability in his officer corps, even if it meant a decline in military capability. In both cases, a state chose to risk domination by an outside army rather than risk having its own army play too large a role in its political system.

Because variants and combinations of these three models have interacted, military coups are relatively rare in modern European history. Although the military has frequently played important roles in European political and social history, it has rarely dominated. Prussia and Germany in the nineteenth and early twentieth centuries are a clear exception. In the years before World War I, German chancellor Theobald von Bethmann Hollweg took his place at the imperial table after the generals, because he had only attained the military rank of major. During that war, Europe experienced one of its few military dictatorships under Generals Paul von Hindenburg and Erich Ludendorff; notably, it failed. The German example scared most Europeans (including the Nazis) into creating even stronger checks against military influence in the interwar period.

Militaries are, if not mirror images, then certainly reflections of the societies they serve. A democratic state will necessarily produce a different military than will a totalitarian one. Similarly, a technologically and bureaucratically sophisticated state will produce a different military than a developing one. Militaries can serve as vehicles for modernization, as the Russian army did under Peter the Great, or they can act as conservative institutions that resist modernization. However constituted, militaries play critical roles in shaping a state's political, social, and cultural patterns.

FROM FEUDALISM TO ABSOLUTISM

The medieval period left three important legacies for the role of militaries in European society. First, European armies were commanded and led by aristocrats. In the face of a changing society, the military became one of the few institutions that the nobility could dominate, resulting in a conservative outlook for most European armies. Even otherwise innovative monarchs like Russia's Peter the Great (1672–1725) and Prussia's Frederick the Great (1712–1786) were reluctant to change the social composition of their officer corps. Peter went so far as to compel noble service in his officer corps. Aristocratic control probably slowed the technological development of militaries and certainly reduced their overall level of expertise by using birth as the prerequisite for entry into the officer corps. Concentrating the officer corps in the nobility served as a subjective control by limiting senior positions in the military to the segment of society seen as being most politically reliable. Despite the limitations it brought about, monarchs saw noble participation in the armed forces as critical to the army's reliability and stability. The pattern of elite control over armies continued into the twentieth century in most European armies. Navies tended to be relatively less aristocratic and more bourgeois.

Nonnoble, "common" soldiers and sailors generally came from much lower social strata; they even included criminals. Mercenaries (defined as men who serve exclusively for money and are foreigners to the system they serve) and men paid on retainers or bounties (different from mercenaries because they are usually subjects of the state they serve) were another common solution to the problem of filling the ranks. Keeping such men motivated and reliable presented its own problems. Sixteenth-century Spain tried to solve the dilemma by creating permanent regiments called *tercios*. Each *tercio* contained about three thousand men and had distinct insignia, uniforms, colors, songs, permanent officers, and, over time, traditions. The *tercio* system created a small-unit dynamic not seen in European armies since the Roman legions. It also created loyalty to individual units and, by focusing men on the problems of their own unit, distracted military units from political participation, creating an early form of objective control. France and England soon developed a regimental system that served much the same purpose. Many contemporary European military traditions date to this period.

Second, feudalism left a legacy that militaries should have a dignity, an ethos, and a sense of duty. This code (derived in part from medieval chivalry) helped to legitimize militaries as institutions and made possible the creation of laws of warfare. The concept of a "just war" separated formal military institutions from other practitioners of violence and gave the military a political and religious basis for existence. This dignity did not, however, necessarily connect the army to any ideas of a nation-state. Noble control and the growth of royal authority meant that most subjects saw the military as an instrument of the king and the aristocracy, not the people. Put simply, when kings were

Swiss Mercenaries. Drawing (1515) by Urs Graf (c. 1485–1527). KUPFERSTICHKABINETT, OFFENTLICHE KUNSTSAMMLUNG, BASEL, SWITZERLAND

despotic, the army became an instrument of despotism (see the example of Oliver Cromwell's England).

Third, the end of the feudal period saw the rise of the state's administrative capacity, in part so that monarchs could better control their own armies. At the end of the feudal period, these capacities allowed some monarchs to broaden the recruitment base of their militaries and allowed them to rely upon their own administrations, rather than the capricious compliance of their vassals, to equip their armies. It also allowed the state to monopolize the right to declare and legitimate war. Spain and France were early pioneers in the creation of larger, less aristocratic militaries directly controlled by the monarch, though the nobility still dominated the officer corps. This trend continued throughout Europe, making the aristocracy more of a royal instrument and less the Crown's rival.

The introduction of gunpowder weapons helped to undermine the feudal order and tip the balance of power toward princes who could afford the new weapons. Gunpowder weapons were expensive and constantly became obsolete, requiring new investments. Few nobles could afford to continually update their armies. Many kings, however, could use their admin-

Military Expertise. In a German military academy of the eighteenth century, cadets study the theory of fortification. Engraving from *Der vollkommene teutsche Soldat* by Hans Friedrich von Fleming (Leipzig, 1726). BILDARCHIV PREUSSISCHER KULTURBESITZ, BERLIN

istrative capabilities and their wealth (itself based in part on their military success) to buy new weapons and hire more soldiers. Monarchs could now force formerly unruly dukes and barons to accept a new, far less equal, relationship. Large artillery pieces, of course, rendered tall castles, once an aristocrat's safeguard against the king's armies, much less secure. Armies thus became connected to the monarch and to his evolving state apparatus.

The state's enlarged administrative and fiscal capabilities led to increasing links with associated civilian fields of expertise. Increased sophistication in banking and other areas gave states the power to place armies in the field far from home, but most states still had financial difficulty keeping those armies in the field. Mercenaries and men paid by bounty were too expensive to keep on a permanent or semipermanent basis, and could turn on the king if he demobilized them. Much of the destruction of the Thirty Years' War (1618–1648) resulted from armies seeking loot or sustenance from local areas when regular payments from kings failed to materialize. War was no less expensive in the eighteenth century. French assistance to the American rebels led to a debt that required the dedication of almost half of the royal treasury to debt service.

Although most historians argue that this period did not represent one of great "skill transferability" between the military and civilian spheres, important links were created between the army and navy on the one hand and science and engineering on the other. Artillery weapons necessitated new siege techniques and forms of fortification and defense that required skills outside the army's own ability. Engineers like France's Sébastien Le Prestre de Vauban (1633–1707) became highly valued in an era of limited warfare and attempts to limit the impact of war on civilians by focusing military operations around forts.

Navies also built on links to civilians, especially in areas like navigation and, of course, shipbuilding. As European warships grew larger and substituted sails for rowers, they became capable of carrying more food and cannon. By the fifteenth century, European navies were becoming more powerful in African and Indian waters as well as in the Mediterranean and the North Seas. By 1518 Portuguese galleys could carry 35 guns, impressive for the time but soon dwarfed by later warships. By 1759, Great Britain had a ship that carried 104 guns capable of firing 1,100 pounds of iron every 90 seconds.

THE AGE OF NATIONALISM

Though few saw it at the time, Great Britain's unsuccessful war to subdue a rebellion in the American colonies was a watershed. Relying heavily on mercenaries, the British tried to defeat an opponent motivated more by nationalism (or at least regionalism) than by money. The French Revolution brought this same change to the European continent. Throughout the "long nineteenth century" (1789–1914) armies became less an instrument of monarchs and more an instrument (and reflection) of nations. Militaries also became larger, more sophisticated, and capable of extending European imperialism to almost any place the state wished.

France's *levée en masse,* issued in 1792, established (in theory at least) the idea that all citizens, regardless of age and gender, owed service to their nation's army because it was a representation of them and their general will. The Jourdan Law of 1798, passed to meet the demands of the War of the Second Coalition, established the principle of conscription in France and required all young men to register with the state. By 1815, more than 2 million Frenchmen had joined the army through conscription. The French Revolution changed the prevailing justification of war as an instrument of society. This connection between the military and society weakened the link between the military and the *state* and created a new link between the military and the *nation.* The difference is critical. Over the course of the nineteenth century armies became instruments of the citizenry in ways not seen in Europe since Roman times.

This connection brought fundamental changes. The logic of mercenaries as both operationally effective and cost-effective no longer made sense. The nation now had to be defended by citizens, not foreigners. Few Europeans argued that nonprofessional citizen-soldiers made better tactical soldiers. The distinction was more moral than military. The citizen, Europeans now presumed, brought élan, morale, and patriotism that more than compensated for any lack of military discipline or operational skills.

That logic led to another important change: the further opening of the officer corps to nonnobles. In most armies, nonnoble officers were concentrated in technical fields like artillery and engineering. Napoleon opened the officer corps much further with a famous call to his troops that all of them carried the baton of a marshal in their haversacks. While nobles still served disproportionately in the officer corps, a greatly increased number of bourgeois and former enlisted men became officers. Prussia followed suit in 1808, defining its officer corps by talent instead of birth and opening new institutions for the training and educating of officers. Two years earlier, Prussian reformers attempted to create an army on the "Jacobin" model, based on national devotion generating close links between the soldier and his society. Napoleon and his imitators radically changed the military to improve its esprit and, they hoped, its battlefield performance. In the process, they radically changed the connection that militaries had to their nations.

The connection of armies to their societies meant that they only derived legitimacy when citizens viewed them as representing the nation. Throughout the nineteenth century, various crises diminished that legitimacy by making the military again seem like an instrument of the state, sometimes against the peoples' will. We have already seen the Prussian model and the changing balance of civil-military relations there. In Prussia, France, and elsewhere, the military's role in breaking the revolutions of 1848 and the crushing of the Paris Commune in 1871 seemed to many to renew the links between military and monarchy as did scandals like the Dreyfus Affair, in which many republicans saw a nefarious military acting to erode the same liberties it was supposed to defend. The very term "militarism" dates to French republican opponents of Napoleon III and his use of the army as a sword of Damocles to reduce the power of the legislature, control the press, and threaten dissidents.

Fears of the military put the late-nineteenth-century expansion of continental conscription in a new light for people on both the right and the left. Marxists and other leftists saw a larger military as an instrument of capitalism and imperialism and inherently threatening to domestic liberty. Those on the right sometimes resisted conscription as well. Prussian and German Junkers occasionally called for lower conscription levels out of fear that a larger army would mean a larger officer corps, incorporating many nonnobles. Of all the European great powers, only Great Britain, due to its geography, its residual fear of standing armies from the Cromwell era, and its unrivaled navy, avoided conscription in this period.

European militaries also created general staffs in this period to coordinate and plan military activity. Originally devised by the Prussians to manage mobilization, general staff planning and centralization seemed to show its utility to Europe in the Prussian-German victory in the Franco-Prussian War of 1870–1871. In the following decades, most major military systems in Europe created staffs of their own. These staffs concentrated expertise in a variety of auxiliary fields from technology to diplomacy. Although most historians argue that the period before World War I followed the pattern of relatively little direct skill transferability between the military and civilian worlds, the staff system meant that militaries now had large numbers of officers with expertise in civilian areas.

Armies and navies played central roles in expanding European imperialism. Superior technologies like steamships and machine guns made imperialism cheap. In the First Opium War (1839–1842), one British sloop sank fifty-eight Chinese junks without suffering a single hit. Most military planners and general staffs, however, were much more concerned with the immediate problems of power projection and security on the European continent itself. Militaries also had to deal with the dizzying array of new weapons systems that European industry provided in the fin de siècle period. By 1910, these included artillery powerful enough to reduce any existing fort, machine guns capable of firing 250 rounds per minute, all-big-gun battleships, and torpedo-carrying submarines. The inability of generals and admirals fully to comprehend these technologies partially explains the unprecedented carnage of the twentieth century.

THE WORLD WARS

The two world wars brought nightmares to Europe. From German devastation of Belgian cities in 1914 to the firestorms and Holocaust of World War II, European militaries became instruments of a level of violence that horrified the world. Each of the elements of the European military system discussed above (and for that matter the state and cultural systems as well) contributed to the carnage of World War I. The vaunted general staff system created inflexible war plans that did not permit states to respond with levels of violence proportionate to either the enemy's perceived offense or immediate threat. Germany, the birthplace of the general staff, authored the most cataclysmic of these plans, the Schlieffen Plan. The plan tried to account for Germany's unfavorable geographic position between France and Russia, which were allied through the Triple Entente. At the moment of hostilities, the plan called for German forces to move through Belgium (thereby defying Great Britain, the main guarantor of Belgium's neutrality), seize Paris in six weeks, then move east by rail to meet the Russians. Better than any other single factor, it explains how the assassination of an Austrian archduke in Bosnia set an entire continent to war for four years.

The nineteenth-century creation of mass, conscript armies meant little more than mass targets for the new weapons at the disposal of World War I armies. Despite the mass casualties, nationalism kept nationally based armies like the French, British, and German in the field. Even a French mutiny in 1917 proves the point. French soldiers refused to attack defended German positions, but they did not fraternize with the enemy (indeed, somehow the Germans never found out that a mutiny was in progress) and they did not leave their positions: they knew that they were the only force between the Germans and Paris. Armies that were not nationally cohesive broke down more fully. These included, most obviously, the Austro-Hungarian, where training was conducted in eleven languages and four different religious services were performed by army chaplains each week. They also included the multiethnic Ottoman and Russian armies as well as the Italian army, where northern-southern identities often overrode still-nascent Italian nationalism.

World War I also altered the relationship between the military and society. On the one hand, large groups of veterans, proud of their service, now claimed the right to make special demands on the state as a result of that service. On the other, the war did little to inspire popular faith or confidence in Europe's military leaders. Even among the victors, few generals emerged from the war with sparkling reputations. As a result, the public's faith in the military to resolve, or even correctly define, security problems waned. The widespread disarmament movements of the 1920s were partly rooted in a desire to keep militaries as small as possible. In effect, Europeans had come to argue that smaller, not larger, armies were the pathway to peace. That logic represented a radical change from the logic of the prewar period.

The political instability of the interwar period led to a period of relatively frequent military involvement in European politics. Most famously, army support was critical to fascist takeovers in Italy, Germany,

and Spain. In the latter case, a former army chief of staff, Francisco Franco, took power, while in the former two, Mussolini and Hitler derived much of their appeal from army support of their cause. In Greece, a military coup in 1935 restored King George II to the throne and in France major military appointments always had an overtly political dimension. Chief of the General Staff Maurice Gamelin was a political ally of the socialist Édouard Daladier. His commander-in-chief, A. J. Georges, was closely connected to Daladier's political nemesis, Paul Reynaud. The political rivalry between the generals and their political supporters impeded decision making in the French high command in the 1930s, with disastrous results. Gamelin actively opposed the return of Reynaud to power after the German occupation of Norway in April 1940. As a compromise, Daladier stayed on as defense minister. In the tense month of May, Reynaud replaced both Gamelin and Daladier with men closer to his own politics.

In both world wars, mass mobilization and mass suffering blurred the line between military and civilian. Especially in the World War II period, civilian and military skills "fused" as the formerly sharp distinction between the two spheres melted. So many people wore uniforms (including large numbers of women in Britain and the Soviet Union) that maintaining a military-civilian dichotomy proved difficult. Long-range aviation allowed militaries to take war into their enemy's heartland. The incredible sacrifices of the Soviet people underscored how warfare in the twentieth century affected civilians.

World War II also marked the decline of Western Europe as the world's main center of military power. Close links to the increasingly powerful United States military help to explain the Anglo-Soviet victory. Germany, on the other hand, was much less successful in creating synergy with its non-European ally, Japan. Throughout the war American industrial capability and manpower translated into an increasingly large voice in strategic and operational decision making. After bearing the brunt against Germany in 1940 and 1941, Great Britain had to accept second (some argue third) power status in the Grand Alliance. This diminution of European military power and prestige resulted in problems across their empires as well, including the "Quit India" movement and the growth of anti-imperial groups like the Viet Minh.

THE COLD WAR AND AFTER

The dominant theme of the post–World War II period is, of course, the cold war. No European military could escape the reality that their power in relation to

Soviet Military. Parade in Red Square. ©CORBIS

the Americans and the Soviets had diminished significantly. What, then, were militaries to do? Three possibilities soon emerged: alliance with either the USSR or the United States; neutrality (usually implying only defensive military activity); or military action largely independent from the superpowers. For some Europeans, reestablishing empires (and in some cases, the nation itself) was often a higher state priority than choosing sides in the cold war.

Most European militaries became involved in one of the two cold war alliances, the North Atlantic Treaty Organization (formed in 1949) and the Warsaw Pact (formed in 1955). NATO involved active members of the World War II coalition alongside former enemies of that coalition like Italy and, later, West Germany. The 1954 decision to rearm West Germany, under the leadership of many Nazi-era officers, stirred considerable controversy. In August of that year France rejected the proposal, but under American pressure later accepted it. The lingering problems, including NATO's 1957 naming of a German general to command forces in Central Europe, contributed to France's

alienation from NATO (see below). The militaries of Eastern Europe, of course, had little choice. Largely as a response to NATO and a rearmed West Germany, the Soviet Union codified its relationship with its satellite states' militaries in the Warsaw Pact. Austria, Yugoslavia, Ireland, Sweden, Finland, and Switzerland tried to remain outside the superpower alliance system, with varying degrees of success.

The existence of nuclear weapons represented a fundamental change in the logic of alliances and of military strategy itself. England's explosion of an atomic bomb in 1952 (followed by an explosion of a hydrogen bomb in 1957) and France's successful nuclear test in 1960 did not change the fundamentally unequal power relationships between the superpowers (in this case the United States) and their allies. America's role in ending the 1956 Suez War against England's and France's wishes underscored the nature of that relationship. European militaries thus faced very real credibility problems when they were seen by their citizens as mere instruments of the superpowers. This problem particularly plagued Eastern European militaries as the policies they helped to enforce were so evidently contrary to the wishes of the people.

Striving to create a more independent military policy could help to solve the problem of legitimacy. Of course, this option was simply not open to the Eastern European militaries until the collapse of the Soviet Union. Ironically, the end of the cold war may not have solved the problem, as many Eastern European nations soon applied for membership in NATO. France typified the model of independent military action. In 1959 France withdrew its fleet from NATO, refused to stockpile American nuclear weapons on its soil, and asked the United States to remove its warplanes. In 1966, shortly after revealing its own long-range nuclear delivery capability, France formally withdrew from the military operations of NATO. The alliance subsequently moved its headquarters from Paris to Brussels and other key facilities to Maastricht and Rome.

Allegations that national armies were primarily serving the superpowers combined with several militaries' unpopular roles in trying to reestablish empires. The French experiences in Indochina and Algeria tore the country apart, leading to the collapse of the Fourth Republic and fears of revolution or even civil war. The French war in Algeria (1954–1962) led to ten thousand French casualties, an army mutiny, and even an assassination attempt on France's greatest hero, Charles de Gaulle. Belgium's experiences in the Congo, Portuguese operations in Angola, and Dutch operations in Indonesia also met significant opposition at home. Depending on one's point of view, European militaries looked to be either ineffective in reestablishing colonialism or antediluvian in trying to restore empires that properly belonged to a bygone era. Significantly, European militaries did not support the American war in Vietnam as they had the war in Korea. To do so would have further fed charges of both neoimperialism and inappropriate action as an instrument of the United States.

The end of the cold war did not end the essential dilemma of European militaries. Although the Warsaw Pact dissolved, NATO expanded. Britain and France both joined the coalition that defeated Iraq in the Persian Gulf War, though the war was not as popular in Europe as it was in America. Europeans also participated in military operations in Bosnia and Kosovo under the aegis of NATO. The latter operation saw the largest German military effort since 1945. British prime minister Tony Blair called the operation in Kosovo an example of a new ideology: the imperialism of morality. European military operations, he suggested, would derive legitimacy from their defense of the weak and their protection of human rights. In doing so he was both addressing the still powerful need to legitimate the actions of European militaries and recalling medieval notions of just warfare.

Exactly what role Europe should play in the military arena of the post–cold war world remains of great debate. In the absence of an immediate threat, many European nations have eliminated or greatly reduced unpopular universal (male) military training laws. Relying exclusively on volunteers, including larger numbers of women, may lead to increased legitimacy, as may European attempts to move away from American leadership. In 1999 several Western European nations took final steps toward the creation of a joint European military force designed to be able to act independently of the United States. Eastern Europe's military future appeared to be in even more doubt. Some of the former Soviet republics became important nuclear powers. Several former Warsaw Pact nations looked to NATO membership as a way to guarantee their security and gain access to advanced Western weapons technology.

CONCLUSIONS

War, according to the famous dictum by Carl von Clausewitz, is an extension of politics by other means. To paraphrase Clausewitz, militaries are an extension of their societies by other means. As such, they merit attention from social historians. Military history ought to do more than examine generalship and tactics. It ought also to explore the connections between military institutions and the social, cultural, and political patterns of European history. Here, of course, social historians have much to contribute. The result of such a contribution will be a better understanding of the ways that the military has influenced, and been influenced by, large patterns of social history.

See also **Military Service; War and Conquest** *(volume 2);* **Social Control** *(in this volume).*

BIBLIOGRAPHY

Bushnell, John. *Mutiny amid Repression: Russian Soldiers in the Revolution of 1905–1906.* Bloomington, Ind., 1985.

Cobb, Richard. *The Peoples' Armies: The Armées Révolutionnaires, Instrument of the Terror in the Departments, April 1793 to Floreal Year II.* Translated by Marianne Elliott. New Haven, Conn., 1987. Analysis of what the military as an institution meant to revolutionary France.

Déak, István. *Beyond Nationalism: A Social and Political History of the Habsburg Officer Corps, 1848–1918.* New York, 1990.

Ellis, John. *The Social History of the Machine Gun.* Baltimore, 1986. See his argument on the responses of European militaries to technological change.

Herwig, Holger. *The German Naval Officer Corps: A Social and Political History, 1890–1918.* Oxford, 1973.

Horne, Alistair. *To Lose a Battle: France 1940.* Boston, 1969. Insightful discussion of the domestic roles of the French military between the world wars.

Huntington, Samuel. *The Soldier and the State: The Theory of Politics and Civil-Military Relations.* Cambridge, Mass., 1957. Remains an important starting point for discussions of civil-military relations.

Wildman, Allan K. *The End of the Imperial Russian Army.* 2 vols. Princeton, N.J., 1987. Provides a good complement to Bushnell.

ARTISANS

Peter N. Stearns

Artisans form a key category in European social history, from before the early modern period into the early twentieth century. Many of the most perceptive studies of workers and working-class movements have been devoted implicitly or explicitly to artisans. Distinguishing between artisanal experience and that of a larger working class, but also relating the two groups, forms a vital topic in modern European history.

Artisanal history focuses primarily on western and central Europe. Even in this region, important studies show contrasting artisanal reactions, based on distinctive legal and economic contexts, despite shared components. In eastern Europe, an artisanal category began to develop in the later nineteenth century, fed by imported workers from central Europe. Until communist takeovers, this belated artisanal experience replicated some of the features seen in western Europe earlier on.

Artisans are craft workers. They share a high degree of skill, the result of substantial and usually fairly formal training. Depending on the trade, apprenticeships could last up to seven years. Acquisition of mature skill was often demonstrated by some kind of exemplary production, a "masterpiece." After apprenticeship, most artisans went through a stage of service as journeymen, working for an artisan master and receiving wages plus, often, housing and board. In some cases, the journeyman phase proved lifelong. In principle, however, journeymen sought opportunities to become masters in their own right, by saving to buy a shop or by marrying a master's daughter and/or acquiring through inheritance. Masters were owners, but unlike modern employers they typically continued to work with their hands, alongside their journeymen.

Artisanal work depended on rather simple, often manual technology, which brought the skill component to the foreground. Artisans participated in various stages of production, from raw material to finished product, and often had a sense of artistry and a high degree of identification with their work. Traditionally, artisans sold their own wares.

Prominent artisanal trades included food processing (bakers, butchers), fine metal and jewelry work (smiths, goldsmiths), construction (masons, carpenters, cabinet makers), printing, and clothing (tailors, shoemakers). While the classic artisanal centers were urban, rural artisans existed as well—like village blacksmiths or millers. Rural artisans typically stood apart from peasants, often playing a key role in organizing rural protest or taking advantage of new opportunities for education and literacy. But the skill definitions for rural artisans were less clear and their

Artisans' Workshop. A cutler's family workshop. From the codex of Balthasar Behem, early fifteenth century, Cracow.

An Artisan's Skill. A basketmaker. From *The Book of English Trades and Library of the Useful Arts* (1824).

group experiences were less coherent than among the urban cohort.

EARLY MODERN PATTERNS

The European artisanal tradition formed during the Middle Ages. This is when most crafts emerged (printing was of course a later development). This is when the guild organization emerged as well. Artisanal guilds, often compulsory for major crafts in a given city, attempted to defend artisanal status and economic position on a noncapitalist basis. Guilds regulated the number of apprentices, to prevent oversupply and so a reduction of income and also to constrain the opportunity for individual masters to advance too rapidly over their colleagues by employing too many assistants. The type of training apprentices were to receive was stipulated as well, although enforcement varied. Standards of production were regulated, which inhibited rapid technological change but in principle protected the quality of goods pro-

duced. Guilds often wielded considerable urban political power. They provided a rich associational life, participating in urban festivals with distinctive costumes. Many guilds sponsored social events and also assisted members or their families in sickness or death. Guilds also facilitated travel, particularly by younger journeymen. A year or more—the *Wanderjahre* in Germany—was often spent wandering from town to town, with guilds helping the journeyman to obtain appropriate jobs. Wandering provided unusual experience for many artisans, even across loose political boundaries. It also helped prevent gluts in labor, serving as part of the security protection that artisans valued so highly. Traditionalism and group orientation, rather than change and individual maximization, characterized the artisanal tradition.

Within this context, several developments focus historical attention during the early modern centuries. Change is one. With an increasingly commercial economy and some population growth, artisanal ideals became harder to achieve. More and more journeymen found access to masterships difficult, if not impossible—particularly if there was no possibility of inheritance. Journeymen sometimes organized separately from masters in this situation. Strikes occurred, the first in European history—for example, among early printers in the sixteenth century. The artisanal economy was not yet overturned by the eighteenth century, but it was often challenged. At the same time, however, opportunities for more distant sales, even exports to such new customers as the Russian aristocracy after Peter the Great's westernization, provided growing opportunities for master craftsmen in such fields as fine furniture.

Change often had a gender component. In the Middle Ages, women as well as men participated in some crafts, even in guilds. This was most common among widows of master artisans, but there were female crafts, such as lace making, as well. In early modern Europe women tended increasingly to be excluded from the major crafts and from guilds, and a great deal of misogyny developed among some journeymen's organizations. On the other hand, the wives of master artisans often played a key commercial role, supervising the sales counter; in some cases they were more literate than their husbands.

Variety is a final early modern theme. Different parts of Europe maintained different degrees of guild cohesion. Guild traditions relaxed substantially in Britain, permitting unusual rates of technological change without obliterating the artisanal tradition. Guild traditions were far tighter in Germany, ultimately promoting a more conservative artisanal approach in economics and politics alike.

THE INDUSTRIAL REVOLUTION

Individual artisans contributed to the industrial revolution in various ways. Particularly in Britain and France, key industrial inventions, like the Jacquard loom in France, typically emanated from artisan-tinkerers. Some artisans masters gradually evolved their operations into more modern, capitalistic forms of employment, increasing their workforce and separating their own managerial activities from manual labor. This was particularly true in textiles. Other artisans migrated to early factories, adjusting their skills to serve as machine-installers and other skilled operatives.

On the whole, however, the industrial revolution was a shock to artisans and the artisanal tradition. The emphasis on profit, production, and often lower quality all conflicted with artisanal values. Ironically, given the gradual installation of industrialization, artisanal opportunities often continued to increase, particularly in fields like construction, where urban and overall population growth was not initially matched by technological change. But artisans knew or sensed that they were losing control of the manufacturing economy. Simultaneously, legal changes, often derived from the French Revolution, eliminated guilds or at least weakened their control over technological change and the size of the labor force. Economic and political developments in tandem led to reductions in formal apprenticeship. Many artisans encountered efforts to speed up work and reduce artistic quality, even when the factory system had not yet arrived. This was true in furniture making, for example.

Artisans reacted in various ways. Some opposed industrialization altogether. Artisans were among the leading Luddites, protesting and sometimes destroying new machinery. Many artisans formed the key audience for utopian socialists who urged a return to idealized cooperative production. Artisans led in the formation of early unions, using their skilled position, their frequent literacy, and their organizational experience. Some unions were purely local, but several national efforts were ventured under artisanal leadership, from England to (later) Russia. Everywhere in Europe, artisans sponsored the first phases of what turned out to be the modern labor movement. Artisans were key participants in the great European revolutions, from 1789 through 1848 and the Paris Commune of 1871. From artisanal ranks came early socialist activists, such as August Bebel in Germany.

But artisans also sought to improve themselves individually through education and by imitating some of the habits of the middle class. Many sought "respectability," for example, by leading in temperance movements (against what was usually a heavy-drinking artisanal tradition). Many artisans picked up the new middle-class work ethic, which insisted on an unprecedented attention to clock time and maximizing productivity, in place of older artisanal traditions, such as taking off "holy Monday" to recover from weekend revels. Many tried to protect their position by marrying late and/or limiting their birthrates. Many were vociferously hostile to factory workers, whom they viewed as degraded and dangerous.

Impulses toward collective and individual improvement often combined. Artisans played a key role in the British Chartist movement, particularly in southern England, but in it they sought better educational opportunities and the vote. Artisanal unions often turned to narrow-group protection at the expense of larger working-class unity. In the 1860s, New Model unionism in Britain reacted against Chartist radicalism by stressing gains based on skill. Craft un-

A Shoemakers' Guild. A sign representing the shoemakers' guild in Nürnberg, Germany, in 1600. The inscription was added in 1786 when the sign was restored. GERMANISCHES NATIONALMUSEUM, NÜRNBERG, GERMANY/SCALA/ART RESOURCE, NY

ions were often quite successful, locally and even nationally, in winning higher pay and shorter hours and even pushing back efforts to speed up production through the spread of piece-rate wage systems. In all their reactions—radical, conservative, and mixed—artisans had a key impact on European society throughout most of the nineteenth century.

Artisanal history fades, however, by the later nineteenth century. The growth of the factory labor force equaled and then surpassed artisanal numbers; in England the parity point occurred as early as 1850. Labor movements continued to have identifiable artisan components, but mass unions and marxist socialism increasingly predominated by the 1890s. New technology cut into artisanal specialties. With new printing equipment, old skills were displaced and even semiskilled women workers entered the field. Sewing machines unseated artisan tailors and shoemakers. Electric and gasoline motors, plus new materials, destroyed or at least modified artisanal work even on construction sites. By 1900, distinctions between skilled workers and other workers remained, but the skilled workers were not really artisans.

Still, echoes of artisanal separatism and tradition continued into the early decades of the twentieth century. Some artisans turned to the political right in defense of their identity. Artisanal support for Nazism in Germany was considerable, and guildlike entities were revived in response (though without significant economic powers). This was a last hurrah, however. Further industrialization, plus the advent of communism in postwar east central Europe, ended all but the memory of a distinctive artisanal identity in Europe, once and for all.

See also other articles in this section.

BIBLIOGRAPHY

Crossick, Geoffrey, and Heinz-Gerhard Haupt. *Shopkeepers and Master Artisans in Nineteenth-Century Europe.* New York, 1984.

Farr, James R. *Artisans in Europe, 1350–1914.* Cambridge, U.K., and New York, 2000.

Merriman, John, ed. *Consciousness and Class Experience in Nineteenth-Century Europe.* New York, 1985.

Stearns, Peter N. *1848: The Revolutionary Tide in Europe.* New York, 1974.

Steinberg, Mark. *Moral Communities: The Culture of Class Relations in the Russian Printing Industry, 1867–1907.* Berkeley, Calif., 1992.

Thomis, Malcolm. *The Luddites: Machine-Breaking in Regency England.* Hamden, Conn., 1970.

Thompson, E. P. *The Making of the English Working Class.* New York, 1964.

Volkov, Shulamit. *The Rise of Popular Antimodernism in Germany: The Urban Master Artisans, 1873–1896.* Princeton, N.J., 1978.

Wiesner, Merry. *Working Women in Renaissance Germany.* New Brunswick, N.J., 1986.

THE PETTY BOURGEOISIE

Daniel T. Orlovsky

In his diaries, Victor Klemperer, a survivor and a remarkable observer of daily life under the Nazi regime, from time to time described his commonplace surroundings in a Dresden suburb. He referred to the banal decoration schemes of his neighbors and their herdlike passivity in accepting the daily outpourings and policies of the regime. When he wished to describe those people negatively, he frequently called them and their attitudes "petty bourgeois." Herein lies a story with deep roots in European history. Klemperer was after all a university professor, a professional, a member of the intelligentsia, and a converted Jew married to a Protestant. In education and income he was several notches above the traditional artisans and white-collar workers who in the twentieth century were thought of as belonging to the lower middle class. It has been all too easy to overlook the petty bourgeoisie or to follow Klemperer and dismiss or mock them. But the historian does this at great risk.

DEFINING THE PETTY BOURGEOISIE

One of the more fascinating and hard to define topics of European social history is the role and evolution of the petty bourgeoisie. This was a social group or groups that occupied the space between the peasantry and later the factory wage laborers on the lower end of the social spectrum and the capital owning, higher status professionals of the bourgeoisie. It is a hard group to define precisely because it was composed of many groups that changed over time, from the master artisans and shopkeepers of the eighteenth and nineteenth centuries to the white-collar workers, lower- and middle-ranking civil servants, and technical personnel of the late nineteenth century and the twentieth century. The petty bourgeoisie comprised a variety of occupations and social and cultural outlooks but was generally in a precarious economic and social situation. Generally, however, too much has been made of this precariousness. The petty bourgeoisie bore the brunt of industrialization and modernization in all

their forms. Yet at the same time they furthered the process of industrialization and in the twentieth century were essential cogs in the vast projects of Soviet-style socialism, fascism, the European interventionist welfare state, and even the conservative, promarket regimes, such as that in Great Britain in the 1980s under Margaret Thatcher.

The results of the early challenges of industrialization were seen in the politics of the large numbers of people who filled lower-middle-class occupations. Most often it was a defensive politics of interest or corporation that shifted uneasily between left and right by the mid-nineteenth century. Nonetheless, to overemphasize the weaknesses of this social formation misses the important social and political power generated by the functions of the petty bourgeoisie within both socialist and capitalist societies. The occupations of the petty bourgeoisie were crucial to all the major state-building projects of the twentieth century. Through these occupations, the lower middle classes became a powerful social force despite the fact that they had to fit into the cultural and political hegemonies of classes to which they were in most respects alien, that is, the proletariat and the bourgeoisie.

It is hard to study the petty bourgeoisie or "lower middle classes." Scholarship made great strides in the late twentieth century, but the groups and layers have been understudied compared to the more attractive histories of the workers, peasants, entrepreneurs, and professionals. The petty bourgeoisie were attacked vehemently by Karl Marx and Friedrich Engels, who predicted their disappearance. Their history does not seem at first glance to shed much light on the profound historical movements and events of modern Europe. But that is the paradox, for these middling people in fact played key roles in the major revolutionary events. Petty bourgeois groups were in the forefront of the politics of "antimodernism" and hostility to liberalism. They formed part of the electoral support for fascist parties in Italy and Germany and fed various right-wing movements in France as well. In Russia, however, the lower middle strata leaned toward the left, an essential social base for the Populist and Socialist Parties, and helped build the world's first socialist state, the USSR.

Thus it is no longer possible to maintain the dominant ideas associated with the petty bourgeoisie in earlier historical writings. The first idea was that the group was nonconcrete, that the petty bourgeoisie had no consistent social or cultural characteristics, lacked definition, and therefore was not a class in a marxist or any other sociological sense. The second idea was that the group emerged out of the concrete guild institutions of the Middle Ages and the early modern period and that its trajectory was inevitably toward a class within "modern" capitalism. Marx and Engels predicted that, despite its high point in the eighteenth and nineteenth centuries, the petty bourgeoisie must inevitably lose its confrontation with capital and disappear. The last image of the petty bourgeoisie was that its discontents fueled and became a mainstay of fascism. According to this view, a straight line existed between the confrontation of artisans and shopkeepers with late nineteenth-century capitalism and twentieth-century fascism. However, the petty bourgeoisie survived and indeed reinvented itself several times during the long history of its confrontation with capitalism. Artisans could and did play an important role in electoral and corporate politics even in the twentieth century. Adding the Russian and Soviet experience to the mix, clearly the lower middle occupational groups in the right circumstances could just as well become state builders on the left as well as active elements of corporatist or fascist movements and politics on the right.

FROM CORPORATE TRADITIONS TO INDIVIDUALISM

Beleaguered shopkeepers seeking to defend older forms of commerce and turning to the right were not the whole story, however. In Britain the rise of shopkeepers was vital to the consumer revolution of the eighteenth century. There, too, shopkeepers were intermediate between middle and working classes, often supporting the latter, on whom their businesses might depend. Concern about department stores and other innovations developed. But British shopkeepers never coalesced politically, certainly not on the right. They hoped for some government protection but with fewer partisan overtones.

The German term *Mittelstand* (middle class) originated in the Middle Ages in the estate society of central Europe and the orderly world of handicrafts and artisanship. The meaning changed significantly during the nineteenth century. The middling or mediating nature of these groups was captured in the definition, yet the *Mittelstand* increasingly represented the space between the bourgeoisie and high professionals on the one hand and the proletariat and peasantry on the other. Far from lacking a firm set of characteristics, the classical petty bourgeoisie derived their livelihoods from their own capital and labor. They earned income from small-scale property that they worked with the help of family or limited wage labor. As Geoffrey Crossick and Heinz-Gerhard Haupt put it, petty bourgeois economic activity in both form and manner of operation centered on the family. The foundations of the preindustrial petty bourgeoisie were corporations and guilds of medieval and early modern Europe. These corporations, which organized craft production and trade, were powerful everywhere in Europe except England through the mid-eighteenth century. Monopoly and order were the corporate goals, reinforced and maintained by strict entrance requirements, family origins, and conservative social norms. It was easier for the sons of master artisans, for example, to reach that status, though the typical path was through a formal apprenticeship, followed by journeyman status, and eventually independent practice in the trade as a master, having won the approval of the jury of the corporation. This approval was based on expertise in the craft. The path involved symbolic rituals buttressing the notion of the corporation as a harmonious community that protected its members and looked after its member families in time of need. These corporations in turn were part of the hierarchy of the towns, so citizenship and a place in the guild and family were part of the social identity of the master artisan.

Early challenges to this order came even before the French Revolution and the rise of liberalism and capitalism. Challenges came from the state, stratification within the guilds, and dissatisfied journeymen, who wished to strike out on their own. Corporate structures were strongest in Germany. Though weaker in France, even there small-scale enterprises and artisan life persisted into the late nineteenth century. The corporate traditions were weakest in England, where individual small-scale enterprises developed and flourished much earlier than on the Continent. The corporate traditions permitted German master artisans to organize to defend themselves and their idealized way of life against industrialization, free trade, and liberalism in politics.

In France the shopkeepers organized much later in the century and with volatile, rapid shifts from left to right in politics. The petty bourgeoisie and lower middle classes saw the power of organized labor yet

Skilled Craftsmen. Cannon founders at work in Renaissance Florence. Biblioteca Riccardiana MS. 2669, fol. 110v. BIBLIOTECA RICCARDIANA, FLORENCE/SCALA/ART RESOURCE, NY

wanted to maintain their separateness from labor, and they were susceptible to the appeals of nationalism. Though French shopkeepers moved to the right, the shift was by no means simple. It involved a thorough transformation of shopkeepers' place socially and politically, their relationship to the state and its various branches of government, and their relationship to other interests, especially big business and employees. After several unsuccessful attempts to organize shopkeepers, the Ligue pour la Défense des Intérêts du Travail, de l'Industrie, et du Commerce was created in Paris in 1888. Quickly growing to 100,000 members, it lasted until the outbreak of World War I. At first the league's political view was radical socialist, and its main demands centered around punitive taxation of the threatening department store. Its code word was "specialization," summarized in the following 1896 appeal in the league's official newspaper, *La Revendication:*

> The money you bring from all over Paris and spend in those commercial agglomerations is absolutely lost to you. . . . If on the other hand, the hatter did business with her neighbor the shoe merchant, and the shoe merchant reciprocated, then both would make money and be all the more willing to do business with the neighborhood butcher, *charcutier* [pork butcher] and wine-seller. In helping your neighbors to earn a living, you are making customers for yourself and creating an environment of mutual respect. If centralization is bad in political matters, it is even more harmful from an economic point of view. (Nord, 1986)

The enemy was defined as all that threatened the economic independence of the local community—the department stores, financial institutions, cooperatives, and bureaucratic state. In common with representatives of the petty bourgeoisie elsewhere in Europe, the league considered itself a defender of the family, the locality, and the workplace. Foreign competition and by extension foreigners were viewed with hostility. French shopkeepers were protectionists, and as Philip Nord put it, they detested economic liberalism and were not in fact individualists. Rather they saw the family and workplace as "little communities organized hierarchically and cemented by ties of sentiment," not as institutions of free and equal individuals bound by contractual relations. The league spoke of "direct democracy" and invoked the traditions of the revolution of 1789. But the larger political context came into play as the radical right began to use rhetoric that appealed to the shopkeepers.

In addition Christian democracy after 1891 launched a defense of the small shopkeeper as a victim of the anarchy of free market individualism. According to this view, laissez-faire policies imposed by a cabal of Jews and Freemasons threatened the family, small shop, and other natural associations. The cure

Individual Small-Scale Enterprise. A Scottish shopkeeper. Anonymous drawing, eighteenth century. GLASGOW MUSEUMS: THE PEOPLE'S PALACE, GLASGOW, SCOTLAND

turn inspired creation in 1904 of the Institut International pour l'Étude du Problème des Classes Moyennes, a permanent body, headquartered in Brussels, to study the problems of the petty bourgeoisie. Interest in the petty bourgeoisie on the part of large capital and conservative politicians derived from a desire for stability and a fear of socialism, similar to the motivations behind fascism later in the twentieth century. The smallholder and artisan were considered virtuous, and most important they occupied a "strategic social location, at the juncture where labor and capital met. The small shopkeeper, by virtue of his middling rank, blurred the lines of social cleavage and tempered the shock of class struggle." This rapid shift in the outlook and political alignment of the shopkeepers illustrates the unique characteristics of the petty bourgeoisie as a whole that cannot be reduced to simple political and social formulas.

was economic and political decentralization, which would reenergize local bodies as the source of Christian values. The move to the right was abetted by the need to become more effective politicians. The shopkeepers, insofar as they were small propertyholders, were caught between the socialist movement and the bourgeoisie. Shopkeepers as propertyholders and more importantly as believers in the traditional ideology described above did not necessarily support and were not necessarily supported by the emerging layers of commercial employees and white-collar workers, who saw collectivism in the form of cooperatives, for example, as salvation. The Dreyfus affair solidified the shift to the right. Nationalist electoral victories in 1900 and 1902 were in part blamed by the left on the shopkeepers, whom they now saw as enemies of the working class.

Shopkeeper engagement in nationalist politics had its downside, as the league and other bearers of traditional values lost leadership of the movement. The torch passed to syndicates, professional organizations, and new forms of corporatism that persisted after World War I. The ideology of the movement also was transformed as the syndicate took precedence over the local community in the retailer's life. State protection became less important than demands for a consultative role within the executive branch. Finally, shopkeepers identified less with the "people" and more with the *classes moyennes* (middle classes). Such notions and the idea of a full-scale mobilization of the middle classes owed much to the Belgian Catholic publicists Hector Lambrechts and Oscar Pyfferoen, who in 1899 and 1901 organized International Congresses of the Petty Bourgeoisie. These congresses in

WHITE-COLLAR WORKERS AND ARTISANS

A quiet social revolution was taking place alongside the evolution of traditional petty bourgeois social groups. A new social stratum defined as white-collar workers organized by occupation developed. The white-collar workers and the closely related technical personnel were clearly the offspring of late-nineteenth-century capitalism and technological changes. White-collar workers and technical personnel were situated just below the professions in the social hierarchy, though often they adopted and displayed educational and organizational characteristics similar to those of the higher-status professions. The prospects of social mobility for the children of the traditional petty bourgeoisie were limited. The young rarely made it into the higher world of the big bourgeoisie or high-status professions. By the end of the nineteenth century the sons and sometimes the daughters of the petty bourgeoisie, however, were drawn into the new white-collar occupations in commercial or industrial firms, the government bureaucracy, and lower-status professions such as elementary and secondary school teaching. This was one more indication of adaptability and of the new phenomenon of layering within the petty bourgeoisie itself. Henceforth occupation was a more defining characteristic, and place in the layered hierarchy within and among occupations and professions became the essence of social identity.

The rise of white-collar workers raises a host of interpretive questions. The group differed from workers, if only in being nonmanual. But they had routine jobs, often governed by new technologies, such as typewriters and cash registers. Yet they valued their tentative links with the middle class, taking pride, for example, in wearing business outfits to work. Employers also made every effort to keep them distinct from workers, offering salaries instead of wages and often separate benefit plans. This combination helped keep white-collar workers from significant unionization, though some movements developed. The same combination explains why marxists often berated clerks for their false consciousness. The presence of many women in white-collar ranks, as salesclerks and telephone operators, was another distinctive feature of this rising segment. Eager to protect their standard of living, white-collar families were often at the forefront in limiting family size by the late nineteenth century. Finally, many white-collar workers led in developing novel leisure forms and habits, such as cigarette smoking, that might compensate for the routine nature of their work without seeming to proletarianize them.

World War I came as a watershed both for tradespeople and artisans and for the new lower middle class of white-collar workers, commercial employees, technical intelligentsia, and mid- to lower-level bureaucrats. The petty bourgoisie in Germany and Russia exhibited the volatility and capacity for changing allegiances from right and center to left and from left to right that became the hallmark of the lower middle classes in the twentieth century. In Germany, in a major shift during the decades leading up to World War I, traditional artisans adopted a politics and culture of "antimodernism," a term coined by Shulamit Volkov. Reacting to industrialization and the growing power of capitalism, the artisans responded negatively to liberals and socialists alike. They expressed a mood of hostility to democratic institutions and politics linked to a capitalism that was destroying their way of life. These attitudes changed to some extent during the war, as some artisans identified more with wealthier factory owners and store owners under the pressures of the mobilized state.

The ambivalence if not hostility of artisans toward what they loosely labeled "modernity" formed a ready reservoir of support for antidemocratic and fascist movements in the Weimar Republic, including the Nazis. White-collar workers, on the other hand, were more numerous and more powerful as a result of the war and the expansion of capitalist and government institutions. The lower middle classes (or *Mittelstand*) were split. A good number leaned heavily to the left and identified with the social and economic plight of factory workers and organized labor. In fact organization of white-collar workers was the order of the day, and numerous large associations were created.

The war pressured white-collar workers with inflation and stagnant or falling wages.

In France, where the structure of the economy was more conducive to the traditional petty bourgeoisie, the *artisanat* (craftsmen) virtually recreated their structure after the war in what has been termed an artisanal renaissance. In March 1922 representatives of artisanal groups met in Paris and formed the General Confederation of French Artisans (CGAF). Skilled tradespeople earlier had formed syndicates and federations that established lines of demarcation from both unskilled labor and capital, but the creation of the CGAF was a major shift from a traditional corporate trade consciousness to a class idea that posited the *artisanat* as a group with common interests based on skills and limited property. The Artisanal Charter of 1923 presented the *artisanat* as a *tampon social,* a "social buffer in a troubled tumultuous time, as a group based on the quality of work, on individualism and regional diversity" (Zdatny, 1990).

The French artisanal movement was unusually cohesive. At its core was the notion of the "profession," or "human activity . . . productive as opposed to speculative . . . manual, full of personality, as opposed to anonymous, mechanical and schematized" (Zdatny, 1990, p. 123). This was music to the ears of corporatists who, like the more radical fascists, believed in the idea of social harmony, an anti–class war notion of society, based on occupation, "the shared skill and holistic labor experience." The occupation or profession was the antidote to class identity and the threat of bolshevism. The occupation was, of course, closely linked to the family. The *artisanat* in the 1930s was drawn to both corporatism and syndicalism as political movements hostile to market capitalism. Al-

White-Collar Worker. A clerk types in an office in Cadiz, Spain, 1917. JULIAN OSLE MUÑOZ/©ARCHIVIE OSLE/ CORBIS

though a significant number of artisans opted in the late 1930s for the rightist utopias of corporatism, they never accepted the authoritarianism of fascism itself.

RUSSIA AND THE SOVIET UNION

In Russia the lower middle classes played a crucial role in the development of economic institutions, in three early-twentieth-century revolutions, and in building the world's first socialist state, the USSR. The Russian lower middle strata were truly a "hidden class" both before and after the revolutions of 1917. Their powerful social movement was instrumental in the growth of capitalism in the late nineteenth and early twentieth centuries. The Russian experience combined political volatility and ambiguity with economic and institutional staying power, a relevant model for lower middle strata experiences elsewhere in Europe.

In Russia the lower middle strata leaned heavily and quickly to the left and saw factory workers and the peasantry as their natural allies. Russian commercial employees, cooperative workers, shop personnel, teachers, and medical assistants never formed a solid alliance with the liberal parties of the left center or center, such as the Kadets, Progressists, or Octobrists. The magnetism of bourgeois life remained weak, largely because the bourgeoisie was small and fragmented but also because the antibourgeois ideologies of the left, both marxism and populism, were strong. Instead, the Russian or petty bourgeoisie remained well hidden to historians and even to contemporaries because of the dominant marxist paradigm of society that emphasized workers and peasants and their struggles against capital and the nobility. The lower middle strata were full participants in the social and political movements that produced the February and October Revolutions in 1917. They organized according to occupation and profession in a prolific manner and assumed leading roles in professional organizations, congresses, political parties, and the Soviets. The Russian provisional government leaned on them heavily, especially the cooperative movement, in its half-baked attempt to transcend the market amidst the revolutionary turmoil of 1917. This mass of educated and skilled personnel was largely invisible in political discourse, a lesson in how language can obfuscate as well as shape or create social realities.

When the Soviets came to power in 1917 at the head of what was loudly proclaimed as a socialist revolution guided by a workers' and peasants' state, it was convenient to de-emphasize the powerful role of the lower middle strata in the revolution and in building the Soviet state and society. Yet in fact the entire infrastructure of administrative and economic institutions that had grown up in the early twentieth century and had reached maturity during World War I and the revolutions of 1917 was staffed by the burgeoning masses of white-collar workers. Vladimir Lenin and the Bolsheviks seized and maintained power and built a vast bureaucratic state quickly due to the organizational prowess of this underrecognized social group and the social revolution in which they participated as equal members with the striking factory labor, the armed forces, and the peasantry. Throughout the 1920s the Soviet lower middle class tried to fit in, to become mediators in the new socialist state and society, while avoiding the opprobrium of birth outside the proletariat. Their greatest fear was rejection as members of the socialist commonweal. They fit in and became indispensable. The social revolution continued with the addition of large numbers of women to the white-collar workforce, a feature of the new lower-middle-class life and occupations that was duplicated elsewhere in Europe. Joseph Stalin's revolution from above at the end of the 1920s and throughout the 1930s again created great instability for employees yet increased opportunities in a vastly expanding industrial economy, collectivized agriculture, and the building of new cities. All required armies of white-collar personnel.

THE SELF-IMAGE OF THE LOWER MIDDLE CLASS

Elsewhere in Europe the petty bourgeoisie were influenced by the dominant models of politics emerging from under the rubble of World War I and the Russian Revolution. In all countries some visible patterns were observable and similar questions were framed. Were the new strata of technical and protoprofessionals full members of the middle class, or were they subordinate to those higher up in the professional hierarchies and mediators between capital and labor?

With the Soviets the power of the new lower middle class in twentieth century history is clearer. For example, the self-image of the emerging technocratic lower middle classes was expressed by a twenty-four-year-old industrial chemist in June 1939:

I belong to the lower middle class. From the financial consideration, I should limit this to income ranges of about 200–300 pounds per annum. . . . In a word, the middle class man must be a black coated worker. . . . Although I belong to the blackcoated middle class, I do not think this classification is very hard and fast. For I belong to another division of the middle class, what I may call the "technologically educated" class. This division I consider very important—and interesting from a historical point of view. Soon after the Industrial Revolution when Marx made his classical analysis, and it appeared as though society would divide in the main between the rich capitalist class and the poor, uneducated, unskilled machine-minding proletariat. But there has been an increasing growth of this "technological class" . . . as well as the clerical classes, accountants and the like. This technical class does show differences from the working class, and also from the purely "blackcoated" section of the middle class. Its members are highly trained specialists, with or without (generally without) wide cultural interests. It is more independent than the "blackcoated" section . . . but it has not the independence and social solidarity of the almost defunct "skilled artisan" class. And it has less power, and more opportunities for power, than any other class in the modern world. (Jeffery, p. 70)

This group's social parameters are revealing. This lower middle class of public servants, teachers, bank and insurance officials, technicians, draftspeople, and clerical workers in the private sector earned between 250 and 500 pounds per year and received pensions, sick benefits and holidays with pay in generally secure posts. A skilled worker by contrast might earn 4 to 5 pounds per week and a university professor 1,000 pounds per year. They established a considerable social weight and political power by the end of the 1930s. During the 1920s and 1930s the lower middle class adhered to the national governments of the conservatives. The lower middle class was never proletarianized, nor did it find the fascism of Sir Oswald Mosely appealing. A generational shift in the 1930s and threats in the foreign arena radicalized some younger people.

FASCISM AND NATIONAL SOCIALISM

The social history of fascism in Italy only joined historians' agendas in the late twentieth century. Nevertheless, the petty bourgeoisie, particularly the lower middle classes and the intelligentsia, were deeply embedded in the fascist movement. The Italian historian Luigi Salvatorelli labeled them "literate illiterates," and Antonio Gramsci applied the term "monkey people" to this group. Salvatorelli identified a "humanistic lower middle class" found in "bureaucratic offices, scholastic halls and petty professional activities" among the supporters of fascism. According to him these people were half-educated possessors of a "smattering of formulaic and grammatical culture, the literacy of the illiterate." They lacked the critical and synthetic abilities to use their knowledge to evaluate the contemporary political scene. Gramsci described fascism as "the urban petty bourgeoisie's latest performance in the theater of national political life." He warned that the monkey people "supply daily news,

they do not create history, they leave traces in the newspapers, they do not offer materials to write books." Teachers, civil servants and white-collar employees became ardent supporters of Italian fascism, turning to the rhetorical ideals of the nation and the utopias of occupational hierarchies directly linked to the state to overcome the threat of class conflict.

In July 1929 the liberal German newspaper *Vossische Zeitung* claimed that the National Socialists represented "the petty bourgeoisie gone mad." (Crossick and Haupt, p. 224). Similarly in 1930 the German sociologist Theodor Geiger called Nazi electoral success the result of "a panic in the *Mittelstand*" induced by economic crisis. Indeed many others linked the petty bourgeoisie, romanticism, and irrationality with fascism, defined as an "extremism of the middle." These views repeat the antimodernism arguments of the late nineteenth century. Insofar as such arguments are teleological and monocausal, ignoring the role of other social groups in supporting the Nazis, they can be dismissed readily. As to actual lower-middle-class support of the Nazis, the picture is more ambiguous.

As demonstrated above, specific occupations and trades and their contexts are decisive in determining the actual political behavior of the lower middle class. Evidence, especially in local and regional studies, shows that owners of small retail shops and artisanal enterprises were attracted strongly to the Nazi movement and that the Nazis had entered their organizations by the end of the Weimar Republic. Although both the traditional petty bourgeoisie and the new lower middle class joined the Nazi party in numbers larger than their share of the laboring population as a whole, the majority by far remained outside the party. The German lower middle class was "preoccupied with the power and ritual of voluntary organizations" (Koshar, 1990, pp. 34–35). The party had to mobilize the lower middle class through such voluntary associations, which were often locally based. Nationalism, which in Germany also had strong local foundations, played well into the process of co-optation and mobilization. Still the new lower middle class in particular was well represented among party members. Distinctions are necessary. For example, shopkeepers voted for Nazis more often than did artisans, and Protestant areas in the north did also compared to Catholics in the south.

The Nazi Party benefited only from "shifting support among white collar and civil service groups; collectively these groups were not good predictors of the Nazi vote 'even after the calamities of the world economic crisis descended on the Republic.'" (Koshar, 1990, p. 43). The Nazis had a nucleus of support among artisans and shopkeepers as noted above, but they relied on large votes from elites outside the lower middle class as well as approximately 3.5 million workers in, for example, the Reichstag elections of July 1932.

Nazism used marketing principles to appeal to particular groups. Lower-middle-class political activity emerged out of the particular contexts set in motion by the upheavals of World War I and its aftermath. In a way the Nazis exploited a gap in language. For the more traditional members of the *Mittelstand* the Weimar experience meant neglect from the state and favors for interest groups representing large economic and social blocs. Most parties of the new democracy did not attempt to win traditional petty bourgeois support. In ideological terms, social democracy could not connect with a retrograde *Mittelstand,* the Center Party focused on the Catholic population, and the Democratic Party was too weak to effectively represent them. The Communists tried to connect with the traditional petty bourgeoisie, but the latter felt uncomfortable with them because of their nationalism and because the Communists were too closely linked to the Soviet Union. The parties and rhetoric of the right had an open field. The Nazis exploited the gap, but only through the filter of politics and only over time.

CONCLUSION

The lower middle class or petty bourgeoisie was clearly a dynamic and positive force in European history. It was capable of frequent reinventions and expansions to include new occupations and skilled, semiprofessional positions within the technology and information-driven economies of the twentieth century. Though their appeal and self-conception often were couched in traditional language and their values looked to an idealized "pre-modern social order," they organized for modern mass politics and affected the larger political frameworks in which they operated. Culturally they readily blended in, sometimes to imitate the prevailing cultural norms, whether bourgeois or proletarian, but also as major components of a mass consumer society. Its members were never just the passive victims of larger historical forces such as industrialization. Their attraction to retrograde movements such as fascism was never complete, uniform, or foreordained. Their collective social power in fact grew exponentially in the twentieth century, as they anchored regimes and economic and social systems across the political spectrum. They were, along with the working class, an important vehicle for labor opportunities for women, as entire sectors of the clerical workforce, shop personnel, and professions such as teaching brought in female labor and became feminized.

Members of the twentieth-century lower middle class set themselves apart from factory laborers in appearance, status, and outlook and were located astride sometimes permeable boundaries in relation to the big bourgeoisie and high-status professions. Most professions in fact had lower-ranking analogues, such as paramedical personnel in medicine; technical personnel, draftspeople, or statisticians in engineering; and elementary teachers in education, whose members fit securely into the lower middle class. Much remains undiscovered about these layers of society, their culture, the relative importance of occupational and professional associations and political parties, their relationship to matters of gender and family, and their relationship to the dynamics of post–cold war ethnicity and nationalism.

See also other articles in this section.

BIBLIOGRAPHY

Anderson, Gregory. *Victorian Clerks.* Manchester, U.K., 1976.

Bechhofer, Frank, and Brian Elliott, eds. *The Petite Bourgeoisie: Comparative Studies of the Uneasy Stratum.* New York, 1981.

Berezin, Mabel. *Making the Fascist Self: The Political Culture of Interwar Italy.* Ithaca, N.Y., 1997.

Cocks, Geoffrey, and Konrad H. Jarausch, eds. *German Professions, 1800–1950.* New York, 1990.

Crossick, Geoffrey, ed. *The Lower Middle Class in Britain, 1870–1914.* New York, 1977.

Crossick, Geoffrey, and Heinz-Gerhard Haupt. *The Petite Bourgeoisie in Europe, 1780–1914: Enterprise, Family, and Independence.* London and New York, 1995.

Crossick, Geoffrey, and Henz-Gerhard Haupt, eds. *Shopkeepers and Master Artisans in Nineteenth-Century Europe.* London and New York, 1984.

Gellately, Robert. *The Politics of Economic Despair: Shopkeepers and German Politics 1890–1914.* London and Beverly Hills, Calif., 1974.

Kocka, Jürgen. *Facing Total War: German Society, 1914–1918.* Translated by Barbara Weinberger. Cambridge, Mass., 1984.

Kocka, Jürgen. *White Collar Workers in America, 1890–1940: A Social-Political History in International Perspective.* London and Beverly Hills, Calif., 1980.

Koshar, Rudy, ed. *Splintered Classes: Politics and the Lower Middle Classes in Interwar Europe.* New York, 1990.

Lebovics, Herman. *Social Conservatism and the Middle Classes in Germany, 1914–1933.* Princeton, N.J., 1969.

Mayer, Arno. "The Lower Middle Class as Historical Problem." *Journal of Modern History* 47, no. 3 (September 1975): 4.

Morris, R. J. *Class, Sect, and Party: The Making of the British Middle Class: Leeds, 1820–1850.* Manchester, U.K., 1990.

Morris, R. J., ed. *Class, Power, and Social Structure in British Nineteenth-Century Towns.* Leicester, U.K., 1986.

Nord, Philip G. *Paris Shopkeepers and the Politics of Resentment.* Princeton, N.J., 1986.

Orlovsky, Daniel. "The Hidden Class: White Collar Workers in the Soviet 1920's." In *Making Workers Soviet.* Edited by Lewis H. Siegelbaum and Ronald Grigor Suny. Ithaca, N.Y., 1994.

Orlovsky, Daniel. "The Lower Middle Strata in Revolutionary Russia." In *Civil Society in Late Imperial Russia.* Edited by E. Clowes, S. Kassow, and J. West. Princeton, N.J., 1991.

Orlovsky, Daniel. "State Building in the Civil War: The Role of the Lower Middle Strata." In *Party, State, and Society in the Russian Civil War: Explorations in Social History.* Edited by Diane P. Koenker, William G. Rosenberg, and Ronald Grigor Suny. Bloomington, Ind., 1989.

Parker, D. S. *The Idea of the Middle Class: White-Collar Workers and Peruvian Society, 1900–1950.* University Park, Pa., 1998. Excellent discussion of theoretical issues.

Pedersen, Susan. *Family, Dependence, and the Origins of the Welfare State: Britain and France, 1914–1945.* Cambridge, U.K., 1993.

Pennybacker, Susan D. *A Vision for London, 1889–1914: Labour, Everyday Life, and the LCC Experiment.* London and New York, 1995.

Speier, Hans. *German White-Collar Workers and the Rise of Hitler.* New Haven, Conn., 1986.

Volkov, Shulamit. *The Rise of Popular Antimodernism in Germany: The Urban Master Artisans, 1873–1896.* Princeton, N.J., 1978.

Winkler, Heinrich August. *Mittelstand, Demokratie und Nationalsozialismus: Die politische Entwicklung von Handwerk und Kleinhandel in der Weimarer Republik.* Cologne, Germany, 1972.

Zdatny, Steven M. *The Politics of Survival: Artisans in Twentieth-Century France.* New York, 1990.

WORKING CLASSES

Dick Geary

FROM WORKERS TO
WORKING CLASSES, 1750–1850

The term "working classes": a modern category.
All societies have depended on the labor of "workers"
in various forms, yet the *Oxford English Dictionary*
records the first use of the term "working classes" in
1789. It only entered into broader parlance after
1815. In the works of Daniel Defoe, Gregory King,
and Edmund Burke, social divisions were categorized
as "ranks" and "orders," not "classes." Eighteenth-
century references to "manufacturers" included both
employers and employees in a particular trade, but
by the 1830s "manufacturer" and "craftsman" often
meant "capitalist" and "wageworker" respectively. In
Germany the term "worker" (*Arbeiter*) was used rarely
before 1800. *Arbeitende Klassen* (working classes)
was known but denoted artisans, including the self-
employed, domestic servants, agricultural laborers, and
even peasants. From the 1830s, however, the term was
applied more specifically to manual wage laborers, as
the self-employed were gradually excluded, though
this exclusion took several decades. In Britain, France,
and Germany in the 1830s and 1840s the designation
"worker" became a form of self-characterization. This
article is concerned with that modern category of
employment.

The late appearance of class terminology reflected a social order in which wage labor for life was
far from universal and in most European countries the
exception rather than the rule. Much agricultural production in eastern Europe, where serfdom was prevalent, was for subsistence rather than the market as in
large parts of France, Spain, and Italy and in southern
Germany. Even where free workers labored for a landowner, their remuneration often was nonmonetary,
that is, housing, food, and fuel. In urban Europe, especially where guild regulations remained in place,
each trade retained a distinct identity, and its members
fought with those of other trades. In England in 1801
many employed in manufacture had double occupations, weaving and farming, for instance, and others

returned to husbandry at harvesttime. Furthermore
family economies were often mixed, with children and
women tending smallholdings while men worked in
manufacture. Rural trades and industries did not share
a common interest with their urban counterparts, for
the spread of manufacture beyond the control of urban regulation could be a major source of grievance
for urban craftspeople. A complex pattern of local particularities further obviated collective identities.

***Working classes and the changing shape of pro-
test.*** The shift to a language of classes corresponded
to changes in the nature of labor and collective action.
Until the 1820s in Britain, the 1850s in France, and
the 1860s in Germany the most common form of
popular protest was the riot or demonstration against
high food prices, conscription, and taxation. These
actions were not shaped by conflict between employers and their workers but rested on communal solidarities, which embraced women and children. They
were joined after 1800, however, by a new repertoire
of protest that both reflected and promoted the creation of working-class identities. The new repertoire
included the destruction of industrial machinery or
Luddism. In many respects Luddite actions resembled
riots. They were localized, they lacked formal organization though they often required considerable planning, and they rested on the use or threat of violence.
However, although Luddite crowds often included
other members of the community, they were primarily
made up of workers from the trades threatened by
industrial machinery, and their actions were against
merchants and industrialists. By promoting the notion that workers had a set of separate and definable
interests, Luddism and other, similar actions helped
create new identifications based on class.

The strike promoted this type of identification
even more strongly. Strikes were far from unknown
in eighteenth-century France and were common in
preindustrial Germany. In Britain industrial action
was relatively frequent before 1800. However, strikes
occurred much more often after 1800. The strike dif-

fered significantly from earlier forms of protest in its social composition and its reliance on the withdrawal of labor as its principal weapon, though violence often accompanied early strikes. It was clearly a struggle between workers and their bosses and demonstrated the increasing importance of wage-dependency in the most advanced European economies.

The first working class organizations. From the 1820s in Britain and the 1830s in France workers also developed a rich organizational life of discussion clubs, cooperatives, trade unions, and in some cases political organizations. The most common organization was the friendly society. England had over 1 million such societies by 1815, and France had some two thousand in the 1840s. Skilled workers founded friendly societies in most other European countries later in the nineteenth century, for example in Spain in the 1840s and in Russia in the 1870s. These societies provided against the misfortunes of accident, sickness, and old age in the days before the welfare state. Sometimes they expressly forbade any involvement in politics. However, they could become a focus for collective action in a single trade, serve as a cloak for radical politics in repressive regimes, and on occasion develop into trade unions.

Producer and consumer cooperatives were more clearly related to dissatisfaction with the prevailing economic order. These were created not only to provide workers with cheap and reliable goods but also to bypass the capitalist merchant in manufacture. In some cases they aimed to reestablish the craftsperson's control over the product and the labor process through collectively purchasing raw materials and selling the finished goods. By 1832 Britain counted five hundred cooperative societies with over twenty thousand members. Some were only concerned with retailing, though their contribution to working-class welfare should not be ignored. Others had more sweeping aims to combat unemployment and to provide their workers with remuneration commensurate with their labor. In France the movement toward cooperative associations was the principal form of working-class activity in the 1830s and 1840s.

Simultaneously trade unions increased in significance, especially in Britain. Wool combers, shoemakers, hatters, shipwrights, and tailors had an organizational history that reached back into the eighteenth century and was by no means terminated by repressive legislation after 1800. However, the partial legalization of union activity in 1824 led to a proliferation of trade societies capable of organizing strikes. Until the 1820s the most common union was formed by a single trade in a single town. Such unions often func-

tioned additionally as friendly societies, and they usually attempted to restrict apprenticeship and entry into a trade. English cotton spinners, for example, excluded hand loom weavers from their organization. In the 1830s most British unions remained exclusive, despite some famous but abortive attempts to found general national unions. They also remained small. The masons' union, which was one of the largest, had only 5,500 members in 1851. Not until the advent of the New Model Unions, especially the Amalgamated Society of Engineers (ASE) around the middle of the century, did effective national confederations of trade unions came into existence, though these too usually restricted membership.

In France masons, carpenters, tailors, printers, and engineering workers organized under the July Monarchy (1830–1848) despite repressive legislation, and they continued more overtly in the 1848 revolution. In the Rhineland craft associations came into existence in the 1840s, while during the revolutionary upheavals of 1848, German cigar makers, printers, and engineering workers formed trade associations. Skilled workers created trade unions in the 1860s and 1870s in Russia, Italy, Spain, and most of western Europe.

Often these early unions refused to become involved in radical politics. In Britain, for example, unionized miners did not wish to be associated with Chartist political agitation, and print unions in Britain, France, and Germany turned their backs on politics. Though unions were not exclusive to workers in an economically strong position, most unskilled laborers found it almost impossible to sustain combination in periods of high unemployment or against employer offensives. Stable unions were created by those with skills, a strong bargaining position, and relative job security, whereas the journeymen of the depressed trades of weaving, tailoring, and shoemaking often provided the fuel for radical Chartism, revolutionary secret societies in Paris, and the Brotherhood of German Workers in 1848.

Yet union organization and political radicalism were not necessarily at odds. The state's frustration of attempts to form economic unions could force even moderate unionists into the ranks of political protest. To a certain extent that was the case in Britain in the early years of the nineteenth century. In France the repression of working-class industrial action in the 1830s and the 1840s led to insurrections in Lyon and Paris as well as the formation of revolutionary societies. The increase in strikes and trade unions provides evidence that growing numbers of workers identified a conflict between their interests and those of their employers, even though their solidarity usually failed to extend beyond the individual trade. In some cooperatives and political organizations, however, a broader critique of capitalism and a language of class appeared.

Between 1815 and 1850 European workers adopted a discourse of class. Some British workers espoused the cause of radical Chartism, often because they came from depressed artisan trades and possessed little industrial muscle or because other forms of protest, such as petitions and Luddism, had failed or had been thwarted by laws of association. In the 1840s radical Chartists, such as Ernest Jones, deployed the language of class interest and a more diffuse populist and cross-class rhetoric. Advocates of cooperative socialism, including Robert Owen, George Mudie, Francis Bray, and Thomas Hodgskin, developed a critique of market economics centered on a labor theory of value and a concept of parasitical capitalism. In Paris workers read the publications of the utopian socialists, such as Étienne Cabet and Charles Fourier. Despite the fantastical nature of many of their projects, these socialists produced a trenchant critique of capitalism and recurrent economic crisis, although they did not speak to an exclusively working-class audience. They also had a profound effect on Karl Marx. In Germany the formation of the Brotherhood of German Workers in 1848 marked the point at which many journeymen broke with their masters and categorized themselves as workers. By 1850 therefore some workers in the economically advanced economies of Europe had engaged in strikes, joined unions, and embraced radical politics, though not necessarily all three.

Throughout the early industrial period the definition of the urban working class is complicated by the deep divisions between artisans and the less coherent groups of factory workers, only a few of whom had artisanal backgrounds. Most organized working-class activity, such as unions, was in fact artisanal. Only the Chartists and some of the 1848 uprisings suggested the existence of shared interests and perceptions between these segments of the working class.

A second issue that runs through working-class history is the relationship between protest history and a larger but definable working-class experience or culture. Many workers enjoyed the same leisure interests, including social drinking. Most held a highly masculine value system that relegated women to domestic functions, at least in principle. They also shared characteristics as consumers and had some sense of cooperation, bailing each other out in hard times. While a few workers strove for upward mobility, the majority were attached to a more traditional idea of work that clashed with employer attempts to increase pace and output. Some of these values were more widely shared than the ideas promoted by specific organizational or protest efforts.

The origins of working-class identity. A classic argument about the rise of Luddism, strike action, union organization, and the language of class links these phenomena directly to the growth of an industrial economy and to the resultant material deprivation and social upheaval. This view derives some support from the fact that the nation with the largest labor movement in 1850—Britain—was also the most advanced economically. Whereas France, the German states, most of the Iberian Peninsula outside Catalonia, all but the north of Italy, and virtually the whole of eastern Europe remained predominantly agrarian at mid-century, almost 43 percent of the British labor force was employed in manufacturing in 1851. Furthermore the chronology of strikes and labor organization tended to follow that of industrialization, with its first appearance in Britain, followed by Belgium, France, and Germany with eastern Europe trailing. It also seems perfectly rational to believe that low wages, long working hours, unsanitary and dangerous working environments, and appalling and overcrowded housing conditions explain working-class protest. The personal upheaval involved in the transition to impersonal factory labor and migration to unfamiliar urban environments also has been seen as alienating workers and causing protests. However, the relationships among industrialization, living standards, social upheaval, and class identity are not simple. Examinations of these different aspects follow below.

Poverty and the formation of working-class identity. Regarding impoverishment as an explanation of labor protest and organization, what was happening to working-class living standards in the first half of the nineteenth century is far from clear or uniform. Standards varied from country to country, from region to region, and from one occupational group to another. Most calculations suggest that material conditions in Britain improved between 1790 and 1850 as average real wages probably rose by 25 percent. However, this global figure hid enormous variations. Compositors, craftspeople in the building trades, engineers, and boilermakers were especially fortunate, whereas Black Country nail makers, faced with machine competition, and Lancashire hand loom weavers, whose livelihood was threatened by Irish, female, and rural labor, experienced a dramatic decline in living standards. What made this situation worse was that earlier economic expansion had actually benefited these workers. Thus

Workers' Housing. Kitchen of a building at Grossbeerenstrasse 6, Berlin, 1905. AKG LONDON

changed circumstances rather than simple poverty generated bitter protest among hand loom weavers. Clearly factory workers were not always in the worst circumstances. Factory hours were certainly long, but they were often less so than in nonfactory and rural occupations. Moreover, for good or ill, work became more regular and less dependent on the seasons for those in manufacture in Britain between 1800 and 1850. Even for better-placed workers, however, the inflationary crisis of the 1790s and subsequent slumps in 1815, 1819, 1829 had deleterious effects on real wages or employment prospects respectively. A crisis of the scale of 1842, when a downturn in the trade cycle was accompanied by harvest failure, could not help but depress the condition of workers. In summary, British industrialization did not entail any universal fall in living standards.

In less industrial continental Europe real wages may have declined more generally. A combination of cyclical unemployment and harvest failure devastated the German textile town of Krefeld, where three out of every eight looms were idle, and Cologne, where a third of the population was dependent on public assistance in 1847. Both Luddism and political radical-

ism were fueled as much by memories of better days and traditions of association as by poverty. The permanently poor, those who had known nothing but low living standards, were likely to be absent from protests. In any case, many strikes and virtually all stable unions were the product of the strength of skilled workers with increasing rather than declining resources. The absence of a necessary connection between poverty and industrial militancy or political radicalism will become even more apparent in the subsequent discussion of class identity after 1850.

SOCIAL UPHEAVAL AND THE FORMATION OF WORKING-CLASS IDENTITY

One argument states that social upheaval and uprooting contributed to alienation, grievance, and protest and that strikes were the result of a pathological crisis connected with the dissolution of traditional ties and with a generation of workers unaccustomed to urban and factory environments. However, strikers were rarely uprooted outsiders but tended to be well integrated into their local communities. In addition the later stages of industrial growth after 1850 exhibited higher, not lower, strike rates. Furthermore the centers of working-class protest before 1850 were usually older sites of manufacture, including Paris, Marseille, Berlin, and Leipzig, with strong craft traditions, not new industrial areas. In Halifax, England, the operatives of the new factories distanced themselves from Chartism, which had a much greater attraction among the craft trades of Huddersfield. Family units often worked together in the textile factories of Lancashire. In Germany distance migrants rarely traveled alone. In Russia factory workers in an individual plant often came from the same village.

Thus the concept of individual uprooting and anomie needs qualification. Distance migrants and new industrial workers needed time to adapt to the rhythms and disciplines of industry, which were prerequisites of union formation, and time to learn the lessons of the trade cycle as to when was the best time to strike. In many parts of eastern and southern Europe this learning process was at best just beginning on the eve of World War I.

Mechanization and the formation of working-class identity. It may seem more likely that class identity was a consequence of mechanized factory labor, which supposedly created a more homogeneous working class. However, the language of class and new forms of protest emerged in Britain, Belgium, France, and Germany before factory production had become widespread. Even Britain had fewer than 100,000 male factory operatives in 1830. Twenty years later domestic outworkers and artisans still outnumbered factory workers. Moreover unskilled factory labor did not form unions, rally to Chartism, or join the Parisian societies and the Brotherhood of German workers. Unions recruited from craft workers in relatively stable employment, while radical politics found strong support among the degraded artisanal trades of tailoring, furniture manufacturing, and shoemaking.

Some have argued that the centrality of the artisan experience rather than the factory experience to the growth of class awareness does not contradict the significance of industrialization in the genesis of working-class identity, for supposedly mechanized production deskilled artisans. For some workers, including nail makers and framework knitters, the problem indeed was mechanization. However, these cases were exceptional. Many artisans, wheelwrights, shipwrights, hatters, watchmakers, jewelers, barbers, and butchers, were wholly or partially insulated from new techniques. Others, such as Birmingham metalworkers and Sheffield toolmakers, adapted to factory production without a loss of skills and earnings. Even in the trades most vulnerable to expansion and degradation, such as tailoring and shoe-making, elite groups of workers continued to produce for the luxury end of the market. The trades most strongly represented among radical Chartists, French revolutionaries, and the Brotherhood of German workers—tailors, shoemakers, and furniture makers—were from trades not affected by mechanized production.

Merchant capitalism and the formation of working-class identity.

If mechanization, social upheaval, and poverty did not generate working-class protest, what factors did? One of the most serious threats was not industrial capitalism but capitalism in its merchant form. In Britain, France, and Germany in the first half of the nineteenth century merchants began to relocate industries in rural areas and to deploy low-wage outworkers, a process often labeled protoindustrialization. Dispersion often brought a greater division of the labor process and the use of cheaper materials and labor. The growth of outwork led to substantial overmanning in tailoring, shoemaking, woodworking, and hand loom weaving. In textiles, craftspeople, even where they remained nominally independent and worked at home, became increasingly dependent on merchants, who purchased and supplied the raw materials and marketed the finished product.

In addition to protoindustry, work simplification extended into the urban strongholds of craftspeople. Large parts of the British woodworking and clothing trades were taken over by garret masters and sweating workshops. In Paris artisan tailors were undercut by sweatshop competition and the production of off-the-peg clothing. Shoemaking and tailoring were becoming sweated trades in Marseille in the 1840s, and German cabinetmakers became de facto employees of large furniture manufacturers. Many artisans, often with high expectations and traditions of organization, thus became increasingly dependent upon merchants, who owned the raw materials, the final product of their labor, and in certain trades like hosiery, even their tools. This dependence explains the growth of artisan socialism and cooperation and led to the denunciation of capitalists as parasites.

Political variables and the formation of working-class identity.

The emergence of artisan socialism and the search for political remedies was no automatic response to changes in the labor process, however. It was driven by political variables. The European state, which previously had regulated the conditions of craft labor, increasingly encouraged the development of free market forces after 1800. In several countries between 1780 and 1850 apprenticeship, entry into a trade, and the introduction of machinery were deregulated, and wage controls were abolished. This explains why major aims of artisan agitation in Britain in the early nineteenth century were first the strict observation of the Elizabethan Statute of Artificers and Apprentices (1563) and, after its repeal in 1814, its reintroduction. The run-down condition of public relief in Britain, France, and the German states between 1800 and 1850 and an increasingly free market in grain also were perceived as infringements of the rules of a moral economy and an abandonment of the state's duty. German artisans demanded restrictions on apprenticeship and entry into the manufacturing trades, especially where guild regulations had been abolished, as in Prussia.

British political protest and awareness of workers' common interests after 1800 was also a consequence of increasing repression. The Combination Acts of 1799 and 1800, the use of the military against Luddite actions, and the use of yeomanry volunteers against demonstrators, most infamously in the Peterloo Massacre in Manchester in 1819, gave rise to an acute sense of discrimination and politicized grievances. A French law, the *loi le Chapelier,* which took effect in 1791, proscribed combinations and contributed to the growth of revolutionary societies in Paris and to insurrections there and in Lyon. Strikes and combinations were also illegal in most of the German states until the 1860s except for the brief revolutionary interlude of 1848.

WORKING-CLASS IDENTITY IN 1850

The emergence of a sense of class arose from the interaction of worker expectations, merchant domination in the workplace, the state's retreat from paternalism, and repressive legislation. That identity, however, remained fragile and extremely limited in 1850. Many workers were unaffected by merchant capitalism, and factory labor was mostly quiescent. Moreover most of the skilled workers who formed unions were as anxious to protect their own interests against other workers as against their employers. Industrial militancy and trade union organization did entail conflict between the employer and worker and required some degree of solidarity. In this sense they indicated a degree of class awareness.

This solidarity was usually restricted to an individual craft and did not necessarily imply any shared identity with workers as a whole. What is more, those who became radical Chartists, joined Parisian clubs, and went to the barricades in parts of Europe in 1848 were not only journeymen craftspeople but also small masters. Consequently some historians have preferred to see radical Chartism in Britain and republicanism in France as forms of popular rather than class protest. For Gareth Stedman Jones, for example, Chartism arose from a populist political discourse rather than from a new class structure.

As a counterweight to the skeptical position, John Breuilly has shown that artisan socialism had an international structure in the 1840s. Workers in different cultures responded in similar ways to increasing dependence on merchant capitalism, suggesting that ideas of class arose from the conflict between traditional artisan expectations and merchant capitalism. The discourse of class made sense to certain workers in different countries and cultures precisely because of the economic reality of dependence and because restrictive practices were no longer feasible.

Within this economic framework, the presence of small masters in radical artisan movements is explained by the fact that they, like their journeymen, were losing their independence. Master tailors in Cologne and cabinetmakers in Paris were increasingly tied to a single merchant in the 1840s. The Birmingham metal trades carried out their activities in small workshops, but in the 1830s and 1840s these became dependent on larger firms. Masters divided into two groups. Those with capital resources became merchants, but others became increasingly proletarianized. Channels of mobility for journeymen were blocked by overmanning, and more capital was required to set up as a master. Consequently the interests of masters and journeymen splintered.

As it became increasingly difficult for journeymen to become masters, issues of journeymen's rights, wages, and working conditions set masters and journeymen in conflict. German masters and journeymen together desired restrictions on the import of foreign manufactures, entry into a trade, and the introduction of machinery, but only masters demanded the reintroduction or enforcement of guild regulations, which gave them power over journeymen. This conflict of interests became apparent in the 1848 revolution, when Berlin journeymen formed the Brotherhood of Workers. Similar conflicts had become increasingly bitter in the London tailoring trades in the 1820s and 1830s. In the 1850s and 1860s a growing separation of shopkeepers and masters from workers was evidenced by increasingly endogamous marriage patterns and a separate associational life in Britain and France. By the 1890s in Germany *Handwerker* (artisan) had come to mean a self-employed craftsperson, who organized separately from and often against the burgeoning labor movement.

The solidarity between petty bourgeois and working-class communities took much longer to fracture in some places and in some trades than in others. In Saint-Étienne, for example, the fracture had to wait until the last two decades of the century. Small shopkeepers, master craftsmen, and journeymen often inhabited a popular rather than a proletarian social milieu. This common milieu was reinforced by intermarriage between working-class and petty bourgeois groups. Thus the consolidation of separate worker-employer identities was far from complete in 1848 and remained far from universal in 1914, but it constituted the dominant trend.

THE GROWTH OF WORKING-CLASS IDENTITY, 1850–1914

Signs of identity. Between 1850 and 1914 ever more European workers went on strike, joined trade unions, and supported political parties that claimed to speak for the working class. France experienced over five hundred industrial disputes between 1900 and 1914. In Germany 1 million workers downed tools in 1912. Between 1911 and 1914 a strike wave of unprecedented proportions hit the United Kingdom. The increase in strike action involved the greater mobilization both of more members of the same trade and of more trades. It was also far from unilinear, depending partly on the trade cycle and partly on the learning process of new and less-skilled workers. But strikes did come to incorporate these groups, including match girls and dockers in Britain in 1888 and 1889 and female textile workers in Saxony in 1903. This extension of strike action to new categories of employees was especially noticeable in strike waves, such as those of 1869 to 1871 and 1889 to 1891 in Germany and Britain, 1910 to 1912 in Germany, and 1911 to 1913 in the United Kingdom. The growth of strike participation encouraged a massive increase in the number of trade union members between 1850 and 1914. Britain had over 4 million trade unionists, Germany had over 3 million, and France had roughly 1 million on the eve of World War I. German Austria also possessed a high trade union density, but growth on a mass scale was yet to come in Italy and Spain and was effectively proscribed in tsarist Russia.

Above all the working classes announced their presence in political parties that expressly claimed to articulate the interests of labor. By the end of 1910 the British Labour Party held forty-two seats in the House of Commons. The French Socialist Party (SFIO) could count on the support of 1.5 million voters, and its Italian counterpart (PSI) was making considerable headway in local elections in the north of the peninsula. Most successful of all was the German Social Democratic Party (SPD) with over 1 million members, 4 million voters, and a massive empire of ancillary leisure and cultural organizations by 1914. The SPD became a model for social democratic parties in Sweden, Denmark, Norway, Austria, Finland, and Russia. Workers also made their presence felt in more dramatic and violent ways in the Russian Revolution of 1905–1906; in the "tragic week" in Barcelona in 1909, when anarchosyndicalists fought with the authorities; and in armed clashes in Italy in the "red fortnight" of June 1914.

Explanations of the rise of labor. That more workers went on strike, joined unions, and voted for labor or socialist parties between 1850 and 1914 is indisputable. Why they did so and how typical these workers were of European labor as a whole, however, is less clear. It is certain that industrial conflict and unionization cannot be explained by working-class impoverishment. Britain continued to witness the most strikes and to have the largest trade union membership, yet British real wages were between one-third and one-half greater than those in France and Germany in the 1860s. A Board of Trade investigation in 1905 concluded that money wages in France were only two-thirds and in Germany no more than three-quarters of their British counterparts at a time when the price of rent, food, and fuel was actually higher on the Continent, by some 20 percent in Germany. Moreover the standard of living of British workers increased substantially between 1850 and the outbreak of World War I. The average length of the working week declined substantially between the 1860s and 1914 from over sixty hours to approximately forty-eight hours. In 1850 workers on average spent 75 percent of their wages on food. By 1914 the figure had dropped to 50 percent. Their diet became more varied and included corned beef, cakes, eggs, cocoa, and even fruit purchased from cooperative and chain stores. Housing conditions remained deplorable by later standards but certainly improved after 1850. By 1914, 80 percent of British families with three or more members occupied at least three rooms, and many enjoyed the benefits of piped water and gas lighting. The single-family terraced house enabled a better-off worker's family to enjoy a "modest domesticity" (McKibbin, 1990, p. 307), for which virtually no equivalent existed in the densely occupied industrial cities of continental Europe. Rates of child mortality fell and life expectancy rose, reflecting the general improvements in living standards. Most notably, real wages rose, according to one index from 100 in 1850 to 190 in 1913–1914. This enabled British workers to travel to the seaside, go to the races and the music hall, and watch football matches in huge numbers.

Of course such working-class prosperity was not universal. Regional variations in wages were vast. Carpenters earned ten and a half pence an hour in London but only four and seven-eighths pence an hour in Falmouth in 1908. Between 1840 and 1880 the differential between skilled and unskilled wages probably increased. Subsequently it declined in some trades but still remained substantial. Unskilled building workers received 64 percent of the wages of their skilled colleagues in 1885. The differential between male and female wages was even greater. According to Charles Booth 30 percent of the London population lived below the poverty line in 1886. Irish immigrants tended to live in the worst housing conditions, where typhus, called "Irish fever," was common. Accidents, illness, periodic unemployment, and old age remained sources of insecurity.

The economies of continental Europe exhibited similarities. The living standards of French and German workers rose steadily between 1850 and 1900, precisely when industrial and political labor movements began to recruit in large numbers. Again the benefits were spread unevenly. In the fourteen years before the outbreak of World War I, however, some of the gains were eroded in France, and real wages stagnated in Germany as a result of price inflation.

In addition to uneven prosperity, a set of new developments created problems for even skilled workers. The emergence of an increasingly numerous class of white-collar workers standing between management and the shop floor produced both more impersonal labor relations and an obstacle to the mobility prospects of the skilled manual worker. A range of technological innovations eroded the status and security of some groups of skilled laborers by facilitating the employment of semiskilled workers. Mechanical saws, prefabricated wooden units, and iron and concrete building materials revolutionized the construction industry. Milling machines, specialized lathes, and mechanical drills and borers intensified the labor process in engineering. By the 1890s the hand manufacture of shoes was displaced by a new technology. In general, however, the problem confronted by skilled workers had less to do with technological innovation, which lagged behind that in the United States, than with an intensification of work stemming from greater supervision, the premium bonus system of remuneration, and "scientific management." Growing numbers of workers demanded a shorter workweek, and workers in France, workers at Bosch in Stuttgart, and print and engineering workers in the United Kingdom went on strike against the reorganisation of production. Some German engineering workers even complained of nervous exhaustion. The emergence of engineering workers in the forefront of industrial protest between 1910 and 1920 may well have reflected these developments. That emergence reinforces the position that factors other than poverty drove working-class mobilization.

Skilled workers: the backbone of labor mobilization.
Many workers remained poor, and even skilled workers were not affluent or completely secure before 1914. Again, however, increasing resources facilitated widespread strike action, a growth in trade union membership, and to some extent membership of labor and socialist parties. This becomes clear when the timing of strikes at upturns in the economic cycle and the membership of trade unions is examined. Trade unions were strongest throughout Europe among workers who had served apprenticeships and who, through their skills, had considerable bargaining power, such as printers, skilled woodworkers and metal workers, masons, plumbers, and bricklayers. Unions were weakest among the unskilled and poorly paid, such as agricultural laborers, domestic servants, unskilled textile workers, and women. This was not true just of

Britain. Most French unionists in the 1870s were skilled, while printers, engineers, bricklayers, and carpenters formed unions in Germany in the 1860s. In Austria typesetters and watchmakers established successful craft associations by 1867, while artisans provided the backbone of labor organization in Milan and Turin in the 1870s.

In contrast, unskilled factory workers in France and Germany did not usually join unions or go on strike. Semiskilled laborers were increasingly involved in strikes after 1889. General unions formed in the United Kingdom, and industrial unions formed in Germany. However, the great majority of members were still skilled and male in 1914. The membership of the unskilled was more fragile and often declined at times of economic recession. The strike waves of 1889 to 1891 and especially 1910 to 1912 attracted greater numbers of the semiskilled and unskilled workers to industrial action. Nevertheless, the unskilled in general and women in particular, though capable of strike action, faced much more difficulty in sustaining organization.

Patterns of political mobilization were slightly different. Impoverished outworkers often played a role in the early history of socialist parties. Depressed textile workers in Roubaix, Reims, Roanne, and Lyon supported French anarcho-syndicalism. In Germany, August Bebel, the leader of the SPD, was first elected to a Reichstag seat not by the factory workers of Chemnitz, the German equivalent of Manchester, but by the depressed domestic weavers in Glauchau-Meerane. By 1913 the scale of social-democratic electoral support was so great in Germany's large Protestant cities, over 70 percent in Berlin and over 60 percent in Leipzig, that some unskilled and semiskilled workers must have voted for the party.

However, from the beginning skilled workers also took charge, and by 1914 the British Labour Party, the French and Italian Socialist Parties, and the German and Austrian Social Democratic Parties were organizations of skilled men in the building, metal, and woodworking trades. Parisian artisans formed the backbone of French anarcho-syndicalism, and skilled workers in printing, metalwork, and clothing manufacture took the lead in the creation of the Italian Workers' Party in the 1870s. The Spanish Socialist Party drew its first support from printers in Madrid. These skilled workers experienced rising living standards in the main. They enjoyed a strong bargaining position against their employers and had the resources, time, and energy to invest in union and party activities. Their ability to assert their identity thus stemmed from strength, not weakness. They also possessed a culture that, through apprenticeships, incul-

Rural Laborers Protest. *The Human Tide,* painting (1895–1896) by Giuseppe Pellizza da Volpedo (1868–1907). PINACOTECA DI BRERA, MILAN, ITALY/THE BRIDGEMAN ART LIBRARY

cated the worth and dignity of labor. They had expectations and aspirations that the unskilled and impoverished either did not share or could not realize. They also possessed long traditions of craft association that sustained industrial militancy and organization. In many cases, however, these skilled men remained concerned solely with their own sectional interests and failed to identify with the working class as a whole. This was especially so in Britain, where most enfranchised working-class voters stayed away from the Labour Party before 1914. The politics of class thus depended on factors outside the labor market.

Industrialization and identity. Rising living standards, the spread of strike action, and the growth of trade union membership related manifestly to changes in the occupational and residential structure of European society. The more rural the society, the less pronounced these developments were. In general few rural workers went on strike, joined unions, or voted socialist between 1850 and 1914. Sometimes prevented from organizing by repressive legislation, as in parts of Germany and in tsarist Russia; tied to landlords by law or by nonmonetary types of payment, like tied housing, food, and fuel; with very low wages, few expectations, and little bargaining power, rural labor did not possess the resources to mobilize in any sustainable way.

Significant exceptions existed, however. The French and Italian Socialist Parties and the Spanish anarchists had some success at recruiting support from rural areas. In Emilia and the Po Valley landless la-

borers and some sharecroppers protested against agrarian capitalism and benefited from labor exchanges, through which the Italian Socialist Party exerted influence on the hiring and firing of rural labor. In France agrarian socialism recruited not only from the landless woodcutters of Cher and Nièvre but also from landowning peasants in parts of the Midi. These peasants had access to urban ideas and enjoyed a collective social life around the local bar and cafè. Most important, they engaged in market agriculture, in particular viticulture; often experienced conflict with commercial intermediaries; and were subject to the fluctuations of the market, as in the agricultural depression of the 1870s and 1880s. In rural southern Spain anarchists recruited landless laborers who lived together in large agrotowns. In general, however, the industrial and political mobilization of European workers was a product of industry and the town.

The growth of wage labor and urbanization. In 1811, 30.2 percent of the British workforce was employed in manufacture, mining, and industry. A century later the figure had risen to 46.4 percent. At the same time employment in trade and transport increased from 11.6 percent to over 21 percent. In Germany approximately 35 percent of the labor force was still employed in agriculture in 1907 but by then 40 percent worked in crafts and industry and 25 percent in the tertiary sector. Dependent wage labor became the norm, especially in factory employment, though this development was more extensive in Britain and Germany than in the rest of Europe. In Germany the percentage of wage earners, as distinct from the self-employed, in industry grew from 57 percent in 1875 to over 76 percent in 1907. Russian industrial labor also expanded rapidly between 1875 and 1914, although it constituted a small minority within the population as a whole. In Spain 11 percent of the labor force worked in industry, rising to almost 16 percent in 1910.

At the same time an ever greater percentage of the European population moved into towns. In 1800 only 23 European towns housed over 300,000 people. By 1900 135 such towns existed. In the same period London grew from a city of 1 million to one of 4.5 million. In Britain urban dwellings outstripped rural dwellings in 1851, in Germany in 1891, but not until 1931 in France. In Germany, where a strong correlation existed between size of town, trade union density, and support for the SPD, a large migration of population from the rural east in to Berlin, Saxony, and the Ruhr took place. The percentage of the Reich's population living in towns of over 100,000 inhabitants grew from 4.8 percent in 1871 to 21.3 percent in 1910. Even in countries with lower overall levels of urbanization, individual cities experienced dramatic growth. Thus between 1897 and 1914 the population of Saint Petersburg rose from 1.26 million to 2.11 million, though Russia as a whole remained overwhelmingly rural. In France 16 cities had over 100,000 inhabitants by 1911, and Paris increased its population by 345 percent between 1800 and 1900, from 547,000 to 2.8 million.

That some correlation existed between industrialization-urbanization and strikes–trade union membership seems indisputable. However, industrial workers from rural backgrounds, distance migrants, and workers new to factory conditions took longer to organize than longer-term factory workers. Where employers were strong, as in heavy industry in the Ruhr Valley, or where the labor force was largely unskilled, industrial organization and strike action were difficult to sustain. They were also difficult where the state intervened to repress industrial conflict, obviously in Russia, to a significant extent in Germany, and much less in the United Kingdom. On the other hand, unions were strong where labor was skilled and organized, where employers were relatively small and disorganized, and where the state or employers promoted collective bargaining, as in Britain in the decade before 1914. Notwithstanding these caveats, the correlation between the chronology of industrial union and trade union growth seems clearly positive. It is often overlooked, however, that the uneven development of the industrial economy fragmented rather than united labor in a single class.

UNEVEN INDUSTRIALIZATION AND WORKING-CLASS FRAGMENTATION

Obviously industrial growth and technological modernization took place at different times in different countries. Agricultural labor as a percentage of the total workforce dropped to 8 percent in Britain but still stood at 31 percent in Germany, 42 percent in France, and 57 percent in Spain in 1920. It still constituted 46 percent of Russian and 53 percent of Polish labour in 1950. The early but relatively gradual industrialization of Britain, where craft associations already existed, facilitated the development of powerful sectional unions and gave rise to a system of collective bargaining. In contrast, later but more rapid and more capital-intensive industrial change in Germany after 1850 spawned powerful but intransigent employers and a labor force that was far less likely to be successful in the arena of industrial conflict. Consequently labor turned to the politics of social democracy.

Equally significant was the uneven development within national boundaries. In France most of the Midi was free of modern industry before 1914, and Languedoc actually deindustrialized. In northern Italy industry expanded, while the south remained overwhelmingly agrarian and impoverished. The spectacular economic growth of Saxony, the Ruhr Valley, and Berlin was not vouchsafed to Germany's eastern provinces or most of the Reich south of the Main River. Catalonia and the northern Basque provinces were much more economically developed than the rest of Spain, while Austria-Hungary boasted of both dynamic industrial cities, such as Prague, Vienna, and Budapest, and the most primitive rural economies in the Balkans. In consequence the structure of the labor force was regionally variable, which may in turn explain the persistence of regional traditions in working-class behavior and identity.

Unevenness was also sectoral. In France a large artisanal sector survived beyond 1914 but coexisted with the modern exploitation of hydroelectric power, technologically advanced artificial fiber (rayon) production, a modernized automobile industry, and the most innovative retail sector in Europe. Germany's Second Reich housed giant firms in electrotechnology and chemicals yet still possessed a domestic textile and shoemaking industry. Even within a single industry technological modernization did not breed a homogeneous workforce. Different sectors of the same industry, for example, engineering, modernized at different rates.

Such modernization did far less to "deskill" European workers than is often imagined. The huge expansion of engineering actually created more, not

Die Welt ist unser Vaterland! Und alle Menschen Brüder!

Gruss von der Maifeier!

Class Identity. A postcard (1903) celebrates the International Working Day. AKG LONDON

fewer, jobs for skilled engineers, as in Bielefeld, which became a center of German bicycle manufacture. Even where modern machines facilitated the deployment of semiskilled labor, that labor was rarely recruited from the ranks of the formerly skilled. Instead, as in the case of the French textile industry, labor came from those new to industry, often from rural backgrounds. Skilled men still set up and tended the new machines, but the invention of gas and electric motors together with the need for bicycle and motorcar maintenance afforded mechanics new opportunities for self-employment. On the shop floor labor was divided further by differential payment systems. As a result a common identity remained the exception rather than the rule. In fact factors exogenous to the labor process created cross-occupational solidarity, among them the rise of exclusively working-class residential communities, increasingly endogamous marriage patterns, and the emergence of a hereditary proletariat, that is, a generation of workers not new to the factory and the urban environment. The autocratic behavior of employers, the relative weakness of middle-class liberalism, and political repression and discrimination forged a class identity among some European workers.

The fragmentation of working-class politics. As demonstrated, economic development did as much to divide as to unite workers. In creating solidarity, the state's role was crucial in the generation of a radical politics of class. When the state relied on indirect taxes

or agricultural tariffs, it demonstrated its hostility to urban consumers. When it interfered violently in industrial conflict, deprived workers of full citizenship rights, and rested on nonparliamentary foundations, working-class grievances were often politicized and marxist parties were likely to be strong, as in Russia, Austria, and Germany. That liberal and parliamentary regimes were best able to create legitimacy among workers was demonstrated at the end of World War I, when labor overthrew the old autocracies in Russia, Austria-Hungary, and Germany but not the democratic polities in Britain and France.

Workers in similar occupations often displayed similar forms of behavior and identity across national boundaries, but this correlation did not include politics. Miners possessed a strong sense of occupational identity almost everywhere, but printers were almost always the first to form stable unions and to engage in collective bargaining. Dockers in Hamburg, Livorno, and Liverpool had difficulty organizing and often leaned toward direct action. Males dominated the industrial organizations of labor well into the twentieth century in virtually all European countries. In Britain, France, Germany, Austria, Czechoslovakia, and Hungary engineering workers rose to prominence in various forms of protest, often involving tensions between cautious trade union leaders and a restive rank and file.

As noted, however, these international similarities usually were restricted to the sphere of industrial behavior and did not extend to politics. This is clear even in the postulate that "labor aristocrats," skilled workers with high earnings and job security, such as printers and skilled engineering workers, provide a key to the reformism of the British labor movement. In England the labor aristocrats dominated the unions and voted Liberal, but in Germany they joined the SPD, and in Russia they appeared at the barricades in 1917 and 1918. Thus their politics cannot be explained by their place in the labor market.

Even the role of the state is not enough to explain working-class politics. Within the boundaries of a single state, workers in the same occupation often displayed marked differences in political outlook and identity. Miners in Pas-de-Calais, for example, gave their support to reformist socialism, whereas their counterparts in the southern Massif tended toward syndicalism. Syndicalism in Spain was supported by the workers in small-scale textile production in Barcelona but not in Guipúzcoa. Moreover the political identity of the same group of workers in the same place could change over time. For example, in Spain Asturian miners supported primarily reformist labor organizations until the 1920s then engaged in insurrectionary violence. The change was clearly dictated by shifts in the political conjuncture, perhaps at the local level, and not at the workplace.

Support for political parties, which spoke the language of class, was stronger in some states than in others; but even in imperial Germany, which had the largest socialist party in the world with a marxist program, the SPD could never claim to speak for the German working class in its entirety. Even among dependent wage laborers, other identities cut across and fragmented that of class. Women and the unskilled were largely absent from the membership, as were Catholics, Poles, and those who belonged to company unions and voted National Liberal, such as senior workers at the Krupp steelworks in Essen. In Britain and France significant numbers of workers preferred the collaborationist politics of liberalism to class confrontation and voted for the Liberal Party or the Radical Party respectively.

It was also not unusual for workers to give their support to nationalist or conservative political parties. That happened in the "working-class Tory" districts of industrial Lancashire, where hostility to Irish immigration and to Liberal mill owners played a role. This last instance also suggests that class identity and political conservatism were not invariably incompatible. Indeed the French wool shearers of Mazamet sustained lengthy strikes against their employers but gave their votes to conservative parliamentary candidates. At Krupp in Essen workers who belonged to the company union, sang in the company choir, and lived in company housing voted National Liberal before 1914, Nationalist in the 1920s, and Nazi in the depression of 1929–1933.

A sense of class could also be fractured by religious and denominational variables. Socialism in France, Spain, and Italy went hand in hand with anticlericalism, and the parties of the left were weak in areas of high religious observance. In Germany, Holland, and Flemish Belgium, Catholic workers formed their own Christian Unions and voted for Catholic parties. Ethnic differences were as divisive and potentially more explosive than those of religion. In Austria-Hungary, Czech and German workers split into separate organizations. Poles in imperial Germany stayed away from both the Catholic Center Party and the SPD, formed their own unions, and voted for the cause of Polish nationalism. No love was lost between English and Irish laborers. Workers in the north of France resented the employment of Belgians, and Marseille dockers displayed even greater hostility toward North African workers.

Gender and working-class fragmentation. The European working classes were further fragmented along the lines of gender. Women were grossly underrepresented in the membership of trade unions and labor and socialist parties. Even in the SPD, which had a women's organization with 170,000 members in 1914, females only constituted 16 percent of the total party membership. Significantly these women were usually not employed outside the home but were the housewives of Social Democrats. Part of the reason for female absence from the ranks of organized labor lay in the distribution of female employment. In Germany in 1907, 4.5 million women worked in agriculture, and 3.75 million worked in domestic service. Only 1 million found jobs in trade and commerce and 2 million in manufacturing. In Britain in 1911 almost 40 percent of the females in paid employment worked in personal and domestic services, 16 percent in textiles, 15 percent in clothing manufacturing, 3 percent in metals manufacturing, and 2.1 percent in agriculture. Of those employed in manufacturing, many worked in poorly paid domestic production. Female factory occupations were usually unskilled and badly rewarded. Thus women were the archetype of unskilled labor, and unskilled, poorly paid men did not form unions or join political parties either.

The difficulties of mobilizing women were compounded by other, more gender-specific factors. A woman's time was taken up by labor in and outside the home, the so-called "double burden." Furthermore the great majority of women in factory employment were unlikely to keep their positions for life. In

Germany in 1895 over 52 percent of employed females were single, 40.2 percent were divorced, and only 9.1 percent were married. In the United Kingdom sixteen years later the figures were respectively 69.3 percent, 29.4 percent, and 9.6 percent. Most women working outside the home would not do so for the rest of their lives. They were usually young and single, and at around age twenty-four they left for marriage or childbirth. Since the home and not the workplace was the locus of their activities for much of their lives, investment in factory-based organizations made little sense.

Religious observance was much higher among European females than males by 1900. Continued religious commitment may have kept women away from "godless" socialist organizations. Women also faced gender-specific discrimination. They suffered verbal and physical abuse, low wages, and proletarian antifeminism, which could become quite vicious in times of recession. Trade unions often were not interested in the problems of female workers, who were considered wage-cutting competitors rather than comrads. Also, as women did not yet possess the vote, many labor politicians in Britain and France showed little interest in their mobilization.

Of course working-class wives and daughters indispensably supported striking brothers, fathers, and husbands by caring for their offspring and providing sustenance on picket lines. The work of women in the home that created the space and time for the union and party activities of males. Though relatively few female workers joined unions, many women went on strike.

White-collar workers were generally absent from the unions, and their numbers in the total workforce increased rapidly by 1910. They constituted 36 percent of all wage earners in France in 1906, though under 40 percent of the French workforce were wageworkers at that time, and they were 18 percent of the total German labor force. In Germany, where the "collar line," the division between white-collar and blue-collar workers was especially great, the former displayed considerable hostility toward socialist organizations. Most did not organize, but those who did usually joined the German National Union of Commercial Employees, which was antisocialist, nationalist, imperialist, and anti-Semitic. The political identity of white-collar workers, however, was less clear in many other European societies and underwent significant changes during World War I.

Working-class identity in 1914.

On the eve of World War I more workers went on strike, belonged to trade unions, and voted for labor or socialist parties than ever before, in part an indication of class identity. However, that identity was fragile and was not shared by all. In fact the great majority of European workers, even in Britain, never went on strike, formed a union, or voted socialist. Uneven economic development and religious, ethnic, and gender differences complicated, obscured, and sometimes undermined the class solidarity the socialist parties hoped to create. However, those who considered their skill, gender, religion or ethnicity important might still have some perception of themselves as workers. The Christian (Catholic) Unions in Germany, for example, were increasingly involved in industrial action. Polish workers were proud to be Polish, but they joined the Free (socialist) Unions in the strikes of 1905 and 1912 in the Ruhr Valley. In fact to be a Pole in the Ruhr was to be a worker. National and class perspectives in this case reinforced one another.

The possibility of the coexistence of different identities raises another important point. Support for the national cause in 1914 did not necessarily imply the demise or absence of class consciousness. Not only was proletarian patriotism different from the jingoism of the nationalist right, but the same Welsh miners who volunteered to fight for king and country in August 1914 were back on strike the following year. Studies of various European cities, including Brunswick, Hamburg, and Vienna, have suggested that workers did not demonstrate the same nationalist fervor as their middle-class compatriots in the first days of the war. Patriotism and a sense of class could go hand in hand. German workers marching off to the front sang patriotic and socialist anthems. That working-class men and women were divided in various ways in 1914 is not surprising, but remarkably many of them had overcome such divisions by 1914. The story of the European working classes after that date is also a story of solidarities and divisions.

EUROPEAN LABOR FROM 1914 TO 1950

World War I. World War I is best remembered for its human sacrifice and its material deprivation that formed the background to revolutions in central and eastern Europe at its end. Yet the experience of European labor during the war was in some ways ambiguous. In the belligerent nations civilian politicians and army generals realized they could not sustain the war effort without the support of organized labor, a clear statement of how far the working classes had come since 1800. In the democratic states, France and Britain, members of the Labour Party and the SFIO were taken into the war cabinets. Although the semi-autocratic German state went nowhere near as far, it granted some degree of recognition to trade union leaders and their wishes. Union officials were exempted from conscription and were given a role in the organization of food supplies and welfare. The unions were for the first time allowed to recruit rural laborers and state employees, and a law in 1916 established workers' councils with elected labor representatives in all large firms. This effectively obliged previously authoritarian employers to deal with the unions and gave a massive spur to the growth of union membership from 1917.

State recognition of and consultation with trade union leaders gave the unions greater legitimacy in other countries too, and national systems of pay bargaining began to erode local particularities. It now made sense to be in the union because the union might be able to achieve something. At the same time shortages of labor in the dominant munitions industries placed workers in a strong bargaining position. Government intervention to control prices and rents and the supply of foodstuffs and raw materials together with an acceptance of new welfare obligations brought to the public's attention the possibility of controlling private capital and the advantages of planning. It was no accident that the British Labour Party first adopted clause IV, nationalization of industry, in 1918.

The consequences of these developments were paradoxical. Unions benefited from recognition, yet the collusion of trade union leaders and labor politicians with systems of national wage bargaining gave rise to shop floor discontent. Radical shop stewards who were often hostile to the official union leadership emerged in Clydeside, Berlin, and Turin. The divide that separated restless workers from trade union bureaucracies was widened by massive food shortages and high levels of inflation in central and eastern Europe, above all in Russia. In Austria, Germany, Hungary, and Russia food riots involving women and children became common. So did strikes throughout Europe caused by food shortages and inflation but facilitated by severe labor shortages in the munitions industries. On top of all this, the war forced longer working hours and an intensification of labor with the suspension of protective labor legislation and a marked increase in industrial accidents.

The war years also witnessed a restructuring of the workforce. Increasing numbers of women and youths were recruited to fill the shortage of labor in the arms industry. They came to work in the large engineering and electrical concerns in Berlin, and the foundries of Krupp and Thyssen in the Ruhr, in large factories on the outskirts of Paris, in the giant engineering concerns of Turin and Milan, and in the Putilov munitions factory in Saint Petersburg. The newer factories, manned by semiskilled workers, employed serial techniques in production. Trained on the shop floor to perform a specialized task, the workers had not experienced apprenticeships but were far less quiescent than unskilled workers. They played a major role in the revolutionary upheavals at the end of the war in Saint Petersburg, Moscow, Vienna, Berlin, Budapest, Turin, and Milan, where the focus of industrial militancy shifted to the large factories.

At the same time more workers became involved in industrial protest and union organizations. Women, rural laborers, and the unskilled in chemical and steelwork appeared on the historical stage between 1917 and 1924 but were largely quiescent again after 1924, by which time political and employer controls had been reestablished. The deteriorating situation of white-collar employees in Germany encouraged some of them to join socialist unions and to vote for the SPD at the end of the war.

Material deprivation and a restructuring of the labor force generalized economic discontent. The war transformed that discontent into a political issue, for material deprivation was manifestly caused by war waged and ended by governments. Thus strikers in central Europe demanded peace and democratic reform. They failed to see why they should make sacrifices for states that treated them as second-class citizens. The inability of the old regimes to guarantee peace was the immediate cause of revolutions in February and October 1917 in Russia and in Austria and Germany a year later. The war thus had a massive impact on labor and actually prepared the ground for the exercise of power by workers' parties in some states after 1918 by temporarily demobilizing or destroying their enemies, especially where the old regimes were held responsible for defeat.

However, many of the upheavals were not unmediated consequences of the war alone. Revolutions took place where radical working-class cultures had developed before World War I and were absent in democratic Scandinavia, Britain, and France. The years immediately before 1914 had seen waves of labor militancy in Germany, Italy, and Russia, often associated with conflicts between trade union leaders and a radical rank and file of engineering workers. Most of the socialist parties in continental Europe, such as the SPD, the SFIO, and the PSI, had revolutionary and reformist elements before 1914. In the course of the war and in the wake of the Russian Revolution and the foundation of the Third International, these split into social-democratic and communist wings. This split therefore had a prewar history and was not simply a consequence of war and inflation between 1914 and 1923. The absence of a revolutionary movement in Britain before 1914 partly explains communism's failure to take hold there after 1918.

Postwar revolutions. The overthrow of autocratic regimes in 1917–1918, the sacrifices workers made during the war, the increasing legitimacy of labor politicians, and the continued shortage of labor at the end of World War I led to the greatest upsurge in international working-class industrial militancy and political radicalism that Europe had seen. The October Revolution brought the Bolsheviks to power in 1917 and saw the first attempts to create a socialist society. Admired by many workers at the time as a model of workers' government, it inspired the creation of significant communist parties in France, Germany, and Italy. Yet revolutionary socialists did not successfully seize power anywhere outside of Russia. Social structure in western Europe lacked a revolutionary peasantry but produced a large and powerful bourgeoisie, which was effectively absent in Russia owing to the dependence of its industry on foreign capital or tsarist initiatives. This Western bourgeoisie was temporarily weakened in the revolutionary upheavals at the end of the war but rapidly reconstituted its control over labor during the economic downturn in 1921 in the United Kingdom, France, and Italy and in 1923 in Germany. Particularly in Germany and Italy the defeat of the revolutionary left was the work of armed counterrevolutions by right wing paramilitary groups, the *Freikorps* and the fascist *squadristi,* respectively. From 1922 in Italy and from 1933 in Germany fascist regimes destroyed the industrial and political labor organizations.

The failure of the revolutionary left to deliver liberation to the European working classes, compounded by the split between democratic socialists and communists, most obviously in Germany, should not obscure the fact that social-democratic welfarism did much to improve the workers' lot in several European states. In the Weimar Republic, national governments with SPD participation extended welfare benefits massively, built public housing, and initiated a sea change in industrial relations by enforcing trade union recognition and collective bargaining. In Britain the fact that the Labour Party was in office only briefly did not prevent measures to subsidize council housing and improve unemployment benefits. Social-democratic participation in the governments of Denmark, Norway, and Sweden impressively extended social welfare. In Sweden the all-socialist government of Per Albin Hansson established a public works pro-

gram of jobs, created a system of pensions and unemployment relief, reduced working hours, set up maternity benefits, and developed a national medical service. The Popular Front government, a communist-socialist-liberal alliance, in France in 1936 increased wage rates, introduced paid holidays, and obliged employers to recognize trade unions.

The absence of a successful socialist revolution outside Russia therefore did not mean the abandonment of working-class interests. However, social-democratic reformism was only possible where it found allies among democratic liberals and where the middle class was prepared to tolerate it. It made no headway against authoritarian regimes in eastern Europe or against fascist dictatorships. Furthermore the great upsurge of labor militancy between 1917 and 1920 rested on conditions of economic expansion and job security. High levels of unemployment after 1921 (1923 in Germany) demobilized and fragmented the labor movement. The search for jobs or the desire to keep them set the employed against the unemployed, factory against factory, men against women, and the young against the old in disputes regarding who should keep the jobs. The 1930s were a period of authoritarian government in eastern Europe, fascist rule in Italy, and Francisco Franco's triumph in Spain but also of Conservative Party domination in Britain. Left-wing governments in France were shortlived in this decade.

The European working classes, 1924–1950. The general models used above to account for variations in working-class politics continued to hold true in this period. They varied enormously from country to country, often depending on earlier traditions, as in the case of communist party support. It is true that socioeconomic factors go some way toward explaining the split between democratic socialists and communists. Germany exhibited a strong correlation between unemployment and the size of communist party support, for example. In Germany, France, and Italy political radicalism was particularly marked among young and semiskilled workers in large factories. Yet the British and the Swedish unemployed and semiskilled did not turn to communism. Again political traditions and the preexistence of revolutionary labor were crucial. No simple correlation emerged between economic position and electoral behavior.

The number of wageworkers increased generally between 1914 and 1950, from 4.7 million to 6.5 million in France, from 17.1 million to 21.4 million in the United Kingdom, and from 9.3 million to 9.7 million in Italy. Between 1913 and 1950 the average rate of growth of nonagricultural employment was 1 percent per annum in Western Europe and 1.5 percent in Eastern Europe, reaching as much as 2.6 percent in Russia, though Eastern Europe was still overwhelmingly rural. In Britain 70 percent of the active population were workers in the 1950s. Furthermore national systems of wage bargaining and decreasing differentials between skilled and unskilled workers helped create a working class that was economically more united than previously. Though union density increased from 23 percent in 1914 to 44.1 percent in 1950 in Britain, from 17 percent to 39 percent in the Netherlands, and from 15 percent to 76 percent in Sweden, the combined vote for the parties of labor rarely rose above 35 percent in most European countries. Only infrequently did socialists form majority governments before 1944, and Sweden was the most obvious exception to this rule. This may have been partly because of the enfranchisement of women in several states between the wars, though Italy and France did not enact woman suffrage until the end of World War II and it produced Catholic mass politics. Women remained less likely to vote for the left in this period, not least because the division between work and home remained as complete for married working-class couples as it was before. In 1931 only 16 percent of married British women were employed outside the home, and the evidence is overwhelming that women placed a positive value on housework and child rearing at this time. They also voted for parties that proclaimed the sanctity of traditional family values.

The increase in waged labor also should not obscure the fact that much of that labor was nonmanual. By 1933 white-collar workers made up approximately 25 percent of the active population in Germany. In Britain the proportion of nonmanual workers in the labor force rose from 18.7 percent in 1911 to 30.9 percent in 1951. Paid by seniority and thus guaranteed rising incomes where they remained loyal to the firm, they often acted as intermediaries between management and the shop floor, and they were conscious of their status. Not until the 1960s and 1970s did the rates of unionization of female and white-collar staff began to catch up with those of males in manual employment. Furthermore the unemployment of the interwar years often decimated precisely those sectors of the economy where working-class militancy had been strong, such as coal mining.

Again support for the labor parties and trade union membership were not consequences of impoverishment, except possibly the unemployed, many of whom fell into apathy and resignation rather than militancy. For those employed, real wages continued to rise, and levels of poverty were reduced according to all the British surveys. The life expectancy of workers continued

to improve, but it still did not reach that of the middle class. Working-class consumption, typified by visits to the cinema, the dance hall, and sports events, increased significantly. This was especially true in Britain, but France and Germany experienced similar developments between the wars. Extensions of welfare and especially public housing made a huge contribution to working-class living standards. However, homogenous working-class residential areas became more common than before, while the mobility prospects of even skilled manual workers remained extremely limited into the 1960s. Hence significant numbers of European workers, increasingly self-confident in the democratic states, held collective values. The extent of embourgeoisement before the 1960s was truly limited.

EPILOGUE:
EUROPEAN LABOR AFTER 1950

As early as the 1950s some commentators feared the demise of traditional working-class culture at the hands of mass entertainment in Britain. Those fears heightened in the recession of the 1970s and the political triumph of Thatcherism. The postwar welfare state and massive rises in real wages in the 1950s and the 1960s, the time of economic miracles, stimulated huge increases in working-class consumerism. From the 1960s working-class ownership of houses and cars expanded dramatically. Radio, already popular before 1950, and television enhanced the possibilities of private, home-based leisure. Slum clearances sometimes disrupted working-class residential communities. The recession of the 1970s and 1980s laid waste to many of the traditional heartlands of labor and deindustrialised large parts of Europe.

Simultaneously white-collar employment outstripped that of manual labor. By 1981, 52.3 percent of the active British population was employed in nonmanual jobs. In Holland 1,042,000 worked in manufacturing but 2,943,000 worked in trades and services at the same date. Simultaneously a feminization of the labor force occurred. Whereas the number of women workers in 1950 was 7.1 million in the United Kingdom, the figure rose to 22.9 million by 1990. In 1951, 32.7 percent of women and 87.6 percent men of working age were gainfully employed, but by 1980 51.6 percent of women and 77.9 percent of men were working. Working-class support for labor politics eroded in Western Europe, and socialist parties survived only where they appealed to the middle ground and to voters outside the traditional working class.

Historians and sociologists have debated the extent of embourgeoisement of the working class amid undeniable affluence in the postwar decades. The

Solidarity. Union leader Lech Wałęsa and Solidarity strikers at the Lenin Shipyards, Gdansk, Poland, August 1988. ©SYGMA

growth of an immigrant lower working class in most Western European countries also created internal tensions and disparities within the working class. Many workers no longer displayed distinctive culture or behavior, even aside from the dilution of working-class politics and the decline in unionization. But the working class was still less likely than the middle class to strive for upward mobility or to send children to universities, reflecting social barriers and distinctive expectations. Most people of the working class view their labor in fiercely instrumental terms, judging it on the basis of earnings, in contrast to those of the middle class, who usually seek some meaning in the work. The boundaries of the working class have definitely become less defined, but the concept continues to have some real utility in European social history.

The lot of workers in Soviet-controlled Europe was, of course, very different. Workers played a role in the collapse of Communist regimes, most obviously in the Solidarity organization in Poland. This was far from a universal phenomenon, however. Until the 1970s many workers in Eastern Europe enjoyed rising living standards, though not on a Western scale. Some,

miners in particular, enjoyed special privileges, so it is not surprising that they supported the old regime in Romania and did not initially participate in Solidarity in Poland. The collapse of the old system and the triumph of market forces created massive inequalities and a decline in living standards for the great majority. In western Europe the old working class became only a shadow of its former self, and in eastern Europe it seemed powerless.

CONCLUSION

For much of the nineteenth and twentieth centuries the working classes possessed a distinct identity, but that identity was never uniform. In some cases workers did show allegiance to a broad concept of class, though this was more often the case in autocratic than in liberal states and was rarely a consequence of economic variables alone. Class identity was always fragile and contested by other loyalties of nation, race, gender, and occupation. Since 1960 it has arguably been in a state of dissolution. However, the struggles of working men and women have done much to change

European society, especially in the form of the welfare state, though some would see even this achievement as threatened in the early twenty-first century. Furthermore, cross-national comparisons of working-class behavior and identity do suggest that much can still be explained in terms of structures—be they economic, social, or political, whatever the postmodernists may tell us.

See also **Technology; Capitalism and Commercialization; The Industrial Revolutions; Communism** *(volume 2);* **Collective Action; Moral Economy and Luddism; Labor History: Strikes and Unions; Socialism** *(in this volume);* **Gender and Work; Factory Work** *(volume 4); and other articles in this section.*

BIBLIOGRAPHY

Berger, Stefan, and David Broughton, eds. *The Force of Labour.* Oxford, 1995.

Bourke, Joanna. *Working Class Cultures in Britain, 1890–1960.* London, 1994.

Breuilly, John. *Labour and Liberalism in Nineteenth-Century Europe.* Manchester, UK., 1992.

Cronin, James E., and Carmen Sirianni. *Work, Community, and Power.* London, 1983.

Geary, Dick. *European Labour Politics from 1900 to the Depression.* Basingstoke, U.K., 1991.

Geary, Dick. *European Labour Protest, 1848–1939.* London, 1981.

Geary, Richard, ed. *Labour and Socialist Movements in Europe before 1914.* New York, 1992.

Haimson, Leopold H., and Charles Tilly, eds. *Strikes, Wars, and Revolutions in International Perspective.* Cambridge, U.K., 1989.

Hobsbawm, E. J. *Labouring Men.* London, 1964.

Hobsbawm, E. J. *Worlds of Labour.* London, 1984.

McKibbin, Ross. *The Ideologies of Class.* Oxford, 1990.

Marks, Gary. *Unions in Politics.* Princeton, N.J., 1989.

Mitchell, Harvey, and Peter N. Stearns. *Workers and Protest.* Ithaca, N.Y., 1971.

Stearns, Peter N. *Lives of Labor: Work in a Maturing Industrial Society.* London, 1975.

Stedman Jones, Gareth. *Languages of Class.* New York, 1983.

Tilly, Charles, Louise Tilly, and Richard Tilly. *The Rebellious Century, 1830–1930.* Cambridge, Mass., 1975.

SERVANTS

Bridget Hill

For a large part of the period from the sixteenth to the early twentieth century, servants were ubiquitous throughout Europe. The largest concentrations were in the cities and towns, but servants were also found in rural villages and on farms. In rural France, for example, between 2 and 12 percent of the population was in service (Hufton, 1993). It constituted the biggest employment after agriculture. Indeed the smaller proportion of servants in France and Germany as compared with Britain was the result of a larger number of women still working in agriculture. Thus, servants formed a significant occupational group in Europe. Numbers probably peaked in the late nineteenth century, declined steadily in the following years when in both France and Britain new job opportunities opened up for women, and slumped in the period following World War I. Yet until World War I, domestic service remained throughout Europe the largest category of female employment (Hufton, 1997). As late as 1911 in Britain, 35 percent of working women were employed as domestic servants.

In part it is the large number of servants in the population, especially in urban areas, that makes them an important subject of research for social historians. In the eighteenth century they constituted something like 12 percent of the population of any European city or town (Hufton, 1993). In Paris at the end of the eighteenth century there were one hundred thousand servants—that is, 15 percent of the population (Fairchilds, 1984). In France as a whole there were two million servants, which meant that 8 percent of the population earned their living in service (Fairchilds, 1984). According to Patrick Colquhoun, London in 1806 had two hundred thousand servants of both sexes, with twice as many women servants as men (Hufton, 1993). Given that such a sizable proportion of the population of European countries was in service, one must ask why. Where did the demand for servants originate? Where did servants come from and why did they choose (if "choose" is the appropriate word) service as an occupation?

Servants were unique among the lower classes in their contact with their employers. This was the nearest most masters and mistresses came to the laboring class. Indeed, one function servants performed was to shield their employers from contact with the working class. The diaries and journals of employers tell us a great deal about master-servant relations, the work servants were expected to do, the conditions under which they carried it out, and the conditions of hiring and firing. Accounts written by servants themselves are rare, but some do exist. Other members of the working class were suspicious of and even hostile to the close, even intimate, relations between many servants and their employers. An analysis of these relations provides a fascinating insight into the complexities of class. Because most domestic servants were not natives of the town or city in which they worked, the history of service is also intimately linked to the history of rural-urban migration and, on a wider scale, to international migration.

With the exception of France and England, comprehensive studies of domestic servants are lacking. One reason this subject of research has been ignored is that, as part of the lower orders, servants and their work were regarded as unimportant. Only in the late twentieth century did historians see them as a fit subject for study. Another reason is that from the end of the seventeenth century servants were increasingly women, and, some historians would say, therefore of little significance. That the vast majority never wrote about their experiences also presents real difficulties in learning about servants. They constitute an elusive and nearly silent group of the population. Some were visible, but most were not. If historians were to rely only on the many accounts written by employers they would rapidly conclude that servants constituted a necessary evil, as they were generally the subject of criticism and abuse from employers.

Information about servants is also available in the many courtesy books telling servants how to behave toward their mistresses and masters and how best to perform their tasks, but these tell us little of how

Servant and Employers. *While the Sunday Lunch Is Laid (Interior of the Architect Carlsberg's Home)* by Pehr Gustaf von Heideken, c. 1835. A servant sets out the lunch *(left)*. STADSMUSEUM, STOCKHOLM, SWEDEN

in fact they did behave or exactly what work was demanded of them. Many of these books were written by men and emphasize the dependent role of servants and their duty of unquestioned obedience, loyalty, and absolute discretion. One of the worst sins a servant could commit was to discuss the lives and behavior of his master and mistress outside his household.

DEFINITION OF SERVANTS

"Servant" is a term that has been used very loosely. In England in the seventeenth and early eighteenth centuries the term covered all servants in husbandry—that is, both farm servants and domestic servants. Although now the distinction between live-in servants and day laborers who lived in their own homes and worked only part-time for an employer is clear, in earlier periods people did not distinguish between the two (Hill). Apprentices were frequently referred to as "servants," as were undertenants in the seventeenth century.

In France the term *domestique* or *serviteur* could cover a great range of occupations and people from very different social backgrounds. *Domestique* was used not to describe the work done as much as the conditions of employment: a *domestique* lived in an employer's household in a state of dependency. Those considered *domestiques* might include gardeners, musicians, teamsters, shop clerks, silk weavers, and lawyers (Fairchilds, 1984).

WHO BECAME A SERVANT

During the eighteenth century the demand for domestic servants increased as urban development cre-

ated a growing affluence among the middle classes. Who were the servants who responded to this demand and from where were they recruited? Most women entering domestic service came from the countryside. It has been estimated on the basis of urban censuses that in the preindustrial period 13 percent of the total population in any city north of the Loire were country girls in service (Hufton, 1997). Only a minority of those employed in cities and towns were natives of the towns in which they worked.

The link between domestic service, rural poverty, and unemployment for women was a close one. In southeast England, where agricultural changes had limited the nature of employment available to women, the sheer inability of single women to earn sufficient funds for economic independence made migration an important option. In France girls living in the poor and backward agricultural regions of the Massif Central regularly made the journey to Montpellier and Béziers. In Toulouse in the eighteenth century girls were recruited from the poor agricultural land of the surrounding hill areas.

In general, women entered service when young. The censuses of Wurzburg and Amsterdam show a steady influx of female adolescents. Domestic servants in Amsterdam came from the northern provinces, where family poverty forced many girls into service at a very young age (Hufton, 1993). After 1820 in the area of the Netherlands, where there was a heavy concentration of textile work but where the industry was in decline, parents decided between factory work or domestic service for their daughters. Eighteen percent of domestic weavers' and 28 percent of factory workers' daughters decided to enter domestic service and left home at a very early age (Janssens). In England it was normal for girls aged thirteen to fourteen to enter service, and many started much earlier. In nineteenth-century Italy children as young as ten or twelve were brought into a family as maids. They grew up with the family and lived in intimacy with their mistresses. Often they were expected to serve all their lives in the one family (Robertson).

According to Danish landowners the very low level of wages on farms persuaded maidservants to migrate to the nearest provincial town or to Copenhagen in the hope of finding better conditions of employment (Dahlsgård). During the first half of the nineteenth century, unmarried girls aged twelve to thirteen flocked to Antwerp and the other chief towns of Antwerp province. Most of them came to be housemaids of Antwerp families. As the city's director of poor relief wrote in 1843, these migrants did not come to Antwerp "in order to set up in business or to carry on their former trade but quite simply to find in another community one way or another the means of existence denied them in their birthplace" (quoted in Lis, p. 45).

The middle classes in towns usually preferred to recruit their servants from the countryside. They were regarded as better and more virtuous workers. It is interesting to note that nearly one in two of female immigrants to Antwerp left the city in the period between 1817 and 1830. At least one-third returned to their places of birth, hoping no doubt that the meager savings they had made in service would enable them to marry. Similarly, seasonal migration from Massat, a village in the Pyrenees, was essential to the survival of the inmates. Most young girls migrated to Spanish cities, but however long they were away, ultimately they tended to return home with the little capital they had accumulated (Hufton, 1997).

CHANGES IN DOMESTIC SERVICE

During the eighteenth century domestic service was changing. In the first place it was fast becoming feminized. Increasingly, only wealthy masters could afford to employ men at twice the wages of women servants. They did this to display their wealth; also, as the streets were unsafe for women, men served in public as pages, coachmen, and porters. This process first affected urban servants in Britain, Holland, Germany, and France, and later in Spain and Italy. In addition, and perhaps most notably in postrevolutionary France, there was a marked decline in the number of servants employed by the nobility and an increase in the number employed by the middle classes. Another change was the increasing mobility of servants. In response to the chance of a wider experience, better wages or conditions, or the hope of more sympathetic employers, domestic servants constantly changed places.

With the expansion of the middle class in the eighteenth century many more households than formerly were able to employ servants. Given the differential between the wages of male and female domestics most of these households—some quite humble—employed a woman. There was a marked increase in the number of single-servant households. Male servants tended to opt out of service, resenting the close personal supervision. There were far more employment opportunities available to them that allowed them to live in their own homes. In the massive migratory flow from country into towns women were predominant. Many of them ended up in domestic service, so that cheaper female servants became readily available.

Thus, noble households became smaller and more feminine not only because female domestics

were cheaper but because male domestics were increasingly attracted out of service by alternative occupations. Apparently the proportion of male servants in noble households peaked around 1750 and then declined. In England in the mid-eighteenth century, the duke of Bedford's household numbered forty servants of both sexes (Hill). While earlier in the seventeenth century households of over fifty had been common, by the late eighteenth century they frequently numbered twenty or less.

Even so the hierarchical structure of servant households often remained. In servant-households in nineteenth-century Germany, for example, individual workloads were carefully defined according to gender, and a rigid hierarchy was maintained between upper and lower servants both in their work, at mealtimes, and in periods of rest. A lady's maid, for instance, was carefully defined in a German dictionary compiled by the Brothers Grimm as "a maiden in the service of a princess or a noblewoman . . . distinct from the chambermaid, often also from the maids-in-waiting who are below her in rank, and distinct also from the housekeeper who runs the household" (quoted in Joeres and Maynes, p. 65). On the whole the bottom of the hierarchy was occupied by women, the top by men (Fairchilds, 1984).

The Scullery Maid. Painting by Jean-Baptiste Chardin (1699–1779). GLASGOW ART GALLERY & MUSEUM/THE BRIDGEMAN ART LIBRARY

By the end of the eighteenth century, most middle-class households employed one servant, usually a woman. Increasingly, lowly families could afford to employ servants. Maids-of-all-work were cheap enough to attract new employers who wanted help with the burden of the family wash or someone to serve in a shop when the mistress was occupied. Servants had moved into the category of wage earners and were no longer regarded as part of the families who employed them. They were contracted to work and no longer used to denote status or for show. In consequence service was seen by some as increasingly menial and the condition of service considered degrading.

SERVANTS' WORK

Beginning in the nineteenth century in larger households, the labels attached to individual domestics described the work they did and distinguished them from other domestics. Thus terms like "butler," "coachman," and "postilion" bore a close relationship to the work performed by the servants in these positions. In the eighteenth century such labels were more arbitrary. Servants, however they were labeled, moved between roles in response to their employer's current needs. This is reflected in advertisements for servants that appeared in mid century. In 1755 the *Ipswich Journal,* for example, carried an advertisement for "a Livery Servant who has been used to wait at Table, and knows something of Horses, and if he has any Knowledge of Gardening it will be the more agreeable." It was the same when it came to employing a woman servant. One advertisement for a female servant in the same journal ran "Wanted immediately. A Cook Maid in a large Family, who must look after two Cows" (Hill, pp. 23–24). For the majority of single-servant-employing households the label attached to them was of little consequence. Most were females, maids-of-all-work, whose range of duties might have little or nothing to do with housework.

SERVANT HIRING

Normally it was women who both hired servants and supervised their day-to-day tasks. In Germany, however, husbands not only did the hiring but sometimes also the supervising. Similarly, in middle-class households in nineteenth-century Rome it was common for the husbands to deal with the servants and even arrange for the delivery of supplies (Robertson). In England hiring fairs were held at the Whitsuntide and Martinmas fairs when all kinds of servants paraded before their future employers prepared to hire themselves out for six months' service or a year.

Around the middle of the eighteenth century in England registry offices were established to provide exemplary servants with places. Almost immediately they were accused of fraud and deceit. There were servants prepared to pay for good references, and the registry offices responded willingly. In Scotland John Lawson set up a registry office, calling it Lawson's Intelligence Office as early as 1701. He offered to provide households all over the country with reliable servants. But employers found that servants recruited through registry offices did not stay any longer than those recruited by other means (Plant).

Servants were more commonly recruited through friends, relations, or tradesmen. Although servants in search of a position were expected to offer good references, it soon became clear that employers could not trust their authenticity. Employers were urged to seek out former mistresses in order to inquire about their past servants. Some mistresses resorted to advertising for servants, although that method presented difficulties when it came to checking up on applicants. In Spain it was often the village priest who established a line of contact with a particular city and would act as a reference for a girl taken on by a family. Therefore Galician girls migrating as servants tended to predominate in Madrid (Hufton, 1997).

WORKING CONDITIONS

The conditions of employment varied according to the size of the household and the individual employers. Hours were always long—frequently twelve to eighteen a day. Servants rose early to light fires and start the drudgery of cleaning the house. While employers might define their servant's duties carefully, there was no set time schedule. Free time was minimal—perhaps one day off a month. Often there was no clear agreement about off-duty time, so that servants could be on call every hour of the day and night. A German essayist, Fanny Lewald, wrote in the mid-nineteenth century of how the German domestic servant was " 'in service' day and night. On workdays and holidays, at any hour, the master and mistress have a right to her services" (quoted in Joeres and Maynes, p. 68). This was typical. Samuel Pepys's female servants were frequently expected to stay up until he returned home drunk, and then to undress him and put him to bed.

Accommodation varied greatly. It could consist of a space on the kitchen floor, the area under the stairs, a cupboard, cellar, or by Victorian times, an

Servants for Hire. The market for hiring children at Spitalfields, London, 1850. MANSELL COLLECTION/TIME INC.

unheated and unlit attic equipped with a trundle bed and little else. It could consist only of a space in a bed. In seventeenth-century France, masters and mistresses thought nothing of having servants of the same sex sleep two or three to a bed. Often all that was provided was a space on a landing. Danish servants often occupied minute rooms adjacent to the kitchen and without windows. A Neapolitan servant maid in the twentieth century still slept in a dark cupboard under the stairs. In the larger noble households of prerevolutionary France, male servants at the top of the hierarchy might have rooms of their own, but most servants lived in houses with two dormitories—one for men and the other for women. Lack of privacy was guaranteed by the failure to provide any keys to servants' rooms. This was just one factor that made female servants vulnerable to the attention of the male members of the household. Pepys regularly watched his female servants undressing. Victorian houses were often designed with separate staircases to separate servants from their master and mistress and to prevent those unfortunate confrontations, but they still occurred.

The standard of food given to servants also varied. Some servants ate the same food as their employers, although not necessarily of the same quality; others did not. The British feminist author Mary Wollstonecraft, visiting Scandinavia in 1795, was horrified to find that employers gave their servants food different from what they ate themselves. This was, however, the usual practice in Scotland in large households. In 1829 Lady Breadalbane ordered that no butter was to be served in the servants' hall but that all their pies and puddings must be made with dripping (Plant, p. 171). On the whole servants' food in Scotland was dull but not unwholesome. In smaller households the servants ate the same food as their employers. As there was little meat, most of the week they lived on porridge, broth, and bannocks.

WAGES

Throughout Europe, the wages paid to servants varied enormously—both among different areas of each country, and between towns or cities and the rural countryside. For example, while in general female servants' wages were half those of men in Denmark, there were wide variations between one manor and another (Dahlsgård, p. 63). There was also a striking contrast between wages in Scotland and England in the early eighteenth century. Maximum wages were fixed by the Lanarkshire justices in 1708 at £24 Scots a year or £2 sterling for any male servant able to perform "all manner of work relating to husbandry" (Plant, p. 165). In England, the equivalent wage could be at least five times greater.

What has not always been fully appreciated are the large number of servants who were paid no wages at all but were taken on to work in exchange for board and lodging. In Denmark until the late twentieth century it was customary for daughters who became maidservants on farms to receive practically no cash wages at all (Dahlsgård). In England many pauper servants were placed by the parish authorities with employers. Foundlings who survived tended to go into service. Unemployed daughters of those claiming parish relief were liable to be forced into service on the same terms. Not only were no wages paid to them, but the parish authorities usually gave their employers an allowance toward the maintenance of the servant. Young boy-servants, or "livery boys" as they were called, might be given a suit of clothes, but rarely, if they were paid at all, were they paid more than a pittance—more pocket-money than a wage (Hill).

From the sixteenth to the early eighteenth century the wages of French domestic servants are accurately described as "in general so low as to be almost nonexistent" (Fairchilds, 1984, p. 54). Most servants were paid à récompense—that is, they received board, lodging, and some sort of present at the end of their service. Such a system was widespread among both farm and house servants. The alternative was hiring à gages, when servants were in theory paid a yearly wage, although very often it was paid at least partly in kind. In 1705 François Louradour was hired by the Chevalier de la Renaudie at a yearly wage of "eighteen livres, two shirts, and one of my old hats" (quoted in Fairchilds, 1984, p. 55). But wages often went unpaid—sometimes for as long as six years. In eighteenth-century Madrid, many servants in times of hardship were prepared to work for their keep alone—at least until times improved. Most expected to be able to profit a little from the sale of food, and even in modest households servants expected to be able to sell "dripping from meat . . . to street vendors for candles" (Hufton, 1997, p. 86).

In general women servants earned less than men, often no more than a half, even for the same kind of work. Wages varied not only according to gender but also by skill and by geographical location. In France, Paris was by far the highest-paying city for servants. But all servants, except the most highly skilled upper servants, earned wages that were uniformly extremely low, even taking into consideration the value of their board and lodging. Things changed when servants' wages began to rise gradually in the period 1730–1750 and then sharply in the 1770s and 1780s. All wages were rising in France in this period, but servants' wages rose more than those for other occupations. The wages of an unskilled female servant rose 40 percent between the periods 1726–1741 and 1771–1789. For male servants the rise was even greater. In these circumstances hiring à récompense died out (Fairchilds, 1984).

If wages of domestic servants were universally low there were perks from which servants could benefit. We do not know the exact origin of these perks, but by the beginning of the seventeenth century they were a firmly established practice to which servants attached great importance. As the relationship between employers and servants became less paternalistic and more contractual, such practices came under increasing criticism, but attempts to abolish them were met with frenzied opposition. As Samuel Richardson's heroine learned in Pamela, it was usual for employers to pass on clothes to their servants. In England there were often tea allowances made to female domestics and beer to males. Some employers gave special washing allowances to their servants. Cooks and housekeepers were in a position to benefit from tradesman's perks given to confirm their employers' continued use of their services. But by far the most valuable of perks were vails or tips. This custom survived from a time when guests of a household were expected to tip the servants. Vails amounted to a generous supplement to wages for those servants who benefited from them—that is, mainly male servants who were on public view, such as footmen, postilions, and butlers.

SERVANTS AND SEX

One thing common to all female domestic servants was their vulnerability to advances made by their employers, their employers' sons, or fellow servants. Away from their families and friends, in strange households, these young girls lacked all protection from sexual exploitation. Absence of privacy in households (as has been noted, if a servant was lucky enough to have a room of her own she would not possess a key) meant frequent cases of pregnant servant girls. In France ecclesiastical court records reveal masters who impregnated three maids in succession but managed to negotiate marriages for each (Hufton, 1997). We know most about the situation in France, where the déclarations de grossesse (statements required by law of unwed mothers detailing the circumstances surrounding their pregnancies) provide an invaluable source of evidence. Even so, the threat to servant maids was almost certainly much greater than the evidence suggests. To many it seemed perfectly natural that masters should have sexual access to their servants. It is clear that in France affairs between servants and masters were commonplace. It seems probable that most female servants experienced some form of sexual harassment from their masters at one point or another (Fairchilds, 1984).

For the majority of the servant girls who became pregnant, employers had made promises of money or gifts, or threatened dismissal or the use of force. Often male servants promised marriage and abandoned the women when they became pregnant. In eighteenth-century Nantes, for instance, 40 percent of women reporting illegitimate pregnancies were domestic servants. In Marseilles it was as high as 90 percent (Maza). There is no reason to think the situation in England was all that different. In France it appears to have been easy for a well-to-do master to unload the maid he had made pregnant on some single male in need of money. Often this was done with the full connivance of the wife-to-be. Such a marriage cost one French seducer one hundred florins and a new set of clothes (Hufton, 1997).

Such marriages notwithstanding, the fate of the pregnant servant maid was dire. As soon as her condition was known, instant dismissal followed. The opportunities for her reemployment were few, particularly if she had the child. Shame and fear of returning to their families caused many to take to the road. A town provided more anonymity than a rural village. But they had to be very careful, for anyone harboring a traveling pregnant woman in England could find himself in court and fined (Hufton, 1997). Wherever they were discovered, they were harassed and moved on. Occasionally evidence of some humanity toward such traveling women appears. Anne Frie of Broad Hinton told the magistrates in 1610 that when she found " 'a walking woman . . . in travail of child in the open street' she took her in 'for womanhood's sake' " (Hufton, 1997, p. 269).

While there is some disagreement about the scale of recruitment of domestic servants into prostitution, two groups constituted regular sources. One was unemployed domestic servants (Fairchilds, 1984). As Daniel Defoe's *Moll Flanders* suggests, in such cases the choices were simple—either prostitution or starvation. Often such prostitution was short-term and the women returned to regular employment as servants at a later stage. In France that was the recurring experience of women employed in the silk manufac-

ture in Lyon. Whenever trade was bad the *servantes* would be dismissed. Their only recourse would be a period in prostitution. The same thing happened in the lace industry in Belgium when bad trade left women workers unemployed. They made their way to Dutch ports and for a spell became prostitutes (Hufton, 1997). The second source for the recruitment of prostitutes was inn servants, who received no regular wages but were expected to survive on the basis of tips. It is not surprising that they attempted to supplement their earnings by prostitution (Fairchilds, 1984, p. 75). In Amsterdam, where prostitution was particularly common, most prostitutes were migrants from the north Netherlands and Germany, and 15 percent of the total number of prostitutes had been servants (Hufton, 1997, p. 326).

SOCIAL MOBILITY

What chances existed for upward social mobility among domestic servants? For the minority in larger households it was possible to ascend the servant hierarchy by learning new skills and accumulating experience. As Olwen Hufton writes, "a kitchen skivvy after a few years might even advance to parlourmaid." She might achieve the status of chambermaid or, more exceptionally, lady's maid, but this was far from usual, and required a large dose of good luck (Hufton, 1993, p. 21). So for a minority of servants of status there was some career structure to their lives in service. In the large houses of the rich, where a strict hierarchy of servants existed, an experienced servant could enjoy a measure of autonomy, a comfortable standard of living, and some authority over others. This was especially true of male servants. Given the decline in the number of male servants there was a decreasing opportunity to marry men in service. Many female servants married tradesmen or craftsmen. Others were lucky if they won the affections of the lowest paid laborer. Much depended on what dowry a female servant had managed to accumulate from her earnings. Real social advancement from marriage, however, was rare. If the estimate of John Rickman, the chief statistician employed on the early nineteenth-century British census, was right—that is, that one-third of servants were upwardly mobile, one-third remained static, and one-third were downwardly mobile—then two-thirds of servants experienced no social betterment (Hill). For the majority of servants there was no such career structure. This in part explains the great mobility of eighteenth- and nineteenth-century domestic servants who were constantly changing places, to learn new skills, to increase their wages or improve their working conditions, and often just to get away from an unpleasant master or mistress.

Most young girls entering into service had little or no education. There is evidence that by the eighteenth century in Britain and the Netherlands better-off employers were demanding a degree of literacy from servants above the level of kitchen maid. It has been argued that servants were more literate than the rest of the working population and that a high proportion married above their social origins (Smith). Of course literacy varied; in France and the Mediterranean countries, literacy rates were much lower. In the departments of Provence and Normandy, for example, the literacy rate in the eighteenth century was barely 30 percent. Employers of servants in Spain did not expect them to be literate. In northwest Europe in the eighteenth century, employers demanded some sophistication and education in their servants (Hufton, 1997).

What was the attitude of servants to service? Of eighteenth-century London female servants, D. A. Kent wrote, "domestic service was an occupation which allowed women a measure of choice and relative economic independence" (quoted in Hill, p. 107). In sharp contrast is the comment from a German novel of the brother of a German woman entering service. "You have no idea of the dependent status that awaits you, or of the moods to which you will be exposed" (quoted in Joeres and Mayne, p. 66). One historian confidently states that most French women employed as domestics would have been anxious to get out of service as soon as they possibly could. For thousands of French women service was an unpleasant but necessary experience that lasted ten years before a dowry was earned to make marriage a possibility (Maza). In fact many servants married and left their employment. At least in theory the head of the household would expect to be consulted, if not about the groom, then about when the marriage was taking place. If the girl hoped to stay on in service the approval of the head of household was essential. There is evidence that, by the end of the eighteenth century, French domestic servants found service more and more intolerable as it involved loss of independence. Service at its best was regarded as a temporary bridge to better things (Fairchilds, 1979).

In their anomalous position between masters and mistresses and the rest of the laboring class, servants belonged nowhere. They were an isolated group.

In the Kitchen. Kitchen maids, c. 1890. ©HULTON GETTY/LIAISON AGENCY

Female domestic servants in particular were consistently objects of hostility, as indeed were unmarried woman generally. Their unmarried status was seen as threatening by a society that saw marriage as the foundation of social stability. They were assumed to be promiscuous, debauched, and wanton, and were often accused on the barest of evidence of being prostitutes. Their ambiguous position was seen as menacing and a threat to social order (Maza).

In the twentieth century, as employment opportunities for women increased, the number of women choosing to enter service declined. Women wanted better wages than was possible in service, and more independence and freedom to live in their own homes and to spend their spare time as they chose without the close supervision of their employers.

In 1849 the *Westminster Review* published an article looking forward to a time when women would refuse to enter domestic service. The growth of more attractive alternative occupations for women in the late twentieth century made domestic service a rarity except among the very wealthy. But in a subtly different form domestic service thrived in the shape of home-helps, baby-sitters, and *au pairs*. These occupations appealed mostly to women, often single parents with young children, who needed part-time employment. The great difference from domestic service of the past is that they lived in their own homes and led lives independent of their employers.

See also **Estates and Country Houses** *(volume 2);* **Prostitution** *(in this volume);* **Illegitimacy and Concubinage** *(volume 4); and other articles in this section.*

BIBLIOGRAPHY

Boxer, Marilyn, and Jean Quataert. *Connecting Spheres: Women in the Western World 1500 to the present.* New York, 1987.

Bridenthal, Renate, and Claudia Koonz, eds. *Becoming Visible.* 2d ed. Boston, 1987.

Dahlsgård, Inga. *Women in Denmark Yesterday and Today.* Selskab, Denmark, 1989.

Fairchilds, Cissie. *Domestic Enemies: Servants and Their Masters in Old Regime France.* Baltimore, 1984.

Fairchilds, Cissie. "Master and Servants in Eighteenth-Century Toulouse." *Journal of Social History* 12 (1979): 367–393.

Hanawalt, Barbara, ed. *Women and Work in Preindustrial Europe.* Bloomington, Ind., 1986.

Hecht, Jean J. *The Domestic Servant Class in Eighteenth-Century England.* London, 1956.

Hilden, Patricia Penn. *Women, Work, and Politics: Belgium 1830–1914.* Oxford, 1993.

Hill, Bridget. *Servants: English Domestics in the Eighteenth Century.* Oxford, 1996.

Hufton, Olwen. *The Prospect Before Her: A History of Women in Western Europe.* Vol. 1. 1500–1800. London, 1997.

Hufton, Olwen. "Women, Work and Family." In *A History of Women III: Renaissance and Enlightenment Paradox.* Edited by Natalie Zemon Davis and Arlette Farge. Cambridge, Mass., 1993. Pages 15–45.

Janssens, Angélique. *Family and Social Change.* Cambridge, U.K., 1993.

Joeres, Ruth-Ellen, and Mary Jo Maynes, eds. *German Women in the Eighteenth and Nineteenth Centuries: A Social and Literary History.* Bloomington, Ind., 1986.

Kent, D. A. "Ubiquitous but Invisible: Female Domestic Servants in Mid-Eighteenth-Century London." *History Workshop Journal* 28 (1989): 111–128.

Lis, Catharina. *Social Change and the Labouring Poor: Antwerp 1778–1860.* New Haven, Conn., 1986.

Maza, Sarah C. *Servants and Masters in Eighteenth Century France.* Princeton, N.J., 1983.

Plant, Marjorie. *The Domestic Life of Scotland in the Eighteenth Century.* Edinburgh, 1952.

Robertson, Priscilla. *An Experience of Women: Pattern and Change in Nineteenth-Century Europe.* Philadelphia, 1982.

Smith, Bonnie G. *Changing Lives: Women in European History Since 1700.* Lexington, Mass., 1989.

PEASANTS AND RURAL LABORERS

Cathy A. Frierson

From the North Atlantic to the Urals in the 1500s, peasants and rural laborers made up 80 to 90 percent of the population. Peasant men and women were part of a population expansion that began with the ebb of the Black Death in the late fifteenth century and extended into the second half of the seventeenth century. Geographic location set the first boundaries. Peasants who lived west of the river Elbe in the German northeast were among the more fortunate of Europe's rural laborers; those born to the east of the river Elbe faced limits more restrictive and more persistent.

In western Europe, most peasants lived on small farms, for which they paid the lord of the manor rents in money or in kind. Although they were not free of obligations, they did have some autonomy in developing strategies for meeting them. They decided how best to cultivate the land and tend their animals to produce goods they either paid to the master or sold at a local market for the cash they then paid as rent.

In France in the 1500s, most peasants were legally tenants of lords, or seigneurs, to whom they owed monetary payments. There were some peasants who owned their land outright, but their numbers diminished in the 1500s and continued to decline thereafter, especially near urban areas, where population increased and wealthier members of society bought land as an investment. By the middle of the seventeenth century, only a very small number of French peasants owned enough to feed their families, much less prosper. This made the French peasantry a population of renters, who paid rents, taxes, and tithes to landowners, the state, and the church.

The lord was closest at hand and figured most prominently in the local imagination, as he exacted rent on the land and fees for fishing in his streams, hunting in his forests, or milling grain in his mills. The lord also controlled the local markets and could charge fees on peasant trade there. Finally, the lord controlled the local courts and political system, setting the parameters for justice and governance in the local communities that constituted the peasants' world. Some French peasants were able to go beyond meeting

the lord's demands to expand the lands they rented and become minor employers themselves, hiring less prosperous neighbors to work in their fields. This practice increased during the sixteenth and seventeenth centuries, creating a majority population of agricultural laborers who might dig a fellow villager's soil as a hired worker or sharecropper. By the end of the seventeenth century, agricultural laborers might make up as much as 90 percent of a village's population. Relative opportunity and social differentiation thus went hand in hand in the early modern French village.

Rural agriculturalists in England in the 1500s enjoyed a degree of autonomy on the land they worked and security in their tenancy that would have been the envy of peasants east of the Elbe. With the population recovery from the Black Death, lords needed peasants as much as peasants needed access to the lords' land. Lords were constrained not only by demographic trends and their labor needs, but also by an emerging royal judicial system that entered into their relationships with the peasants on their manors. While lords were certainly the masters of their land and retained considerable powers to exact fines, fees, and rents, they found themselves granting forms of tenancy that enabled a peasant to contemplate long-term farming on a particular plot of land and not only the prospect of paying the lord his due, but also opportunities for going beyond subsistence and obligation through successful farming.

Short of outright ownership of the land in perpetuity, English peasants sought a form of tenancy termed copyhold in inheritance. A peasant who secured a copyhold in inheritance for the land he tilled paid an annual rent, but could pass the land to another peasant (not only a family member) who in turn had to pay an entry fine to the master in order to receive the copyhold. Both rents and entry fines varied according to the landlords' whims, injecting some insecurity in the relationship for the peasant and opportunities for revenue and exploitation for the lord. Manorial court records reveal both that lords' courts were mimicking new royal court procedures and that

The Landed
Estate

- ■ Core zone of the landed estate
- ■ Eastern periphery of the landed estate
- ■ Western and southern peripheries of the landed estate

The Landed Estate. Adapted from Werner Rösener, *The Peasantry of Europe,* translated by Thomas M. Barker (Oxford and Cambridge, Mass.: Blackwell, 1994), p. 104.

peasants were successfully disposing of their land to individuals of their choice, who received the preferred tenancy through copyhold in inheritance. Less preferable forms of tenancy were prevalent in the Midlands and the south of England, including copyhold for lives (not heritable) and beneficial leases, which gave lords considerably more power over the peasants and subjected the peasants to more insecurity in their relationship to the land and the master. All three forms of tenancy (copyhold in inheritance, copyhold for lives, and beneficial leases) determined what the peasants owed to the masters, but the peasants determined how they met the terms of tenancy.

Even in Spain, where poverty was the primary experience of the 80 percent of the population who were peasants, those working on the land were legally free. The economic condition of the Spanish peasantry in the sixteenth century and beyond closely resembles that of agriculturalists east of the Elbe, but the Spanish retained legal freedom of movement. As in France, town dwellers bought up land, forcing farmers who had held their land in tenancies for life to enter short-term tenancies, with all the insecurities and periodic reminders of their economic dependency that entailed. Everywhere, peasants paid taxes, rents, and dues to noble, church, and royal lords. In the northern mountains, peasants lived on small plots of land in miniature villages, paying their dues largely in kind, but increasingly in cash from the sixteenth cen-

tury forward. In Catalonia, situated on France's southern border and along the Mediterranean coast, peasants were able to secure long-term tenancies starting in the sixteenth century; some used these opportunities to expand their holdings until they themselves rented their land to other peasants. Further south, peasants were more likely to be day laborers on large manors, or latifundia, which dated to the reconquest of Spanish land from the Moors in the thirteenth century. There, fewer peasants could be called proprietors and most were either renters or hired hands. Over all of Spain, half of the peasants had to hire themselves out to their wealthier neighbors for at least part of the year, either because they had no land at all or too little to enable them to feed their families from one harvest to the next. Across Western Europe, as in Europe east of the Elbe river, those who tilled the soil did so not only for individual lords, but also for institutional lords such as religious institutions, the state as a major landowner, universities, and foundations. Further, peasants dependent on individual lords might find themselves transferred from labor on the land to labor in the lord's other enterprises, such as mining or agricultural processing.

Peasants born on the west bank of the river Elbe in the sixteenth century entered a trajectory leading some to individual proprietorship, freedom of movement, and expanding expectations for personal prosperity beyond subsistence. In the west, peasants had secured heritable land tenures and fixed rents by the sixteenth century. While they still had to pay the lords of the land their due, peasants could plan for a future because they knew they had the land they cultivated for as long as they wished, and they knew what their financial obligations would be. These certainties enabled a class of middle peasants to emerge and expand as they moved onto lands that had been abandoned during the Black Death. The family farm situated in a compact village became the peasants' foundation for moving beyond subsistence. They were fortunate in the fertile soil they farmed and the dynamism of towns and cities, which created both markets for any surplus they might want to sell and a class of burghers who kept the aspirations of the landed nobility in check.

These advantages enabled the agriculturalists in German states west of the Elbe to enjoy a steady recovery through the sixteenth century up to the Thirty Years' War (1618–1648). A generation of warfare depleted both population and resources, threatening the gains the west German peasants had made in the previous century, yet the foundation of those gains seems to have carried them through to both financial recovery and confirmation of the personal freedom and secure land tenures their forebears had acquired. With an eye to tax revenues, rulers in the west German states intervened on behalf of the middle and more prosperous peasants, protecting them from noble lords' efforts to render them more dependent and less mobile. As the eighteenth century approached, peasants along the Rhine, Weser, Main, and western reaches of the Danube owed regular taxes to their political rulers, but farmed and lived as community members relatively free of the heavy hand of their noble neighbors and landlords. The most prevalent forms of tenancy were ownership, for which the peasant still paid rent to a lord; and hereditary leasehold, so-called "steward tenancy" or *Meierhof* in the northwest. Much less prevalent were lifetime leasehold and tenancy at the will of the lord, who could recall it without warning. The latter faded from the German landscape as tenancy became hereditary in practice, even if not legally recorded as such. This is not to say that the peasants of west German principalities and duchies were free of domination. They were still captives in a web of obligations and hierarchies (*Herrschaft*) that provided channels for the intrusion of church, state, and nobles into the life of the village. But in the larger European framework, peasants in the west had a wider range of possibilities and actions than their fellows to the east.

Peasants born east of the Elbe in the sixteenth century entered a downward spiral toward the loss of mobility, increasing dependence, economic stagnation, and vulnerability to natural and man-made calamities. From Brandenburg to Moscow, through Poland, Hungary, Bohemia, and Romania, noble lords and ruling princes responded to the demographic crises of the fourteenth century and the political and military crises of the sixteenth and seventeenth centuries by joining forces to bind peasants to land and master, locking them into a series of dependencies and insecurities. Throughout these regions, noble lords were able to secure the legal restriction of the mobility of peasants living on their lands, which they had often acquired through the beneficence of the ruling prince or king. The result was large landed estates, populated and cultivated by plowmen and their families, whose former freedom to move from one estate and master to another was criminalized and subject to punishment.

The obligations of peasants in eastern Europe and Muscovy also became more restrictive, shifting from payments in money and kind to labor services. When east European peasants greeted the day, it was as likely that their activities were already defined and assigned to the lord's land and barns as it was likely that they could work for themselves according to their own priorities. Lords were not only taskmasters; they also acquired the roles of local judges, juries, tax col-

A Peasant Goes to Market. A farm wife bringing fowls to market (from MS. Eger 1222, fol. 73; 1598). BY PERMISSION OF THE BRITISH LIBRARY, LONDON

lectors, and often human barriers that peasants were forbidden to pass in order to appeal directly to the prince or king. Furthermore, as peasants were bound to lord and land, the lord viewed them as part of an estate's inventory, to be bought, sold, or traded as he saw fit. The estate was the lord's patrimony; peasants were patrimonial possessions; patrimonial lords became local petty autocrats over the people who labored beneath them. The reach of the laws that enforced these regimes was, of course, limited, and peasants continued to flee whenever they could in search of better conditions of life and labor. But the fact was that fleeing within the eastern half of Europe usually only led to another master with similar expectations and prerogatives.

COMMUNITY AND MENTALITIES, 1500–1750

Through the early modern period, all peasants and rural laborers in Europe, from Moscow to Glasgow, answered to another master or mistress beyond their earthly superiors in the shape of landlord, cleric, or state official: nature. Peasants cultivated the land in the traditions of their ancestors, using implements little changed over the previous centuries. The energy available to them came from the sun, the wind, food, water, and animals. Their ability to forecast the weather, to anticipate frost, flood, or drought, rested on folk wisdom and memory. Their understanding of diseases that struck human, plant, and animal populations offered little or nothing that would help them prevent or treat them. This subordination to weather, soil, water, and microorganisms joined their subordination to secular and religious masters to inform the bonds they created with each other and the belief systems they embraced and defended in the communities they inhabited and imagined.

Before the technological age, nature set the parameters of cultivation and production, determining which crops to grow, animals to raise, foods to eat, clothes to wear, housing to construct, and fuel to provide heat and light. Soils, temperatures, and precipitation created a different set of boundaries in Europe, cutting across the tenancy line at the river Elbe. Peasants in central Norway and northern Russia were equally likely to be planting barley; peasants in northern Germany, Poland, Lithuania, and Muscovy shared in the experience of cultivating rye and oats; while those around Dijon, Munich, Budapest, and Kiev were growing wheat. Until the middle of the eighteenth century, peasants largely ate what they grew, without imported tastes or ingredients from other regions. Before the advent of railroads, steamships, and an extensive network of weatherproof roads (still lacking in late-twentieth-century rural Russia), the costs of transporting foodstuffs and the risks of spoilage over long journeys inhibited an interregional market in grains or meat and dairy products, and the differentiation of diets, urban or rural.

Peasants in early modern Europe devised social and agricultural strategies to meet environmental demands, while their belief systems and identities reflected their interpretation and attempts to accommodate those demands without yielding to them completely. Scattered plots in open field farming provided a form of insurance for peasants who recognized that diversifying their crops and distributing their fields over relatively broad areas meant that total crop failure was unlikely in the event of some natural misfortune. From insect infestations and blight to local flooding, drought, or hailstorm, natural assaults on cultivated fields were less likely to wipe out one peasant's or even an entire community's subsistence when numerous plots were spread out, usually with strips of uncultivated land ("balks" in England) to act as the equivalent of a firebreak, protecting each field from the misfortunes of a neighbor's. Scattered plots also enabled peasants to plant multiple crops, as for example winter and spring wheat, sequentially, moving from one to the next while avoiding simultaneous tasks on all of them.

Family life reflected economic considerations. In the north and west of Europe, families were nuclear by the mid-sixteenth century, comprising husband, wife, children, and hired hands who worked together as a labor unit on the land they cultivated. On the southern periphery along the Mediterranean, through the Balkans and into Russia, the household comprised extended, multigenerational and multibranched families who likewise constituted a labor unit. In the west small farms and the relative autonomy peasants enjoyed in organizing their labor encouraged independent households of nuclear families, which took shape when young people had worked long enough to set up a separate home. Kin networks continued to be of primary importance in establishing personal identity, but the larger social and economic structure of western Europe made it possible for a nuclear family to farm on its own and hire hands if its labor needs exceeded familial capacity. In the east, where peasants had to render significant labor to their lords, nuclear families might often be short of the working hands they needed to meet external obligations and feed their families. In areas where poor soils joined significant labor obligations and premodern technologies, extensive farming encouraged extended families or the addition of hired hands to ensure household survival. The trend toward larger households quickened in the late seventeenth century as the grip of lords on bound peasants tightened.

Families were everywhere the primary community and source of identity. Through membership in a family or a household, the individual peasant had access to the land and its products and to shelter, and held a position in the next larger community—the village. Gender, age, marital status, blood ties, and relationship to the household head established a peasant's place in the world. In this framework the distinction between peasants and rural laborers emerged across Europe. Almost everywhere, peasants within families whose household head had established tenancy or serf's terms with the external lords were both more secure in fact and in status within village communities. Those whose families did not have an adequate combination of land, equipment, and labor to support themselves through farming had to hire themselves out to subsist. In Spain and Portugal, such rural laborers lost not only autonomy in their farming lives, but also access to common village pastures and other lands, which was reserved for peasants who could support themselves and their families on the land they cultivated. In southern Iberia, these laborers had reached 75 percent of the rural population by the eighteenth century, and for the entire region, 50 percent of the total.

In Germany west of the Elbe, the ranks of the village poor grew in the sixteenth century, prompting the development of local systems of poor relief and charity. So-called "cottagers" had only their houses

A Peasant Family. *Peasant Family,* painting (c. 1640) by Louis Le Nain (1593–1648). Musée du Louvre, Paris/Erich Lessing/Art Resource

and a small plot of land for a cottage garden. While not landless, they had to seek subsistence beyond their land, either through hiring themselves out as workers for other, more prosperous peasants, or through practicing some supplemental trade, such as pottery, smithing, carpentry, or cobbling. In the German states east of the Elbe, the numbers of the rural poor expanded after the Thirty Years War, with more and more villagers falling into the category of landless labourers or householders with inadequate land, who had to work for their fellow peasants as well as the lord to feed self and family. Everywhere in the German states and elsewhere in Europe, this was disproportionately women's fate when they were widowed with children. At this largely pre-industrial era, stratification in rural communities defined layers of prosperity by access to the land and the capacity for household subsistence. Within peasant society, prosperous peasants were thus in a position to assume the status of local "betters" vis à vis their more dependent peasant neighbors.

Stratification within village communities bred resentment and visions of a social reckoning among the poorer peasants and rural laborers, as well as fear and a consequent effort to impose social discipline among the more prosperous and powerful peasants. Historians have detected the tensions within village communities in "epidemics" of witchcraft, court re-cords of local conflicts, and testimonies before officials of Christian churches from those accused of heresy. Accusations of witchcraft fell most frequently on women, and sometimes men, who lived on the margins in rural communities. Women living outside the disciplined order of the patriarchal household fell under suspicion when disorder came to local communities in the form of human or animal epidemics, family disputes, or excessive sexual activity outside the bonds of marriage. Sometimes church officials joined with village leaders in the campaign to restrict the power of women, whose traditional practices in healing threatened both the monopoly of church doctrine and local social hierarchies. Similarly, church and local peasants could join together to bring a maverick in the community to heel if he or she failed to attend church services regularly or to take communion while there.

Rural laborers who challenged the local hierarchy or the larger social and political order sometimes offered tales of personal encounters with angels or supernatural beings who, they said, articulated alternative visions of a more just and equitable society. Within these oral traditions, captured for historians in the testimonies of those accused by their neighbors or local priests, marginal members of Europe's early modern villages left their record of disabilities and discomforts on the edge of their communities.

EMANCIPATION: FROM BONDSMEN AND BONDSWOMEN TO FREE CITIZENS: 1770–1861

In the late eighteenth century, princes, kings, emperors, and revolutionary leaders began to set the peasants of land free from obligations to their lords and bonds to their land. Emancipation came through a combination of influences, ranging from the ideals of individual liberty and property to revolutionary upheaval and warfare, which illuminated the hazards of maintaining an order perceived to be unjust, unproductive, and a brake on economic development. The decisions by the prince of Savoy in 1771 and Austria's Emperor Joseph II in the 1780s to abolish serfdom anticipated the watershed resolutions in revolutionary France between 1789 and 1793. When France's National Assembly and National Convention eliminated all noble prerogatives and peasant duties to their lords, then granted peasants the right to divide up the land they cultivated without any compensation to their former lords, they set in motion a total program of emancipation without compensation that was not matched or fully achieved elsewhere in Europe for more than a century. Individual liberty and rights in property became the hallmark of the French Revolution's gains for those peasants who held land; landless laborers and tenant farmers gained individual liberty in principle, but continued economic dependency on their wealthier neighbors. Even so, France set the standard for emancipation and exported it either on the bayonets of Napoleon's soldiers or by example to the rest of Europe.

Across the German states and into the Russian Empire, reforming bureaucrats placed peasant emancipation above noble prerogatives in the name of economic and military progress. For the Prussians, defeat at the hands of Napoleon's army led the Hohenzollern rulers to launch an incremental process of granting peasants personal liberty and freedom of movement in 1809, which expanded two years later to the granting of rights in land to peasants, who had to compensate their former masters and the land's former owners with a third or a half of the land they were cultivating. By 1838, the process of turning peasant renters into property owners and full citizens was largely complete in Prussia.

In Russia, military defeat in the Crimean War enabled reform-minded bureaucrats to implement Alexander II's decision to emancipate the Russian serfs who dominated the rural landscape in the empire's European provinces west of the Ural mountains. Through the Emancipation legislation of 1861 for proprietary serfs and subsequent decrees for state and crown peasants, tens of millions of Russian peasants gained their personal liberty from their masters and property in land, for which they were to pay compensation over the next four decades. They did not gain full liberty of movement, however, as legislation bound them to their communities absolutely for the next decade, and made departure from their communities thereafter contingent upon the granting of permission by the communal assembly of household heads. In principle, they gained equality before the law with other Russian subjects; in fact, the vast majority of their legal concerns remained within the jurisdiction of the caste-specific cantonal court, over which peasant judges presided and ruled according to customary law. The compromises evident in Russia's emancipation process illustrated on the largest scale in Europe the challenges emancipation had posed to rulers everywhere: how to grant individual liberty and property to the majority population of peasants while maintaining economic stability and social order.

Behind emancipation lay the rulers' and bureaucrats' goal of economic progress, now understood to be a prerequisite for membership in the European community of modern states and for military power to defend the interests of those states. The very concept of modern economic and military power was itself in transition during these years, shaped by the process of industrial revolution in Great Britain, which coincided with the political and social revolution in France, and vied with it for influencing both agrarian policies and the experience of Europe's peasants and rural laborers.

PEASANTS UNBOUND: ENCLOSURE, PROFIT, AND THE LOOSENING OF THE BOND TO THE LAND

Between 1800 and 1850, Europe shifted from a world in which roughly 80 percent of the population continued to live and labor in the countryside to one in which the push of agricultural reform and the pull of industrial development and urbanization was displacing, rearranging, and in some cases, destroying the parts making up the preindustrial village. Great Britain set the standard for the emergence of the modern European countryside. Social and economic processes played out there were repeated across the continent.

The push of agriculture. The new element was the prospect of steady agricultural surplus, which could bring both profit to landowners and a ready food supply to towns and cities. The consolidation and enclosure of scattered plots from open fields into

Nineteenth-Century French Peasants. *Paying the Harvesters* by Leon Lhermitte (1844–1925), 1882. Musee d'Orsay, Paris/Erich Lessing/Art Resource

hedged spaces has long been the hallmark of Great Britain's shift from early modern to modern agriculture and the rural social relations it engendered. Hailed initially by agricultural reformers of the Scottish enlightenment, including Adam Smith, "rationalizing" the open fields by gathering scattered plots together, fencing them in, then subjecting them to profit-oriented farming was understood to be the absolute prerequisite for economic progress. This agricultural transformation was mirrored by a social transformation in which peasants trapped in the narrow expectations of subsistence were replaced by farmers who managed their consolidated holdings with an eye to profit on the commercial market, incorporating profit-maximizing developments in crops, animal husbandry, fertilizers, and technologies.

In this mix of technological, economic, agricultural, and social transformation, the social group denoted by the label "peasants" was a de facto endangered species en route to extinction in Europe's development into a modern, industrial, market, consumer society revolving around cities and their activities. As early as 1896, the French observer Jean-Gabriel de Tarde referred to the peasant as a "fossilized creature." Rural laborers were those countrymen and women who provided the hired labor to the entrepreneurial agriculturalists termed farmers. Thus, the

peasantry ceased to be a social group or class bound by the traditional concepts, practices, and horizons of the early modern period. While the term and the phenomenon persisted into the second half of the twentieth century from France through Eastern Europe, both "vanished," to use Henri Mendras's expression, much earlier in Scotland and England. One may still visit the village of Laxton, a functioning open field village in Nottingham, to observe peasant practices in England, but one does so as a tourist or a historian peering into an archaic social and economic form.

The features of the transformation of subsistence farmers/peasants into farmers, rural laborers, or urban workers included dispossession, dislocation, and disintegration both social and moral for the peasants and rural laborers who were its victims, and conversely expansion of property, prosperity, and opportunity for those who became farmers and major landowners. As land was consolidated and fenced in, rents increased, labor decreased, agriculture became more intensively commercial, and animal husbandry grew. Enclosures were both voluntary and state enforced through acts of Parliament. In the sixteenth and seventeenth centuries village communities voted through unanimous decisions required under common law thus, voluntary enclosure could be frustrated by as few as one peasant unwilling to relinquish land in his use. In the eigh-

155

Steward and Tenant. *The Rapacious Steward, or Unfortunate Tenant,* engraving (c. 1803) by H. Gillbank after a painting by William Redmore Bigg (1755–1828). POLESDEN LACEY, SURREY, U.K./THE BRIDGEMAN ART LIBRARY

teenth century acts of Parliament, which required only majority consent, dominated the process. Enclosure by Parliamentary decree, therefore, is the more notorious in the literature for compelling unwilling smallholders to give up their land to the process, and for granting formal property rights to those who received consolidated plots.

Enclosure produced one of the great human dramas of social history. Marxist historians, interested in distributive justice, have focused on the inequities in property distribution enclosure produced. Furthermore, because enclosure commissions in individual communities were typically dominated by large local landowners, the process itself earned E. P. Thompson's sobriquet, "a plain enough case of class robbery." Among the most damaging aspects of enclosure was the loss of free access to common lands in pasture and woods, which deprived the rural poor of traditionally free fodder for their horse or cow and fuel for their fireplace or stove. Fences, hedgerows, and ditches constructed to demarcate consolidated fields kept out not only wandering animals, but also the women and children of the poor who had previously gleaned the harvested fields for whatever leavings they could find to add to their meager larders.

When smallholders received lands through the enclosure process, they also received the obligation to fence them in at their own expense, primarily to keep their animals contained, thus to prevent their trespass and damage on their neighbors' crops. This cash expense was disproportionately high by comparison with fencing expenses for the larger holdings; sometimes it alone was adequate to convince a smallholder to leave the land altogether. Rural laborers who had earlier been able to supplement their wages with access to common lands and perhaps to garden on a small strip of land assigned to their cottage now found themselves genuinely landless and reliant solely on the labor of their hands and backs. Enclosure, meant to consolidate land and increase production, thus had a broad effect of alienation for the rural poor in England, who were separated first from common lands, then, through the combination of high rents and fencing prices, from the land itself and the subsistence farming they had practiced.

This experience was especially bitter when they observed the benefits larger farmers gained, as enclosure did indeed increase profits for those with land sufficient to compensate for the costs of enclosures. There can be no doubt that this social and economic transformation subjected large numbers of the English population to harsh psychological, physical, and social trauma, which surfaced in such rural crimes as arson, maiming of farmers' animals, and theft of harvested crops. Beyond individual acts of protest and desperation, full-scale rural revolts broke out as the most striking demonstrations of the human costs of enclosure and the agricultural revolution it represented. The preponderance of rural laborers among those accused and convicted of crimes against the property of the beneficiaries of the agricultural revolution pointed to their frequent inability to maintain subsistence for themselves and their families in the new order, as well as to their profound sense of alienation from the communities that developed around profit-oriented, prosperous farms.

Like the witchcraft epidemics of the early modern era, the epidemiology of rural crimes in the nineteenth century pointed to stratification in rural communities. As the village population segregated into farmers, rural laborers, and those who departed to become urban workers, the farmers and rural laborers remained on their former lands on transformed terms. Land and labor were now commodities. Farmers possessed the land and commanded labor on terms designed to generate profit in the larger market, while rural laborers became atomized individual labor units, alienated from both the land and the products of their labor. Laborers protested their reduced status and means by seizing goods they needed for subsistence, or by destroying those same goods through maiming livestock and torching hayricks when farmers denied them access to these sources of their income in commercial farming.

And yet, England did not suffer in macroeconomic terms from this process. On the contrary, enclosure coincided largely with the great leap forward in England's economic history, when the industrial revolution created opportunities for employment and mobility to compensate for the lost insurance of open field, community-based farming. When they found themselves outside the figurative and literal fences of England's agricultural revolution, the displaced agriculturalists had new occupations to explore, new residential centers to inhabit, and new forms of transportation to use to get there. Whereas the undeniably traumatic character of enclosure in those areas where it was imposed from above constituted the "push" of this great transformation, external markets, urban employment, and accelerated economic processes constituted the "pull."

The pull of industry. The bond to the land was broken not only by forced enclosure and state decrees, as in England, but also by the attractions and opportunities offered by Europe's shift from the rural and agricultural to the urban and industrial. Peasants not only "lost" the rural way of life they had known for

centuries because their way of life was undermined by state decrees and commercial farming; they also discarded it in search of opportunities beyond the constraints of climate, land, family, and local community.

From Laxton in England to Erdobenye in Hungary to Soligalich in European Russia, this push and pull generated greater mobility for peasants and rural laborers. Social structures, work routines, and geographic boundaries gave way, yielding hybrid labor experiences and social identities throughout the eighteenth and nineteenth centuries. Those who continued to farm incorporated new crops, production and processing techniques, and fertilizers, and often combined their agricultural labor with seasonal work for emerging markets and the industrial sector. Those who shifted to commercial farming in England and elsewhere also invested in new technologies to speed up agricultural labor, simultaneously threatening the manual skills of the rural laborers and setting new time standards for the performance of daily tasks. Timepieces, such as clocks and pocket watches, became markers of the farmers' higher status and new expectations, as intensely resented by their laborers as the farm equipment in their more prosperous neighbors' barns. Enterprising farmers turned to cash crops for the market, abandoning traditional crops and crop rotation, disrupting seasonal cycles and altering familiar landscapes. The technologies of western Europe made their way through eastern Europe all the way to Russia, where British steel plows competed on the local market with Swedish steel plows for the purchasing power of Russia's most innovative farmers.

Eighteenth-century Flanders provides a particularly vivid example of the combination of agricultural and nonagricultural pursuits by peasants and rural laborers, as well as of the social stratification that accompanied that combination. Flemish peasants planted flax, then transformed it into cloth over the winter months. Flax farming and linen production through home-based spinning and weaving enabled peasants to supplement their agricultural income when population increase and the fragmentation of landholdings threatened subsistence. Family-based linen production for town merchants fed an international textile market, primarily in the American colonies, where Flemish cloth held coffee beans, covered the backs of slaves, and decorated windows in colonial homes. Labor came from every able family member, but rural laborers also hired themselves out to families who had the looms they could not afford on their own. For both the hired hands and the family weavers, the income their participation in the international linen market brought was quite low. For many it staved off indigence, however, while providing a safety valve of sorts in the period between the shift to commercial farming and the full-blown development of industry.

Once industry entered the equation in full force, such tenuous adaptations to demographic and macroeconomic developments faded before the more stunning prospects and pressures of industrialization and urbanization. Before the industrial revolution, peasants combined farming and nonagricultural home-based occupations, such as weaving, smithing, lace making, pottery, or tanning, producing goods to trade in their local or neighboring communities largely as a seasonal supplement to subsistence farming. Once steamboats and trains opened up broader transportation opportunities, towns became centers of industry and commerce, and markets expanded in town for labor and in the countryside for urban products. Non-rural locations and occupations exerted a magnetic pull so forceful that it dislodged many elements in the rural structure, breaking up old patterns and drawing people away from the land. The emigrants included gentry landowners, who sold their land to garner capital to invest in the commercial, industrial economy. Peasants thus gained opportunities to become small-holders themselves. People, products, and information began to move back and forth between town and country.

This process displayed great regional variation, of course, in its tempo, with England and the Low Countries moving most rapidly away from agricultural dominance toward industrial, capital economies. In France in the nineteenth century, tenant farmers leased their lands from wealthy urbanites who invested the capital they had gained in banking and industry in land in the countryside. These former peasants were able to accumulate extensive landholdings of their own and become powerful local employers who hired neighboring peasants. In some regions, peasants rose above their neighbors not through tenant farming, but through their own labor, prudent saving and control over expenses, and family planning. The French village also included peasants who were able to support themselves and their families on their own lands, neither expanding their lands with an eye to profits nor falling behind or risking the loss of any of their holdings. Still other peasants held onto their family land only by supplementing their income with periodic labor through jobs in town or local factories. Sharecroppers and migrant rural laborers in France constituted the lower elements in village stratification. They typically had no land of their own and lived lives of forced subservience as long as they remained in the countryside. In 1892, there were 2.5 million rural laborers in France, who were the group most likely to contribute to the 650,000 rural inhab-

itants who left for the cities and towns between 1896 and 1901. France and Germany were slower to embrace technological changes (from the use of mineral fertilizers to the purchase of farming equipment), and Russia lay at the geographic and chronological extreme of the spectrum. But even in imperial Russia, so late to embrace industrial development and so constrained by officials fearful of a landless rural proletariat whom they associated with Europe's revolutions, the emergence of industrial centers and a consumer economy by the 1890s wrought upon the countryside the same changes experienced as much as a century earlier on the other end of the European continent.

Four "types" among the peasantry in European Russia in the late nineteenth century illustrate the experience, however belated, of the European peasantry and rural laborers in the transition from agricultural to industrial societies: the peasant proprietor, the migrant agricultural laborer, the peasant-worker male, and the peasant woman who departed for the city or factory town. Peasant proprietors were those who bought land from the departing gentry, who had given up farming when they no longer had access to free labor as they had before the emancipation of their serfs. Peasant proprietors' numbers expanded after 1883, when the state established the Peasant Land Bank, with loans available at affordable rates to the enterprising agriculturalist. These peasants invested not only in land, but also in recently introduced mineral fertilizers and steel plows imported from Sweden and England. They hired their less fortunate or less enterprising fellow peasants, purchased cloth and factory-made clothes in town or from itinerant traders, replaced their thatched roofs with tile or tin, drank tea from samovars, and illuminated their homes with kerosene lamps. They might well be literate, and thus able to read both popular chapbooks and the state's newspaper targeting the aspiring peasant farmer with news of agrarian methods and reforms. They might also join a peasant cooperative, thus entering an institutional arrangement signifying their larger involvement with the market and state beyond their village's boundaries. In sum, their economic and social existence reflected a series of choices and decisions about how to shape their agricultural existence, which was no longer the product of their involuntary bondage to the land, but of their preferences and dreams.

Migrant peasant laborers might well be property owners, too, who farmed the land they had received as part of the emancipation settlement, but who needed to seek income elsewhere to supplement subsistence farming, in order to pay off their various tax obligations or to purchase items for their households. Some traveled far to the south of the empire to large labor markets where wealthy landowners sent their stewards to hire enough hands to bring in their commercial crops. They traveled by train and by riverboat, as well as by cart or wagon, often covering remarkable distances in their search for cash income. The existence of an export market in grain was critical to their employment, however, so they too were involved in the larger market economy, despite the fact that they continued to labor on the land. Once in the hiring markets, they met their counterparts from all over the European provinces of the Russian Empire, whom they recognized as fellow laborers, but not as members of one community.

Peasant-workers were those who left their villages seasonally to work in cities and towns. Often they traveled in village groups as a labor cooperative, hiring themselves out annually to the same employer, living together in factory barracks or city apartments in social groupings that resembled village structures. Like the migrant laborers, they sought cash income, some of which they sent home to family members still in the village and some of which they used to purchase city clothes and goods, which would make them desirable in the eyes of peasant girls when they returned to the village. They, too, traveled by riverboat, railroad, or wagon, part of the Europe-wide movement of peasants into cities, human agents of the transition from the agricultural to the industrial society. The railroads they traveled were themselves funded in no small part through loans from major French banks, who had invested the savings of French peasants in the great Russian construction projects.

The magnet of the city also attracted peasant women, many of whom followed the men of their village and assumed traditional roles as housekeepers and cooks for their transposed community. Others entered domestic service for urban families or became factory workers, usually in the textile industry, moving into factory housing or communal apartments. Like their male covillagers and relatives, many of these peasant women followed a circular pattern of migration, moving back and forth between village and town. Along the way, they gained not only cash, but also new tastes in clothing and entertainment, a sense of mobility as they rode the imperial rails, and a sure knowledge of alternatives to the traditional tasks of the peasant woman. By 1900 in the central industrial region of Russia, which comprised seven provinces, roughly one-fifth of the peasant population requested and received the internal passports they needed to migrate for labor. Somewhat more than half the peasants who immigrated to Moscow and St. Petersburg for labor were women. Thus, at the far eastern reaches of Europe, the processes of transition away from the in-

voluntary bondage to the land that had marked the peasant experience 150 years earlier across the continent had accelerated even in Russia, and had come to include women as well as men. By the end of the nineteenth century, former peasants in some countries were beginning to depart from their insular worldview by participating in collective organizations, movements, and, to a smaller extent, political parties. Collective organizations included cooperatives for the purchase and use of farming equipment, mutual insurance programs, volunteer firefighting brigades, and some farmers' trade unions. There were also parties founded by members of the intelligentsia who became advocates for the peasants and encouraged their political engagement. In Russia, peasant-focused politics had already gone through several party formations by 1900, from the Populists of the 1870s through the People's Will and Black Repartition of the 1880s to the Socialist Revolutionaries of the turn of the century. In Bulgaria the Agrarian Union, formed in late 1899, was on the verge of being the dominant political force in the country. These embryonic forms of economic and political organization would expand in the twentieth century. Full-blown, they would signify both the end of the autarkic peasant mentality and the need for agriculturalists to fight for the preservation and subsidization of their way of life in an industrial age.

PEASANTS IN THE TWENTIETH CENTURY

Most peasants in Europe at the beginning of the twentieth century had a dim concept of the state or of their identity as citizens of a national political culture. The expansion of their mental horizons had occurred largely in the last decades of the nineteenth century through instruction in churches and schools, military training, and the reading of newspapers and the popular press. The very creation of the nation state was recent for citizens of Italy, Germany, and Serbia, and peasants in central and eastern Europe had every reason to be skeptical about any lasting territorial polity. Even in France, with its long tradition of consciously constructed nationalism, peasants often entered the army uncertain about the identity of their enemies or the political order they were to defend. Yet the state has been the critical player in determining the fate of the European peasantry in the twentieth century. The state most brutally invaded the lives of rural people through the failed politics embodied in two world wars fought across the farmlands of France, Belgium, Germany, Italy, Poland, Hungary, Yugoslavia, and the

Hungarian Collective Farm. Collective-farm workers return from the fields, Hungary, 1956.
ERICH LESSING/ART RESOURCE

Soviet Union. The Russian and Spanish civil wars brought similar visitations of destruction upon the Russian and Spanish peasants. The trench warfare of World War I left mines and shells deep in the fields, still to be located and defused a hundred years later by state-employed *demineurs,* or worse, to detonate under the tractors of French farmers who unwittingly come upon them during spring planting. Invading German troops and tanks in World War II laid waste to the farmlands of Belorussia and Ukraine, when soldiers paused long enough to burn hundreds of villages to the ground. These wars also forced peasant men into the service of the state through conscription. From a vague notion associated with a distant capital city or a local tax collector at the beginning of the twentieth century, the state became an unavoidable entity and element in the rural consciousness.

The state became alternately the agent of forced transformation or the object of political activism. Most dramatically in the Soviet Union in the late 1920s and 1930s and in the states the Soviet Union dominated after World War II, the state determined the nature of agriculture and the socioeconomic position of the people who practiced it on consolidated collective farms, forcing a twentieth-century version of enclosure and binding the peasants to the land again through a system of internal passports, and eliciting popular resistance that repeated the traumas of a century earlier in England. Collectivization in the east also reproduced the divisions between the tightly bound and the relatively free along a line running through Germany that followed the boundaries of the early modern era. To the west of that line, states have stepped in to protect those who farm through state subsidies, tariff systems, and social welfare programs, which make it possible for the individual farmer to prosper in an industrial age. On the eve of World War II, a distinct minority of the population was engaged in agriculture in western Europe, as the percentages for the following countries indicate: France, 32.5 percent; Germany, 29 percent; Belgium, 17 percent; Britain, 5.7 percent. The pull of industry and the power of market economies ensured that peasants would indeed "vanish" in the twentieth century. Everywhere in the West, those who worked the land did so as part of national and international economies, with their work experiences and financial lives as likely to be shaped by regional associations, the International Labor Organization, national ministries and departments of agriculture, import and export regulations, international trade treaties, and state subsidized grain and dairy prices as by their individual or family ties to the land. From the crops they plant to the goods they buy and sell in the marketplace, contemporary agriculturalists must reckon with national and international policies and economic trends far beyond the reach of household, village, or region.

Enclosure on a massive scale, dubbed agrobusiness, made even those independent small farmers attuned to the market seem irrational vestiges of an earlier age. To defend the farming way of life, agriculturalists of the twentieth century formed numerous associations, such as those in France: the Cooperative for the Collective Ownership of Farm Equipment, Societies for Land Management, Associated Farm Interests, Movement for the Organization and Protection of Family Farms, Farmers' Organization for Communal Land Use, and others. French farmers were the most notorious for taking collective action to defend their way of life against international competition and policymaking, with their tractors processing through Paris and their assaults on trucks importing cheap produce from Spain being emblematic of their effort to command the attention of the state to protect their interests. In Hungary, independent farmers participated in post-communist politics with the goal of prohibiting the sale of Hungarian farmland to international interests. From tractors to the ballot box, farming people seized modern technologies and systems to keep rural interests in play, to maintain some power in a world defined by cities and industries.

Farming people of the second half of the twentieth century thus abandoned by necessity or choice much of what sociologists, anthropologists, and historians have described as the "peasant way of life": insularity; dependency on or forced subservience to powerful lords; distance from the dominant systems and values of the larger society beyond the village; primary bond to the land and localities; a cyclical view of time; an aversion to innovation and profit; and profound conservatism in economic, social, and po-

litical decisions. And, yet, the word "peasant" has not disappeared from the vocabulary of European cultures or from the mental landscapes of their citizens. Peasants continue to be viewed as the somehow still essential figures in national distinction. *Paysans* still sell their grapes, garlic, cheese, and lavendar sachets in the market at Ferney Voltaire, where the city folk from Geneva crowd on Saturday mornings to touch base with the fundament of old French culture. In Budapest, a few genuine people of the countryside sell their honey and flowers at the Vasarcsarnok, the central market otherwise dominated by traders. In Moscow, *muzhiki* still pass through the major train stations, with heavy packs on their backs filled with farm produce in the morning when they arrive and city goods in the evening when they head home.

While cityfolk may disdain such "peasants" for their rough ways, urbanites still fill the trains and highways as they make their own pilgrimages back to the countryside, where many of them till small garden plots, gather mushrooms and berries, and thereby connect with the land of their ancestors' primary experiences. When asked in the year 2000 if Russian people would still rush to their summer cottages at the first moment spring planting becomes possible, even after a fully modernized system of agricultural production and distribution is in place in all cities and towns, two young law professors in their twenties laughed and said, "Of course, we will! We go to plant not just to produce food for our pantry. We go because of our connection with the soil. It restores us

***Muzhiki* Selling Produce.** Street market in Krasnodar, Russia, 1990. SOVFOTO/EASTFOTO

and makes us whole after a winter in apartments, buses, subways, and cars in the city." At the opposite end of Europe, in England, urban people display the same impulses and attachment to the earth in their gardening and lobbying for continued free access to walking paths across farming properties in the countryside. Everywhere in Europe, "peasants" are entrepreneurial farmers or hired laborers whose insular world has given way to the industrialized market. But the peasant past continues to hold emotional meaning and definition for an urbanized society which maintains its tenuous bond with the land. States have also everywhere provided the infrastructures of communication and rapid transportation that make the rapid movement of agricultural goods to market and of industrial goods to the countryside possible.

See also **Land Tenure; Peasant and Farming Villages; Serfdom: Eastern Europe; Serfdom: Western Europe** *(volume 2); and other articles in this section.*

BIBLIOGRAPHY

Archer, John E. *By a Flash and a Scare: Incendiarism, Animal Maiming, and Poaching in East Anglia, 1815–1870.* Oxford, 1990.

Avrich, Paul. *Russian Rebels 1600–1800.* New York, 1976.

Brooks, Jeffrey. *When Russia Learned to Read: Literacy and Popular Literature, 1861–1917.* Princeton, N.J., 1985.

Burds, Jeffrey. *Peasant Dreams and Market Politics: Labor Migration and the Russian Village, 1861–1905.* Pittsburgh, Pa., 1998.

Braudel, Fernand. *Capitalism and Material Life, 1400–1800.* Translated by Miriam Kochan. New York, 1973.

Brettell, Caroline. *Men Who Migrate, Women Who Wait: Population and History in a Portuguese Parish.* Princeton, N.J., 1986.

Clarke, Colin, and John Langton, eds. *Peasantry and Progress: Rural Culture and the Modern World.* Oxford, 1990.

Darnton, Robert. *The Great Cat Massacre and Other Episodes in French Cultural History.* New York, 1984.

Davis, Natalie Zemon. *Society and Culture in Early Modern France.* Stanford, Calif., 1975.

Engel, Barbara Alpern. *Between the Fields and the City: Women, Work, and Family in Russia, 861–1914.* Cambridge, U.K., 1994.

Fitzpatrick, Sheila. *Stalin's Peasants: Resistance and Survival in the Russian Village after Collectivization.* New York, 1994.

Frank, Stephen, and Mark Steinberg, eds. *Popular Culture in Late Nineteenth-Century Russia.* Princeton, N.J., 1987.

Ginzburg, Carlo. *The Cheese and the Worms: The Cosmos of a Sixteenth-Century Miller.* Translated by John and Anne Tedeschi. Baltimore, 1980.

Ginzburg, Carlo. *The Night Battles: Witchcraft and Agrarian Cults in the Sixteenth and Seventeenth Centuries.* Translated by John and Anne Tedeschi. Baltimore, 1992.

Hammond, J. L., and Barbara Hammond. *The Village Labourer 1760–1832: A Study in the Government of England before the Reform Bill.* London, 1913. Reprint, New York, 1967.

Hobsbawm, E. J., ed. *Peasants in History: Essays in Honour of Daniel Thorner.* Calcutta, 1980.

Hobsbawm, E. J., and George Rudé. *Captain Swing.* Harmondsworth, U.K., 1973.

Hoch, Steven. *Serfdom and Social Control in Russia: Petrovskoe, a Village in Tambov.* Chicago, 1986.

Holmes, Douglas, and Jean Quataert. "An Approach to Modern Labor: Worker Peasantries in Historical Saxony and the Friuli Region over Three Centuries." *Comparative Studies in Society and History* (April 1986): 191–217.

Johnson, Robert. *Peasant and Proletarian: The Working Class of Moscow in the Late Nineteenth Century.* New Brunswick, N.J., 1979.

Jones, Eric L. *Agriculture and Economic Growth in England, 1650–1815.* London and New York, 1967.

Kingston-Mann, Esther, and Timothy Mixter, eds. *Peasant Economy, Culture, and Politics of European Russia, 1800–1921.* Princeton, N.J., 1991.

Lehning, James R. *Peasant and French: Cultural Contact in Rural France during the Nineteenth Century.* Cambridge, U.K., 1995.

Le Roy Ladurie, Emmanuel. *The French Peasantry, 1450–1660.* Translated by Alan Sheridan. Berkeley, Calif., 1987.

Melton, Edgar. "Proto-Industrialization, Serf Agriculture, and Agrarian Social Structure: Two Estates in Nineteenth-Century Russia." *Past and Present* 115 (May 1987): 69–106.

Mendras, Henri. *The Vanishing Peasant: Innovation and Change in French Agriculture.* Translated by Jean Lerner. Cambridge, Mass., 1970.

Parker, William N., and Eric L. Jones, eds. *European Peasants and Their Markets: Essays in Agrarian Economic History.* Princeton, N.J., 1975.

Potter, Jack M., May N. Diaz, and George M. Foster, eds. *Peasant Society: A Reader.* Boston, 1967.

Rosener, Werner. *The Peasantry of Europe.* Translated by Thomas M. Barker. Oxford and Cambridge, Mass., 1994.

Sabean, David Warren. *Power in the Blood: Popular Culture and Village Discourse in Early Modern Germany.* New York, 1984.

Schulte, Regina. *The Village in Court: Arson, Infanticide, and Poaching in the Court Records of Upper Bavaria, 1848–1910.* Translated by Barrie Selman. Cambridge, U.K., 1994.

Scott, James C. *Seeing Like a State: How Certain Schemes to Improve the Human Condition Have Failed.* New Haven, Conn., 1998.

Scott, Tom, ed. *The Peasantries of Europe: From the Fourteenth to the Eighteenth Centuries.* London and New York, 1998.

Segalen, Martine. *Love and Power in the Peasant Family: Rural France in the Nineteenth Century.* Chicago, 1983.

Shanin, Teodor. *The Awkward Class: Political Sociology of Peasantry in a Developing Society: Russia 1910–1925.* Oxford, 1972.

Shanin, Teodor. *Peasants and Peasant Societies: Selected Readings.* Harmondsworth, U.K., 1971.

Simoni, Peter. "Agricultural Change and Landlord-Tenant Relations in Nineteenth Century France: The Canton of Apt (Vaucluse)." *Journal of Social History* 13, no. 1 (Fall 1979): 115–135.

Stichter, Sharon. *Migrant Laborers.* Cambridge, U.K., 1985.

Weber, Eugen. *Peasants into Frenchmen: The Modernization of Rural France, 1870–1914.* Stanford, Calif., 1976.

Worobec, Christine. *Peasant Russia: Family and Community in the Post-Emancipation Period.* Princeton, N.J., 1991.

Wylie, Laurence William. *Village in the Vaucluse.* Cambridge, Mass., 1974.

SLAVES

Richard Hellie

The slave is typically, with some exceptions, at the bottom of society. This was true in Renaissance and later Europe from the Urals to the Atlantic as well as in nearly all other times and places. Other constants also apply to nearly all slaves throughout history. For one, the slave is nearly always an outsider, someone whose race, religion, or nationality is different from that of the slaveowner. The slave typically is socially dead, excluded from participating in society, whether through voting, office holding, access to the slave-owning society's burial rituals, or simply joining in festive activities. All slaves are legally owned by someone or a corporate organization, and the powers of the state are available to slaveowners to enforce their claims to their chattel. These state powers range from registration of chattel to providing court services for the resolution of disputes over whether a person really is a slave or over which owner has the right to possess the chattel. In the eyes of the law, the slave is universally an object, never a subject.

World history knows basically two types of slaves: household (domestic) slaves and slaves owned because they produce value in agriculture, mining, industrial, or other production for their owners. Production slaves are relatively rare in world history, confined to classical Greece and Rome and in the New World after 1500. Europe after 1250 knew almost nothing but household slavery until the Nazis enslaved "subhumans" to man their factories and the Soviets enslaved "political undesirables" as well as common criminals in the Gulag, the vast penal system of labor camps. Probably even including these two episodes, slavery was never central for European economic development.

Because slavery in Europe is partly a political phenomenon defined by states in their laws as well as a nationality phenomenon in deciding who is an "insider" and who an "outsider," slavery can be discussed in terms of the major political entity in which the slaves lived, the country or nation in which they were enslaved, and under whose laws they were held in bondage. The discussion is best conducted from east

to west, from Russia to England and Ireland—that is, from countries with more extensive and enduring slavery practices to places with less extensive slavery that was abolished much earlier. Thus this essay begins with Russia, then moves to the Slavic countries and the Ottoman Empire; Italy, Iberia, and France; and northern Europe; and ends with England, Scotland, and Ireland. It does not deal with Europe's role in the slave trade of non-Europeans or in the abolition movement involving non-Europeans.

RUSSIA

From earliest known times in the areas that are now Russia and Ukraine, slaves were relatively common. Russia and Ukraine had the most developed system of slavery in all of Europe; its impact there was the most prolonged in all of Europe, with the twentieth-century Soviet system of slavery lasting longer than any other country's. After 1132, whatever political unity in Rus' had existed in the previous quarter millennium evaporated as smaller and smaller principalities were created that warred with one another. Slave raiding became one of the major objects of warfare, and some of those war slaves were housed in barracks and forced to farm in an attempt to give value to land that otherwise had none for the social elite, other than as a source of taxes on the agricultural population. This situation was only made worse by the Mongol conquest of 1237–1240, for the Mongols enslaved at least 10 percent of the East Slavic population. This initiated the process of making Slavdom into one of the world's two great slave reservoirs, the other being Africa. Indeed, in many European languages the word "slave" comes from the word "Slav." The Mongols and their heirs the Crimean Tatars "harvested" Slavs (Russians, Ukrainians, and Poles) and sold them throughout Eurasia, the Middle East, and North Africa, where buyers inspected them along with black Africans.

After Moscow put an end to the anarchy on the East European Plain by creating Muscovy, a unified

Great Russian State, in the late thirteenth century, slavery, perhaps unexpectedly, continued to play a major role. A perceived labor shortage was a major feature of most of Russian history, with the years 1870–1917 being perhaps the sole exception. In such an environment the demand for slaves and slavelike chattel was intense. In the mid-sixteenth century a central bureau, the Slavery Chancellery, was created to record slaves, slave transactions, and disputes over slaves. Muscovy was the sole country in the world ever to have a single, centralized office for the recording of slaves. At least eight kinds of slavery existed there: for debt (which was worked off by females at the rate of 2.5 rubles and by males at the rate of 5.0 rubles per year); for indenture (a young person, typically male, agreed to work for an owner for a number of years in exchange for training and some cash upon manumission, or release); pawnship (a special category of urban slaves); special military captives (who had been seized as military booty by Muscovite soldiers but might have to be released upon the signing of a peace treaty); hereditary slaves (the offspring of slaves, who could never look forward to manumission regardless of how many generations they had been enthralled); reported slaves (elite slaves who managed estates); military slaves (men who sold themselves to cavalrymen to accompany and to assist their owners in warfare—their price was considerably higher than that of other slaves); and limited service contract slaves.

About half the slaves in Muscovy were limited service contract slaves, who violated the social scientific norm that slaves were supposed to be outsiders. Prior to the 1590s, in a limited contract, slaves signed a contract to work for someone for a year in lieu of paying interest on a loan (a form of antichresis); upon default, they became full slaves whose offspring would become hereditary slaves. After the 1590s they could not repay the loans—which they almost never did—and were freed upon the death of their owners. For the slaves, this was a form of welfare in which the slaveowners agreed to feed and clothe their chattel. All of these types of slaves were registered in the books of the Slavery Chancellery, and they were all treated alike, for example, in case of flight or ownership disputes. Except for limited service contract slaves after the 1590s, manumission was rare for Russian slaves. The numbers of slaves cannot be calculated with any precision, but they may have composed 10 percent of the population, certainly a much higher percentage than anywhere else in Europe after 1300.

In Europe after 1300 slave rebellions occurred solely in Russia. Khlopko was a slave who led others on the southern frontier in an uprising against the government in 1603. Bolotnikov, the leader of the vast uprising of 1606 under his banner, was a runaway military slave (many of the rebels were not slaves). After these experiences the government diminished the role of elite slaves in the army, thus depriving them of combat training. After Bolotnikov no slave led a rebellion in Russia, although fugitive slaves are known to have participated in the Us and Razin uprisings of 1667–1671. They also participated in the 1682 uprising in Moscow led by musketeers against Sophia, Ivan, and Peter, the sibling trio of rulers, during which they made sure to burn the records of the Slavery Chancellery. There were probably no such episodes elsewhere in Europe because of the low concentrations of slaves in Christian Modern Europe.

Slavery served as the model for serfdom in Muscovy, even more so than was the case in the territories of the decaying Roman Empire. The major difference was that the serf was still the subject of the law and owned things that his owner legally could not claim. He also had to pay taxes, whereas the slave, as chattel, generally did not. Serfdom was consolidated by the Law Code (*Ulozhenie*) of 1649, after which peasants began to sell themselves as slaves with increasing frequency so as to avoid paying taxes. After a census was taken in which the government discovered what was happening, all farming slaves in 1679 were converted back into serfs. Being a household slave offered one other tax dodge. Serfs, peasants, and others began to convert themselves into household slaves, whereupon the government in the early 1720s converted all household slaves into household serfs and, with the new soul tax (a head tax on every male), put them all on the tax rolls. This essentially abolished slavery in Russia, although its impact lived on in the institution of serfdom, which after the middle of the eighteenth century was increasingly slavelike in that the serf owners could dispose of serfs as though they were slaves: move them around, sell them without land, force them to work demesne lands, and control them as though they were their personal chattel. The Nazimov Rescript of 1857 proclaimed the intention to free the serfs from their owners' control, but they were to remain bound to the land until they had paid for it (over a period of forty-nine years). The slavelike element of serfdom—personal dependency on a serf owner—was abolished in 1861, but the serfs were not fully freed until 1906, when, with the cancellation of the redemption payments, they were allowed to move wherever they wanted and became almost full citizens.

By many definitions the extensive Russian use of penal servitude was another form of slavery. Exile for criminals was introduced in the seventeenth century with the twin purposes of "cleaning up" the central areas and populating the frontiers, especially

Soviet Forced-Labor Camp. Deported peasants and political prisoners building the Stalin–White Sea Canal, c. 1933. DAVID KING COLLECTION

the southern frontier south of the Oka and the Siberian frontier east of the Urals. Classic exile demanded that a felon, who was either a common criminal or, increasingly, a political dissident resettle involuntarily from a desired locale to an undesirable locale. After 1700 this typically meant sending someone out of Europe into Asia. Over a million were so relocated between 1649 and 1917. A slavery element entered into the equation when the felon was forced to work. Gold mining was a frequent occupation chosen for the forced-laborer exiles in Siberia and the Russian far east.

The Russian heritage of slavery was revitalized in an example of path dependency in the Soviet period. The peasants were again bound to the land in 1930 as part of the collectivization of agriculture (sometimes called "the second enserfment," in which they were not issued passports, with the result that they could not move from their collective farms) and in the Gulag system of forced labor. The NKVD (secret police) got into the business of operating huge slave labor camps as part of the intensified industrialization drive of the Five Year Plans. Soviet central planners in Moscow relied on the slave miners in Vorkuta, for example, for 40 percent of Leningrad's coal. Again, this system was unusual from a world perspective, for most of these "slaves" were not outsiders but native Soviet citizens who were made artificially into "outsiders" by the heaping on of derogatory apposi-

tions: enemy of the people, exploiter, wrecker, traitor, scum, insect. (They were supplemented by genuine "outsiders," Poles and people from the Baltic states, as the Soviet Union expanded in 1940 and the NKVD arrested and sent to the Soviet forced labor camps anyone who was considered capable of opposition. They were followed by Germans POWs during World War II.) The Gulag slaves were freed only upon closure of the concentration camps after the death of Stalin in 1953. Most were freed by 1957, and allegedly there were few slave laborers in the Gulag when the Soviet Union collapsed in 1991. The exact total number of Gulag slaves is unknown, but numbers up to twenty million are mentioned in the literature. The Gulag was known for high death rates until Stalin's death, which made the Soviet institution look much like the Nazi dual-purpose camps—extraction of labor until the victim was exterminated.

SLAVIC COUNTRIES AND THE OTTOMAN EMPIRE

Other Slavic countries in Central Europe also had slaves. Poland had privately owned slaves in the Middle Ages, peaking in the twelfth and thirteenth centuries, but they blended into serfs as the "second serfdom" expanded in the late Middle Ages. Slaves originated primarily from capture in war but also from punishment for criminal activity, indebtedness, and self-sale. Polish slaves were freed by owner manumission, by the slave's working his way to freedom, or as a punishment of the master (who was deprived of his property). A slave turned out by his owner during a famine automatically gained his freedom. Slavery was abolished in Lithuania by the Lithuanian Statute of 1588.

The Balkans (Byzantium, which fell to the Ottoman Empire in 1453, Albania, Bosnia, Bulgaria, Croatia, Greece, Macedonia, and Serbia) present insuperable problems for a short essay. About 40 percent of Byzantium, the Eastern Roman Empire, lay in Europe; it was Orthodox Christian and used Roman law. Slavery in Byzantium yielded to serfdom and essentially died out in the Middle Ages, after 1100. On the other hand, the Ottoman Empire's faith was Islam, and slavery was revived there by the Turks. The Ottoman Turks by 1500 conquered most of the rest of the Balkans and imposed the slave norms of the Qur'an and the Shari'a (the fundamental code of Islamic law) where they could. The result was a revitalized system of household slavery as well as military slavery in the form of the infantry janissaries and galley slavery in the Mediterranean. In addition to the janissaries, there were elite slaves—as many as 100,000 in 1609—who belonged to the sultan and worked in the palace. State slaves were also used in large construction projects such as marketplaces, schools and mosques, and hospitals. Household slaves fulfilled their traditional roles—domestic service, cleaning, cooking, running errands, standing guard, tending children, and so forth. Islam permitted slave women to be concubines, which was the assured destination of almost every young female slave. Slaves were also used in the silk and textile industries and other small businesses.

Ottoman slaves were outsiders. Taken by the Crimean Tatars from the neighboring Russians, Ukrainians, Poles, and some Hungarians, they were almost always Christians, sometimes animists, and typically Slavs. Up to 2.5 million slaves are calculated to have passed through the Crimean market in Kaffa (Kefe) alone in the years 1500–1700, most of them destined for the Ottoman Empire. The Muscovites set up a special tax to ransom their nationals taken by the Crimeans into slavery, and individuals paid such monies as well. Muscovite attempts to keep out the Crimeans were the major factor motivating the first Russian service-class revolution and the creation of a garrison state—in which the autocrat ruled supreme—that had serfdom as one of its major constituents. The Polish government did not engage in the ransom of its subjects, although occasionally individuals did. In

1607 a Polish-Ottoman treaty required that Polish slaves be returned without the payment of ransom, but that had little impact on the Crimeans. In spite of the treaty, Poles continued to be taken into captivity, especially after the Russians completed in the years 1636–1653 the construction of the Belgorod fortified line, which kept the Crimean predators out of Muscovy and deflected them into the Rzeczpospolita (the commonwealth). Catherine the Great liquidated the Crimean Khanate in 1783, which put an end to Crimean slave raiding. After that slaves in the European parts of the Ottoman Empire were so-called "white slaves" kidnapped from the Caucasus (Circassians and Georgians) or black slaves imported through Egypt from Africa. Turkey increased its number of galley slaves in the seventeenth century, most being from Muscovy and some from Italy. Galley slaves had one advantage over others: while in port, when not chained to their oars or benches, they could jump ship and make their way to freedom; but the number who did was very small. The Crimean War brought the trade in Christian Georgians to the attention of the British, who in the 1850s convinced the Ottomans and Russians to suppress it. The trade in Islamic Circassians was suppressed four decades later. The Ottoman slave trade was abolished officially only in 1909. As always, the abolition of the trade did not signify the abolition of slavery itself. Slavery in the Ottoman Balkans was extinguished only by the collapse of the Ottoman Empire after 1878 and World War I. The modernizing reforms of Kemal Atatürk, who proclaimed the state of Turkey with himself as president in the early 1920s, fully brought slavery to an end.

Census records indicate that, in spite of the huge numbers of slaves known to have been imported, slaves never exceeded 5 percent of the total population of the Ottoman Empire because Islamic practice encouraged frequent manumission by slaveowners. In other words, the "outsiders" were considered to be "insiders" after a very brief period of time. On the other hand, the Islamic world was addicted to slaves. Social relations were established so that the society could not function without slaves. Frequent manumission meant that it was necessary to replace those manumitted either by frequent slave raids or frequent trips to the slave market. Slavery became a form of involuntary migration marked by the high death rates of those who resisted capture into slavery or died en route to their final destination of enslavement. These high death rates (often only one in ten reached a slave destination) prefigured the high death rates in Soviet and Nazi slave systems.

Roma (Gypsies) comprised an interesting subset of the slaves in the Balkans, primarily in Romania,

Wallachia, and Moldova. Many of them were brought there from India by the Ottomans and remained into the twenty-first century. As a visible minority, a number of them were converted into slaves, and their enslavement was recognized by law. They were probably first enslaved by the Ottomans, who viewed them as outsiders. This view was adopted by the indigenous peoples as the Turks allowed them significant local control. As usual, the slaves can be divided into field and household slaves. Among the latter the Roma were valued as slaves in the sixteenth century as artisans and laborers. A Moldovan law code of 1654 referred to the Roma as slaves. The monarch, private individuals, and the church all could own slaves. An Ottoman Wallachian penal code included all the Roma among the slaves. When the Russians moved in (1826–1834), they tried to limit Romanian slavery. In 1837 and 1845 some slaves were freed in Moldova, and in 1847 the church in Wallachia freed its chattel. In 1855 the Moldovan parliament and in 1856 the Wallachian parliament voted to free the slaves, and in 1864 the ruler declared all Roma to be free people.

After the Ottoman conquest of the Balkans, the northern part of what was to become Yugoslavia (especially Croatia) remained Catholic and fell under the domination of the Habsburgs in Vienna. While slavery was being revitalized south of the Sava River under the Muslim Ottomans, in Croatia it yielded to serfdom and did not reappear again until the Nazi conquest. Here Austria set the tone. In Austria slavery was largely irrelevant in the modern era.

ITALY, IBERIA, AND FRANCE

In Italy the slavery of the Roman Empire merged into serfdom, but nevertheless Renaissance Italy was well acquainted with slavery, which persisted at least until the seventeenth century. In the period 1300–1700 slaves probably composed 5 percent of the population at any given time. Until the merchants of the Italian city states were driven out of the Black Sea by the Ottomans in 1475, a number of them engaged in the slave trade. Particularly noteworthy were the Genoese, who dispatched any number of Slavs to Italy. Italian merchants of the late Middle Ages were the most active in the slave trade. Florence in 1363 permitted unrestrained import of non-Roman Catholic slaves. Besides Genoa and Florence, slavery flourished in Venice, where thousands of Slavic slaves were sold in the first quarter of the fifteenth century alone. In Italy Slavic slaves were joined by Africans, and both were employed in domestic slavery, where females were typically preferred and sometimes used as concubines. A small minority of slaves were used as artisans in handicraft production, both on estates and in the thriving towns. Male slaves occasionally were used as business agents to extend the family firm, and they also traded on their own account.

Although wars were frequent on the Italian peninsula, the losers were rarely enslaved by the victors. Other factors had a greater impact on slavery practices. In areas close to Islamic lands of the Ottoman Empire and North Africa slavery was reinforced by virulent Muslim slavery, especially in Italy and Spain, where Islamic merchants with their slave merchandise and morality had a definite impact. Also important in the maintenance of slavery in Italy was the heritage of Roman law, in which slavery was one of the most evident social institutions. The Black Death of 1347–1348, following famine in the earlier 1340s, killed up to a third of the population in much of Europe, creating a labor shortage and therefore increased demand for slave labor in Italy. (Elsewhere in Europe the labor shortage led to the freeing of serfs and other servile workers as rising wages created an intense demand for free, mobile labor.) The cultivation of sugarcane in the Canary Islands prompted transference of slavery there from the eastern Mediterranean islands. Italian states with navies employed slaves, primarily purchased in North Africa, in their Mediterranean galleys into the eighteenth century. Other galley slaves came from Russia, the Rzeczpospolita, Greece, and from captured enemy ships.

Spain and Portugal both experienced slavery during the Renaissance and beyond. Spain was in regular combat with the Moors, who were subject to enslavement upon capture. Both countries also imported Africans for household employment. During the Renaissance and into the modern era, household slavery continued, as did the use of slavery to retain valued artisans. Córdoba, the leading city in Spain and one of the major cities in Europe, had a flourishing slave trade and slave community. Seville later became Spain's leading slave city in terms of slaves' percentage of the city's population. The king of Castile before 1265 ordered the law compiled in the *Las Siete Partidas,* which was based on Roman law and was confirmed by the *Leyes de Toro* in 1505. Thus Roman law entered Spain and subsequently much of the New World, including Louisiana. Spain owned the Canary Islands and transferred slave sugar cultivation from there to the New World. Given these factors, it was easy for Spain to develop slavery in its New World possessions. Up to half of the crews of Spanish galleys in the sixteenth and seventeenth centuries were slaves. Slaves were also employed in agriculture as shepherds, and household

Slave in Portugal. A slave waits at the family table. Illustration for the month of January from the Book of Hours of D. Manuel I (early sixteenth century) attributed to António de Holanda. MUSEU NACIONAL DE ARTE ANTIGA, LISBON/JOSÉ PESSOA

slavery persisted into the beginning of the nineteenth century.

Portuguese slavery became significant in the second half of the fifteenth century and peaked in the sixteenth century, when slaves constituted a significant portion of the population. Subsequently it declined and by the eighteenth century was reduced to occasional household slavery. Slaves in Portugal originated in the late Middle Ages from conflicts with Muslims, but became significant only when the Portuguese began to play a significant role in Africa after 1450. The economic pull, as elsewhere, was a perceived labor shortage resulting from wars and epidemics. Most Africans were reexported to northern Italy and Spain, but sufficient numbers remained to compose 2.5 percent of the total population. Besides Africans, slaves were imported from China, Japan, Brazil, and elsewhere. Slaves were primarily an urban phenomenon, where they were valued for their household service and their income-generating activities as employees in the iron and prepared-food industries, as artisans, clerks, and merchants. As was true in Russia, owners legally did not enjoy automatic sexual access to their female slaves, and the church regarded slave marriage as a sacrament. Slavery was abolished in Portugal in 1869.

France was the European country seemingly least affected by slavery in this period. It epitomized the processes at work after the collapse of the Roman Empire. Slavery survived into the twelfth century in the Loire Valley on a few monastery estates and elsewhere.

The absence of state power had made the enforcement of slave laws nearly impossible, with the result that magnates preferred to retreat to their manors and rely on more tractable sources of labor that needed less compulsion and were probably cheaper besides. The demand for slave labor was also reduced by technological improvements including improved heavy plows, the horse collar and harnesses that permitted draft animals to pull heavier loads, and horseshoes, which gave horses (which were improved by selective breeding) more traction. Water mills replaced slave labor in such activities as grinding grain. More effective crop rotation improved yields. These factors combined to make slaves an inefficient form of rural labor. As was true in much of western Europe, by the eleventh century most slaves were assimilated into the class of serfs. On the other hand, in Marseille both slavery and the slave trade flourished in the Middle Ages but declined in the city as they had declined in the countryside. France had galley fleets in the seventeenth and eighteenth centuries, but no more than 20 percent of the oarsmen were slaves. When the French jurist Jean Domat compiled the law in the years 1689–1697, slavery was not mentioned because it did not exist in France. In the early modern period in France, "slave" was primarily a derogatory epithet rather than a reality.

NORTHERN EUROPE

In Norway, Iceland, and Denmark, slavery was extinct by the thirteenth century, in Sweden by the fourteenth. During the Viking era, circa 750–1050, the Norwegians, the Danes, and Swedes went "a-viking" (became pirates) throughout Atlantic Europe in search of loot and human booty. After that era household slavery existed in Scandinavia on a very small scale, with Celts (Irish) being the most common slaves in Norway and Iceland. The word "thrall" was the Old Norse word for slave. It is assumed that increasing population density and church pressure combined to terminate Scandinavian slavery.

The modern Dutch Republic had no slaves. In 1648 it was explicitly illegal, and attempts to establish slave markets in the major seaports were vetoed by local officials. Dutch merchants, however, were prominent in the international slave trade in both Asia and the New World, and overseas Dutch were prominent slaveowners wherever Holland had colonies. Intellectually, the Synod of Dort in 1618–1619, a gathering of Calvinist theologians from northwestern Europe, was noteworthy for its statement that baptized slaves were entitled to the same liberties as other Christians and should not be sold to non-Christians. The dogma did not require Calvinists to convert their chattel and thus effectively did not compel the manumission of slaves. The Synod's dictum was important in northwestern Europe in holding that anyone was capable of conversion to Christianity and thus capable of freedom. This ran counter to the belief that certain persons, for example because of their race, were suited for slavery and thus unsuited for freedom.

The Germanies had thriving slave systems in the High Middle Ages. German eastward expansion, the *Drang nach Osten* (press to the east), turned many Slavs in the conquered lands into slaves. Around the year 1000 there was a full range of slaves in Germany, with the majority of course on the bottom as household dependents. Some slaves, however, were even "slave ministers," figures who had positions of responsibility in the government, just as they did in the Byzantine Empire and in late medieval Muscovy. In the Germanies slavery where it existed and while it lasted tended to be a rural phenomenon, for the famous doctrine *Stadluft macht frei* (town air makes one free) put a damper on urban slavery, something that was not true throughout most of the rest of Europe. Anyone who was not a native was subject to enslavement in the Germanies. A kinless, "outsider" slave at emancipation was subject to various forms of clientage and a transitional status to freedom that might last as long for his heirs as three or five generations. As elsewhere in Central Europe, so in the Germanies slavery in the productive sphere tended to be pushed aside by serfdom, especially east of the Elbe. The reason for this phenomenon was clearly economic: the owner

Nazi Slave Workers. Jews from the Warsaw ghetto being taken for forced labor, 1941. NEED CREDIT

was responsible for his slave, whereas the serf was typically expected to fend for himself. In the household, of course, the situation was different. While the household slave worked, his or her output was not monetizable.

Germany shares with Soviet Russia the dubious distinction of being one of the nation states of the twentieth century that revitalized slavery in a major way between 1938 and 1945. Unlike the Soviets, who preferred to enslave their own, the Nazis had a marked preference for "outsiders"—Jews, Slavs, communists, Roma, all of whom were called *Untermenschen,* subhumans who were suited for slave labor. French and other POWs were also added to the millions in the slave labor force. Over 7.5 million non-German civilians were transported to the Third Reich to work as slave laborers. Fritz Sauckel, Hitler's Plenipotentiary General for the Utilization of Labor, was the major organizer of this importation of millions of slave laborers. The Nazi choice of occupation for their slaves was somewhat different from the Soviet choice. Rather than logging and mining, canal and railroad building, the Nazis employed their slaves in manufacturing and

Nazi Slave Workers. Inmates of the Dachau concentration camp working in a munitions factory. MARY EVANS PICTURE LIBRARY

agriculture, wherever there were labor shortages to meet World War II military needs caused by the drafting of 13 million men into the Wehrmacht. The Hitlerite labor shortage was aggravated by the Nazi mystique that women should stay at home and not replace in field and factory their men who had been inducted into the Wehrmacht. By 1945 nearly a quarter of Germany's labor force was non-German, and in agriculture it was close to half. A number of the biggest, most famous German companies, including I. G. Farben, Volkswagen, Mercedes, Friedrich Flick, BMW, Bayer, Hoechst, Siemens, Thyssen, and Krupp, used slave labor they leased at the bargain rate of four Reichsmarks per day per slave from Heinrich Himmler's SS; survivors in 1999–2000 were still suing those companies in an attempt to gain recompense for their labor. The Nazis in numerous cases followed the same noneconomic, extermination-through-labor policy that was employed in the Soviet Gulag. The Nazis also placed extraordinary priority on making their female chattel into sex slaves of the Wehrmacht.

ENGLAND, SCOTLAND, AND IRELAND

In both England and Ireland after the year 500, Celtic and Germanic (Anglo-Saxon) peoples considered each other fair game for enslavement. Just before 1000 slavery was revitalized, and it endured throughout the eleventh century. In 1102 a church council at Westminster forbade the sale of slaves, a sign that slavery was on the wane. By 1500 it is probably accurate to say that slavery had died out in England, although not in Scotland. In 1569 (the eleventh year of Elizabeth's reign) occurred one of the most famous legal decisions of all time. In a suit brought by Cartwright, who was going to flog a slave he had imported from Russia (the slave might have been a Russian, Tatar, Pole, or Finn), it was held that "England was too pure an air for slaves to breathe in." After that time, the issue of white slaves (other than indentured laborers) did not arise in England. A possible major source of slaves was ruled out when in 1601 Elizabeth ordered the expulsion of blacks from England. Early in the eighteenth century Lord Chief Justice Holt opined that "as soon as a negro comes into England, he becomes free." Nevertheless, a few black slaves were brought into England by their owners.

Throughout most of the eighteenth century English newspapers contained advertisements to sell slaves and to recover runaways. Then in 1772 the Lord Chief Justice Baron Mansfield ruled in the famous *James Somerset v. Charles Stewart* case that a slave essentially gained his freedom by landing in Britain. The plaintiff, a former Virginia slave, could not be shipped against his will back into slavery in Jamaica. Mansfield wrote that "a notion had prevailed, if a negro came over, or became a christian, he was emancipated." Henceforth slavery in England was unsupportable by English law. Although Englishmen subsequently were the major players in the international slave trade out of Africa and were the major slaveowners of the sugar islands of the Caribbean and the tobacco plantations of the South, slaves themselves had little or no physical contact with England.

See also **The Balkans; Russia and the Eastern Slavs; Roma: The Gypsies** *(volume 1);* **Serfdom: Western Europe; Serfdom: Eastern Europe; Military Service** *(volume 2); and other articles in this section.*

BIBLIOGRAPHY

Bloch, Marc. *Slavery and Serfdom in the Middle Ages: Selected Papers.* Translated by William R. Beer. Berkeley, Calif., 1975.

Borkin, Joseph. *The Crime and Punishment of I. G. Farben.* New York, 1978.

Dallin, David J., and Boris I. Nicolaevsky. *Forced Labor in Soviet Russia.* New Haven, Conn., 1947.

Erdem, Y. Hakan. *Slavery in the Ottoman Empire and Its Demise, 1800–1909.* New York, 1996.

Hancock, Ian. *The Pariah Syndrome: An Account of Gypsy Slavery and Persecution.* 2d rev. ed. Ann Arbor, Mich., 1987.

Hellie, Richard. *Enserfment and Military Change in Muscovy.* Chicago, 1971.

Hellie, Richard. *Slavery in Russia 1450–1725.* Chicago, 1982.

Hellie, Richard, trans. *The Muscovite Law Code* (Ulozhenie) *of 1649.* Irvine, Calif., 1988. See especially chapter 20.

Herbert, Ulrich. *Hitler's Foreign Workers: Enforced Foreign Labor in Germany under the Third Reich.* Translated by William Templer. Cambridge, U.K., and New York, 1997.

Homze, Edward L. *Foreign Labor in Nazi Germany.* Princeton, N.J., 1967.

Inalcik, Halil. "Servile Labor in the Ottoman Empire." In *The Mutual Effects of the Islamic and Judeo-Christian Worlds: The East European Pattern.* Edited by Abraham Ascher, Tibor Halasi-Kun, and Béla K. Király. Brooklyn, N.Y., 1979. Pages 25–52.

Karras, Ruth Mazo. *Slavery and Society in Medieval Scandinavia.* New Haven, Conn., 1988.

Ka-Tzetnik 135633. *House of Dolls.* Translated by Moshe M. Kohn. New York, 1955. Describes Nazi slave practices with regard to female captives.

Origo, Iris. "The Domestic Enemy: The Eastern Slaves in Tuscany in the Fourteenth and Fifteenth Centuries." *Speculum* 30 (1955): 321–366.

Phillips, William D., Jr. *Slavery from Roman Times to the Early Transatlantic Trade.* Minneapolis, Minn., 1985.

Pryor, Frederick L. "A Comparative Study of Slave Societies." *Journal of Comparative Economics* 1, no. 1 (March 1977): 25–50.

Samson, Ross. "The End of Medieval Slavery." In *The Work of Work: Servitude, Slavery, and Labor in Medieval England.* Edited by Allen J. Frantzen and Douglas Moffat. Glasgow, Scotland, 1994. Pages 95–124.

Saunders, A. C. de C. M. *A Social History of Black Slaves and Freedmen in Portugal, 1441–1555.* Cambridge, U.K., and New York, 1982.

Solzhenitsyn, Aleksandr I. *The Gulag Archipelago, 1918–1956*. 3 vols. Translated by Thomas P. Whitney. New York, 1974–1978.

Stuard, Susan Mosher. "Ancillary Evidence for the Decline of Medieval Slavery." *Past and Present* 149 (1995): 3–28.

Swianiewicz, Stanislaw. *Forced Labour and Economic Development: An Enquiry into the Experience of Soviet Industrialization*. London and New York, 1965.

Verlinden, Charles. *The Beginnings of Modern Colonization*. Translated by Yvone Freccero. Ithaca, N.Y., 1970.

Verlinden, Charles. *L'esclavage dans l'Europe médiévale*. 2 vols. Brugge, Belgium, 1955–1977.

Wergeland, Agnes Mathilde. *Slavery in Germanic Society during the Middle Ages*. Chicago, 1916.

MARGINAL PEOPLE

Timothy B. Smith

During the first three quarters of the twentieth century, as Europe overcame subsistence problems and constructed massive welfare states, the problem of poverty and social marginality seemed to have receded into the background. Unemployment was down to 1 percent in Germany by 1960, and it remained below 2.5 percent in most of western Europe until 1973. But during the last twenty years of the century, the marginal people of Europe once again became visible: the homeless (an estimated 500,000 in France and 930,000 in Germany alone in 1996), illegal immigrants (up to 1 million in France); the unemployed (20 million unemployed in Europe in the mid-1990s), and the estimated 6 to 8 million Sinti and Roma (commonly known as Gypsies) who for so long have been living on the margins of society. Except for a brief respite between about 1960 and 1975, during Europe's golden age of full employment, vagrants, beggars, and economic marginals of all sorts have always been a visible and significant feature of western European society.

Until the twentieth century, the economies of Europe were not strong enough to support the vast majority of the population at a level of comfort on a regular basis. Plague and famine periodically paralyzed the economy, pushing people to the margins of society. Until the eighteenth century, when Europe escaped from the Malthusian trap, population ebbed and flowed according to the rhythms of the harvest and pestilence cycles. Although England had escaped from the specter of famine by the early nineteenth century, France had its last nationwide subsistence crisis in the 1850s, and in eastern Europe the threat of crop failure persisted decades longer. Starvation was still a real threat to the peasants of eastern Europe and Russia through World War I and, in some cases, after.

The harvest was the lifeblood of the early modern economy; when it failed, as it did so frequently (one in six harvests in England failed during the seventeenth century), a large part of the population would be forced to scramble to make ends meet. Only when European populations became more urban and more commercial and less peasant based and agricultural—would prosperity increase. Those nations which underwent an agricultural revolution first (Britain) would be the first to enjoy widespread material prosperity. But the processes associated with modernization—agricultural improvements, rural exodus, urbanization, mechanization of artisanal industry, and so on—would, in the short (or intermediate) term, push millions of people to the margins of society. East of the Elbe River, millions of peasants remained mired in serfdom until the mid-nineteenth century.

The typical western European peasant family lived in poverty right into the early nineteenth century, but with one unsettling event—a crop failure, an injury or illness, a rise in bread prices, the death of a spouse or a child, a foreclosed debt—they could be pushed from poverty into destitution and would have to seek charity or public assistance or else take to the road to beg or steal. For example, during the period 1840–1842, some 84 percent of those entering three major *dépots de mendicité* (beggars' prisons) in Belgium were first-time offenders, members of the casual labor force who were ineligible for public assistance.

Women would sometimes resort to prostitution in a last-ditch effort to spare the family from the shame of seeking assistance, or simply to make ends meet: "morals fluctuate[d] with trade" (Leeuwen, 1994 p. 601). Minor forms of illegality such as smuggling, poaching, and petty theft were common. Banditry persisted in parts of Europe (Italy) well into the nineteenth century. Everywhere, the distinction between poverty and indigence was blurred, and until some point in the eighteenth or nineteenth century (depending on the nation) perhaps half of the continental European population risked falling into indigence or destitution at any given time. Within this wider context of general poverty, however, it is possible to identify certain particularly vulnerable and/or marginal groups.

SOURCES

For the most part, our knowledge of marginal people stems from three sources: court and police records, where the otherwise elusive marginal people left their scarce and faint traces in the historical record; the archives of hospitals, poor relief agencies, and charities; and from the observations of elite contemporaries. Scholars have been interested in the study of poverty and marginality not only because of its intrinsic importance, but also because it provides a good window into many other issues: class relations, trends in religious observance and practice, political and social ideologies, the growth of state penal powers and social spending, and so on.

Thanks to several detailed studies of the clientele of hospitals, prisons, and workhouses, we know that some social groups were more at risk of falling into indigence than others: casual farm laborers (*journaliers,* as they were known in France), the elderly, widows with children, workers with large families, and casual urban laborers. Child beggars could be seen everywhere in London. In 1816, Lionel Rose reminds us, 50 percent of the three thousand inmates in London's twenty jails were under seventeen years of age. In 1848 Henry Mayhew estimated there were thirty thousand to forty thousand young "street Arabs" wandering in London.

RURAL MARGINALS

Many rural marginals were attracted to the large capital cities, as were youth, who were drawn to places like London and Paris by the thousands. Few young provincials, Arthur Young noted in 1771, could resist the allure of London. But the medium-sized regional centers—Lyon, Grenoble, Turin, Toulouse—were usually closer to home. Seasonal migration within a region was also common, especially in Alpine areas. For example, every year during the period 1780–1820 roughly twenty thousand peasants would leave their spartan mountain villages in Piedmont (today part of Italy) to eke out an existence in nearby cities or in France for six or even nine months.

These people, like their elders, lived in what Olwen Hufton has termed an "economy of makeshifts." Agricultural laborers, those who lived on the margins of rural society, with no firm roots or legal claims to the land, accounted for roughly 40 percent of those who entered the Charitè hospital in Aix-en-Provence, France, during the eighteenth century; up to one-half of those assisted by some charities in the 1890s; and 20 percent of patients in the hospitals of Mantes-la-Jolie, outside Paris, around 1900. Typically, landless rural laborers were the largest single component of any given nation's floating, vagabond population, but textile workers, artisans, soliders and sailors, servants and apprentices were also commonly found among the wayfaring poor.

Most villages also contained a marginal population, as opposed to older images of village solidarity and rough equality. Many villagers lived hand to mouth, easily victimized by disease, periodic bad harvests, or simply overlarge families. As European agriculture became more commercialized, with inroads on community resources such as common lands, the marginal village population increased.

The debate over the social consequences of enclosure (the process whereby the English—and, later, other Europeans—cleared and enclosed common lands and forests and set about using the land more productively, with fewer laborers) has divided historians for generations. Undoubtedly, enclosure was good for the economy in the long term, leading to more productive use of land, but it hurt several social categories, in particular small owners and casual farm hands, who drifted to the margins of rural (and urban) society. The historian Deborah Valenze has argued that in England women were hurt more than men. The modernization of agriculture during the eighteenth and early nineteenth centuries eliminated women's traditional role in growing and gathering food as well as other customary activities such as tending livestock. Women were forced into domestic service, factory work, marriage, and quite often into begging and prostitution. Some enterprising people, like the English landowner John Warren of Stockport, were not unaware of the consequences of their actions: having enclosed a commons in 1716, he set up a prison and a workhouse in one corner of his lot. As Roy Porter concludes in his acclaimed survey, *English Society in the Eighteenth Century,* the eighteenth-century agricultural revolution created a landless proletariat, many of whom remained on the margins of society for decades before being integrated (if they ever were) into new positions in society.

THE MARGINS OF URBAN SOCIETY

Many cities engaged in significant efforts to help both the working and the unemployed poor. Between 1829 and 1854 in Amsterdam, for example, a quarter of the population received assistance on a regular basis. But as Marco van Leeuwen shows, the elderly and workers with large families were favored. In an age of limited resources, a sharp line between different categories of poor served to ration relief. Poorly paid artisans and textile workers were among the luckiest of the poor,

A Flemish Vagrant. *The Prodigal Son,* painting (detail) by Hieronymus Bosch (1450–1516). AMSTERDAM MUSEUM/ART RESOURCE, N.Y.

in the sense that their somewhat respectable occupations gave them a chance of receiving public assistance from urban authorities. Lyon geared its relief system to unemployed silk workers; Florence geared its poor relief system to unemployed shoemakers, textile workers, woodworkers, and the like; and Antwerp favored unemployed textile workers (27 percent of those assisted in 1855 were in the textile trade).

A wide stratum of urban society was never fully integrated into the civic fabric or the regular economy and would have had a harder time getting relief: young journeymen, apprentices, casual day laborers, hawkers, porters, ragpickers, haulers, dustmen, charwomen, and domestic servants. These last were particularly vulnerable. Most were unmarried, and many lived in damp basements or cramped attic apartments. Many slipped into prostitution, begging, or vagrancy at some point in time.

This state of affairs had not changed much by the late nineteenth century. The lack of full-time, reliable, adequate wages was the root of the problem. When the city of Hamburg was engaged in a public-health crusade against cholera in the 1890s, it did background checks on the laborers employed in "disinfection columns." Of some 671 men who had their backgrounds checked, 82 had criminal convictions, often several. But most of these convictions were for minor contraventions, indicating, as Richard Evans concludes in *Death in Hamburg,* "the extent to which the poor of Wilhelmine Germany habitually broke the law in order to survive" (Evans, 1987 p. 322). These

were working men, not professional vagabonds or beggars. Catharina Lis observes that the vast majority of those interned for petty crimes in early-nineteenth-century Antwerp were of the poorest stratum of the lower classes.

Surveying a wealth of literature on European urban and social history since 1750, Peter Stearns and Herrick Chapman estimate that the typical large European city in the nineteenth century had a floating, marginal, casually employed labor force which might amount to 20 percent of the population. These unskilled transient laborers searched for new work every day or every week—dock work, ditch digging, hauling, carting, construction work. Paid low wages, they were often hired by the day by a hiring boss in a city square. Many drifted from city to city in search of work, and along the way they might be forced into begging or petty crime. Deprived of the strong neighborhood support networks enjoyed by permanent residents of the city, they lived on the margins in every sense. And yet their very numbers suggest that they were indispensable to the running of the cities—they performed work which no one else would. In a world without the eight-hour day, with little or no labor protection, no welfare state, and low expectations, "marginals" could pick up society's crumbs by taking on a handful of odd jobs at any given time.

Indeed, Barrie Ratcliffe has argued that to be marginalized from mainstream society during the nineteenth century did not necessarily mean that one was also alienated and more prone to criminality. Indeed, as he suggests, when one adds up the various categories of "marginal" people even in early-nineteenth-century Paris, one approaches such a large number that one may be able to speak of the mainstream. Certainly these "marginals" were more integrated into the casual economy than today's unemployed marginals. Still, workers in the early stages of industrialization were often lumped together in the minds of elites with vagrants and other unsavory characters. As the French *Journal des débats* put it in 1832, "workers are outside political life, outside the city. They are the barbarians of modern society." The same was true, John Merriman argues, for workers in the new faubourgs. Suburban workers were relegated, in Merriman's term, to "the margins of city life."

HONOR, BLOOD, AND RELIGION

In the Germanic areas of central Europe, the loss or lack of honor, a value enforced by the urban guilds, was a barrier to entry into society. It could even be a permanent condition, passed on to one's unlucky offspring. This sort of inherited dishonor was less common in western Europe. Honor could be lost in the first instance through illegitimate birth, a criminal record, or racial "impurity," such as having Slavic blood. Lack of honor might mean permanent marginalization, which would force people into a lifetime of begging, theft, smuggling, and/or vagrancy.

The religious divide was often impenetrable. Numerous large European cities had important religious minority communities: Muslims in Venice, Moors in Spanish cities (until they were expelled), Protestants in predominantly Catholic cities, and so on. Of course Jews were marginalized throughout European history in every nation. Indeed, as Christopher Friedrichs notes, "perpetual marginalization was the norm for non-Christians" in Europe in the period 1450–1750—and beyond (Friedrichs, 1995, p. 239).

The Jews were first granted full civil rights in France during the Revolution, but social and economic discrimination continued in the early nineteenth century and then increased later in the century, as the traditional religious recipe for anti-Semitism was made more virulent with the addition of racial, biological anti-Semitism. Jews were dispersed throughout Europe, but everywhere they lived they were conspicuously marginalized, often as a matter of local or central government policy. Jews were often forced to wear markers on their clothing so that they would not be mistaken for Christians. The concept of the Jewish ghetto was first introduced in Venice, but it reached its zenith in Frankfurt, where Jews were confined to a single street, walled and gated off from the rest of the city, and restricted in their movement. If there was one caste-like division in European society in the early modern period, this was it: the towering wall between Jews and Christians.

Walled free cities in central Europe usually denied full citizenship rights to foreigners of all sorts. But money could serve as a passport to social acceptance, if not full citizenship. Some foreigners were prized for their skills or assets (Italian bankers and silk weavers in Lyon, foreign merchants in Polish cities, Italian master craftsmen in France); others were feared as dangerous marginals (Italian peasant migrants in nineteenth-century Marseille). Impoverished foreigners who arrived in distant cities seeking casual labor or charity might be lucky enough to be tolerated, but often they were sent packing with the crack of a whip. A steady flow of Irish beggars was redirected from London back to Ireland in the eighteenth century, but most managed to elude authorities long before their ship set sail, returning to London to start all over again. In addition to the usual social and economic obstacles thrown in the way of immigrants, non-Christians and foreigners had to cope with hostility toward their different religion, language, and customs. They accounted for a large proportion of any given city's beggars.

BEGGARS

The problem of begging and vagrancy decreased significantly between the two world wars (there were, for example, only 4,760 prosecutions in Britain in 1934, as compared with up to 25,000 per year in the period 1900–1914). Still, beggars could be seen in European cities until the 1950s or 1960s, and in the 1980s they reemerged in a dramatic fashion. The question, as always, is one of magnitude. In the early modern era (1450 to 1750), and in many places right into the late nineteenth century, beggars could often swamp cities.

German court records from the early modern period provide a glimpse into this complex and colorful underworld: there were *Stabülers* (professional beggars with several children); *Klenckner* (beggars who positioned themselves near churches and marketplaces with broken limbs and other deformities, whether real or feigned); and *Grantner* (beggars who feigned illness, often using soap to induce foaming at the mouth). The fifteenth-century Italian writer Teseo Pini listed forty different "occupational groups" within the world of begging in his book *Speculum cerretanorum* (1484). The Englishman John Awdeley listed nineteen in his 1561 study of the issue, *Fraternity of Vagabonds*. Marginals inspired fear in the minds of many people, and many imaginary traits were ascribed to them. As Keith

Wandering Beggars. "These are not brave messengers who wander through foreign lands," engraving by Jacques Callot (1594–1639) of beggars during the Thirty Years' War. ©BETTMANN/CORBIS

Thomas has shown, in early modern England vagabonds were often seen as filthy, scavenging dogs, beasts who lived from one scrap to another, slaves to their empty stomachs. Often portrayed as subhuman, marginals were sometimes treated as such.

Despite the misconceptions and fears that surrounded marginals, the image of the "professional beggar" was in fact grounded in reality: one could cite the unofficial beggars' guild in fifteenth-century Cologne; the thousands of beggars who paid taxes in German cities in the early modern period; or, more recently and specifically, a certain Hubert Nicolourdat, a sixty-eight-year-old Parisian arrested for begging at least fifty-six times by 1899, or Louis-René Pasquer, a sixty-year-old with fifty-four arrests to his credit. Every European town had its share of occasional and professional beggars. As is the case today, some had their fixed spot—on a certain street corner or opposite the church—which they "owned." In eighteenth-century Marseille, beggars bequeathed their spots to their impoverished relatives, who would come in from the countryside to claim their deceased relative's corner. In some smaller cities, like those of Brittany as late as 1900 or like Aix-en-Provence, in southern France, the streets were overrun by beggars:

> They squatted on street corners, swarmed near the city gates, and crowded the churches, disrupting services with their piteous pleas for alms. Once in the troubled days of of the 1620s, more than 2,000 beggars crowded the courtyard of the Hôtel-de-Ville [city hall]; when they tried to climb a staircase to beg outside the chamber of the municipal council, it collapsed under their weight. (Fairchilds, 1976, p. 100)

This type of scenario was still being played out in the nineteenth century, for instance in Florence, where begging and poverty were widespread. A census of 1810 recorded 36,637 poor persons, of whom 22,838 were deemed to be indigent, out of a population of only 69,000. Vagabonds who hailed from outside the city were threatened with a prison term of up to ten years if they were caught by officials. A new workhouse-prison, the Pia Casa di Lavoro, awaited them.

WANDERERS

Socially marginal groups in the early modern period were often made up of itinerants who practiced a number of precarious occupations. Some even peddled quack medicine. When this precarious "economy of the makeshift" failed—as it did so often—they might resort to other forms of legal activity; failing that, they would turn to begging, swindling, and theft. It was in all rural marginals' best interests to keep their options open. A typical landless wanderer was Edward Yovell, a vagrant whose story has been told by the historian Paul Slack. Yovell was born in London in the sixteenth century. After an apprenticeship in Worcester ended, he began wandering. Twice in a two-year period he took up casual work in London. He helped out at harvest time at his uncle's farm in Surrey, worked at various inns in Chichester, and followed a circuit leading back to Worcester via Salisbury, Bristol, and Gloucester, where he begged and took casual work when he could find it. Like most vagrants, he often took on work—when it was available.

Many wanderers tended to try to make it on their own in the summer by foraging, hunting, and mushroom picking in forests, and by traveling. The forests were their safety valves. In winter, however, demands for charity and public assistance would increase significantly, especially in northern Europe. The roads would become more dangerous at this time of year. In some countries, such as France, marginals would head south for the winter. The city of Nice was overwhelmed with this type of seasonal migrant in the late nineteenth century. Hospital admissions would double in some towns during the winter months and at the low points of the harvest cycle, when marginal people would suffer more than others.

Peddlars—a more enterprising lot than simple vagabonds—roamed the rural roads selling their wares: repair services, odds and ends, almanacs, chapbooks, and medical potions. They were at once marginal and indispensable, in that they helped to spread news and knowledge.

ILLNESS AND DISABILITY

Edme Gardy, a twenty-seven-year-old from Auxerre, France, was condemned in 1775 in Paris to stand in the pillory for two hours, to pay a small fine, and to be banished from Paris for three years. His crime? He had been arrested for begging. His road to the pillory had begun shortly before his arrest, when he had sustained an injury while doing some casual farm work in the Brie region. He had been forced to beg, he pleaded to the magistrate, while he nursed his injury. At a time when Paris was overrun by several thousand beggars (there were up to eight thousand detained beggars alone in prisons in the region in 1784), there was little sympathy to be found. Gardy's story, recounted by Jeffrey Kaplow, speaks volumes about life at a time when the slightest injury (for a manual laborer especially) could spell a trip to the poorhouse or to prison.

In the absence of effective and widely available medical treatment, illness, disability, and serious injury were three sure tickets to a life on the margins of society. Disease and deformity meant shame—and shame meant marginalization. Lepers are the most obvious example of such a marginalized group. Similarly, victims of venereal disease were often treated by special hospitals, cut off from the mainstream, or even relegated to the margins of city boundaries. But there were many others. In Toledo in 1598, for example, 15 percent of arrested beggars and poor-relief recipients were lame, 12 percent had broken or missing limbs, 7.5 percent were blind, and most others had some other form of illness or disability (5 percent were without a tongue). In Lower Saxony in the period 1659–1799, 24 percent were lame; in Aix-en-Provence in 1724, the figure was 25 percent. The elderly infirm without familial support or social patrons often ended up being dumped into beggars' prisons in nineteenth-century France, or else they ended up in the hospital or hospice. Until the second half of the twentieth century, when European governments finally began to provide meaningful assistance to the physically handicapped as a sort of social right, physical disability almost certainly led to a life on the margins of society. In the French city of Saint-Étienne 83 percent of beggars arrested in 1858 had some form of physical disability. Epileptics and persons with severe skin diseases formed a disproportionate number of French beggars and vagabonds into the early 1900s.

STIGMATIZATION

Many marginals were forced to wander because they had been branded (sometimes literally) as outcasts. Stigmatization is a product of scarcity and low expectations: stigmata mark off the unworthy from the worthy and ease the claims on public resources. The branding of vagrants with hot irons is perhaps the utmost form of stigmatization. It was indeed practiced, but it was certainly not a routine affair in most areas of Europe. David Underdown uncovered only one branding of a "rogue" in an eight-year period in seventeenth-century Dorchester, England. The practice appears to have been more common in central Europe. Nonetheless, the practice of branding—from England to France to the German lands—suggests that European elites generally shared the idea that poor marginals were some sort of subhuman species, to be treated like livestock. Indeed, in his study *Man and the Natural World,* Keith Thomas unearthed much evidence to suggest that marginal people were often deemed worthy of the same (harsh) treatment as animals.

WOMEN, INFANTS, AND THE ELDERLY

Olwen Hufton estimated that among the wandering poor in eighteenth-century France, men outnumbered women by six to one. This figure, as she notes, is skewed in that men were more threatening and therefore more likely to be reported to police. Still, there were fewer opportunities for women to take to the road. Their safety would be at risk, and the need to care for children often anchored them to a particular city, where they might beg or receive charity. Men forced to live on the margins of society were arrested at ten times the rate of women in late-nineteenth-century France.

Despite men's higher rate of conviction for begging and vagrancy, few social groups were as vulnerable as young single pregnant women or elderly widows. A pregnant village girl might escape to the city to bear her child far from the watchful eyes of her fellow villagers, or she might become pregnant by some young man (or her employer, if she were a domestic servant) in the city and be left to fend for herself. As Rachel Fuchs has shown in her book on child abandonment in urban France, illegitimate birth and child abandonment were perhaps the most pressing social problems of the early nineteenth century in several major French cities. In the 1830s over thirty-two thousand infants were officially abandoned each year, and the actual figure was much higher. At times up to one-third of all live births were abandoned. As recently as the 1890s, over thirty-three thousand Italian newborns were abandoned by their mothers each year. Similar patterns of child abandonment have been found in Russia and Spain. By the late nineteenth century one-third of newborns in Milan and Florence were left at foundling homes. In Italy and in other Catholic countries, the Catholic Church deprived illegitimate children of a social identity and branded their unwed mothers as sinners, relegating both to the margins. Until the advent of child and maternal welfare benefits in the twentieth century, pregnancy for young, poor, or single women almost certainly spelled poverty and often social marginalization.

Elderly men and women, especially those who had toiled away at physical labor throughout their rough lives, were particularly prone to begging and vagrancy. The old and retired vineyard workers of the Gironde, near Bordeaux, are a case in point. As an inquiry during the French Revolution revealed, when these men could no longer work, they became prisoners of their worn-out bodies, often totally dependent on public charity or begging (or both) to survive. Elderly, impoverished widows were a common sight at street corners, as well as in hospitals and hospices (where they often constituted a majority of residents) and at charities, many of which devoted as much as half of their resources to the elderly. A wide but insufficient array of charitable institutions was set up to assist these people. Elderly *journaliers* (casual farm hands) in France and English farm hands dispossessed by enclosure were overrepresented on the relief rolls and in the begging and vagrancy statistics.

ATTITUDES TOWARD MARGINALS AND REPRESSIVE MEASURES TAKEN AGAINST THEM

Europeans have usually held conflicting views of the poor and have accordingly prescribed contradictory measures to deal with poverty. This is as true for the sixteenth century as it is for the nineteenth. If, on the one hand, marginals were to be chased out of town after having their ears bored, their noses cropped, their backs lashed, or the letter V (for vagabond) or R (rogue) inscribed on their arms with a branding iron, the worthy poor served, on the other hand, as what Hufton called "the linchpin in the salvation of the rich" (Hufton, 1974, p. 132). They were to be assisted, and those who administered the institutions which assisted them would gain social, political, and spiritual capital.

Early responses to begging and vagrancy. A wave of reform swept across Europe starting in the 1520s, prohibiting indiscriminate public begging. The concept of the "deserving" and "undeserving" poor gained ground at this time and was officially incorporated into many municipal poor-relief systems. Badges were introduced to distinguish the worthy poor from all others. This had the effect of further marginalizing those who were not recognized as the local worthy poor. Vagrancy and begging were on the rise at this time, and reform was designed to cope with these problems, which seemed to be getting out of hand. Banditry, for example, had become so severe on the Italian peninsula that in 1572 Milan and Venice concluded a treaty regarding punishment of bandits: They were not to live within fifteen miles of the places from which they had been banished. If found within these limits, they could be attacked and killed without penalty. Bandits were preferred dead to alive; there were no extradition provisions in the treaty. Authorities took remarkably repressive measures to combat the problem of banditry, but bandits and vagabonds also inspired sympathy among the common people. Some marginals, such as Cartouche, the legendary French criminal, or Geronimo Tadino in sixteenth-century Veneto, became folk heroes, to be revered as well as feared.

The creation of a rural proletariat in Europe, beginning (slowly) in England in the seventeenth century, in France and elsewhere in the eighteenth century or later, exacerbated the problem of vagrancy. Already in 1688 Gregory King's crude demographic study of England (only a rough sketch of reality) estimated a population of 400,000 cottagers and paupers as well as 849,000 vagrants. Historians are generally in agreement that vagrancy and begging became more acute problems over the course of the eighteenth century. All statistics point in this direction—arrests, admissions to hospitals and charities, and so on. London and Paris were never more overrun by beggars than in the period from 1770 to 1820, but the problem persisted into the twentieth century. Kathryn Norberg provides ample evidence of the increasing geographic mobility of the population, coupled with the rise in vagrancy in and around eighteenth-century Grenoble. Bands of thieves and vagrants terrorized the

French countryside in the eighteenth century and well into the late nineteenth. In 1820 thirty-nine thieves led by a certain "Bruno" wreaked havoc in the Auvergne. The notorious vagabond-murderer Vacher terrorized France in the 1890s, killing up to two dozen people. Bands of so-called *apaches* terrorized Parisians at about the same time. These seemingly rootless marginals from the suburbs, living on the margins of the city and the world of work, struck fear in the hearts of polite society. Stern repression was seen as the only solution.

But official proscriptions against begging were not always received sympathetically by the general population. In many parts of Europe, a certain "moral economy of begging" persisted, whereby people, particularly the common people who must have realized that they might one day be forced to beg, recognized that beggars were not necessarily lazy, immoral shirkers. In her study of Aix-en-Provence, Cissie Fairchilds found numerous occasions in which the common people prevented city officials from enforcing the laws against beggary. In July 1749, for example, an angry crowd forced the officials of the Charité hospital to set free a group of beggars they had arrested. The poor in eighteenth- and even nineteenth-century England and France embraced the "moral economy" which defended their customary rights, including a notion of the right to subsistence. Food riots in defense of a "just price" were common.

With the advent of liberal political economy in the period from 1780 to 1850 (depending on the nation), this old "moral economy," which provided certain benefits to the respectable poor, was attacked by economists and politicians alike. As the market eroded the old paternalistic society, the tendency to marginalize the poor and blame them for their poverty increased. Those who failed to live up to the notion of self-help espoused by Samuel Smiles (in *Self-Help,* 1859) were deemed doubly responsible for their lot in life. Vagrancy laws and urban police forces were introduced in Britain between 1815 and 1830, which turned the screws of the law tighter on the nation's marginal population. A more concerted approach to "eradicating" mendicity was (once again) introduced in France in the 1830s. Belgium followed the same path once it won its independence. In an age which celebrated individual self-improvement, marginals became less tolerable: they stood as a threat to the ethos of the age. The penitentiary was born, and beggars' prisons got a second life in the period from 1820 to 1850.

Attitudes in the late nineteenth and early twentieth centuries. Late in the nineteenth century, attitudes toward marginals hardened in several countries, as the issue became entangled in the growing concern over national depopulation and the "degeneration" of racial stock. In light of the heightened military competition that preoccupied politicians and elite opinion, marginals were seen as a sort of cancer on the body politic, a threat to the military, economic, and demographic virility of the nation. This was particularly the case in France, Germany, and Italy—three countries whose cities were being overwhelmed by rural migrants, vagabonds, and beggars at this time.

In the countryside, vagabonds and migrant workers were a regular sight into the early twentieth century. There were still an estimated 200,000 to 500,000 vagabonds (up to 1 percent of the population) roaming the roads of France in the two decades before World War I. Guy Haudebourg estimates that 9 percent of Bretons were beggars in the eighteenth century, and 6 percent of the population still begged in parts of Brittany in the nineteenth century. The problem was also acute in Germany, which was in the grips of a process of rapid and massive internal migration, with only half of Germans living in the place of their birth in 1907; in Italy, where the southern population was being "pulled" up toward the northern cities out of hope for a better future; and in Belgium. Over fifty thousand people were arrested for vagrancy and begging each year in France during the 1890s.

In the thirty years before World War I, France took remarkably repressive measures against marginals. In 1885 the "relegation" law was passed, empowering judges to deport certain categories of recidivist and violent vagabonds. France deported over five thousand vagabonds to its colonial prisons in the tropics each year in the 1890s, and in 1902 alone the figure topped 9,900. Prussia had an agreement with Russia to send vagrants and criminals to Siberian prisons. Hamburg sent criminals to Brazil. The Belgians constructed what was arguably western Europe's most draconian beggars' prison at Merxplas.

Repression toward the Sinti and Roma (or Gypsy) populations in central and eastern Europe was stepped up shortly before and during World War I. Europe's largest marginal group, at the end of the twentieth century with a population of up to 8 million scattered across the continent, the Sinti and Roma were repressed as a matter of state policy in several countries. Attempts were made to stamp out their itinerant culture, to force them to settle down. By 1906 Germany had bilateral agreements to "combat the Gypsy nuisance" with Austria-Hungary, Belgium, France, Italy, Russia, and several other nations. The Danes began to expel them beginning in the 1870s.

In an age of nationalism, an age which emphasized the need for a single unifying national culture within state boundaries, those who did not belong to the dominant ethnic group might be further marginalized. This was particularly the case in the Austro-Hungarian empire (with the Romanian minority population in Hungary, for instance) and above all in Russia, where a wave of brutal pogroms (public anti-Jewish campaigns of harassment and often extreme violence, including murder) was encouraged by authorities in the final decades of the nineteenth century. Russia's 5 million Jews were compelled to live in a region of western Russia and eastern Poland known as the Pale of Settlement. As repression increased beginning in the 1880s half a million Jews migrated to western Europe and North America. By 1900 foreign populations were being harassed out of or even expelled from several nations: the German government, for example, forced thousands of ethnic Poles across the German border into Russia in the 1880s and 1890s. In Russia, a state program of "Russification" attempted to wipe out the Ukrainian language. Poles in Russia were targeted for discrimination. Russification was paralleled by Magyarization, as Hungarians attempted to spread their language and root out minority languages in the portions of the Austro-Hungarian empire under their control.

Since World War I. In many ways World War I marks the beginning of a new era. It disrupted traditional seasonal migration patterns, as many marginals were drafted into the war effort. After the war, in France (and possibly elsewhere in the West) the population settled down and became more urban. During the 1920s and 1930s, workers in many countries made important gains—higher wages, better working conditions, paid vacations, more bargaining power, more stable work conditions, and so on. But the Depression turned the clock back again (especially in Germany and Britain), and marginal people suffered immensely. Post–World War II prosperity did not really materialize in western Europe until the mid-1950s, and cities like Paris and Turin were still encircled by squalid shanty towns into the 1950s, the result of the rural exodus, the influx of immigrants, and the deplorable and insufficient housing stocks of France and Italy. Here as elsewhere the urban poor lived, literally, on the margins of urban society, banished to the *banlieu* (suburb).

After the bloodshed and Holocaust of the 1940s, the golden age of prosperity which fell upon Europe during the 1950s and 1960s helped most people finally to join the economic mainstream—but not permanently. The bubble of prosperity burst in the mid-1970s. Unemployment inched up to as much as 13 percent in the European Community by the mid-1990s. Hard times affected all, but the marginals of the 1980s and 1990s were most likely to be young people: one-third of Italians under the age of thirty were unemployed, as were one-fourth of French youth, and almost one-half in Spain. Non-European immigrants—North Africans and French citizens of North African descent who live in the suburban ghettos of Paris, Lyon, Marseille, and other large French cities; Turkish "guest workers" in Germany; Africans in Italy; immigrants from the Caribbean in the United Kingdom; and so on—were also particularly vulnerable. They accounted for a disproportionate number of the long-term unemployed and were often the victims of racial violence and discrimination.

There were over one hundred suburban housing ghettos in France, containing hundreds of thousands of immigrants and their children. Complexes like Sarcelles and Les Tartarets were plagued by unemployment rates of over 30 or even 50 percent. In several European countries, including France, Italy, and Spain, the long-term unemployed (those without work for over one year) accounted for up to 40 percent of the unemployed at times in the 1990s. In Spain and Italy, the rate of female unemployment was markedly higher than the average. In the mid-1990s, the unemployment rate of Italian women under the age of thirty was over 43 percent. One-half of Arab youth in France (under age twenty-five) were unemployed.

The existence of marginal populations is of course nothing new. But there was a new dimension the situation of the late twentieth century. Before the twentieth century, most major western European cities would also have contained a marginalized immigrant community or communities, whether it was the Irish in Liverpool or London or, later, Jews and other migrants from eastern Europe. But the situation in the last decades of the twentieth century was in many ways different. Although historians once argued that migrants were, by definition, "uprooted" and alienated, research in the 1980s and 1990s showed that migrants to nineteenth-century cities were often welcomed into supportive networks by members of their community who had already put down roots in their new homes. Provincials and foreigners alike created "urban villages," crude mini–welfare states, providing the charity of the poor toward the poor, with a strong self-policing element as well.

This world was dying by the end of the twentieth century, especially in suburban ghetto housing complexes. The separation of home and work, the uprooting of younger generations from their parents and grandparents in vibrant, densely populated slums,

Shelter for the Homeless. Reading the scripture in a night shelter. Print (1871) by Gustave Doré (1832–1883). LIAISON AGENCY

and the advent of high-rise public housing units eroded sociability and support networks among the poor. Over the course of the twentieth century, as work became more structured, routine, and full-time, falling out of the job market acquired graver, more long-lasting consequences. The fine gradations of rank and status and the numerous types of footholds on the occupational treadmill that accompanied a more casual labor market disappeared. As Roy Porter stresses throughout *London: A Social History,* the widespread availability of casual work until the 1960s and 1970s facilitated the social and economic integration of most newcomers to the city. This process stopped, and in the 1990s the city was embarrassed by the sight of a shanty town erected by the homeless on Lincoln's Inn Fields.

Europe's marginals were, by the end of the twentieth century, a distinct minority, denied the fruits of consumerism and leisure which most people were able to enjoy, cut off geographically from the economic and social mainstream, often denied full citizenship rights, and shut out of a more stable and formalized labor market. The integration of economically marginal peoples into the mainstream of European society was surely one of the greatest challenges facing Europe at the century's end.

See also **Roma: The Gypsies; Immigrants** *(volume 1);* **Migration** *(volume 2);* **Social Control** *(in this volume); and other articles in this section.*

BIBLIOGRAPHY

Adams, Thomas McStay. *Bureaucrats and Beggars: French Social Policy in the Age of Enlightenment.* New York, 1990.

Beier, A. L. *Masterless Men: The Vagrancy Problem in England, 1560–1640.* London, 1985. The definitive study.

Chesney, Kellow. *The Victorian Underworld.* London, 1970.

Evans, Richard. *Death in Hamburg.* Oxford, 1987.

Evans, Richard J. *Tales from the German Underworld.* New Haven, Conn., 1998.

Evans, Richard J., ed. *The German Underworld.* London, 1988.

Fairchilds, Cissie C. *Poverty and Charity in Aix-en-Provence, 1640–1789.* Baltimore, 1976.

Farge, Arlette. *Fragile Lives: Violence, Power, and Solidarity in Eighteenth-Century Paris.* Translated by Carol Shelton. Cambridge, Mass., 1993.

Friedrichs, Christopher R. *The Early Modern City: 1450–1750.* London, 1995. Important chapters on the poor and marginals in the city.

Fuchs, Rachel G. *Abandoned Children: Foundlings and Child Welfare in Nineteenth-Century France.* Albany, N.Y., 1984.

Gueslin, André, and Dominique Kalifa, eds. *Les exclus en Europe, 1830–1930.* Paris, 1999.

Haudebourg, Guy. *Mendiants et vagabonds en Bretagne au XIXe siècle.* Rennes, France, 1998.

Hufton, Olwen H. *The Poor of Eighteenth Century France, 1750–1784.* Oxford, 1974. Unparalleled rich study.

Jutte, Robert. *Poverty and Deviance in Early Modern Europe.* Cambridge, U.K., 1994. A very useful survey of secondary literature.

Kaplow, Jeffrey. *The Names of Kings: The Parisian Laboring Poor in the Eighteenth Century.* New York, 1972.

Kertzer, David I. "Infant Abandonment and Gender Ideology in Nineteenth-Century Italy." *Journal of Interdisciplinary History* 22 (summer 1991): 1–25.

Lees, Lynn Hollen. *The Solidarities of Strangers: The English Poor Laws and the People, 1700–1948.* Cambridge, U.K., 1998.

Leeuwen, Marco H. D. van. "Logic of Charity: Poor Relief in Preindustrial Europe." *Journal of Interdisciplinary History* 24 (Spring 1994).

Leeuwen, Marco H. D. van. "Surviving with a Little Help: The Importance of Charity to the Poor of Amsterdam 1800–1850, in a Comparative Perspective." *Social History* (October 1993).

Lis, Catharina. *Social Change and the Labouring Poor: Antwerp, 1770–1860.* New Haven, Conn., 1986.

Lis, Catharina, and Hugo Soly. *Poverty and Capitalism in Pre-industrial Europe.* Brighton, U.K., 1982.

Merriman, John M. *The Margins of City Life.* New York, 1991.

Porter, Roy. *English Society in the Eighteenth Century.* 2d ed. London, 1990.

Porter, Roy. *London: A Social History.* Cambridge, Mass., 1995.

Rose, Lionel. *"Rogues and Vagabonds": Vagrant Underworld in Britain, 1815–1985.* London, 1988.

Schwartz, Robert M. *Policing the Poor in Eighteenth-Century France.* Chapel Hill, N.C., 1988.

Slack, Paul. *Poverty and Policy in Tudor and Stuart England.* London, 1988.

Smith, Timothy B. "Assistance and Repression: Rural Exodus, Vagabondage, and Social Crisis in France, 1880–1914." *Journal of Social History* 32, no. 4 (1999): 821–846.

Snell, K. D. M. *Annals of the Labouring Poor: Social Change and Agrarian England, 1660–1900.* Cambridge, U.K., 1985.

Stearns, Peter N., and Herrick Chapman. *European Society in Upheaval.* 3d ed. New York, 1992.

Swaan, Abram de. *In Care of the State.* New York, 1988. Important chapter on vagrancy.

Woloch, Isser. *Eighteenth-Century Europe.* New York, 1982. Important chapter on poverty.

Section 11

SOCIAL PROTEST

COLLECTIVE ACTION

Charles Tilly

Collective action applies pooled resources to shared interests. In European social history, collective action has ranged from communal bread baking to electoral campaigns, from idol-smashing to revolution. Much collective action actually consists of conflict or cooperation, which imply two or more interacting parties. To treat an episode as "collective action" is therefore an analytic simplification; it singles out the perspective and behavior of just one participant in complex interactions. Collective actors sometimes include corporate bodies such as craft guilds and religious confraternities, but on occasion they also include friendship networks, neighbors, and participants in local markets. Collective action rarely involves all members of such ongoing social structures at the same time, but often draws currently active participants disproportionately from one or more existing structures.

Participants in collective action, furthermore, regularly claim to speak in the name of such structures—our guild, our confraternity, our lineage, our neighborhood, and so on—or in the name of more abstract collectivities such as workers, women, Huguenots, pacifists, or environmentalists. Some of European social history's most vivid moments centered on this sort of claim making: Florentine workers rising against the oligarchy in the name of crafts excluded from municipal power; newly converted mountaineers resisting demands of their Catholic lords in the name of Protestant sects; Parisian residents attacking the Bastille in the name of the whole citizenry. Over that same history, nevertheless, the great bulk of collective action took less spectacular forms such as local celebrations, jury deliberations, or the everyday production of goods or services by households and workshops.

NARROW VERSUS BROAD DEFINITIONS

Social historians and social scientists often reserve the term "collective action" for episodes engaging participants who do not routinely act together or who employ means of action other than those they adopt for day-to-day interaction. Collective action in this narrow sense resembles what other analysts call protest, rebellion, or disturbance. It differs from other collective action in being discontinuous and contentious: not built into daily routines, and having implications for interests of people outside the acting group as well as for the actors' own shared interests. When those implications are negative we can speak of conflict, whereas when they are positive we can speak of cooperation. The narrower definition of collective action refers to discontinuous but collective contention, whether conflict-bearing or cooperative.

No one should adopt the narrower definition without recognizing four important qualifications. First, no sharp dividing line exists between "routine" and "extraordinary"; demonstrating and attacking ethnic rivals, for example, sometimes become everyday activities. Second, exceptional bodies of participants and unusual modes of action always depend in part on previously existing social relations and known models of making claims. In old-regime Europe, for instance, the unauthorized popular courts that repeatedly formed to judge violators of the public interest always drew their members from previously established political networks and regularly mimicked routines of royal courts. Third, even in apparently repetitive, everyday forms of collective action such as tending a village's common lands or establishing defenses against infectious diseases, participants were incessantly negotiating, improvising, and applying group pressure to reluctant contributors. Fourth, both exceptional and everyday episodes of collective action therefore pose essentially the same problems of explanation.

Nevertheless, social historians who have adopted the narrower definition of collective action have rightly sensed that something sets off discontinuous, contentious collective action from its continuous and noncontentious forms. Discontinuous, contentious collective action always involves third parties, often poses threats to existing distributions of power, and usually incites surveillance, intervention, and/or repression by political authorities. As a consequence, it also generates more historical evidence in the form of chronicles, memoirs, administrative correspondence, judicial proceedings, military reports, and police records than do continuous and noncontentious varieties of collective action. Accordingly, social historians who seek to reconstruct collective action can generally do so much more easily for its discontinuous, contentious forms. The following discussion therefore draws disproportionately on studies of discontinuous collective contention. It also deals primarily with popular collective action rather than collaboration among the rich and powerful. Finally, because historians of northern, central, and western Europe have so far done the bulk of European research on popular collective action, the arguments and conclusions that follow qualify as no more than working hypotheses for southern and eastern Europe.

CONDITIONS FOR COLLECTIVE ACTION

From the perspective of individual self-interest, collective action (especially its narrower form) presents a logical puzzle. Much collective action produces goods from which all members of a group benefit whether or not they participate in the action. Cleaning up a local water supply, building a new market, and raising the minimum wage for a whole category of workers provide obvious examples. Since participation takes effort and often exposes participants to risks, any particular member of the beneficiary category therefore has an interest in standing by while others do the essential work and take the crucial risks. To the extent that collective action is discontinuous and contentious, furthermore, costs and risks generally increase. In such circumstances, individual costs loom large compared with likely individual benefits. If everyone stands by, however, nothing gets done. This collective-action problem helps explain why many populations that would have been collectively better off if they had coordinated their action to produce shared benefits—for example, most women in cottage textile production—rarely acted together on a large scale. One of the most important findings of social history, early on, was the necessity of existing community structures and goals for protests, which means also that the poorest sectors of the population can rarely mount collective action.

Yet Europeans frequently did manage collective action. Some special circumstances reduced collective-action problems. If the number of potential participants and beneficiaries in a collective action was quite small, for example, each member would gain a substantial share of the benefits, could easily gauge whether others would contribute their shares of the effort, and could readily put pressure on would-be slackers. In the presence of shared interests, small numbers thus promoted collective action. At times one of the potential beneficiaries (for example, a merchant household contemplating construction of a bridge across a forbidding river) had so much to gain from collective action that it invested a large share of the resources to produce the collective good and to reward other people's participation in production of the good. Other favorable circumstances for collective action included serious, simultaneous threats to group survival, extensive communication among parties to a shared interest, and opportunities to make substantial individual gains (for example, through looting or acquisition of inside information) while serving collective ends.

Europeans still repeatedly acted collectively in the absence of such favorable circumstances. Why? Like other peoples, Europeans accomplished most of their collective action through institutions and practices they invented, borrowed, or adapted in the course of historical experience. Some of those institutions and practices emerged from more or less deliberate attempts to coordinate collective action; labor unions and revolutionary associations qualify in this regard. But many came into being as by-products of local, routine social interaction, as when unmarried village males who drank, fought, and played sports together formed organized bands that also collected wood for holiday bonfires, conducted shaming ceremonies outside the houses of cuckolds, and ritually barred the way to wedding processions for local brides who were marrying men from other parishes.

Institutions and practices promoting collective action varied significantly in their mixes of coercive, material, and solidary incentives. States, for example, generally employed significant coercion to produce collective action; they conscripted soldiers, forced reluctant taxpayers to contribute their shares to collective endeavors, and seized privately held land for public purposes. In contrast, although workshops and factories used plenty of coercion, they generally organized much more directly around quid pro quo material rewards than states did. Meanwhile, kin groups, religious congregations, sewing circles, and similar institutions offered substantial solidary incentives to their participants in addition to whatever coercion and material reward they dispensed. They provided opportunities for intimacy, affirmation of identity, mutual aid, social insurance, information, and participation itself—backed by the threat of shaming, shunning, or utter exclusion for those who violated their fellows' expectations.

For most of European history, most Europeans carried on risky, emotionally engaging, and delayed-payoff activities such as procreation, cohabitation, long-distance trade, and pursuit of the afterlife by means of institutions and practices centering on solidary incentives, with coercion and material reward playing a lesser part. Kinship groups, neighborhood networks, and religious congregations figured importantly in these institutions and practices, but so did more specialized organizations such as devotional and penitential confraternities, lodges, and mutual-aid societies. On the whole, Europeans insulated such structures from interference by outsiders and public authorities; they did so either by keeping the structures inconspicuous or by relying on protection from powerful members of the same structures.

SHIFTING REPERTOIRES OF COLLECTIVE ACTION

One of European history's greatest changes was a massive shift from such solidarity-bound structures toward governments, firms, unions, specialized associations, and other organizations emphasizing coercion and material rewards as sites of high-risk, emotionally engaging, long-term activities. The shift occurred in most of Europe during the nineteenth and twentieth centuries. To be sure, it did not obliterate institutions and practices centering on solidary incentives. Europeans still find their sexual and marriage partners, for example, chiefly through networks of friendship, kinship, and neighborhood that are typically homogeneous with respect to class, religion, and/or ethnicity. Some groups, like poor housewives and working women, continued to find it easier to mobilize through these kinds of daily networks. Still, as compared to the fifteenth or sixteenth century, the average twentieth-century European conducted a much wider range of risky, important business through institutions and practices centered on coercive and material incentives.

That large transformation of institutions and practices interacted with substantial shifts in collective action. To understand these shifts, we must recognize four profound features of collective action, wherever it occurs. First, it always takes place as part of interaction among persons and groups rather than as solitary performance. Second, it operates within limits set by existing institutions, practices, and shared understandings. Third, participants learn, innovate, and construct stories in the very course of collective action. Fourth, precisely because historically situated interaction creates agreements, memories, stories, precedents, practices, and social relations, each form of

collective action has a history that channels and transforms subsequent uses of that form. The form of collective action we call a strike has a distinctive history, as do the forms we call coup d'état, feud, and sacred procession. For these reasons, collective action falls into limited and well-defined repertoires that are particular to different actors, objects of action, times, places, and strategic circumstances.

Any collective actor employs a far smaller range of collective performances than it could in principle manage, and than all actors of its kind have sometimes managed somewhere. Yet the performances that make up a given repertoire remain flexible, subject to bargaining and innovation. Indeed, precisely repetitive performances tend to lose effectiveness because they make action predictable and thereby reduce its strategic impact. The theatrical term "repertoire" captures the combination of historical scripting and improvisation that generally characterizes collective action.

Europe's collective-action performances changed incrementally as a result of three classes of influences: shifts produced by learning, innovation, and negotiation in the course of collective action itself; alterations of the institutional environment; and interactions between the first two. In the first category, eighteenth-century Britain's petition march mutated from the humble presentation of a signed request borne by a few dignified representatives of the petition's many signers to the clamorous march of thousands through streets to confront authorities with their demands. The campaigns of John Wilkes on behalf of rights to public dissent during the 1760s figured centrally in that change.

Alterations of the institutional environment—notably suppression of civic militias as national armies formed—lay behind the widespread disappearance in western Europe during the sixteenth to eighteenth centuries of collective action by means of armed local bands marching under elected captains marching in military order. (The century beginning in 1789, however, saw widespread revival of similar performances by centrally authorized but sometimes independent militias such as the French National Guard.)

Examples of interaction are more common. An instructive case is the legalization of strikes in most western European countries during the nineteenth century. That legalization typically protected rights of workers to assemble, deliberate, and withdraw from work collectively, but simultaneously declared a wide range of previously common worker actions (such as coercion of nonstrikers and attacks on employers' houses) illegal. It also subjected strikers to scrutiny of governmental specialists in industrial relations. Similarly, governmental interventions in public health,

Religious Action. Engraving commemorating the pilgrimage to the shrine of Our Lady of Montaigu in Brabant (northeast of Louvain in present-day Belgium). At left, a legless man gives thanks to the Virgin for saving his life; at right, behind the kneeling figure, a possessed man is cured; in the background at left, a procession approches the shrine church. BIBLIOTHÈQUE NATIONALE, PARIS, RC 36D

education, water control, and other local production of collective goods generally standardized organization from place to place, reduced the autonomy of local institutions, and subordinated local efforts to top-down control.

The shift from eighteenth- to nineteenth-century repertoires.

Although incremental change in repertoires never ceased, in some periods interaction between internal alterations of performances and transformations of their institutional environments accelerated. In those periods, massive transformations of repertoires occurred. The best-documented transformation of this sort affected much of western Europe during the century or so after 1780. At least in Great Britain, the Low Countries, France, Germany, and Italy, a large net shift in popular collective action occurred. At the shift's beginning, we might characterize prevailing repertoires as parochial, particular, and bifurcated: parochial in orienting chiefly to local targets and issues rather than national concerns; particular in varying significantly with respect to format from setting to setting, group to group, and issue to issue; and bifurcated in dividing sharply between direct action in regard to local targets and requests for intervention by established authorities (chiefly priests, landlords, and officeholders) when it came to national questions. In contrast, we might call the repertoire that came to prevail during the nineteenth century cosmopolitan, modular, and autonomous: cosmopolitan because it covered a wide range of targets and issues, emphatically including national ones; modular because people used essentially the same forms of action (such the public meeting) over a broad range of issues; and autonomous because participants addressed objects of their claims in their own names via interlocutors from their own ranks.

The last observation requires qualification. The very changes that produced the new nineteeth-century repertoire also opened unprecedented opportunities for a variety of brokers who spoke, or claimed to speak, for popular constituencies. Those brokers included labor leaders, organizers of popular societies, and substantial peasants, but they also sometimes included alliance-making priests, officeholders, and bourgeois. Such brokers often played significant parts in popular collective action, especially in connecting interactions of disparate groups. They also frequently competed with each other for recognition as valid representatives of their claimed constituencies.

Table 1 summarizes contrasting principles in the earlier and later western European repertoires. We may call them "eighteenth-century" and "nineteenth-century" with the warnings that transitions from one to the other took decades everywhere and occurred at different times in different regions, that each collective-

A Strike. The London Dock Strike of 1889. Private Collection/The Bridgeman Art Library

May Day. Workers in Dresden, Germany, celebrate international socialist solidarity on 1 May 1890. Woodcut by E. Limmer. AKG LONDON

action performance had a somewhat different history and timing from the others, and that various segments of the population moved from "eighteenth-century" to "nineteenth-century" repertoires at their own paces. Powerful people and local authorities, for example, typically assembled at their own initiative long before the nineteenth century. Some of the repertoire change, indeed, consisted of generalizing just such elite privileges to ordinary people. Gender also shaped available repertoires of protest, since rights available to women expanded on different timetables than those of men, and expectations of female and male behavior differed as well.

With these provisos, note how closely western Europe's eighteenth-century collective-action repertoires adapted to local conditions. They depended heavily on prior daily connections among participants in collective claim making. They also drew heavily on local knowledge of personalities, symbols, and sites. Well-documented examples include shaming ceremonies (such as "rough music"), popular interventions in public executions (to attack a maladroit hangman, to jeer at the victim, or sometimes to rescue him),

sacking of houses occupied by persons accused of wrongdoing, and invasions of enclosed common fields. In less overtly conflict-filled domains, local celebrations, water control systems, and use of communal ovens likewise depended heavily on dense personal connections and local knowledge. The exact forms, personnel, and circumstances of these performances varied greatly from place to place. Later repertoires sacrificed some of that local knowledge and connection but offered the possibility of coordination among multiple sites and ready transfer of learning from one site to another. The public meeting, the demonstration, the voluntary special-purpose association, and the electoral campaign all generalized easily from one place or occasion to another.

As they created the new repertoire, Europeans were inventing what later generations called social movements. Although historians sometimes apply the term indiscriminately to all sorts of popular collective action regardless of time and place, it refers especially to sustained challenges of constituted authorities in the name of wronged populations, challenges backed by public displays of activists' worthiness, unity, numbers,

TABLE 1
CONTRASTING PRINCIPLES OF EIGHTEENTH- AND
NINETEENTH-CENTURY REPERTOIRES IN WESTERN EUROPE

Eighteenth Century	*Nineteenth Century*
Frequent employment of authorities' normal means of action, either as caricature or as a deliberate, if temporary, assumption of authorities' prerogatives in the name of a local community	Use of relatively autonomous means of action, of kinds rarely or never employed by authorities
Convergence on residences of wrongdoers and sites of wrongdoing, as opposed to seats and symbols of public power	Preference for previously planned action in visible public places
Extensive use of authorized public celebrations and assemblies for presentation of grievances and demands	Deliberate organization of assemblies for the articulation of claims
Common appearance of participants as members or representatives of constituted corporate groups and communities rather than of special interests	Participation as members or representatives of special interests, constituted public bodies, and named associations
Tendency to act directly against local enemies but to appeal to powerful patrons for redress of wrongs beyond the reach of the local community and, especially, for representation vis-à-vis outside authorities	Direct challenges to rivals or authorities, especially national authorities and their representatives
Repeated adoption of rich, irreverent symbolism in the form of effigies, dumb show, and ritual objects to state grievances and demands	Display of programs, slogans, and symbols of common membership such as flags, colors, and lettered banners
Shaping of action to particular circumstances and localities	Preference for forms of action easily transferred from one circumstance or locality to another
Summary: *parochial, particular, and bifurcated*	Summary: *cosmopolitan, modular, and autonomous*

and commitment. The social movement's preferred performances were (and still are) demonstrations, processions, public meetings, petition drives, print pronouncements, and interventions in electoral campaigns. Social-movement activists commonly formed special-purpose associations devoted to promotion of their causes. They also typically created identifying names, banners, badges, and slogans.

Little of the social movement repertoire would have been possible without extensive interaction between internal changes in collective action performances and transformations of their institutional contexts. Social-movement activists pushed accepted

boundaries of association and assembly but also took advantage of changes in legal controls brought about by others. Thus popular associations proliferated in French cities after the Prussian victory, and the very bourgeois revolution of 1870 brought down Louis Napoleon's empire. Those popular associations then coupled with National Guard units as frames for activism in the 1871 insurrectionary Communes of Paris, Lyon, and other cities.

Regimes and regime changes exerted significant influence over collective-action repertoires. At any given moment each regime made rough, implicit, but often effective distinctions among performances that

Rough Music. Neighbors ridicule a tailor who is dominated by his wife. Engraving by William Hogarth (1697–1764). BIBLIOTHÈQUE NATIONALE, PARIS/JEAN-LOUP CHARMET

it promoted (such as participation in public ceremonies), tolerated (petitioning), or forbade (sacking of toll gates). Regimes backed these distinctions by means of rewards and punishments for potential and actual collective actors: honors, entertainment, food, and drink for promoted performances; imprisonment, execution, shaming routines, or military attack for forbidden performances. Generally speaking, democratic regimes tolerated a wider range of collective-action performances. That toleration actually sharpened the distinction between tolerated and forbidden performances, made forbidden performances the province of political outcasts, and encouraged a wide range of actors to make their claims by means of tolerated or promoted performances. Undemocratic regimes, on the average, drew sharper lines between promoted per-

formances and all others, with the paradoxical effect that collective action frequently consisted either of subverting promoted performances (for example, shouting antiregime slogans during official ceremonies) or adopting clearly forbidden means (for example, assassinating public officials or collaborators). Undemocratic regimes narrowed the tolerated middle.

While the transition from eighteenth- to nineteenth-century protest forms is most studied, other points of change in the history of European collective action deserve attention. These include the decline of the great rural revolt against landlord and manorial controls, which began in the late Middle Ages and tapered off after the great risings of 1648. The decline of strikes and unions in the later twentieth century raises questions about changes in protest goals and participants.

METHODS OF STUDYING COLLECTIVE ACTION

Social historians know much more about the detail of popular collective action in western Europe because students of that region have more often studied popular collective action systematically. Elsewhere, most published information on the subject comes either as illustrative material in general political histories or as documentation of major conflicts. Whatever their region and period of specialization, however, serious students of European collective action generally adopt a combination of three rather different procedures: collection and analysis of relatively homogeneous catalogs of events; reconstruction of one or a few crucial or characteristic episodes; and recasting of previous political narratives by inclusion of popular collective action, often as seen through experiences of one or a few localities or groups.

Systematic catalogs of collective action episodes require extensive effort but offer significant rewards for social history. Because many European governments started collecting comprehensive reports of strikes during the nineteenth century, students of industrial conflict have often concentrated on systematic catalogs of strikes and lockouts. Other historians, however, have used administrative correspondence, periodicals, and other sources to construct catalogs of events they have called riots, protests, or contentious gatherings. Catalogs of this kind have the advantage of facilitating comparison and detecting change, but they remain vulnerable to reporting biases.

Closely studied episodes offer the possibility of attaching participants and actions more firmly to their social settings than most catalogs do. They have therefore attracted many students of crises, revolutions, and rebellions. Pursued alone, they have the drawbacks of extracting the event from its broader historical context (including its relation to previous, subsequent, and even simultaneous collective action) and of making comparison more difficult.

The augmented narrative has two signal advantages. First, it makes clear what bearing the study of collective action has on conventional interpretations of the political history in question. Second, it provides direct answers to the question: why should historians care about these sorts of events? All too easily, however, it lends itself to the supposition that the questions built into previous narratives were valid. Since the questions addressed by existing narratives (for example, did people support the regime or not?) often actually mislead investigators (for example, where participants in collective action are strongly attached to local leaders who maintain only contingent commitment to the regime), it is always prudent to undertake close examination of collective action for its own sake.

CASE STUDY: THE LOW COUNTRIES, 1650–1900

We can see the advantages of synthesizing catalogs, specific episodes, and augmented narratives by looking at popular collective action in the Low Countries from about 1650 to 1900. During those two and a half centuries, the regions now known as the Netherlands, Belgium, and Luxembourg underwent major changes of regime and of popular politics. Seen from the top, the Low Countries moved from dynastic struggles to intermittently revolutionary politics mobilizing substantial blocs of the general population in bids for control over central governments.

Suppose we recognize as revolutionary situations those instances when for a month or more at least two blocs of people backed by armed force and receiving support from a substantial part of the general population exercised control over important segments of state organization. By that rough test, likely candidates for revolutionary situations in the Low Countries between 1650 and 1900 include the following events:

1650	Failed coup of William II
1672	Orangist seizures of power in many towns
1702	Displacement of Orangist clients in Gelderland and Overijssel
1747–1750	Orange revolt in United Provinces, after French invasion precipitates naming of William IV of Orange as Stadholder
1785–1787	Dutch Patriot Revolution, terminated by Prussian invasion
1789–1790	Brabant Revolution in south
1790–1791	Revolution in principality of Liège, terminated by Austrian troops
1792–1795	French-Austrian wars, culminating in French conquest of Low Countries, installation of variants of French and French-style rule
1795–1798	Batavian Revolution in north
1830–1833	Belgian Revolution against Holland, with French and British intervention

In detail, to be sure, these clustered events consisted of much meeting, marching, petitioning, confronting, fighting, sacking, arguing, and organizing. The largest changes in texture consisted of shifts from the mobilization of aristocratic military clienteles and burgher militias to the sustained integration of ordinary householders into national struggles for power. In conformity with our general argument, increases in state capacity promoted shifts toward mobilization on the basis of detached identities and by means of nationally standardized repertoires.

Cataloging "eighteenth-century" repertoires in Holland. Seen from a local perspective, collective contention occurred far more frequently, and changed character even more dramatically. Rudolf Dekker has cataloged dozens of "revolts"—events during which at least twenty people gathered publicly, voiced complaints against others, and harmed persons or property—in the province of Holland during the seventeenth and eighteenth centuries. By comparison with all of Europe's contentious repertoires from 1650 to the present, the events in question generally qualify as small, local, variable in form from one place or group to another, and bifurcated between (many) direct attacks on local targets and (few) mediated appeals to higher authorities. Concretely, Dekker's catalog emphasizes four sorts of events: forcible seizures of marketed food or attacks on its sellers; resistance to newly imposed taxes; attacks by members of one religious category on persons, property, or symbols of another; and attempts to displace political authorities.

By and large, qualifying events falling outside those four categories involved a fifth category: collective vengeance—for example, sacking of houses—on figures who had outraged public morality. Sacking of houses also often accompanied protests against tax farmers and other public figures targeted in the first four categories of violent events. In that regard, Dutch eighteenth-century popular actions greatly resembled their French, British, and North American counterparts. Like students of old-regime contention in these other areas, Dekker calls attention to the festival atmosphere of many such rituals: "A participant in an Orangist disturbance of 1787 declared," he reports,

"'I've never had so much fun at a fair as in tearing down that sacked house'" (Dekker, 1982, p. 92). More generally, Dekker's events conformed recognizably to prevailing old-regime repertoires of popular contention in western Europe as a whole. Along the standard range from petitions and parodies through local vengeance, feuds, and resistance to mass rebellion, they clustered at the edges of prescribed and tolerated forms of public politics. Nevertheless, in such times of general political struggle as the Orange revolt of 1747–1750, they merged into open rebellion.

So far as Dekker's catalog indicates, Holland's struggles over food concentrated from 1693 to 1768 in market towns and in periods of rising prices when local authorities failed to guarantee affordable supplies to the local poor. His catalog's tax rebellions (which Dekker worries may only have been "the tip of the iceberg") focused on farmed-out excise taxes rather than direct taxation, and clustered in times of general struggle over political authority such as 1747–1750. In a Holland where about half the population belonged to the established Dutch Reformed Church, perhaps 10 percent to other Protestant denominations, 40 percent to the Roman Catholic church, and a small number to Jewish congregations, ostensibly religious conflicts often included struggles for voice in local affairs as well as responses to religiously identified external events—for example, the duke of Savoy's persecution of Protestants in 1655. Like tax rebellion, however, religious contention appears to have surged in times of general political struggle such as 1747–1750. At such times, every political actor's stake in the polity faces risk. As a result, a wide range of place-holding and place-taking action occurs, regardless of how the cycle of contention began.

Events that Dekker classifies as openly political pivoted on the house of Orange. Under Habsburg rule, the absent king had typically delegated power within each province of the Netherlands to a Stadhouder (state-holder = lieu-tenant = lieutenant or deputy). From their sixteenth-century revolt against Habsburg Spain onward, Dutch provinces had commonly (although by no means always or automatically) named the current prince of the Orange line their Stadhouder, their provisional holder of state power; that happened especially in time of war. Whether or not a prince of Orange was currently Stadhouder, his clientele always constituted a major faction in regional politics, and opposition to it often formed around an alliance of people outside the Reformed church, organized artisans, and exploited rural people. During the struggles of 1747–1750, contention over the Stadhouder's claims to rule merged with opposition to tax farmers and demands for popular representation in provincial politics. Such events underwent greater transformation between 1650 and 1800 than did food-, tax-, and religion-centered events.

Defining the emergence of "nineteenth-century" repertoires in Holland.

During the later eighteenth century, we see emerging concerted demands for broad participation in local and provincial government, so much so that R.R. Palmer's *Age of the Democratic Revolution* (1959–1964) bracketed the Dutch Patriot Revolt of the 1780s with the American Revolution (1775–1783) as significant representatives of the revolutionary current. Wayne te Brake's systematic analysis of the Dutch revolution in the province of Overijssel identifies the 1780s as a historical pivot in popular claim making. Public meetings, petitioning, and militia marches did much of the day-to-day political work, but in company with older forms of vengeance and intimidation. In the small city of Zwolle, te Brake reports, for example, that in November 1786,

> A gathering of more than 1,000 persons in the Grote Kerk produced a declaration that a scheduled election to fill a vacancy on the Sworn Council by the old method of co-optation would not be recognized as legitimate. When the government nevertheless proceeded with the election in mid-December, the chosen candidate was intimidated by Patriot crowds and forced to resign immediately. (te Brake, 1989, p. 108)

When Prussian troops ended the revolution with an invasion in September 1787, however, the Patriots' Orangist opponents took their own vengeance by sacking the houses of Patriot activists. Speaking of nearby Deventer, te Brake concludes that

> the "People" of Deventer had entered politics to stay. Not simply the rhetorical invention of self-serving Patriot pamphleteers or constitution-writers, "*het Volk*" had in the course of the 1780s become an armed and organized reality which proved to be easily capable, when united, of breaking into the urban political space. As unity gave way to division and conflict at all levels of society, however, the force and significance of the new popular politics was by no means extinguished. Thus, as we have seen, the counter-revolution in Deventer represented the victory of one segment of a newly politicized and activated "People" over another—not simply a restoration of aristocratic politics as usual. Indeed, the Orangist counter-revolution in Deventer unwittingly consolidated two momentous changes in the politics of this provincial city, the combination of which suggests that the character of urban politics was forever transformed: the private, aristocratic politics of the past had been shattered and the foundation had been laid for the public, participatory politics of the future. (te Brake, 1989, p. 168)

In public politics at a regional and national scale, both repertoire and participation in contention were changing noticeably.

During the later eighteenth century, organized workers and their strikes also became more prominent in Dutch political struggles. A significant transformation of contentious repertoires was under way even before French conquest so profoundly altered the Low Countries' contentious politics. On balance, newer performances in the Low Countries' repertoires mobilized more people from more different settings, built on detached rather than embedded identities, targeted more regional and national figures and issues, adopted forms that were more standardized across the whole region, and involved direct rather than mediated presentation of claims. Specialized political entrepreneurs (as opposed to established local and regional authorities) were emerging as critical actors in popular contention.

Cataloging collective action in early Belgium.

In a parallel study to Dekker's, Karin van Honacker has cataloged about 115 "collective actions" directed against central authorities farther south, in Brabant—more precisely, in Brussels, Antwerp, and Louvain—from 1601 to 1784. Some actions took place in a single outing, but many consisted of clusters spread over several days or weeks. Honacker classifies her events under four headings: resistance to violation of local political rights, fiscal conflicts, civil-military struggles, and fights over food supply. The first two categories overlap considerably, since in Brussels the dominant guilds (the Nine Nations) frequently resisted taxes on the basis of what they claimed to be their chartered rights. Religious struggles of the sort that figured prominently in Holland escape Honacker's net because they did not typically set members of the urban population against authorities. With Brabant under Spanish, then Austrian, control, struggles of civilians with royal soldiers, disputes over their quartering or payment, freeing of captured military deserters, and competition of urban militias with royal troops for jurisdiction all loomed much larger than in Holland. Fights over food supply, however, greatly resembled each other in north and south; repeatedly city dwellers attacked merchants who raised their prices and outsiders who sought to buy in local markets.

On the whole, Honacker's catalog of events from seventeenth- and eighteenth-century Brabant reveals less change in the character of popular demands than Dekker's findings from Holland. In the three southern cities we see repeated resistance to royal centralization in the name of established privilege, but no obvious swelling of demands for popular sovereignty. Claim making followed western Europe's characteristic old-regime repertoire; in Honacker's account it featured frequent employment or parody of authorities' own

political means and symbols; participation of people as members of established communities and corporate groups; concentration of claim making in holidays and authorized gatherings; rich symbolism, often including shaming ceremonies; and orientation of avenging actions to dwellings of perpetrators and to places where alleged offenses occurred.

Defining the emergence of the new repertoire in nineteenth-century Belgium.

The eighteenth-century repertoire did not last much longer. Gita Deneckere has assembled a catalog of "collective actions" in Belgium as a whole from 1831 through 1918 from a wide range of archives, official publications, periodicals, and historical works. Her catalog includes about 440 occasions on which people gathered and made collective demands "in the socio-economic field of conflict," which means largely workers' actions and actions concerning work. Within that field, her evidence demonstrates a significant alteration in Belgian repertoires of contention.

Or, rather, two alterations. Up to the revolution of 1848, Deneckere's contentious events feature workers' assemblies and marches to present petitions, attacks on the goods or persons of high-priced food merchants, and work stoppages by people in multiple shops of the same craft. Workers' actions frequently took the form of turnouts: occasions on which a small number of initiators from a local craft went from shop to shop demanding that fellow craft workers leave their employment to join the swelling crowd. The round completed, turnout participants assembled in some safe place (often a field at the edge of town), aired their grievances, formulated demands, and presented those demands to masters in the trade (often through a meeting of delegations from both sides), staying away from work until the masters had replied satisfactorily or forced them to return.

Between the revolution of 1848 and the 1890s, turnouts practically disappeared as demonstrations and large-firm strikes became much more frequent and prominent. Although strikes and demonstrations continued apace into the twentieth century, from the 1890s onward regionally and nationally coordinated general strikes emerged as major forms of contentious action. As Deneckere says, workers and socialist leaders designed general strikes to be large, standard in form, coordinated across multiple localities, and oriented toward national holders of power. These new actions built on public identities as socialists or as workers at large. They represented a significant shift of repertoire.

Of course these changes reflected major nineteenth-century social changes such as rapid ur-

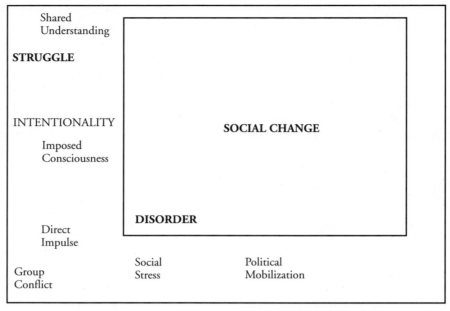

Figure 1. Competing descriptions and explanations of European popular collective action.

banization and expansion of capital-intensive industry. But the changing repertoire of contention also had a political history. Deneckere sees increasingly tight interdependence between popular contention and national politics. In the 1890s,

> The correspondence between successive socialist mass actions and the parliamentary breakthrough to universal suffrage is too striking for anyone to miss the causal connection. On the basis of published and unpublished correspondence from ruling circles one can conclude that the general strike had a genuine impact, in fact more significant than contemporary socialists themselves realized. Time after time socialist workers' protests confronted power-holders with a revolutionary threat that lay the foundation for abrupt expansion of democracy. (Deneckere, 1997, p. 384)

Thus, in Belgium, street politics and parliamentary politics came to depend on each other. Deneckere's analysis indicates that both before and during democratization, major alterations of repertoires interact with deep transformations of political power. It identifies confrontation as a spur to democratization.

However, this interaction between protest repertoires and political transformation was also powerfully gendered, since both sides of the equation affected largely male citizens. That is, the breakthrough to universal suffrage in the 1890s in fact applied only to men, just as the majority of socialist workers in the

streets were also men. Thus a masculine-dominated form of collective action spurred gendered forms of political transformation.

Evaluating the catalogs. Methodologically, the analyses of Dekker, Honacker, and Deneckere offer us both hope and caution. All three use catalogs of contentious events to gauge political trends and variations in the character of conflict. Clearly, such catalogs discipline the search for variation and change in contentious politics. But comparison of the three catalogs also establishes how sensitive such enumerations are to the definitions and sources adopted. Dekker's search of Dutch archives for events involving at least twenty people in violent encounters, regardless of issues, brings him a wide range of actions and some evidence of change, but it excludes smaller-scale and nonviolent making of claims. Honacker's combing of similar Belgian archives for collective challenges to public authorities nets her plenty of smaller-scale and nonviolent episodes but omits industrial and intergroup conflicts. Deneckere's sources and methods, in contrast, concentrate her catalog on industrial events.

None of the three choices is intrinsically superior to the others, but each makes a difference to the evidence at hand. When trying to make comparisons over time, space, and type of setting, we must make allowance for the selectivity of all such catalogs. We are, nevertheless, far better off with the catalogs than without them. The Low Countries are among the few regions where scholars have inventoried contentious events on a substantial scale before the twentieth century. France and Great Britain are two of the others. For most of the rest of Europe we must settle for pickings from general histories and for occasional specialized studies of particular localities, issues, and populations.

THEORIES OF CAUSALITY

Significant historical questions are at issue in such investigations. As figure 1 indicates, historians' descriptions and explanations of popular collective action vary significantly along two dimensions: intentionality and precipitating social processes. With respect to intentions, some authors emphasize impulse: hunger, rage, or fear. In such a view, ordinary people burst into public politics only when driven by irrepressible emotions. Other authors argue that various available agencies and programs impose consciousness on ordinary people, as when churches, political parties, or local power holders dominate popular views. More populist or radical historians commonly counter impulse and imposition accounts with the assertion that popular collective action arises from shared understandings of social situations—whether those shared understandings develop from daily experience or result in part from exposure to new ideas.

Along the dimension of precipitating social processes, historians sometimes emphasize social stress (for example, famine, epidemic, war, or geographic mobility) as the chief precipitant of popular collective action. Their investigations typically explain collective action as response to crisis. Others single out political mobilization by organizations committed to change or by local consultation within dissenting segments of the population. Their investigations center more directly on organization and consultation among aggrieved people A third group of historians treat popular collective action chiefly as an expression of group conflict. Such conflict may align class against class, but it also forms along religious, ethnic, linguistic, kinship, gender, or local cleavages. Although the third group of historians resembles the second in examining organization and consultation, they also study intergroup relations in daily contacts.

The two dimensions correlate. Where direct impulse and social stress coincide, we have historians' analyses of collective action as disorder—as temporary disruption of the political order maintained by established authorities. Imposed consciousness and political mobilization likewise pair with each other in analyses of social change, where competing movements and leaders articulate changing popular interests more or less effectively. Finally, historians who see struggle as history's motor characteristically attribute shared understandings to ordinary actors and portray group conflict as the motive force. Rarely, in contrast, do historians who consider social stress to be the chief precipitant of popular collective action also impute shared understandings—except perhaps in the form of wild beliefs—to its participants. Similarly rare are historians who explain collective action as a consequence of group conflict, yet read the consciousness of participants as unmediated impulse; the largest exception to this rule is the explanation (almost always wrong) of intergroup struggle as direct venting of age-old hatreds.

More is at stake in disputes over the description and explanation of collective action than mere differences in opinion among historians. On the whole, analyses in the disorder zone deny historical effectiveness to ordinary people; instead, they treat history as the product of great individuals, slowly changing mentalities, or impersonal forces. They also treat at-

Ordinary People. "The Headscarf Is Our Honor." Muslim women defend wearing the headscarf, Paris, October 1989. AP/WIDE WORLD

tributes of individuals (rather than, say, their social locations or their relations to other individuals) as the fundamental causes of their behavior, including their participation in collective action. Within the zone of social change, historians typically consider large-scale social processes such as secularization, urbanization, or the development of capitalism to cause a wide range of effects, including transformation of incentives and opportunities for collective action. Here reorganization of everyday social life and of politics plays a significant part in explanations of collective action. Historians who emphasize struggle commit themselves to views of individual social life as inextricably embedded in relations among individuals and groups. In classic marxist analyses the crucial relations form within the organization of production, but nonmarxist social historians have also studied relations of conflict and co-

operation based on gender, race, ethnicity, nationality, and locality.

A dwindling number of social historians treat Europe's popular collective action as the expression of direct impulses incited by social stress. Social historians have contributed significantly to moving prevailing historical explanations of popular collective action toward social change and struggle. As they have done so, they have uncovered increasing evidence of the influence of existing institutions on the form, frequency, and outcome of collective action. One significant contribution of European social historians, indeed, has been to show how extensively local institutions mediate between people's individual impulses, on one side, and collective action, on the other. Here the histories of conflict, of cooperation, and of social institutions converge.

See also other articles in this section.

BIBLIOGRAPHY

Birnbaum, Pierre. *States and Collective Action: The European Experience.* Cambridge, U.K., 1988. Lucid, energetic essays on connections between collective action and states' organization.

Blickle, Peter, ed. *Resistance, Representation, and Community.* Oxford, 1997. The bottom-up experience of state formation in early modern Europe.

Bonnell, Victoria. *Roots of Rebellion: Workers' Politics and Organizations in St. Petersburg and Moscow, 1900–1914.* Berkeley, Calif., 1983. Bonnell establishes the importance of trade unions, artisans, and skilled workers, thus increasing the similarity between Russian and western European workers' collective action.

Charlesworth, Andrew, et al., eds. *An Atlas of Industrial Protest in Britain 1750–1990.* London, 1996. Historically informed mapping of workers' collective action and strike activity.

Dekker, Rudolf. *Holland in beroering: Oproeren in de 17de en 18de Eeuw.* Baarn, Netherlands, 1982. Careful documentation of rebellious activity in Holland before 1800.

Deneckere, Gita. *Sire, het volk mort: Sociaal protest in België, 1831–1918.* Antwerp, Belgium, 1997. Similar in conception to Dekker's study, but concentrating on work-related conflicts in Belgium.

Franzosi, Roberto. *The Puzzle of Strikes: Class and State Strategies in Postwar Italy.* Cambridge, U.K., 1995. Perhaps the most successful marriage of econometric analysis and historical treatment of industrial conflict ever consummated.

Goldstone, Jack A. *Revolution and Rebellion in the Early Modern World.* Berkeley, Calif., 1991. Sweeping comparison and connection of sixteenth- to eighteenth-century revolutions, with glances forward to our own time.

Hanagan, Michael P., Leslie Page Moch, Wayne te Brake, eds. *Challenging Authority: The Historical Study of Contentious Politics.* Minneapolis, Minn., 1998. What happens when scholars take time, place, and social process seriously.

Honacker, Karin, van. *Lokaal Verzet en Oproer in de 17de en 18de Eeuw: Collectieve Acties tegen het centraal gezag in Brussel, Antwerpen, en Leuven.* Heule, Belgium, 1994. Popular collective action in cities of the southern Netherlands during the seventeenth and eighteenth century, closely documented.

Jarman, Neil. *Material Conflicts: Parades and Visual Displays in Northern Ireland.* Oxford, 1997. How competing militants have acted out their claims to priority since the seventeenth century.

Koenker, Diane P., and William G. Rosenberg. *Strikes and Revolution in Russia, 1917.* Princeton, N.J., 1989. Built around a statistical collection, the book provides a detailed history of workers' collective action during a revolutionary year.

Levi, Margaret. *Consent, Dissent, and Patriotism.* Cambridge, U.K., 1997. How senses of a regime's fairness or unfairness affect citizens' collaboration with military conscription.

Lis, Catharina, Jan Lucassen, and Hugo Soly, eds. "Before the Unions: Wage Earners and Collective Action in Europe, 1300–1850." *International Review of Social History* 39 (1994), supplement 2, entire issue. Journeymen associations, seamen's organizations, miners, and much more.

Nicolas, Jean, ed. *Mouvements populaires et conscience sociale, XVIe–XIXe siècles.* Paris, 1985. Sixty-three reports of work in progress on popular contention, mainly in France.

Olzak, Susan. "Analysis of Events in the Study of Collective Action." *Annual Review of Sociology* 15 (1989): 119–141.

Ostrom, Elinor. "A Behavioral Approach to the Rational Choice Theory of Collective Action." *American Political Science Review* 92 (1998): 1–22. Compact, if complex, introduction to general theories and methods.

Palmer, R. R. *The Age of the Democratic Revolution.* 2 vols. Princeton, N.J., 1959–1964. A classic synthesis.

Rucht, Dieter, Ruud Koopmans, Friedhelm Neidhardt, eds. *Acts of Dissent: New Developments in the Study of Protest.* Berlin, 1998. "New developments" refer especially to methodological and conceptual innovations.

Tarrow, Sidney. *Power in Movement.* 2d ed. Cambridge, U.K., 1998. Powerful synthesis of ideas and materials concerning social movements and related forms of collective contention.

te Brake, Wayne. *Regents and Rebels: The Revolutionary World of the Eighteenth-Century Dutch City.* Cambridge, Mass., 1989. Another eighteenth-century revolution, less well known than its French cousin, firmly seated on its social base.

te Brake, Wayne. *Shaping History: Ordinary People in European Politics, 1500–1700.* Berkeley, Calif., 1998. Synthetic, sweeping, smart analysis of regional and social variation.

Tilly, Charles. *Popular Contention in Great Britain, 1758–1834.* Cambridge, Mass., 1995. Analysis of social change and collective action centering on a large catalog of contentious episodes.

Traugott, Mark, ed. *Repertoires and Cycles of Collective Action.* Durham, N.C., 1995. Theoretically informed analyses, both historical and contemporary.

MORAL ECONOMY AND LUDDISM

John G. Rule

Although the concept of a moral economy has older uses, in the twentieth century historians' use of the term "moral economy" largely followed an influential article written in 1971 by the English historian Edward Thompson. In "The Moral Economy of the English Crowd in the Eighteenth Century," reprinted in *Customs in Common* (1991), Thompson sought to explain the actions of the English who rioted against high food prices. Focusing on the eighteenth and early nineteenth centuries, a time of rapid change, he presented food rioters as resisting the cold logic of the "market economy" by asserting an alternative "moral economy" based on a sense of justice and entitlement to procure food at affordable prices. The rioters appealed to a disappearing tradition of paternalist regulation of the food market by the state.

MANIFESTATIONS OF MORAL ECONOMY

Backed by a powerful sense of legitimacy, the typical food-rioting crowd indulged in premeditated, controlled behavior against what it saw as unjust, self-interested attempts to profit from food scarcities. The protesters especially targeted middlemen, who were seen as enhancing food prices by imposing themselves between the food producers and the consumers. Crowds, which often included women, took direct action in marketplaces, at fairs, or at bakers' shops by seizing food from sellers, publicly selling it themselves at a "just" price, and returning money and sacks to the sellers. They usually took wheat or barley in the form of grain, flour, or bread but sometimes took meat and cheese. Merchants who transported grain from areas where it was in short supply, in order to sell it in markets offering higher profits, especially London, were also likely to have it seized in this way. Crowds visited farmers suspected of hoarding grain while prices climbed even higher and ordered them to bring their grain to the nearest local market.

Food riots occurred in more than a dozen years between 1714 and 1815, and they continued sporadically later in the nineteenth century. They were widespread in the so-called wartime famine years of 1795–1796 and 1800–1801 (see Wells, 1988). With more than four hundred outbreaks between 1790 and 1801 alone, examples are plentiful with which to illustrate the patterns Thompson included in the moral economy. Although some changes emerged, such as the north was affected later than the south, for the most part the main characteristics of these protests endured, and the compact contemporary account of more than fifty riots in the *Annual Register* of 1766 provides models. Not many of these took place in the north, which that year had a better harvest than the south.

In Gloucestershire and Wiltshire cloth workers destroyed flour mills, taking grain and distributing it among themselves. In Exeter, another center of woolen manufacture, protesters seized cheese and sold it at a reduced price. Cornish miners forced butchers to lower meat prices, as did metalworkers at Wolverhampton. In Derby a crowd took cheese off a riverboat before it could be shipped from the town. Similarly cheese intended for transport to London was seized from a wagon. In Devon protesters seized corn from the barns of farmers, sold it openly at a market for a fair price, and returned the money and sacks to the farmers. In Malmesbury, "They seized all the corn, sold it at 5s a bushel and gave the money to the right owners." In Nottingham a crowd seized all the cheese being sold by the factors (middlemen) but, significantly, left untouched that being sold directly by the farmers.

Such rioting recurred from one place to another over wide lapses of time, a response from the popular memory when pressure situations arose. In some places the proclivity for riot was stronger than in others. For example, riots intended to stop the outward movement of corn happened at transport networks, such as seaports and inland waterways. Manufacturing and mining communities exhibited an especially robust tradition of food rioting because crowds formed easily in their dense populations and because, unlike the farming population, miners bought most of their food

Food Riot. Crowd attacking a farmer accused of hoarding grain, Devonshire, August 1800.
©THE BRITISH MUSEUM

in markets. Inhabitants of market towns felt invaded when, for instance, Cornish tin miners entered Penzance, Redruth, or Truro or when colliers from neighboring villages entered Bristol, Coventry, or Newcastle. Often anonymous letters served notice of the intention to lower food prices, like this one received by a magistrate at Norwich in 1766, "This is to latt you to know and the rest of you Justes of the Pace that if Bakers and Butchers and market peoppel if thay do not fall the Commorits at a reasnabel rate as thay do at other Markets thare will be such Raysen as never was known."

The letter's eccentric spelling hardly lessens its impact, and serious rioting did indeed follow. However, actual violence was rare, whatever threats were issued. Food rioters deliberately killed no one over the whole period, although a small number of rioters was shot by those defending their premises. John Bohstedt, in *Riots and Community Politics in England and Wales, 1790–1810* (1983) argued that food riots worked best in smaller communities, where the magistrates had authority to offer negotiation and even reciprocation rather than outright suppression. In general harsh retributory sentences were not imposed, and once order was restored magistrates often went some way toward meeting the wishes of the crowd by encouraging lower prices and initiating or participating in relief measures. Eighteenth-century crowds rioted

over food prices in part because they could expect some short-term remedy.

Thompson's article attracted significant critical response, to which he replied at length in "The Moral Economy Reviewed" (*Customs in Common,* 1991). Some objected that Thompson's moral economy implied that the defenders of the corn market, especially Adam Smith and his major discussion in *An Inquiry into the Nature and Causes of the Wealth of Nations* (1776), were immoral or at least had no moral vision about access to food. Thompson's critics pointed out that Smith in fact believed that the free operation of the market was the best defense against food shortages because it evened supply and, through the rationing effect of high prices, restrained consumption until the next harvest.

Thompson welcomed the examination by John Walter and Keith Wrightson, in their 1976 article "Dearth and the Social Order in Early Modern England," of the implementation of regulation of prices and marketing activities. The government achieved this regulation through such means as the issuing, at times of dearth, of the *Book of Orders,* first done in 1597. The book reminded justices of the peace of their powers to take action over price and supply (such actions became the objectives of the eighteenth-century crowds). The government also resorted to the prosecution of offending traders, a course of action

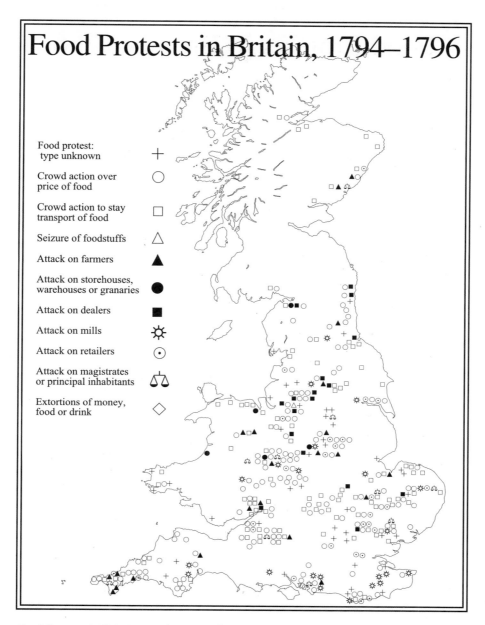

Food Protests in Britain, 1794–1796. Adapted from Andrew Charlesworth, ed., *An Atlas of Rural Protest in Britain* (Croom Helm, U.K., and Philadelphia: University of Pennsylvania Press, 1983), pages 98–99.

that had been part of the response of the authorities in the seventeenth century. This reinforced the authority of justices in times of dearth. Years of high prices were more frequent in the eighteenth century, but rioters drew a sense of a moral economy from a longer expectation of regulation, much of which was still part of the common law and statute law, although it was increasingly disregarded by government. In the popular memory a belief in regulation remained strong, and as Douglas Hay demonstrated in "The

State and the Market in 1800: Lord Kenyon and Mr. Waddington" (1999), it persisted among some of the more traditional justices.

Thompson cautiously did not extend his concept of a moral economy beyond the English experience, but to a marked extent the same essential features appeared in food protests across Europe. Indeed the British historians Richard Rose and George Rudé, who pioneered the study of food rioting in England ahead of Thompson, both first studied riots in revo-

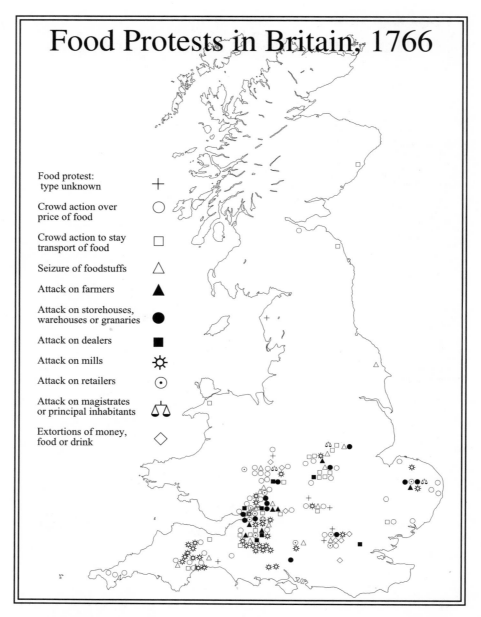

Food Protests in Britain, 1766

Food protest:
type unknown

Crowd action over
price of food

Crowd action to stay
transport of food

Seizure of foodstuffs

Attack on farmers

Attack on storehouses,
warehouses or granaries

Attack on dealers

Attack on mills

Attack on retailers

Attack on magistrates
or principal inhabitants

Extortions of money,
food or drink

Food Protests in Britain, 1766. Adapted from Andrew Charlesworth, ed., *An Atlas of Rural Protest in Britain* (Croom Helm, U.K., and Philadelphia: University of Pennsylvania Press, 1983), pages 90–91.

lutionary France. In that country, too, the government abdicated from paternalist control of the food market and came to believe in laissez-faire. This switch was especially marked under the finance minister Anne-Robert-Jacques Turgot in 1775, when disturbances around Paris were the largest of the pre-1789 period. But in 1768, an earlier dearth year, France experienced a full medley of food-rioting actions, including people seizing grain to sell at just prices, known in France as *taxation populaire*, or popular price control.

The riots of March and April 1775 were widespread and serious enough to earn the title *la guerre des farines* or the "flour war." The change of regime brought about by the Revolution did not end food riots, which continued on a considerable scale in 1789, 1792–1793, and 1795. During these years the riots were widely scattered. In the provinces, the riots for the most part targeted grain or flour, as in 1775. In Paris the main targets were meat, butter, and eggs, but even sugar, coffee, and soap became the objects

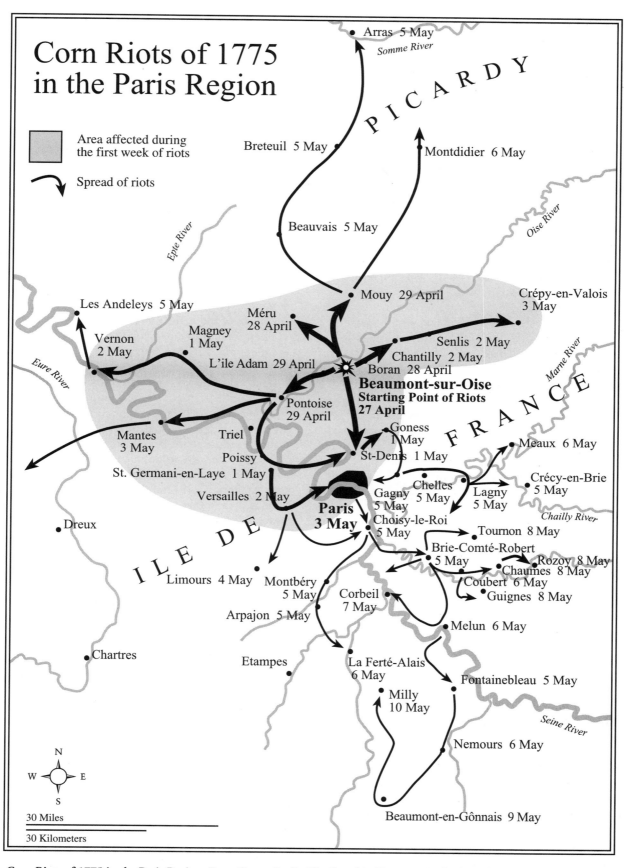

Corn Riots of 1775 in the Paris Region

Area affected during the first week of riots

Spread of riots

Arras 5 May
Somme River

PICARDY

Breteuil 5 May

Montdidier 6 May

Oise River

Beauvais 5 May

Epte River

Les Andeleys 5 May

Mouy 29 April

Crépy-en-Valois 3 May

Méru 28 April

Magney 1 May

Senlis 2 May

Vernon 2 May

L'ile Adam 29 April

Chantilly 2 May

Boran 28 April

Eure River

Beaumont-sur-Oise Starting Point of Riots 27 April

Marne River

Pontoise 29 April

FRANCE

Goness 1 May

Mantes 3 May

Triel

Meaux 6 May

St-Denis 1 May

Poissy

Chelles 5 May

Crécy-en-Brie 5 May

St. Germani-en-Laye 1 May

Lagny 5 May

Versailles 2 May

Gagny 5 May

Chailly River

Dreux

Paris 3 May

Choisy-le-Roi 5 May

Tournon 8 May

ILE DE

Brie-Comté-Robert 5 May

Rozoy 8 May

Chaumes 8 May

Limours 4 May

Montbéry 5 May

Coubert 6 May

Guignes 8 May

Corbeil 7 May

Arpajon 5 May

Melun 6 May

Chartres

La Ferté-Alais 6 May

Etampes

Fontainebleau 5 May

Milly 10 May

Seine River

Nemours 6 May

N
W   E
S

30 Miles

30 Kilometers

Beaumont-en-Gônnais 9 May

Corn Riots of 1775 in the Paris Region. From George Rudé, *The Crowd in History: A Study of Popular Disturbances in France and England, 1730–1848* (New York: John Wiley, 1964), page 25.

of riots. The crowds were as insistent on the tradition of *taxation populaire* as they had been under the ancien régime, but now protest over food prices also involved political slogans. These protests were at least partly successful in securing a short-term (fifteen months) return to the days of regulation as the Convention imposed price controls under the law of the General Maximum of 1793. After the 1790s food rioting was never again so widespread or so insistent, but the moral economy of *taxation populaire* persisted to some extent into the disturbances of 1848. Protests in the depression year of 1817 called for *taxation populaire,* as did the disturbances of 1845 through 1847, when the traditional bogeymen of corn hoarders, grain exporters, and bakers were again targeted and women led demonstrations to force sales in the markets at just prices.

In Spain the riots of 1766 followed the removal of controls over the grain trade in the previous year. Those protests expressed a sense of a just price with expectations that authorities would lower prices. But unlike in England and France, the Spanish riots were an unusual occurrence in a country where food riots remained rare. In Germany food riots against the resented commercial operations of grain dealers remained a feature of the widespread disturbances of the 1840s, when food riots in Berlin and elsewhere produced government intervention and the sale of bread and grain at reduced prices. Prussian Germany experienced two hundred food riots in 1847.

More than twenty years after his original article, Thompson remarked that, even if he did father the term "moral economy," it had come of age in historical discourse and he was no longer responsible for its actions. He had misgivings about its application away from the special moral and entitlement context of the food supply. He was uneasy, for example, about extending it generally to expectations from traditional systems of poor relief, such as the pre-1834 Old Poor Law in England. He conceded that in carefully considered contexts some actions of industrial protest could have a moral economy dimension.

In this regard Thompson approved the work of Adrian Randall, who analyzed both the food riots of 1766 and the industrial dispute of 1756 within the same woolen-working communities of Gloucestershire in "The Industrial Moral Economy of the Gloucestershire Weavers in the Eighteenth Century" (1988). Both protests were informed by the same values and displayed the same community solidarities and sanctions. Industrial protestors, like food rioters, appealed both to custom and to the regulative legislation of the labor market in Tudor and Stuart statute law. They appealed also to the authority of magistrates, seeking their intervention as conciliators and arbitrators. No firmly bedded reactionary opposition to the market economy as a whole, these disturbances reflected resistance at points where the market operations broke down or threatened to break down customary standards and expectations.

Other historians, equally influenced by Thompson's insight, have presented eighteenth-century industrial disputes as legitimized within assumptions of rights and entitlements. William Reddy in *The Rise of Market Culture* (1984), his important study of French textile workers in dispute, even suggested that "something like a moral economy is bound to surface anywhere that industrial capitalism spreads" (Reddy, p. 334), developing as much from lived experience as from traditional culture. Yet viewing any version of the moral economy as capable of generally embracing early forms of industrial protest presents problems. It implies resistance to a particular set of capitalist market operations affecting wages or employment, but not all and possibly not even most industrial disputes in eighteenth-century and early-nineteenth-century Europe were defensive. Smith, discussing English workers' strikes in 1776, recognized the existence of "offensive" strikes intended to take advantage of favorable situations in the labor market to increase wages or otherwise improve workers' conditions. In such actions allied artisans frequently employed strategies more explicable in the modern language of industrial relations than in that of an industrial moral economy. However, that not all disputes can be explained by moral economy does not mean that the concept does not apply in some measure to a significant population of conflicts at points where innovating capitalist employers were breaking down the ingrained traditions and expectations of occupational communities and trades. No more than in the food market was customary culture in the labor market the simple antithesis of market culture. The culture of the wage-dependent artisan, cloth worker, or miner presumed that the labor market was not fully free but operated under the restraints of custom and claimed rights. In short, the workers understood as "fair" a market that recruited only from those with an entitlement to a particular trade and that employed neither unskilled labor, especially female, nor machinery simply to enhance the profits of capital.

LUDDISM

In England. The best-known example of such community-based resistance is the Luddite disturbances of 1811–1813. The machine-breaking activi-

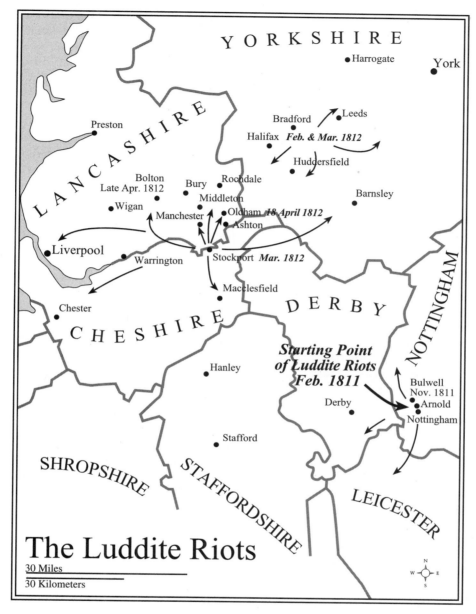

The Luddite Riots. Adapted from George Rudé, *The Crowd in History: A Study of Popular Disturbances in France and England, 1730–1848* (New York: John Wiley, 1964), page 82.

ties of workers across much of England's industrial north and Midlands seriously alarmed the government and gave a new word, "Luddism," to the language. Luddism can be linked to the moral economy in at least two ways. First, it was based on the resistance of occupational communities, where networks of kin and neighborhood interlocked with those of employment to provide a rich texture of customary expectations about ways of working and living. Second, it came at what Thompson, in *The Making of the English Working Class*, called the "crisis point in

the abrogation of paternalist legislation and in the imposition of the political economy of laissez-faire upon and against the will and conscience of the working people" (1968, p. 851).

Machine-breaking and other attacks on employers' property had a long history in the repertoire of workers' actions against employers in times of dispute. Eric Hobsbawm called this "collective bargaining by violence" (1964, p. 7) in his article "The Machine Breakers." At times the attacked machinery was seen as a grievance for bringing unemployment to skilled workers and hunger to their families. At other times machines were broken as a means of putting pressure on employers or as acts of revenge.

The English disturbances of 1811–1812, however, were without precedent in their extent and seriousness. They seemed to pose a threat not just to capitalist employers but to government itself. A prelude had succeeded in the woolen industry of the west country, the same area of manufacturing where Randall claimed to identify an industrial moral economy behind the strike of 1756. The shearmen, who cut the nap from a woven piece of cloth with heavy hand shears, a vital role in finishing cloth, had attacked the newly introduced shearing frames that threatened to displace their skill. Their action effectively deterred clothiers in that region from persisting with their innovations.

The name "Ludd" first appeared in the stocking manufactures of the East Midlands, where framework knitters produced hosiery on stocking frames. In 1811, a time of market contraction due to the war with Napoleonic France, the capitalist hosiers, who employed the framework knitters by putting-out the yarn to their homes, began a series of measures to reduce labor costs. Essentially they resorted to "colting," that is, to the employment of young unskilled labor to make stockings by the cheaper method of "squaring." Squaring is knitting on wide frames a square of cloth from which stockings were subsequently cut and sewn instead of knitted in the traditional fully fashioned way. Work was the issue, not new machinery as such. A Nottinghamshire folk song of the time, "General Ludd's Triumph," expresses the grievances of the trade and of the community in which it was enmeshed along with the determination to continue the struggle:

Till full-fashioned work at the old fashioned price
Is established by Custom and Law.
Then the Trade when this arduous contest is o'er
Shall raise in full splendour its head.
And colting and cutting and squaring no more
Shall deprive honest workmen of bread.
(Hammond and Hammond, 1979, p. 212)

At first the knitters concentrated on traditional action within the context of a paternalist state. They petitioned Parliament for an act of regulation to preserve just wages and fair employment. This produced nothing, and local magistrates refused to intervene when hosiers continued to cut wages. Attacks on knitting frames began. The framework knitters were no more indiscriminate in their targets than were the food rioters. Their attacks by night were said to be led by a mythical "Captain" or "General Ludd," whose name appeared at the bottom of a host of threatening letters. But as another verse of the ballad points out,

"His wrath is entirely confined to wide frames/and to those that old prices abate" (Hammond and Hammond, 1979, p. 212). At its most active phase in Nottinghamshire and Leicestershire, from March 1811 to February 1812, the movement destroyed one thousand wide frames in one hundred separate attacks. A worried government reacted, making machine breaking a capital offense and dispatching six thousand troops to Nottingham.

The name "Ludd" appeared elsewhere. It spread to woolen manufactures of the West Riding of Yorkshire, where shearmen, or "croppers" as they were known locally, began a series of attacks on newly introduced shearing frames. As conflict intensified, an organization formed that was capable of attacking larger mills, and lives were lost. The fears of the skilled croppers were not unfounded. By 1817 only 860 out of 3,625 croppers had full employment. Ludd also appeared in Lancashire and adjacent parts of Cheshire, where the development of cotton weaving by power looms created a machinery issue. But few manufacturers were at that time attempting power cotton weaving, and the disturbances were part of a medley of protests that included the food riots of 1812.

Luddism is not an easy phenomenon for historians to accommodate within traditional labor history. Its early historians, especially J. L. Hammond and Barbara Hammond in *The Skilled Labourer* (1927), called it a regrettable but understandably desperate response by workers who, in the face of the growing influence of the economic ideology of laissez-faire, had failed to persuade government to redress their grievances by invoking paternalist regulation. Machine breaking was the final act in the traditional craftsworkers' struggle to maintain or revive customs and laws that the new breed of capitalist employers was eager to evade. Increasingly the state seemed on the side of capital rather than labor. For the Hammonds and some others the true line of descent for the labor movement in Britain was through the "constitutionalists," who had organized the petitioning of Parliament. Without any strong evidence, they insisted that the constitutionalist movement developed parallel to but entirely separate from the direct actions of the machine breakers.

Such compartmentalization of protests works even less well for Yorkshire and Lancashire than for Nottingham. Government spies reported that the Luddites in the northern counties were moving beyond industrial protest into political action and were even linking to an underground Jacobin revolutionary movement. The Hammonds dismissed these reports as the fabrication of self-interested professional spies. In 1964 Thompson, in *The Making of the English*

Working Class, was the first modern historian to argue that the government was right to take the threat of revolution in the Luddite districts seriously.

Some historians agree that Luddism or its failure convinced at least some of the artisan population that the old regime was no longer willing to play a paternalist role and intervene to redress the balance of power between employer and worker. This view was reinforced by actions outside the Luddite areas. Calico printers, cotton workers, and others petitioned fruitlessly over working and hiring conditions. Possibly the Luddism of 1811–1813 was the last major episode of industrial protest that can be accommodated within the idea of an industrial moral economy and hold parallels to actions in the food market. Indeed in *The Question of Class Struggle* (1982) Craig Calhoun suggested that the events of 1811–1813 were in essence a "populist reaction" legitimated by the senses and beliefs of community rather than a revolutionary movement based on the concept of class conflict. The innovating capitalist was viewed less as a person exploiting labor than as a person breaching the norms of the occupational community. In fact the protest had elements of both.

The community basis of resistance to machinery was evident in earlier periods. The introduction of spinning jennies into the cotton districts, threatening the traditional cottage-based wheel spinning, led to attacks on the machinery of the inventor James Hargreaves at Blackburn as early as 1768. Much more widespread and serious were the disturbances that erupted across Lancashire in 1779, when not only the jenny but carding and roving machinery were coming into use. The most notable attack was on the factory at Chorley of the inventor and industrialist Richard Arkwright. An idea of the social justice expectations of the moral economy clearly emerges in this episode in the protesters' distinction between large jennies of twenty spindles or more, which were taking the site of yarn production from the cottage to the workshop or factory, and the smaller, hand-operated jennies, which were considered fair. Although smaller jennies displaced the wheel, they had been accommodated within the cottage economy and had offered enhanced earnings. What was fundamentally at issue was the viability of the family economy, which was the economic and moral building block of the community.

Women carried out domestic spinning, and as the ratio of spinners to weavers was 6 to 1, more women than just the wives of hand-loom weavers were employed. In addition to male and female cloth workers, colliers, nail makers, joiners, and general laborers were among the eight thousand or more who participated in the disturbances of 1779.

In France. Moral economy protests and equivalents of Luddism characterized many early industrial settings. In 1788, when the spinning jenny was introduced into the Rouen district of France, the resulting disturbances suggested the existence of an industrial moral economy. The reduction of the rates paid for hand spinning had severely lowered family earnings when food prices were beginning a rapid rise. Protestors claimed that "machines had stolen the bread." Industrial protests merged with food riots by the summer of 1789. In July a mob composed mainly of women attacked a grain store at Rouen, then attacked the workshop of an English artisan where jennies and carding machines were manufactured. After it was fired on, the angry crowd scattered the broken parts of the machinery in the same manner that food rioters sometimes scattered seized grain. In the following weeks protesters frequently attacked workshops where new jennies were in operation in Rouen, Paris, Lille, Troyes, and Roanne. Attacks continued sporadically until 1791. Another round of protests against machinery occurred after 1815, when French industrialization was gaining speed.

The machine breakers of the English north and Midlands gave a generic word to the language with revealing speed. "I have not been able to discover any symptom of 'Luddism,'" the mayor of Preston advised the government in 1816. The following year the cutlery workers from Sheffield were reported to have a "complete system of Luddism." By then the meanings had been conveyed to France, where the prefect of a woolen-manufacturing district urged that manufacturers should consult with him before introducing shearing frames, saying, "It is prudent to spare ourselves the disorders which the Luddites have committed in England." To some extent the events of 1811 and 1812 in the West Riding were repeated in the older woolen districts of France, including Sedan, Reims, Carcassonne, Lodève, and Clermont, in 1816 and 1817. A few manufacturers were introducing shearing frames and gig mills, and they expected the support of the authorities. Earlier the threat of violent protest had been a deterrent, as it had been in the west of England. In 1803 a Sedan merchant explained that the authorities would undoubtedly punish workers who resisted machinery, but "who will return to us our murdered families and burned workshops?"

The more determined introduction of shearing frames in 1816 and 1817 brought resistance from shearmen and from the woolen-working community as a whole. Women again were prominent, reportedly urging the men to be even more vigorous. According to a Vienne police report the crowd shouted "down with the shearing machine" as they removed one from

Luddite Rising. Engraving after Hablot Knight Browne. MANSELL COLLECTION/TIMEPIX

its crates and threw it into the river. Ballads expressed the same moral outrage that had legitimized English Luddism. A petition to the government accused the machinery of offering the "pernicious means of shearing, glossing and brushing 1000 ells of cloth, while being directed by only four men." It was an "evil" that would destroy and divide the community because it would be "beneficial only to the owners." The prefect of Hérault, while recognizing his duty to suppress riots and protect manufacturers' property, called the machines "an inevitable and almost irreparable evil." Whether as part of a strategy or as a persistence of belief in the old moral, regulated economy of the ancien régime, the protestors appealed to the recently restored king, hoping, "If he knew this machine would reduce many of us to begging he would not let it be introduced."

The episodes of 1816–1817 involving shearmen and established woolen centers are the closest parallels in French labor history to English Luddism. However, attacks on machinery remained endemic if sporadic in France for another three decades, whereas in Britain, with the noted but idiosyncratic exception of the attacks on threshing machines in the name of "Captain Swing" by the agricultural laborers throughout southern England in 1830–1831, machine breaking did not pose a significant threat in the years after 1820. The slower pace and different character of industrial change in France allowed both artisan attitudes and domestic manufacturing to persist longer, underpinning notions of traditional entitlements to work and to bread.

From the episodes of 1816–1817 to the Revolution of 1848, more than one hundred major incidents of Luddism were recorded, with distinct peaks at times of high food prices and political upheaval, such as 1828–1833 and 1846–1848. Both urban and rural workers were involved. As well as serious food rioting, for example, Paris in 1830 and 1831 experienced Luddite-type actions among female shawl workers and tobacco workers as well as an attack on printing machines at the government's Royal Print workshops. In 1830 around two thousand cutlers were involved in destructive disturbances in Saint-Étienne, as were other workers in Toulouse and Bordeaux. In the period of the political and hunger crises of 1848 silkworkers and tobacco makers attacked machinery in Lyons. River boatmen attacked steamships in Lyons, while at Rouen they damaged railway lines.

In Germany. Such early forms of industrial protest persisted at least as long in Germany, although frequency there was affected by the fact that German states were policed more effectively and determinedly. Traditions went back to the early modern period with attacks on ribbon mills by embittered laceworkers.

214

Cloth Shearing. From *The Costume of Yorkshire* by George Walker (1814).

Other Luddite outbreaks included those of the metalworkers of Solingen in 1826, the silk weavers of Krefeld in 1827, Saxon weavers and Leipzig printers in the 1830s, and most serious and best-known, the linen weavers of Silesia in 1844. During 1848, the "year of revolutions," Germany had episodes with textile workers, as did Italy, especially in Campania.

In *The Rebellious Century* (1975), Charles Tilly, Louise Tilly, and Richard Tilly argued that food rioting, machine breaking, and the protection of rights over woodlands or commons belong to a "reactive" era of European popular protest due—after the mid-nineteenth century, or two decades earlier in Britain—to give way to a "proactive" modern era of organized trade unions and political movements ready to negotiate in different ways with the power of the state. How far notions of moral economy assist in understanding a transitional stage associated with resisting the increasing encroachments of capitalism is debatable. What is clear is that, wherever groups feel traditional entitlements, whether to food or to the right to work as a resource controlled by the members of a particular trade or community, they inevitably legitimized their protests in moral terms. Usually those terms pose at least some measure of opposition to the workings and rhetoric of the "market." It is far too easy to offer the moral economy as a simple antithesis of the market economy, but to a significant extent the former only has meaning when considered against the growth of the latter.

See also **Modernization; Technology; The Industrial Revolutions** *(volume 2); and other articles in this section.*

BIBLIOGRAPHY

Bohstedt, John. *Riots and Community Politics in England and Wales, 1790–1810.* Cambridge, Mass., 1983.

Calhoun, Craig. *The Question of Class Struggle: Social Foundations of Popular Radicalism during the Industrial Revolution.* Chicago, 1982.

Hammond, J. L., and Barbara Hammond. *The Skilled Labourer, 1760–1832.* London, 1927. Reprint, with new introduction, London, 1979.

Hay, Douglas. "The State and the Market in 1800: Lord Kenyon and Mr Waddington." *Past and Present* 162 (February 1999): 101–160.

Hobsbawm, E. J. "The Machine-Breakers." In *Labouring Men*. London, 1964. Pages 5–17.

Magraw, Roger. *A History of the French Working Class*. Vol. 1: *The Age of Artisan Revolution, 1815–1871*. Oxford, 1992.

Randall, Adrian. "The Industrial Moral Economy of the Gloucestershire Weavers in the Eighteenth Century." In *British Trade Unionism, 1750–1850: The Formative Years*. Edited by John Rule. London, 1988. Pages 29–51.

Reddy, William M. *The Rise of Market Culture: The Textile Trade and French Society, 1750–1900*. Cambridge, U.K., 1984.

Rodriguez, Laura. "The Spanish Riots of 1766." *Past and Present* 59 (May 1973): 117–146.

Rose, Richard B. "18th-Century Price Riots, the French Revolution, and the Jacobin Maximum." *International Review of Social History* 3 (1959): 432–445.

Rose, Richard B. "Eighteenth-Century Price Riots and Public Policy in England." *International Review of Social History* 6 (1961): 277–292.

Rudé, George. *The Crowd in History, 1730–1848*. New York, 1964.

Stearns, Peter N., ed. *The Impact of the Industrial Revolution: Protest and Alienation*. Englewood Cliffs, N.J., 1972.

Stevenson, John. *Popular Disturbances in England, 1700–1832*. London, 1992.

Thomis, Malcolm I. *The Luddites: Machine-Breaking in Regency England*. Newton Abbot, U.K., 1970.

Thompson, E. P. *The Making of the English Working Class*. 1964. Reprint, Harmondsworth, U.K., 1968.

Thompson, E. P. "The Moral Economy of the English Crowd in the Eighteenth Century." *Past and Present* 50 (February 1971): 76–136. Reprinted in *Customs in Common*. London, 1991. Pages 185–258. Thompson's lengthy response to his critics, "The Moral Economy Reviewed," appears on pages 259–351.

Tilly, Charles, Louise Tilly, and Richard Tilly. *The Rebellious Century, 1830–1930*. Cambridge, Mass., 1975.

Walter, John, and Keith Wrightson. "Dearth and the Social Order in Early Modern England." *Past and Present* 71 (May 1976): 22–42.

Wells, Roger. *Wretched Faces: Famine in Wartime England, 1793–1801*. New York, 1988.

URBAN CROWDS

Michael P. Hanagan

Urban crowds comprise a large number and great variety of human social interactions. A broad survey of European history reveals that crowd behavior has been shaped by transformations of the state system, the character of urbanization, and the composition of urban populations. Urban crowds have been one of the oldest objects of social analysis. Generally theorists have condemned the crowd as prone to irrationality and violence, although this view has never gone unchallenged.

THEORIES OF CROWD BEHAVIOR

The dominant classical view, based on philosophers such as Plato and the historical accounts of Tacitus and Procopius, portrayed the crowd as an unthinking mob. Almost all the conceptions of crowd behavior articulated by nineteenth-century crowd theorists can be found in Tacitus's analysis of the Roman mob. In the late 1880s the conservative historian Hippolyte Taine's monumental history of contemporary France (*Origines de la France contemporaine;* Origins of contemporary France) drew the attention of the developing social sciences to crowd phenomena. Appalled by the Paris Commune of 1871, Taine delighted in presenting the gruesome details of crowd atrocities during the French Revolution and argued that such behavior was endemic in democracies. Within a decade, the French sociologist Gustave Le Bon had ransacked the writings of a host of innovative predecessors to create the field of "crowd psychology." Le Bon listed three characteristics of crowd behavior: a psychic unity giving the crowd a sense of almost unlimited power, a collective mentality yielding suddenly to powerful emotional appeals, and a very low level of intelligence sinking to the level of the lowest common denominator of its participants. While urban crowds were Le Bon's prime example of crowd behavior, he believed his principles applied to all human assemblies from juries to legislatures. In 1960 Elias Canetti attempted a reconstruction of this intellectual tradition by emphasizing the crowd's transcendence of individualism, but Canetti's ignorance of historical context and penchant for facile generalization limited his influence in the contemporary reshaping of theories of crowd behavior.

A more favorable view of crowd activity originated in the Renaissance in Niccolò Machiavelli's *Discourses on the First Ten Books of Titus Livy.* Machiavelli portrayed the uncorrupted Roman crowd as the last repository of civic virtue and the only recourse against tyrants and a degraded aristocracy. His views influenced Montesquieu, who celebrated the English crowd's role in maintaining that country's mixed constitution. In the nineteenth century, the great French historian Jules Michelet was a foremost exponent of the Machiavellian view. Posing the rhetorical question of who participated in the siege of the Bastille, Michelet responded, "The people, the whole people."

Only in the twentieth century did historians and sociologists such as George Rudé and E. P. Thompson introduce a new perspective on crowd behavior based on the actual study of crowds, primarily in turn-of-the-eighteenth-century England and France. The result was a striking early achievement of the "new" social history. Uncovering a variety of records about the individual identity of crowd participants, Rudé examined the composition of protesting crowds, while Thompson concentrated on crowd demands and their social context. Their investigations challenged images of the crowd as primal and irrational and also the view of the crowd as the collective conscience of an entire society; instead they portrayed protesting crowds as composed of relatively better-off members of popular communities responding to specific threats to their communities and acting according to widely shared popular cultural assumptions. Sociologists studying contemporary crowds have also challenged some of the basic postulates of earlier crowd theorists. Questioning images of the "lonely crowd," Clark McPhail has shown that crowds are not generally composed of isolated, atomistic individuals subject to the manipulation of talented orators; rather,

Claim-Making Crowd. A demonstration of students in Petrograd, October 1917. ©HULTON GETTY/LIAISON AGENCY

small groups of friends generally join together in the formation of crowds. Small group ties persist within crowds and condition an individual's response to speakers and the actions of other crowd components.

THE CROWD IN HISTORY

Begun by Rudé and Thompson, the study of historical crowds became an important theme of historical analysis, and works at the end of the twentieth century have enabled historians to discover secular patterns in crowd behavior. For a survey of some of the findings of crowd historians, a few definitions are helpful. An "urban crowd" refers to a number of people, say ten or more, who are not part of government, assembled for some common purpose in a publicly accessible place within a densely settled site of three thousand or more inhabitants. The three chief types of crowds are extrinsic, claim-making, and commemorative. "Extrinsic crowds" are the unintended but inevitable consequence of time- and space-restricted services, usually connected with commerce, entertainment, or routine religious observance. Crowds thronging to markets, fairs, or balloon ascensions are examples, as are concert audiences and attendees at Sunday religious services. With an extrinsic crowd the services in question could be provided privately without serious decline in the value of the services. Thus, in the nineteenth century the replacement of open stalls by private shops lessened the crowd character of many grow-

ing market towns without affecting the fundamental purpose of commercial exchange. A Catholic mass retains its full meaning with only the celebrant present.

In contrast, numbers are necessary to claim-making and commemorative crowds, and poor attendance amounts to failure of the claim. "Claim-making crowds" make claims on at least one person outside their own number, claims that if realized would affect the interests of their object. Claim-making crowds have taken many different forms. At one time or another, the seizure of grain, cessation of work, pulling down of houses, mass demonstrations, invasions of common land, rough music, and naval mutinies were all recognized forms of claim making. Recognizing a claim-making process required familiarity with the social and cultural context on the part of both claim makers and the objects of their claims. When employers first saw most of their workers withdraw in concert from work, often leaving unfinished material to ruin in stilled machines and, subsequently, marching around factory gates with signs, shouting insulting names at loyal workmen, these actions struck many of them as personal betrayal, criminal disruption, or attempted extortion. Only in time did the "strike" become a recognized form of claim making, with laws distinguishing legal from illegal actions and with both employers and workers carefully scrutinizing each other's behavior to distinguish routine from nonroutine behavior in order to gauge relative strength or weakness.

"Commemorative crowds" pay tribute, witness events, or assert an identity openly. Examples are sports rallies, religious revival meetings, and coronation processions. Because the political purposes of commemorative crowds are not always explicitly stated and the intentions of their organizers may differ considerably from the mass of participants, they deserve special attention. Commemorative crowds often demonstrate the extent of support for a particular identity and may implicitly support political claims; insofar as it discusses commemorative crowds, this essay deals with implicitly claim-making commemorative crowds.

The ritual actions of commemorative crowds and authorities' attitudes toward them may implicitly express claims more effectively than explicit claim making. In Northern Ireland in the 1990s, sectarian Protestant determination to preserve a "Protestant state for a Protestant people" was asserted publicly through parades commemorating battles such as those of the Boyne (1690) and the Somme (1916) and Protestant holidays such as Reformation Day. To demonstrate their predominance, hard-core Protestants insisted on their right to march through both Protestant and Catholic communities, and Northern Irish authorities generally supported their claims. Meanwhile Catholics, who emulated the Protestants in the use of parading, were allowed to celebrate such holidays as St. Patrick's Day and the anniversary of the Easter Rebellion (1916) by marching only through Catholic areas. In an effort to resolve the conflict resulting from Catholic resistance to Protestant parades through their neighborhoods, British politicians attempted to work out impartial procedures for granting parade permits. In turn, this led to confrontations between political authorities and sectarian Protestants who opposed both the limitations on their parading and, much more important, the concept of a nonsectarian political administration in Northern Ireland.

As in the case of Northern Irish parades, a clear line cannot always be drawn between various categories of crowds. Until the nineteenth century, almost all claim-making crowds emerged from extrinsic and commemorative crowds. Market days, fairs, Sunday church, processions, and carnivals were the only legitimate public assemblies and offered the best opportunities for the development of claim-making crowds. In early modern European marketplaces, Monday was often a favorite day for bread or grain riots. Grievances were discussed and participation pledged after Sunday church services that brought together community members; the actions were carried out the next day, which many urban workers took off or on which they worked irregularly.

From 1500 on, population growth combined with urbanization increased both the average size and frequency of extrinsic urban crowds. Nineteenth-century social theorists proclaimed their own time as preeminently the "age of the crowd" and insisted that the crowd was becoming the dominant force in modern society. Yet such claims cannot be sustained, for in fact crowds played an important political role at almost all stages of European history after 1500.

Perhaps the single most important factor affecting the character of claim-making crowds was the nature of the political regime. Since commemorative and claim-making crowds are significantly shaped by state transformation, this essay examines their characteristic features in the era of composite monarchies, sovereign states, and consolidated states. It also looks at how changes in urban population and its distribution caused by commercialization and industrialization affected the character of crowds.

COMPOSITE MONARCHIES AND CROWDS

In 1500 composite monarchies dominated Europe. These were cobbled-together unions of previously separate political units that retained the important political institutions of preceding regimes and were typically territorially dispersed. Fragmented sovereignty and overlapping jurisdictions were characteristic features of composite monarchies. The claims to legitimacy on the part of the central authority were frequently weighed against the competing claims of regional or local authorities, and small territorial units often strengthened their positions by playing off the rival claims of king and emperor.

Already by 1500 the European state system was characterized by permanent military competition, and military success was strongly affected by economic development; money fueled western European war machines, and the search for money inevitably brought tax collectors and royal financial agents to town. In the sixteenth century, towns in western Germany, northern Italy, the Netherlands, and the Baltic used their financial power to mobilize troops and maintain a large degree of independence from the territorially large but capital-poor states surrounding them. The autonomous power of many cities combined with conflicts among rival polities about their respective rights led to the emergence of political spaces for direct negotiations between authorities and crowds. These spaces tended to disappear with the rise of the sovereign state in the seventeenth and eighteenth centuries, but were revived and expanded with the growth

Commemorative Crowd. Crowds gather in Budapest to hear the proclamation of the Hungarian republic, 23 October 1989. AP/WIDE WORLD PHOTOS

of consolidated states in the nineteenth and twentieth centuries.

In the era of composite monarchies, the distinctive features of claim-making crowds, both commemorative crowds with implicit claims and explicitly claim-making crowds, were their origin in non-claim-making crowds combined with their ability to negotiate directly with rulers or to take independent authoritative action.

For a look at a commemorative crowd, Mardi Gras 1580 in the Dauphiné region of southeastern France, as described by Le Roy Ladurie in *Carnival in Romans* (1979), offers a representative case. At the

time France was in the midst of its seventh religious war since the accession in 1560 of ten-year-old Charles IX under the regency of his grasping mother, Catherine de Médicis. In the chaos produced by the confrontation between Catholics and Protestants, normally quiescent popular forces organized to influence power. In the Dauphiné peasant leagues mobilized to protest unjust taxation, and in the city of Romans, urban artisans challenged the oligarchical elites' monopoly of urban political power and also protested the incidence of urban taxation. The monarchy's preoccupation with the religious wars forced local elites to act directly on their own behalf; to reassure the king about the propriety of their own actions, they exaggerated the Protestant ties of their artisanal enemies. Elites used the Mardi Gras crowd to articulate a response to popular demands. Mardi Gras provided a public forum for assembling their party, expressing their concerns, and declaring their intentions. Antoine Guérin, royal judge and political boss, organized the celebrations; by means of parade floats and dramatic performances, he expressed the elite's hostility to rebellious artisans, their fear of artisan cooperation with rebellious peasants and local Protestants, and their determination to use violence against the insubordinate artisans. Toward the end of Mardi Gras, the elites called on their henchmen to put into practice the murderous intentions expressed initially in carnival.

Turning from western Europe in the midst of religious wars, one finds a good example of a claim-making crowd in eastern Europe and the Baltic region in the period immediately after the Thirty Years' War. Although the situation of divided allegiances that marked Mardi Gras in Romans represented a thirty-five-year break in the continuity of the French monarchies' drive toward centralized power, dual allegiance was a permanent condition in the independent city-state of Reval (modern Tallinn) in the second half of the seventeenth century. In terms of everyday politics, a mercantile oligarchy ruled the city but recognized the Swedish king's overlordship. Oligarchical rule was far from absolute. Public petitions presented to the city council were the normal method for presenting artisanal demands, and artisans had real bargaining power. City rulers generally depended on the urban population to enforce the law, and adult males often possessed arms as members of the city militia. Artisanal petitions were seriously considered and rejected only when they conflicted with the interests of the merchant oligarchs, which they often did. Merchants were willing to loosen or remove restrictions on the entry of nonguild, migrant workers to the urban market, a move that would make the goods that merchants sold cheaper by reducing the cost of labor. Serious divisions arose due to the merchants' stance, and artisans rioted. In 1662 a group of artisans attacked twenty soldiers that the city council had brought in to repress such riots. Artisans also appealed to the Swedish king, who, in response, made concessions to them as a way of retaining popular support in the distant city.

Together, the commemorative Mardi Gras crowd in Romans and the claim-making artisans in Reval capture essential features of crowd action in the composite monarchies of early modern Europe. Claim-making crowds generally emerged only from extrinsic or commemorative crowds, and the conditions of their emergence powerfully shaped the character of their claims. Claim-making crowds frequently employed violence. Mardi Gras parodies hardly encouraged compromise, and petitioning often assumed the character of an ultimatum because it was unconnected with the give and take of daily political interaction.

The dual sovereignty of Reval, with an urban oligarchy close at hand and a distant but powerful Swedish king, represented a very common feature of European urban life; in such situations, crowds were able to manipulate competing sovereignties. The diversity of structures and the fragmentation of sovereignty within composite monarchies allowed for the creation of "political spaces" in which popular crowds could actually negotiate with authorities and extract political concessions; but the possibility of popular political power contained a threat that might move elites to respond with terrible violence, as evidenced by the incidents in Romans. Even in France, local elites' control of the most powerful administrative positions allowed them a great deal of room for independent maneuver, especially when the monarch was occupied elsewhere. While the conditions for the emergence of claim making did not promote compromise or conciliation, the political context for claim-making crowds provided favorable opportunities for concessions; these contradictory situations often resulted in violence and, in the long term, created pressures for the limitation of popular claim making.

SOVEREIGN STATES AND CROWDS

Under the pressure of war, conflicting claims to sovereignty were resolved by the emergence of sovereign states, mainly constitutional or autocratic monarchies but also confederations and independent city-states. In these states, sovereignty tended to be concentrated in a single geographic and institutional location, although the central power continued to operate through a variety of intermediary institutions, autonomous municipal councils, freewheeling legal institutions, and quasi-independent clerical establishments that all acknowledged the central power's ultimate dominance but still possessed a great deal of decision-making leeway. Major political thinkers of the period such as Jean Bodin and Thomas Hobbes championed the view that sovereignty should be located unambiguously in a single institution, preferably a monarchy. Their insistence that sovereignty could not be divided, however, was easily refuted by a simple survey of the contemporary European state system. Thus their views were not so much assessments of what existed as the founding propositions of the ascendant sovereign state.

As composite monarchies collapsed, the formation of the Dutch republic and the Swiss confederation represented the triumph of confederations of independent cities and small autonomous regions. But if cities dominated the Dutch and Swiss territory, territorial states dominated cities in England and France. Ultimately, territorial states proved more successful in mobilizing troops than were city-states or confederations. Although they succeeded in dominating cities, however, English and French monarchs also had to come to terms with urban financial elites. The power of these elites grew as an expanded international trade linked urban consumers to colonial markets and encouraged the growth of urban networks linking cities throughout states.

The development of networks of cities in western Europe provided a dramatic contrast with eastern Europe, where cities were few and urban elites weak both politically and financially. The weak commercialization of the eastern European countryside and the orientation of eastern European landlords toward selling their grain directly on international markets gave eastern European urban elites much less of a commercial role and consequently much less bargaining power than their western European counterparts. The military monarchies that emerged in the area depended on the forced recruitment of serf labor, not on paid mercenaries or conscripts; lacking wealthy urban bankers, these monarchs depended on coercion. The annexation of Reval in 1710 by Peter the Great ended that city's dual sovereignty and lessened the opportunities for independent crowds. In England and France commercial ties and financial concerns tightly connected cities, and channels of communication that served commerce could also effectively transmit political information throughout the nation and indeed throughout all western Europe.

In the era of sovereign states, commemorative and claim-making crowds changed in important ways. Claim-making crowds were less likely to negotiate directly with rulers; instead they allied with or sought to enlist powerful intermediaries who might intervene on their behalf. Crowd action typically focused on remedying immediate grievances and often employed violence, but having carried out their actions, crowds typically appealed humbly to powerful local figures to confirm their actions.

Harris's study, *London Crowds* (1987), presents a splendid example of a commemorative crowd used in implicitly claim-making ways. He studies attempts to rally support for and against the Exclusion Bill, a proposal to deny the royal succession to the Catholic

duke of York, later James II. In November 1680, on a day celebrating the accession of Elizabeth I, a London crowd, supported by a Whig club, carried an effigy of the pope seated in his chair of state through the City. At Temple Bar the effigy was burned on a giant bonfire. Urban crowds were able to carry out such symbolic actions because urban policing largely rested with part-time, unpaid local officers, constables, beadles, and watchmen, who served in rotation. In theory these officers were property holders, but some hired replacements. As a result many local officers represented the poorer rather than the richer urban population. In an emergency these officers were entitled to call on any passerby for support. If worse come to worst, six regiments of trained men could be called on; in practice, however, it was impossible to coopt passersby to repress a procession with which they sympathized, and even the regiments' loyalty was far from totally reliable. In the weavers' riot of 1675, some regiments even seem to have gone over to the weavers.

Although urban crowds acknowledged the monarch's sovereignty, they still reserved the right to express their opinion. But the issues at stake were no longer demands that could be settled directly by negotiations between crowds and rulers; the fate of the Exclusion Bill proposed in Parliament depended on divisions within the English elite. While crowds could not exert their influence directly, crowd opinion still represented a legitimate expression of opinion as acknowledged even by its opponents. The Tory response to Whig efforts to mobilize crowds against the duke of York was to mobilize crowds in his favor. A variety of crowds and popular political perspectives existed in the City of London. While many in London were disappointed by the restored Stuart monarchy's failure to reduce taxes, the London population was not notably sympathetic to religious sectarians. As the government tightened its grip on the government of the City of London, Tory crowds mobilized. In 1681 at Westminster, a crowd organized by the scholars at St. Peter College dressed up and burned "Jack Presbyter" in effigy.

In 1795 in Exeter, Devonshire, an English claim-making crowd can be seen in action as described in Bohstedt's *Riots and Community Politics* (1983). On market day forty or fifty people assembled and forced a farmer to sell wheat and potatoes considerably below market price. Two days later, at the next market day, the crowd reappeared to seize wheat and potatoes; but this time the mayor intervened, and under his auspices the commodities were sold at compromise prices somewhere between their market price and that set by the previous crowd. In the same region, other crowds

Food Riots. Bread riot, London, 1830. From *The Looking Glass.* By PERMISSION OF THE BRITISH LIBRARY

mobilized during this period and events like those in Exeter were repeated.

Bohstedt's study locates the Devonshire crowd in the larger framework of English popular protest and reminds us that crowd action depended on far more than a shared sense of popular grievances—it hinged as well upon the existence of social and political structures that facilitated popular mobilization. Bohstedt shows that southwest England was the favored location for such food riots. The area was heavily commercialized and was the major supplier for the English fleet. Thus, at a time when food prices were rising, the inhabitants of the area's small towns, who purchased their food in the markets, witnessed large food convoys supplying the fleet. More important, the prosperity of the small-town economy of the area was a product of a population of prosperous farmers who served as an intermediate social layer between day laborers and artisans and the great landlords who leased land to the farmers and controlled the local administration. Food riots presented an opportunity for landlord officials, the mayor, or the justice of the peace to intervene and secure local popularity by championing the people against gouging farmers and urban traders. Such tactics depended crucially on the presence of an urban economy and of middle-class buffers between great landlord and landless laborer. In the

Yorkshire countryside dominated by villages and lacking strong intermediary classes, landlord justices of the peace could not condone food riots because such actions would directly challenge their rule. Accordingly, repression of riots was fierce, and agrarian discontent was liable to manifest itself in anonymous letters rather than food riots.

While rulers increased their control over territorial states, crowds were confined to the margins of state politics. In the era of composite monarchies crowds could find political space to bargain directly with authorities; in the era of the sovereign state such possibilities dwindled. As in London, the closest a crowd could come to challenging politically the central authorities was in the great capital cities, the seats of centralized sovereign power, but even here the challenge was indirect, confined to demonstrations of implied approval or disapproval, and strongly influenced by powerful elites.

Although the relationship between crowds and central authorities had become attenuated, crowds still played an important role in local politics where political authorities yet possessed considerable leeway to respond independently to crowd demands. In Europe and the Americas, much protest involved attempts to take on-the-spot action to put right a perceived violation of popular morality; violence was

223

often an implicit or explicit element in such actions. Hungry urban crowds invaded bakeries to sell bread at a just price. Crowds protesting tolls destroyed tollgates. Unpopular administrative actions resulted in attacks on administrators. Protest was typically bifurcated, with vigorous popular action at the local level combined with humble appeals to higher authorities to support crowd actions. At the local level crowds acted militantly, but the crowd's political role was usually restricted to local struggles for traditional rights; crowds were seldom in a position to raise completely new demands or to seek the incorporation of their demands into the law.

CONSOLIDATED STATES AND CROWDS

Finally, after 1700 consolidated states developed that were territorially continuous, centralized, and differentiated and that monopolized coercion within their borders. These enjoyed a new and more direct relationship with their populations. The consolidated state abolished intermediary institutions and governed directly through its own officials. Initially, the consolidated state came into the daily life of ordinary Europeans in the form of the tax collector and the recruiting officer, but it slowly established itself as educator, health officer, and caretaker. In return for the increasingly heavy burden of taxation and conscription, the state conferred citizenship on its population and bestowed a whole series of new rights as well as a new sense of national identity. As states expanded their fiscal demands and widened conscription, citizens in turn demanded expansion of their rights. Among the most important rights that citizens demanded was the expansion of suffrage.

Meanwhile the character of cities was changing; industrialization created new cities and transformed the artisanal and commercial core of many old ones. A casual proletarian labor force emerged, permanently settled in the city. This growing proletarian labor force lacked both the personal and collective resources of the artisan; they often did not even own their tools and lacked guild organizations. While artisanal protest dominated most of the period under consideration, the problems of urban proletarians came to the fore in the twentieth century.

Consolidated states affected profoundly the character of commemorative and claim-making crowds. Unlike the crowds previously discussed, crowds within consolidated states were able to constitute themselves and to take action on their own initiative. They had considerable freedom to select the conditions under which they would mobilize and an increased ability to select their tactics. They also were able to make demands directly on those in power. At the same time, crowds were less likely to be able to act autonomously, and their actions were limited by the political parties and formal organizations that were often instrumental in organizing them.

May Day represents an important example of the commemorative crowd in the era of the consolidated state. In 1889 the founding meeting of the International Socialist Congress in Paris set the date as an international labor day. Like so many of the affairs of the "International," May Day celebrations were organized at the national level by national political organizations. The earliest May Day celebrations also involved claim-making crowds, as formal demands for the eight-hour day and other socialist reforms figured heavily in the celebration. Strikes for an eight-hour day often were launched on 1 May and settled in the days and weeks following. Legal enactments in the wake of World War I made the eight-hour day a reality in many countries. Long after their original demands had been won, however, labor organizations and socialist parties continued to organize massive demonstrations on 1 May to demonstrate working-class strength. So powerful had May Day become in popular consciousness that rivals of the socialist movement sought to coopt it. The Catholic Church proclaimed 1 May the Feast of St. Joseph the Worker, and in Germany the Nazi regime proclaimed it National Labor Day to encourage the incorporation of workers into their own ranks.

Strikes and demonstrations are the best examples of claim-making crowds in the era of the consolidated state. In August 1969 Italy was on the eve of its "hot autumn" of massive working-class upheavals. As analyzed in Tarrow's study, *Democracy and Disorder* (1989), production workers in the industrial zone of Mestre, Venice's link to the mainland, went on strike against the petrochemical giant Montedison. They demanded reorganization of the company's incentive plan and an equal pay increase for all grades of workers. Students joined workers on the picket line to demonstrate their support. New tactics were introduced: workers struck every second day, thus avoiding a loss of pay, but at the same time totally disrupting the plant's integrated functioning. When the company finally resorted to a lockout, a huge column of workers and students occupied the train tracks and the station, proclaimed a general strike, and announced their intention of closing off railway access to Venice. Within a day the company settled the strike with a generous across-the-board pay increase.

May Day crowds in France and the petrochemical strikes in Venice illustrate the new features of

The Army and Crowd Control. Troops storming a barricade in the Döngesgasse in Frankfurt on 18 September 1848. Wood engraving from a contemporary German newspaper. THE GRANGER COLLECTION

crowd activity in the era of the consolidated state. Tilly has labeled the characteristic features of modern protest as autonomous, cosmopolitan, and modular. Neither May Day parades nor strikes typically originated in extrinsic crowd celebrations or in commemorative crowds formed for other purposes, but rather were autonomous protests in that the protesters took the initiative in setting the time and place of their action. The form of the protest was also different from that of earlier crowds. Both May Day and the strike were cosmopolitan forms of claim making in that their participants regularly exceeded a single locality. In the form of general strikes, the protest form could extend through an entire nation, and the range of the May Day parades was international. Both strikes and May Day parades were also "modular" forms of protest in that they could represent a variety of kinds of claims. Where grain riots were almost inevitably associated with a rise in bread prices, the new forms of protest could be used to demand extensions of the suffrage or an end to imperial rule in European colonies, as well as to demand higher wages and the eight-hour day. Indeed, one of the first challenges faced by authorities and trade union leaders confronted with the French general strike of May–June

1968 was to find out exactly what it was the workers wanted.

A key element of both May Day parades and strikes that distinguishes them from previous manifestations of crowds was the presence of an organized police force. No longer relying on unpaid watchmen recruited from the population to enforce the law, states instead hired professionals who began to develop tactics of crowd control. Police having become the urban authorities charged with handling crowds, policing profoundly affected the character of crowd activity. The difference can be seen partly in the official responses to the revolutions of 1848 and to the mass protests of 1919–1921. In 1848 most European cities lacked a large professional police force. When large crowds gathered demanding reform, the only force large enough to respond was the army. Unfortunately, armies were not trained in crowd control. Shoot or do nothing were pretty much the options available to them. Almost always, the soldiers shot, and the resulting deaths produced the revolution's first martyrs as well as the proximate cause for building barricades. Police handling of general strikes and mass demonstrations in 1919–1921 was often brutal, but in western Europe it lacked the murderous violence of 1848 and helped to prevent revolutionary situations from becoming actual revolutions.

If claim-making crowds gained enormous freedoms within consolidated states, they were also constrained in entirely new ways. Increasingly, formal organizations served to coordinate crowd protests and to formulate collective demands. Legally recognized trade unions, social movements, and socialist parties often possessed independent connections to power that helped to protect crowds from threats of police brutality; yet crowds also lost a great deal of freedom to articulate their own demands. More and more, crowds served as the mute witness for the popularity of claims formulated by others. The negotiations between the political leaders standing on the balconies of city halls and the crowds assembled below—either roaring their approval or bellowing dismissal, as was characteristic of 1848—was replaced by disciplined demonstrations, previously coordinated between formal organizations and police authorities and limited in their political expression to slogans and posters preapproved by sponsoring formal organizations. Insofar as claim-making crowds continue to play an important role in modern politics, they are relatively domesticated crowds, quite different from those of Reval in 1662 or Paris in 1848. Having acquired new rights vis-à-vis the state, crowds have increasingly been subordinated to the purposes of formal organizations.

Every European age has been the age of the crowd. Over five centuries, crowds have played an important role in European history; it is only their structure and orientation that have changed.

See also **Absolutism** *(volume 2);* **Festivals** *(volume 5);* **Police** *(in this volume); and other articles in this section.*

BIBLIOGRAPHY

Barrows, Susanna. *Distorting Mirrors: Visions of the Crowd in Late Nineteenth-Century France.* New Haven, Conn., 1981.

Bohstedt, John. *Riots and Community Politics in England and Wales, 1790–1810.* Cambridge, Mass., 1983.

Canetti, Elias. *Crowds and Power.* Translated by Carol Stewart. London, 1973. Reprint, New York, 1998.

Favre, Pierre. *La Manifestation.* Paris, 1990.

Harris, Tim. *London Crowds in the Reign of Charles II: Propaganda and Politics from the Restoration until the Exclusion Crisis.* Cambridge, U.K., 1987.

Harrison, Mark. *Crowds and History: Mass Phenomena in English Towns, 1790–1835.* Cambridge, U.K., 1988.

Le Roy Ladurie, Emmanuel. *Carnival in Romans.* Translated by Mary Feeney. New York, 1979.

McClelland, J. S. *The Crowd and the Mob: From Plato to Canetti.* London, 1989.

McPhail, Clark. *The Myth of the Madding Crowd.* New York, 1984.

Ozouf, Mona. *Festivals and the French Revolution.* Translated by Alan Sheridan. Cambridge, Mass., 1988.

Tarrow, Sidney G. *Democracy and Disorder: Protest and Politics in Italy, 1965–1975.* Oxford, 1989.

Rudé, George F. E. *The Crowd in History: A Study of Popular Disturbances in France and England, 1730–1848.* New York, 1964.

Te Brake, Wayne. *Shaping History: Ordinary People in European Politics, 1500–1700.* Berkeley, Calif., 1998.

Thompson, E. P. "The Moral Economy of the English Crowd in the Eighteenth Century." *Past and Present* 50 (1971): 76–136.

Tilly, Charles. *Popular Contention in Great Britain, 1758–1834.* Cambridge, Mass., 1995.

REVOLUTIONS

Michael D. Richards

Revolutions form one of the principle elements of European history after 1500. If they generally begin with issues of political power, they nearly always quickly come to include social, economic, and cultural issues, and have contributed in fundamental ways to the transformation of European politics and society.

Under the influence of Karl Marx, many social historians approached revolutions as examples of class struggle. Social classes were the major actors and the outcome of a revolution affected the composition of society, as well as distribution of economic and political power within it. In the 1960s historians challenged the use of class. Did all bourgeois, for example, see life the same way? What led some factory workers to join unions and support political parties and others to concentrate on personal interests? Also, social historians sometimes neglected the political entirely in their concern with describing and analyzing the way people lived.

Later scholarship emphasized an analysis of political culture, ideology, representation, symbols, and images. It often presented ideas about the origins and results of revolution in terms of social class, but in ways different from the Marxist analysis. Some of the revisionists stressed the futility of revolution and the danger that its attempts at reform would lead to a powerful and oppressive state. By the turn of the century, the state of the historiography of revolution was quite fluid. The Marxist position had been undermined but not eliminated. The revisionists, not a particularly united group to begin with, faced numerous different approaches, which had in common an interest in reconnecting the political and the social.

The impact of revolution on society, of course, varied from revolution to revolution. Challenges to the existing social order appear in each of the revolutions under consideration. As a generalization, it might be asserted that these challenges were unsuccessful in the sixteenth and seventeenth centuries and only partially successful in the eighteenth and nineteenth centuries. One result is that after the Revolutions of 1848, most members of the middle classes believed revolution was no longer a useful tool for reform or change. In the twentieth century, revolutionary challenges to the social status quo, beginning with the Russian Revolution of 1917, frequently resulted in a fundamental reordering of society. These massive attempts at social engineering, associated in nearly every case with Communism, without exception resulted in appalling social disasters.

Three European revolutions in particular stand out: the English in the seventeenth, the French in the eighteenth, and the Russian in the twentieth century. Each created a revolutionary tradition that heavily influenced revolutions that followed. The English Revolution furnished an example of the ways in which religious issues and political questions came together in explosive ways in the sixteenth and seventeenth centuries. The French Revolution brought to the fore not only questions of political arrangements but also issues concerned with social structure. However, the ways in which people lived did not change much, although for women the Revolution was undoubtedly a step back. Perhaps the most important result of the Revolution was to unleash the force of nationalism, a force that did more to change how people lived over the following two centuries than any other. Finally, the Russian Revolution, as already noted, produced an expanded idea of revolution, which called for remaking every aspect of life. It is perhaps not accidental that the utopian tradition began at the same time as the revolutionary tradition. At the heart of revolution is an aspiration toward utopia.

There is no agreement on what a revolution is, but a minimal definition includes calls for substantive change in the political system. A change in personnel is not sufficient. A revolution can also entail changes in economic arrangements, social structures, or cultural assumptions. The use of force or at least the potential for the use of force is necessary but, again, not sufficient. Finally, a revolution need not involve innovation. Attempts to preserve what is in existence or what people believe once existed can have revolutionary repercussions. There are also failed revolutions

EUROPEAN REVOLUTIONS, 1500–2000: A SHORT LIST

Italian City-State Revolutions (1494–1534)
Spanish *Comuneros* Revolt (1520–1521)
German Peasant War (1524–1526)
Netherlands Revolt (1568–1609)
The Bohemian Revolt (1618–1648)
British Revolution (1638–1660)
The Catalan Revolt (Spain) (1640–1659)
The Fronde (France) (1648–1653)
Revolution of 1688 (Britain)
Dutch Patriot Revolution (1785–1787)
Brabant Revolution (Belgium) (1789–1790)
French Revolution (1789–1799)
Italian Risorgimento (1789–1870)
Polish Revolt (1794–1795)
Batavian Revolution (Netherlands) (1795–1798)
Revolutions of 1820
Revolutions of 1830
Revolutions of 1848
Greek War of Liberation (1821–1832)
Decembrist Revolt (Russia) (1825)
Belgian Revolution (1830–1833)

Polish Revolt (1863–1864)
Paris Commune (1871)
Revolution of 1905 (Russia)
Irish Revolution (1916–1923)
Russian Revolution of 1917
German Revolution (1918–1919)
Hungarian Revolutions (1918–1919)
Spanish Civil War (1936–1939)
Yugoslavian Communist Revolution (1941–1945)
Hungarian Revolution (1956)
"Prague Spring" (Czechoslovakia) (1968)
"Events of May" (France) (1968)
Irish Revolt (Northern Ireland) (1969–1998)
Portuguese Revolution (1974)
"Solidarity" (Poland) (1980–1989)
Bulgarian Revolution (1989)
"Velvet Revolution" (Czechoslovakia) (1989)
German Revolution of 1989 (German Democratic Republic)
Romanian Revolution (1989)
Albanian Anticommunist Revolution (1990–1992)
Implosion of the Soviet Union (1991)

The list does not include the extensive involvement of European countries in colonial liberation movements and revolutions outside Europe. Based on tables in Goldstone, ed., 1998, pp. xxxix and xl; and in Tilly, 1993, pp. 74, 82–83, 94–95, 114, 151, and 203.

---

or revolutionary situations that never develop further. And, finally, the line is often quite thin between revolution and many other phenomena that have characteristics in common with it.

REVOLUTIONARIES BEFORE THE CONCEPT OF REVOLUTION

In the sixteenth and seventeenth centuries, even though the concept of revolution as a radical way of doing politics did not exist, there were events that should be seen as revolutions. A combination of religious and political issues drove most of the revolutionary events of the sixteenth century. Religion and politics continued to be major factors in the seventeenth century. In addition, economic, social, and demographic issues added fuel to the revolutionary fires. While most of the events had limited results, the Netherlands Revolt

and the British Revolution had important consequences for those two nations.

The Netherlands Revolt (1568–1609). Participants in the Netherlands Revolt against the Spanish crown did not begin with the intention of gaining independence. Like many other revolutionary movements in this period, the Netherlands Revolt developed mainly out of religious conflict and political disagreement. It resulted in the establishment of the Dutch Republic, which enjoyed world-power status in the seventeenth century.

Important Dutch leaders were appointed to the Council of State under the regent, Margaret of Parma, but they had little influence on the formation of policy. Instead Philip II of Spain reorganized the church to increase royal control and to continue attempts to stop the growth of Calvinism. The form of opposition varied according to the group involved. The Confederation of Nobles in 1565 was a protest against royal policies, while the sacking of Catholic churches by lower-class crowds the following year was directed against religious policies.

The duke of Alva, sent to repress the rebellion, was successful militarily, but he was not able to convince the States-General to grant new taxes. Attempts in 1571 to collect taxes by force led to revolt in 1572. By July 1572, the rebels had conquered many of the towns in Zeeland and Holland and others had joined the revolt voluntarily. The States of Holland offered William, prince of Orange, military command. William, the mainstay of the revolt, emphasized the rights of the provinces and the wrongs committed by the Spanish authorities. Where revolt in the south had largely ended, revolt in the north took positions on political and religious matters that made compromise difficult. Also, by this time the Netherlands Revolt had become part of international conflicts involving France, England, and Spain.

The Pacification of Ghent, approved by the States-General on 8 November 1576, attempted to assert the leading role of the States-General in the affairs of the Seventeen Provinces of the Netherlands and religious freedom for Protestantism. It was not possible, however, to hold all the provinces together. In the Union of Utrecht, January 1579, the Dutch-speaking areas of the north separated from the southern provinces. The latter reconciled with Philip II. In part this was in reaction to radical Calvinism among the lower classes. The northern provinces formed the United Provinces of the Netherlands.

William the Silent worked to keep the Netherlands together in the early 1580s. On 10 July 1584, however, he was assassinated. English intervention the following year proved crucial in preserving the United Provinces. Additionally, Spanish preoccupation with England and France helped the Dutch survive. In 1609 Spain agreed to the Twelve Years' Truce. Formal recognition of Dutch independence came only in 1648.

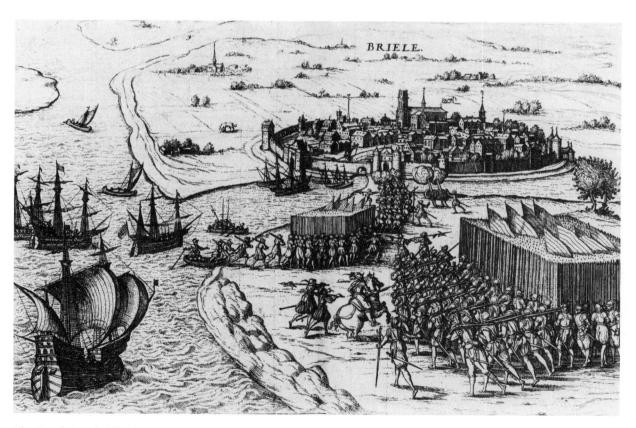

The Dutch Revolt. The Sea Beggars, privateers loyal to William the Silent, capture Brielle (The Brill), April 1572. Engraving by Frans Hogenberg from Michael von Aitzinger's *De leone belgico* (Cologne, 1583). BY PERMISSION OF THE BRITISH LIBRARY, LONDON

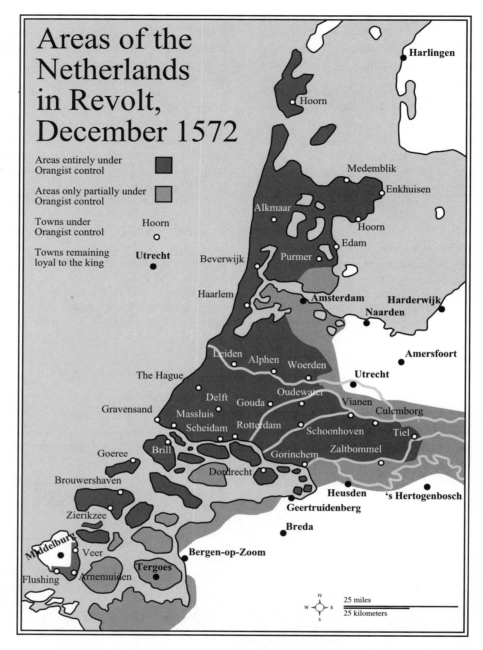

Areas of the Netherlands in Revolt, December 1572. Adapted from Geoffrey Parker, *The Dutch Revolt*, p. 143.

The Netherlands Revolt led to a society tolerant of religion and favorably disposed to commerce and manufacture. The large number of refugees from the south added greatly to the success of the Dutch Republic. Although urban elites continued to dominate politics, the bourgeoisie found ample scope for business. The lower classes also enjoyed some of the fruits of the seventeenth-century golden age.

The British Revolution (1638–1660). The British Revolution, as it is now called in recognition of the importance of the overall British context, also involved a mixture of political and religious issues. Unlike the continental revolutions it was not affected by external problems or by widespread peasant revolts.

By the twenty-first century, historians no longer saw the British Revolution as a long defense of English political rights against royal tyranny. Some profess to see little political conflict before 1638 and the emergency situation created by the Scottish uprising. Others see political opposition forming in the 1620s and coming to a head in the Petition of Right in 1628 and in the dissolution of Parliament by Charles I in 1629. Although no revolutionary group formed after these events, the policies of the crown were unpopular and widened the gap between the court and the country. The ship money tax (a special tax that had previously been levied only on coastal areas to help pay

for defense) in 1638 was especially unpopular. Complicating the matter was the Scottish Revolution, which forced Charles I to call in 1640 first the "Short Parliament," which, however, refused to vote funds for war with Scotland, and then the "Long Parliament."

The immediate goal of the parliamentarians was the end of measures associated with the Crown's eleven years of rule without the help of parliament. The parliamentarians benefited from the support of both merchants and the poor. By 1642 opposing sides had formed, each claiming to defend the true English

DRIE OKTOBER

Drie Oktober (3 October), a municipal holiday in the university town of Leiden, celebrates the relief of the siege of the town in 1574. The relief of Leiden not only had considerable military significance but probably even more psychological impact in the struggle of the Dutch to regain political and religious freedoms.

The Spanish forces took up positions during the night of 25–26 May and sealed off the city from outside aid. They planned to starve Leiden out as they had done earlier with Haarlem. If successful, they would drive a wedge between supporters of the Dutch Revolt in the northern part of Holland and the main concentration of strength in Zeeland.

Most in Leiden were loyal to William the Silent and the Dutch cause, but the town had failed to reprovision after an earlier siege. Compounding this, town officials did little to ration provisions the first two months.

On 30 July, the States of Holland, meeting in Rotterdam, decided to flood two water control areas to the south of Leiden in the hope of eventually flooding the area around Leiden itself and drowning "*la vermine Espagnole.*" There were many reasons why the plan would not work. Nevertheless, the slogan advanced was "*Liever bedorven dan verloren land*" (better a drowned than a lost land).

As preparations began for the fleet that was supposed to rescue Leiden, the town questioned its ability to hold out. It even sent messengers to William toward the end of August to ask him to release its citizens from their oath to him if he could not come to their aid. The mes-

sengers returned on 30 August with news that help was being readied and the town celebrated by parading musicians through the streets.

Reduced in September to a ration of 1,000 grams of meat (bones included) every four days, the citizens of Leiden seriously considered accepting Spanish offers of mercy and amnesty. The fleet was on its way, however, as people in Leiden learned on the 15th. Two weeks later, however, although the fleet was close, the water had not risen sufficiently for it to relieve Leiden.

The night of 29 September, a gale drove the North Sea into the mouth of the Maas River, sending it back in floods through the cuts in the dikes. By 1 October the water had risen high enough for the fleet to move toward Leiden. On the 2d there was only one more strong point to be taken. Early on the 3d a party of men left Leiden, determined to attack the strong point from their side. The story goes that an orphan went ahead to see what he could see and found the Spanish had abandoned the fort and even left behind a pot of *Hutspot,* an unbelievable feast for anyone who had not eaten well in weeks.

The fleet moved into Leiden and distributed food to the starving inhabitants. Afterwards all went to the Pieterskerk for prayers and hymns. The town had suffered greatly, with the death of some 6,000 of the 15,000 inhabitants, but it had endured. Observing the way in which nature itself seemed to have intervened, the God-fearing Dutch could hardly help but interpret it as a sign of favor for their cause.

political system and the Protestant religion. Both factions were similar in social composition: support from the gentry with leadership furnished by aristocrats. In the civil war between 1642 and 1647, the parliamentarians (or Roundheads) defeated the royalists (or Cavaliers) at Marston Moor and at Naseby.

The parliamentarians favored disbanding the army as soon as possible. Soldiers worried not only about pay but also about the religious and political settlement proposed by Parliament. The Putney debates in 1647 showed the influence of the Levellers, a middle-class group interested in popular sovereignty and social equality. This group, moving away from doctrines that looked to the past, looked toward universal ideals and revolutionary change.

Civil war broke out again in 1648, but this time the royalist cause was quickly crushed and a republic established. Charles was tried, sentenced, and then beheaded on 30 January 1649. In December of the previous year, the military command had carried out a purge of the House of Commons, leaving "The Rump" to carry on.

The new Commonwealth survived the popular unrest of the early 1650s and Oliver Cromwell reestablished control over Ireland and Scotland. In 1653 Cromwell forcibly removed "The Rump" from office. After the failure of the "Barebones" Parliament, he became lord protector. In effect a personal dictatorship, it collapsed soon after Cromwell's death in 1658. Following an interval of confusion and crisis, Charles II was invited to return.

The British Revolution was not a bourgeois revolution in the Marxist sense of a revolution produced by the growth of a capitalist economy. Nor can it be said it was caused by a "crisis of the aristocracy" or by rising or declining gentry. Cultural changes associated with Puritanism played a prominent role, but these cut across the lines of social division. Social discontent helped generate radical democratic movements during the Revolution, but these did not triumph. Late twentieth-century historians emphasized continuity and also argued against any decisive victory for constitutional monarchy. It is true, of course, that it took the Revolution of 1688 to make Parliament supreme. One can even argue that a process of political evolution continued into the nineteenth century. Nonetheless, the British Revolution of the mid-seventeenth century was an important step in the creation of a durable political system, a constitutional monarchy based on widespread participation and recognition of political and civil rights. It played an important role in establishing a political culture that many British took for granted by the beginning of the twentieth century.

The Revolution of 1688.

Was the Revolution of 1688 actually a revolution? It may have been little more than a coup against the government of James II, but it did what the earlier British Revolution had been unable to do: establish the supremacy of Parliament and put Britain on the road to constitutional monarchy.

Although much of the political nation stood ready to support James II when he came to the throne in 1685, he squandered that support by engaging in what was perceived as a weak foreign policy, that is, a foreign policy that favored Louis XIV. He was also seen as conducting a domestic policy that did not appear to respect the law. Many distrusted his attempt to promote religious toleration, which was seen as threatening the Church of England. By 1688 many Whig and Tory politicians, ordinarily opponents, united behind the idea of inviting William, prince of Orange, *stadhouder* (chief executive) of the United Provinces of the Netherlands and also the son-in-law of James II, to invade England. According to some historians, this plan had widespread support among merchants, gentry, and aristocracy.

After James II and his family fled to France, a Convention was elected, and in February 1689 debated what should be done. It was agreed that James II had abdicated and that Mary and William had inherited the throne. The Convention further issued the "Declaration of Rights," essentially a restatement of English law. This document underlined a position that had not been fully accepted before, the concept that the nation, not the monarch, was sovereign. These were, as one historian has it, "reluctant revolutionaries." In fact, John Locke's *Two Treatises of Government* (1690) was largely ignored at the time as too radical.

The Fronde (1648–1653).

Under the heading of "The Fronde" (from *fronde*, French for slingshot), historians have grouped protests by royal officials, aristocratic revolt, urban disorders, and rebellion in the countryside. Contemporaneous with the British Revolution, the Fronde lacked an institution such as Parliament to serve as a focus for opposition to the crown. Also, no leader of the same caliber as Cromwell or William the Silent emerged. The situation of the monarchy was precarious, with a regent, Anne of Austria, ruling for the boy king Louis XIV with the help of an unpopular first minister, Cardinal Mazarin. Nevertheless, the Fronde failed because of a lack of unity, purpose, and leadership.

The Fronde began in the summer of 1648, but it was the product of years of high taxes and attempts to establish an absolutist form of monarchy. Almost all groups in France, from the great nobles to peasants

The English Revolution. In a royalist engraving of the seventeenth century, a diabolically inspired Oliver Cromwell directs the cutting down of the royal oak of Britain. ©THE BRITISH MUSEUM

in the countryside had grievances. The breakthrough came when the regent and Mazarin attempted to end the ability of the Parlement of Paris (a judicial body, not to be confused with the English Parliament) to obstruct royal business by arresting two of its judges. This led to the "days of the barricades," 26–28 August, when officials, merchants, artisans, and other urban dwellers took to the streets.

The Treaty of Reuil in the spring of 1649 settled many of the issues with the Parlement of Paris and other bodies of officials, but not with the nobility, who wanted Mazarin dismissed and their right to participate in governmental affairs recognized. In the first part of the Fronde, the commander of the royal army had been Louis, prince of Condé, a royal cousin. In the civil war beginning in 1649 Condé switched to the side of the Frondeurs and became their main leader. Although a talented military leader, he lacked political skills. The Fronde became increasingly fragmented.

When Louis XIV declared his majority in 1651, this created a dilemma. Most of the protest had been directed against Mazarin, and not the king. Now that he was ruling directly, it was no longer possible to claim to be rebelling against the regent and Mazarin.

In fact, much of France did not rebel. Of ten parlements, only four rebelled. Many cities remained quiet. Nonetheless, the concessions the Parlement of Paris gained initially from the crown might easily have led to a very different style of monarchy in France. France after the Fronde took a path quite different from that of Britain or the Netherlands.

THE ERA OF THE FRENCH REVOLUTION

The French Revolution dwarfed the other events associated with it. It also inspired or made possible some of those events. Nonetheless, it is useful to consider the period from roughly 1770 to 1850 as an era of rebellion and revolution, a time of rapid change and dislocation. Whether one looks at demographic trends, price series, intellectual currents, political developments, or diplomatic events, change rather than continuity is the prevailing theme. The French Revolution introduced the main elements of modern politics, including the idea of constructing the political system from the ground up. It also raised many social issues. For some the revolution became an instrument for refashioning men and women into citizens.

In the decades after the Napoleonic Empire there were three successive waves of revolution. The first, in 1820, was relatively minor. The second, in 1830, had significant repercussions. The last, in 1848, involved most European nations and initially appeared to introduce fundamental changes to European politics. In the end, however, it led only to compromise and reaction.

In addition to the waves of revolution, there were individual revolutions of some note. These included, among others, the Decembrist Revolt of 1825 in Russia, the Greek liberation movement (1821–1832), an ensemble of events in Britain in the early 1830s, and the Risorgimento in Italy. Theorists as well as activists abounded. The most important theorists of the period were Karl Marx and Friedrich Engels. The anarchists were also prominent in this period. By the end of the century, hundreds of thousands of Europeans were organized in revolutionary parties or groups, but, paradoxically, only a relatively small number actually looked forward to revolution.

The French Revolution.

The beginnings of the French Revolution lie in the fiscal problems of the monarchy. Where the nation as a whole was prosperous, the government was deeply in debt because of its involvement in past wars. A reform of the tax system seemed the obvious solution.

The ministers of Louis XVI hoped an Assembly of Notables would agree to the new taxes, but this group deferred to the Estates General, an institution that had not met since 1614. As soon as it was decided the Estates General would meet, a controversy broke out that split those planning to use tax reform to widen the governing process. The group identified with the aristocracy appeared to want to monopolize political influence. The other, identified with a national or patriotic position, seemed to want broader participation in the political process. Voting in the Estates General had been by estate, the first being the clergy, the second the nobility, and the third everyone else. The "patriots," drawn from the liberal aristocracy and the bourgeoisie, wanted to double the third and vote by head. This opened the possibility of obtaining a majority. In the pamphlet war before the elections, Abbé Sieyès argued forcefully in "What Is the Third Estate?" that the third estate, as the backbone of the

nation, deserved to be an important part of the political process.

During the elections, voters composed *cahiers,* lists of grievances. The *cahiers,* while noting many particular complaints, also expressed loyalty to the monarchy and satisfaction with the established church and hierarchical society. Delegates expected change, but within the confines of the established system.

A series of events in the summer of 1789 plunged France into revolution. When the crown failed to lead, the third estate declared itself on 17 June the National Assembly and invited members of the other estates to join it. It planned to write a constitution, which implied sovereign political power vested in the people. This was the first move toward revolution.

The next was mostly symbolic. On 14 July, a crowd composed mostly of the lower-middle class and lower classes, stormed the Bastille, long a symbol of royal tyranny. This action was part of a municipal revolt that overturned governing bodies in many cities around France. It may also have forestalled plans by the monarchy to disperse the National Assembly.

In response to peasant disorders in the countryside, the National Assembly abolished nearly all privileges on the night of 4–5 August, providing a new meaning for the word "Liberty" (which, not capitalized, had been a synonym for privilege) and also creating a situation of equality before the law. Finally, on 26 August, the National Assembly enshrined "Liberty" and "Equality" in the "Declaration of the Rights of Man and Citizen," a statement of principles meant to be attached to a constitution.

When a mob composed mostly of women forced the king and his family to move to Paris in October, the first part of the revolution was complete. The National or Constituent Assembly followed the monarchy to Paris and worked there on defining a constitutional monarchical system.

Attempts to construct a constitutional monarchy floundered because of two major problems. One was the place of the church in the new revolutionary system. The Civil Constitution of the Clergy (1790), which established a state church, divided the clergy into those who refused to take an oath of loyalty ("Refractors") and those who took the oath ("Constitutionals"). This created a dilemma for many French. How could they support the Revolution and remain Catholics?

The other major problem concerned the monarchy. Louis XVI, uncomfortable with the arrangement for constitutional monarchy, was under pressure from his wife, Marie Antoinette, and many nobles to bargain for more power. The attempt by the royal family to flee the country in June 1791 effectively ended the possibility of constructing a workable system.

By 1792 the major groups opposing the Revolution were the aristocracy, large numbers of clergy, and many peasants. The latter often took their cue from the local notables and the clergy and were naturally suspicious of anything originating in the towns. The main support for the Revolution came from the urban middle and lower-middle classes. Many belonged to revolutionary societies of which the Jacobin club was the best known and most powerful. The Jacobin club in Paris, which met in a former monastery, was connected to Jacobin clubs throughout France. The urban lower classes also supported the Revolution and intervened sporadically.

France went to war in April 1792 as both opponents and supporters of the Revolution maneuvered to gain advantage. On 10 August, the war going badly and the king's loyalty uncertain, a crowd stormed the royal residence in Paris and overthrew the monarchy. With the election of a new representative body, the Convention, the Revolution moved into a more radical phase. Initially, the main question was what to do about the king. Eventually he was placed on trial and by the narrowest of margins—one vote—sentenced, and later executed. The execution took place on 21 January 1793.

Although there were no political parties, factions developed in the Convention. The execution of the king eliminated any reason for monarchists to remain in the Convention. Among the supporters of the republic and democracy, almost all middle class, two groups stood out. The group associated with Jacques-Pierre Brissot, the Girondins (several came from the department of Gironde), had been reluctant to vote to execute the king. It also had difficulty meeting the demands of the lower-middle and lower class Parisians, the so-called *sans-culottes* (those who wore trousers and not the knee breeches favored by the aristocracy). The Mountain, which sat up high on the left in the Convention, favored property and order just as the Girondins, but found they could make those decisions the Revolution seemed to require. Most deputies were part of an unorganized mass known as the "Plain" or the "Belly." Even those identified as part of the Mountain or the Girondins by their opponents did not always see themselves as members of one or the other group.

By the middle of 1793, France was fighting a coalition of European powers and a civil war. Furthermore, the lower and lower-middle classes in Paris, now the driving force of the revolution, demanded a maximum on prices and a minimum on wages. In a tense atmosphere such as this, some saw the reluctance

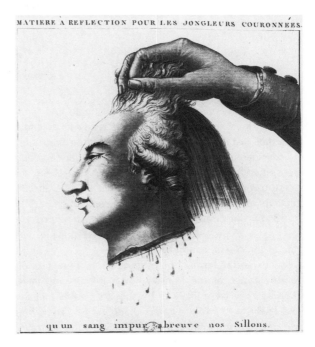

Louis XVI. "Something for crowned jugglers to think about": the head of Louis XVI after his execution, 21 January 1793. Below, a line from *The Marseillaise,* "Let impure blood irrigate our furrows." BIBLIOTHÈQUE NATIONALE, PARIS/©ROGER-VIOLLET

of the Girondins to take radical measures as traitorous. At the beginning of June, Girondins were driven from the Convention and arrested.

Over the next few months, the Committee of Public Safety, formed that April, became the main locus of power in France. Maximilien de Robespierre, who became a member of the committee in July, quickly became the leading figure, and was responsible for much of the Reign of Terror (1973). But a number of others, including Georges Danton, Lazare Carnot, and Louis-Antoine Saint-Just, also played important roles.

In the late summer and the fall, several extraordinary measures were passed. First, the nation was called to arms in August with the *levée-en-masse.* In September a *maximum* on prices was enacted. More draconian measures followed. Still, some historians argue that the Terror was mostly an effort to preserve France and the revolution. Much of the horror associated with the revolution actually took place in the civil war. Also, some of the representatives-on-mission went far beyond their orders, as was the case, for example, in the mass drownings at Nantes.

Robespierre and other revolutionaries wanted to use revolution to transform humanity and spent time discussing various architectural and educational

SANS-CULOTTES

The *sans-culottes* saw themselves as simple and hard-working, loyal to the revolution and ready to defend it with their last drops of blood. In political terms they might be considered the victors of the great revolutionary *journées,* the storming of the Bastille on 14 July 1789, the overthrow of the monarchy on 10 August 1792, and the removal of the Girondins from the Convention on 31 May 1793. For historians influenced by Marx, they were the forerunner of the working class, who were playing their role in the classic bourgeois revolution.

In social terms, the *sans-culottes* were broadly representative of the Parisian lower-middle and lower classes. They were likely to be shopkeepers or artisans, less likely to be wage-earners or domestics. They were certainly not marginal figures, although often portrayed as such in nineteenth-century accounts of the revolution, not people without sources of income or fixed residences.

The *sans-culottes* were, above all, social animals. Fraternity was the watchword and they customarily presented themselves as part of a group or committee or as speaking for their section. They despised those who wanted to set themselves apart, whether through manner of speaking, dressing, or behaving. One dressed as everyone dressed, in pantaloons, sabots (wooden shoes), a red cap, and a tricolor cockade. The opposite of the *sans-culottes* were the aristocrats, by definition proud and selfish and not fully human.

In economic terms, the *sans-culottes* did not believe in absolute equality but rather in social justice. Everyone should have enough on which to live. Prices of the most necessary items as well as wages and profits should be fixed.

The *sans-culottes* were most prominent in the Year II (1793). In part, this was due to the radicalization of the revolution. But it must also reflect the increasing political involvement of some of the *sans-culottes.* The overthrow of the monarchy in August 1792 and the new circumstances this created resulted in more continuity in political involvement than before. The execution of the king in January 1793, an economic crisis that spring, and the division between the Girondins and the Mountain increased the significance of popular militancy. By the fall of 1793, the *sans-culottes* had gained two important goals: the *maximum,* or price controls; and the revolutionary armies, a people's militia. Many *sans-culottes* could read and write or were in any case influenced by revolutionary publicists and even by some of the *philosophes,* especially Jean-Jacques Rousseau. They saw themselves more and more as playing a historical role.

It has been estimated that only five to ten percent of those eligible to participate in the political life of the forty-eight sections of Paris actually did so. A small minority of this group, perhaps 3,000 to 4,000, made up the functionaries of the sections. It was this small group that worked with the Mountain to channel the political energy of the *sans-culottes,* to make that energy more regular, formal, and predictable. By the time Robespierre was executed on the 10th of Thermidor (July 1794), the *sans-culottes* had lost much of their revolutionary power. Or perhaps they were only exhausted from their revolutionary labors. In any case, they had lost the power to push the revolution forward. For the time being, they stepped back out of politics.

schemes. Little came of this, however. The *sans-culottes,* long in the habit of sending delegations and petitions to the Convention, were gradually cut out of political life. They still exerted considerable influence, however, on dress, behavior, language, and forms of entertainment, emphasizing the plain, the simple, the sentimental, and the moralistic.

Robespierre and his fellow revolutionaries were constantly on the alert politically in the first part of 1794. Robespierre turned first on Jacques-René Hé-

bert and the Enragés, once hugely popular with the *sans-culottes.* He then ordered Danton put on trial. By the early summer everyone in the Convention worried about Robespierre's next move. Several representatives-on-mission, fearing prosecution for their crimes, helped organize an opposition. Robespierre, taken into custody on the 9th of Thermidor (27 July 1794), was guillotined the next day.

The Revolution ended with the death of Robespierre. No one had the energy after years of intense political activity to restart the machinery of the Terror. The Thermidorian Reaction, a gaudy reaction to the puritanism of the Revolution, replaced the Terror. The Convention gave way to the Directory, a complicated system that, over the next four years, worked mostly through occasional coups. Finally, Napoleon carried out one last coup on the eighteenth Brumaire (November 1799). The Directory began the work of consolidating the revolution; Napoleon finished it in brilliant style in the first years of his rule. While there is dispute over how much social tensions, as opposed to political and ideological issues, generated the French Revolution, there is little doubt about some key social results. While revolutionary chaos disrupted economic development, revolutionary legislation—for example the abolition of the guilds—favored a more capitalist economy in the long run. The end to manorialism and the establishment of equality under the law undermined the position of the aristocracy. The legal context of peasant life also changed sub-

INTERPRETING THE FRENCH REVOLUTION

For much of the twentieth century, historians viewed the French Revolution from a marxist perspective. They saw it as the classic example of a bourgeois revolution clearing the way for the development of capitalism. The high-water mark of the marxist approach came with Georges Lefebvre's study of 1789, published in 1939, the sesquicentennial of the French Revolution.

The first important challenges to the marxist view came in the 1960s. Historians focused on the early leaders of the revolution, the definition of the word bourgeois, and the extent to which the revolution cleared the way for the development of capitalism. Alfred Cobban was one of the most prominent revisionists. He and other historians showed that many of the early leaders were aristocrats, that many bourgeois identified with and aspired to become aristocrats, and that the revolution actually retarded the growth of capitalism.

Although no longer a marxist interpretation, the revisionist position remained a social interpretation. It now featured a crisis of social mobility. More people within the ranks of an elite of aristocrats and bourgeois sought to improve their social positions. The elite split, creating the opportunity for revolution, but later reappeared as notables after having learned the high price of revolution.

Revisionists concentrated on learning more about political culture. This ranged from festivals and images to the use of language. The new concentration on the political recognized that political activities shaped social relations and identified the development of a new political culture as the most important result of the revolution. Even if society seemed much the same after the revolu-

tion, the new political culture was not forgotten and continued to influence social development.

The person most prominently associated with the revisionist interpretation in the latter part of the twentieth century, François Furet, believed the French Revolution led unavoidably to the Terror. Politics in the revolution was, according to him, simply a means for reshaping society. Many revisionists, however, do not take that view.

The bicentennial marked the peak of the revisionist interpretation. Observers in the 1990s saw a fluid situation in which neither the revisionist position nor the marxist position was dominant. By 2000, much of the work being done focused on connections between the political and the social. For example, one approach emphasized the idea of apprenticeship or political acculturation. What kinds of networks, previous associations, and local circumstances helped to draw one into revolutionary politics? What is involved in the actual practice of politics? The result is a political interpretation informed by an extensive knowledge of social history.

It may be that these approaches seek to extend the work on ideology, representation, imagery, and symbolism of the revisionists. Or it is possibly a more pragmatic, local approach to politics that makes reference to social history. It is no longer possible to interpret the revolution in terms of large social categories. By the same token, the revolution cannot be understood in political terms alone. Social conditions place certain parameters on political action. In turn, political action and the development of a political culture change social conditions. How these interactions work will likely be the focus of much historical scholarship in the near future.

stantially. Attacks on the church created new social and cultural divisions. The revolution's impact on family life was less dramatic, though divorce was briefly tolerated. Disparities between revolutionary ideas and a rather conservative approach to gender had important consequences in the nineteenth century.

Revolution had spread to other parts of Europe even before Napoleon began his string of conquests. In some instances revolution took place either before or at the same time as the French Revolution. Even countries such as Prussia, opposed to Napoleon and the tenets of the Revolution, changed considerably in order to preserve its independence. Modifications of guild and manorial systems spread throughout Europe.

Dutch Revolutions (1780–1800).
The Dutch Revolutions at the end of the eighteenth century provide a good example of the other revolutionary events occurring around the time of the French Revolution. The initial Dutch Revolution, the Patriot Revolution from 1786 to 1787, grew out of involvement in the American Revolution. This led to war with England and criticism of the government for its handling of the war. A Patriot group formed in opposition to Prince William V, the *stadhouder* of the Netherlands. The Orangists organized to defend the prince. In 1781, J. D. van der Capellen, one of the Patriot leaders, called on the Dutch to imitate the Americans in seizing control of their affairs. In 1783 the Patriots organized citizens' committees and militias. Even the regents, powerful figures on the municipal level, joined the anti-Orangist popular movement.

By 1787 the Patriots had succeeded in gaining power on the municipal level in Utrecht. Then the movement, radically democratic and revolutionary, took control of the provinces of Overijssel and Holland. Just at the point of success, however, artisans and shopkeepers, worried about new regulations passed by municipal councils dominated by the Patriots, switched allegiance to the Orangists. The Orangists also imitated the Patriot organizational efforts. Prussian intervention in 1787 sealed the fate of the revolution and restored William V to power.

If the first Dutch Revolution anticipated the French Revolution, the second came largely as a direct result of the French Revolution. Popular forces had remained concentrated in the voluntary associations and militias. With the help of French forces, the Patriots came to power again in the mid-1790s. The Batavian Republic, however, experienced increasing problems with the French, especially after Napoleon came to power. Finally, in 1813 the Patriots were driven from power and William I, son of the last *stadhouder*, became king.

The Revolutions of 1830.
Of the several revolutions in 1830, by far the most important took place in France. The origins of the revolution owe something to the effects of the economic crisis of 1826–1827, but it was largely a product of the provocative policies of Charles X and his reactionary aristocratic allies, the "Ultras." The liberal opposition disliked what it viewed as an alliance between "throne and altar." It also believed the electoral franchise was too narrow. The July Ordinances of 1830, which dissolved the newly elected and liberal Chamber of Deputies, disenfranchised three-quarters of the electorate and provided for new elections, was meant to produce a pliable Chamber. It also called for a harsh policy of press censorship. This brought apprentices and journeymen from the print shops out into the streets of Paris. The demonstrations on 26 July 1830 escalated the following day to barricades and battles with troops. Charles abdicated 2 August and Louis-Philippe, duc d'Orléans, became "king of the French." The tricolor again became the national flag and in April 1831 the franchise was doubled. A variety of groups, peasants, artisans, workers, and socialists, viewed the revolution as permission to voice grievances. The first few years after the revolution were marked by disorder and repression and in the 1830s and 1840s republicanism and socialism developed rapidly.

The July monarchy was considered liberal and more favorably disposed to business than Charles X's government had been. Land, however, was still the main basis for wealth and the bourgeoisie, if more prominent than before, were divided into groups with differing interests.

Elsewhere, the Belgian revolution was successful in defeating the Dutch and creating an independent state. Great power interest in the strategic importance of Belgium played an important role. The reverse was true in Poland. An uprising in November in Warsaw created popular support among artisans at first. The Polish nobility, however, hesitated to ally with the peasantry, the only real chance for the revolution to succeed, and it collapsed in August. In this case, some great powers, namely France and Great Britain, had no particular reason to intervene, while others, Prussia, Russian, and Austria, had every reason to suppress the revolution. There was also some activity in Italy, which the Austrians dealt with easily, and in Germany.

The Revolutions of 1848.
The Revolutions of 1848 formed the major instance of revolution in Europe between the French Revolution and the Russian Revolution. They began in France, where for several reasons they took on a character different from revo-

The Revolution of 1830 in Belgium. A painting by Gustave Wappers illustrates the popular nature of the Belgian uprising. IRPA, BRUSSELS

lutions elsewhere. Eventually, most of the continent was involved in revolution.

Three factors helped create the possibility of revolution in 1848. First, economic crises in 1846–1847, stemming from bad harvests and leading to high prices and unemployment, produced tensions in much of Europe. Next, the transition to an industrial economy brought problems for many, particularly among artisans, priming a large number of people for protest. Finally, the legacy of the French Revolution and unfinished business from the Revolution of 1830 created a particular situation. Political banquets meant to press for the expansion of the franchise easily spilled over into violent confrontation.

In Paris the government decided in February 1848 to ban a demonstration supporting electoral reform but could not control the protest that followed. Louis-Philippe and his prime minister quickly lost support. A provisional government formed after the collapse of the government and established a democratic republic. Almost immediately a gulf appeared between the moderate republicans making up the government, mostly drawn from middle-class professional men, and those who had supported it on the street, drawn largely from the artisans and skilled workers and from the lower-middle class. The latter groups often wanted simply to return to the old ways of living and working, ways that economic change was destroying.

The Second Republic's major response to the needs of the lower classes was the National Workshops, basically relief measures for the unemployed. This was not what Louis Blanc, an important French socialist and member of the government, wanted. He favored something closer to producers' cooperatives.

Since France was already an independent nation, the social question appeared almost immediately. For their part, the moderate republicans feared the electoral power of urban artisans and workers under the new arrangements for universal manhood suffrage. The situation finally came to a head in June when the government ruthlessly used the army, the National Guard, and the Mobile Guard to suppress protests against the dismantling of the National Workshops.

The social question existed in Germany as well, but the more pressing question was national unity. When Frederick William IV refused the Frankfurt Parliament's offer to head a new German Empire, this ended the major thrust of revolution in Germany. Frederick William, having recovered his confidence and reestablished support in Prussia, easily defeated the revolution in Prussia and in several other German states as well. By 1849, the Austrians, too, had regained the initiative in Vienna and had crushed Czech revolutionaries in Prague and Hungarian revolutionaries in Budapest, the latter with the aid of the Russian Empire. They had also prevailed in the Italian peninsula, where Italian revolutionaries had been temporarily successful.

The most important results from the Revolutions of 1848 were negative. France failed once again to find a workable political system, either in the Second Republic or in the Second Empire of Napoleon III that followed. The direction that Italian unification took over the next two decades, however, owed much to experiences in 1848–1849. Finally, while the movement toward German unification owed little to 1848, it may be argued that many German liberals responded to unification as they did because of their perceived failure in 1848.

After 1848 the middle classes ended their interest in revolution, even in a moderate political revolution for a constitution and representative government. Already fearful of the urban lower classes, the lesson they learned from 1848 was that revolution was too unpredictable a phenomenon to be safely used. The urban lower classes, especially the emerging proletariat, were now wary of allying with the middle classes in a revolutionary movement. Some were attracted to the idea of proletarian revolution that Marx and Engels put forward after 1848 or the ideas of the anarchists, but many others preferred reform and trade-union work. As for the countryside, in Germany, Austria, and Italy, the end of manorialism tended to reduce peasant discontent.

The Paris Commune (1871).

The Paris Commune was the last major revolutionary event of the century and an isolated one at that. It ended the tradition of the French Revolution. It was mainly a product of municipal pride, the bitter experience of the siege of Paris by the Prussians between September 1870 and January 1871, and the possibility that the royalist National Assembly elected in February 1871 would attempt to restore the French monarchy. The catalyst was the attempt by the French government to disarm the Parisian National Guard on 18 March 1871.

The Paris Commune was meant to recall directly the revolutionary Paris Commune of 1792. It even adopted the revolutionary calendar, which meant it was now Year LXXIX. Those who made up the Commune were largely socialists and neo-Jacobin radicals drawn from the middle classes and white-collar and skilled workers. The main ideas were to defend the republic against the return of the monarchy and to protect the autonomy of Paris. The Commune was also against the church, the army, police, and bureaucracy. Relatively few social changes were made, however, since the overwhelming reality was the civil war.

On 21 May, French troops broke through the defenses and began a week of street fighting. Many prisoners were slaughtered or executed after a perfunctory court-martial. Estimates are that 20,000 Communards died. Marx and Engels hailed it as the dawn of an age of proletarian revolution. Late twentieth-century historians saw it more as the end of an era of revolution and the product of a particular location and circumstances.

Karl Marx and Friedrich Engels.

Once the French Revolution established the idea of revolution as another way of doing politics, many sought to develop theories of revolution. The two most prominent nineteenth-century theorists were Karl Marx (1818–1883) and Friedrich Engels (1820–1895). They developed a theory of scientific socialism to distinguish their ideas from those of the Utopian Socialists. History, they stated in the *Communist Manifesto* (1848), consisted of class struggles. At mid-century, they saw economic life dominated by the bourgeoisie. As the bourgeoisie changed all aspects of European life, it created the class—the proletariat—destined to destroy it, according to Marx and Engels.

Underlying the class struggle was economic life itself, which involved the means for carrying on economic life, that is, the forces of production, and the ways in which economic life was organized, that is, the relations of production. All else was superstructure, a reflection of economic life. Invariably, the forces of production developed to the point where the relations of production constricted them. Marx and Engels thought this would soon result in conflict between the proletariat and the bourgeoisie. Eventually, the proletarian revolution would usher in a new historical situation, a classless society in which there was no longer a conflict between the means of production and the relations of production.

Marx and Engels played a role both in the founding of the First International, a grouping of socialist parties and trade unions, and in its destruction, rather than see it controlled by the anarchists. They also oversaw the founding of the German Social Democratic Party (the SPD). After Marx's death in 1883, Engels played a prominent role in SPD politics for more than a decade.

Although Marx and Engels believed in the historical inevitability of their ideas, they continued to emphasize organization of the working class. Historical conditions had to be ripe for a revolution to take place, but, in the meantime, workers achieved class-consciousness through activism and prepared for the new era after the revolution. They speculated that revolutionary change might come through peaceful means. Engels, in his introduction to *Class Struggles in France,* wrote about the possibility of achieving power through the ballot box and the difficulties of mounting the barricades. Even so, he was unsure the bourgeoisie would surrender power peacefully and warned social democrats to be prepared if necessary to defend the revolution.

Marx and Engels strongly influenced revolutionaries in Europe and beyond in the last part of the nineteenth century and throughout the twentieth century. Their understanding of revolution had a powerful, even fateful, impact.

Anarchism.　Anarchism, a major rival to Marxism in the second half of the nineteenth century, advocated abolition of the state and formation of cooperative institutions. Anarchists, however, differed over means. The major current thought in terms of peaceful change through the power of the example of cooperatives. The person most closely associated with this tendency was the Russian, Pyotr Kropotkin (1842–1921). Another important current stressed the need to use violence to destroy the state and found its most important advocate in another Russian, Mikhail Bakunin (1814–1876). A wave of terrorist violence at the end of the nineteenth century led to the stereotype of the anarchist as a bomb-throwing, heavily bearded madman.

Anarchism found a good reception in France, Switzerland, Italy, and Spain, particularly among peasants in large-estate regimes, as in Andalusia, and among artisans. In the twentieth century it was briefly prominent in the Russian Revolution and Civil War. It also had many supporters in the Spanish Civil War. Finally, it enjoyed something of a revival in the 1960s among student radicals.

THE ERA OF THE RUSSIAN REVOLUTION

There is no comparison between the Russian Revolution and similar events in twentieth-century Europe. The German Revolution of 1918 and other revolutionary events in central Europe after World War I were minor events. Italian Fascism and German National Socialism proved to be major factors in twentieth-century history, but it is difficult to consider either a genuine revolution. Each contained revolutionary elements, but it would be more accurate to see the two phenomena as parasitical. German National Socialism challenged the established order in Europe because it controlled the resources of the German nation.

The Russian Revolution, although measuring itself against the French Revolution, set the new standard for revolution in the twentieth century. Especially in the form of the Stalinist Revolution of the 1930s it appeared to offer a blueprint for independence, freedom, urbanization, and industrialization. Its influence continued nearly to the end of the century and declined only with the collapse of the Soviet Union.

The Russian Revolutions of 1917.　The February Revolution ended the Romanov dynasty. Over the next few months, the Provisional Government struggled to solve Russian problems. Its failure led to the October or Bolshevik Revolution that brought V. I. Lenin and his party to power.

The February Revolution was more a collapse of the Russian Empire than an organized effort to seize power. Russia, battered by defeats in World War I, was close to economic disintegration early in 1917. For a variety of reasons, large numbers of people thronged the streets of Petrograd (St. Petersburg) on 23 February o.s. (8 March). Over the next few days, the crowds grew larger. Eventually the soldiers, sent to control the crowds, made common cause with them.

A Provisional Government was organized at the end of February to deal with the political vacuum caused by the government's disintegration. Its most influential members were Alexander Guchkov, an Octobrist and minister of war, and Paul Miliukov, a Constitutional Democrat (Kadet) and foreign minister. At the same time, the Petrograd Soviet of Soldiers and Workers appeared. People spoke of "dual power," the idea that the Soviet represented public opinion and therefore had considerable leverage on the Provisional Government.

The Provisional Government overestimated the patience of average Russians and insisted on continuing the war effort. To do this, it was necessary to postpone decisions on the form of government and land reform. Eventually, the government's failure to end Russia's participation in the war and to take action on major questions doomed it.

For several months, however, the Provisional Government maintained power in Russia. Alexander Kerensky, a moderate socialist, quickly became the most powerful figure in the government, becoming prime minister in the summer of 1917. Kerensky seemingly had no rivals by the summer of 1917.

Lenin returned to Russia in April and set out in the April Theses a position that distinguished his party, the Bolsheviks, from all others in Russia. He called boldly for a peace without annexations or indemnities, land to the peasants, and all power to the Soviets. The Bolsheviks at this point were a very small party.

By the fall of 1917 Lenin believed Russia was ripe for revolution. The Central Committee (CC) of

The Russian Revolution. Lenin addresses workers and soldiers at a meeting of the Petrograd soviet, 6 November 1917. Painting by V. Serov, 1940s. SOVFOTO

the Bolsheviks was reluctant to take action, but Lenin persuaded them to put the idea of revolution on the agenda. Leon Trotsky, a major figure in the Bolshevik Party and also an influential figure in the Petrograd Soviet, made preparations to protect the revolution. Red Guard units, workers' militias, and soldiers and sailors in the area overthrew the Provisional Government in October when it appeared it was beginning a counter-revolution. The Second All-Russian Congress of Soviets, meeting then in Petrograd, approved a Bolshevik government. The seizure of power was accomplished with relatively little bloodshed, but the civil war that followed was bloody and cruel. For

many historians, the civil war period shaped the party and its leaders in important ways. Institutions such as the Cheka (the secret police), state control of the economy, and political dictatorship were products of the civil war. Communist leaders also dealt with intervention by several great powers.

Socially, the Russian revolution depended heavily on discontent among factory workers and urban artisans, heightened by the pressures of early industrialization and rapid urbanization, and among peasants angered by the existence of large estates. Marxist leaders meshed readily with worker groups, but ultimately bypassed some of the main peasant demands. With regard to social structure, however, the revolution affected countryside and city alike, with the expropriation of foreign owners, the abolition of the aristocracy, and a host of new educational and political opportunities for members of the former lower classes.

The Stalinist Revolution (1928–1938).

A little more than ten years after the October Revolution, Stalin took the Soviet Union through what was, in effect, a revolutionary experience. The first two Five-Year Plans (the third was interrupted by war) were heroic efforts to industrialize the Soviet Union. The plans, which emphasized heavy industry and centralized economic planning, were intended to create the economic basis for socialism. Stalin also wanted to prepare the Soviet Union for the possibility of war.

The First Five-Year Plan, officially dated from the latter part of 1928, called originally for difficult but not impossible goals. Stalin insisted on raising the already high targets. He emphasized large-scale projects and speed. Magnitogorsk, a new metallurgical complex near the southern end of the Ural Mountains, is a good example of the Stalinist approach to industrialization in that its goals were raised repeatedly.

The Soviet Union became a major industrial power in the 1930s. The labor force more than doubled, from about eleven and a half million to nearly twenty-three million. A large number of peasants left the new collective farms to work in factories in the cities. One of the main features of the Stalinist Revolution was rapid social mobility. Consumer goods were scarce and housing crowded, but many Soviet citizens took great pride the new Soviet Union.

Collectivization, which began in 1928, resulted in approximately fifty percent of peasant families joining collective farms by early 1930. Many had been forced to join. The level of resistance was so high Stalin was forced to retreat. His article in March 1930, "Dizzy with Success," blamed problems on overzealous subordinates and reassured peasants they would not be forced to join. Many left at that point, but continuous pressure meant that by 1933 over ninety percent of peasant families had joined collective farms or state farms. One feature of collectivization was the hunt for kulaks, so-called rich peasants. Often these were simply the most independent peasants in a village. They were sometimes summarily shot, or they might be shipped to some desolate spot.

Collectivization was a failure as an economic policy. In 1932 there was a massive famine in the Ukraine and the northern Caucasus region. About seven million peasants died. Intended to mechanize agriculture and to increase productivity, collectivization became the Achilles heel of the Soviet economy.

The Stalinist Revolution also included the great purges, a series of show trials and purges of various institutions. It is conventionally dated from the assassination of Sergei Kirov in December 1934. The purges are the most controversial part of the Stalinist Revolution. The heart of the purges, the *Yezhovshchina* (after Nikolai Yezhov, the head of the NKVD, the secret police) was in 1937 and 1938 when the army was purged and two of the three main show trials took place. The issues in dispute concern, first, who was responsible and what were their motives, and, second, how many died in the process. Stalin and some of his associates clearly played major roles, but there is also evidence that many subordinates went beyond orders either because they were zealous, fearful, or simply opportunistic. The numbers are difficult to sort out, but it appears the NKVD executed less than a million prisoners during the purges. Labor camps in the Gulag (the acronym for the NKVD prison system), while harsh, were not comparable to the Nazi death camps during World War II.

Finally, the Stalinist Revolution has also been seen as a "Soviet Thermidor" (Leon Trotsky). The Stalinist Revolution industrialized the Soviet Union, but it also created a group of privileged bureaucrats who adopted many aspects of life from the tsarist period. This may be seen most strikingly in the educational system, where experimentation was dropped in favor of rote learning, school uniforms, and other trappings of the tsarist educational system. Workers, while far less privileged, did have access to free education and health care and low-cost housing and food. Those who remained in the countryside were the major losers.

The postwar fear of the Soviet Union and the development of the cold war encouraged the acceptance among social scientists of the concept of totalitarianism. Supposedly, the Soviet Union, Nazi Germany, and Fascist Italy were comparable in the desire of each to control all aspects of life. The Soviet Union had done far more than Nazi Germany or Fascist Italy to change the way its citizens lived, but even it did not succeed in creating a totalitarian society. Although there was some political value in emphasizing the similarities of the three regimes, comparison invariably broke down on close examination of actual conditions and practices. Totalitarianism eventually came to be seen as a social science construct of limited explanatory value.

Post-war Revolutions.

The German Revolution was the most important of the postwar revolutions. It began in November 1918 with the refusal of sailors at the naval base in Kiel to take part in a last engagement against the British navy. In Kiel and several other cities in northwestern Germany, sailors, soldiers, and

ROSA LUXEMBURG, MARXIST REVOLUTIONARY

In 1898, Rosa Luxemburg moved to Berlin to seek her fortune in the German Social Democratic Party (SPD). New to the SPD, she was, however, no novice. The year before she had earned a doctor of law degree from the University of Zurich with a thesis on the development of capitalism in Poland. She was also one of the founders and leaders of the Polish Social Democratic Party (SDKPiL).

The SPD wanted Luxemburg to work in the Polish areas controlled by the German Empire, but she almost immediately began playing a prominent role in the Revisionist controversy. Revisionists, particularly Eduard Bernstein, stressed the importance of bringing Marx up to date. Luxemburg defended marxist orthodoxy, particularly in her pamphlet *Social Reform or Revolution?* A brief quotation may sum up her argument:

> The legislative process and revolution are . . . not various methods of historical progress that one can choose at the buffet of history like hot or cold sausages according to inclination, but various *factors* in the development of class society that qualify and complement one another.

Virtually an overnight success in the SPD, Luxemburg spent the next several years writing articles and giving speeches on the necessity of working toward the eventual outbreak of revolution. At the same time, she worked to create a personal life, with a comfortable apartment, a few close friends, and, most important, the companionship of her lover and coleader of the SDKPiL, Leo Jogiches.

The Russian Revolution of 1905 seemed to offer a new political direction. She succeeded in traveling to Warsaw, in the Russian part of Poland, only in December 1905, when the main part of the revolution was over.

Nevertheless, for a few months, she lived the life of a full-time revolutionary. In March 1906, she and Jogiches were arrested. Her health deteriorated alarmingly in prison and friends and family worked to secure her release on bail. In August she was allowed to leave the country.

She wrote a pamphlet, *The Mass Strike,* setting out her ideas on revolution, but by the time it appeared the SPD and most other European social democratic parties had lost interest in the possibilities for revolution. The SPD showed little interest in Luxemburg's idea that the working class would gain class consciousness through historical experience in mass strikes. Luxemburg found the period between the Russian Revolution of 1905 and the outbreak of World War I very difficult in personal terms as well. She broke with Jogiches after hearing he had had an affair with another woman.

Rosa Luxemburg spent most of the war in prison. From there she hailed the Russian Revolution as "the mightiest event of the World War," but she believed its fate depended on what the countries of the West did.

Luxemburg was released from prison on 9 November 1918, the day the German Revolution began. She and her friends had little influence on German politics over the next two months. She participated in the formation of the German Communist Party (KPD), but this changed little more than the name. In January 1919 she became involved in the so-called Spartacist Rebellion. Arrested on 15 January, Rosa Luxemburg was beaten, shot to death, and tossed in the Landwehr Canal in Berlin. Her body was recovered in the spring. And so ended the life of a brilliant, orthodox marxist revolutionary, someone who likely would have made an important difference in the interwar period had she lived.

---

workers formed the equivalent of the Russian soviets in 1917, Workers' and Soldiers' Councils. A second center of revolution appeared in Munich when social democrats formed the Bavarian Republic on 8 November. The following day the Kaiser left Berlin for exile in the Netherlands and social democrats formed a coalition government.

When the Congress of Workers' and Soldiers' Councils met in mid-December, it supported government efforts to provide food and oversee the demobilization of the army. Radical elements formed the Communist Party of Germany (KPD) late in December of 1918. Early in January 1919 some members of the KPD tried unsuccessfully to overthrow the government. The main result was the arrest and murder of two prominent leaders of the KPD, Rosa Luxemburg and Karl Liebknecht. Sporadic attempts from the left and the right to overthrow the government characterized the period from 1919 to 1923, but the Weimar Republic survived and seemed to take on new life by the mid-1920s.

Elsewhere, a radical center of revolution emerged in Hungary, now an independent state. In March 1919 a coalition of left socialists and communists proclaimed a Soviet Republic. The most prominent figure in the regime, Béla Kun, immediately began establishing socialism in Hungary. The regime lasted only until 1 August 1919, however. Beyond Germany and Hungary, there were few echoes of 1917 in Europe.

The Hungarian Revolution (1956).

Most of the revolutionary activity after World War II took place in the Soviet bloc. As was the case with the Hungarian Revolution, it provided clear indications of how deeply unpopular the Soviet-style regimes were. In 1956 Hungary, like Poland, questioned the failure to address consumer needs, the practice of police terror, and the reasons for the show trials of the early 1950s. Unlike Poland, however, Hungary could not find a path that would provide it autonomy without provoking the Soviet Union.

On 23 October 1956, Imre Nagy, a popular, reform-minded communist leader, was again appointed prime minister. His appointment led to a surge of popular enthusiasm. In the next several days, Hungary moved toward a more democratic political system, a mixed economy, and neutrality. The Soviet Union, particularly once the Suez Canal crisis began to preoccupy the United States and its allies, decided to send in troops. Despite weeks of resistance, it crushed the Hungarian Revolution. Some 2,700 died fighting or were executed. More than 200,000 fled the country. The Soviet Union demonstrated the narrow limits of experimentation it would accept. The United States and NATO showed their unwillingness to risk nuclear war in order to help the Hungarians.

Student Revolts in Europe (1965–1968).

In the last half of the 1960s, students and intellectuals questioned every aspect of the established system in what appeared to be a new wave of revolutions. They accused governments of ruling in an authoritarian style at home and aiding counterrevolution abroad. Some saw themselves as part of a worldwide revolutionary movement. Others had more limited aims, the reform of elitist educational systems. The impact varied. Britain and the Netherlands had important movements, but limited results. Germany and Italy contended with larger movements, but escaped major crises. Only in France did student radicalism lead to the possibility of revolution.

May 1968 in France occurred because of dissatisfaction with the authoritarian style of government and uneasiness with rapid and uneven change, but mostly because of complaints about conditions at the new University of Nanterre. It began almost accidentally. On 22 March a meeting to protest the arrests of students for protesting the involvement of the United States in Vietnam produced the 22 March movement. On 2 May, members of the movement, locked out of Nanterre, went to the Sorbonne, part of the University of Paris. The next day, police broke tradition by coming into the Sorbonne and arresting hundreds of students. This began a series of demonstrations between students and police in the Latin Quarter. By the 13th, in support of the students, hundreds of thousands of people demonstrated in Paris against the government. The next day workers seized the Sud-Aviation plant. Eventually ten million workers all over France went on strike. The French government seemed in serious trouble.

Toward the end of May, the French government finally took hold, dissolving the National Assembly and setting a date for new elections. Charles de Gaulle, president of France, appealed for "civic action" against a "totalitarian plot." The possibility of a communist takeover frightened many. Parisians, initially sympathetic to the students, had tired of disruptions. Workers generally only wanted modest changes. Student radicals themselves were divided as to goals. Faced with a choice between stability and revolution, most voters opted for the former.

The "events of May" were never close to succeeding. The "system" was the enemy, but no one could agree on what to put in its place. Daniel Cohn-Bendit, a German studying in Paris, caught the imagination of many, but most radicals distrusted leaders. Operating mostly on the level of tactics, the students

Hungary, 1956. Hungarians destroy a statue of Stalin. THE DAVID KING COLLECTION

were lost once the government seized the initiative. In addition, labor organizations impeded potential links between students and factory workers.

Radicalism continued in the 1970s and led to the formation of terrorist organizations in Germany and in Italy. These groups were the source of much drama in the 1970s, but the fulcrum of politics moved back toward the right-center in the 1980s.

The Prague Spring (1968).

The Prague Spring encompassed efforts to create a "socialism with a human face" in Czechoslovakia. Although crushed by the August invasion of troops from the Warsaw Treaty Organization (WTO), it left a legacy that was revived in the revolutions of 1989.

By the mid-1960s, Czechoslovakia was ripe for change. Reformers in the Czechoslovak Communist Party called for reform in the neo-Stalinist party and for new economic policies. Writers, filmmakers, and people working in theater had already begun daring artistic experiments.

In January 1968, Alexander Dubček replaced Antonín Novotný as first secretary of the party. Dubček represented the moderate reform element in the party and also spoke for Slovak interests. Reforms began cautiously. An "Action Program," announced in April, called for concentration on consumer-goods production and the expansion of political freedom.

The pace of events was too rapid for many in the party. Quasi-political clubs appeared and the Social Democratic Party was revived. A radical declaration, "2,000 words," signed by many intellectuals and cultural figures, appeared in June. By then, not only students and intellectuals but also the working class supported the reforms. Conservative elements in the Czechoslovak Communist Party, however, began to wonder if the party could maintain its political monopoly.

The WTO also grew nervous. Czech leaders met with their counterparts from the WTO in July and again in August. Dubček believed he had successfully convinced the WTO the Czechoslovak Communist Party had the situation under control. On the night of 20–21 August, WTO troops and tanks crossed into Czechoslovakia. The Czechs followed a policy of nonviolent protest, but this did not stop the invasion. Over the next few years the "normalization" of Czechoslovakia took place. Some half million members of the Czech Communist Party were thrown out of the party. People who had been officials or doctors now worked as janitors, construction workers, or window washers.

In the west the invasion was seen by many as one more example of counterrevolution destroying the hopes of reformers and revolutionaries in a year filled with disappointments. The Prague Spring was also presented as a lost opportunity for Communism to show what it could do. Leonid Brezhnev, head of the Communist Party of the Soviet Union, asserted in the "Brezhnev Doctrine" that the USSR had an obligation to intervene in Czechoslovakia to preserve the continued existence of socialism.

The East European Revolutions of 1989.

By 1989 the "Brezhnev Doctrine" was a dead letter and the Soviet bloc faced a period of change and reform. Mikhail Gorbachev, secretary-general of the Communist Party of the Soviet Union, was largely responsible for the new situation. Gorbachev had begun a process of reform in the Soviet Union that, while unsuccessful, influenced reformers and dissidents throughout the Soviet bloc. He had stated pointedly that the Soviet Union would no longer intervene in domestic affairs of other Soviet bloc nations. Finally, Gorbachev opened a new era in the cold war, resulting in much better relations between the Soviet Union and the United States.

The reemergence of Solidarity, the trade union movement begun in 1980, as a major factor in Polish politics in 1989 added to the new situation. In the elections in the summer of that year, Solidarity won a stunning victory. The first non-Communist premier in more than forty years headed the new coalition government. In Hungary, too, there were important changes in 1989. That summer Hungarians candidly discussed the Revolution of 1956, and in a moving ceremony they reburied martyrs from that event.

In each of the countries that experienced revolution in 1989, domestic factors played important roles. The German Democratic Republic (GDR) began to collapse first simply from a hemorrhage of people. Thousands of East Germans crossed the border between Hungary and Austria, which Hungary opened in mid-summer. East Germans also crowded into the West German embassies in Prague and Warsaw and eventually traveled to West Germany on special trains. Finally, the uncontested march on the ring road around Leipzig on 9 October began a process in which the government responded to events rather than initiated them. Each week demonstrations in Leipzig, Berlin, Dresden, and other cities grew larger and bolder. The attempt by the government to regain its footing by dumping party leader Erich Honecker was insufficient. The more-or-less accidental opening of the Berlin Wall, long the symbol of the standoff between communism and democracy, doomed the government. By this time, thousands of ordinary East Germans had decided they no longer were interested

LEIPZIG AND THE BEGINNING OF THE GERMAN REVOLUTION OF 1989

On Monday, 9 October 1989, rumors abounded in Leipzig, the "Second City" of the German Democratic Republic (GDR). The authorities were stockpiling medical supplies. Police and militia groups were taking up positions near the Nikolaikirche in the city center. All signs pointed to a showdown between the government and the demonstrators, who planned to march around the city after the weekly peace prayer services that evening. Now that the official ceremonies marking the fortieth anniversary of the founding of the GDR had taken place, the government had no reason to avoid a confrontation.

For many years, there had been a weekly prayer service at the Nikolaikirche. In the fall of 1989, when the services started up again after a summer recess, a new element appeared. After the service, people met outside the church to talk about current events, including the large number of East Germans who had crossed the Hungarian border to Austria and, subsequently, to West Germany. Many people talking outside the church after the service had not attended it, but knew they could find people to talk with after the service. In September and the first Monday in October there had been demonstrations. The weekend before the 9th, during the celebrations of the fortieth anniversary of the founding of the GDR, people had been arrested. Everyone expected that this Monday there would be some kind of confrontation between demonstrators and the authorities.

On Monday, 9 October, in addition to the usual peace prayer service at the Nikolaikirche, several other services were scheduled to accommodate the expected crowds. At each service someone read an appeal from six prominent citizens of Leipzig. The appeal noted the need for discussion of the serious questions now facing the nation and called for all in attendance to refrain from provocative behavior.

After the services, the demonstrators began walking the ring road that encloses the center of the city. Unlike the week before, the police, the militia, and the *Stasi* (the political police) merely watched. The crowd chanted *Wir sind das Volk* (we are the people, that is, the people for whose benefit the government was supposed to be ruling) as it walked around the city center. And also, very important for that particular moment, it chanted *Keine Gewalt!* (no violence).

It is still not clear why the government chose not to confront the demonstrators that evening. Probably the decision was made on the local level to avoid violence. On whatever level the decision was made, it was of tremendous importance. The peaceful demonstration by thousands of ordinary people that Monday evening marked the beginning of the German Revolution of 1989. From then on, no matter how quickly and radically the government responded to a particular initiative of the crowds of demonstrators in Leipzig, Berlin, Dresden, and other cities of the GDR, it always found itself one step behind. Exactly one month after the successful demonstration in Leipzig, the Berlin Wall opened on November 9th. Over the next few months, the revolutionaries moved from a desire to reform the GDR to the idea of merging the GDR and the Federal Republic of Germany (FRG). Negotiations for unification moved rapidly and in 1990 the GDR and the FRG came together as a united Germany.

---

in reforming the socialist system. To the dismay of the activists in the civic movements, they embraced the appealing idea of entering the social market economy of the Federal Republic of Germany. The elections of 18 March 1990 made it clear that most East Germans wanted unification with West Germany.

In Czechoslovakia, demonstrators in Prague filled Wenceslaus Square in November. At first, police tried to break up the demonstrations, but over the next few days the crowds swelled to overwhelming numbers. The Czech government remained always a step behind. The center of political gravity shifted to the Magic Lantern Theater, where Václav Havel and others worked to direct the revolution. In December, the old government resigned and a new government headed by Havel formed. Alexander Dubček, hero of the "Prague Spring," returned from years of obscurity to take part in the "Velvet Revolution."

The revolutionary wave swept away the Communist government in Bulgaria without violence. In Romania, however, Nicolae Ceauşescu, who had ruled in an increasingly arbitrary way since the 1960s, tried to stay in power. Captured by revolutionary forces, he and his wife were tried, declared guilty, and shot. Television pictures of the dead couple flashed around the world.

In a few short months, the unthinkable had happened. The "Iron Curtain" was no more. New governments began experiments with market economies and democratic political systems.

CONCLUSIONS

The dissolution of the Soviet Union in 1991 marked the end of the long Russian Revolution. Gorbachev's attempts to reform the system had inadvertently caused its demise. It was not likely it would have survived much longer in any case. It was ironic that Gorbachev, a true believer in the communist system, was the prime mover in its dissolution. It was also fortunate in that he ended the system in a way that caused little damage.

Five hundred years of revolutions did much to shape European political, economic, and social systems. Paradoxically, one major conclusion may be that failure leads to success. Those revolutions that eventually resulted in enduring systems—for example, the Dutch, the British, and the French—each involved a series of revolutionary efforts to achieve a consensus durable and flexible enough to sustain itself into the future. The Russian Revolution of 1917, however, turned into a system that, while hardly ideal, worked well enough for a time, but lacked any capacity for dealing with new circumstances.

The Hole in the Flag. A soldier makes a victory sign through a flag from which the communist symbol has been removed, Russia, 1991. ©FILIP HORVATH/SABA

In politics, systems capable of responding to changing circumstances have the best chance to endure. Revolutions seem prone to create systems that resist moderation and compromise. Nonetheless, in the future change may still come through revolution. Almost no one foresaw the Revolutions of 1989. That series of events also calls into question any easy connection between revolution and the desire for utopia. The temptation in revolutionary situations has been to want to change human nature dramatically, but there are examples of revolutions where the moderates have not moved in the direction of large-scale social engineering. So much depends on circumstances and the weight of the past. In the end there are no iron laws of revolution.

See also other articles in this section.

BIBLIOGRAPHY

General

Billington, James H. *Fire in the Minds of Men: Origins of the Revolutionary Faith.* New York, 1980. An intellectual history of the concept of revolution from the late eighteenth to the early twentieth century. Wide-ranging and authoritative.

Brinton, Crane. *The Anatomy of Revolution.* Rev. and expanded ed. New York, 1965. First published in 1938. A highly influential comparative study of revolution. Brinton, an expert on the French Revolution, used it as the basis for his paradigm of revolution.

Cohn, Norman. *The Pursuit of the Millennium: Revolutionary Millenarians and Mystical Anarchists of the Middle Ages.* Rev. and expanded ed. New York, 1970. The classic study of millenarianism. It covers sixteenth-century millenarianism and the medieval background as well.

Forster, Robert, and Jack P. Greene, eds. *Preconditions of Revolution in Early Modern Europe.* Baltimore, 1970. Very useful essays by experts on the Netherlands Revolt, the English Revolution, and the Fronde.

Goldstone, Jack A., ed. *The Encyclopedia of Political Revolutions.* Washington, D.C., 1998. A well-organized resource with contributions from leading experts in the field.

Goldstone, Jack A. *Revolution and Rebellion in the Early Modern World.* Berkeley, Los Angeles, and Oxford, 1991. A wide-ranging study of revolution that suggests demographic pressures on limited resources as the primary cause of revolution.

Moore, Barrington Jr. *Social Origins of Dictatorship and Democracy: Lord and Peasant in the Making of the Modern World.* Boston, 1966. A highly original and influential study that focuses on reactions by aristocracy and peasantry to changing economic and social circumstances as a means for explaining the transition to a modern political and economic system.

Skocpol, Theda. *States and Social Revolutions: A Comparative Analysis of France, Russia, and China.* Cambridge, U.K., 1979. The most important comparative study since Brinton. Skocpol stresses the central role of the state and the importance of the international context.

Tilly, Charles. *European Revolutions, 1492–1992.* Oxford, 1993. A study of revolution over the long term, primarily in the Netherlands, Britain, France, and Russia. Highly recommended.

Todd, Allan. *Revolutions 1789–1917.* Cambridge, U.K., 1998. An introduction to various aspects of revolution including origins, ideology, and personnel. Includes brief excerpts from relevant documents.

Van Creveld, Martin, ed. *The Encyclopedia of Revolutions and Revolutionaries: From Anarchism to Zhou Enlai.* New York, 1996. Comprehensive coverage chronologically and geographically.

Zagorin, Perez. *Rebels and Rulers, 1500–1660.* 2 vols. Cambridge, U.K., 1982. A comparative discussion of the Netherlands Revolt, the British Revolution, and the Fronde, among others, by a scholar thoroughly familiar with the era.

Studies of Particular Revolutionary Periods

Agulhon, Maurice. *The Republican Experiment, 1848–1852.* Translated by Janet Lloyd. Cambridge, U.K., 1983. A thorough study by one of the leading experts on the period.

Banac, Ivo, ed. *Eastern Europe in Revolution.* Ithaca, N.Y., 1992. Scholarly studies of the various revolutions.

Berlin, Isaiah. *Karl Marx: His Life and Environment.* 3d ed. Oxford, 1963. The best biography of Marx.

Carsten, Francis L. *Revolution in Central Europe, 1918–1919.* Berkeley, Calif., 1972. A good introduction to the topic.

Chartier, Roger. *The Cultural History of the French Revolution.* Durham, N.C., 1991. Chartier stresses the importance of cultural practices in shaping the ideas of the participants in the French Revolution.

Conquest, Robert. *The Harvest of Sorrow: Soviet Collectivization and the Terror-Famine.* New York and Oxford, 1986. A careful study of the famine of 1932 and collectivization policies.

Cust, Richard, and Ann Hughes, eds. *Conflict in Early Stuart England: Studies in Religion and Politics, 1603–1642.* London, 1989. An important series of studies intended to revise the revisionists without, however, returning to a class-based analysis of the English Revolution.

Doyle, William. *The Oxford History of the French Revolution.* Oxford, 1989. A knowledgeable synthesis of the history of the French Revolution.

Ferro, Marc. *October 1917: A Social History of the Russian Revolution.* London and Boston, 1980. A readable and solid history by a leading French scholar.

Fink, Carole, Philipp Gassert, and Detlef Junker, eds. *1968: The World Transformed.* Cambridge, U.K., and New York, 1998. Wide-ranging and excellent scholarly essays on 1968.

Fitzpatrick, Sheila. *Stalin's Peasants: Resistance and Survival in the Russian Village after Collectivization.* Oxford, 1994. An examination of peasant response to collectivization based on new archival material.

Furet, François and Mona Ozouf, eds. *A Critical Dictionary of the French Revolution.* Translated by Arthur Goldhammer. Cambridge, Mass., 1989. A very useful and authoritative reference work, the book is divided into sections on "Events," "Actors," "Institutions and Creations," "Ideas," and "Historians and Commentators."

Garrioch, David. *The Formation of the Parisian Bourgeoisie, 1690–1830.* Cambridge, Mass., 1996. An ambitious study that indicates the Parisian bourgeoisie may have been in some sense ready to support an event like the French Revolution and were further shaped by their experience in the Revolution.

Gati, Charles. *Hungary and the Soviet Bloc.* Durham, N.C., 1986. Places the Hungarian Revolution in the context of the experience of the Soviet bloc.

Gelderen, Martin van. *The Political Thought of the Dutch Revolt, 1555–1590.* Cambridge and New York, 1992. A thorough study of an important topic.

Hill, Christopher. *Century of Revolution, 1603–1714.* Wokingham, U.K., 1980. Although Hill's marxist interpretation of the seventeenth century is no longer widely accepted, his study of the period is nevertheless interesting and highly readable.

Hunt, Lynn. *The Family Romance of the French Revolution.* Berkeley, Calif., 1992. An original study dealing with ways in which the French understood the Revolution by references to family dynamics and images of mothers and fathers.

Israel, Jonathan, *The Dutch Republic: Its Rise, Greatness, and Fall, 1477–1806.* Oxford, 1995. A massive and indispensable survey of the history of the Dutch Republic.

Jones, J. R. *The Revolution of 1688 in England.* New York, A useful overview of the revolution.

Keep, John L. H. *The Russian Revolution: A Study in Mass Mobilization.* New York, 1976. One of the few books that looks at 1917 outside of Petrograd and Moscow.

Kotkin, Stephen. *Magnetic Mountain: Stalinism as a Civilization.* Berkeley, Calif., 1995. An important study of Magnitogorsk, on of the show projects of the First Five-Year Plan.

Kusin, Vladimir. *The Intellectual Origins of the Prague Spring: The Development of Reformist Ideas in Czechoslovakia, 1956–1967.* Cambridge, U.K., 1971. An excellent source for tracing the roots of the reform movement.

Landes, Joan B. *Women and the Public Sphere in the Age of the French Revolution.* Ithaca, N.Y., 1988. An important study that demonstrated that the French

Revolution actually provided less room for women in the public sphere than the Old Regime had.

Maier, Charles S. *Dissolution: The Crisis of Communism and the End of East Germany.* Princeton, N.J., 1997. The best single book on the topic.

Parker, Geoffrey. *The Dutch Revolt.* Rev. ed. New York, 1988. A recent survey by an expert in the period.

Pilbeam, Pamela. *The 1830 Revolution in France.* London, 1991. A recent scholarly study of 1830 in France.

Price, Roger. *The French Second Republic: A Social History.* Ithaca, N.Y., 1972. An excellent book on French society in the Second Republic.

Ranum, Orest. *The Fronde: A French Revolution, 1648–1652.* New York, 1993. A useful overview of the Fronde.

Rosenberg, W. G. and L. H. Siegelbaum, eds. *Social Dimensions of Soviet Industrialization.* Bloomington, Ind., 1993. Scholarly essays on workers and workplaces in the 1930s.

Rudé, George. *The Crowd in the French Revolution.* Oxford, 1960. A careful and fascinating study of who made up the crowd in the various revolutionary *journées*.

Russell, Conrad. *The Fall of the British Monarchies, 1637–1642.* Oxford, 1991. Russell, in addition to downplaying political conflict and restricting the revolutionary period to the late 1630s and early 1640s, stresses the extent to which the English Revolution was a British problem.

Schama, Simon. *Patriots and Liberators: Revolution in the Netherlands, 1780–1813.* New York: Alfred A. Knopf, 1977. The best study of the Dutch Revolutions at the end of the eighteenth century.

Siegelbaum, L. H. *Stakhanovism and the Politics of Productivity in the USSR, 1935–1941.* Cambridge, U.K., 1988. An interesting study of the Stakhanovite movement in particular and labor relations more generally.

Sonn, Richard David. *Anarchism and Cultural Politics in Fin-de-Siècle France.* Lincoln, Neb., 1989. A scholarly study of anarchism at the peak of its influence.

Tackett, Timothy. *Becoming a Revolutionary: The Deputies of the French National Assembly and the Emergence of a Revolutionary Culture (1789–1790).* Princeton, 1996. A very useful study of how the movement for change and reform became a revolution.

Tilly, Charles. *Popular Contention in Great Britain, 1758–1834.* Cambridge, Mass. and London, 1995. The best book available on this controversial topic.

Tilly, Charles, Richard Tilly, and Louise Tilly. *The Rebellious Century 1830–1930.* Cambridge, Mass., 1975. A wide-ranging study that provides useful perspectives on political violence in the nineteenth century.

Tombs, Robert. *The Paris Commune 1871.* New York, 1999. A recent survey.

Tucker, Robert. *The Marx-Engels Reader.* 2d ed. New York, 1978. A convenient collection of the most important works by Marx and Engels.

Williams, Kieran. *The Prague Spring and Its Aftermath: Czechoslovak Politics, 1968–1970.* Cambridge, U.K., 1997. An analysis of the reform movement and its suppression by the Soviet Union using archival sources available since the events of 1989.

LABOR HISTORY: STRIKES AND UNIONS

Michael P. Hanagan

Labor history studies the history of class relationships in societies where wage labor predominates. It is inevitably bound up with strikes, the major forms of wage-labor protest, and trade unions, the major organizations for mobilizing wage laborers. One scholar noted, "Strikes and unions appear to be the only universal characteristics of industrial societies" (Roberto Franzosi, unpublished paper, 1992).

EUROPEAN LABOR HISTORY BEFORE THE 1960s

Labor history has flourished in countries with some perceived anomaly in labor movement development requiring explanation. For a long time most scholars viewed labor movement growth as following a necessary path of development from the foundation of the first local trade unions to the organization of national unions, culminating in socialist parties composed of class-conscious workers. Expectations about the "necessary path" of labor development were powerfully shaped by Karl Marx and Friedrich Engels's *Communist Manifesto*. Marx and Engels portrayed economic concentration and mechanization as promoting a movement from dissatisfaction with local conditions on the part of workers within specific trades, to a generalized class consciousness. For early generations of labor historians a glance around the Continent seemed to warrant such a generalization. By 1914 national trade unions and socialist parties had formed in almost every continental European state and were making rapid electoral progress wherever workers possessed the suffrage. France and Germany, where class-conscious labor movements began to emerge in the late nineteenth century, did not see the first growth of serious labor history. Instead, labor history developed in England, where the moderate Trades Union Congress gradually rallied to a Labour Party that adhered, very tentatively, to socialism in 1918. For some time the most important questions in labor history were implicitly comparative. Why did the labor movement in an individual country not follow a path pursued by labor in other countries?

British labor history. Among the first classics of labor history were the study of British trade unions by Sidney and Beatrice Webb published in 1894 and the series of studies of laborers and skilled workers between 1780 and 1840 by John and Barbara Hammond, the first of which appeared in 1911. The Webbs' trade union history emphasizes the democratic character of trade unionism and its commitment to bargaining at a time when the enfranchisement of a substantial section of the male working class worried many middle-class Britons. In Russia the newlywed Vladimir Ilich Lenin and his young wife, Nadezhda K. Krupskaya, celebrated their honeymoon by translating the Webbs' history. The Hammonds' much-reprinted portraits of the industrial revolution as a catastrophic visitation on the proletarianized laborers shocked many Britons, who gloried in their pioneering industrial role. The Hammonds portrayed Chartism as a native English variety of radicalism. They set off a controversy about the standard of living in the industrial revolution that endured into the twenty-first century and lastingly concentrated the attention of British labor historians on this period of the nation's history.

The Hammonds and the Webbs produced an analytical labor history based on archival research that dealt with broad social conditions of the population and the effects of industrial change on their daily lives as well as with trade unions as institutions possessing unique organizational characteristics and capacities. They brought social history concerns into labor history from the outset. Although neither the Hammonds nor the Webbs were traditional academics, their arguments developed according to academic standards and almost immediately stimulated academic debate. They were extremely fortunate that their successors in the interwar years included historians as remarkable as G. D. H. Cole and R. H. Tawney.

In the 1950s and 1960s British scholarship in labor history was brilliantly advanced by historians of the caliber of Eric Hobsbawm, George Rudé, and E. P. Thompson. Like their predecessors these historians did not occupy prestigious academic positions but still exerted major influence within academia. Surely the Hammonds and the Webbs would have been surprised to discover that their successors apprenticed in the Communist Party Historians Group between 1946 and 1956. They would also have been surprised by the transformations in labor history these scholars wrought. Hobsbawm and Thompson particularly expanded the Hammonds' focus on the changes in the daily life of workers caused by the industrial revolution and stressed the influence of violent protests against capitalism in the formation of broader reform movements instead of democratic integrationism. Hobsbawm advanced some basic ideas that labor historians debated in the 1960s and 1970s. His elaboration of the role of the "labor aristocracy" in labor movements, debated by Lenin and other socialists at the turn of the century, and his conception of the "rules of the game" as a set of standards, mutually understood by workers and employers and subject to change over time, were widely influential.

Still more important was Thompson's emphasis on the role of popular culture and political conflict in the development of a worker identity. In his classic account *The Making of the English Working Class* (1963), Thompson acknowledged the marxist argument that economic forces created a new industrial proletariat but insisted on the importance of popular culture and social conflict in the development of class consciousness. Unlike earlier labor historians, Thompson portrayed class consciousness and class conflict as more than reflections cast by economic structures. He insisted on their independent roles in class formation. In particular Thompson challenged the view that British class formation in the early nineteenth century was incomplete because it did not achieve the kind of socialist consciousness found in France. Thompson denied that consciousness could be ranked and insisted on its variety and complexity.

Thompson's work provoked a great deal of controversy among British labor historians, but even those who challenged him betrayed his influence. Scholars such as Gareth Stedman Jones increasingly focused on the role of cultural and ideological factors in the molding of popular identity, stressing that class was only one possible construction of popular experience and arguing for the independent role of ideology and culture in identity formation. Only a minority of historians pursued Thompson's emphasis on the role of conflict in shaping identity formation.

Class Conflict. Capital pummels Labor during the Scottish coal miners strike of 1894. Cartoon on the front page of *The Labour Leader,* a journal edited by James Keir Hardie, 22 September 1894. BY PERMISSION OF THE BRITISH LIBRARY, LONDON

French labor history.   The contrast between the timing of the evolution of labor history in Britain and in France is remarkable. In 1913 the scholar Maxime Leroy published a pioneering work, *La coutume ouvrière,* dealing with labor's influence in the regulation of nineteenth-century French industry. It found no echo in academia or in the labor movement. Never reprinted, Leroy's book survives in only a handful of libraries around the world. Pre-1914 France produced popular narratives recounting the history of the labor movement from the point of view of particular socialist factions or by concerned middle-class outsiders. These histories were seldom based on extensive research, simply reinterpreted familiar events, and never paid attention to the condition of the great mass of French workers or the transformations in the labor force under way as the country industrialized in the late nineteenth century.

As a field of academic study, French labor history began at least a generation later than English labor history. Founding figures like Maurice Dommanget, Georges Duveau, and Jean Maitron moved easily between socialist movements and historical research projects. Dommanget possessed a prodigious knowledge of the history of the French Socialist movement, Duveau's studies of working-class life and educational theories under the Second Empire prefigured the later turn toward social history, and

Maitron was personally familiar with many labor activists. French labor history tended less toward comparison, either explicit or implicit, than did English or German labor history. France's revolutionary heritage and early embrace of socialism often was taken for granted, as if that country followed a predestined path of development. French historians perhaps remained unaware of the unique features of their country's evolution.

As in England the growth of labor history in the French academy resulted from a need to explain unexpected developments within the labor movement during World War I. Despite the denunciation of war by the Socialist Party and the revolutionary pretensions of the Confédération Générale du Travail (General Confederation of Labor), the main French trade union, both party and union entered into the war effort with hardly a demurrer. Why did French leftists follow one course of action and Russian leftists another course? After World War I the movement split into communist and socialist factions, and as the split hardened historians sought to understand the basis of this profound division within the working classes. Why did French intraclass political divisions prove so irreconcilable? Responding to these questions was an important problem facing French labor history. To understand why revolutionary political rhetoric had concealed nationalist sentiments, French labor historians examined the social conditions of trade unions and political parties. In the 1960s and 1970s France produced a brilliant constellation of academically trained labor historians to address these questions, including Claude Willard, Annie Kriegel, Michelle Perrot, Rolande Trempé, and Yves Lequin.

German labor history. In Germany the advent of dictatorships delayed or interrupted the growth of labor history scholarship until the post–World War II period. In the 1950s and 1960s German historians, preoccupied with the rise of fascism, explored Germany's "special path," the particular mixture of traditional institutions and rapid industrialization that produced both mass socialism and fascism. German historians were particularly interested in comparative history, focusing in particular on comparing German development with that of England. Like French historians German historians were interested in why self-proclaimed revolutionary socialists had embraced the war so eagerly. Of course, marxist East Germany was especially concerned with labor history. East German labor historians typically concentrated on the history of socialism and trade union organization, but innovative historians drew on Western labor history, which was interested in broader social and cultural aspects of workers' experiences. Perhaps the best-known labor historian of the immediate post–World War II period was Gerhard Ritter, who produced an important study of the labor movement in Wilhelmine Germany. In the 1960s and 1970s a large number of talented German historians emerged, including Werner Berg, Dieter Groh, Jürgen Kocka, Klaus Tenfelde, and Hartmut Zwahr.

EUROPEAN LABOR HISTORY AFTER THE 1960s

The 1960s and 1970s were a period of rapid growth in labor history throughout Europe. In these years, the growth of politically independent radical youth movements and spontaneous explosions of worker protest led to a reappraisal of labor movement history by many militant young historians. In general these young historians sought new approaches to answer old questions. Addressing the classic question of why the London working classes became quiescent in the late nineteenth century, historians abandoned their focus on the character of marxist leaders and studied the deindustrialization of the London urban economy in the second half of the nineteenth century. To answer why French trade unionists supported the war effort in World War I, historians rejected the old emphasis on traitorous leaders and looked at the undermining of artisanal militancy by waves of industrialization. To explain the German socialists' participation in the war, historians explored the cultural isolation of socialist workers and the wholesale acceptance of mainstream cultural assumptions by German socialist organizations. Young scholars began to label themselves "labor historians" and, though established historians remained doubtful, to explore the social and political bases of class formation. Almost every European country produced serious works of labor history, and some academic traditions, such as those of the Netherlands and Sweden, yielded their own distinctive historical approaches to the field. Americans, too, contributed significantly to European labor history, but they often were as much influenced by American labor historiography, an interesting subject in its own right. They are not discussed in this essay.

Increasingly, current events mocked attempts to claim "exceptional" status for a national labor movement or to argue that any nation had followed a "special path." The dominant questions in labor history lost their significance as the sense of labor as an international movement declined. Everywhere in Europe labor movements adapted to the national political environment. Although this accommodation began during the interwar and war years, its reality became clear after World War II, as European labor movements developed different patterns of strike militancy and varied relationships with states. Strikes diminished in some countries, while worker militancy continued in others. Some trade unions participated in industrial planning alongside employers, while other national unions balked. Some trade unions gave socialist parties considerable leeway to negotiate labor demands, while others refused or kept party leaders on a tight leash. In the 1970s labor union membership declined in many European countries, and the bargaining positions of trade unions almost everywhere deteriorated. Many labor historians shared Hobsbawm's sense of *The Forward March of Labour Halted?* (1979). Few any longer saw labor as an international movement with a common strategy and an incontestable claim on the future. The marxist paradigm that privileged workers as the "world-historical" class seemed less convincing.

Faced with the dissolution of old assumptions, the decline of labor movements, and labor's varied efforts to adapt to national politics, labor history reconfigured itself. Some historians argued for a more institutional labor history that would place labor organizations more precisely within national political structures. Most labor historians chose to cast their nets more broadly, looking at class and the ways in which class interacted with culture, gender, and race—a vital contact with social history generally. No longer preoccupied with manifestations of class consciousness, historians stressed how class interpenetrated, shaped, and was shaped by other social and cultural contexts. Other labor historians, focusing on discourse and the ways language constructs meaning, sought to look at how class was discursively constructed and deconstructed. The 1980s and 1990s witnessed an explosion of exciting labor history and a dramatic expansion of research agendas. Scholars such as Anna Clark, Patrick Joyce, Alf Lüdtke, Hans Medick, Gérard Noiriel, and Pascal Ory indicated the continuing richness of this research tradition. However, it became increasingly difficult to locate them within a unified field of study because labor history entered a postparadigm fluidity.

As labor history gave up its concern with "exceptionalism" or "special paths," it also abandoned its concern with internationalism. But in an age when trade unions confront globalization and states come under pressure from both the European Union and international organizations, it may be necessary to consider international issues again without the teleological blinkers of common paths and shared strategies.

STRIKES

One of the oldest concerns of labor history has been the study of strikes. More than any other, this area has produced interdisciplinary exchanges between historians and social scientists, but these exchanges have not been as complete as they might. A look at studies of strike propensity by sociologists and economists may bear more on debates among historians than is generally realized.

While the origins of the strike can be traced to far antiquity, strikes did not become a routine form of protest until the nineteenth century. The rise of the strike form of protest is roughly correlated with the growth of the wage labor force that became the focus of labor historians. In all European countries the collective cessation of work became the universal weapon of labor protest. Whether demanding higher wages, the eight-hour day, the suffrage, or the end of colonialism, workers struck.

While labor historians have studied strikes extensively, most research on the rhythms of strike activity is by sociologists or economists. Unlike many other aspects of labor history, strikes are susceptible to precise measurement in terms of participation, duration, and length, and many scholars have detected a tendency for strikes to occur in waves. Systematic records of strikes maintained by national governments or culled from other sources have been subjected to quantitative analysis. While willing to consider the findings of social scientists, labor historians have, with only a few exceptions, generally proven reluctant to undertake anything but the most elementary quantitative analyses.

Theories of strike causation abound. Some scholars stress the role of supply and demand for labor, others see strikes as dependent on the interactions of workers and employers, and still others emphasize the need to place strikes within a political context. Early social scientific explanations of strike activity sought a single universal cause, either searching for a single general principle that explained all strike activity or positioning labor movements within a comprehensive stage theory of development. While some once-prominent theories of strike causation have been seriously challenged, a sophisticated theory of strikes probably depends less on accepting or rejecting competing theories than on combining various theories and specifying the circumstances in which different explanations apply or refining them to take into account additional factors.

Strikes and business cycles. One of the most commonly employed explanations of strike activity is an

Labor Demonstrators. Cooperative and Trade Union members demonstrate against profiteering, Hyde Park, London, 21 September 1919. ©HULTON GETTY/LIAISON AGENCY

economic model that links strikes to business cycles. In good times, when labor markets are tight, workers are likely to strike for higher wages, while in bad times, when unemployment makes it easy to replace workers, they are less likely to strike. Such explanations depend on a highly instrumental interpretation of labor relations, but strike waves are loosely correlated with economic cycles. More intriguing is the relationship of strikes to longer Kondratieff waves, cycles of approximately fifty years' duration. James Cronin has argued their importance in understanding large-scale changes in the structure of the British labor movement.

While most scholars agree that business cycles play a role in strike activity, much remains that economic conditions cannot explain. Most notably they cannot explain international variations in strike propensity, and these differentials have become more important with time. The variations in strike propensities among leading European countries increased significantly during the twentieth century. Because strikes vary along national lines, the development of different regimes of industrial relations or political factors are liable to be of more importance.

Strikes and unions. The presence of trade unions is another factor associated with strike activity. By pro-viding workers with collective resources and experienced organizers, trade unions increase the likelihood of strikes. Undoubtedly trade unions contribute to strike propensity, but on some occasions unionization increases after strike activity rather than before it as trade union theories of strikes would suggest. Trade unions are sometimes the products of strikes rather than their causes.

While unions may facilitate strikes, they also play an important role in shaping them. Michelle Perrot's study of strike activity in France explores the era of spontaneous strikes. Between 1870 and 1890 most strikes occurred without prior notice. Frequently the notification of a paycut resulted in an unannounced strike. Upon reading the posted notifications, a band of workers might roam the shop floor, singing revolutionary songs and calling their fellows out on strike. Next a committee of workers would be elected to represent workers' grievances to their employers and to report their employers' responses to general assemblies of workers. These workers' assemblies made all the basic decisions, often unanimously. Gradually, Perrot argued, trade unions took over the strike, requiring workers to propose concrete demands and organizing them in disciplined demonstrations. In the process, Perrot suggested, strikes often lost touch with the sentiments of the rank and file.

While most students of strike activity agree that business cycles and trade unions encourage strike activity, stage theories of trade union development that once enjoyed considerable support generally have been abandoned. In the 1950s and 1960s a well-known American study by Clark Kerr, John T. Dunlop, Frederick Harbison, and Charles A. Myers emphasized the existence of a variety of forms of evolution beginning with societies controlled by dynastic elites. They contended that under special circumstances revolutionary intellectual elites used worker militancy to take power. But revolutionary elites were only temporary custodians of power. In the long run only middle-class elite regimes proved really stable and compatible with the requirements of modern industrialization. Middle-class elites were willing to bargain collectively with workers if necessary to accomplish their economic goals. For Kerr and his collaborators, 1960s America was a model of advanced industrial relations, while European unions with their communist and socialist affiliations were only hindrances to the development of genuine industrial relations. Supporters of this view may take comfort from the collapse of the USSR but only cold comfort, since American collective bargaining collapsed almost as completely. Most European trade union movements remained more vital than those in the United States at the end of the twentieth century.

Strikes and industrial relations. Other interpretations relying on industrial relations stress international variations in factors such as employer organization, repression, or the organization of labor. The component factors of industrial relations may differ in degree across Europe and are better candidates for explaining the manifest variations in the character of strikes. Although labor history is based on the study of class relationships, workers have been studied far better than employers. Only in the late twentieth century did historians begin to analyze employers' roles in labor conflicts. Much can be learned. For example, the mysterious short-term cycle of Italian strike activity that had puzzled some scholars is explained by the three-year contracts that prevailed in large-scale Italian industries. Over time the ability of employers to organize and collectively oppose strikes has varied greatly. Peter Stearns demonstrated that French strike activity declined in the years before World War I, as employers successfully organized to resist militant unionists. Roberto Franzosi showed that the anticommunism of immediate post–World War II Italy allowed the state and employers to carry out repressive actions against communist activists.

Franzosi offered the most daring argument of all and presented well-documented evidence about the ways class conflict influences the formation of the working class and industrial organization. He posited that labor militancy in large factories resulted in the transformation in the character of Italian heavy industry. Responding to the waves of strikes that swept Italian industry in 1969, industrialists reconfigured their industrial sites, abandoning the strike-prone, large, continuous-process plants operating under intense time discipline. They trimmed the workforces at large factories and subcontracted to more flexible, smaller plants that were also less likely to unionize. Franzosi argued strongly that labor militancy influenced the choice of technology and plant selection at the highest level.

Strikes and the political context. Another series of powerful arguments contributing to the understanding of strikes and strike waves stresses the political context of labor relations. In this literature political parties are seen as shaping strike militancy and thus as influencing the character of class conflict. Among the best-known arguments in this vein are those that contrast countries like Germany, Sweden, the Netherlands, and Switzerland, where strikes have been infrequent, with countries like Belgium, France, Italy, and the United Kingdom, where strikes have been common. According to this interpretation, countries with large Social Democratic Parties that have close relations with trade unions incorporate trade unions' demands into political bargaining and, by exerting pressure at the national political level, avoid strikes. In contrast, countries such as the United Kingdom, where trade unions and the Labour Party are not intimate, or France, with multiple trade unions and politically marginal left-wing parties, have been unable or unwilling to diminish strikes.

A more sophisticated political interpretation of the origin of strikes is that of Edward Shorter and Charles Tilly. Like Franzosi they maintain that industrial conflict produces unique repertoires of protest and that such repertoires can have enduring influence on class antagonisms and their expression. A "repertoire" of protest is a cultural creation that describes how people act together in pursuit of shared goals. Shorter and Tilly described how a particular type of political strike became a part of French workers' repertoire. They suggested that the precarious political position of the Third Republic led republicans to intervene to protect workers, who were generally republicans, from large employers, who were often antirepublican. Eventually republican intervention shaped French industrial relations. Instead of gathering resources for long strike struggles, French workers engaged in temporary but massive strikes to win the at-

The French General Strike of 1936. Workers dance during a sit-down strike at the Thomson factory in Paris, 3 June 1936. ©HULTON GETTY/LIAISON AGENCY

tention of politicians. They were most likely to strike when prolabor administrations took power. The massive strikes of June 1936 that followed the election of the Popular Front can be seen as the climax of this tendency.

Strike outcomes. While theories about the causes of strikes proliferate, much less work has evaluated the primary concern of strikers and employers, that is, the outcomes of strikes. The most important work in this area is that of Samuel Cohn. Looking at French strikes between 1890 and 1935, Cohn found that unions engaged in frequent strikes produced higher wages, even when strikes failed. In addition strikes over working conditions and political issues won more in the long run than strikes over wages. Short strikes yielded greater gains than long strikes, and bureaucratized, centralized unions produced smaller gains than decentralized unions. But strikes only yielded these results when unions competed against one another, as they frequently did in pre-1914 France, to establish their militancy. Once a trade union established its identity as reformist and decidedly moderate, trade union competition discouraged militancy. Employers channeled benefits to the moderate trade unions to reward them and to punish radicals. In such circum-

stances radicals could be made scapegoats and punished when strikes occurred.

The analysis of strike conflicts has produced a rich and diverse literature concerned primarily with the causes of strikes. Much of this debate was conducted by social scientists using quantitative methods to analyze strike behavior. The full weight of their findings has not yet been integrated into mainstream labor history. Certainly, social scientists have been more willing than labor historians to suggest that labor conflict plays an important role in shaping industrial organization and protest repertoires. More fully than many labor historians realize, the work of social scientists suggests that industrial conflict is an important determinant of class formation and identity.

TRADE UNIONS

In every European industrial country workers organized into trade unions, which played an important role in generating strikes. Trade unions are legal institutions regulated by governments, economic institutions that claim jurisdiction to represent different sections of the labor force, and political organizations that often have formalized relations with national political parties and sometimes with organized industrialists. Trade unions are one of the characteristics that distinguish labor movements from other social movements seeking to influence government for social reforms. They have a base in ongoing organizations that represent workers in their everyday work life. Because they usually have a professional staff, organize at the national level, and control substantial resources, trade unions provide the sustained support to working-class social movements that enables them to endure the inevitable ebb and flow of popular support characteristic of many social movements.

Trade unions vary considerably according to

1 the type of workers they seek to organize,
2 their power to establish an organizational monopoly in an occupation or an industry,
3 state regulation, and
4 their ability to develop a centralized national structure.

Although students of industrial relations recognize the importance of different forms of labor organization in collective bargaining, the full range of causes of international differences in the structures of trade union organizations has been studied little.

Origins of trade unions.

The earliest trade unions organized highly skilled workers, and some historians have argued that early trade unions were shaped by the ideological perspectives of the failing guilds or corporations. Both organizations sought to regulate trade, and early trade unions often provided death benefits and sometimes pension plans reminiscent of the services that guilds provided for their members. William Sewell Jr. suggested that in France early mutual aid societies inherited guild traditions and transmitted them to the nascent trade union movement. Sewell's view has been challenged by French historians who found little relationship between the first mutual aid societies and collapsing guilds, and not much evidence indicates that elsewhere in Europe mutual aid societies perpetuated guild outlooks. In any case the democratic character of western European mutual aid societies in contrast with typical guild practices should raise doubts about the continuity of their views. In Germany, where guilds retained a legal or semilegal basis into the mid-nineteenth century, the influence of guild spirit may have shaped attitudes. Scholars have suggested that the provision for elected workers' representatives to supervise the insurance funds that Otto von Bismarck incorporated into his insurance laws was a response to the older practice of guilds controlling and supervising their members' funds.

While they may not have inherited the practice from guilds, highly skilled urban artisanal trades, invariably the earliest centers of craft trade unionism, were everywhere dominated by males. The strength of trade unionism has always depended on informal solidarity among workers created and maintained in the social world outside the workplace. The first unions were invariably unions of highly skilled workers based on male recreational networks formed in cafés, bars, and taverns and shared residence in working-class neighborhoods. Mary Anne Clawson described these informal male ties as constituting a "fraternalism" that, while underwriting worker solidarity, also preserved gender discrimination within the working class. Gender discrimination in early craft trade unions also reflected a desire to preserve skilled craft jobs, especially in the textile industry, from "deskilling," a frequent synonym for feminization.

Industrial unions.

Although the industrial revolution threatened the positions of many craft unions, the sense of shared interests that produced industrial unionism took much longer to develop, in contrast to Marx's original expectations. The industrial revolution influenced artisans by bringing many of them into large factories, but even behind factory walls these workers maintained their characteristic independence. In many instances they remained a self-conscious elite, separate and independent from the majority of factory workers. The industrial revolution also increased the numbers of coal miners, who represented a new group of workers, the semiskilled workers. Unlike artisans, most miners acquired their skills by assisting or working alongside older, more experienced workers. But like artisanal labor, underground coal mining depended on the spirit of teamwork and off-the-job recreation. Such images of camaraderie aboveground and belowground could only be accepted in a gendered form, usually as masculine characteristics.

Eventually the second industrial revolution, with its large-scale capital accumulation and new disciplinary techniques, brought new opportunities for women. But progress was hardly immediate. At first the great power accumulating in the hands of employers enabled them to remake the labor force, and by and large they made it in their own image, masculine. A new family economy arose around the fledgling industries of the second industrial revolution. This family economy was based on increased earnings of male workers in heavy industry and decreased opportunities for female employment, as homework declined and unskilled factory work grew more slowly than semiskilled. Working-class males increasingly found stable, long-term employment, while their wives performed domestic labor at home but not commodity production.

As the militancy of workers crested during the 1920s, a result of the vast expansion in metalworking during World War I, trade unionists attempted to embed the assumptions of this new family economy within the bargaining process by demanding a "family wage" sufficient for adult males to adequately support a family. The significance of the demand for a family wage differed from nation to nation and from occupational group to occupational group. In some nations, such as Great Britain, many male skilled workers actually attempted to maintain nonworking wives even though budgetary constraints often foredoomed their goals. In France male coal miners demanded a family wage on the assumptions that women's work was unsteady and subject to more fluctuations than men's work and that family maintenance depended on the preservation of a stable, high male wage. In both cases male workers based wage demands on assumptions about males' predominant responsibility for wage earning, but such assumptions did not always require married women's absence from the workforce, even as an ideal. The family wage model justified a dual wage structure for men and women whether or not women were in fact supplemental earners.

The vision of the male proletarian breadwinner did not prove prophetic. Partly as a result of war work during both world wars but also because of recurrent labor shortages, employers were forced to accept a growing number of female workers in heavy industry. Many of these organized women rejected the assumptions behind the family wage and its implications for trade union action. As the twentieth century wore on the division of labor once more changed. By the late nineteenth century white-collar unions formed in some European countries, and their expansion was general in the post–World War II period. White-collar work always had a larger proportion of women than artisanal or semiskilled labor. At first a rough equality prevailed among male and female clericals. As the number of clerical workers grew, most women were tracked into gender specific pools of female secretaries, while male workers occupied better-paid positions with chances for promotion. In the twentieth century the gendered division of labor within many areas of white-collar work and the associated unions began to break down. When schoolteachers, engineers, designers, or bank clerks organized, women were as likely to organize as men. Fraternalism was least likely to dominate in the expanding white-collar unions, although a gendered division of labor remained characteristic of many trade unions in most industrial countries.

Competing union movements.

The preceding discussion of unions as bargaining agents presumes that unions successfully established their claims to represent workers. In many European nations rival unions competed for workers' allegiances. In some cases employers or repressive states tacitly supported the creation of company unions to prevent the growth of independent trade unions or as vehicles to enhance surveillance of workers. Paternalistic unions sometimes offered financial inducements for membership. After the encyclical *Rerum Novarum* (1891), Catholics organized their own trade unions, and in Belgium, France, the Netherlands, Germany, and Italy these unions became minorities to reckon with. Originally many of these religious unions adopted paternalistic principles and sought to conciliate employers, but over the long haul they became more militant and independent of employers. As they did so Catholic units also tended to become more secular and sometimes provided militant competition for established socialist or communist trade unions. In addition Catholic unions often successfully organized women workers. The church's original insistence that men and women workers meet separately sometimes fostered the growth of Catholic female trade union activists more successfully than did secular socialist unions, with a few exceptions, like those associated with the Sozialdemokratische Partei Deutschlands (German Social Democratic Party) when socialist women also organized separately. In France in the 1960s and 1970s the formerly Catholic Confédération Française Démocratique du Travail (French Democratic Confederation of Labor) often criticized the communist CGT from the left.

While leftists denounced the division of the trade union movement between religious and secular unions, in the end the most serious divisions in the European labor movement were produced by leftist factions. Before 1919 socialist unions were the majority unions in almost all European countries. Exceptions included France and Spain, where revolutionary syndicalists or anarchists were dominant, and England, where after 1906 the Labour Party, not at that time socialist, was the official party of most trade unions. Although trade unionists publicly expressed opposition to war, the enthusiastic participation of the majority of trade union organizations in the World War I war effort and divergent responses to the Russian Revolution of 1917 split the trade union movement in many countries right down the middle. Communists won the majority of the trade union movement, at least temporarily, in France and Italy and possessed a substantial minority in German and Austrian trade unionism. Until 1989 communists re-

Sit-Down Strike. Workers block the entrance to the Austin factory in Longbridge, Birmingham, England, 1956. ©HULTON GETTY/LIAISON AGENCY

tained a powerful hold over the major unions in France and Italy, and opposition between socialist and communist trade unionists proved divisive in national trade union movements. In one of the most dramatic examples, the socialist-communist divisions in Germany in the 1930s contributed to the Nazi Party's rise to power.

Unions, parties, and the state. The spread of radical ideas into the trade union movement or in some cases the ideological resistance to radicalism has attracted much attention. Trade unions as institutions regulated by the state have received less attention. Strikes in Europe became legal but also subject to greater regulation. The same laws that recognize some strikes prohibit unauthorized, sit-down, and wildcat strikes. The modern strike is powerfully influenced by legal regulations. Long after trade unions were recognized legally in Great Britain, judges found it difficult to distinguish between unions and criminal conspiracies and awarded civil damages to employers that would have resulted in a prohibition on strikes. Laws passed in 1859, 1871, and 1875 to legalize peaceful strikes were invalidated by court decisions declaring strikes breaches of contract and, as such, conspiracies against employers. These decisions forced trade unionists to intervene politically to protect their organizations. The Taff-Vale decision of 1901, which held that trade unions were conspiracies of civil law, was the

breaking point that stimulated British trade unionists to form the Labour Party to obtain relief. The French law of 1884 that seriously restricted the right of unions to own property and forbade unions to have relations with political parties encouraged the growth of a revolutionary syndicalist movement stressing militancy rather than building strike funds or performing social insurance functions.

The relationship between trade unions and socialist parties also powerfully influenced the bargaining strategies pursued by trade unions. Countries where trade unions developed early, in advance of or separate from socialist parties, often found it difficult to construct industrial unions. The United Kingdom and Denmark had early trade union movements, and craft unionism retained significant strength. When socialist parties played an important role in the construction of trade unions, they almost always built industrial unions and favored centralized trade union organizations. Socialists preferred centralized industrial unions because they facilitated relationships with national socialist political parties.

In the 1960s and 1970s the presence of such organizations was practically a precondition for labor's participation in "neocorporatism." "Neocorporatism" refers to the extraparliamentary cooperation between the state and private interests by which the state confers legal authority to private groups in return for their self-regulation. According to Colin Crouch, Austria, the Netherlands, Sweden, and West Germany were among the leading neocorporatist states. While the study of the neocorporatist phenomenon was a favorite research topic of the 1970s, interest subsequently slackened because of the phenomenon's decline in the face of global competition.

Just as important for the evolution of industrial relations was the trade unions' formal relationships with socialist parties. Perhaps the most striking position on their relationship is that first taken by Seymour Martin Lipset. He argued that in countries like Great Britain and the United States, where suffrage expanded before the growth of socialist parties, craft unions developed ties to liberal parties, inhibiting the growth of socialist parties and ties between trade unions and socialist parties. In contrast, in countries like Germany and Scandinavia, where mass socialist parties developed in advance of national trade unions, socialist parties dominated the trade union movement, encouraged industrial unionism, and coordinated economic policies with trade unions.

In a work comparing Britain and Sweden, James Fulcher stressed the importance of the relationship between trade unions and socialist parties. Fulcher argued that in countries like Sweden, where socialist parties dominate trade unions, it is much easier to develop an active labor market policy. In countries like Britain, where relations between trade unions and socialist parties require negotiation and bargaining, it is politically difficult to impose an active labor market policy and possible only to secure pledges of support for wage-price guidelines. Because active labor market policy is a flexible and efficient economic tool, it tends to win public support and to sustain cooperation between party and union. In contrast, because wage-price guidelines tend to incite union hostility, these policies maintain the tense relationship between party and union characteristic of Britain. Thus the party-union relationship in both countries has a self-sustaining character, but the equilibrium status is more favorable to workers in Sweden than in Britain.

Unions in national and international perspective.

In the late twentieth century the focus among students of labor history shifted from a preoccupation with explaining national peculiarities or "exceptional" behavior to a concentration on the adaptation of labor movements to national environments. Scholars began to recognize that differences in political contexts and the relationships between industrialization and democratization exerted long-standing influences on trade unions and class formation. Much work has stressed the open-ended character of the interaction between politics, industrialization, and trade union organization. At any given point in time militant workers must chart their course within a context of labor movement structures, party and labor relations, and political alignments inherited from the past and

The First International. The first congress of the International Working Men's Association (the First International), Geneva, 1866. ©HULTON GETTY/LIAISON AGENCY

263

not easily changed. To understand this interaction, it is necessary to examine historical processes.

Considerable evidence points toward another shift within labor movements that poses important questions for labor history. The collapse of Communist regimes in Eastern Europe in 1989 revealed that the Eastern European working class had abandoned its long-standing socialist commitments. That tradition produced revolution in Russia and greatly facilitated the Soviet takeover of Eastern European governments in the post–World War II period. Although the USSR is gone, socialists and communists have remained split, and relatively little has been done to overcome the internal division of the international labor movement.

The persistence of this division when it seems to lack all justification has been particularly puzzling given the widespread recognition of the new importance of an international organization. Increasingly labor movements are concerned about global economic trends and the effects of European Union policies on their members. Such concerns are ironic. In the nineteenth century the labor movement was the most international of movements. Labor leaders were among the first concerned with establishing international ties to prevent the importation of strikebreakers and to discourage cheap foreign labor by helping laborers organize. In the nineteenth century business leaders questioned the loyalty of socialist leaders because of the socialist connection to international organizations. In late-twentieth-century Europe matters were almost reversed. Capital took the initiative in forming the European Union and in enrolling European states in international organizations from the World Trade Organization to the International Monetary Fund. In contrast, European labor leaders were notably slow to organize internationally. Increasingly students of labor movements have sought to understand how the most international of social movements has become so nationally oriented.

Labor history has revealed the multiple ways labor movements have interacted with national governments and national employers' organizations. A pressing issue is the extent to which adaptation to national environments has incapacitated labor for international organization. The varying structures of trade union organizations, the array of national strike repertoires and strike frequency, and the different cultural practices of national trade union movements pose serious problems for effective international coordination and collective action. In the past class conflict served as a potent force for mobilizing workers to recognize new circumstances and to adapt to new organizational forms. Will the advent of globalization and the greater transnational organization of capital produce a new sense of transnational class identity? Addressing this question may well become the next major item on the agenda of labor history.

See also **Marxism and Radical History** *(volume 1);* **The Industrial Revolutions; Communism** *(volume 2);* **Social Class; Working Classes** *(in this volume);* **Gender and Work; Factory Work** *(volume 4); and other articles in this section.*

BIBLIOGRAPHY

Labor History

Berg, Werner. *Wirtschaft und Gesellschaft in Deutschland und Grossbritannien im Übergang zum "organisierten Kapitalismus."* Berlin, 1984.

Clark, Anna. *The Struggle for the Breeches: Gender and the Making of the British Working Class.* Berkeley, Calif., 1995.

Groh, Dieter. *Negative Integration und revolutionärer Attentismus: Die deutsche Sozialdemokratie am Vorabend des Ersten Weltkrieges.* Frankfurt, Germany, 1973.

Hammond, J. L., and Barbara Hammond. *The Village Labourer.* London, 1911.

Hobsbawm, E. J. *The Forward March of Labour Halted?* Edited by Martin Jacques and Francis Mulhern. 1979. Reprint, London, 1981.

Hobsbawm, E. J. *Labouring Men: Studies in the History of Labour.* New York, 1965.

Hobsbawm, E. J., and George Rudé. *Captain Swing.* New York, 1968.

Joyce, Patrick. *Visions of the People: Industrial England and the Question of Class, 1848–1914.* Cambridge, U.K., 1991.

Kaye, Harvey J. *The British Marxist Historians: An Introductory Analysis.* New York, 1984.

Kocka, Jürgen. *Klassengesellschaft im Krieg: Dt. Sozialgeschichte 1914–1918.* Göttingen, Germany, 1973.

Kriegel, Annie. *Aux origines du communisme français: Contribution à l'histoire du movement ouvrier français.* 2 vols. Paris, 1970.

Lequin, Yves. *Les ouvriers de la région lyonnaise (1848–1914).* 2 vols. Lyon, 1977.

Lüdtke, Alf, ed. *Alltagsgeschichte: Zur Rekonstruktion historischer Erfahrungen und Lebensweisen.* Frankfurt, Germany, 1989.

Ory, Pascal. *La belle illusion: Culture et politque sous le signe du front populaire, 1935–1938.* Paris, 1994.

Perrot, Michelle. *Les ouvriers en grève, France 1871–1890.* 2 vols. Paris, 1974.

Ritter, Gerhard Albert. *Die Arbeiterbewegung im Wilhelminischen Reich.* Berlin, 1959.

Rudé, George. *The Crowd in the French Revolution.* Oxford, 1959.

Stedman Jones, Gareth. *Languages of Class: Studies in English Working Class History, 1832–1982.* Cambridge, U.K., 1983.

Tenfelde, Klaus. *Sozialgeschichte der Bergabeiterschaft an der Ruhr im 19. Jahrhundert.* Bonn, Germany, 1977.

Thompson, E. P. *The Making of the English Working Class.* New York, 1963.

Trempé, Rolande. *Les mineurs de Carmaux, 1848–1914.* 2 vols. Paris, 1971.

Webb, Sidney, and Beatrice Webb. *The History of Trade Unionism.* London, 1894.

Willard, Claude. *Les guesdistes: Le mouvement socialiste en France, 1893–1905.* Paris, 1965.

Zwahr, Hartmut. *Zur Konstituierung des Proletariats als Klasse: Strukturuntersuchungen über das Leipziger Proletariat während der industriellen Revolution.* East Berlin, Germany, 1978.

Strikes

Cohn, Samuel. *When Strikes Make Sense—and Why: Lessons from Third Republic French Coal Miners.* New York, 1993.

Cronin, James E. *Industrial Conflict in Modern Britain.* London, 1979.

Franzosi, Roberto. *The Puzzle of Strikes: Class and State Strategies in Postwar Italy.* Cambridge, U.K., 1995.

Friedman, Gerald. *State-Making and Labor Movements: France and the United States, 1876–1914.* Ithaca, N.Y., 1998.

Kerr, Clark, John T. Dunlop, Frederick Harbison, and Charles A. Myers. *Industrialism and Industrial Man.* Cambridge, Mass., 1960.

Shorter, Edward, and Charles Tilly. *Strikes in France, 1830–1968.* London, 1974.

Stearns, Peter N. "Against the Strike Threat: Employer Policy toward Labor Agitation in France, 1900–1914." *Journal of Modern History* 40 (1968): 474–500.

Trade Unions

Clawson, Mary Ann. *Constructing Brotherhood: Class, Gender, and Fraternalism.* Princeton, N.J., 1989.

Crouch, Colin. *Industrial Relations and European State Traditions.* Oxford, 1993.

Fox, Alan. *History and Heritage: The Social Origins of the British Industrial Relations System.* London, 1985.

Frader, Laura L., and Sonya O. Rose, eds. *Gender and Class in Modern Europe.* Ithaca, N.Y., 1996.

Fulcher, James. *Labour Movements, Employers, and the State: Conflict and Co-operation in Britain and Sweden.* Oxford, 1991.

Kassalow, Everett M. *Trade Unions and Industrial Relations: An International Comparison.* New York, 1969.

Katznelson, Ira, and Aristide R. Zolberg, eds. *Working-Class Formation: Nineteenth-Century Patterns in Western Europe and the United States.* Princeton, N.J., 1986.

Linden, Marcel van der, ed. *Social Security Mutualism: The Comparative History of Mutual Benefit Societies.* Bern, Switzerland, 1996.

Lipset, Seymour Martin, and Stein Rokkan. "Cleavage Structures, Party Systems, and Voter Alignments: An Introduction." In *Party Systems and Voter Alignments: Cross-National Perspectives.* Edited by Seymour Martin Lipset and Stein Rokkan. Munich, 1967. Pages 1–64.

Marks, Gary. *Unions in Politics: Britain, Germany, and the United States in the Nineteenth and Early Twentieth Centuries.* Princeton, N.J., 1989.

Tilly, Chris, and Charles Tilly. *Work under Capitalism.* Boulder, Colo., 1998.

SOCIALISM

Eric D. Weitz

Socialism is a word that has inspired great hopes and dread fears. It became the preeminent ideology of the labor movement in the industrial age, even if it never won the majority support of workers, let alone the rest of the population. Amid the harsh realities of industrial society, when poverty and insecurity were often the fate of workers, when society seemed riven by intense class conflict and an obsession with productivity and material success, socialism's promise of a world infused with liberty, equality, and prosperity proved immensely appealing. Socialism gave to its largely working-class advocates an enhanced sense of identity as workers, the opportunity to improve themselves through education and political activity, organizations through which they could fight for their ideals, and associations in which they and their families could enjoy their leisure. In many countries in Europe, the socialist movement played the key role in establishing or widening the democratic system and contributed greatly to the expansion of the social welfare state. It promoted women's participation in politics and the economy and gave a more open and liberal tenor to society.

At the same time, socialists fostered the enhanced discipline and regulation of modern society, both through the expanded role of the state that most socialists demanded and through the ideal of the self-disciplined, dedicated, male socialist militant. Socialists were often blind to forms of oppression that were only partly rooted in the class character of industrial society. In the heyday of the socialist movement, roughly from 1880 to 1960, women were accorded secondary status and socialist parties rarely challenged the gender division of labor or even the overt discrimination against women in the labor market and in wage scales. Too often, the socialist movement degenerated into sterile controversies over what precisely constituted "true" socialism. Factionalism—one group leaving to form a new party, another group expelled by party leaders—became a fixed feature of modern socialism. In its worst forms, the belief that the future society would come about through armed revolution and a vigilant state resulted in authoritarian systems in central and eastern Europe that systematically violated democratic liberties and, at times in the Soviet Union, engaged in mass killings of defined population groups, all in the name of socialism.

Socialism has been most commonly studied from the standpoint of intellectual or political history. Social history has also made important contributions, by turning its attention to the movement's social composition and its significance for working-class life and culture. In their studies, social historians have examined the variety of social groups that were drawn into the movement—artisans in the utopian socialist phase, students, discontented professionals, and, certainly in some cases, peasants. The social history perspective has illuminated the fact that socialism has never been a purely working-class phenomenon, and it has helped to explain why the movement failed to attract some workers, such as British textile workers, long drawn to the Conservative Party. Social history has also sought to assess what socialism meant for the workers involved, both in terms of practical politics and individual and group identities. For many workers, socialism was a means of reinforcing their efforts to improve wages and working conditions—a view of the movement which tended to promote a revisionist, rather than a revolutionary, ideology. Others, however, found real meaning in socialist revolutionary ideology, which sustained them in agonizing work situations and motivated them for political action when they could find no other place within the existing political system.

ORIGINS AND IDEOLOGIES OF SOCIALISM

The words "socialist" and "socialism" appeared first in German in the eighteenth century and have Latin roots. The immediate derivation of the words lay with the natural-rights philosophers of the seventeenth and eighteenth centuries, notably Hugo Grotius, Samuel Pufendorf, Thomas Hobbes, and Christian Wolff, who made "society" or the "social" an object of rational investigation and a source of sovereignty. The term "socialist" was first used as a pejorative, especially by Catholic philosophers who attacked natural-rights theorists as heretics. By the 1790s, "socialist" had become a more neutral term of description for them, chiefly for Pufendorf and his intellectual descendants. Often, they were called interchangeably "naturalists" or "socialists." In 1802 came the first recorded instance of the word "socialism," again in reference to Pufendorf and his teachings. Around the same time, the philosopher G. W. F. Hegel used the term "antisocialist," by which he meant, oddly enough, the same group of thinkers whom others had labeled socialist. For Hegel, natural-rights theory, especially in its French variants, was individualistic, hence antisocialist.

Into the 1830s, the terms were only common in the intellectual discourse of the very few members of the educated elite, especially in Germany and Italy. Conservative philosophers and theologians would continue to see a direct line of descent from Grotius, Pufendorf, and Hobbes and their concern with the social to the socialist thinkers and organizers of the modern period. But around the 1820s and 1830s, the meaning of the words became transfigured, and their usage became vastly broadened. The sources for the change were the French and industrial revolutions of the late eighteenth and nineteenth centuries, the great transformations that ushered in the modern era. Both revolutions gave an entirely new meaning to the social. In the first half of the nineteenth century, the word "social" conjured up images of masses in motion, the popular classes going to the barricades in Paris and Lyon or joining the revolutionary and Napoleonic armies as they crossed the Continent, spreading the ideas of liberty and fraternity. "Social" also signified the new factory system, with scores and hundreds of workers toiling away behind the gates in a factory and giving a new density to urban life. The "social question" emerged, signifying a new realization of the poverty and the dangers to the social order that industrialization brought in its wake.

"Utopian" socialists.

For the first time in the 1820s, "socialist" was used self-consciously and in a positive sense by a political group, namely, the followers of Robert Owen in England. They seemed to have no knowledge of the word's usage in German, but obviously adopted it from the term "social," now widely current to designate both English versions of natural-rights theory and the entire complex of transformations associated with the French and industrial revolutions. In the 1840s Karl Marx and Friedrich Engels would pin the term "utopian socialists" on the

Owenists and their French and (a few) German counterparts, notably the writers, ideologues, and organizers Charles Fourier, Étienne Cabet, Flora Tristan, and Claude Henri de Saint-Simon and their followers. The term has stuck ever since, though not always with the disparaging sense used by Marx and Engels. These first socialists were by no means all alike; a number of them postulated ideas that definitely ran toward the wild (and sometimes endearing) end of the political spectrum. Fourier's belief that men and women in the future socialist society would live among oceans of lemonade is only one of the more bizarre examples.

Still, it is possible to identify certain common elements among the utopian socialists. All of them believed that industrialization had created a crisis in human existence that required radical solutions. As heirs of the Enlightenment and the French Revolution, they believed that the new society could be created by self-conscious acts of will, by human beings, rational in nature, dissecting the problems around them and conceiving the correct course of action. In opposition to the conflict and anonymity of the new industrial society, people would live in small-scale, face-to-face, self-governed communities. Production would still be largely artisanal in nature (though Owen's communities were based on factories). The early socialists did, indeed, imagine their solutions to be utopian in the sense that they would solve for all eternity the problems of human existence. The mutual ownership of wealth would unleash great prosperity, precisely because wealth would not be squandered by the excesses of the few who could afford to indulge their whims and desires. Common ownership would also abolish the jealousies that arose from social inequalities, which had caused so much conflict and so many wars in all of past time. But the utopian socialists firmly believed that their promised society was not only about economics. It would also be about liberty and the creation of a true fraternity (and, in the minds of a few, like Tristan, a new sorority as well) that had been promised by the French Revolution but that had gone unfulfilled. Socialism would be the stage of the "loving and productive society," in the words of the Saint-Simonians. Warm and affectionate relations would emerge among people, perhaps underpinned by the recognition that their interests lay in harmony with one another. Artistry and innovation would flourish, and true liberty—self-government and individuality—would at last prevail.

A number of the utopian socialists also engaged in a radical critique of the patriarchal family and were among the first to articulate a call for the equality of women and men. A few of them, like Fourier, also envisaged more open and experimental sexual lives in

A Utopian Community. View of New Lanark, founded by the reformer Robert Owen (1771–1858) as a workers' utopia for cotton mill employees. THE ART ARCHIVE/EILEEN TWEEDY

their communities. Particularly in the sphere of family and gender relations, the utopian socialists promoted more diverse and radical ideas than the marxist parties and trade unions that came to dominate the socialist movement later in the century. In this sense, marxism, while playing a key role in the explosive growth of the movement, also represented a narrowing of the social critique and of the political possibilities represented by socialism.

Alongside the emancipatory strains, there was, no doubt, also a strong tenor of control and regulation in utopian socialism. The Owenite communities in Scotland and the United States, notably New Lanark and New Harmony, were carefully supervised by Owen, who was, after all, an industrialist, albeit an atypical one. The Icarian communities, founded by Cabet and his followers in France and the United States, were more completely collectivist than the Owenite ones, but by their very nature they too were not exactly amenable to expressions of individuality. Fourier thought each socialist community should house precisely 1,620 members.

But even organization and control could prove appealing to people whose lives were being battered by the advance of the market system and the factories. Both the timing and the message of the utopians held particular appeal for anxious urban craft workers. The utopian socialists began to attract popular support in Britain and France between the 1820s and 1840s, and somewhat less so, but also significantly, in Germany.

They were tireless organizers and thereby helped create the pattern of ceaseless political activism that would be a major characteristic, for good and bad, of the socialist movement well into the twentieth century. Much of their energies (and resources) went into the establishment of model autonomous communities, which they believed would become replicated throughout society. Utopian socialists also engaged in political activism in the existing systems. Owen, Cabet, Tristan, Fourier, and others lectured, wrote pamphlets and books, and published newspapers. Their followers agitated around the country, distributing the printed word and learning to speak whenever an audience could be found. They formed the first trade unions and producer and consumer cooperatives in working-class communities. They helped generate the climate of opposition to the prevailing order that fed into the revolutions of 1848. The cause in 1848 was not theirs alone, by any means, but the early activists inserted a minority, socialist strain into the agitation surrounding the revolts that spread all over Europe.

These engagements generated intense hostility from the forces of order, governments, industrialists, and the churches. The dreary run of arrests, prison sentences, exile, and, sometimes, execution became a feature of the activist life. For the representatives of order, the utopian socialists represented dangerous, even perverse, ideas, and they went to great lengths to paint the socialists as destroyers not just of the political and social order but of the family and morality as well.

The marxian impulse. The utopian socialists suffered in the widespread repressions that followed the revolutions of 1848. But there were inherent weaknesses in their ideas that also contributed to their decline (though not disappearance) in the second half of the nineteenth century. The biggest problem was the small-scale orientation of utopian socialism at a time when industrial units were becoming ever larger and the wave of nationalism was superimposing national upon local and regional identities. By 1880 or so, utopian socialism seemed somewhat quaint, the product of an earlier, now largely surmounted, era. Marxian socialism could meld far more easily with nationalism than could utopian socialism. Moreover, the Owenite and Icarian communities suffered the fate of so many communal organizations that set themselves apart from society. A kind of sterile infighting set in, along with severe economic difficulties. A few of the communities would survive into the twentieth century, carrying along traces of their original egalitarian ideas. But almost no one could imagine them to be the pioneers of new forms of social and political organization.

Instead, over the course of the second half of the nineteenth century, the ideological direction shifted to marxism. One should not imagine that marxism became easily and completely the single or even dominant expression of socialism. Various strands of anarchism had strong followings, especially in the Mediterranean regions of Europe and in Russia. Moderate socialists, especially in Great Britain, explicitly rejected marxism. Even in Germany, syndicalist-type socialism, rooted in the trade unions and contemptuous of politics and the state, had significant support in particular regions and trades, notably in the Berlin construction trades, among others. The supporters of Marx and Engels fought long and hard in France and Russia to establish their own parties and their domination over other groups, and they were never completely successful. The majority of workers all across the Continent remained outside the socialist camp and affiliated with Catholic, conservative, or liberal parties.

Nonetheless, it was marxism that became the dominant ideology of the socialist labor movement. Marxism offered militants and workers a clear perspective on contemporary society and a sense of history. For those who engaged the ideas, even on a cursory level—and Engels's "Socialism, Utopian and Scientific," was probably the most accessible and widely read summation—marxism gave people an understanding of how capitalism had emerged and how it would be, inevitably, superseded. By accepting and even promoting industrialism and the nation-state and, at the same time, ruthlessly critiquing them, marxism accorded with the lived realities of many workers, who lived within these structures yet chafed at their oppressions. Marxism also promised, in essence, a developmental dictatorship to the more backward parts of Europe—that is, a system that would bring more underdeveloped areas into the era of the factory and the nation-state, and then would go beyond them.

Still, marxism retained many of the impulses of the utopian socialists who both preceded and were contemporaries of Marx and Engels. Like the utopians, marxism promised an end to history, a point at which all the bloody, ceaseless conflicts that had defined history would truly be surmounted. Society would be harmonious, egalitarian, and democratic. Self-government in a world of equality would create the substratum that would allow individuals to develop freely their own talents and interests. The clash between individual and society would be forever erased. And that essential contradiction of capitalism—social production coupled with private ownership of the means of production—would also be surmounted, leading to unparalleled riches for all.

Marxist arguments continued to appeal to many artisans, who, along with intellectuals, often provided the leadership for the political movements that resulted. (The German socialist leader August Bebel, for example, was from an artisanal background.) But the ideology and above all the strong emphasis on solid political organization also attracted factory workers and miners, many of whom, by the last third of the nineteenth century, became durable supporters. Finally, it was at this point that peasants in certain regions, because of tensions over landownership or traditions of regional dissent, moved toward socialist commitment. This was the case in the countryside around Bologna, Italy, for example, and also in southeastern France.

THE SOCIAL HISTORY OF SOCIALISM

Marxism provided a heady vision, and it helps explain why a new surge of the socialist movement began in the 1860s and then took off, especially from the 1880s, and continued well into the twentieth century.

Organization and the movement before World War I. The socialist upsurge began more or less concomitantly in all the countries of central and western Europe and then spread more slowly into eastern

Europe, where the economies were less developed and the political systems more repressive. The socialist upsurge did not occur easily, and it was not a simple creation of political ideologues. Socialism as a movement was shaped not just by the ideology of marxism but also and very profoundly by the proletarian milieu in which it was anchored.

Around the 1860s in central and western Europe, that milieu was still largely artisanal in nature despite the tremendous growth of factories. The first socialists tended not to be factory proletarians, those idealized by Marx, but skilled, male craft workers who labored in small shops, some of which they owned. They had not been subject to the difficulties of factory labor, but had very definitely felt their livelihoods and ways of life threatened by the advance of factory production and the capitalist market. Some of these people became the key rank-and-file militants of the socialist movement, those who spread the word, organized cooperatives and trade unions, and helped found, in the 1870s, the first marxian socialist parties that would last long into the twentieth century. Increasingly, they began to attract factory workers to their side as well, though many of those workers first entered the trade unions, especially when the so-called "new unionism" of the 1890s emerged, with mass unions in large-scale enterprises like the docks, coal mines, and steel factories. New unionism was clearly tied to the contemporaneous "second industrial revolution" based on very large-scale production and on the high technology of the day and typified by chemicals production, electric-power generation, steel manufacturing, and deep-shaft mining.

Germans succeeded in creating the largest socialist party in this era, the Social Democratic Party of Germany (SPD). This feat alone would warrant attention to the SPD. In addition, the SPD became the model party of the Second International, the association of socialist parties formed in 1889. Because of its size and ideological sophistication, and because, after all, Marx and Engels were German, the SPD was seen as their filial descendant.

Around 1900, the model socialist in Germany, as well as in Britain and soon also in Russia, was a male skilled worker, self-disciplined at work and at home and dedicated to the cause. In this period the "cradle-to-grave" concept—the notion that one would be involved in the party through the entire life course, and that the party would also take care of its members—became firmly ensconced. Children and youth would spend their free time in the libraries and clubs accommodated in union or party halls. They would distribute party leaflets and sell its newspapers on street corners. As apprentices, they would be prepared

to enter the union along with learning a trade. As adults, they would distribute party writings; demonstrate in support of free suffrage, higher wages, and peace; wander to different localities and workplaces as agitators for the party; stand for election as union delegates; and, if they lived in a country where democratic norms prevailed, run for the local city council. They might also learn to administer the arcane rules of state-supervised health plans, or learn how to counsel workers to obtain their accident insurance or old-age pensions. Their free time might be spent in the socialist choir or bicycle club. After a Sunday outing with the family, they might retire to the party hall for beer and a hot meal.

The situation for women was more complex, and everywhere women were a distinct, and sometimes minute, proportion of the organized socialist movement. Despite the socialist call for equality between men and women, the male "family wage" had become a fairly common ideal in the socialist movement. By demanding that working-class families be able to live on male wage earning, the socialist parties absorbed the common dual-spheres rhetoric of the age, which charged women with maintaining and developing the domestic sphere. In this manner, socialism supported patriarchal power. Moreover, socialists were enamored with heavy metal, the coal and steel industries that were the very epitome of industrialism and that employed few female workers. Socialists could not imagine a movement that organized only textile and commercial food workers, sectors in which women were much more prevalent, let alone those in domestic service. Yet at the same time, socialists sought to organize women into the movement, most successfully when women were allowed to join separate female groups. Some women, like Clara Zetkin and Adelheid Popp, countered the intense male prejudice of the movement. Like male militants, they found in socialism a setting where they could develop their talents and interests and give meaning to their lives.

Socialism was never, then, simply a political movement. It became inscribed in the social and cultural life of workers and militants, male and female, in very profound ways. There were towns and neighborhoods in Germany, France, Britain, and Scandinavia that acquired a pronounced socialist tone by the time of World War I. Clearly, the movement itself depended upon the tight intertwining of workplace and community that marked the age of high industrialization. There were always competing and overlapping identities—of religion, region, gender, and nationality. But an identification with class was probably strongest in Europe between 1880 and 1960, when workers encountered one another in the factory, on the streetcar or train commuting to work, and on the sidewalks and in the courtyards and pubs of the neighborhood. Upon that social reality, socialism provided an added layer of identity, one that gave ideological meaning to the status of worker.

Farther east on the Continent, socialism was far less rooted in society, if for no other reason than that industry was much less developed. Still, significant socialist parties had emerged in Bulgaria, Macedonia, Poland, and Russia, and they too won at least a few pockets of support. The harshly repressive political conditions, especially in Russia, resulted in a more militant, still angrier tone to the socialist parties. Almost every leading socialist in the Russian Empire endured the horrendous conditions of tsarist prisons and Siberian exile. They had little opportunity and fewer resources to provide the recreational programs and representation that socialists gave to workers in the western countries. They also competed with more peasant-based parties that represented a nonmarxian, populist form of socialism. A more typical form of contact between socialist militants and regular workers in these areas was literacy groups, in which socialist militants, often intellectuals, strove to teach workers, many of them only weeks removed from the villages, to read, and thereby introduce them to socialist teachings. Surreptitious trade unions were another form of organization, as was the establishment of underground couriers, who would distribute pamphlets and other literature.

Sometimes the rigors of underground life brought out the worst aspects of conspiratorial mentalities—sterile ideological conflicts, authoritarian dealings with others, arrogant confidence in the righteousness of one's own cause, and acts of terror against opponents. Indeed, in his famous tract *What Is to Be Done?* (1902) Vladimir Ilich Lenin turned many of the aspects of party life specific to the authoritarian conditions of Russia into the model organizational form for all socialist parties. Lenin wrote rhapsodically about the most severe discipline and most complete devotion required of party members, who were to be professional revolutionaries. Going further than most contemporary socialists and sharply modifying standard marxism, Lenin also argued that workers would not automatically develop revolutionary class consciousness. Instead, the revolutionary socialist party had to bring class consciousness to the proletariat.

Lenin's views were by no means universally accepted even within the marxian wing of the Russian socialist movement. Nor were the conflicts restricted to the east. The socialist movement, always diverse, faced severe internal dissension in the two decades before World War I. The "revisionist controversy," be-

gun in the 1890s, can be seen as the precursor to the great divide that would open up between socialists and communists in the wake of World War I. Initially fought out within the SPD, the conflict soon spilled over to the other member parties of the Second International. Eduard Bernstein, a leading figure in the SPD, argued that capitalism was not dividing into two classes, the bourgeoisie and the proletariat, as Marx had predicted. Instead, the middle class was expanding. Socialist parties had to win the backing of the members of the middle class as well as proletarians if they were ever to come to power with majority support. Socialism would then be implemented gradually and democratically. An accumulation of reforms, not armed revolution, would create the socialist future. Bernstein was opposed by Karl Kautsky and Rosa Luxemburg, who would later have their own differences, but for a time at least were united in upholding the marxian orthodoxy of revolution against Bernstein's more accurate sociological analysis of capitalism.

Most socialist workers, it can safely be estimated, were closer to the revisionist than the revolutionary position. Despite all the fire and brimstone of marxian rhetoric, which the socialist parties happily reproduced, in Germany, France, Britain, and Scandinavia socialists were increasingly drawn into the administration of the state. If not at the very top levels, at least in the municipalities, welfare agencies, and state-supervised labor markets, socialists worked ardently to improve the daily existence of the working class. They had successes, and the revolutionary impulse waned, at least in central and western Europe. At the same time, in the years just before World War I, class conflict grew exceedingly intense. Strikes and demonstrations became ever more prevalent, inspiring great unease among the upper classes, great hopes among workers and socialist militants. Luxemburg gave voice to this view with her idealization of mass spontaneous strikes, which was based on her observations of the 1905 Revolution in the Russian Empire.

World War I and socialist movements. On the eve of World War I, socialism had become a powerful movement in many countries. As political and diplomatic tensions accelerated in Europe in the summer of 1914, socialists made concerted efforts to prevent the advent of war. In every country they held great rallies in favor of peace, and the national leaderships convened for deliberations under the rubric of the Second International. But the SPD, attracted by the force of nationalism, fearful of government repression and a Russian invasion, voted in support of war credits in the German parliament—in contradiction to the antiwar position that both the German party and the

Rosa Luxemburg. The German socialist speaking at a meeting of the Socialist International in Stuttgart, August 1907. AKG LONDON

International had expressed for years. With very few exceptions, the other socialist parties followed suit. Contrary to long-held opinions, however, the most recent research has shown that workers did not all march enthusiastically off to war. The vote for war remained controversial among the rank and file, and many went off to war bitter at their own leaders and fearful of the realities of warfare.

World War I, the first total war in history, had unprecedented consequences for the working class and the socialist movement. As states directed resources, human and material, into the war-related industries, the working class became more concentrated in heavy industry and the more urbanized industrial areas. By and large, this was not the first time that women were drawn into the industrial labor force, as the most recent research has shown, revising another long-standing myth from the war era. But there were important sectoral shifts in women's labor, out of textiles, commercial food processing, and small-scale production generally and into the metalworking and munitions factories. Female workers were also becoming more highly skilled. The working class became more concentrated, accentuating those links between community and workplace, the sense of a common destiny, that underpinned the rise of the socialist movement.

This restructuring occurred in the midst of the enormously high death rate suffered by soldiers at the front and the intense losses and hardships endured by the population at home. Moreover, the state, since it had assumed such enormous powers during the war, became the object of hatred and the target of protests.

With increasing breadth moving west to east across Europe, a chasm opened up between populations and governments and between workers and their socialist representatives who supported the war effort. In many places, notably the metalworking and munitions factories of Düsseldorf, Berlin, Turin, Petrograd, and elsewhere, incremental change seemed a rather unsatisfying program as food supplies and official rations plummeted, the number of working hours grew incessantly, and increasing numbers of soldiers never returned or came back physically and psychically wounded.

The result of popular discontent was a wave of strikes and revolutions on a scale not seen since 1848. Typically, strikes broke out first over wages and food rations. Workers were often able to extract concessions from employers and the state. Quickly, though, strikes became more overtly politicized as workers raised demands for an end to the war and for democratization. In Russia, the strikes in February 1917 led almost seamlessly to revolution when the troops began to follow the sentiments of workers, many of them female, and Tsar Nicholas II realized that he had virtually no support. Elsewhere, in Germany and the Austro-Hungarian Empire, revolution would erupt more or less concurrently with the end of the war.

Two critical factors emerged out of this vast wave of popular protest. In the course of strikes and revolutions, workers invented the "council" ("soviet" in Russian), a democratic form of representation initiated in the workplace during mass demonstrations. Typically, at the end of a great rally workers would

Socialism in Russia. Bolshevik tracts being distributed on the streets of Petrograd, August 1917. THE DAVID KING COLLECTION

elect delegates to represent their interests to employers and the state. The councils from different factories in a city would convene and constitute the city council. Usually workers elected well-respected local leaders, shop stewards or other union representatives, to the councils, and most of those elected were members of one or another socialist party. The councils presented an often chaotic and confused form of governance and could not easily be assimilated into the existing state structure. Leon Trotsky famously labeled the situation in Russia between the February Revolution and the October Bolshevik Revolution as the period of dual power, when the executive of the councils and a more regular state ministry existed side by side. At first, the councils were rather submissive to the government, but in the course of the year they became far more assertive, and each body began jockeying for power.

However chaotic the situation, however unfulfilled the leaders' promises went, the councils represented the potential for a more democratic form of governance than that which prevailed both in the Soviet Union and in the West. The councils represented a distinctively twentieth-century model that emerged out of the disastrous conditions of war, out of the long-term process of capitalist development that concentrated a good segment of the working class in the heavy industries, and out of the decades of socialist organization that had intensified the sense of class identity and promoted the ideas of democracy and

socialism as the solution to the travails of life under capitalism.

But the struggle over the councils, which lasted in many countries until 1921, also revealed the limits of socialism's democratic promise. Men were not the only workers who went out on strike, nor were strikes the only manifestation of workers' protests in the World War I era. Women initiated strikes in many factories, and they launched demonstrations and riots designed to force merchants and government officials to lower food prices. Yet all across Europe, women were forced out of the factories at war's end as the men returned from the front. Socialists, trade unionists, employers, government officials—all were united in the belief that men deserved priority in the job market. The vain, desperate search for a return to "normalcy" meant that women were to return to home and hearth and men were to regain their supposedly rightful place at the workbench. All of the politically active groups could envisage, with hopes or fears, depending on the perspective, a new order arising out of the workplace and the councils. None of them could imagine the contours of a future society based on female drill press operators or demonstrations and riots in the marketplace.

The Bolshevik Revolution. The second enormous consequence of World War I was the fatal, irreparable division of the labor movement into communist and socialist wings. The February Revolution that had toppled the tsarist system had inspired nearly universal support among socialists and great hopes for a future democratic Europe. The Bolshevik Revolution aroused almost immediate criticism, which became ever more fervent as the Bolsheviks undertook antidemocratic measures, such as dispersing the Constitutional Convention because Bolsheviks were in the minority of those elected to the body. When counterrevolutionaries launched a civil war that lasted from 1918 to 1920, the Bolsheviks responded with the organization of the Red Army and the open advocacy of terror against political opponents. To many Western socialists, the Bolsheviks merely mirrored the traditional authoritarianism and violence of tsarist Russia. "Russian conditions" became a watchword for avoiding experiments like the council system and a term that conjured up images of chaos, violence, and backwardness. A good deal of prejudice against Slavs, so deep that it approached a racialized hostility, was bound up with these views. To many well-schooled marxists, the Bolsheviks had violated the laws of history by trying to push Russia from its peasant-based underdevelopment to the socialist future without bothering to linger in the intermediary stage of bourgeois capitalism.

Yet to many workers and socialists, the Bolshevik Revolution became a great rallying point. After the long, dreary, miserable years of war, a war that so many socialist leaders had supported, the audacity of the Bolsheviks, their willingness to seize and defend power in the name of socialism and their unbridled opposition to the war, proved inspiring. The Bolsheviks promised the socialist future in the here and now, and that was enough for many people. Many of these hopes would be dashed over the course of time—the disillusionment with communism is a pronounced literary genre of the twentieth century, resulting in shelf loads of epochal novels and memoirs. Arthur Koestler's *Darkness at Noon* (1940) is simply one of the most famous, but it was hardly the first of its kind.

Nonetheless, communism would continue to draw powerful support, even in its most undemocratic, murderous periods under Joseph Stalin. Like the socialists before them, communists proved dedicated and tireless organizers. In particular neighborhoods and towns all over Europe—in Wales and Scotland, in Berlin, in the Paris suburbs, in Turin—communism became a part of everyday culture, structuring and giving meaning to the lives of its supporters. Despite a few lapses, notably the period of the Nazi-Soviet Non-Aggression Pact from 1939 to 1941, in the 1930s and 1940s communists proved the most consistent opponents of Nazism and fascism. Their prominent and effective roles in the resistance against

German occupation led to the high tide of communism from around 1943 to 1956, when the Soviet leader, Nikita Khrushchev, revealed publicly the immense crimes of Stalin. In that same year, the televised images of Soviet tanks crushing the Hungarian revolt, combined with the impact of Khrushchev's revelations, destroyed for many people the allure of communism, although communist power remained in place for another thirty-five years.

Despite the virulence of the communist-socialist split and the growing competition from mass consumer culture, the 1920s were the high point of a specifically socialist culture in Great Britain and the German-speaking countries. "Red Vienna" became a model socialist municipality. Socialists implemented extensive social-welfare and cultural programs, organized giant festivities, and built well-run city housing for workers. On a smaller scale, similar programs were initiated in a number of German cities that had significant socialist representation in the municipal governments. Socialist ideals were woven through daily life, which also now became the object of discipline and reform by socialist leaders who found the unruly aspects of working-class life distasteful and an expression of the moral degeneration of life under capitalism.

The social democratic model. Socialist culture in central Europe was effectively quashed by the rise of Nazism. But in Sweden socialists came to power in the 1930s in alliance with the rural population and established a successful system that combined an extensive social welfare program with democratic participation. This was the archetypal social democratic model that, in one fashion or another, was followed by other socialist parties that came to power after World War II. Its attraction was so great that even conservative parties modeled some of their programs along similar lines, if only to outcompete their socialist rivals.

The success of the social democratic system went hand in hand with the decline of socialism and the working-class subculture that had sustained it. Socialists in central and western Europe were now deeply entwined with liberal capitalism. By the 1960s, the utopian impulse of socialism had all but disappeared. Socialism now meant trade union officials who negotiated wage increases and improved benefits and government leaders who raised old-age pensions. The progress here should not be underestimated. After the upheavals of two world wars, worldwide depression, and fascist violence, the postwar decades offered workers, for the first time, a measure of economic security and material improvement. Without the force of socialism, these improvements would never have occurred, certainly not on the scale that enabled work-

Socialists in Government. H. Branting, prime minister and foreign minister *(seated in the middle),* with his Social Democratic cabinet, which governed Sweden from December 1921 to April 1923. ROYAL LIBRARY, NATIONAL LIBRARY OF SWEDEN, STOCKHOLM

ers, by the 1960s, to enjoy four-week vacations and the pleasures of the automobile.

Yet the mobility offered by the automobile symbolized the breakup of working-class communities. Since World War II capitalist expansion has displaced the once-tight linkages between residency and workplace. Highways, automobiles, and urban renewal dispersed working-class populations. Most recently, work itself has sometimes been dispersed into cyberspace by computers and all over the globe by the hyperactive mobility of capital. The influx into Europe from the late 1950s onward of large numbers of immigrants from Africa and Asia has sometimes made ethnic and national identities seem far more salient than class identities. Consumerism and mass, popular culture have provided alternative sites of leisure and entertainment and, most definitely, values different from those invoked by the socialist and communist parties.

Historians and sociologists continue to debate what socialism or communism meant to workers in affluent European consumer societies. Proclamations about the "end of ideology" in postwar Europe seemed premature. But it is true that the lives of workers moved beyond the confines of socialist organizations and that attention to consumer goals diluted political activism. These pressures pushed for greater pragmatism in socialist and communist parties alike.

Socialism, then, grew in tandem with industrialization and nation-building, two central features of Europe's modern epoch. Socialism's tide ran high in the period from roughly 1840 to 1960; its decline is symptomatic of Europe's move into a postmodern age. Work and workers remain, but a specifically socialist class consciousness is ever harder to find. Yet socialism's past provides a storehouse of democratic ideas and promises that may still find its advocates.

See also **Marxism and Radical History** *(volume 1);* **The Welfare State; Communism** *(volume 2);* **Social Class; Artisans; Working Classes** *(in this volume);* **Gender and Work; Factory Work** *(volume 4); and other articles in this section.*

BIBLIOGRAPHY

Barclay, David E., and Eric D. Weitz, eds. *Between Reform and Revolution: German Socialism and Communism from 1840 to 1990.* New York, 1998.

Berlanstein, Lenard R., ed. *Rethinking Labor History: Essays on Discourse and Class Analysis.* Urbana, Ill., 1993.

Cole, G. D. H. *The History of Socialist Thought.* 5 vols. London, 1953–1960.

Daniel, Ute. *The War from Within: German Working-Class Women in the First World War.* Translated by Margaret Ries. Oxford, 1997.

Eley, Geoff. "Reviewing the Socialist Tradition." In *The Crisis of Socialism in Europe.* Edited by Christiane Lemke and Gary Marks. Durham, N.C., 1992. Pages 21–60.

Frader, Laura L., and Sonya O. Rose, eds. *Gender and Class in Modern Europe.* Ithaca, N.Y., 1996.

Gruber, Helmut. *Red Vienna: Experiment in Working-Class Culture, 1919–1934.* New York, 1991.

Gruber, Helmut, and Pamela Graves, eds. *Women and Socialism, Socialism and Women.* New York, 1998.

Hobsbawm, Eric. *Workers: Worlds of Labor.* New York, 1984.

Joll, James. *The Second International, 1889–1914.* Rev. ed. London, 1974.

Katznelson, Ira, and Aristide R. Zolberg, eds. *Working-Class Formation: Nineteenth-Century Patterns in Western Europe and the United States.* Princeton, N.J., 1986.

Kocka, Jürgen. *Arbeitsverhältnisse und Arbeiterexistenzen: Grundlagen der Klassenbildung im 19. Jahrhundert.* Bonn, Germany, 1990.

Kriegel, Annie. *Le pain et les roses: Jalons pour une histoire des socialismes.* Paris, 1968.

Lidtke, Vernon. *The Alternative Culture: Socialist Labor in Imperial Germany.* New York, 1985.

Lindemann, Albert S. *A History of European Socialism.* New Haven, Conn., and London, 1983.

Manuel, Frank E., and Fritzie P. Manuel. *Utopian Thought in the Western World.* Cambridge, Mass., 1979.

Maynes, Mary Jo. *Taking the Hard Road: Life Course in French and German Workers' Autobiographies in the Era of Industrialization.* Chapel Hill, N.C., 1995.

Moss, Bernard H. *The Origins of the French Labor Movement, 1830–1914: The Socialism of Skilled Workers.* Berkeley, Calif., 1976.

Sassoon, Donald. *One Hundred Years of Socialism: The West European Left in the Twentieth Century.* New York, 1996.

Schieder, Wolfgang. "Sozialismus." In vol. 5 of *Geschichtliche Grundbegriffe: Historisches Lexikon zur politisch-sozialen Sprache in Deutschland.* Edited by Otto Brunner, Werner Conze, and Reinhard Koselleck. Stuttgart, Germany, 1984.

Taylor, Barbara. *Eve and the New Jerusalem: Socialism and Feminism in the Nineteenth Century.* London, 1983.

Thompson, E. P. *The Making of the English Working Class.* New York, 1963.

GENDER AND POPULAR PROTEST

Anna Clark

Eighteenth-century observers of popular protests often characterized food riots as female. As popular protest evolved into more organized forms, such as strikes and political demonstrations, did the female presence fade? Indeed, late nineteenth- and early twentieth-century crowds were depicted as a masculine sea of sober dark suits and hats. But a closer look reveals women's persistent presence. Food riots reerupted in the years around World War I, a time of crisis. As historian Temma Kaplan argues, women expressed "female consciousness," drawing on neighborhood bonds to defend their families and communities. Does this mean that personal, local, and familial ties motivated women, rather than the impersonal, formal, organizational bonds that attracted men? The historical record shows that domestic obligations kept many women from joining trade unions or other political organizations, but male hostility also deterred women. Even without formal organizations, however, women did not riot only as mothers of families; they went on strike as workers, joined radical processions, and even triggered revolutions.

THE SYMBOLISM OF GENDER

Eighteenth-century observers often dismissed riots as the work of disorderly "women and boys." It is important therefore, when analyzing popular protest, to consider masculinity as well as femininity in a gender analysis. The association of women and boys with disorderliness derived, in part, from the fact that both groups were excluded from the formal power structures of towns and villages. Indeed, young men could threaten a community's order by rioting and carousing simply for entertainment. But young men also played an important role in the informal means by which small communities regulated themselves, such as "rough music" and other moral rituals. In "rough music," villagers would rebuke those who violated community norms—for instance, by inflicting domestic violence—through congregating at their house at night, banging pots and pans. Popular protests often adopted rough music's repertoire.

Women also played an important symbolic role in popular protests when they drew upon the carnivalesque tradition. In carnival, the world could be turned upside down for a day: women could rule men, the young the old, and servants the master. Protests also borrowed the ritual and display of carnivals, such as processions bearing effigies of hated authorities or celebrated heroes. In more organized community protests, such as mass processions, young girls dressed in white and carrying flowers often served as symbols of family, purity, and unity. But women were also emblematic of defiance, female nature being seen as more disorderly and irrational than the male: sometimes men who rioted or engaged in nocturnal terrorism would take on a female persona, such as "Queen Sive," the mythical queen of the fairies in eighteenth-century Ireland, or "Lady Lud" in the Luddite riots against machinery in Nottingham in 1811–1813.

Popular protests were not, of course, simply irrational, carnivalesque outbursts of disorder. Rather, popular protests occurred when authority failed to live up to its obligations, or even disintegrated. Women defended their communities alongside men when outside forces threatened them. For instance, during the sixteenth-century Peasant Wars, women went on mass deputations to plead for the freedom of husbands who had been conscripted or captured; in 1522, fifty women invaded Basel's city hall demanding recognition for a Lutheran preacher. During wartime, villages might send out women to confront soldiers, hoping that the military men would hesitate at shooting females.

During the seventeenth and eighteenth centuries, contemporaries often identified food riots with women. In food riots, inhabitants of a community would protest the high prices or scarcity of food. Rather than just rampaging and seizing food, however, they often appealed to authorities to enforce old laws against hoarding or profiteering. If such protests went unheeded, crowds would appropriate grain or bread;

the ringleaders would then sell the food at what they considered to be a "just price." E. P. Thompson identified this practice as the defense of a "moral economy," in which prices were based on need, against an encroaching market economy. Women played an essential role in the moral economy because they were chiefly responsible for feeding their families, and because they daily went to market to purchase provisions, thus easily assembling for protests. But as the historian John Bohstedt has pointed out, most food rioters were not women; in eighteenth-century England, for instance, it is estimated that they composed between 14 and 33 percent of food rioters. And women did not only participate in riots as consumers but also as workers and as members of communities, alongside men. For instance, women were more likely to participate in food riots in industrial towns, where they were often employed in new industries.

FOOD RIOTS AND THE FRENCH REVOLUTION

Food riots could also have a wider impact when they occurred in the context of a breakdown in state authority, as in the French Revolution. Food riots were endemic during subsistence crises in eighteenth-century France; in fact, women's right to protest food shortages and high prices was implicitly recognized, although authorities would arrest women who attacked persons or destroyed property, as in the Flour War in Paris of 1775. Such riots acquired a political dimension in 1789. Women were excluded from the Estates General, the formal assemblage of representatives of the clergy, the nobility, and the people, which was called in 1789, but as the third estate (the people) transformed itself into the National Assembly, the common people of Paris became more and more interested in political affairs. Orators denounced the king in Paris streets and cafés, and blamed his foreign mercenaries and aristocratic hoarders for the food crisis that plagued the city. While women played only a minor role in the fall of the Bastille prison on 14 July 1789, they helped to transform the position of the monarchy in October. On 5 October, the fishwives, market women, and female consumers of Paris, accustomed to spreading the news of the day as they bought and sold provisions, decided they needed to take action to ensure that the people of Paris were fed. A huge crowd of five to six thousand women marched from Paris to Versailles, sweeping up passersby in their wake. Once the weary and footsore women arrived in Versailles, they crowded into the palace and sent a delegation to the king. Fearing for their lives, the next day the king and queen and their children returned to Paris, their coach led by a crowd of women who chanted that they were bringing back the baker, the baker's wife, and the baker's children.

The women of the sansculottes played a pivotal role when crowds erupted and changed the direction of the Revolution. They spread rumors, incited hostility to aristocrats, and attended not only club meetings but executions with enthusiasm. In 1793 women of the popular classes joined male sansculottes in calling for an insurrection against the moderate Girondins. They also protested and even rioted to enforce a maximum on the price of bread, sugar, soap, and candles; by conceding to their demands, the Jacobins gained sansculotte support in their struggle to attain power. Female revolutionaries organized women's groups in thirty cities around the country, most notably the first feminist organization: the Society of Revolutionary Republican Women, founded by Pauline Léon and Claire Lacombe, a chocolate maker and actress respectively, in 1793. This society discussed women's rights, but their public political protests mainly stemmed from their militant Jacobinism. They vehemently supported the war effort, and even patrolled the streets of Paris, allegedly in trousers, urging women to sacrifice for the war, forcing passersby to don the tricolor, denouncing aristocrats, and demanding a maximum on prices. However, the Society of Revolutionary Republican Women clashed with other, less militant women, especially the market women, who did not support the price maximum. And their fierce feminism clashed with the Jacobins' domestic ideology, derived from Jean-Jacques Rousseau. Jacobins denounced the revolutionary women as harridans who had no place in politics; women, they proclaimed, should remain in the home and raise good republican citizens. Some prominent feminists, such as Olympe de Gouges, were executed in the Terror, and Léon and Lacombe were imprisoned. After the Terror, poor women increasingly turned against the Revolution, instead rioting in support of the Catholic Church, which they saw as consoling them for the hardships that the Revolution had failed to ameliorate.

NINETEENTH-CENTURY LABOR ISSUES

By the early nineteenth century, popular protest focused on labor issues. Women sometimes participated in labor protests as workers and as members of working-class communities, but trade unionism tended to be dominated by a tradition of male bonding and a concomitant hostility to female workers. Trade unions descended originally from the artisanal associations of the early modern period. As guilds disintegrated and the interests of masters, apprentices, and journeymen diverged, male workers formed their own associations. Journeymen, especially, formed groups known in France as *compagnonnage* and in Germany as *Wandervogels;* in Britain they were often called friendly societies. As members of such groups, men could find work in any city. As they traveled, they also transmitted a heritage of song, legend, and resistance to masters' work discipline through drinking customs and labor organization. They based their identity as workers on fraternal bonding and often on a hostility to women, which had roots in both personal and labor relations. Journeymen could no longer expect to attain the status of mastership in their late twenties, acquiring a wife and a workshop at once; instead, they were condemned to a perpetual adolescence, marrying or cohabiting without earning enough to support a wife. Their ties to their fellow workmen competed with the claims of home. In addition, journeymen traditionally kept up their wages by insisting that all craftsmen go through a strict apprenticeship, but they faced increasing competition from unapprenticed labor, especially from women. During the late eighteenth century, journeymen often struck against the competition of female labor, especially when women ran machines, which undercut male skill.

Textile workers, however, followed a different pattern of popular protest, since their labor process was based on the family rather than the masculine workshop. The father might weave and the wife and children card and spin. As the handloom weaving industry expanded once mechanization increased the supply of yarn, women increasingly wove as well. Textile workers, such as weavers, sometimes attempted to follow artisan traditions in keeping out unapprenticed workers, such as women, but the artisan tradition was not particularly suited to an industry in which over half the workers were women and children. Weavers therefore had to organize on the basis of community as well as workplace bonds.

As textile processes became mechanized, first in spinning, then weaving, this gender division of labor translated into factories. Skilled men, such as cotton spinners or power loom mechanics, would oversee the work of women and children, who usually composed over half of the workforce. To strike effectively, therefore, male workers also had to draw upon kinship and neighborhood ties, and gain the support of female and child piecers and power loom weavers. When they did so, their strikes could be quite formidable. For instance, in 1818 a strike wave broke out in Lancashire, England, as male and female factory workers violently protested against the introduction of lower-paid female workers who were used to undercut the wages of skilled men. Male and female workers viciously attacked the rival female workers, threatened to burn down factories, and also rioted against high food prices.

In areas where women worked as wage earners, they were also much more likely to participate in collective political action. To be sure, radical republican ideology regarded men as more rational, disciplined, and suited to public life, while women, it was thought, should look after home and family. However, radical women could turn these notions to their own ends, claiming that as wives and mothers they had a right to protest, to strike, to appear on platforms, to speak in radical causes, in order to defend their families. While the middle-class notion of domesticity restricted women to their homes, working-class women could combine a domestic identity with participation in popular protest. Their bold actions belied their modest words. For instance, in 1819 in northern England, women formed Female Reform Societies to support the cause of male suffrage and radical reform. They embroidered banners and carried them in the great reform procession to Manchester on 16 August 1819. When the yeomen cavalry charged the crowd, women fell alongside men in the massacre known as Peterloo.

REPUBLICAN IDEOLOGIES AND INSURRECTIONS

In general, radical organizations defined republican ideologies and worker consciousness in masculine terms. However, radicals espoused varied visions of masculinity. For instance, the British Chartist movement for the vote split into "moral force" and "physical force" wings in the late 1830s and early 1840s. Those who advocated "moral force" believed that radicals must denounce violence and organize in a peaceful, disciplined manner to prove their respectable manhood. Although the "moral force" wing also usually denounced women's wage earning as destructive to the working-class family, their moral reform efforts also opened up some space within the movement for women. Chartists often tried to create alternatives to the pub, sponsoring Chartist churches, temperance societies, and soirees that could appeal to women as well as men.

Yet frustrated by peaceful efforts for reform, radicals sometimes turned to a more insurrectionary tradition in which physical, military prowess took precedence and excluded women. Men could imagine themselves as conspiratorial heroes fomenting revolution. In the Chartist movement for the vote of the 1830s and 1840s, for instance, the "physical force" wing often marched and drilled, and mounted a few abortive insurrections. They justified their activities as defending their wives and families, proclaiming, "For child and wife, we will fight to the knife!"

The early nineteenth-century French republican tradition also celebrated revolutionary violence, seen in masculine terms as the brave citizen able to fight on the barricades. Often driven underground by monarchical repression, republicans covertly congregated in cafés, largely frequented by men. So even when repression forced radical organizations to base themselves on informal community networks rather than legal organization, this informality did not incorporate women. Instead, republican ideology celebrated fraternal bonding and ignored women.

When open insurrections broke out, however, as in 1848, a few women fought on the barricades, and more incited men to action or planted flags on cobblestones, especially in areas where women were very active in industry, such as Rouen's textile mills. And 1848 stimulated the formation of women's political clubs such as the Société de la Voix des Femmes. The 1848 revolution in France, of course, triggered radical and nationalist uprisings in Germany and elsewhere. In Germany, the insurrection had been preceded by the potato riots of 1847, in which women took a significant part. In October 1848, democratic women presented a petition demanding women's right to vote. Wearing revolutionary colors, women fought on the barricades in Dresden. The year 1848 also witnessed the formation of many women's political and charitable associations, including newspapers and schools, but the repression of the 1840s crushed the women's movement in the German states until the 1860s.

Women also played a highly visible role in the Paris Commune of 1870–1871. The Prussian army came to the brink of invading Paris in 1870; Napoleon III had capitulated to the invaders, quickly offering peace terms. But the working people of Paris, organized along anarchist and socialist lines, refused to surrender to the Prussians. Instead, they seized the cannons of the national army and took over the government of Paris themselves. The working-class women of Paris either fraternized with government soldiers to distract them or threw rocks at troops and cut the traces of horses' harnesses. Rumors spread that prostitutes urged a mob to lynch two French generals at the inception of the Commune. During the Commune's regime, hundreds of women evoked the heroic role played by women in the October Days of 1789

by marching to aid the Commune and the National Guard. As in the earlier revolution, they also assembled in a few debating societies, discussing issues such as divorce, women's rights, and peace. However, the national army attacked and overcame the Commune in May 1871. Many women perished as thousands of Communards died defending the city, or were executed as they were captured. The press denounced the women of the Commune as bloodthirsty, anarchistic harridans, depicting them as *pétroleuses* who set Paris alight as the Commune collapsed. Women thus symbolized the threat the Commune posed to bourgeois France.

In Britain during the same era, workingmen's protests became much more disciplined and controlled, as skilled men organized themselves into legal associations and trade unions. They would assemble in large, peaceful demonstrations with elaborate trade union banners, demanding their political rights as manly workers. However, when moderate action failed, occasionally the hint of disorder could impel the government to act. In 1867, when Parliament delayed passing the Second Reform Bill, enfranchising urban working men, working men illegally assembled in Hyde Park, breaking down iron railings and trampling on flower beds. Parliament quickly passed the bill.

WOMEN'S SUFFRAGE

Women agitating for female suffrage in Britain emulated the workingmen's campaign for the vote. After decades of lobbying, pamphleteering, and organizing, to no avail, feminists were told by politicians that they must prove that large numbers of women wished for the vote. To do so, by 1905 the suffragettes (militant advocates for the vote) began more public, mass demonstrations of women and their supporters. As had male trade unionists, they marched with banners and adopted their own iconography of colors (purple, green, and white), as emblematic of the purity and righteousness of their cause. Workingwomen, especially in Lancashire, also began organizing for suffrage. But when peaceful protest failed by 1912, suffragettes turned to more violent means of popular protest, blowing up postboxes, smashing windows, hectoring politicians, and chaining themselves to railings. They intended to gain attention for their cause, to force politicians to act, and to court martyrdom. In prison they went on hunger strikes to demand the status of political prisoners, only to be force-fed. Released when dreadfully ill, their gaunt faces declared their determination to gain the vote.

Mrs. Pankhurst Arrested. Policeman removes Emmeline Pankhurst (1858–1928) from a suffragette meeting, London, 21 May 1914. ©HULTON GETTY/LIAISON AGENCY

On the Continent, the women's movement for the vote faced much more formidable obstacles. In France, the Radical Party believed female suffrage would lead to clerical dominance, but a few feminists nonetheless engaged in spectacular activities, such as burning the discriminatory Civil Code in public, overturning ballot boxes, and breaking the windows of polling booths, although the feminist movement never engaged in widespread property destruction as in England. In Belgium, sections of the socialist movement had supported women's rights, but when socialists abandoned protest politics and entered the government with the Liberals in 1902, they gave up their support for women's suffrage. In Germany, women were prohibited from joining political parties or indeed from attending political meetings altogether until 1908 under the Prussian Law of Association.

WOMEN AND TRADE UNIONS

During the late nineteenth century, socialist and trade union movements were quite hostile to middle-class feminism. Although some socialists wished to organize and support women as workers or mothers, labor movements generally refused to acknowledge women as workers. Male trade unionists often assumed that women were unorganizable as workers because work did not provide the center of their identities, being only an interval before marriage and child rearing.

Especially in areas such as Russia, they often depicted women as ignorant, illiterate, and in thrall to priests.

In the mid to late nineteenth century, trade unionists all over Europe increasingly adopted the ideal of the breadwinner wage, the notion that a man should be able to feed his family; concomitantly, they often demanded that girls and women be excluded from the workforce, or at least from factories and mines, to preserve the working-class family and keep up male wages. Did this notion of the breadwinner wage lead to women's exclusion from popular protest? Male workers feared that employers would use cheap female labor to undercut their wages. For instance, after Milanese ribbon weavers successfully struck against wage cuts in the 1860s and 1870s, employers substituted female for male ribbon weavers. But the male ribbon weavers did not try to incorporate the women into their trade union organization or to impel them to go on strike. As a result, the trade became low-waged and feminized.

Some historians, however, have argued that working-class women went along with demands for the exclusion of women workers and for the breadwinner wage for men because they wanted their husbands to earn enough so that they could stay at home instead of working long days in a noisy factory. Even if wives and mothers did not work for wages, they joined in protests for their husbands, brothers, and fathers because their family survival depended on it. For instance, in 1869, the women of La Ricamarie, France, rallied around their husbands, brothers, and sons, who were coal miners striking against wage cuts. Crowds of frenzied women insulted and even threw rocks at the soldiers who defended the mines, stirring the men to further militance. As they shared in the community mobilization, the women also shared in its vulnerability, as soldiers shot two women and a baby as well as ten men.

Women workers in late nineteenth-century industry, furthermore, were not necessarily passive and quiescent. Although women tended to compose a very low percentage of unions and socialist organizations, they often struck spontaneously not only over wage grievances but against sexual harassment and other issues. For instance, Dundee jute workers occasionally engaged in wildcat strikes against unfair labor practices, but male trade unionists never supported their actions. In trades where married women continued to work, such as tobacco in Spain, Russia, and France, and textiles in Germany and France, they were more likely to engage in strikes or even to join unions, since they had longtime ties to their workplaces and communities and a sense of pride in their skill. Tobacco workers were especially known for their militancy. In

1895, when thirteen hundred "cigarette girls" struck the Laferme factory in St. Petersburg against new machines that took away women's jobs, the women broke windows and threw the tobacco and even furniture out of the building. But female tobacco workers' militance differed from their male counterparts. While willing to strike, they hesitated to join unions, in part because their identities were bound up in their neighborhoods and communities, not just in their work; they were just as likely to act as consumers in the marketplace, defending their families, as they were to act as workers in the factory and union. German women textile workers also built upon their identities as both women and workers to engage in collective action. They sometimes rioted against sexual harassment or engaged in wildcat strikes in solidarity when a sick woman was fired.

By the 1890s, however, some trade unions and socialist organizations did attempt to harness women's willingness to engage in collective action. Many women joined trade unions in Germany after the Prussian Law of Association was repealed in 1908. The Social Democratic Party supported women workers in 1903, when they struck at Crimmitschau demanding ten-hour days on the basis that they needed an extra hour for home life. In the 1890s Milan tailors, realizing they could not restrict access to skill in their trade, admitted women to their union, and both men and women struck in 1892. A union also organized women in a Pirelli rubber plant in 1898, a year when Italy was wracked by strikes, demonstrations, and food riots.

Male trade unionists sometimes tried to take advantage of women's energies for their strikes, but they often found them difficult to control. For instance, in 1913 men and women joined together in the Constancy textile strike in Barcelona, protesting low pay for women both in factory and sweated labor. For the first time, a leftist trade union group, the National Confederation of Labor (CNT), demanded higher wages for women, not just the breadwinner wage for men. But unlike male workers, women organized themselves by neighborhood, not by trade, and defined their demands to include cheaper food prices as well as higher wages. They battled authorities at the workplace and in the streets. Appalled, the men of the CNT asked them to stop, but the women kept on confronting the authorities.

WORLD WAR I

The era of World War I witnessed an upsurge of women's strikes and food riots. During World War I,

women entered the workforce, especially in munitions, to substitute for the men at the front. During the first years of the war, most trade union, socialist, and suffrage organizations, with some significant exceptions, supported the war effort, exhorting all to sacrifice. But by 1916–1917, long hours, food shortages, and the endless slaughter of their men at the front increased discontent among women workers. In 1916 women in the war industries often engaged in spontaneous strikes. They would first meet outside the factory, in halls, even movie houses, to organize themselves into committees, to write their grievances, and to raise strike funds, and only then would they contact syndicalist trade union leaders. (Syndicalists believed that a general strike would enable labor unions to take over government and society.) Once they struck, their actions would often take on a festive, carnivalesque atmosphere as they marched around cities turning out women in other factories. As Laura Lee Downs points out, these were not just parochial strikes over local concerns, but soon linked up to wider issues as the general crisis spread. Food riots broke out, and vast crowds demonstrated against the war. Similarly, in Milan in 1917, women workers in textile factories first struck over sexual harassment and piecework, but soon broadened their concerns as they rioted for food and closed down munitions factories to protest the war.

The persistence of food riots in a time of crisis belies the conventional chronology that food riots disappeared with modernization. Rather, their reappearance signified the fragility of the modern state. When Germany faced food shortages in 1915, housewives mounted peaceful demonstrations simply requesting that the government intervene to lower prices and ensure supplies, but when local governments failed to respond, housewives began to articulate more explicitly socialist goals, demanding that the state take over all food and clothing supplies and distribute them equally to all, especially the poor. Governmental responses to these demands, while inadequate, staved off revolution. In France, just after the war, women's agitation over food combined traditional and modern elements: they drew upon their traditional neighborhood networks, but they also cooperated with syndicalists and socialist organizations and set up their own committees.

In Russia, however, women's strikes and food riots became symptomatic of a general crisis that resulted in the Bolshevik takeover of 1917. As early as 1905, women participated in the huge strike wave that swept through both peasants and workers in the context of political agitation and war. Along with their men, women workers and housewives demonstrated

International Women's Day. Textile workers carry a sign saying "Praise to Women Fighters for Freedom" during an International Women's Day demonstration in Petrograd, Russia, 23 February 1917. DAVID KING COLLECTION

before the Winter Palace to petition the tsar on Bloody Sunday. As the Russian polity broke down under pressure of war, women and men began dozens of protests all over Russia against shortages of bread, soap, and other essentials. Peasant women also used their status as mothers to defend their communities, using their children as shields in demonstrations so that soldiers would not shoot. But by 1913–1915, women became more confident and assertive as workers as well; textile workers, predominantly female, actually became somewhat more apt to strike than workers in male-dominated industries such as metalworking. Women's actions on International Women's Day, 23 February 1917 (Russian calendar), are widely seen as triggering the February revolution. Defying instructions by labor unions and social democrats to remain calm, both housewives and women workers demonstrated against high prices and shortages of food, pouring into the streets to urge workers to strike. This strike wave soon erupted into a massive protest against the war, which soldiers refused to suppress.

Immediately after the Bolshevik revolution, however, the Communists remained ambivalent about the place of women. They gave women legal equality and promised to collectivize childcare and housework. But some male Communists depicted strikes and demonstrations by discontented women workers and soldiers's wives as counterrevolutionary, regarding them as *babas,* ignorant and conservative peasant women who hindered the revolution. But women themselves could exploit this stereotype, drawing upon the tradition of the *bab'i bunty,* or peasant women's riots. These were outbreaks of violent peasant opposition, which authorities viewed as irrational and hysterical. When the Communist Party introduced collective farms in the late 1920s and early 1930s, women were especially opposed to collectivization of livestock because women raised cows and hens to provide eggs and milk for their children, and to sell. Peasant communities often thrust women to the forefront of their protests against collectivization, knowing that women enjoyed a certain, if limited, immunity from punishment.

THE INTERWAR PERIOD

In some ways, gender tensions increased in the interwar years. Hardened by their service at the front, frustrated by the failure of abortive socialist insurrections, and embittered by wage cuts, inflation, and unemployment, German men, especially communists, tended to organize in a militaristic, confrontational style, marching in formation in uniforms through the streets and engaging in street battles with fascists. Women had misgivings about this increasingly violent form of politics, writes Karen Hagemann, and preferred organized cultural activities such as parades, festivals, International Women's Day, and agitation around reproductive rights.

285

The General Strike, 1936. Paris restaurant workers join the strike. ©HULTON GETTY/ LIAISON AGENCY

In postwar France, conventional politics still marginalized voteless women. To make the French suffrage campaign even more difficult, all street demonstrations were banned in Paris in the early 1930s, a time of great political instability. So feminists carried out spectacular, symbolic actions, such as secretly entering the Senate public gallery and tossing pamphlets onto the politicians, hoisting banners on buses and taxis, silently demonstrating, and postering Paris. Although few women joined trade unions and the Socialist and Communist Parties (they were not even allowed to join the Radical Party until 1924), many women workers, such as factory workers and even clerks in department stores, participated in the strike wave following the election of the Popular Front in 1936. Contemporary pictures showed women workers knitting as they occupied factories, while men smoked and played cards. Even as women workers struck, however, Popular Front parties focused on a maternal, pronatal feminine image.

The Spanish Civil War between 1936 and 1939 provoked an unusual efflorescence of women's political activities. Enfranchised by the republic in 1931, anarchist, socialist, communist, and republican women leapt to its defense when the civil war began. The anarchist group Mujeres Libres (free women) combined militant support for the republic with a demand for female emancipation. In the first months of the civil war, the armed militia woman even became a potent symbol of republican resistance, even though she was more important as a symbol than as a representation of the number of women fighting at the front. In fact, after the initial outburst, those women who were fighting at the front were sent back to support the men through working in munitions, nursing, and propaganda. However, in 1937, when the National Confederation of Labor took over Barcelona factories in the name of the workers, female workers resisted labor discipline and protested food shortages. The fascist triumph pushed women back into the home, as in Germany and Italy.

WORLD WAR II AND AFTER

Fascist regimes and occupying forces banned trade unions and socialist organizations, of course, but the abolition of formal politics made space for women's participation in the resistance in Italy and France. Women could smuggle and spy for partisan groups, but they also overtly demonstrated against food shortages and protested against the deportation of their husbands, brothers, sons, and neighbors to labor camps in Germany. During the 1950s, however, both left and right parties espoused a domestic role for women, once again marginalizing them in politics.

During the 1960s the New Left criticized traditional social movements for their emphasis on the workplace as the only locus of struggle; instead, the New Left engaged in spontaneous, theatrical, nonviolent protest suited for a media age. While the New Left appealed to women, it also romanticized the masculine rebel's defiance of authority. In response, the women's liberation movement invented its own form of spectacular protest, such as disrupting the Miss World contest. One wing of the women's movement also declared that women were more nurturing than men, and should therefore engage in their own autonomous protests against war. Most notably, between 1981 and 1991 women encamped around Greenham

Common, a cruise missile base in England, surrounding the base with thousands of women linking hands and blowing whistles in a form of "rough music" against nuclear missiles.

From the sixteenth century to the twentieth century, as popular protests became more organized into formal associations such as trade unions or political parties, women faded from view. But the persistence of women's strikes, food riots, and feminist actions in the twentieth century undercuts the notion that women were reluctant to engage in public political protest because of an essential feminine nature, a preference for fluid, spontaneous, personal actions. Instead, when popular protests became formalized, political actors were defined in masculine terms, which marginalized women.

See also other articles in this section.

BIBLIOGRAPHY

Aminzade, Ronald. *Ballots and Barricades: Class Formation and Republican Politics in France, 1830–71.* Princeton, N.J., 1993. Discusses masculine nature of republicanism and women's participation in politics in areas where they worked.

Barzman, John. "Entre l'émeute, la manifestation et la concertation: la "crise de vie chère" de l'été 1919 au Havre." *Mouvement Social* 170 (1995): 61–84. Food riots after World War I in France.

Bohstedt, John. "The Myth of the Feminine Food Riot: Women as Proto-Citizens in English Community Politics, 1790–1810." In *Women and Politics in the Age of the Democratic Revolution.* Edited by Harriet B. Applewhite and Darline G. Levy. Ann Arbor, Mich., 1990.

Bouton, Cynthia. "Gendered Behavior in Subsistence Riots: The French Flour War of 1775." *Journal of Social History* 23 (1990): 735–754.

Canning, Kathleen. *Languages of Labor and Gender: Female Factory Work in Germany, 1850–1914.* Ithaca, N.Y., 1996. Discusses women's strikes in the 1890s and 1900s, as well as men's attitudes toward women's work.

Davis, Belinda. "Reconsidering Habermas, Gender, and the Public Sphere: The Case of Wilhelmine Germany." In *Society, Culture, and the State in Germany, 1870–1930.* Edited by Geoff Eley. Ann Arbor, Mich., 1996. Food riots during World War I. Pages 397–426.

Downs, Laura Lee. "Women's Strikes and the Politics of Popular Egalitarianism in France, 1916–1918." In *Rethinking Labor History.* Edited by Lenard R. Berlanstein. Urbana, Ill., and Chicago, 1993. Pages 114–148.

Engel, Barbara. "Not by Bread Alone: Subsistence Riots in Russia during World War I." *Journal of Modern History* 69 (1997): 696–721.

Hagemann, Karen. "Men's Demonstrations and Women's Protest: Gender in Collective Action in the Urban Working-Class Milieu during the Weimar Republic. *Gender and History* 5 (1993): 101–119.

Glickman, Rose. *Russian Factory Women.* Berkeley, Calif., 1984. Women and strikes in Russia.

Gullickson, Gay. *Unruly Women of Paris: Images of the Commune.* Ithaca, N.Y., 1996.

Gordon, Eleanor. "Women, Work, and Collective Action: Dundee Jute Workers, 1870–1906." *Journal of Social History* 21 (1987): 27–47.

Kaplan, Temma. "Female Consciousness and Collective Action: The Case of Barcelona, 1910–1918." *Signs* 7 (1982): 545–566. Important article defining female consciousness.

Radcliff, Pamela. "Elite Women Workers and Collective Action: The Cigarette Makers of Gijón, 1890–1930." *Journal of Social History* 27 (1993): 85–108.

Rogers, Nicholas. *Crowds, Culture, and Politics in Georgian Britain.* Oxford, 1998.

Taylor, Lynne. "Food Riots Revisited." *Journal of Social History* 30 (1996): 482–496. Revisits debate over women's role in food riots.

Tickner, Lisa. *The Spectacle of Women: Imagery of the Suffrage Campaign, 1907–1914.* Chicago, 1987.

Tilly, Louise. *Politics and Class in Milan, 1881–1901.* New York, 1992. Covers women, trade unions, and strikes.

Viola, Lynne. "*Bab'i bunty* and Peasant Women's Protest during Collectivization." *Russian Review* 45 (1986): 23–42.

Wiesner, Merry E. "*Wandervogels* and Women: Journeymen's Concepts of Masculinity in Early Modern Germany." *Journal of Social History* 24 (1991): 767–782.

Weitz, Eric D. "The Heroic Man and the Ever-Changing Woman: Gender and Politics in European Communism, 1917–1950." In *Gender and Class in Modern Europe.* Edited by Laura L. Frader and Sonya O. Rose. Ithaca, N.Y., and London, 1996. On masculinity in communist protests, especially in interwar Germany.

Wood, Elizabeth A. *The Baba and the Comrade: Gender and Politics in Revolutionary Russia.* Bloomington, Ind., 1997. Covers hostility to women workers and peasants.

NEW SOCIAL MOVEMENTS

Gisela Kaplan

Social movements in Europe are a phenomenon of the modern era. Indeed, although there were many movements before the nineteenth and twentieth centuries, they were not called movements or analyzed as such because they generally failed to be based on important seminal ideas or ideologies. Instead, they tended to focus on specific grievances or specific goals. Such actions lacked any conscious intention of overturning the status quo. It is worth remembering that the Latin word *revolutio* signified the *restoration* of order, not its overthrow (as turning about, a return of the same). The term gained its new meaning only after the French Revolution. Nevertheless, in social history it can be very important to ascertain when and how a new idea started and so be able to answer the question why it became relevant and significant at a certain time in history.

The French Revolution (1789–1791) created an important baseline for modern social movements because of two very important ideas. One revolutionary idea argued that vested interests were not in the interest of the people and therefore should not be the foundation of the state. While the French Revolution did not succeed in overturning class divisions it succeeded in challenging the interests of the aristocracy and, in particular, their political power. It also challenged the church, which provided the other most powerful representatives of parliament. The "third estate," the people, were hence to be considered as gaining new status in the politics of their nation. The second important idea, originating in seventeenth-century England, discredited, then to be later supported by the French Revolution, was to issue a Declaration of Human Rights. The important element of this declaration was the assumption that people had rights rather than just duties and that they had equal rights, no matter what their status might have been at birth. Jean-Jacques Rousseau's point well before the Revolution that "man is born free but everywhere he is in chains" referred to the social and political ills of his time, as he perceived them. However, to "unshackle" each individual, as revolutionary idealism desired, proved to be difficult in practice. This was so partly because vested interests are not given up without a fight and partly because the broad restructuring of Europe in the nineteenth century favored a politics of oppression, domination, and imperialsim, fought out also in two world wars and driven by fascism. It took well into the second half of the twentieth century before democracies in western Europe were on a firm footing and the ideals proposed before and during the French Revolution could be raised again.

THE ROOTS OF SOCIAL MOVEMENTS: SEVENTEENTH-CENTURY REVOLTS

The first events that we may see as precursors of social movements occurred in the seventeenth century, a century of great instability and of a particularly long-drawn-out war (the Thirty Years' War, 1618–1648). These first movements of the 1640s and 1650s questioned the authority of the aristocracy and the kings. Sometimes more generally referred to as the "seventeeth-century crisis," they affected England, France, the Spanish Empire, the Ottoman Empire, and Poland. They had in common that, for fleeting and yet impressive moments, the world turned upside down and traditionally accepted social orders were suddenly overturned. When, in Catalonia and Naples, the populace took to the streets to fight against the aristocracy, led in Naples by a mere fisherman (Masaniello), contemporaries felt that these disturbances were qualitatively different from the riots of years earlier.

More ominous to the aristocracy (and even the common people) of Europe than this were the events simultaneously taking shape in England. Here it was not just a revolt but a battle cry by radical clergy and learned burghers, who claimed that great changes were required in England, not just in politics but across the entire spectrum of society. The rebellion succeeded insofar as it led a king to the executioner's block. The beheading of Charles I of England in 1649 stirred an immediate controversy, in which completely new concepts were debated by a small but powerful minority. Groups like the Diggers and the Levelers advocated something akin to a public health insurance system, maintenance of common land, communal life as opposed to individual ownership, and a participatory democracy based on the idea of equality. Between 1647 and 1649 the Levelers drafted an *Agreement of the People*, a type of constitution that was to form the basis for the American *Declaration of Independence* (1776)—perhaps the best index of the "modernity" of their ideas. By 1660 the Levelers and their ideas had been driven underground, but they would find an echo in the ideals of the French Revolution, which would change social and political thinking in Europe forever.

THE AGE OF SOCIAL MOVEMENTS: 1789–1945

Large-scale unrest arose again with the Enlightenment period and the French Revolution. In the eighteenth century the French philosophes as well as English and Scottish thinkers developed the confidence to think that everything could be ascertained and explained by reason. The belief that human institutions and systems of government could be rationally analyzed, assessed, and reformed gave new justification for overturning the status quo. One group receptive to these ideas was the bourgeoisie, which emerged along with a new economic system and thinking: capitalism. In England and France, in particular, economic developments had led to the strengthening of a group of people who did not fit well the traditional three-tiered society composed of the king, the church, and the people. The "third estate" had consisted of powerless peasants, but the growth of cities and of trade in western Europe saw the rise of a class who were city dwellers, businessmen, merchants, traders, professionals (particularly lawyers). Increasingly they felt ignored by a political system entirely run by church and aristocracy. The bourgeoisie demanded more space, more freedom, and greater participation.

While some scholars no longer view the French Revolution as primarily class-based, in the classic interpretation it was led and motivated by the bourgeoisie while the common people of Paris and rural France were coopted to secure the numbers. A charter of human rights was declared, embodying the principles of the *Liberté*, *Egalité*, and *Fraternité* that were the catchwords of the Revolution. Maximilien de Robespierre, later executed, pronounced the right to work, and the first feminists argued for equal rights for women. Despite countless backlashes after the Revolution, the brief revolutionary Reign of Terror, and Napoleon's dictatorship, the idea and expression of individual rights were to become the ethical benchmark for Europe and later for the industrialized world in general. Moreover, the forms that political action took during the Revolution defined the shape of social movements for the next century and more.

Several European uprisings and revolutions took place after the French Revolution—one set between 1830 and 1831 and another, involving large numbers of people across all of Europe, in 1848, fought over the principles of individual and national rights. These revolutions were crushed, but the social movements associated with them began to address new issues, no longer just those of a politically frustrated bourgeoisie. By the mid-nineteenth century the industrial revolution had taken off in many western European countries and, in the advanced case of England, had shown its first stark fatalities. A new social group made its entry into the history books: the factory workers. Their often appalling living and working conditions were described by Karl Marx's collaborator, Friedrich Engels, in *The Condition of the Working Class in England in 1844*. The labor movement coalesced around the struggle to improve these conditions and establish basic rights for workers. This movement, influenced by the writings of Marx and Engels and fanned by the socialist parties of western Europe and then Russia, put forward the most popular and powerful program for political and social change between 1870 and World War I. Its influential powers as a liberatory force for the working classes and as an advocate for an experimental egaliatrianism in Europe began to decline in the 1920s, due to rising fascism and, in the East, to Stalin's totalitarianism.

One other major movement developed in the nineteenth century—the women's movement. Women's movements emerged at various times and in various places throughout Europe, culminating in most western European countries (led by England) in the suffragette movement toward the end of the nineteenth century. Suffragettes demanded the vote, as Olympe de Gouge had during the French Revolution, changes in property laws and marriage laws, and a right to work.

For most Scandinavian countries, the cause of women's rights was associated with an almost continuous agenda of social change throughout the nineteenth century. In Sweden in 1810, well before anywhere else, women gained permission to enter trade and sales occupations. In 1845 they obtained the right to inherit property. Other milestones followed, including the right to attend universities as fully enrolled students in 1873. Although many of these

Marx and the Labor Movement. International Working Men's Association membership card showing receipt of dues for 1869. Karl Marx's signature appears on the line for Germany. AKG LONDON

rights were implemented before the rise of a significant social movement, its emergence in the late nineteenth century spurred even more change. Before it died down in the 1920s, divorce by mutual consent was made possible (1915), women gained the vote (1919), and a new family law of 1920 abolished the husband's guardianship of wife and children. Norway was the first sovereign state in Europe to give full citizenship rights to women, a process that began in 1901 and ended with full suffrage for all women in 1913. As early as 1908 the country passed a law granting women equal pay for equal work. Many of these improvements, including amendments to family law that granted women rights to control and inherit property, were the result of a widespread suffrage movement which had been active since the mid-1880s.

Another noteworthy case of very early consideration of women's rights and issues was Italy, despite its strict Catholicism. Italy had developed a strong bourgeois city culture during the Renaissance, when women filled with distinction several of the most important chairs in the universities of Italy. This past became a model for Italian women much later. After the unification of Italy in 1870, women played an active role in politics, whether in grassroots workers' movements or (usually) on the political left, even before the existence of an organized women's movement.

Before the elections of 1897, the socialist Anna Kuliscioff gained fame by calling for an end to the dehumanizing working conditions of 1.5 million Italian women. Anna Maria Mozzoni, by contrast, stressed the need for the liberation of women. As early as 1864 she advocated the right to divorce, and in 1881 she founded a league for the promotion of women's interests. In 1897 the first National Women's Union was formed in Rome, followed by other local and national organizations. One organization, Unione Donne Italiane, founded in 1944, existed throughout the post–World War II years and retained an important voice even at the time of the "new" women's movement of the 1970s.

Since universal suffrage was eventually achieved in all European countries, the issue of citizenship receded into the background, even though its importance was not entirely lost. Almost naturally, because of the idea of women's moral superiority that was common among the movements, many of the national women's movements joined together prior to World War I and became internationally associated in peace movements. Renewed feminist and libertarian ideas were proposed between the world wars, but they were largely confined to the brief period between the end of World War I and the rise of fascism. Renewed feminist and liberationist ideas were proposed long before the two world wars. Although their expression was driven underground by fascism, ideas of earlier generations never died and resurfaced in the second-part of the twentieth century. Historically, then, with a couple of exceptions, it is rather incorrect to conceive of the women's movements of the late 1960s to 1980s in Europe as "second" or "new" women's movements. It is possible to trace back feminist ideas to the nineteenth century or even earlier.

Europe has had a dual legacy of revolutions and authoritarian traditions, and throughout the modern era these forces have been played out against each other. In the nineteenth and twentieth centuries tradition prevailed more often than radicalism, but progressive ideas and the social movements associated with them flourished in particular periods. It is impossible to understand how the "new" social movements after World War II would have taken place without the humanism of the Renaissance and the revolutions attempting to unshackle the chains that traditions, vested interests, and even the church had foisted upon the individual. It is especially difficult to think of the new social movements without the Enlightenment and the rise of the ideological left, with its dreams of equality, liberty, and a social contract to gain and maintain personal freedom. In a sense, the new social movements are the logical extension of the long-drawn-out Enlightenment projects. The Enlightenment and the French Revolution made slavery and serfdom unsavory, inequality problematic, and a self-sustaining wage a basic right.

POST–WORLD WAR II LIBERATORY MOVEMENTS AND IDENTITY POLITICS

The "newness" of the social movements after World War II has to do with the focus of their grievances. There had always been uprisings by poor farmers and poor urban dwellers in times of famine but their revolt was usually not aimed at the political and social fabric. By the early twentieth century, Europe had also become familiar with protests by workers against bosses and by the working class against the ruling classes. However, it was entirely new to see protests for specific issues forging alliances across class and even political parties. The old revolutionary dictum of justice, equality, and liberty for all was supplemented by a new awareness of one's neighbor, community, and world. Indeed, the new movements forged, temporarily at least, a new sense of community and new identities. The threat of nuclear armament, the many problems of the environment, and, since the beginning of the twenty-first century, the perceived threats of globalization, repeatedly gave rise to strong protests and to

protest movements. Other new concerns of the late twentieth and early twenty-first centuries were movements concerned with celebrating and wishing to protect individuals and individual differences. Laws were challenged as unjust if they were found to discriminate against individuals on the grounds of sex, age, able-bodiedness, sexual orientation, ethnic background, religion, or any other social markers. In other words, from the 1960s to the 1980s, in particular, but also thereafter, the new movements were concerend with turning the table on society and its norms and values.

After World War II, a number of movements arose that some thought were qualitatively different, to be discussed in their own right, and thus should be labeled "new." Others have claimed that these new movements were really continuing and concluding unfinished business of the nineteenth century. The emphasis on historical processes characteristic of social history would support the latter view, at least to some extent. The French Revolution and the European working-class movements were certainly precursors of the various women's movements in the nineteenth and twentieth centuries. Most autonomous women's movements of the postwar era were associated with the left. Some called themselves marxist and others socialist. The Korean War and the Vietnam War also brought into sharp relief the role Western societies played in the affairs of people far from their own legitimate bases of power. Through their activities, the new movements addressed questions of citizenship, the possible trajectory of personal freedom, and the nature of the communal good to which they hoped to contribute.

The first set of these movements of the 1950s and 1960s involved the labor movement, the anti-Vietnam War movement, nuclear disarmament, and the student movements. These movements were characterized by claims concerning class, race, anti-imperialism, and the power of the state. Later they were to be called the "classical" movements, while the movements of the 1970s and 1980s are generally referred to as the "new" social movements. The new social movements included the peace movement, the environmental movement, the women's movements, and the disability movement. While these two sets of movements have been distinguished by different names, certain continuities in social criticism, driven by a desire for a new orientation of society at large, can be observed. All "new" movements went through several phases, from a preparatory incubatory stage (usually in the mid-1960s) to a revolutionary phase (from the end of the 1960s to the mid-1970s), ebbing to reformist phases thereafter and to a diffuse phase of pragmatic politics from the mid-1980s to the present.

The features specific to the new movements included, first, a new identity politics that was defined not by class but by the self-identification of the movements' members as women, as gay, as disabled, and so on. Second, such identity politics made it possible to combine forces with groups whose individuals were formerly separated across class lines and at times also across political affiliations.

The economic and welfare context was also important. Notably, the new movements occurred within a context of full employment. For the fifteen years between 1948 and 1963 unemployment in most European countries averaged around 1.9 percent or rose, at the most, to about 5 percent. In short, this period was one of "entrepreneurial euphoria," uninterrupted by crises. The postwar years also saw an expansion of the welfare state. Service industries underwent a boom period and heralded the growth of the service sector throughout the remaining decades of the twentieth century. Sweden was hailed as the model welfare state, and most European countries had some policies in place to protect the individual from personal hardship and to offer support services of some kind for specific life situations. There were two additional factors, at least for the onset of the postwar women's movements. One had to do with the fact that during World War II women were asked to fill men's places in manufacture and most other civilian positions once thought to be the prerogative of men. The same women were not always entirely satisfied with returning to home duties. Their daughters were well aware of the tensions and conflicts and took up the fight that their mothers could not or would not fight. A second decisive factor was provided by an unlikely source: the pharmaceutical industry. The invention and sale of birth-control pills in the early 1960s delivered into women's hands freedom from worry about unwanted pregnancies. A side effect of the pill was a promise for women of greater social freedom, even the option of having careers without premature pregnancies. Family planning became a new field of service support for women and young couples.

The impetus for the movements hence did not arise from hunger and want. Germany experienced an economic "miracle" and was for many years in a state of boom. Even economically troubled Spain experienced its own "Spanish miracle" in industry. Between 1950 and 1956 its industrial production tripled, and in the 1960s Spain's industrial growth rate was exceeded only by that of Japan. Not all European countries were in quite such a privileged position. Portugal was still poor. Greece was also predominantly an agrarian society, with more than 50 percent of the labor force still employed in agriculture in 1960. But here and in Portugal the new movements were considerably weaker. In that sense, the movements were the last vestiges of an unusually long and comforting economic summer. The quest for careers, independence, and fulfillment of one's abilities fell on fertile ground. Shortages of labor, expressed in guest-worker conscription and a rising demand for female labor, created favorable circumstances for discussions of women's equality with men in the workforce.

However, crises fell upon the movements in almost all countries with a change of economic fortunes. By the early 1970s inflation was the chief concern, having jumped from 2 or 3 percent in the immediate postwar decades to over 10 percent in most and over 20 percent in some European countries. These increasing signs of an imminent crisis were coupled with fiscal disasters in 1973 and 1974, caused by the oil embargo. Stock-market declines greater than those in the Wall Street crash of 1929–1932 were recorded. From 1976 to 1983 unemployment for women in member states of the European Economic Community rose by 15 percent, as compared to a rise in unemployment for men of only 0.6 percent. In all, a total of 7 million women in eighteen western European countries lost their jobs in less than a decade.

Student movements. The influential American civil-rights movement of the 1950s and 1960s had substantial repercussions throughout Europe. Then, in the 1960s, student movements and hippies created an atmosphere of general upheaval against the state. The entire basis of western European life came under review. Student demonstrations took place in Madrid and Barcelona as early as 1965. Like other countries, Spain had massively enlarged its educational institutions, opening eleven new universities since the 1950s. Britain had opened a total of twenty-eight, and throughout Europe the number of student enrollments had risen astronomically, growing by more than sevenfold in some countries in the span of less than fifteen years. The student movement, particularly in France, was strongly associated with the union movement and to some extent (as in Italy) with political parties of the left. Ironically, the German student uprising of 1968 originated from the Free University of Berlin, the one West German university which had been founded after the war as an explicitly democratic institution. The students understood that the ideals were not translated into practice.

The student uprisings in France, Italy, and West Germany were not just campus revolts but uprisings against the establishment and the state generally. Ultimately, they were not just "student" uprisings but represented the discontent of an entire generation, the generation mostly born after World War II and the Holocaust. They were not going to take the lead from their parents and grandparents, who, they felt, had given them no reason for pride. They wanted to see substantial changes, not just at the level of university administration, but in society at large so that they would see democracy in practice, transparent politics, and a complete abolition of traditional social hierarchies. Their influence on other movements was significant, partly because some of the same people who had been active in the student movement would later emerge in one of the other movements.

The "new" women's movements.

The new wave of women's movements arose simultaneously in European countries, as in the United States, Australia, and Canada, often within just a few years of each other and, at times, without knowledge of the others. In national analyses, one finds quite often that specific triggers for the mass-scale movements were unique to one country. For instance, Norway had the resistance movement of the Lapps, who were fighting for self-determination (as they were also in Finland and Sweden). Denmark had a movement against joining the European Community that led to the so-called people's movement against the EEC in 1972. Finland's first movement for women's liberation occurred in the context of Finnish nationalism and calls for secession from Russia. In Berlin, it was the visit of the shah of Iran, general imperialism, and the fight against outmoded institutions that gave rise to the student movement there, and this merged almost seamlessly into the autonomous German women's liberation movement. In all the above-named cases women actively participated in these movements and hence learned to organize politically. It was easier to shift people from one cause to another than to mobilize politically inactive or inexperienced groups. But such a national analysis cannot account for the enormous similarity and the timing of movements across national and continental boundaries.

It is generally agreed that the so-called new women's movements in western Europe began in France and West Germany around 1968. By the end of the international Decade of Women (1985), every western European country had had some exposure to women's protests and demands, sometimes leading to a drastic revision of thinking on individual liberty and political participation. In 1988 leading women declared that the European Community was, legislatively, the most progressive political community for women in the world. Credit for these advances was primarily due to the tens of thousands of women who developed a keen eye for strategy, for the impact of

protest, and for political organization. They mobilized in sometimes spectacular protest events (Reclaim the Night, smile strikes, or the dramatic strike actions by 90 percent of Icelandic women, refusing to do their chores). However, the European political powers were also keen to take some credit for this apparent achievement. They argued that the foundations for gender-fair legislation were laid in 1957 in the Treaty of Rome, which sealed the formation of the EEC. The Treaty of Rome espoused the principle of economic parity and fair competition, and this included the rights and costs of female employment. Equalization was to avoid any distortion of competition stemming from a lower-paid female workforce. The second wave of the movement happened well after these politico-economic European networks were in place. Although grassroots movements did not at first take much notice of this European framework, nor did officialdom take note of grassroots movements, both levels of activity moved in the same direction of change.

All women in western Europe are now formally equal before the law, a right that in most countries existed before the second-wave movements started. They all have a right to equal opportunity in education and to careers once thought to be the sole domain of men. The problem was, and partly still is, that the gap between formal legal and political equality and daily practice has not been entirely bridged. Thus a culture of dissent and protest spread throughout western Europe and, to a point, became respectable. Such a culture of dissent was stronger in central Europe than in the Scandinavian countries, where much had been achieved in a quiet step-by-step program of reform over most of the twentieth century. The protests were nearly absent in countries behind the Iron Curtain because women's demands so much fought for in the West had already been fulfilled, in a fashion.

Abortion and the women's movement.

Abortion was clearly the issue around which the greatest support in the women's movement was collected in the 1970s. Women marched in their tens of thousands, including many women who otherwise took no active part in the women's-movement activities. Abortion and reproductive technologies have been themes since the nineteenth century. New antiabortion and anticontraception regulations, perceived as necessary to boost populations, were enforced either toward the end of the nineteenth century, or at the beginning of the twentieth. Most western European countries introduced antiabortion laws for the first time in the twentieth century. Antiabortion laws occurred at a time of nationalism and racism, fascism, and preparation for war. Many countries had criminalized abortion by the time World War I broke out in 1914, and several others, such as Germany and Italy, had tightened the laws by the 1920s or 1930s, introducing strict penalties and long prison sentences for offenders and for those who volunteered to become accessories.

In such areas as sexuality, contraceptives, and family counselling, the Scandinavian countries, except for Norway, were in general far ahead of other Western nations, both in legislation and in policy initiatives. The issue of abortion was also decided earlier there and usually with far less public uproar than in other countries. Thus, in Scandinavia, abortion never became the catalyst for women's movements that it did in other western European nations. Iceland, Sweden, and Denmark liberalized their abortion laws in the interwar period (1918–1939), Finland in 1951, and Norway in 1965. Abortion on demand was introduced in Denmark in 1973 and in Sweden in 1975. One of the main reasons, one suspects, why Sweden never developed a strong new feminist movement is that most demands that brought women together in other countries had actually been met in Sweden.

Elsewhere in Europe, the case was different. Although the abortion issue was hardly new in Europe, it was "novel" again in the 1960s and 1970s because the issue began to acquire new meaning through the rise of the women's movement, which viewed the right to abortion as a necessary condition for the liberation of women. Eastern European countries provide a useful contrast. Abortion was freely available and encouraged, but in the absence of methods to prevent conception.

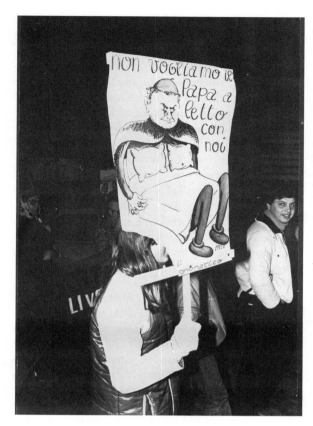

Abortion and the Women's Movement. Italian feminists demonstrate for the legalization of abortion, Rome, 10 January 1981. A marcher's sign reads "We don't want the pope in bed with us." GIANSANTI/SYGMA/©CORBIS

Gay liberation. The new gay liberation movement started some years after the women's movements in Europe, but it, too, had a long history of struggle. Broadly, in western Europe the existence of libertinism among the European aristocracy had traditionally enabled the maintenance of a permissive subculture. In this sphere secret expressions of a sexual diversity were possible and not uncommon, especially in a bawdy and celebratory court culture of the seventeenth century and thereafter. There were rituals and occasions both for women and men to seek and maintain same-sex lovers. The aristocracy generally deemed itself to live above the strict moral laws of its age. Such practices and favors were occasionally extended to members of the bourgeoisie, usually when these were either wealthy or beautiful. The most famous of these affairs became scandals not because they existed but because they had been flaunted in public, as in the case of George Sand (1804–1876), especially in her affair with Marie Dorval, which Sand conducted

while dressed in male attire. Then the full force of nineteenth-century French laws, written largely by the aristocracy for the "lower classes" (including the bourgeoisie), had to descend on her. In another famous case, which led to the conviction of Oscar Wilde for homosexual offenses in 1895, Wilde's unforgivable error had been to have stepped outside his class. But these scandals aside, a gay subculture never stopped flourishing. An openly gay woman like Rosa Bonheur (1822–1899) or Collette (1873–1954) would have been unthinkable in Australia or the United States. Women such as Sylvia Beach (1887–1962), Gertrude Stein (1874–1946), and her lifelong companion Alice B. Toklas (1877–1967) moved from the United States to Paris in order to live a life that was possible in Paris but still rather unlikely or impossible in New World countries.

Legally, homosexuality was not always forbidden. The situation was extremely uneven between countries, and policies changed within countries from one regime to the next. For instance, the French criminal code of the Napoleonic era permitted any sexual activities between any consenting adults. Repression occurred only with the Vichy government during World War II, when the age of consent was raised to twenty-one. Prosecutions for anyone below that age were then conducted on the basis of pedophilia, and women were usually not prosecuted. In the Soviet Union of the 1920s homosexuality was considered normal, and Soviet legislation stated so explicitly. However, with the Stalinist reaction also came severe repression. Likewise, the Netherlands had persecuted and executed hundreds of homosexuals in the early part of the eighteenth century. But following the French Revolution, the law penalizing sodomy (under which any male homosexuality fell) was abolished in 1811, removing all restrictions on consenting adults. German occupation of the Netherlands under the Nazis imposed a brief reign of terror, but immediately after the war (1946) there was a Dutch campaign to liberate gay people from the oppression. As early as 1944 homosexuality was decriminalized in Sweden, and about ten years later the High Court ruled that sexual preference was an irrelevant criterion for parental fitness. Unparalleled anywhere else in the world, the Swedish Riksdag actually decreed in 1977 that two people of the same sex living together "shall be fully accepted by Swedish society." Between 1951 and 1960 there existed an International Committee for Sexual Equality, which many western European countries joined.

Explicit mention of lesbians occurred much later, largely because it was believed that homosexual relationships between women either did not exist or were not possible. Lesbians suffered from the veil of invisibility so completely that they often did not come to the attention of the public and very little was known about them. Radclyffe Hall's novel *The Well of Loneliness* (1928), which dealt openly with lesbianism, was widely translated into European languages in the late 1920s, and it had a major impact on local subcultures by testifying to their existence.

Despite the ongoing existence of a gay subculture in the large cities of Europe, the degree of oppression against homosexuality should not be downplayed. In the 1950s and 1960s homosexuality was considered a perversion within internationally defined disease models. When offenders were not sent to prison, they came to the attention of the medical profession for treatment, which usually entailed an attempt to "cure" them. Aversion therapy was practiced in most Western countries from the 1950s to the 1970s, using electric shock or administering emetic agents that caused prolonged bouts of vomiting.

Surprisingly, despite the long French tradition against criminalizing homosexuality, France did not lead the way to gay liberation. The Stonewall riots of gays against police in New York in 1969 gave the impetus for change throughout the entire Western world. In France, the beginning of the gay liberation movement is commonly identified as the protest on 1 May 1971 that interrupted the May Day celebrations. A small group of people participated in that protest, but a decade later, in 1981, there were mass demonstrations (over 10,000) against legal discrimination. A gay liberation movement began in Spain in 1977. In Italy the most successful gay and lesbian organization was ARCI-Gay, a wing of ARCI (Associazione Ricreative Culturale Italiana), a cultural association affiliated with the Communist Party. By 1989 they had a national office in Rome.

However, the fight for rights of gays and lesbians was not without severe problems and violent reprisals. The first (post-Stalinist) underground gay organization in Leningrad lasted for just two years (1984–1986) before the KGB disbanded it, exiling, firing, or imprisoning its members. But Stalinist draconian laws were dropped between 1991 and 1993 in Latvia, Estonia, Lithuania, the Ukraine, Kazakhstan, Moldova, Uzbekistan. In 1993, under Boris Yeltsin, the criminal penalties against homosexuals in Russia were dropped, freeing over a thousand prisoners convicted on homosexual charges. In Greece, it was found that the Greek gay organization AKOE and its journal "offended public morality," and in 1991 the editor was sentenced to imprisonment. In Cyprus and Turkey the laws on sodomy were declared invalid in 1992, but gay organizations had suffered police attacks, bashings, systematic beatings, and prosecution (1987–1992), and not only there. Gay bashings were on the increase through the early 1990s in other countries that had decriminalized homosexuality.

The HIV and AIDS crisis of the 1980s and early 1990s gave new impetus to the movement, which was becoming increasingly international. The gay liberation movement was never a uniform or politically clearly demarcated group. It was diverse in social composition and consisted of competing schools of thought, nationally and internationally. Since 1995 gays and lesbians have obtained full legal rights throughout Europe, although social rights have not been achieved everywhere, let alone with the same breadth as in Sweden or Denmark.

Environmentalism. Environmentalism encompasses not just conservation but also broad issues of lifestyle. From the mid-1990s onward, for instance, urban activism sought to reclaim cities from the car. It is generally agreed that the oil crisis of 1973 sparked the European environmental movement, although other events were important. In 1972 the Norwegian philosopher Arne Naess began the "deep ecology" movement, and Greenpeace staged its first major action against whaling. Rachel Carson's book *Silent Spring* (1962) alerted the public to the dangers of DDT and the rampant use of pesticides. The rise of the environmental movement is reflected in the substantial shift from traditional to nontraditional associations that occurred in the period from 1980 to 1994. Membership in unions and in established political parties declined, while organizations working for third-world countries, refugees, and human rights increased their membership twofold in this period. Organizations dealing with nature and the environment experienced a fourfold increase. In 1994 Greenpeace had 600,000 members, Amnesty International 164,000, Medecins sans Frontier 500,000, and World Wildlife Fund 600,000 members.

Like the women's movements, the green movement consisted of many different groups and political persuasions. It is difficult to speak of "left" or "right" political positions or to assign a specific class profile. Under the single heading of environmentalism we may find strains as diverse as pop ecology, mysticism, and economic rationalist approaches to "resource management." There were deep ecologists, supporters of Earth First!, spiritual Greens, bioregionalists, spiritual ecofeminists. And like the women's and gay movements, they too resorted to unconventional, extraparliamentary forms of mobilization.

In most countries "green" ideas were readily translated into political parties. The Greens, founded as a party in Germany at the beginning of 1980 and in Austria and Switzerland in 1986, quickly gained a respectable number of seats in Parliament. The Greens argued for an entire renewal and revision of society, economy, and politics. They argued that the ideology of profit and the economic principles of growth had inbuilt the seeds of its own destruction because, if proceeding unchecked, this thinking was destroying the physical basis on which economic success was built. With hindsight, the Greens have been extremely successful insofaras modern economies have at least introduced the concept of sustainable development and have begun to seriously deal with a series of environmental problems. Their founders were former leaders of the student movement and thus represented an ambivalent mix of a traditional leftist revolutionary orientation and a new "catastrophism." The new catastrophism was fanned by people who believed that the planet was doomed unless something was changed very quickly. They argued that human societies came perilously close to destroying their own world by orchestrating the largest wave of extinctions since the

age of the dinosaurs and the wholesale destruction of forests, particularly rain forests. They were usually regarded as doomsday prophets and dismissed as too radical although, today, we know their predictions were largely correct. They revealed the potentially disastrous consequences of a bigger-is-better philosophy and urged societies to revise their destructive practices. Increasingly, however, the Greens acquired a mandate from the population to deal with environmental issues. By the late 1990s they were no longer regarded as alternative lifestyle and marginal. The Green Party of the United Kingdom made the sudden "greenness" of European politics visible when, in 1989, it won over 14.5 percent of votes in the elections for the European Parliament.

While in Britain the movement was aided specifically by people with a concern for the remaining wildlife, in Eastern European countries it contributed to a sense of liberation from overbearing state power. In Eastern European countries the environmental movement started to become a cause célèbre, largely because environmental protest could be closely identified as a protest against the power of the state. A Bulgarian environmental group called itself Ecoglasnost. Charter 77 in Prague, a human-rights dissident organization, turned green. The Polish Ecological Club became active in 1980, and demonstrations were held in Hungary in 1988. Mikhail Gorbachev's repudiation of the Brezhnev Doctrine led to a rapid liberalization throughout the countries of the communist bloc. With the disintegration of communist regimes in 1989, nongovernment organizations rose to new prominence in the East. In short, by the late 1980s the environmental movement had spread throughout all of Europe. Moreover, it had become a recognized international concern. In 1987 the Brundtland Report, called *Our Common Future,* was published by the World Commission on Environment and Development. In 1992 Rio de Janeiro hosted the world's first global environmental summit.

The peace movement. If the environmental movement makes it difficult to tease out the political and class affiliations of its members, the peace movement adds a problem of categorization as "new" or "classic" movement. The modern post–World War II peace and antiwar movements began their mobilization in Europe in the 1950s and were generally very active throughout the 1950s and early 1960s but then died down, to reemerge as a strong "new" movement in the 1980s. Antiwar sentiments were directed against actual military interventions (Korea, later Vietnam) and oppression (the 1956 uprising in Hungary), while peace movements tended to look closely at security

The Peace Movement. Protesters march on the American military base at Torrejone, 30 kilometers (20 miles) from Madrid, 20 March 1983. CHRISTIAN VIOUJARD/GAMMA/ ©HULTON GETTY/LIAISON AGENCY

policies and the nature and purposes of armament. There were also marked differences between East and West. In Eastern Europe, peace movements were at first undifferentiated and broadly anti-imperialist, directed against those outside the Soviet bloc. Western movements, by contrast, put their own governments and policies under scrutiny.

In the late 1950s Britain was one of only three nuclear powers in the world. By 1957 there was noticeable opposition to the path that Britain had chosen, evident in the formation of a National Committee for the Abolition of Nuclear Weapons Tests (NCANWT) and a British Peace Committee, which presented a case against any use of nuclear weapons at the Stockholm Peace Appeal. The important Campaign for Nuclear Disarmament (CND) was formed in 1958, with the philosopher Bertrand Russell as its first president. In 1972 the first Strategic Arms Limitation Treaty (SALT 1) between the United States and the Soviet Union was signed. Although it was

considered a flawed agreement by many, it drained the peace movement and the CND of some of their urgency and momentum.

The rekindling of the peace movement's concerns in the early 1980s followed two very different routes and was sparked by different events. One was the 1979 election of Margaret Thatcher, who, in concert with President Ronald Reagan, publicly expressed her belief in increased arms spending. Then there was the war between Britain and Argentina over the Falkland Islands in 1982, with its inevitable military rhetoric. Another source of revitalization came from the women's movements, particularly from Germany, where the government proposed in 1978 that women should be conscripted into the army in the same way as men, for a compulsory military service of eighteen months. In May 1979 this resulted in a series of demonstrations. In Germany it signaled, in fact, the beginning of a new peace movement. By 1980 the West German contribution to the international women's peace movement was substantial.

During the United Nations world women's conference in 1980, "Women for Peace" organizations presented General Secretary Waldheim with 500,000 signatures of European women against nuclear weapons and militarism. This opposition, particularly to nuclear power stations and nuclear weaponry, steadily drew wider support and began to spread across Western Europe, involving men and women alike. The largest mass demonstrations against nuclear weapons and the arms race were held in October 1981 and again in October 1983. From Helsinki to Brussels, from London to Rome, and from The Hague to Madrid, vast numbers of people took to the streets at the same time. Over 3 million participants were estimated to have taken part, clearly suggesting that the environmental and peace movements had become truly European rather than just national events. It is important to add that the end of the cold war ushered in a period in which the tense "stand-off" tactics between East and West diminished. The processes that led from the Stockholm Peace Appeal to the 1992 environmental summit in Rio de Janeiro indicate the long road that had to be traveled from local and national protest to mainstream international summit meetings.

The twentieth century saw humanity degenerating into practices of large-scale planned elimination of human life and into the most destructive warfare in human history. Yet in response there emerged strong liberatory movements that remembered the Renaissance, humanitarianism, the individual conscience, and the French Revolution. At no time, as at the beginning of the twenty-first century, have the peoples of Europe enjoyed so much personal freedom.

See also other articles in this section.

BIBLIOGRAPHY

Bobbio, Norberto. *The Future of Democracy. A Defence of the Rules of the Game.* Translated by Roger Griffin, edited by Richard Bellamy. Minneapolis, Minn., 1987.

Byrne, Paul. *The Campaign for Nuclear Disarmament.* London, 1988.

Cant, Bob Han, and Susan Hemmings, eds. *Radical Records: Thirty Years of Lesbian and Gay History, 1957–1987.* London, 1988.

Conca, Ken, Michael Alberty, and Geoffrey D. Dabelko, eds. *Green Planet Blues: Environmental Politics from Stockholm to Rio.* Boulder, Colo., 1995.

Grünewald, Guido, and Peter van den Dungen, eds. *Twentieth-Century Peace Movements: Successes and Failures.* Lewiston, N.Y., 1995.

Hayward, Tim. *Ecological Thought: An Introduction.* Cambridge, U.K., 1995.

Heller, Agnes. *Renaissance Man.* Translated by Richard E. Allen. London, 1978.

Hill, Christopher. *The World Turned Upside Down: Radical Ideas during the English Revolution.* New York, 1972.

Kaltefleiter, Werne, and Robert L. Pfaltzgraff, eds. *The Peace Movements in Europe and the United States.* London, 1985.

Kaplan, Gisela. *Contemporary Western European Feminism.* London, 1992.

Lauritsen, John, and David Thonstad. *The Early Homosexual Rights Movement (1864–1935).* New York, 1974.

Lovenduski, Joni. *Women and European Politics: Contemporary Feminism and Public Policy.* Brighton, U.K., 1986.

Lubasz, Heinz. *Revolutions in Modern European History.* New York, 1966.

Melucci, Alberto. "Social Movements and the Democratization of Everyday Life." In *Civil Society and the State.* Edited by John Keane. London and New York, 1988. Pages 245–260.

Minnion, John, and Philip Bolsover. *The CND Story: The First 25 years of CND in the Words of the People Involved.* London, 1983.

Pateman, Carole. *The Sexual Contract.* Stanford, Calif., 1988.

Sartori, Giovanni. *The Theory of Democracy Revisited.* Vol. 1. Chatham, N.J., 1987.

Steinberg, S. H. *Five Hundred Years of Printing.* New ed. London, 1996.

Tourraine, Alain. *Return of the Actor: Social Theory in Postindustrial Society.* Translated by M. Godzich. Minneapolis, Minn., 1988.

Wallerstein, Immanuel. *The Modern World System.* Vol. 1 of *Capitalist Agriculture and the Origins of the European World-Economy in the Sixteenth Century.* New York, 1974.

STUDENT MOVEMENTS

Brendan Dooley

When French students took to the streets once again in October 1998, they brought to a close a thirty-year period of academic unrest that has left an indelible mark on modern culture. To the extent that students as a group and student movements as a category of social action can be identified throughout European culture from the Renaissance to the present, this most recent period in the history of student movements has been unique. Nonetheless, coordinated behavior on the part of those enrolled in educational institutions has always played an important role in larger processes in society. Students alone, as a social elite with specific requirements and specific connections to the institutions of power, have created episodes of protest with a lasting impact on the lives of subsequent generations of students as well as on their societies at large. And students as intellectuals have contributed a crucial ideological element to larger movements for social change.

To be sure, the demands of the students in 1998, mainly of high-school age, were far more modest than those of the student protestors in both Spain and France in 1986. All they wanted were more teachers and better school facilities; whereas their predecessors demanded modifications in university entry requirements and other reforms aimed at leading their societies ever farther along the path to democracy. Similar to the latter were the protests of Italian university students in 1977–1978, sparked by grievances concerning plans for changes in university curriculum that were then before the government.

All these student protest movements in western Europe paled by comparison with the movements in Eastern Europe in 1988–1989, in Czechoslovakia, Hungary, Poland, East Germany, and Yugoslavia, which helped bring about the collapse of their Soviet-backed regimes. Closer in kind to the movements in Eastern Europe, at least from the standpoint of the link between academic grievances and more or less profound social and political ones, as well as from the standpoint of the depth of the impact on contemporary culture, were the student movements of 1968.

These were briefly brought to mind in the waves of antinuclear protest that hit Western Europe in 1980 and 1983.

Social scientists have offered several explanatory models for the recurrence of student protest throughout European history. Some have given a prominent role to generational conflict. For instance, Lewis Feuer states that members of a rising generation imbued with notions of modernity and change may wish to vent on the one preceding it all the frustrations accumulated during their young lifetimes. Some observers have pointed to identity and personality crises due to problems of socialization affecting large groups of individuals. According to Erik Erikson, especially in periods of social upheaval, many young people may refuse to enter adult roles on the terms set for them by adult society. Others such as Kenneth Keniston have seen the presence of alienated and at the same time talented leadership types as a major factor determining whether a student population will be given to revolt. Still others such as Gianni Statera have turned attention to class conflict, pointing out that even students from privileged backgrounds may for a time share a status of dependency with, for example, factory workers.

As elements in a larger society, some theorists have pointed out, students may share in generalized social pathologies like the anomie described by Émile Durkheim or the various new threats to individual autonomy that go under the names of "iron cage" (Max Weber) or "the colonization of the Lifeworld by system imperatives" (Jürgen Habermas). Work on political opportunity structures has tried to show how the political and social consistency of a whole society may lend itself more at some times than at others to the expression of widespread discontent, taking into account variables such as social cleavages, institutional stability, and strategies within the movement and the regime.

For the more remote history of student movements, however, it should be kept in mind that almost all explanatory models have been elaborated on the basis of events in the last several decades for which accurate survey data has been available. Moreover, there are some problems with pinning down the specific historical characteristics of students as a group. They share their status for a far shorter period of time than categories like laborers or mothers. Only in the beginning of the nineteenth century did they begin to develop a self-conscious identity. In every case and in every period, the vastly different circumstances make long-term generalizations an imperfect way of analyzing the phenomenon.

THE EARLY MODERN UNIVERSITY

Social historians have shown how universities evolved in the Renaissance into mainly elite degree-producing institutions for entrance into the professions of medicine, law, and the church. It is important to remember that students before the mid-twentieth-century were for the most part not only a social but a gender (male) elite. Typical student organizations at this time included brotherhoods, drinking clubs, and dueling fraternities, intended mainly to extend to students the same corporate protections guaranteed to other groups. These organizations have so far received no more scholarly attention than have the sporadic eruptions of "town versus gown" violence. Disputes with a town were caused as often by ordinary bread riots as by perceived acts of disrespect for the honor of the citizen or noble families to which the students belonged. Occasionally a *translatio studi* resulted, that is, the movement of an entire student body away from a town, the last of which was from Göttingen to a nearby woods in 1790. Especially at Padua, the contested election of a rector could bring about rioting between student factions. As universities came under the control of political officials in the various states, the imposition of discipline was accepted in return for guarantees protecting the universities' privileges and immunities.

By the sixteenth century, governments began to regulate what had been the most common "student movement" of the time, namely, the so-called *peregrinatio academica,* or academic peregrination, whereby students in France, for instance, tested the waters in no less than three universities, on the average, before getting their degrees. Due to religious disputes and, especially in the less-popular places, fears of a decline in the numbers of students, governments began to insist on restricting the exercise of the professions in their states to those who had received their degrees locally. Unwittingly, they set the stage for local organizational activity in the centuries to come.

More incisive student actions affecting religious, intellectual, and political life in the period usually began outside the university and found echoes within, so they cannot be analyzed as products of a particular student culture or ideology. In the religious category may be mentioned the Little Germany organization in early sixteenth-century Cambridge, in support of the Lutheran Reformation. Intellectual movements included the formation of academies, a typical expression of the Renaissance ideals of polite conversation, usefulness, and pleasure, to which university students in Italy made significant contributions. Most likely in order to increase patronage opportunities, law students at the University of Rome founded debating clubs where they gave harangues and disputations in preparation for their exams, inviting prominent local personages to listen in or take part. Political movements were exemplified by the factions at Oxford in the support of the dynasties of Lancaster and York before Edward IV's decisive victory in the Wars of the Roses. Two centuries later, political sympathies at Oxford remained largely with the king even while civil war was going on and Puritan religious ideas had made serious headway among students.

STUDENTS AND REVOLUTION

During the French Revolution, students imbued with late Enlightenment ideas and perhaps less reconciled than their elders to the ancien régime began playing a more radical role in pushing events in new directions. An organization called the Society of Law Students at Rennes devoted itself to studying the deteriorating political situation of the country and engaged in violent protests against the local nobility, side by side with the unemployed laborers in the Young Citizens' society. And after the University of Paris was drastically reduced by the legislation of February 1792, a considerable number of students enrolled en masse as volunteers in the People's Army, proclaiming their adherence to the ideals of equality and freedom. The French Revolution attack on ancien régime corporatism raised serious questions about future university organization even in areas where guilds and corporations were not abolished. Without immediately doing away with the brotherhoods, drinking clubs, and dueling fraternities of old, students began casting about for new forms of organization.

Modern student organization began in Germany with the so-called Burschenschaften, founded in Jena in 1815 but rapidly diffused throughout the country. In this case, for the first time, social historians have identified a real youth crisis, as students began defining a specific public sphere for themselves, distinct from the political establishment of Restoration

Troubles in Rennes. Students fighting troops in Rennes, France, in 1788–1789. Musée Carnavalet, Paris/Photo ©RMN-Bulloz

Europe. Students often shared a radical nationalism drawn from writers such as Johann Fichte, as well as an anti-régime fervor galvanized by disappointment in the Napoleonic wars. And although they often agreed with Wilhelm von Humboldt's new concept of university education as forming civilization rather than imparting mere encyclopedic knowledge, they did not find this ideal embodied in any existing institutions. The Burschenschaften offered an opportunity for self-reform. Against what was viewed as the political and intellectual establishment's effete Francophilia, they set the new image of the physically fit, self-disciplined, and Teutonic youth.

An expression of the new movement was the first student festival at Wartburg in October 1817, where some fifteen hundred students gathered to express their ideas about freedom and fatherland. At Giessen, a radical right-wing version of the movement, called the Giessener Schwarzen (Giessen Blacks), was formed by Karl Follen, whose program supported an interpretation of German nationalism that excluded French, Slavic, or Jewish elements in the country. When certain acts of violence attributed to members of the student organizations brought about their suppression under the Carlsbad Decrees in 1819, they began a more radical and subversive career underground. In Poland, where libertarian and patriotic ideals inspired by the Burschenschaften combined with opposition to the Russian regime, official decrees banned all secret student societies in 1821. To drive home the point, students were arrested and some executed in Wilno in 1823 in connection with anti-Russian statements.

All over Europe, students contributed significantly to the unrest that built up in the 1830s and 1840s, and social historians so far have not distinguished student motivations from the motivations of other elements of the populations involved. Students were as deeply affected as anyone else by the heady mixture of socialist ideas and romantic patriotism that had no room for expression under the prevailing sociopolitical system. In France they took part in the agitation that led to the fall of the Restoration monarchy and the establishment of the July monarchy in 1830. In Göttingen the following year, they were largely responsible for the creation of a communal council that briefly stood ground against the Hanover government of William II in Münster. In 1832 over thirty thousand students and other participants celebrated patriotism and future German unification at the Hambach festival. In 1833, prefiguring the revolutions of 1848, students at Frankfurt belonging to a group called the Vaterlandsverein unsuccessfully sought worker and peasant support in a failed attempt to seize the federal treasury and bring about a universal uprising. Even in Switzerland, a student group known as the Radicals formed in 1839 to advocate a closer union of the cantons and democratic political reforms.

In Paris one of the triggers of the 1848 revolution was the suppression by Louis-Philippe's government of a politically motivated course by Jules Michelet at the Collège de France, which brought the students out in force one month before actual fighting began. Here as elsewhere, what encouraged student participation in the events that were to follow, besides constitutional ideals, was the specter of intellectual unemployment raised by rapidly increasing enrollments in a time of economic stagnation. In Germany the Eisenach Festival was intended to provide a forum to discuss democratically these as well as more specifically German issues. Some twelve hundred delegates from all over Germany presented their resolutions to the National Assembly then meeting in Frankfurt to draw up a constitution for a new German empire. Although no answer was given, the students were somewhat mollified by the establishment of democratic bodies like the Prussian Landtag and by the suppression of the Carlsbad Decrees.

RUSSIAN POPULISM

The failure of the 1848 revolutions in Europe and the defeat of Russian militarism in the Crimean War combined to set the stage in Russia for some of the farthest-reaching student movements of the age. Often from provincial backgrounds, students were quickly acculturated to the latest trends on their arrival at the universities of Moscow and St. Petersburg. Imbued with the ideas of Marx, the French socialists, and Alexander Herzen, they rebelled against what they perceived as the failed modernism of their elders. Rather than capitalism and state authoritarianism, they turned to agrarian socialism as the solution to society's ills, seeing in the countryside, where many of them originated, the seeds of a more complete rebirth than any possible in the rest of Europe. This populist philosophy seemed all the more utopian considering the dismal conditions most peasants in Russia continued to endure, but its promise grew increasingly attractive as students from poor backgrounds poured into the universities under Nicholas I's new enrollment policies. For thirty years it formed a powerful undercurrent in student life, surfacing from time to time in more or less violent conflicts with the imperial authorities, and included many brilliant theorists and activists, from Mikhail Bakunin to Pyotr Kropotkin.

Organizational activity reached fever pitch with Alexander II's liberation of the serfs, but expectations were soon disappointed. The banning of student organizational activity in 1861, together with a reduction in the number of government scholarships, occasioned a major strike at the University of St. Petersburg. As strikes spread to Moscow and elsewhere, many students were jailed and the university was closed for two years. The government's apparent

France, 1848. In France, as elsewhere, many of the 1848 revolutionaries were university students. ©BETTMAN/CORBIS

lapse into political intransigence drove the movement toward more desperate measures. Pyotr Zaichensky at the University of Moscow published the secret paper, *Young Russia,* calling for violent revolution as the only way to bring about constitutional reform, land reform, emancipation of women, nationalization of factories, and the abolition of inheritances. Other students there and elsewhere set up "Sunday schools" to disseminate such ideas among workers and peasants. Dmitri Karakozov, a member of a terrorist faction at the University of Moscow called Hell, advocated and eventually attempted the assassination of the tsar in 1866. The government reaction, known as the White Terror, led to the arrest of the ringleaders and staved off further terrorist action for a time. Soon, frustrated by peasant indifference and plagued by government repression, some participants turned again to terrorist tactics, attempting and actually carrying out assassinations of several public figures. Disagreement about these tactics created a rift within the movement that led to the formation of the People's Will, the group responsible for the assassination of Alexander II in 1881.

The years before the 1905 revolution may be taken to exemplify the way responses to student demands can turn isolated incidents into a rationale for more incisive organizational activity. The disastrous Russo-Japanese war had hardened the students' resolve, although they were not chiefly involved in the 1905 Bloody Sunday event, where soldiers fired on a crowd of about three thousand demonstrators gathered at Moscow University to begin a strike that was to last nine months. In a huge meeting, they drafted the Second Moscow Resolution committing the student movement to "revolutionary" politics. They organized public propaganda programs and encouraged fellow students to do the same at the universities of Odessa and Kiev. When railway and other workers joined the students in a general strike, Nicholas II finally issued the October Manifesto granting freedom of conscience, speech, and assembly and promising franchise and more powers to the Duma. His subsequent reassertion of autocracy set the stage for the Bolshevik Revolution.

WORLD WAR

In Bosnia and Herzogovina too, but slightly later than in Russia, a new intelligentsia began to emerge, and the Russian revolution of 1905 inspired hopes for change. As students, they were exposed to ideas in sharp contrast with the realities of peasant life. Social historians have identified two distinct groups. A few went to university in Vienna or Paris, where they imbibed advanced ideas about universal brotherhood and the socialist future. Typically, though, they stayed at home and never got beyond local high schools, where intellectual prospects were dominated by less sophisticated notions of heroism against the tyrannical oppressor. To the latter group belonged Gavrilo Princip, a student member of the Black Hand movement, who assassinated the Archduke Franz Ferdinand on the eve of World War I.

In western Europe, student movements were also changing by the late nineteenth century, particularly with the rise of student support for right-wing, anti-Semitic movements. Concerns about job prospects and a sense of competition from Jewish students help explain the new divisions in student politics, particularly in some professional schools in countries such as France. Other students retained more traditional leftist attachments.

After the war, the most active student organizations were in Germany. The most effective leaders were as much repelled by the chaotic world of communist revolution immediately to the east as they were by the indecisive Weimar government in their midst. When Weimar called for international cooperation to resolve the issue of war reparations imposed by the Versailles Treaty, they called for a stronger Germany in opposition to the rest of Europe. Their sentiments were confirmed as Germany slid deeper and deeper into economic chaos and the communist revolution began threatening from within. In 1919 the Deutsche Studentenschaft (DS) began to provide a system of representation for students and, through a program called Studentenhilfe, to finance poorer members. Its ideology of pan-Germanism and anti-Semitism, however, came in conflict with the liberal programs of the Weimar government. The anti-Semitic sections, especially those based in Austria, were eventually forced out, but not before the whole organization began to take on a radical nationalistic character.

In analyzing the German movement at this time, social historians have focused on explaining the climate in which Nazism eventually flourished. Even more radically nationalistic than the DS was the Fichte Hochschulegemeinde, formed in 1919 to celebrate the ideas of Johann Fichte. Along with other groups, it went on to form a part of the Hochschulring Deutscher Art (HSR) aimed at promoting the ethnic community. As the leading voice in student politics throughout the 1920s, it represented anti-parliamentarianism, anti-marxism, and authoritarianism. A major influence within the HSR came from the so-called Young Conservatives, especially strong in Berlin, who added the elements of irrationalism, anti-intellectualism, assertiveness in foreign relations, and nationalistic revolution to this heady mix. Some of the more radical members of the HSR were involved in the failed Nazi beer hall putsch of 8 November 1923. In 1924 a militant fragment broke off to form the Deutschvolkische Studentenbewegung, which, allied with an Austrian sister organization, spoke through a newspaper called *Der Student*. In 1926 a Catholic group seceded from the increasingly radical and militaristic HSR, calling itself the Gorres Ring. However, it too swerved increasingly to the right in the 1930s, advocating the Mussolini government as an acceptable alternative to Weimar, and proclaiming ethnic nationalist concepts.

The first Nazi student groups emerged in Munich in 1922 and in Weimar in 1925, but a veritable national movement began only in 1926. Originally founded by the students themselves, they soon came under Nazi party leadership. By 1928 party leaders appointed Baldur von Schirach to lead them and opened recruitment to all elements of the university populations, from disenchanted proletarians to the members of the older dueling fraternities who had already been espousing right-wing political ideals. Soon the Nazi student network began organizing violent

Berlin, 1919. Students at Berlin University protest the handing over of German war criminals to the Allies at the end of World War I. ©HULTON-DEUTSCH/CORBIS

demonstrations against the left. Older groups like the HSR began to lose ground, and soon the Nazis took control over leadership of the DS as well. On 12 April 1933 the DS issued twelve theses "against the un-German spirit," denouncing Jewish and liberal literary works, and it organized the book burnings that took place at German universities between April 26 and May 10. Eventually the DS was placed under the direct authority of a Reichsstudentenführung headed by Gustav Adolf Scheel, who coordinated it with the Nazi German Student Union.

To be sure, the German movement was not entirely Nazi at this time. In the midst of the war effort, students at the University of Munich staged the only public protest against the party since its rise to power in 1933. Led by Hans Scholl and his sister Sophie, they maintained contact with anti-Nazi sympathizers throughout Germany by way of a correspondence network later dubbed the "White Rose Letters." To engage support for a wider uprising they printed and distributed pamphlets. When the pamphlets were discovered by the authorities, the Scholls were arrested, beaten, and hanged, as were many of their correspondents.

In occupied France, social historians have shown, anti-Nazism could become a student ideology. Students staged the Arc de Triomphe demonstration on 11 November 1940, celebrating the World War I armistice and protesting German occupation of Paris.

Demonstrators were either killed or deported to Germany. Later, in 1943, students played an important part in the Forces Unies de Jeunesse Patriotique organized to protest the occupation and to call for egalitarianism and democracy in the universities.

TOWARD 1968

The first postwar movements were provoked by Soviet-backed repression in Eastern Europe, and at first they were isolated reactions to specific circumstances rather than generalized protests. Supported by the Allied occupation forces, students objecting to manipulation and isolation within the Friedrich-Wilhelm University, located in Soviet-occupied Berlin, in 1948 formed the Free University in the Allied zone, with a radical new program and a new antihierarchical structure.

As students became more aware of the gap between political rhetoric and reality in their countries, they contributed to the workers' uprisings in East Germany and Czechoslovakia in 1953, which occasioned the first armed Russian intervention in the satellite states. Fearing a workers' uprising in Hungary that year, the Soviets replaced the repressive Mátyás Rákosi with the more moderate Imre Nagy. What followed has presented social historians with a typical case in which bungled policies provoked a wider movement. When Nagy immediately freed eighty thousand political prisoners and revealed the terror tactics utilized by the previous regime, the Soviets restored Rákosi to power in 1955. As opposition to Rákosi grew, members of the Petöfi club, the university wing of the Communist Youth League, were among the most vociferous. By July the Russians moved in, replacing Rákosi with the even harsher Ernö Gero. Nonetheless, inspired by the October 1956 revolution in Poland, students began organizing for an independent, democratic, socialist Hungary. About five thousand met on October 22 to adopt the Budapest Technical University Resolution, spelling out demands for peaceful change and demanding reinstatement of Nagy and the withdrawl of Russian forces. Some 300,000 demonstrators, led by students, assembled on October 23. But when security forces fired on the students, Hungarian soldiers called in as reinforcements joined the demonstrators, and the Soviet-backed government took flight. Nagy thereupon took over and formed a cabinet, promising freedom and independence from the Warsaw Pact. Soviet control was reestablished only after a full-scale attack on Budapest and severe retaliation, in which some 20,000 rebels were arrested, 50,000 died, Nagy and 2,000 others were executed, and more than 80,000 were wounded. Nearly 230,000 Hungarians escaped to the West, and 10,000 students were deported to Russia.

The last episode of 1950s student activism in the Eastern bloc was the protest at the University of Warsaw occasioned by the closing of the student paper *Po Prostu,* which had taken a liberal line since the October Revolution of 1956, advocating political liberalization. Protesters who called for reinstating the paper were ambushed and beaten by police after a grant of safe conduct. Those who presented the petition to the government of Prime Minister Wladyslaw Gomulka were arrested.

Several episodes, isolated at first, led to the massive student unrest unleashed in both east and west in 1968. All involved leadership structures were perceived to be more interested in global security issues than in promoting democratization at home. At times the protest was mainly confined to university-related issues. For instance, during the Week of Action in November 1963, French students belonging to the Union Nationale des Étudiants de France (UNEF) and several teachers' unions struck to demand better facilities, more scholarships, and larger research accounts. There was also concern about placement prospects in disciplines like sociology, and these could fuel attacks on the social order. At times university issues combined with wider ones connected with differences in worldview between governments and students.

In this period, for the first time, echoes from the United States had an important effect on student action in Europe. Student involvement in the Freedom Summer in Alabama in 1964 and in the Berkeley student revolt that followed, showed the potential of mass action. The Vietnam War, hotly contested in the United States from 1965, seemed to symbolize for many Europeans the worst effects of Western militarization and colonialism. At the same time, young people of both genders were affected by social and cultural trends that had been transforming modern life on both sides of the Atlantic. In spite of increasing affluence, democratic ideas tended to advance beyond the democratizing potential of even the most open societies. Movements that once concerned a tiny vanguard now became part of mass youth culture, not only in politics, but also in other areas of life. Intellectual liberation was inspired by the Situationists, the neoexistentialists, and Jean-Paul Sartre. Artistic liberation was inspired by the Beat poets and by abstract expressionism. Sexual liberation, meanwhile, introduced behavioral patterns that conflicted with the traditional structure of the family. Attacks on modern consumer society highlighted the lifestyle components of the student movement.

A pattern of confrontation emerged and spread rapidly from place to place. In 1964 students at the Free University in Berlin protested the arrival of the Congolese Prime Minister Moise Tshombe, thought to be a pawn of Belgian mining interests. When the administration refused student requests to invite Erich Kuby, a noted left-leaning critic of West German politics in general and of the university in particular, students staged a protest focused on issues ranging from the tenure case of an activist instructor to the Vietnam War.

In France the rift between the government of Charles de Gaulle and student politics had begun to grow from 1960, when the UNEF declared its support for Algerian independence and officially requested that the government begin negotiations with the rebels. After two years of confrontations on this issue, the government banned student public protests. Finally in 1963 rumblings of discontent culminated in the Sorbonne explosion, ostensibly sparked by the breakdown of university structures in the face of growing enrollments. After a day of struggle between 10,000 Sorbonne students and 4,500 police, some 300,000 students in the nation's twenty-three universities went on strike, along with half the professors. The following year, on the occasion of a university tour by the Italian president, accompanied by the intransigent French education minister Christian Fouchet, University of Paris students and the UNEF organized protests calling for democratic reforms within the universities.

In Britain protests in 1965 at the London School of Economics were concentrated against the white community in Rhodesia, which had declared independence from the black nationalist federation. In Italy the first protests, centered at the University of Turin in 1965, began with the question of official recognition for a degree in sociology, and spread out to include student governance, curricular reform, and the relevance of instructional programs to contemporary affairs. Likewise at Turin, a seven-month occupation of the university buildings in 1967 began by focusing on university issues and broadened out to include social issues of national concern.

Student activism in German universities began to reach critical mass in June 1967, when students protesting a state visit by the shah of Iran were subjected to a previously planned police attack involving brutal beatings and the execution of a bystander. About twenty thousand students from throughout West Germany attended the funeral in Hanover on 9 July. The Hanover meeting produced a manifesto connecting police brutality to the authoritarian and exclusionary structure of German government as well as to the general crisis of the university. The meeting and its outcome propelled the student leader Rudi Dutschke and the Sozialistischer Deutscher Studentenbund (SDS) into prominence. The same year, students formed the Kritische Universität in West Berlin as an alternative to the increasingly bureaucratized Free University by offering student-taught courses.

1968 AND BEYOND

The 1968 season of student unrest opened in Czechoslovakia. In January an unpopular neo-Stalinist secretary of the Czech Communist Party was replaced by Alexander Dubček, who introduced far-reaching reforms including democratization within the party, freedom of movement, and freedom of expression. Students played an important role in the Prague Spring of discussion and protest that followed, with calls for a continuation of the reforming line and the dissolution of Communist Party rule. Encouraged by the Prague movement, students in Warsaw took the occasion of the banning of a nationalist drama to demonstrate for more freedoms and democratization in Poland. The brutal repression of both movements would be a point of reference for student leaders in 1989 during the Velvet Revolution.

In the West the power of the student movement in Prague inspired actions chiefly motivated by such issues as NATO demands on Europe, the Vietnam War, and the effects of U.S. policies in the Middle East. In Rome the via Giulia protest led to 250 student arrests. Next came Germany, where Rudi Dutschke was shot and severely wounded during the suppression of the Easter riots, crippling the movement.

In France the expulsion of the student leader Daniel Cohn-Bendit from the University of Nanterre for his organizational activities moved the center of protest once more to the Sorbonne. On May 3 the rector called in police to remove the demonstrators, who responded by erecting barricades and flinging cobblestones. A week-long battle ensued, in which hundreds of students and police were injured and six hundred students were arrested. Police brutality and government intransigence brought the workers over to the side of the demonstrators, though direct contacts were limited in part by union leaders' uneasiness about bourgeois students, and a season of strikes ensued. By late May some ten million workers were on strike, joining labor issues to the political ones, and the De Gaulle government seemed on the verge of collapse. Only quick concessions by De Gaulle on labor issues, weakening the workers' support for the student movement, avoided political disaster; and a successful appeal brought conservative elements in the country to the government's side in new elections. Inspired by the May events in Paris, outbreaks occurred on June 3–10 in Zagreb and Belgrade, Yugoslavia, in Zurich later that month, in London, and still later in Warwick, where students discovered documents showing university administrators' investigations into student political activity.

The significance of the two-year period of protest is still a matter of debate among social historians. Most have agreed that the immediate results were less important than the long-term consequences. At least in the West, the movements produced few concrete gains besides more open enrollments and fewer entrance requirements. Over the long term, some studies have blamed the movement for driving the radical leftist fringe toward a drastic change in tactics. Disappointed by the failure of the movement to bring about a general revolution, these studies say, some organizers resorted to forming a tiny vanguard of violent operatives dedicated to subverting the system—the Red Army Faction in Germany, Direct Action in France. In Italy the rise of the Red Brigades made the student movement of 1977–1978 all the more radical and violent. On the positive side, studies have suggested that the movement drew attention to the persistent class divisions that seemed to prevent realization of the democratic dream, as well as gender divisions that helped create the women's movement, while the postwar political parties began to abandon

Prague, 1968. A student stands atop a Soviet tank during the Warsaw Pact invasion that ended the Prague Spring, 1968. JOSEF KOUDELKA/J.K./MAGNUM PHOTOS

Paris, 1968. Students hurl objects at the police near the Sorbonne, Paris, May 1968. MAGNUM PHOTOS, INC./©BRUNO BARBEY

ideology in the general enthusiasm that accompanied the economic boom. It drew attention to the negative side of capitalist development and modern technology, emphasizing the limits to economic growth and bringing environmental concerns to international attention, culminating in the Greens movement (begun by students in late-1970s Germany). Intellectuals, many of whom had been students or professors in the 1960s, including Michel Foucault and Jacques Derrida, in questioning the very concept of modernity, looked to the emergence of a new intellectual movement that was eventually dubbed postmodern.

From this standpoint, social historians were less stunned than political scientists when workers who had lived through the 1970s in Eastern Europe as well as students who were just coming of age in the 1980s began questioning the technological and economic utopia of socialism, first in Poland and then elsewhere. For two decades, the movements for reform, democracy, and pluralism had run up against increasingly intransigent and entrenched administrations in these countries. Even convinced socialists saw that something had to change.

The Solidarity movement in Poland from 1981 showed that the regimes were not entirely invulnerable; and Gorbachev's reforms sent shock waves throughout the Eastern bloc. Inevitably, students became involved in what followed. They were on hand when the Honecker government crumbled and the Berlin Wall came down. They were in the vanguard of the Velvet Revolution in Czechoslovakia. Prague Spring veterans who had organized themselves in early 1989 spearheaded a large commemorative demonstration that August. Government repression of a large student demonstration the following November pushed the protest over into revolt. The unofficial opposition party thereupon threatened a general strike. When the government realized Russian aid would not be forthcoming, it resigned. Here as elsewhere, the Soviet era was over.

Although the 1989 movements signaled the decisive end of an epoch in European history, they did not signal the end of student protest movements. The long view of university history suggests that the most recent flare-ups are merely foretastes of what may happen when genuine issues join the interests and the passions of the mass of students, sending them into the streets once more, proclaiming the power of youth, the oppression of the generations and of parents, and the desire for change. The long view also suggests that there is no guarantee that the future envisioned by student movements will always necessarily correspond to the liberal ideals of equal opportunity, multiculturalism, and freedom for all.

See also **Students** *(in this volume);* **Higher Education** *(volume 5); and other articles in this section.*

BIBLIOGRAPHY

Burg, David F. *Encyclopedia of Student and Youth Movements.* New York, 1998.

Erikson, Erik H. *Identity, Youth, and Crisis.* New York, 1968.

Feuer, Lewis S. *The Conflict of Generations: The Character and Significance of Student Movements.* New York, 1969.

Keniston, Kenneth. *Youth and Dissent: The Rise of a New Opposition.* New York, 1971.

Lipset, Seymour Martin, and Philip G. Altbach, eds. *Students in Revolt.* Boston, 1969.

Statera, Gianni. *Death of a Utopia: The Development and Decline of Student Movements in Europe.* New York, 1975.

MODERN PROTEST POLITICS

Marco Giugni

Social protest is a permanent, though discontinuous, feature of European society since the dawn of history. It occurs when ordinary people act together to defend threatened collective interests and/or identities or to promote new ones. Historically it has taken various forms: antitax revolts, struggles against conscription, food riots, land occupations, seizures of grain, insurrections, strikes, barricades, public meetings, and many others. At times social protest cascaded into larger cycles of contention involving dense interactions among various groups using different forms of action (Tarrow, 1998). These phases of generalized contentious activity gave rise to revolutions when multiple centers of sovereignty were created, which turned the conflict into a struggle ending in a forcible transfer of power (Tilly, 1993). Most often, however, social protest occurs at a lower scale, involving a limited number of actors who lack regular access to institutions and engage in confrontations with elites, authorities, and opponents. When these actors engage in sustained challenges to power holders based on common purposes and social solidarities, we have a social movement.

European social movements emerged as two large-scale social processes—the emergence of an urban-industrial economy and the consolidation of the national state (Tilly et al., 1975)—interacted to produce fundamental structural changes in history. On the one hand, capitalism—the concentration of the means of production and the separation between those who control these means and those who provide labor—produced new conflicts and oppositions, most notably between capital and labor. On the other hand, state formation—the creation of autonomous, differentiated, and centralized governmental organizations that are territorially bounded and have the monopoly of the legitimate use of violence over that territory—created a concentration of power and of coercive means in the hands of state authorities. Such infrastructure was needed, among other things, to collect taxes and to engage in wars. In due time, the state and its representative institutions such as the parliament became the main target of social protest as national

politics and local contention intertwined to an increasingly larger extent (Tilly, 1995).

The concentration of capital and coercive means that marks the expansion and consolidation of the European national state implied a transformation of the structures of power in society. New collective interests and identities emerged, new opportunities arose, and new forms of group organization (such as the class) appeared. This, in turn, contributed to the birth of modern social movements by remodeling the forms of collective action (see Figure 1). Charles Tilly (1986, 1995) has shown in his masterly accounts of popular contention in France and Britain how the repertoires of contention changed under the influence of these two large-scale processes via the restructuring of interests (and identities), opportunities, and organization.

Social movements are a special form of social protest and contentious collective action, one that emerged out of the shift from the old to the new repertoire of contention as the concentration of capital and coercion transformed its modalities. Sidney Tarrow (1998, p. 30) has described this shift as follows:

> In the 1780s, people knew how to seize shipments of grain, attack tax gatherers, burn tax registers, and take revenge on wrongdoers and people who had violated community norms. But they were not yet familiar with acts like the mass demonstration, the strike, or urban insurrection on behalf of common goals. By the end of the 1848 revolution, the petition, the public meeting, the demonstration, and the barricade were well-known routines, employed for a variety of purposes and by different combinations of social actors.

The national social movement of the late twentieth century was born, indeed invented by Europeans as they created the new collective-action repertoire, as Tilly puts it (see his article on collective action in this volume), and can be defined as:

> a sustained challenge to powerholders in the name of a population living under the jurisdiction of those powerholders by means of repeated public displays of that population's numbers, commitment, unity, and worthiness. (Tilly, 1994, p. 7)

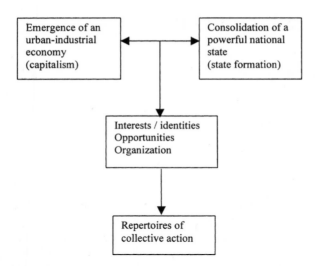

Figure 1. Relationship between large-scale processes and collective action.

Social movements are organized efforts, based on a shared identity, to reach a common goal mainly, though not exclusively, through noninstitutional means. This clearly distinguishes them both from political parties (which engage in elections) and interest groups (which act mainly within the existing institutional channels by way of lobbying and negotiations with the power holders), although at times they make use of forms of action usually adopted by the latter. This definition also emphasizes the action side of movements rather than their organizational basis or their ideology, although the latter two aspects allow us to distinguish between movements and enter the explanation of their mobilization. It therefore excludes purely cultural-ideological movements such as the *Nouvelle Droite* (New Right) in France or cultural-spiritual experiences such as the New Age, as well as religious movements insofar as they do not express themselves through political challenges.

This article deals with social movements as a particular form of the broader category of contentious politics, which includes related phenomena such as riots, rebellions, terrorism, civil wars, and revolutions, and which can be defined as collective interaction among makers of claims and their objects involving government as mediator, target, or claimant and bearing on the interests of claimants (McAdam et al., 1996; forthcoming). Given their origin in the formation of the modern national state, this article focuses on the emergence and mobilization of in western Europe from the mid-nineteenth through the twentieth century, drawing from the work of social historians, sociologists, and political scientists.

SOCIETAL CLEAVAGES AND EUROPEAN SOCIAL MOVEMENTS

The nineteenth century: Traditional lines of conflict. Social movements are the overt expression of latent social conflicts. Their mobilization rests upon societal cleavages, that is, social and cultural dividing lines that oppose the interests and identities of different groups in society. Capitalism and state formation did not only produce a reorientation of the repertoires of collective action. They also modified the structure of dominant conflicts in society and hence the social-structural foundations of social movements. Traditional cleavages constitute the condition for the mobilization of many contemporary movements. In his fundamental geopolitical mapping of Europe, Stein Rokkan (1970) stressed four traditional cleavages, which are particularly important in this respect: the center-periphery, religious, urban-rural, and class cleavages (see Kriesi et al., 1995, ch. 2, for a discussion in relation to social movements).

The center-periphery cleavage forms the basis for the mobilization of regionalist and nationalist movements. Examples are countless: Northern Ireland, Scotland, and Wales in Britain; Catalonia, Galicia, and the Basque country in Spain; Alsace, Brittany, Corsica, Occitania, and again the Basque country in France; Friuli, Sardinia, Southern Tyrol, and the Val d'Aosta in Italy; Flanders and Wallony in Belgium; Jura in Switzerland; and many others. Most of these movements claim have as their final objective the political control over a given territory and are coupled with an ethnically based identity. As such they are ethnic-national movements. The example of the Italian Northern League, however, indicates that this is not always the case. Its claim for an independent or autonomous Padania (the final goal varied over time, shifting back and forth from the quest for more autonomy to full independence) did not rest upon an ethnic identity. It is sometimes framed as such, but there is no basis for a collective identity of the people of Padania in ethnocultural terms. However, regionalist or nationalist claims are typically related to a specific territorial identity and are facilitated by two kinds of cultural resources: religion and especially language. In addition, the strength of this cleavage depends very much on the structure of the state, specifically on its degree of centralization. Regionalist and nationalist claims historically were more frequent in centralized states like France and Spain than in federalist ones like Germany and Switzerland, where the devolution of power to the peripheral minorities tends to institutionalize the conflict between the center and the periphery. They occurred especially when the minority in question has been or felt discriminated against.

The religious cleavage in Europe refers to the opposition between Catholics and Protestants that emerged out of the sixteenth century Reformation. It took different forms in countries where one of the two religions predominates, like France, Italy, and Spain, and in countries that were religiously mixed, like Germany and Switzerland. In predominantly Catholic nations, this cleavage refers to the conflict between the church and the state. In religiously mixed nations it historically opposed Catholics and Protestants. By the late twentieth century the religious cleavage had lost much of its strength and did not often give rise to contentious collective action, although from time to time in predominantly Catholic countries, popular upsurges of protest occurred, typically with regard to education issues. France is a well-documented case in point. Elsewhere, the religious conflict was largely institutionalized into the party system. To be sure, on the world scale the main opposition of the late twentieth century was that between Judaism and Christianity (especially Catholicism) and Islam. Thus, the religious cleavage may be seen as returning in certain western European countries, such as France and Britain, that hosted high numbers of immigrants from the Muslim world. This displacement of the traditional religious cleavage may have facilitated the mobilization of Muslim immigrants in those countries, and indirectly provoked the reaction of racist and extreme right groups.

The urban-rural cleavage opposes Europe's urban and industrial regions to the rural areas where agriculture and the peasant economy prevailed. This line of conflict was dominant during the nineteenth century, forming the basis for the social protest carried on by farmers. In the course of the twentieth century it weakened considerably as the number of farmers shrunk everywhere in Europe and as they became increasingly integrated into national politics. However, in many countries they maintained a strong organization and collective identity, and were able to mobilize in important ways—as they often did in France—often in reaction to the threats posed on them by the process of European economic integration.

The fourth and last of the traditional cleavages is certainly the most important. The class cleavage refers basically to the opposition between the working class and the bourgeoisie. Thus, it obviously underpins the mobilization of the labor movement. The transformation of the class structure that took place with the industrial revolution made this cleavage central from the mid-1800s to at least World War II. The growing role of the service sector in West European countries, however, eroded a large part of the social basis of the labor movement. Furthermore, increased living standards and the expansion of the welfare state weakened the culture and collective identity of the working class. On both these counts (the structural and the cultural underpinnings of labor movements), the strength of the class cleavage diminished in the course of the twentieth century, but kept nevertheless an important mobilization capacity. This holds true especially in countries like France and Italy, in which the industrial conflict between labor and capital was not pacified and therefore remains politically salient.

Twentieth century: New lines of conflict. If the rise of labor and other European social movements stems largely from the profound transformations of the societal conflict structure inscribed in the process of modernization, the same can be said of movements of the second half of the twentieth century. At least in western Europe, the four traditional cleavages highlighted by Rokkan weakened during the twentieth century. At the same time, the weakening of traditional structures and the centrality of the class conflict brought to the fore a new cultural and social cleavage that opposed different sectors within the new middle class (Kriesi 1989): those with a "postmaterialist" value system, stressing individual participation, emancipation, and self-fulfillment; and those with a "materialist" value system, emphasizing socioeconomic needs as well as social order and security. Increased social mobility, the development of a mass education system, and above all the post–World War II economic growth with the related expansion of the welfare state resulted in economic well-being, and may have provoked what Ronald Inglehart (1977) called the "silent revolution," that is, a shift from materialist to postmaterialist values in western societies, leading to the emergence of what came to be known as the new social movements.

New social movements, mobilized around demands for cultural rights and a better quality of life, had three main thematic foci: (1) the criticism addressed to the new risks and threats engendered by economic growth and technological progress; (2) the rejection of all sorts of bureaucratic control over the individual; and (3) the assertion of the right to one's own lifestyle and the right to cultural difference. Thus, the new social movements were situated at the crossroads of the criticism of modern civilization and the search for the cultural emancipation of marginalized minorities. Some prefer to call them left-libertarian movements (della Porta 1995). They are "left" because they mistrust the marketplace, private investment, and the ethic of achievement, and they

Protesting Nuclear Arms. Belgians form a human chain around the U.S. airbase at Florennes to protest installation of cruise missiles on the base, April 1984. The demonstration was organized by the Belgian National Action Committee for Peace and Development and supported by the Socialist Party, leftist movements, and labor unions. MARC DEVILLE/PHOTO NEWS/GAMMA LIAISON

are committed to egalitarian distribution; they are "libertarian" insofar as they reject the regulation of individual and collective conduct by both private and public bureaucracies in favor of participatory democracy and the autonomy from market and from bureaucratic dictates. This label refers to a social movement family that includes the New Left, which prevailed in the 1960s and 1970s; the new social movements, which took the upper hand in the 1980s and 1990s; as well as student movements.

Although there is no clear-cut demarcation between "old" and "new," most observers would call "new" the following movements: peace, ecology, antinuclear, women's, solidarity (humanitarian, antiracist), squatters', and other counter-cultural movements, as well as movements mobilizing for the rights of often-discriminated minorities such as gays and lesbians. Some would add student movements to this list. Others, however, consider them a precursor of the new social movements, which are seen as more pragmatic and less tied to the ideology and organizations of the New Left.

Labor movements (and their ramifications within institutional arenas, most notably social-democratic parties and labor unions) and the new social movements are two dominant areas of social protest—better yet, two political families—of twentieth-century Europe. Both can be classified as leftist forms of social

protest. A third area, located at the opposite end of the political spectrum, comprises conservative and extreme right movements. But, is this a real political family? Can we find a common denominator that allows us to place them in one and the same category? Piero Ignazi (1994) finds at least three different streams within the ideology of the Right: (1) a conservative stream that stresses order and tradition but accepts modernity; (2) a "counterrevolutionary" stream, basically antimodernist and nostalgic for the ancien régime; and (3) a fascist stream, profoundly anticommunist but in its own way revolutionary. (This distinction is only in part drawn from the classical division proposed by René Rémond, which posits a legitimist and traditionalist right, an Orleanist and liberal right, and a Bonapartist and authoritarian right, which is the precursor of fascism.) However, while we may identify certain traits that unite rightist groups and clearly distinguish them from the Left, in particular with respect to the notions of social justice and equality, it is very difficult to put in the same field liberal, conservative, and authoritarian currents. On the one hand, fascism is clearly opposed to liberalism as it emphasizes the superiority of the state over the individual and poses limitations to individual freedoms. On the other hand, with its stress on the creation of a new order and its nationalistic populism, the fascist tradition is also profoundly anticonservative and revolutionary, and hence clearly distinct from the moderate (conservative) right. Furthermore, the fascist ideology is antisystemic, for it displays a fundamental opposition that undermines the legitimacy of representative democracy.

The legitimist (monarchist) and Bonapartist traditions singled out by Rémond form the initial, nineteenth-century ideological underpinnings of the extreme right in the European context (Ignazi, 1994). While the former only rarely gave rise to forms of social protest and was for the most part confined to a marginal space, the latter has been sadly important as it was at the heart of the rise of various fascist movements and regimes in several European countries, most notably Germany, Italy, and Spain, between the two world wars. In addition, various neofascist and neonazi groups, have, explicitly or implicitly, referred back to this ideological tradition. (Whether we can speak of social movements in these cases is doubtful, at least following the definition used here.)

The "traditional extreme right" stems from the conflicts underlying the development of the industrial society and is therefore, in a way, the other side of the coin represented by the class cleavage. Another type of right surfaced in the 1980s and 1990s, which some have called the "postindustrial extreme right" (Ignazi, 1994) and others the "new radical right" (Kitschelt, 1995). Like the traditional extreme right, the new radical right is basically antisystemic. Yet it does not stem from the fascist tradition, and sometimes is even opposed to it ideologically. It is better seen as a response to the transformations that characterized Western Europe after World War II. The weakening of traditional bonds and the emphasis on self-determination and individual freedom are among the outcomes of these transformations. In a way, the structural transformations that have characterized western society during the twentieth century gave rise to new social and cultural cleavages which came to underpin both the new social movements and the new radical right. The movements of the extreme right, in this view, express a deepening conflict between the "winners" and the "losers" of the modernization process (Kriesi, 1999). People adhering to the extreme right would be the "losers," as they would have poor social and cultural resources to cope with rapid social change (accelerated by globalization processes).

While the value system carried by the new social movements was basically social-democratic, libertarian, and emancipatory, that of the extreme right was antisystemic, authoritarian, and antiegalitarian. The discontinuity of the new radical right with the traditional extreme right is seen in the fact that it often has a neoliberal view with regard to economic issues.

According to Kitschelt (1995), the new radical right combines an authoritarian ideology, a market/liberal position toward the allocation of resources, and a particularistic conception of citizenship and membership in the national community. It is therefore not surprising that it has found in immigration and the multicultural society, which it resists on the basis of an ethnocultural conception of the national identity, one of its main grounds for mobilization. Indeed, one of the main characteristics of the new radical right in western Europe, together with its populist appeal, is its xenophobia, which often leads to overtly racist attitudes and behaviors.

The European extreme right, both in its traditional and new radical variants, has usually been channeled into parliamentary politics, taking the form of a party. At the same time, however, these parties have often behaved as social movements, mobilizing people in the streets and challenging the established authorities by means of unconventional protest actions. In addition, especially in the last part of the twentieth century, violence by small extreme right groups surfaced in various countries. Such violence basically took three forms: (1) planned and organized terrorist acts (especially during the 1960s and 1970s, for example by rightist anarchists); (2) more spontaneous activities by various groups of skinheads and naziskins (often addressed against immigrants and asylum seekers, especially during the 1980s and 1990s); and (3), less often, attacks by radical right religious fundamentalists (such as antiabortion activists).

THE HISTORICAL DEVELOPMENT OF EUROPEAN SOCIAL MOVEMENTS

Those who do not fear simplification may think of different historical periods as being characterized by a dominant social conflict that gives rise to a specific type of social protest. According to Alain Touraine (1984), for example, if the labor movement is the central movement of industrial society, the new social movements express the new conflicts inherent in industrial society, whereby symbolic rather than material goods are the crucial stake. In a more systematic fashion, the German sociologist Joachim Raschke (1985) has described as a succession of three political paradigms the shift in the focus of conflict that has taken place since the second half of the nineteenth century. The forms of resistance that characterized Europe in the ancien régime, such food riots and tax revolts, are centered around the "authority paradigm" and reflect the struggle against an unequal distribution of power. The closer we get to the French Revolution, the more this kind of protest concerns the fundamental rights of people and—if these rights are met—citizens: freedom of speech and assembly, voting rights, and so on. In the course of the nineteenth century, and especially after 1848, the crucial conflict shifted toward class conflict, centered around the "distribution paradigm" opposing the owners of the means of production against the labor force. Social rights became the crucial stake, and the main issues had to do with the distribution of wealth in society. More or less since the 1960s, finally, the dominant conflict has come to reflect the "lifestyle paradigm." The centrality of class conflict is undermined, as the defense of interests and identities linked to traditional cleavages, typical of the old politics, has lost significance in favor of nonmaterial issues addressed by the new politics, such as the quality of life, minority rights, unconventional lifestyles, environmental protection, and so forth. Cultural rights and individual autonomy have become the crucial objects of contention.

To be sure, some of the themes raised by the new social movements were already present in the nineteenth century. This holds especially for the women's, ecology, and peace movements, which are among the most important, both quantitatively in terms of political mobilization and qualitatively with regard to the relevance of their claims for twentieth-century. Not incidentally, these precursors of the contemporary new social movements emerged at a time when the national social movement was slowly forming as a major collective actor. Thus, the roots of the women's movement can be found in the *cahiers des doléances* of women during the French Revolution, in which they complained that the only choice left them was between misery and gallantry. The first organizations to defend the interests of women began their activity in Britain in the first half of the nineteenth century. Curiously, French feminists remained quite marginal for a long time. Contemporary environmentalism was pioneered by German romanticism, and the first environmental organizations in Europe were established in the late nineteenth century. These small circles of ecologists *ante litteram* were mainly concerned about the need to protect and conserve certain natural spaces.

The most persistent precursor to the new social movements formed around the issues of peace and war. The origins of modern pacifism can be found in the Enlightenment, or, from an organizational point of view, at the time of the Napoleonic Wars; perhaps the first peace association in Europe, the London Peace Society, was formed in 1816. Similar organizations were created across Europe in the following decades. Their efforts to prevent war, which often contained a

TABLE 1
SIMPLE CLASSIFICATION
OF SOCIAL MOVEMENTS

Paradigm	*Movements*	*Counter-movements*
Authority paradigm	Ethnic movements	Racist movements
	Regional movements	Regional counter-movements
Distribution paradigm	Labor movements	Antitax movement
Lifestyle paradigm	New social movements	Movements defending traditional lifestyles

Source: Kriesi (1988).

strong internationalist dimension, became stronger concomitantly with the intensification of international conflicts, most notably at the end of the nineteenth century and during the two world wars. After the Russian Revolution, the pacifist movement inevitably suffered a split between a radical, communist-oriented wing and a moderate, most often religiously-based wing. This split became most visible during the years of the cold war, when the issue of nuclear arms took center stage.

Just as the repertoires of contention had changed in the shift from the ancien régime to modernity, women's, ecology, and peace issues were transformed in the twentieth century as a result of the "silent revolution" described by Inglehart. Initially, in their archaic forms, the new social movements were generally restricted to small circles of scientific, social, and intellectual elites. Furthermore, issues they were concerned with were not yet anchored in a larger, structural social conflict. The 1960s and 1970s both radicalized and popularized those issues, leading to mass mobilizations on behalf of women's rights, the environment, the maintenance of peace, and other themes related to new societal risks and cultural lifestyles. This shift revived the movement for women's liberation and gender equality, political ecology and opposition to the use of nuclear energy, as well as antimilitarism and the fight against the arms race. They did not, however, fully replace traditional feminism, nature protection and conservation, and peace reformism.

If taken in a synchronic rather than diachronic perspective, Raschke's distinction of three political paradigms lends itself nicely to a simple classification of European social movements according to the claims they articulated. To do so, however, we must add a further distinction, namely that between movements challenging the established authorities and counter-movements, which defend established rights and privileges against those challenges (Kriesi, 1988). This yields six distinct categories of movements (see table 1). Movements asking for more regional autonomy or for the right to a separate state are the most typical expression of the authority paradigm in Western Europe. Racist movements and various forms of resistance to political autonomy can be seen as their corresponding counter-movements, as they defend traditional privileges by denying fundamental political rights to others. Labor movements are at the core of

the distribution paradigm. Indeed, the greatest impact of the transformation from the old to the new repertoire of contention described by Tilly lies in the creation of the conditions for the political mobilization of workers. Antitax and farmers' movements that defend traditional material privileges are examples of counter-movements acting within this paradigm. Finally, the claims articulated by the new social movements concern the lifestyle paradigm. Within this paradigm, they are distinguished, for example, from antiabortion movements, insofar as the latter defend traditional lifestyles.

CYCLES OF CONTENTION

Political conflicts are ultimately rooted in structural and cultural cleavages. These dividing lines, however, create only the potential for social protest and contentious collective action. They remain latent as long

TABLE 2
THE DEVELOPMENT OF WORLD-HISTORICAL SOCIAL MOVEMENTS

	1776–1789	*1848*	*1905*	*1917*	*1968*
Ascendant revolutionary class(es)	Bourgeoisie	Urban proletariat	Rural proletariat	Urban and rural working class	New working class
Emergent organization	Representative assemblies	Insurrectionary parliaments and political parties	Soviets/Councils	Vanguard party	Action committees/ Collectivities
Vision/ Aspirations	Formal democracy; liberty equality fraternity	Economic democracy; trade unions; democratic constitutions	Universal suffrage; unions; freedom from empires	Socialism as the "dictatorship of the proletariat;" land, bread, and peace	Self-management; all power to the people/ imagination
Tactics	Revolutionary war	Popular insurrections	General strike	Organized seizure of power	Contestation of public space/ everyday life

Source: Katsiaficas (1987).

1848: THE FIRST MODERN CYCLE OF CONTENTION

The first modern cycle of contention peaked in 1848, as insurrections spread across Europe in the spring, facilitated by crop failures of 1846–1847, widespread political repression, and the emergence of nationalism. These insurrections combined a variety of claims and aspirations: from the civil war between Catholic and Protestant cantons in Switzerland to the renewed fight against monarchy and for liberal rights in France; from demands for constitutional reforms in Vienna to Sicily's quest for independence from Naples; from the political and social claims of an emerging working class in Britain to the struggle to end Austrian rule in Serbia, Croatia, Hungary, and northern Italy. By the middle of 1848, all major European regimes were threatened or had been overturned under the push of crowds organizing, marching, and erecting barricades in the streets.

The seeds of this phase of generalized social unrest lie in the French Revolution of 1789 and the July revolution of 1830. Strictly speaking, however, this cycle of contention covers the period from March 1847, when the first open conflicts occurred, to August 1848. The peak was reached in February to April 1848 (see Godechot, 1971).

The 1848 revolutionary upsurges represent the crossroads of the two driving forces of the nineteenth century and of modern European history: liberalism and socialism. It was above all a liberal and bourgeois revolution, focusing on political rights, but in which an emerging and increasingly self-conscious working class was gaining its place in history and addressing social issues. These two fronts were fighting to defend different interests and against different enemies, but their destinies were intimately interrelated within the logic of industrial and capitalist society. In addition, nationalistic aims and aspirations, embodied by demands for autonomy, independence, and adhesion to other states, intersected with the class struggle.

The cycle had its highest point in France with the February revolution, but it started at Europe's periphery, most notably in the Swiss civil war (Tarrow, 1998). Echoes from the Parisian July Revolution of 1830 gave rise to a struggle for power in Switzerland, which resulted in a series of political and military conflicts in the cantons. The liberal Protestant cantons wanted to strengthen the central power and impose their will on the mainly Catholic rural cantons, which in response formed the *Sonderbund* (separate alliance), a mutual defense league, in 1845. Civil war was declared in August 1847, after the federal Diet had ordered the dissolution of the Catholic-conservative alliance in July of the same year, which refused to comply and was defeated by before the end of the year. In 1848 the now strengthened Swiss Confederation adopted a new federal constitution, which included the democratic principles declared by French revolutionaries some fifty years earlier.

There had been various revolutionary attempts in the Italian states during the 1830s and 1840s, most of

as they are not politicized—that is, until people develop a collective identity, a sense of solidarity, and a political consciousness, all aspects constitutive of a social movement. When and where these processes have occurred, Europeans engaged in challenges to the constituted authorities in the name of their collective interests or identities. While these challenges often emerged and evolved on their own, sometimes they clustered in broader waves of generalized social unrest which we may call cycles of contention. A cycle of contention is

> a phase of heightened conflict across the social system: with rapid diffusion of collective action from more mobilized to less mobilized sectors; a rapid pace of innovation in the forms of contention; the creation of new or transformed collective action frames; a combination of organized and unorganized participation; and sequences of intensified information flow and interaction between challengers and authorities. (Tarrow, 1998, p. 142)

Social movements form broader cycles of contention as changes in their external political environment present themselves, affecting the mobilization of several challenging groups, and as different movements influence each other, some providing incentives and opening the way to others.

George Katsiaficas (1987) has identified four periods of crisis and turmoil on a global scale—what

them led by secret societies such as the *Carbonari,* the *Filadelfi,* or Giuseppe Mazzini's Young Italy (see Tilly et al. 1975). Revolts broke out across Italy in 1848 and included attempts by peasants and workers to make their claims heard (especially in the south and in Sicily), as well as temporarily successful bourgeois revolutions in Sicily, Naples, Lombardy, Venice, Tuscany, and the Papal States. In the north, just as in the rest of the Habsburg empire, people fought the Austrians, helped there by King Charles Albert of Piedmont-Sardinia. Although the constitutional and republican experiments were cut short after 1848, this period of unrest paved the way for the Italian Risorgimento, which eventually led to the unification of Italy in 1861, after the previous year's spectacular conquest of the Kingdom of Two Sicilies by Giuseppe Garibaldi.

In Germany, liberal revolutions led to the convening of the Frankfurt Parliament (1848–1849), a national assembly whose members were popularly elected and whose aim was the unification of Germany. In the short term, however, the most straightforward effects of the 1848 unrest occurred in France, most notably in Paris, where the "February revolution" of 1848 led to the abdication of Louis Philippe, the overthrow of the monarchy, and the establishment the Second Republic. General dissatisfaction with the reactionary policies of the king and his minister François Guizot had been growing in the pre-

ceding years. Furthermore, the poor conditions of workers worsened in the crisis of 1846–1847, which induced socialist Louis Blanc to propose the *ateliers nationaux* (national workshops), factories managed by the state to provide the unemployed with jobs, to counteract these worsening conditions.

The conflict began within institutional circles and then spread outward (Tarrow, 1998). When the regime rejected the parliamentary opposition's demand for suffrage reform, moderates and republicans allied to launch the campaign of "banquets" to promote reform, and took the issue to the streets, not only in Paris but also in the province. The protest turned to overt rebellion as the initiative passed into the hands of the National Guard and the urban poor, and repression provoked an escalation of violence, especially when protests by workers and radical socialists, known as the June Days, were crushed by the government. The new republic inaugurated in February 1848 lasted for less than five years, as conflicting class interests facilitated the coup d'état by Louis-Napoléon in December 1852 and the establishment of the Second Empire under his lead one year later. In France as elsewhere in Europe, moderates pulled back, eventually allowing military force and conservative reaction to gain the upper hand over popular contention, putting an end to the first major European cycle of contention.

he calls "world-historical social movements"—that have occurred since the historical phase that embraced the American and French revolutions: 1848–1849, 1905–1907, 1917–1919, and 1967–1970. Each had its ascending social class, emergent organizations, dominant social vision, and privileged tactics (see table 2 on page 317). At least two of them qualify as major European cycles of contention. The uprisings that broke out all over Europe in the winter and spring of 1848 represent the first modern cycle of protest. This revolutionary period combined issues pertaining to political rights and claims about social rights with large doses of nationalism. In a way, 1848 was at the same time a bourgeois liberal revolution against the

last gasps of an abdicating monarchy and a proletarian revolution of a nascent labor movement struggling for a place on the stage of history. By the time of the Paris Commune in 1871, the latter had fully gained that place. Another major cycle of contention, with fewer consequences, had its peak in 1968. Student and labor movements were at the core of this phase of unrest. Yet, if traditional cleavages and claims typically underpinned the 1848 cycle, the events of 1967–1970 represent the rise of the New Left and of movements based on new—"postmaterialist"—cleavages; in brief, the shift from old to new politics.

Of course, other moments of generalized social unrest have occurred in Europe, like the post–World

1968: STUDENT PROTEST AND THE NEW LEFT

France in May 1968 symbolizes and represents the peak of a cycle of contention that saw students and workers at center stage, but involved other social groups, issues, and claims as well, such as peace, nuclear arms, women's liberation, and other calls for social and cultural emancipation. In brief, a whole political sector known as the New Left contributed to produce a major phase of turmoil. Students across Europe organized assemblies, held sit-ins, and went into the streets to show their dissatisfaction with the higher education system as well as with political institutions and the functioning of society at large. The mobilization of the student movement was particularly significant in Germany, Italy, and France.

Although the most dramatic memories of 1968 come from Paris, the European wave of student unrest began in Germany. In the early 1960s, the German student movement paved the way to the outbreak of protest by providing their counterparts in other countries with ideological tools and a model for a new type of action based on the separation from institutionalized politics and greater autonomy. West Berlin can be considered the birthplace of European student protest, both chronologically and ideologically (Statera, 1975). There, the protest transcended issues pertaining to the university system, first denouncing the Vietnam War and then imperialism, the repressive nature of capitalism, the authoritarian character of society, the lack of real democracy, and so

forth. Students were massively repressed by the German authorities after December 1966, thus facilitating the rise of a strong extraparliamentary opposition starting from mid 1967. The New Left staged a variety of activities during 1967 and 1968, including a series of attacks against a hostile national newspaper monopoly (Katsiaficas, 1987). The unrest became particularly strong when the parliament passed emergency laws aimed at social control on 20 May 1968. A series of actions, blockades, and mass demonstrations were held that month throughout the country, and included a call for a general strike that was endorsed in several cities.

While the major mobilizations in Germany occurred in 1967, in Italy student masses actively participated only in 1968. Yet in both countries the protest radicalized and spread across the nation during 1967 to peak in spring 1968. The Italian student movement began above all at the Universities of Trent and Turin, where in November 1967 students occupied the headquarters of the arts faculties nearly uninterruptedly for about seven months. The unrest took a broader dimension in spring 1968, involving thousands of people all over the country and leading in March to serious clashes with the police at Valle Giulia in Rome. By the end of the year, the student movement had developed ties with workers, who joined the protest with their own grievances and claims. The mobilization of the labor movement peaked in the so-called "Hot Au-

War I period, with the strike wave and the Popular Front in France, the rise of nazism in Germany, and that of fascism above all in Italy and Spain. Another cycle of contention, this time with tremendous social and political impact, occurred at the end of the 1980s in eastern and central Europe. Spurred by the move toward liberalization made by the Soviet party secretary Mikhail Gorbachev through *glasnost* (openness) and *perestroika* (restructuring), the powerful mix of claims for civil rights and democracy and together with nationalistic aspirations produced one of the more dramatic geopolitical changes of the twentieth century. The democratic "revolutions" that in 1989–1991 led to the fall of the Berlin wall, the collapse of the Soviet Union, and eventually to the birth of a

number of new states also show how processes of diffusion may help social protest spread from one place to another, from one country to another. This, together with diffusion from one sector of society to other sectors, contributes to the creation of a cycle of contention.

Cycles of contention have various outcomes. The radicalization of social protest, which can lead to the overt use of violence, is one; its institutionalization is another. Often radicalization and institutionalization both occur at the same time at the end of a cycle of contention as a result of the selective repression exerted by the political authorities, which exploit and exacerbate the split between radicals and moderates within the movements, and of the dynamics of com-

tumn" of 1969 as major strikes threatened to block the Italian economy and as contention was transforming into class struggle. Students, the New Left, and organized workers all contributed to a major cycle of contention, which declined as various groups of the New Left became increasingly active outside the factories, some turning to terrorist activities.

Student unrest in France was the most intense but at the same time the most short-lived within this cycle of contention. The protest both started and ended more abruptly than in Germany and Italy. Although signs of agitation and dissatisfaction with the educational system had already been present before, the effective rise of collective action began in the fall of 1967 and continued sporadically through the winter and early spring of the following year. It then took an upward turn in March and April 1968, not only in France but in various European countries. In France, the turning point occurred on 22 March, following the occupation of the administration building of the University of Nanterre, which became the center of the protest under the leadership of student activist Daniel Cohn-Bendit. The protest turned into revolt and a near insurrection starting from the night between 10 and 11 May 1968, when barricades and clashes with the police in Paris as well as in other cities nearly led to the collapse of the French government, as President Charles de Gaulle, rumored to be considering

resignation dissolved the parliament. As in Italy, the labor movement joined the protest and engaged in a series of large-scale strikes. The cycle was turning into a near revolution, but de Gaulle's party won the elections in June. After its abrupt rise in May and June 1968, the student movement rapidly demobilized and the working class returned to work with the signature of the Grenelle agreements on 27 May 1968, which closed the crisis as far as industrial relations were concerned. Factory militancy continued, but the May events largely exhausted the mobilization capacity of the other major sectors of the French society.

The student and New Left cycle of contention of 1968 also touched Eastern Europe. The student movement was particularly active in Poland, where it showed characteristics similar to those of its West European counterparts, although its mobilization there did not deal with issues pertaining to the academic structure (Statera, 1975). Protests rapidly spread from Warsaw to the rest of the country in March 1968. The most dramatic images in that part of the Continent, however, come from Czechoslovakia, where the most important popular movement for reform in the East since the one that occurred in Hungary in 1956 was brutally repressed by Soviet arm in August 1968. The Prague Spring thus finished before it could keep its promises, and it was twenty years before revolutionary change came to Eastern Europe.

petition among the groups involved in the protest (della Porta 1995; Tarrow 1989). Yet collective violence is also an outcome of collective action in general, which usually comes in periods of national struggles of power (Tilly et al., 1975).

Terrorism, a special case of violence used for political purposes, is carried out by small, organized, underground organizations. It is not a social movement, but often arises as a result of cycles of contention that involve social movements. In twentieth-century Europe there were three main sources of this highly delegitimized type of political violence: left-wing organizations, right-wing or extreme right organizations, and ethnic-nationalist organizations. Germany and Italy witnessed impressive levels of political

violence in the wake of student and labor unrest that occurred across Europe in the late 1960s and early 1970s (della Porta, 1995). Clandestine armed organizations such as the Red Army Fraction in Germany and the Red Brigades in Italy—to mention only the most famous left-wing terrorist groups—made themselves known during the 1970s. Italy, in particular, suffered from the actions of both left- and right-wing underground organizations. There, the escalation of left-wing violence seems indeed to have been a product of the 1968 cycle of contention. However, this effect is likely to have been exacerbated by a strong left-right polarization and the reminiscences of the harsh confrontations between these two political fronts under the fascist regime in the 1920s and 1930s.

1989: THE DEMOCRATIC MOVEMENTS IN EASTERN EUROPE

When Mikhail Gorbachev became the general secretary of the Communist Party of the Soviet Union in March 1985, no one could imagine that a few years later the Berlin wall and "real socialism" would be only history. Gorbachev's *glasnost* and *perestroika* were a series of reforms and a policy of liberalization that provided new opportunities for people to organize and mobilize. These policies triggered a wave of democratization movements that formed a major cycle of contention, with truly revolutionary outcomes, in east and central Europe in the late 1980s and early 1990s. The symbolic peak of the cycle occurred on 9 November 1989, when East Germany's government announced the opening of the Berlin wall. Although at times and in some places, as for example in Romania, the protest took violent forms, most of this cycle of contention involved peaceful demonstrations, strikes, and protest marches, which has led some to speak of a "soft revolution" or, specifically referring to the case of Czechoslovakia, of the Velvet Revolution.

This cycle of contention was carried in the first place by claims for civil rights and democracy from below. In addition, as in 1848, liberal revolutions intersected with nationalist strife, and the weakening of the Soviet control stimulated nationalist feelings and aspirations that led to civil war, first in parts of the Soviet Union and later in the Balkans. Gorbachev's cycle of reform, especially the proposal to introduce real elections and the removal of the threat of Red Army intervention, spurred protests for more autonomy in several republics of the Soviet Union. The first open signs of revolt appeared in Estonia and Armenia in February 1988 and proliferated in the course of 1989, when in the three Baltic republics (Latvia, Lithuania, and Estonia) people went to the streets to call for independence from Moscow. Social protest remained sustained in the former Soviet Union through 1990 and 1991, and continued even into 1992 (Beissinger, 1998). Indeed, although at the same time, participation diminished, violence increased dramatically in 1992, also as a result of the military intervention of the government in Moscow. The three Baltic republics proclaimed their independence in 1990. Georgia followed in 1991. The Soviet Union collapsed in the wake of the attempted coup d'état by party hardliners in August of that year.

Also in the spring of 1989, conflict emerged in Yugoslavia between the ruling Serbs and the country's other ethnic groups, who demanded more autonomy from Belgrade. This conflict led to the civil wars that shook the Balkan area in the 1990s. First Slovenia, then Croatia and Bosnia fought for and eventually obtained their independence.

Social protest played an especially significant role in East Germany and Czechoslovakia. Concerning the former country, the decision by the Hungarian authorities to open the east-west border and hence to create a breach in the Iron Curtain in the summer of 1989, with the resulting exodus of people from East Germany, precipitated the crisis and further encouraged people to demonstrate first for political reform and then for German reunification (see Oberschall, 1996). The key events occurred in Leipzig, the second-largest city, in fall 1989. In spite of initial repression, increasingly larger crowds staged a series of demonstrations and marches, sometimes with many thousands of people, which peaked in

Other countries were touched less by left- and right-wing terrorism but dealt with violent actions taken by the armed branches of nationalist movements. Britain, France, and Spain certainly suffered from this type of political violence. Terrorist acts respectively by the Irish Republican Army, the ETA Basque organization, and Corsican nationalist groups filled the pages of newspapers for many years. In these cases, terrorism appears less as an outcome of a given cycle of contention than as an endemic feature of those societies, although the pace and intensity of terrorist acts may vary according to the ebb and flow of nationalist protest more generally.

Cycles of contention sometimes evolved into full-fledged revolutions, as in 1789 France, 1917 Russia, or in 1989–1991 Eastern Europe. Historians have identified the major factors that may produce a revolution: the weakness of the state (due to either in-

Democratic "Revolution" in Berlin. Rally at the Brandenberg Gate during demonstrations that led to the dismantling of the Berlin wall, 17 November 1989. ©MARC GARANGER/CORBIS

October of that year. Shortly, thereafter, a weakened government was forced to announce the opening of the Berlin Wall.

The protest spread rapidly from East Germany to Czechoslovakia and the Balkans. The Velvet Revolution that eventually led to the division of Czechoslovakia into two separate countries (the Czech Republic and Slovakia) was successful in short order. Although a peak in mobilization and clashes with the police occurred in January 1989, the democratic movement took a real popular dimension only in the fall of 1989. The strongest mobilization had its center in Prague and lasted only six weeks, including a general strike on 17 November, which proved

to be a crucial event in the challenge to the Communist regime (see Oberschall, 1996). The dissident alliance Civil Forum was founded in Prague on 20 November. By the end of 1989, Václav Havel, the leader of the democratic opposition to the regime, was the new president of Czechoslovakia.

At more or less the same time, in Romania the Communist regime shot at people demonstrating in Timişoara. Previously this would probably have meant the retreat of demonstrators and the "reestablishment of order," but in the changed international context of the late 1980s the inevitable result of this harsh repression was an escalation of violence that led to the arrest and the execution, in December 1989, of president Nicolae Ceauşescu and his wife. These events strongly contrast with the changes that occurred in Hungary and in Poland. In Hungary, social protest in 1988 and 1989 found a divided Communist party, and opposition was facilitated by the erosion of its authority from within. In Poland, negotiations between the government and the free union *Solidarność* (Solidarity) began at the end of 1988, eight years after the latter was outlawed in 1981. The first noncommunist government was freely elected in a Communist country on the following year.

The democratic movements of the late 1990s produced profound changes in Europe's social and political landscape: more than seventy years of applied communism came to an abrupt end as the Soviet Union collapsed and the Warsaw Pact broke up; new states were created, in some cases after bloody civil wars, and Europe's geopolitical configuration was revolutionized with the end of the bipolar system.

ternal or external pressures, or both), the creation of a situation of multiple sovereignty, and the responses by the state to the claims for the control of power made by an increasingly strong and radical collaborative effort to overthrow the state (Tilly, 1993). In brief, revolutionary situations (i.e., open divisions of sovereignty) occurred when a deeply fragmented state was unable to fulfill its basic functions and when there were at least two contenders struggling for power.

These situations produced revolutionary outcomes (i.e. a forcible transfer of power from one contending party to the other) when a weakened state responded to challengers with inconsistent repression. Furthermore, state repression was all the more likely to lead to a revolutionary outcome to the extent that it—and those who perpetrated it—was perceived and evaluated as illegitimate by a large number of people in society.

POLITICAL OPPORTUNITIES AND CROSS-NATIONAL VARIATIONS

State fragmentation and repression thus appear as major determinants of the shift from social movements to cycles of contention and revolutions. This suggests that contentious collective action is not simply the product of grievances or perceived threats. Indeed, among the major contributions of research since 1970 is the idea that, contrary to what breakdown and collective behavior theories postulated, social change impinges only indirectly upon social protest through a restructuring of existing power relations, not directly by creating social stress and deprivation to which protest would be a collective response. Students of social movements have elaborated the concept of political opportunity structures to account for the emergence of contentious collective action and to explain its ebbs and flows. Political opportunity structures capture those aspects of the political context of movements that mediate the impact of large-scale social changes on social protest and either encourage or discourage mobilization.

Doug McAdam (1996) has made an attempt to summarize the numerous dimensions of political opportunity structures found in the extant literature. He came up with the following four kinds of "signals to social or political actors:" (1) the relative openness or closure of the institutionalized political system; (2) the stability or instability of that broad set of elite alignments that typically undergird a polity; (3) the presence or absence of elite allies; and (4) the state's capacity and propensity for repression. Some of these aspects of the external environment of social movements are rather stable (e.g. the institutional structure of the state); others are more volatile and subject to shifts over time (e.g., political alignments). All of them affect people's expectations for success or failure of collective action and either increase or decrease the social and political costs of mobilization.

Political opportunities, however, do not single-handedly produce social movements. Other factors concur to give rise to this form of contentious collective action once processes of large-scale social change have created the structural and cultural cleavages that provide the conditions for their political mobilization. European social movements have emerged due to the interplay of the mobilizing structures by which groups seek to organize, the cultural framing processes by which people define and interpret situations and events, and the political opportunities that provide them with the incentives to act collectively. Tarrow (1998) has aptly summarized the process of movement emergence as follows:

contentious politics is produced when political opportunities broaden, when they demonstrate the potential for alliances, and when they reveal the opponents' vulnerability. Contention crystallizes into a social movement when it taps embedded social networks and connective structures and produces collective action frames and supportive identities able to sustain contention with powerful opponents. By mounting familiar forms of contention, movements become the focal points that transform external opportunities into resources. Repertoires of contention, social networks, and cultural frames lower the costs of bringing people into collective action, induce confidence that they are not alone, and give broader meaning to their claims. Together, these factors trigger the dynamic processes that have made social movements historically central to political and social change (p. 23).

There are few studies that compare the mobilization of European social movements across countries by means of systematic empirical evidence. One of the reasons is that this is a costly and time-consuming endeavor. This state of affairs, however, is changing. Hanspeter Kriesi and his collaborators (1995), for example, have provided a comparative analysis of social movements for a short but significant historical phase. We can use their work to show the extent to which the mobilization of contemporary social movements resembles or varies across nations as a function of different sets of political opportunities. Table 3 shows the distribution of protest actions in four European countries from 1975 to 1989. Even without going into too much detail, we can stress a certain number of interesting patterns. First of all, movements that rest upon traditional cleavages are much stronger in France than in Germany, Switzerland, or the Netherlands, both in percentages and in the numbers of people mobilized. In the latter three countries, traditional cleavages had to a large extent been pacified, whereas in France they kept much of their political salience. As a result, the types of movements and issues based on the four cleavages stressed by Rokkan (regionalist movements, education, peasants', and labor movements) play a greater role in the French context. This, according to the authors, leaves less space for the mobilization of the new social movements; their findings largely confirm this hypothesis. Furthermore, if we look at the number of participants involved in strike activity—the typical means of action used by the labor movement—we realize how strong the class cleavage in France was, compared to the other three countries. In general, a cross-national comparison of both the relative and absolute strength of European social movements shows that, at least for the four countries included in the study by Kriesi et al., their mobilization varies strongly across nations as well as across movements. Such variations depend

TABLE 3
DISTRIBUTION OF PROTEST ACTIONS IN FOUR COUNTRIES, 1975–1989

	Percentage of actions[a]				Number of participants[b]			
	France	Germany	Neth.	Switz.	France	Germany	Neth.	Switz.
New social movements								
Peace movement	4.4	18.7	16.9	6.0	14	111	92	25
Antinuclear energy movement	12.8	12.8	5.1	7.2	9	26	15	24
Ecology movement	4.4	11.3	8.0	10.6	2	11	5	16
Solidarity movement	9.2	15.0	17.7	16.0	15	13	19	19
Squatters' movement	3.0	13.4	14.1	18.4	0	6	5	14
Gay movement	0.8	0.3	2.0	0.7	1	0	4	0
Women's movement	1.5	1.7	1.6	2.1	2	1	3	3
Total new social movements	36.1	73.2	65.4	61.0	43	168	143	101
Traditional movements								
Student movement	4.8	1.5	2.2	0.2	23	4	7	0
Civil rights movement	1.5	1.3	0.6	2.7	0	2	0	3
Foreigners	2.5	4.2	7.1	8.5	1	2	3	8
Regionalist movements	16.6	0.1	0.0	10.6	4	0	0	11
Education	4.0	1.5	1.0	0.2	62	2	2	0
Peasants	6.6	0.3	1.3	0.8	3	2	1	1
Labor movement	10.1	4.3	9.2	3.7	33	19	19	15
Other left-wing mobilizations	2.0	3.9	2.4	2.4	1	3	14	4
Right extremism	3.3	3.8	0.7	0.6	1	0	0	0
Other right-wing mobilizations	2.6	1.9	1.0	2.0	1	7	2	4
Other mobilizations[c]	9.7	4.0	9.2	7.5	9	2	6	9
Total traditional movements	63.9	26.8	34.6	39.0	135	43	55	55
Grand total	100%	100%	100%	100%	178	211	198	156
(n)	(2132)	(2343)	(1319)	(1215)	(2076)	(2229)	(1264)	(1027)
Strikes	—	—	—	—	225	37	23	2
Grand total including strikes	—	—	—	—	403	248	221	158

Source: Adapted from Kriesi et al. (1995), pp. 20, 22.
[a]   Figures for the labor movement do not include strikes.
[b]   Sum of the number of participants in all unconventional actions per million inhabitants. Missing values have been replaced by the national median of the number of participants for a given type of event. Petitions and politically motivated festivals are excluded. Figures on strikes are based on statistics by the International Labor Organization (ILO).
[c]   Also includes countermobilization to new social movements (e.g. all actions directed against them).

very much on the specific political opportunity structures available at a given historical moment, but also on the organizational strength of movements (mobilizing structures), and on the resonance of their claims in the society at large (framing processes). In addition, the level of mobilization of single movements also depends on their relationship with political institutions over time. Certain contemporary movements, such as women's movements, have followed a pattern of institutionalization that has robbed them of much of their mobilization capacity and they therefore either become latent or tend to act through more conventional means, which are not captured by the kind of data gathered by Kriesi and his collaborators.

The prevailing structure of political opportunities in a given nation does not only affect the amount of collective action and the levels of mobilization of social movements; it also encourages the use of certain forms of action while discouraging others. We have an illustration of that by looking again at the data provided by Kriesi et al. (1995). Table 4 shows the distribution of protest in the same four countries broken down by form of action, ranging from the more moderate and conventional actions (the use of direct democratic instruments, petitions, and politically motivated festivals) to demonstrative actions (street demonstrations, rallies, public meetings, etc.), confrontational actions (boycotts, occupations, blockades, etc.), and violent actions (violent demonstrations, destruction of objects, bombing, etc). The action repertoire of social movements is decidedly more radical in France and, conversely, more moderate in Switzerland. This difference, according to the authors, is largely explained by the different opportunity structures in the two countries as yielded by the combination of two of four dimensions highlighted by McAdam (1996): the degree of openness of the institutionalized political system and the state's capacity and propensity for repression. The closed and rather repressive (exclusive) French state has led social movements to make more frequent use of radical and often violent forms of action, while the open and facilitative (inclusive) Swiss state has channeled the protest into more moderate and conventional actions. In this picture, Germany and the Netherlands provide two intermediate cases, as they combine institutional openness and a propensity for repression. The action repertoire of social movements in these two countries, therefore, is more radical than in Switzerland but more moderate than in France.

Although limited to four European countries, this example shows that social movements and the power structures of the national state, which grew together in the eighteenth and nineteenth centuries, re-

main intimately linked. After World War II, as the world became increasingly interconnected and processes of economic globalization and cultural homogenization accelerated, several international and supranational institutions emerged. Like national ones, these institutions provide opportunities and incentives for contentious politics, and scholars have begun to document forms of transnational collective action and transnational social movements (see among others della Porta et al. 1999; Keck and Sikkink 1998; Smith et al. 1997). At least a part of this collective action transcends national boundaries to become transnational social movements, which have recurrently formed in Europe. The creation first of a European Economic Community, then of the European Union undoubtedly opened new opportunities for the mobilization of transnational actors and organizations. Yet, by the late twentieth century, such opportunities remained rather limited and did not stimulate the kind of popular contention that characterized the activity of earlier social movements. National states remained strong in most policy areas and still controlled their borders and exercised legal dominion within them; most mobilizing structures, collective action frames, political opportunities, and repertoires of contention were therefore available at that level. These are resources that even the controversial process of globalization was hardly able to counteract.

CONCLUDING REMARKS

European social movements must be studied as part of a broader spectrum of contentious political actions which includes other forms such as cycles of contention and revolutions. These are related phenomena that originate in similar circumstances but evolve in different patterns as a result of the interaction between social protest, state response, and the larger social and political environment. Jack Goldstone (1998) has elegantly formulated this idea as follows:

> Contentious collective action emerges through the mobilization of individuals and groups to pursue certain goals, the framing of purposes and tactics, and taking advantages of opportunities for protest arising from shifts in the grievances, power, and vulnerability of various social actors. But the *form* and *outcome* of that action is not determined by the conditions of movement emergence. These characteristics are themselves emergent, and contingent on the responses of various social actors to the initial protest actions. (p. 143; emphasis in original)

As Charles Tilly has shown in his many publications on the subject, during the past few centuries Europe has witnessed a long-term structural transfor-

TABLE 4
DISTRIBUTION OF PROTEST ACTIONS BY FORM OF ACTION IN FOUR COUNTRIES, 1975–1989

	France	Germany	Netherlands	Switzerland
Conventional[a]	2.6	4.9	4.2	21.7
Demonstrative	41.7	60.6	49.7	52.5
Confrontational	24.5	19.3	35.0	13.4
Violent	31.2	15.2	11.1	12.4
Total	100%	100%	100%	100%
(n)	(2132)	(2343)	(1319)	(1322)

Source: Adapted from Kriesi et al. (1995), p. 50.
[a]   Direct democracy, petitions, and politically motivated festivals.

mation that involved at least two interrelated processes: the rise of capitalism and the success of the national state over other forms of government and social organization. This transformation fundamentally affected the interests, identities, opportunities, and organizations of Europeans, with two major consequences. On the one hand, the ways Europeans have engaged in contentious collective action, as well as its very targets, have been modified, leading, at some point during the nineteenth century, to the emergence of modern social movements. This change took place in close conjunction with the rise of electoral campaigns and interest-group politics at the national level (Tilly, 1995). On the other hand, the large-scale transformation of European society created a number of structural and cultural cleavages, which underpinned the mobilization of these movements and affected that of later movements.

We may identify four main movement families typical of twentieth-century Europe, most prominent in western Europe, but in part also in evidence in eastern Europe: (1) labor movements, (2) left-libertarian and new social movements, (3) movements of the extreme right, and (4) regionalist and nationalist movements. The lines of conflict underpinning these areas of contention translated into actual social protest when political opportunities gave Europeans the incentives to mobilize and encouraged them to use their internal resources to form social movements. Sometimes the emerging challenges to the constituted authorities clustered into broad and widespread cycles of contention, as in 1848, 1968, or 1989. Sometimes such waves of generalized social unrest produced revolutionary outcomes. Most often, however, people's engagement to defend or promote their interests and identities remained within the boundaries set by the existing cultural and institutional parameters, the very same parameters that account for the similarities and variations in the mobilization of social movements across countries. In either case, by their actions Europeans have shown—and continue to show—that social protest is not an irrational response to situations of strain and deprivation, but is just one of the ways people have to defend or promote their interests and identities, sometimes the only way available. Indeed, as Karl Marx has forcefully shown, conflict is inscribed in the very structure of society.

See also other articles in this section.

BIBLIOGRAPHY

Books

Della Porta, Donatella. *Social Movements, Political Violence, and the State: A Comparative Analysis of Italy and Germany.* Cambridge, U.K., 1995. Comparative analysis of left-wing terrorism and political violence in Germany and Italy based on a creative usage of events, organizations, and individual biographies.

Della Porta, Donatella, and Mario Diani. *Social Movements: An Introduction.* Oxford, 1999. Everything you wanted to know about social movements. Perhaps the best introductory text currently available.

Gamson, William A. *The Strategy of Social Protest.* 2d ed. Belmont, Calif., 1990. Gamson's seminal analysis of the careers of fifty-three American challenging groups active between 1800 and 1945 remains a fundamental point of reference for the study of the effects of social movements and more.

Godechot, Jacques. *Les révolutions de 1848.* Paris, 1971. Provides a detailed chronology of the revolutionary cycle of contention of 1848 for all the major European countries.

Gurr, Ted R. *Why Men Rebel.* Princeton, N.J., 1970. The most sophisticated presentation of the theory of relative deprivation.

Ignazi, Piero. *L'estrema destra in Europa.* Bologna, Italy, 1994. Broad overview of the extreme right in several European countries. Illustrates the origins, ideology, organization, and social basis of parties at the far right of the political spectrum.

Inglehart, Ronald. *The Silent Revolution: Changing Values and Political Styles among Western Publics.* Princeton, N.J., 1977. Inglehart's influential theory of postmaterialism.

Katsiaficas, George. *The Imagination of the New Left: A Global Analysis of 1968.* Boston, 1987. Interesting account of the New Left as a world-historical movement by a sociologically minded New Left activist.

Keck, Margaret, and Kathryn Sikkink. *Activists beyond Borders: Advocacy Networks in International Politics.* Ithaca, N.Y., 1998. Analyzes the formation and role of transnational activist networks.

Kitschelt, Herbert (with Anthony J. McGann). *The Radical Right in Western Europe: A Comparative Analysis.* Ann Arbor, Mich., 1995. Lucid analysis of European extreme right parties, which stresses the impact of structural cleavages, party competition, and coalition formation.

Klandermans, Bert. *The Social Psychology of Protest.* Cambridge, Mass., 1997. Presents the basics of the social-psychological analysis of social movements.

Kriesi, Hanspeter, Ruud Koopmans, Jan Willem Duyvendak, and Marco Giugni. *New Social Movements in Western Europe: A Comparative Analysis.* Minneapolis, Minn., 1995. Uses a systematic collection of protest event data to compare the mobilization of new social movements in four West European countries following a political opportunity approach.

McAdam, Doug. *Political Process and the Development of Black Insurgency, 1930–1970.* 2d ed. Chicago, 1999. Strong statement on the political process approach to social movements, which traces the development of the American civil rights movements to political, organizational, and consciousness change.

McAdam, Doug, Sidney Tarrow, and Charles Tilly. *Dynamics of Contention.* Cambridge, U.K., forthcoming. Threatens to fundamentally shake the study of contentious politics by suggesting, among other things, to shift from the analysis of the conditions for the emergence of contentious action to a more dynamic perspective that stresses the relational mechanisms at work.

Melucci, Alberto. *Challenging Codes: Collective Action in the Information Age.* Cambridge, U.K., 1996. The most comprehensive work of an author who is often considered as the most prominent advocate of new social movement theory.

Oberschall, Anthony. *Social Conflict and Social Movements.* Englewood Cliffs, N.J., 1973. Solid analysis of the sociological conditions that give rise to social movements.

Olson, Mancur. *The Logic of Collective Action.* Cambridge, Mass., 1965. How free-riding can be overcome through selective incentives. This very influential book by the American economist has changed the approach to the study of collective action.

Piven, Frances Fox, and Richard A. Cloward. *Poor People's Movements: Why They Succeed, How They Fail.* New York, 1979. One of the most original and insightful analyses of social movements, including their possibilities for success.

Raschke, Joachim. *Soziale Bewegungen.* Frankfurt, Germany, 1985. Historically informed analysis of the changing forms of social movements.

Rémond, René. *Les droites en France.* Paris, 1982. Rémond's classical distinction between traditionalism, liberalism, and fascism.

Rokkan, Stein (with Angus Campbell, Per Torsvik, and Henry Valen). *Citizens, Elections, Parties.* Oslo, Norway, 1970. Rokkan's fundamental geopolitical mapping of Europe. Not about collective action, but has provided the basis for linking the existence of structural cleavage to the emergence of social movements.

Smelser, Neil J. *Theory of Collective Behavior.* New York, 1962. Classical work on collective behavior by a leading American sociologist.

Statera, Gianni. *Death of a Utopia: The Development and Decline of Social Movements in Europe.* New York, 1975. One of the few comparative sociological analyses of the student movements that shook European countries in 1967–1968.

Tarrow, Sidney. *Democracy and Disorder: Protest and Politics in Italy, 1965–1975.* Oxford: Clarendon Press, 1989. Application of Tarrow's political opportunity theory to the Italian protest cycle of the late 1960s and early 1970s.

Tarrow, Sidney. *Power in Movement: Social Movements and Contentious Politics.* 2d ed. Cambridge, U.K., 1998. Updated and expanded edition of a powerful synthesis of the literature on social movements and related phenomena by one of the most prominent scholars in the field.

Tilly, Charles. *From Mobilization to Revolution.* Reading, Mass., 1978. Milestone of the political process approach, which inspired an entire generation of students of social revolutions and social movements, who worked with some version of the concept of "political opportunity structure."

Tilly, Charles. *The Contentious French.* Cambridge, Mass., 1986. Detailed account of four centuries of popular contention in France. Carefully describes and lucidly explains the shift from the old to the new repertoire of contention.

Tilly, Charles. *European Revolutions, 1492–1992.* Oxford, 1993. Sweeping overview of revolutionary situations and outcomes in Europe since the Renaissance.

Tilly, Charles. *Popular Contention in Great Britain, 1758–1834.* Cambridge, Mass., 1995. Probably Tilly's most important book, which caps more than thirty years of work on collective action. A masterful analysis that illustrates how sociology meets history with the support of a massive data base.

Tilly, Charles, Louise Tilly, and Richard Tilly. *The Rebellious Century, 1830–1930.* Cambridge, Mass., 1975. Focuses on collective violence, but more generally identifies and explains changes in the forms of contentious collective action in France, Germany, and Italy over a century. This book sensitized scholars to the use of systematic catalogs of collective action episodes and events as a way to trace protest activities over time.

Touraine, Alain. *Le retour de l'acteur.* Paris, 1984. Touraine's theory of the postindustrial society and its implications for collective action.

Turner, Ralph H., and Lewis M. Killian. *Collective Behavior.* Englewood Cliffs, N.J., 1957. One of the classical works in the collective behavior perspective.

Edited Collections

McAdam, Doug, John D. McCarthy, and Mayer N. Zald, eds. *Comparative Perspectives on Social Movements: Political Opportunities, Mobilizing Structures, and Cultural Framings.* Cambridge: Cambridge University Press, 1996. Explicit attempt to link the three main sets of variables highlighted by previous research on social movements. See especially articles by Doug McAdam, Anthony Oberschall, and Sidney Tarrow.

McAdam, Doug, and David A. Snow, eds. *Social Movements: Readings on Their Emergence, Mobilization, and Dynamics.* Los Angeles, Calif., 1997. Useful reader on various aspects of social movements. Includes some of the most influential articles on the topic.

Smith, Jackie, Charles Chatfield, and Ron Pagnucco, eds. *Transnational Social Movements and Global Politics: Solidarity, beyond the State.* Syracuse, N.Y., 1997. Examines the development of a wide spectrum of nonstate actors who organize beyond the national state.

Chapter in a Book or Collection of Articles

Beissinger, Mark R. "Event Analysis in Transitional Societies: Protest Mobilization in the Former Soviet Union." In *Acts of Dissent: New Developments in the Study of Protest.* Edited by Dieter Rucht, Ruud Koopmans, and Friedhelm Neidhart. Berlin, 1998. One of the few attempts, based on an impressive wealth of data, to extend protest event analysis outside Western Europe and North America.

Goldstone, Jack A. "Social Movements or Revolutions? On the Evolution and Outcomes of Collective Action." In *From Contention to Democracy.* Edited by Marco Giugni, Doug McAdam, and Charles Tilly. Lanham, Md. 1998. Insightful essay about the relationship between various forms of contentious collective action.

Kriesi, Hanspeter. "The Interdependence of Structure and Action: Some Reflections of the State of the Art." In *From Structure to Action: Comparing Social Movement Research Across Cultures.* Edited by Bert Klandermans, Hanspeter Kriesi, and Sidney Tarrow. Greenwich, Conn., 1988. Introduction to a volume that represents one of the first attempts to integrate European and American approaches to the study of social movements.

Kriesi, Hanspeter. "Movements of the Left, Movements of the Right: Putting the Mobilization of Two New Types of Social Movements into Political Context." In *Continuity and Change in Contemporary Capitalism.* Edited by Herbert Kitschelt, Peter Lange, and Gary Marks. Cambridge, U.K., 1999. The social-structural origins of new social movements and the new radical right.

McAdam, Doug. "Conceptual Origins, Current Problems, Future Directions." In *Comparative Perspectives on Social Movements*. Edited by Doug McAdam, John D. McCarthy, and Mayer N. Zald. Cambridge: Cambridge University Press, 1996. Helpful synthesis of works that have used the concept of political opportunity structures.

McAdam, Doug, John D. McCarthy, and Mayer N. Zald. "Social Movements." In *Handbook of Sociology*. Edited by Neil J. Smelser. Beverly Hills, Calif., 1988. Good introduction to social movements by three prominent scholars.

Oberschall, Anthony. "Opportunities and Framing in the Eastern European Revolts of 1989." In *Comparative Perspectives on Social Movements*. Edited by Doug McAdam, John D. McCarthy, and Mayer N. Zald. Cambridge: Cambridge University Press, 1996. Framing, mobilization, and opportunities in the 1989 democratic movements in Poland, Hungary, East Germany, and Czechoslovakia.

Journal Articles

Kriesi, Hanspeter. "New Social Movements and the New Class in the Netherlands." *American Journal of Sociology* 94 (1989): 1078–1116. Original explanation of the rise of new social movements in terms of class analysis.

McAdam, Doug, Sidney Tarrow, and Charles Tilly. "To Map Contentious Politics." *Mobilization* 1 (1996): 17–34. Redefines the spectrum of events that includes revolutions, social movements, and other forms of social protest and collective action under the single rubric of contentious politics.

Tilly, Charles. "Social Movements as Historically Specific Clusters of Political Performances." *Berkeley Journal of Sociology* 38 (1994): 1–30. Defines social movements as relational and historical phenomena.

Donatella della Porta, Mario Diani, Hanspeter Kriesi, Doug McAdam, Sidney Tarrow, and Charles Tilly gave me valuable insights on previous drafts of this article.

Section 12

DEVIANCE, CRIME,
AND SOCIAL CONTROL

CRIME

Pieter Spierenburg

In the past, no less than today, crime has been seen as a problem and contemporaries have expressed concern about it. Notions of what is criminal and what is not, however, vary over time. These variations are related to changes in both social structure and the material environment. Obviously, an offense like reckless driving can only exist in a world with cars. Similarly, sorcery can only be a crime in a society in which belief in magic is widespread. And the variability of the content of crime extends further. The definition of morals offenses changed as ideas about sexuality and gender and notions of privacy changed. Homosexual activities involving adult men, for example, ceased to be illegal in most European countries since the nineteenth century. Although stealing another's property and assaulting a person are unlawful in almost any society, the meaning and context of these actions greatly differ with time and place. In less developed, feudal regions, for example, cattle rustling was not primarily a means to enrich oneself but a challenge to the power of a rural patron and a test of his capacity for protecting his people and goods. Crime, then, is not a single, straightforward social category but rather a multifaceted phenomenon. Consequently, the historical study of criminality is not just about what some people actually do but also about perceptions, attitudes, and cultural stereotypes.

DEFINITIONS AND SOURCES

Most historians adopt a practical definition of crime, which reflects its diversity. With minor variations in terminology, they define crime as illegal behavior which, if detected and prosecuted, can be punished in a court of law or by some other official agency of law enforcement. Thus crime is simply anything forbidden by the secular authorities. When they determine that blasphemy can be prosecuted and punished in court, it is a crime; should they decide that burglary is no longer punishable, it would not be a crime. Any other definition would be based on the investigator's own sense of right and wrong, bringing the danger of anachronism. Of course, contemporaries never unequivocally agreed with the authorities' demarcation of the range of punishable offenses. Investigating the extent to which various social groups had different views of what is wrong and what is not is an important subject within the historiography of crime. Finally, our definition is not restricted to behavior actually prosecuted: it includes those acts which remain undetected, the so-called dark number.

This practical or institutional definition means that illegality is the sole characteristic all crimes have in common. Criminality is a "container concept." Hence few studies deal with total crime, and if they do, they break it down into categories again. This applies to qualitative as well as quantitative studies. It is not very meaningful to add up figures for theft, fornication, and insulting policemen and present them as a total crime rate. This would be like adding, without specification, corn prices and tax returns and calling them an "economic figure." The diversity of criminal activities also has a distinct advantage: there is a very broad range of historical studies which all, in one way or another, belong to the historiography of crime. Because of the broad range of criminal activities, it is impossible to present a neat chronological account, with crime being like this in the sixteenth century in Scandinavia, Germany, or England, like that in the seventeenth, and so on to the twentieth. The treatment must necessarily be thematic, pointing at change along the way.

By definition, crime is intimately related to the state. Through criminal legislation and court action, the state demarcates the borders of lawful and unlawful behavior. Historically, this implies a parallel relationship between processes of state formation and criminalization. It is only when stronger states emerged that the perception of wrongful acts changed. A number of harmful activities were gradually redefined as being not merely conflicts between private individuals but directed against the state as well. Henceforth they were a breach of the peace, offending the sovereign.

While "classical offenses" like theft and assault were thus redefined, a number of newly created offenses—smuggling, begging, prostitution—were included in this category. Consequently, the activities in question came to be listed under the same heading as crimes. This process extended over a long period, but for most of Europe the sixteenth century was the crucial period of transition. We can term this the beginning of criminalization: the creation of the category of crime itself. From the beginning of the period with which this encyclopedia deals, then, crime was a reality, albeit a reality defined from above.

Crime is what you find when you study court records. In the tradition of legal history, criminal records are studied, if at all, as a supplement to legislative sources. To the legal historian, laws and statutes are of primary interest, and the courts' activities are merely the application of the rules. Social historians, by contrast, are interested in court records because crime is a mirror of society. It reflects, among other things, relations between social classes, submerged tensions, the position of immigrants versus natives, gender relations, and structural change over the long term. More particularly, court records are one of the few sources dealing almost exclusively with common people. They reveal things about the way of life of ordinary men and women, not just of the lawbreakers among them but also their families and neighbors. From the beginning, therefore, the study of historical crime received an impetus from the fashion of writing "history from below." Whereas the first generation of crime historians (from the mid-1960s to the early 1980s) was especially concerned with either the quantitative analysis of property crime or particular offenses which revealed social tensions, the second generation (from the late 1980s) preferred violence over property crime, focusing on issues of ritual, honor and shame, and gender.

The extent to which such issues can be studied in depth depends on the quality of the sources. Much of the earlier work on England, for example, has been done with so-called indictments: brief statements in which the defendant's offense is defined in legal terms and not much more. The prevalence of these documents follows from a peculiarity of the English criminal trial, which remained largely accusatory (allowing only private prosecution by a wronged party) until the early nineteenth century and was based on a jury system. Whereas continental procedure was largely based on written records, the oral element remained more important in England. The main part of the English trial was public and oral before the jury. Examination documents merely served to bolster the prosecution's case at this oral trial and were considered of little worth afterward. Few of these documents have survived. However, later British historians discovered that extensive trial papers have been preserved of some of the lower courts, dealing with neighborly conflicts in urban neighborhoods and rural communities. On the Continent, interrogation protocols have been preserved for many of the higher courts as well, due to the greater importance attached to the written dossier in countries such as France, Germany, and the Netherlands. Incidentally, a Dutch sentence of the early modern period is the opposite of an English indictment: it says what the defendant actually did, often without legally defining the offense.

The records of criminal trials are not the only sources for the historical study of crime. Prison records exist in several countries from the seventeenth century onward, but these are primarily valuable for the history of punishment. When we deal with perceptions of criminality, the contemporary crime literature is an important source, available from the late seventeenth century. From the nineteenth century onward, newspaper accounts inform us about individual cases, but they can also be used to provide supplementary data for quantitative studies. In the twentieth century, finally, police records constitute a source of major importance.

Although no standard categorization of crimes, approved by all scholars, exists, it is common to distinguish four general categories: (1) violence, or crimes against the person; (2) crimes against property, from theft and fraud to robbery; (3) morals offenses, punished either by secular or church courts; and (4) a residual category of offenses against authority, the state, or public order. Historians whose research goes back further in time often add a separate class of religious offenses, such as heresy and blasphemy. With the exception of the third category, especially when prosecution for prostitution was intense, men constituted the majority of offenders. It should be stressed, however, that male preponderance in criminality is much greater in the twentieth century than it was before. In early modern Europe, women often made up 30 to 40 percent of offenders; their share in theft could be considerable. From the late seventeenth century onward, the proportion of women tried in court gradually declined.

PROPERTY CRIME AND THE PROBLEM OF QUANTIFICATION

Quantitative studies of crime mainly deal with violence, in particular homicide, and various types of property offenses. Major issues include the proportional share of categories of offenses, temporary peaks and lows in criminality, trends in property and violent crime, and urbanization and crime. The first of these issues led to the oldest thesis in the historiography of crime. It was developed in the 1960s and early 1970s by French historians, who spoke of a shift *de la violence au vol,* from violence to theft. They argued that the feudal code of honor led to a preponderance of violent offenses, while the central place of the market in bourgeois society produced a larger share of property offenses. Society still was rough and rife with emotions in the sixteenth and seventeenth centuries, but in the eighteenth a more pacified and commercialized society emerged. In this view, the modernization of crime took place during the eighteenth century, as a concomitant of the transition from a feudal to a bourgeois society.

Since the late 1970s, the thesis of a shift from violent to property offenses has been under attack. Although the data from France appear to be congruous with it, a later generation of French historians doubted whether these data reflected a shift in real crime. For one thing, the violence-to-theft thesis refers to the ratios of criminal categories rather than the absolute rates; it is about the share of the two categories of offenses in the total criminal caseload of particular courts. This share is mainly the outcome of decisions at the judicial level; it has to do with the priorities of courts. The courts of prerevolutionary Paris, for example, eagerly prosecuted theft of even the smallest item of food, while they cared less for fights among men and women of the lower classes. It is more likely, therefore, that late-eighteenth-century France witnessed an increase in concern for the protection of property than a peak in real property crime.

Finally, the violence-to-theft pattern has not been found in other countries of early modern Europe. In England property offenses accounted for a large share of the courts' business already in the 1590s, in some cases amounting to three-quarters of all indictments. The proportion of property offenses declined as the seventeenth century progressed, and it remained low during most of the eighteenth. Only in the last decades of the eighteenth century did the prosecution of property offenses again reach the level of the late sixteenth. In Amsterdam the proportion of property offenses rose steadily from about 30 percent in 1650 to about 45 percent in 1750. However, since total prosecuted criminality dropped sharply in this period, the rate of property offenses actually declined. It rose again, also elsewhere in the Netherlands, at the very end of the eighteenth century. With converging data from France, England, and the Netherlands, this last trend appears international: ratios and rates of prop-

erty offenses peaked toward the end of the early modern period.

Determining crime rates. The French studies upon which the violence-to-theft thesis was based remained confined to the the ancien régime. However, for the quantitative study of crime in Europe, the main historical dividing line is between the prestatistical and the statistical periods. During the first half of the nineteenth century, most European countries began to compile criminal statistics. Only from then on is it possible to investigate crime rates on a national scale. Before that period, research is largely restricted to individual courts. The geographic scale constitutes the main difference, rather than the origin of the figures. Well into the twentieth century, national statistics were generally based on figures for prosecuted crimes. This was the case, for example, with the Prussian criminal statistics from 1836 to 1850. From 1857 English criminal statistics included information on main indictable offenses and figures for summary trials before a magistrate; the larger category of crimes known to the police was not reported nationally. The Swedish police did not keep statistics until 1949. Yet most historians accept the opinion of criminologists that every stage of the criminal justice process represents a distortion of the figures and that hence the figures at the first stage, crimes known to the police, are best.

With regard to the quantitative study of crime in both the early modern period and the nineteenth century, then, one methodological problem looms large. How do we know if the level of prosecuted crime reflects the level of real crime? Apart from having police reports available, modern criminologists supplement their statistics with data from victims' surveys. Historians, on the other hand, only have figures based on prosecuted cases. The problem is not the existence of a dark number as such, but the question of whether it remains constant. If the ratio of prosecuted to undetected thefts is always 4 to 2, for example, any increase or decrease in prosecuted theft represents a proportionate increase or decrease in real theft. However, such a situation is unlikely to prevail. If the number of prosecuted thefts rose in a year of hardship, for example, was this because people stole more often or because police and courts were particularly attentive in that year?

One of the earliest answers to that question was based on a negative argument: short-term fluctuations, if not too insignificant, may be taken as meaningful reflections of actual criminal activity, provided that they cannot be due to any legal, administrative, or other change taking immediate effect. This only applies to major fluctuations in crime and in years when the cited counterforces are absent. For the rest, there are two main tools for tackling the problem presented by the dark number. The first is a careful assessment of the influences upon the level of prosecution. For example, English historians emphasize that, in the course of the eighteenth century, concern among the public about the appropriateness of the death penalty for minor crimes against property increased, with a growing reluctance to report and prosecute these offenses as a consequence. This made the rate of indicted property crimes a poorer sample of actual property crime as the century wore on. The second tool is the attempt to look for other indicators to make one's assumptions about the incidence of real crime more plausible. During the crisis years 1771–1772 in Amsterdam, for example, the number of property offenses peaked. Simultaneously, the total amount spent by the various churches on poor relief and the total value of goods brought to the municipal pawn shop were considerably higher than in the years immediately preceding and following.

The two most systematic attempts by historians so far at counting real crime each elaborate one of the tools just mentioned. They refer to the prestatistical and the statistical period, respectively. In his 1982 article "War, Dearth, and Theft in the Eighteenth Century," Douglas Hay examined the impact of war and dearth upon the level of property crime, based on an analysis of Staffordshire cases in the eighteenth century. To distinguish the level of prosecuted from that of real property crime, he referred to the latter as "appropriation." The analysis focused on the influence of two factors, fluctuations in food prices and the alternation of periods of war and peace, upon the level of indictments for larcenies. The data clearly showed peaks in the level of indicted larcenies during the aftermath of war and in years of excessively high food prices.

To show that these peaks reflected increases in the amount of appropriation, Hay argued by way of deduction. In hard years, he noted, poverty was an acute affliction rather than a routine experience for a greater number of people. Consequently, he expected not simply more appropriation in those years but also a change in the nature of the offenses and the offenders. These expectations proved true. Among the offenders, for example, the proportion of women increased in years of high prices, suggesting that more people who did not otherwise run the risk of appearing before the courts stole in those years. The offenses included a disproportionate amount of lesser charges, rather than capital crimes, and the sort of appropriation committed without much planning increased in

frequency. A parallel argument pertained to the alternation between war and peace. Demobilization increased the number of men who were likely to resort to appropriation. In the aftermath of war, then, one would expect the proportion of serious property crime to rise, and indeed professionally committed thefts predominated and the number of women decreased. The traditional factors influencing the level of indicted offenses, such as the formation of associations for the prosecution of felons, were unlikely to have operated to any special extent in years of dearth or following wars.

This analysis has a wider relevance. Studies done in other European countries have revealed similar patterns with respect to peaks and lows in property crime. Even though the data precluded a refined methodological analysis along the lines just described, we may assume that, parallel to the English case, peaks in prosecuted property offenses reflected peaks in appropriation. Generally, years of dearth were years of increased property crime throughout Europe, well into the nineteenth century. Regarding the aftermath of war, matters were a little more complicated. Unlike England, continental countries did not simply send away soldiers and navy men and take them back again. Notably in regions where military operations were held, war itself could equally lead to increases in vagabondage and appropriation, in particular by deserters. For the local population, to be sure, it may have made little difference whether they suffered from robbery by deserters or pillage by regular soldiers.

For the statistical period, V. A. C. Gatrell (1980) assessed the influences upon the level of prosecution over a longer term rather than in peak years. He dealt with property crime and serious violence, two types of offenses about whose heinous character and the desirability of a reaction there was widespread consensus during the period he investigated. In England and Wales, prosecutions for these crimes peaked in the 1840s, but from about 1850 until 1914 the rates, relative to the population, steadily declined. The national scale and longer term of this decline ruled out any influence of incidental or local circumstances. Only two important factors remained: the efficiency and determination of police and courts on the one hand and citizens' cooperation with the law on the other. Both factors had a steadily increasing impact throughout the nineteenth century. As a consequence, the dark number must have steadily decreased, or, as Gatrell put it, recorded and real crime converged. For the period from 1800 to 1850, when recorded crime rose sharply, this convergence can be consistent with either an increase or a decrease in real crime. For the period from 1850 to 1914, however, it necessarily im-

Dealing with a Brigand. *Friar Pedro Binds Maragato with a Rope,* painting (c. 1806) by Francisco José Goya y Lucientes (1746–1828). PHOTOGRAPH ©2000, THE ART INSTITUTE OF CHICAGO, ALL RIGHTS RESERVED/MR. AND MRS. MARTIN A. RYERSON COLLECTION, 1933.1076

plied that actual crime rates declined even more rapidly than the statistical record indicated. Although the method is adequate, Gatrell's "convergence principle" has a limited applicability. It only works when the efficiency and determination of police and courts and citizens' cooperation with the law are increasing, and it only leads to a meaningful conclusion when recorded crime rates decline or at least stay constant.

Again, these British findings have a clear relevance for other European countries, several of which appear to have partaken of the decrease in prosecutions for property crime since the middle of the nineteenth century. In Prussia, for example, prosecutions for theft started to decline in the 1850s. The rates for simple theft declined further in the statistics of imperial Germany from 1882 until 1914, although this trend was offset somewhat by a rise in other property offenses like embezzlement and fraud. In most of Europe, the second half of the nineteenth century was a period of expanding industry and rapid urbanization. Hence the data about criminality in this period are relevant for a debate about the "modernization" of crime, in which historians have engaged for long. The English and German figures contradict earlier notions that urbanization and industrialization brought about a greater preponderance and rising rates of property crime. Hence Eric Johnson (1995) argued against the thesis of Howard Zehr (1976), who stated that modernization led to an increasing preponderance of property crime, not only in Germany but also in France. Johnson believed that his own thesis, that modernization did not necessarily bring an increase in property

crime, holds for Europe generally, but he admitted that more research, in various countries, is needed.

Informal handling of crime. This debate about "modernization" and crime refers to an early phase of urbanization and industrialization, roughly from the 1840s until the 1920s. In the course of the twentieth century, levels of crime, in particular property crime, increased again, especially since the 1960s. Throughout Europe, the level of prosecuted property crime in the second half of the twentieth century was much higher than in the early modern period, in absolute numbers of course but also relative to the total population. Part of the difference probably is real, as the opportunities for theft and fraud are so much greater in the modern world. Another part of the difference, however, is due to a combination of two factors characteristic of the early modern period: the lesser grip of police and courts on illegal behavior and the tendency of private individuals to solve their own problems. The result was that a lot of illegal behavior was dealt with informally at the community level. Historians commonly refer to this world of partly hidden crime and the reactions to it as the infrajudiciary.

Researchers discovered the world of the infrajudiciary because it occasionally surfaces in the judicial records themselves. Some defendants were charged by their neighbors with a long series of offenses, most of which dated back years. The last theft had finally prompted the victim to take legal action. Alternatively, it was simply mentioned that the defendant had a longer history of wrongdoing, which up to then the community had dealt with informally. A particularly illustrative example comes from a nonlegal source, the chronicle which the seventeenth-century yeoman Richard Gough wrote of his parish, Myddle:

> But I must not forgett John Aston, because many in the Parish have reason to remember him. Hee was a sort of silly fellow, very idle and much given to stealing of poultry and small things. Hee was many times catched in the fact, and sometimes well cajoled by those that would trouble themselves noe further with him. Butt at last hee grew unsufferable, and made it his common practice to steal henns in the night and bring them to Shrewsbury, where hee had confederates to receive them att any time of night. Hee was att last imprisoned and indicted for stealing twenty-four cocks and henns. (Gough, 1981, p. 145)

John Aston's neighbors finally took him to court because he had become "unsufferable," but they did not want him to run the risk of hanging, so they fixed the worth of the stolen poultry at eleven pence.

The example from this chronicle highlights a common practice: a complaint to the court often was a last resort. Before it came that far, the neighbors dealt with the offender in an informal manner, as they also did with occasional thieves. Sometimes victims were able to recover their stolen property. Or they acquiesced when, for example, a poor neighbor had stolen their chicken and eaten it. In such cases they might give the thief a beating, as happened to John Aston. These types of informal reaction to crime were typical of an agrarian world in which villagers knew each other well. Well into the nineteenth century, the majority of Europe's population lived in such villages, which means that the informal system was a very common one. Moreover, even in a metropolis like Amsterdam it happened occasionally that victims came to the house of a thief to demand back their stolen goods. The pattern by which charges against fellow villagers often were the culmination of a series of complaints has been found in France, England, the Netherlands, Germany, and Scandinavia, from the beginning of the seventeenth century until the early nineteenth. Although the list of prior complaints can be included in crime figures, these cases are only the tip of an iceberg. For one thing, they only involve habitual malefactors, tolerated for some time but finally prosecuted.

Informal handling explains part of the difference in levels of prosecuted property crime between the early modern and the modern age. Although individual victims of crime were capable of acting on their own, historians assumed, upon discovering the infrajudiciary, that specific persons or institutions were involved in out-of-court settlements. French historians, for example, found that socially recognized arbiters such as the seigneur of a village or the parish priest sometimes acted as mediators. Notaries could be involved, too. In a sample of Parisian notarial acts from the first half of the seventeenth century, 153 acts concerned infrajudicial settlements. However, the overwhelming majority of cases concerned assault or verbal attack, not theft. Similarly, in Dutch notarial archives of the seventeenth and eighteenth centuries one finds depositions about conflicts among neighbors and marital quarrels but hardly anything about stolen property. In three-quarters of the Parisian cases, moreover, the wronged party had started judicial proceedings. Withdrawal of the complaint usually was one of the provisions of the settlement. These cases were not purely infrajudicial; rather, one of the parties had used a judicial complaint as a means of forcing the other to agree to an extrajudicial settlement. Thus, as far as mediation is concerned, we are left with the verbal intervention of local notables and clergymen, which left no trace in written records.

One type of ecclesiastical institution remained where historians hoped to find informal handling of illegal behavior: Protestant associations exercising discipline over church members. In particular, Calvinist consistories were active to promote harmony within the religious community. These institutions dealt with a broad range of activities deemed undesirable, including matters of doctrine, church attendance, morals, sexuality, marital harmony, and the maintenance of friendly relations between neighbors. Sometimes they dealt with violent conflicts among church members, especially in the late sixteenth and early seventeenth centuries. However, studies done so far on Protestant discipline in several countries have hardly disclosed any cases of conflicts arising from theft. In the case of Lutheran Sweden we know that the agencies involved in parish justice were interested in property crime, but the parishioners refused to cooperate. When the ecclesiastical committee visiting the village of Riklea in 1752 inquired about it, the villagers responded that a number of thefts had been committed during the previous year and that they had some idea who were guilty, but they refused to mention names. To conclude, the bodies exercising church discipline in the early modern period were important agencies of social control, but they hardly dealt with crimes, certainly not with property crimes. We know that the subterranean stream of property crime existed, but it is almost impossible to quantify.

VIOLENT CRIME

Whereas most of the important work on property crime was done in the 1970s and 1980s, violence, in particular homicide, is a central concern of today's crime historians. They consider homicide rates as an indication of the level of serious violence generally. Homicide is an attractive subject because the problems of method are less serious than in the case of property crime: it is difficult to hide a dead body, and records exist of bodies found (called coroner's reports in England). Hence in this case it is feasible to count real crime, with only an insignificant dark number. As with property crime, the count is always relative to the population, the homicide rate being defined as the annual average, over a specified period, per 100,000 inhabitants in a specified area.

Yet there is no universal agreement about how to count killings. For one thing, some historians still accept rates of prosecuted homicide instead of only taking figures based on body inspections into consideration. This can make a difference. In early modern Amsterdam, for example, the ratio of detected to prosecuted homicide varied from 9:1 to 3:1. Therefore the homicide rate should always be calculated from re-

Peasants Attacking a Soldier. *Brawl in a Pub,* painting by Marten van Cleve (1527–1581). KUNSTHISTORISCHES MUSEUM, VIENNA/ERICH LESSING/ART RESOURCE, N.Y.

ports about bodies found. For scholars investigating recent periods, this is the standard procedure. In most European countries, medical statistics about the causes of death are available from the end of the nineteenth century or the beginning of the twentieth. A second disagreement concerns the figures for infanticide, commonly defined as the killing of a baby at birth or shortly after. Some historians insist that infanticides should be included in the homicide rate, whereas others reserve the latter concept for the killing of adults and adolescents. This, too, can make a difference, notably for the sex ratio among the killers. The solution adopted by most historians is to present both homicide and infanticide rates. Third, there is the problem of counting homicide in small towns and regions, especially acute for the period before 1500. Because of low population figures, the homicide rate depends too much on chance. For example, if a town has four thousand inhabitants, six killings per decade already make a homicide rate of 15. Because of this, and the great variation in the English medieval rates, J. S. Cockburn (1991) advocated discarding all figures prior to 1500. Twentieth-century rates, on the other hand,

are somewhat less comparable to earlier ones, due to the influence of increased medical expertise and medical infrastructure such as fast ambulances. As a consequence, more people survive an attack, who, in an earlier period, would have died from their wounds.

Trends in homicide rates. The method adopted influences one's conclusions on the long-term trend of homicide, although, in all cases, this trend turns out to be one of decline. England was the first country for which a graph down the centuries could be constructed. The homicide rate in England declined from about 20 per 100,000 in 1200 to about 15 in the later Middle Ages, between 6 and 7 in the Elizabethan period, and then further down (with the most dramatic fall from the late seventeenth to the late eighteenth century), until the figure stood at 1 around 1900. These figures are averages in a double sense, representing the combined rates of several towns and regions, and, moreover, they are partly based on studies which counted prosecuted cases only. If these studies were discarded, the pre-1500 figures, in particular, would end up higher. The available data for the Con-

341

tinent in this period are suggestive. Towns in Italy, the Netherlands, Germany, and Sweden had homicide rates of 50 or more in the fourteenth and fifteenth centuries. In Amsterdam, the rate still approached 30 in the sixteenth century. Thereafter, both the Dutch and Swedish trends resemble the English one. In Dutch cause of death statistics, kept since 1911, the homicide rate was under 0.5 until 1970, except in the 1940s.

For the statistical period, figures are available for all European countries. By the late nineteenth century the long-term decline in homicide had affected the whole of western, northern, and central Europe. The Prussian rates, for example, fluctuated between 1 and 2, and the French rate was under 2 as well. The decline set in later in southern and eastern Europe. The Italian homicide rate still stood at 9 around 1880. In Rome alone, the figure was 12.3 in the years 1872–1879, but then it declined to 4.8 in the years 1910–1914. Throughout southern and eastern Europe, homicide rates declined until they were mostly under 5 in the 1930s. After World War II the rates in most European countries tended to converge, which implied a slight rise for some. Since about 1970, however, homicide has been on the rise throughout Europe (and in the United States), reversing an agelong trend. This rise affects the big cities in particular. In Amsterdam, for example, the figure was 6 in the late 1980s and 1990s, and if correction is made for greater medical expertise it increases to 8. This nearly approaches the figure for the early eighteenth century. It is unclear yet whether the contemporary European-wide rise in homicide is temporary.

Most historians explain the downward trend in homicide from the thirteenth century to 1970 with reference to Norbert Elias's theory of civilization. According to this theory, the increasing differentiation and complexity of society forced people increasingly to control their impulses, violent and otherwise. Several historians paid attention to the social context in which homicide took place in different periods. In every period, this context includes gender. Homicide, and serious violence generally, took place in a male world. In periods of high rates, such habits as knife fighting among men accounted for the majority of cases. Killers as well as their victims were overwhelmingly male. In periods of low rates, on the other hand, while the great majority of killers still were men, women got greater prominence among the victims. The few existing studies counting killer-victim relationships over a longer term confirm this pattern. In Amsterdam a shift occurred by the middle of the eighteenth century, when homicide rates were dropping rapidly: the share of female victims rose, as well as the proportion of victims involved in an intimate relationship with the killer. In England, the long-term decline in homicide was accompanied by a parallel increase in the proportion of cases taking place within the biological family: from 8 percent in the fourteenth century to 45 percent in the second half of the twentieth. As still another way of placing homicidal violence in context, one can distinguish two axes, one with the opposite poles of impulsive versus planned violence, the other with poles of ritual versus instrumental violence. These axes show that the long-term decline in homicide was accompanied by an increasing prominence of instrumentality and planning in violence.

Violence and gender are linked in another way in infanticide. Rather than reflecting aggressive impulses or revengeful desires, this crime tells the story of shame and desperation. The criminal records from England, France, the Netherlands, and Germany confirm that infanticide was committed almost exclusively by unmarried mothers, often servant girls. The interrogation protocols reveal that most of the women involved saw no way out, because of shame but also because of the material consequences. A servant girl who bore a child was dismissed right away, left without a legal income for herself and her baby. The courts considered infanticide a serious offense against Christian morality in a double sense: illicit sexuality and the taking of human life. They were especially severe from the middle of the sixteenth until the middle of the eighteenth century. Then it was even a punishable offense, capital in France and England, for a woman to give birth to a dead baby if she had concealed her pregnancy and refrained from calling upon a midwife. There was no need to prove actual killing. Later, the male judges gradually became more merciful, often paternalistically seeing the accused as poor misled women. In the course of the twentieth century, as the social acceptance and material possibilities of raising children outside marriage increased and, finally, with increased availability of contraceptives, infanticide became a marginal crime.

Arson and minor violence. The attack on and destruction of a person's property is usually classified as a violent offense. Arson occupied a prominent place in the criminality of preindustrial Europe. It was a typically rural crime, facilitated by the material environment. A farmer's house, his barns and haystack, highly flammable, were easy targets for local people who knew their way. No nightwatchmen patrolled in villages, which also lacked public illumination. Arson has been investigated in Germany, France, and England. It was either a form of extortion by wandering groups or, more often, a product of conflicts within rural communities. The motive was to hurt or take revenge on the other party, for which the maiming of cattle sometimes served as an alternative. In the mountainous districts of Bavaria, arson was still a common means of taking revenge in the second half of the nineteenth century. Villagers resorted to it in order to maintain their honor when no other way of redress seemed possible. The perpetrators waited until the wind blew in the right direction, so that only the target farm would burn down. With less flammable material used for the construction of farms and the spread of insurance, arson is less of a threat in the modern world. Today criminal arson is rather the work of the proprietors themselves, wishing to cheat on the insurance company.

Minor violence and conflict in urban and rural communities have received ample attention from crime historians since the 1990s. In this case, the focus is less on quantification than on the character of communal relations. The lower courts in rural areas during the ancien régime dealt largely with petty conflicts among neighbors. Accusations of slander, for example, mostly brought forward by women, were often numerous. Rural lower courts, then, were involved in questions of gender, honor, and neighborliness. An example is the village of Heiden in the German county of Lippe in the seventeenth and eighteenth centuries. The villagers and the local authorities shared a common outlook as far as the sanctity of property and the code of honor were concerned, but their opinions diverged about violence as a means of solving conflicts and such public-order measures as the regulation of alcohol consumption.

POPULAR PERCEPTIONS OF CRIME

For many people in Europe's past, crime was essentially something "the others" did. Contemporaries handled their fears of crime and made sense of it by locating it in specific social groups. Thus the supposed existence of a "criminal class," ready to infect the whole of the working class, haunted the bourgeoisie of Victorian England. At the same time, the French spoke of "the dangerous classes." Older studies saw these French and English fears as largely realistic. They viewed criminality in terms of a professional underworld: a criminal class existing in symbiosis with the working class as a whole and therefore posing a major threat to social order. They saw the urban proletariat as a permanent reservoir of criminality and revolutionary ferment, chaotic and irrational. This view, however, since the 1970s has been criticized by his-

Sensational Crime. "The Ville-d'Avray Affair" from *Le Petit Parisien,* a French tabloid, 7 September 1890. Musée des Arts et Traditions Populaires, Paris

torians of popular protest as well as by crime historians. The former emphasized the rational character of collective action by the lower classes, while the latter showed that nineteenth-century lawbreakers did not form a group acting in conjunction with the working class as a whole. Workers who considered themselves respectable and abided by contemporary standards of morality distanced themselves from the "roughs." There was a widespread acceptance of the legitimacy of the rule of law. In the English Black Country, for example, workers themselves often acted as prosecutors in cases of theft. The public-order panics which occasionally broke out were staged by the media to promote the introduction or expansion of the police.

In the early modern period, vagrants were the group held accountable for a large part of criminality. Early modern Europe indeed knew a marginal population, recruited from the semiemployed and unemployed in towns and the landless proletariat in the countryside. Fears for the criminal potential of vagrants date back to the sixteenth century. Historians who studied the way of life of these marginal groups in France, England, and Germany came up with a nuanced picture. Certainly, vagrants were obliged to steal at times, but they were even more adroit in devising techniques for raising pity when begging. Sometimes this entailed purposely mutilating a child. Marginal people did not live according to the ethics of comfortable society, but they were masters in the art of survival. Although individuals gave alms at times, the majority of the settled population of early modern Europe expressed a hostile attitude to vagrants as a group. France introduced special courts in the eighteenth century to deal with vagrants. If any group in history approached the image of a "criminal class," they did. However, they did so not because all marginal people had the habit of stealing but because begging, vagabondage, and the mere fact of being born as a gypsy were offenses in themselves. Hence it is better to speak of a criminalized class.

The crime literature of the past offers another possibility to study popular perceptions, but in Europe this is still an underresearched subject. Rather than expressing collective fears of crime, we find it mostly concerned with notorious individual cases. In the early modern period, a large part was also punishment literature, since the pamphlets and small booklets of which it mostly consisted were usually published on the occasion of the offender's execution. Examples are the life accounts by the ordinary, or chaplain, of Newgate prison of the criminals hanged in London. This type of literature was highly moralistic in tone, explaining how the offender's ungodly life necessarily led to robbery or murder. Another type of crime literature was primarily sensational. One study (Wiltenburg, 1992) compared broadsides dealing with family violence in early modern England and Germany. While the majority of English ones were about husband murderers, the authors of German pamphlets focused on women and men who slaughtered their entire families in a moment of madness. Newspaper accounts and novels about crime after 1800 have hardly been studied yet by European historians.

CRIME AND SOCIAL PROTEST

Whereas in popular perceptions and literature crime was often portrayed as more fearful and atrocious than in actual reality, some actual criminal activities were not seen as crimes by a large part of the population. Sometimes offenders even enjoyed support. British historians in particular have argued that the offenses in question formed a category in itself, which they called "social crime." Others, while agreeing that popular support for offenders is an important subject, have objected to that term. It implies an antiquated

understanding of the word "social," meaning "for the benefit of the poor or the lower classes" or "in the service of class struggle." In a modern, neutral definition "social" refers to the interaction of people; hence every crime is a social activity. Nevertheless, the question of whether certain crimes were an expression of popular protest is a valid one.

Eric Hobsbawm was the first to posit a link between crime and protest. His *Bandits* (first published 1969) dealt with bandits within a geographically wide range of peasant societies, including preindustrial Europe, and in particular with bands enjoying a measure of support. These bandits, he argued, were peasant outlaws, whom the state or feudal lords regarded as criminals but who actually remained part of the peasant world. The people regarded them as heroes, avengers, fighters for justice, or even leaders of liberation. The relatively long life of many of these bands could only be explained by the active or passive support they enjoyed from the peasant population. Hence their actions constituted an "archaic" form of protest against the prevailing order of society. Hobsbawm's thesis drew an obvious parallel between the bandit and the guerrilla soldier, who, in Mao Tse-tung's famous phrase, found a haven in the peasant population like a fish in the water. Simultaneously, the thesis was inspired by the image of Robin Hood, stealing from the rich and distributing the proceeds to the poor.

We know for sure that the Robin Hood myth played an important role in the popular culture of preindustrial Europe. Noble robbers abound in chapbooks, for example, but most historians doubt whether this type existed in reality. Significantly, Hobsbawm's European data were mostly from eastern or Mediterranean Europe. In ancien régime France, for example, although some rural bands could count on a degree of popular support, this remained largely confined to accomplices. After 1789 it was the counterrevolutionary forces in particular who recruited former criminals and bandits. Neither do the data for eighteenth-century Germany provide much support for Hobsbawm's thesis. Although Carsten Küther (1976) accepted this thesis, distinguishing the peasant bandit, who enjoyed popular support, from the common outlaw, recruited from the marginal population or a minority group, the latter type appeared at least as numerous as the former. Uwe Danker (1988) criticized Küther, pointing out that most bandits were either Jews or people with "infamous" occupations, two groups despised by the peasants. Moreover, the peasants themselves often were victims of the operations of bandits. Danker explained the successes of robber bands primarily by the relative weakness of the German states.

Heroic Bandits. Brigands robbing a French tax collector. The sign on the front of the counter reads "Tax collector who pays the proceeds of his collections straightaway." Engraving, eighteenth century. BIBLIOTHÈQUE NATIONALE DE FRANCE, PARIS/©COLLECTION VIOLLET

Anton Blok provided the most explicit critique of Hobsbawm's thesis. He emphasized the weakness of the peasants in this context. Preindustrial peasants were so powerless that they hardly would have been able to support bands over a longer period. Thus he formulated a counterhypothesis: the more successful a person is as a bandit, the more extensive the protection granted him. This protection primarily came from powerful persons or groups, in the form of acquiescence or tacit support from landlords or regional elites. Bandits' activities often ran counter to peasant interests. Moreover, most members of successful bands were relative outsiders in the peasant world. They had been or were peddlers, skinners, or innkeepers, working in occupations involving a high degree of geographical mobility or offering special opportunities to cover illegal activities. Finally, most bands operated especially in areas where state authority was weak. In the Netherlands, for example, they enjoyed a longer life in border areas than in the urbanized western part. Throughout Europe, the chronology and geography of banditry confirmed its inverse relationship with the growth of state power. After the revolutionary period large bands disappeared from the scene in France, the Netherlands, and Germany, whereas Mediterranean areas remained infested with banditry until the early twentieth century.

Although the homeland of the Robin Hood story, England has been relatively free from banditry since the beginning of the early modern period. Yet the country had its own peculiar offenders who enjoyed local support, in particular in the eighteenth and

first half of the nineteenth centuries. As rule, they were involved in collective activities not viewed as crimes by most of their neighbors. Rather than robbery, the offenses were poaching, smuggling, wrecking, and, in one case, coining. Local people considered these activities as lawful, often as ancient rights. They felt entitled to shoot deer in the nearby forest, for example, but the forest now belonged to the king, and his officials considered the poachers thieves of the king's property. Likewise, the law denied the inhabitants of coastal villages any entitlement to the goods in stranded ships. As in the case of banditry, the research into these crimes was motivated by a desire to find archaic forms of social protest. And again, the results were ambiguous.

For one thing, the protagonists' methods were ruthless at times. The wreckers in Cornish villages, for example, rather than waiting for a ship to run ashore, lured it to the rocks with false lights. This hardly qualifies as protest against social injustice. Generally, wrecking was not so much an activity of the poor as the favorite pursuit of an entire community. When news that a ship had stranded reached the inhabitants of one seaboard village during religious service, they all ran out of church, with the parson yelling after them, "Wait for me." In such cases, support for offenders simply meant local defense of the community's collective complicity against outside agents of law enforcement.

In a similar vein, poachers thought of themselves as defenders of local custom. The Blacks of Windsor Forest, a more or less organized group of deer poachers in the 1720s and 1730s, were experts in age-old privileges. The majority belonged to ancient local families, wealthy and respectable but not of the highest rank. Their opponents were agents of the bureaucracy administering the royal forests. Coining, on the other hand, never was viewed as an ancient right. Yet the so-called Yorkshire Mint, an organized group of counterfeiters and dealers in false gold coins in the 1760s, also enjoyed widespread protection in the county. The coins of this mint were widely accepted, to the advantage of local businessmen operating in a regional market. They were the counterfeiters' staunchest supporters. Other inhabitants of Yorkshire, businessmen and gentry with a concern for their long-term economic interest viewed in a national perspective, cooperated with the law to suppress the illegal mint. Thus the confrontation was between two groups with antagonistic interests, located within a regional and national context, respectively. In a similar vein, poachers, smugglers, and wreckers were locally or regionally bound. The poor never played a leading role in any of these groups of offenders. The laws they impinged upon mainly upheld the fiscal and economic interests of the national state.

A similar clash of interests was visible in other countries, in particular with smuggling. In Dutch cities in the eighteenth century it was a collective enterprise to sneak boats loaded with untaxed grain into town. The smugglers could count on the sympathy of a large part of the urban population. In Prussia's western provinces the smuggling of salt, tobacco, or coffee was a thriving business in the first half of the nineteenth century. Although increasing in intensity during manufacturing slumps, it was no poor man's game. Local merchants were involved, and the Prussian administration tried to counter the practice by setting up antismuggling cartels. The authorities were only partially successful.

The conclusion on smugglers, poachers, and their kind parallels that on bandits. The fact that the people refused to see some offenses as crimes cannot be explained by a simple model of class struggle such as that posited by Hobsbawm. Rather than archaic protest by the poor against the social order, these crimes represented local and regional resistance to the intrusion of the modern state.

CONCLUSION:
THE TRANSFORMATION OF CRIME

Several major trends formed the changing face of crime from the sixteenth century to the twentieth. Foremost among them was the inclusion of certain forms of behavior into the category of crime and the exclusion of others from it. There was a steady increase in criminalization from the sixteenth century until the first half of the nineteenth. At the same time, however, decriminalization took place in certain fields.

The early modern process of criminalization first hit the marginal population of vagrants and beggars. Before the sixteenth century, these groups had been largely tolerated. Both begging and giving alms were viewed in religious terms, the wandering beggar following the footsteps of Jesus and his apostles. From the sixteenth century onward, beggars and vagrants increasingly came to be considered a nuisance or even a threat to public order. Increasingly, they were hunted and often committed to prison workhouses. By the early seventeenth century, vagrancy and unlicensed begging were defined as offenses throughout Europe, and licensed begging was severely restricted. The prosecution of these offenses was largely a matter of summary justice, leaving behind few quantifiable records.

Another wave of criminalization in the sixteenth and seventeenth centuries had to do with the expanding power of the state. As governments increasingly taxed the population and set up tariff barriers, the law defined evasion of the tax as another crime. Smuggling was the result, with smugglers often enjoying support from local communities. Internal tariff barriers largely disappeared after the ancien régime, but in the border areas between European states, smuggling remained a lucrative business until the middle of the twentieth century.

An extension of the range of property crime represented the third wave of criminalization, in the eighteenth and early nineteenth centuries. Taking away small "perks" from the workplace, for example, came to be treated as a criminal activity. Workers themselves thought they were entitled to perks, provided the commodities taken had a low value and it concerned small quantities. The prosecution of workplace offenses was mainly an urban affair, but around 1800 this wave of criminalization hit the rural population in particular. The forces of ongoing commercialization and an expanding state bureaucracy resulted in an intensified prosecution of various activities hitherto considered as the exercise of traditional rights by inhabitants of rural communities.

Poaching, redefined as stealing the game belonging to the owner of the land, has been mentioned already. In the Bavarian mountains, despite vigorous prosecution, poaching remained a favorite pastime of rural youths until the early twentieth century. With increasing urbanization and a dwindling number of wild animals, this crime became relatively marginal. Likewise, gleaning, the collection of leftovers from a harvested field, is no longer a frequent practice. It was a customary practice, usually performed by women and children, well into the nineteenth century. The English Court of Common Pleas declared in 1788 that no one had a right to glean without the permission of the owner of the land. Still, prosecutions for this offense remained infrequent in England. Unauthorized gathering of firewood, on the other hand, was frequently prosecuted in several European countries. A Prussian law of 1821 made the traditional gathering of wood punishable, going into the detail of specifying three types of the offense. The majority of the rural population continued to consider the use of the old common woods and meadows as their traditional right. The level of prosecutions for theft of wood remained high in all Prussian provinces between 1815 and 1848. Nowadays, mainly the rich have fireplaces in their homes, and they buy their firewood at gas stations. Thus this wave of criminalization has rolled back again because most of the activities involved have become obsolete.

Processes of decriminalization date back to the late seventeenth century. In many cases, decriminalization was directly or indirectly related to secularization. Secular courts stopped prosecuting people for blasphemy, for example. With the separation of church and state, most religious offenses disappeared from the books. We can add witchcraft and sorcery here, which the courts in most European countries no longer considered a crime by 1700. Suicide, for a long time punishable by exposing or piercing the dead body, was decriminalized in the eighteenth century. Other sins stopped being crimes, too, with the advent of the liberal state. Offenses such as simple fornication, bestiality, and, in most countries, sodomy have not been prosecuted since the nineteenth century. England and the Netherlands, however, witnessed a revival of criminalization for certain morals offenses around 1900. In the late twentieth century, sexual activities involving children increasingly became a target for prosecution. In 1998 a Swedish law made soliciting a prostitute a punishable offense for men. Criminalization has also extended to a violent offense with sexual overtones, rape. In the seventeenth-century Netherlands, judges made it clear that only forced sex with a respectable woman could attract their attention. Well into the twentieth century, rape victims had a hard time proving they had not provoked the act, but under the influence of the feminist movement since the 1970s this situation has changed.

Apart from social views about which activities are criminal, there were broad changes in the character of crime from preindustrial to modern society. Property offenses became more dominant among total criminality, a development which initially reflected an increasing concern of the courts for the protection of property. In modern society the preponderance of property offenses among total criminality is even more marked. For example, in the Netherlands in the 1980s, the ratio of violent to property crime was 1 to 32. This figure can hardly be the result of prosecution policies alone. The high crime rates of modern society are largely due to higher levels of theft and burglary. In their turn, those levels are related to the greater opportunities for appropriation compared to preindustrial Europe.

In connection with this, the traditional pattern whereby property offenses peaked in years of demobilization and especially economic crisis has disappeared. In England economic depressions still caused peaks in property crime in the nineteenth century, but after 1880 this correlation gradually weakened. French criminal statistics reveal a quite similar pattern: food prices explain most of the variance in theft rates until the 1870s and then no longer. Prior to German unification, Prussian and Bavarian statistics reveal a correlation between grain prices and thefts. This correlation significantly weakened in the statistics of the German Reich, available from 1882 onward. Factors such as ethnic discrimination became more important in explaining concentrations of property crime. In Sweden, finally, the correlation between economic hardship and property offenses decreased from the 1870s onward. Since industrialization came to Sweden much later than to England, factors such as the growth of a social welfare system partly explain the shift. Historians refer to this sea change as the shift from poverty-related to prosperity-related property crime. For ages people had stolen out of sheer necessity, but in twentieth-century Europe this was no longer the case.

The long-term trend in violent crime was unequivocal: homicide rates declined from the thirteenth century to about 1970; among the violence which remained, encounters of an instrumental type and conflicts among intimates occupied a greater share. Even though total prosecuted criminality now consists overwhelmingly of offenses against property, and today's homicide levels are far below those of the sixteenth century, the recent upsurge in homicide constitutes a puzzling countertrend, not yet satisfactorily explained by historians or criminologists. In eastern Europe, the dissolution of the Soviet Union obviously plays a part. Homicide rates in Estonia, for example, moved up from about 7 in 1989 to over 25 in 1994. It is more difficult to explain the rise in homicide in western and central Europe. Some of it is due to the increased availability of firearms, although these are much less common than in the United States. Other possible factors include the immigration of men from societies more accustomed to violence and the spread of organized crime with its violent elimination of competitors.

Finally, modern petty crime differs from its preindustrial counterpart. Minor conflicts in villages and neighborhoods no longer constitute a concern even for the lower courts. Sensitivity to personal honor has decreased. When neighbors are in conflict, it is largely subject to mediation by the police. Today's petty cases are traffic violations, breaches of administrative rules. The result is an intensification of the link between illegal behavior and state control.

See also **Roma: The Gypsies** *(volume 1);* **Modernization; The Industrial Revolutions; War and Conquest; Urbanization** *(volume 2);* **The Military; Marginal People** *(in this volume);* **Honor and Shame** *(volume 5); and other articles in this section.*

BIBLIOGRAPHY

Beattie, J. M. *Crime and the Courts in England, 1660–1800.* Princeton, N.J., 1986.

Beier, Augustus L. *Masterless Men: The Vagrancy Problem in England, 1560–1640.* London and New York, 1985.

Blok, Anton. *De Bokkerijders: Roversbenden en geheime genootschappen in de Landen van Overmaas (1730–1774).* Amsterdam, 1991.

Blok, Anton. *The Mafia of a Sicilian Village, 1860–1960: A Study of Violent Peasant Entrepreneurs.* New York, 1974.

Brewer, John, and John Styles, eds. *An Ungovernable People: The English and Their Law in the Seventeenth and Eighteenth Centuries.* London, 1980.

Castan, Nicole. *Les criminels de Languedoc: Les exigences d'ordre et les voies du ressentiment dans une société prérévolutionnaire, 1750–1790.* Toulouse, France, 1980.

Chevalier, Louis. *Laboring Classes and Dangerous Classes in Paris during the First Half of the Nineteenth Century.* Translated by Frank Jellinek. New York, 1973.

Cobb, Richard. *The Police and the People: French Popular Protest, 1789–1820.* Oxford, 1970.

Cockburn, J. S. "Patterns of Violence in English Society: Homicide in Kent, 1560–1985." *Past and Present* 130 (1991): 70–106.

Danker, Uwe. *Räuberbanden im alten Reich um 1700: Ein Beitrag zur Geschichte von Herrschaft und Kriminalität in der frühen Neuzeit.* 2 vols. Frankfurt, Germany, 1988.

Dinges, Martin. *Der Maurermeister und der Finanzrichter: Ehre, Geld, und soziale Kontrolle im Paris des 18. Jahrhunderts.* Göttingen, Germany, 1994.

Dülmen, Richard van. *Frauen vor Gericht: Kindsmord in der frühen Neuzeit.* Frankfurt, Germany, 1991.

Egmond, Florike. *Underworlds: Organized Crime in the Netherlands, 1650–1800.* Cambridge, U.K., 1993.

Eisner, Manuel. *Das Ende der zivilisierten Stadt? Die Auswirkungen von Modernisierung und urbaner Krise auf Gewaltdelinquenz.* Frankfurt, Germany, and New York, 1997.

Emsley, Clive. *Crime and Society in England, 1750–1900.* 2d ed. London and New York, 1996.

Emsley, Clive, and Louis A. Knafla, eds. *Crime History and Histories of Crime: Studies in the Historiography of Crime and Criminal Justice in Modern History.* Westport, Conn., 1996.

Faber, Sjoerd. *Strafrechtspleging en criminaliteit te Amsterdam, 1680–1811: De nieuwe menslievendheid.* Arnhem, Netherlands, 1983.

Feeley, Malcolm M., and Deborah L. Little. "The Vanishing Female: The Decline of Women in the Criminal Process, 1687–1912." *Law and Society Review* 25 (1991): 719–757.

Frank, Michael. *Dörfliche Gesellschaft und Kriminalität: Das Fallbeispiel Lippe, 1650–1800.* Paderborn, Germany, 1995.

Gatrell, V. A. C. "The Decline of Theft and Violence in Victorian and Edwardian England." In *Crime and the Law: The Social History of Crime in Western Europe since 1500.* Edited by V. A. C. Gatrell et al. London, 1980. Pages 238–370.

Gough, Richard. *The History of Myddle.* Edited with an introduction and notes by David Hey. Harmondsworth, U.K., 1981.

Hay, Douglas. "War, Dearth, and Theft in the Eighteenth Century: The Record of the English Courts." *Past and Present* 95 (1982): 117–160.

Hay, Douglas, et al. *Albion's Fatal Tree: Crime and Society in Eighteenth-Century England.* New York, 1975.

Hobsbawm, Eric. *Bandits.* 1969. Rev. ed. New York, 1981.

Hoffer, Peter C., and N. E. H. Hull. *Murdering Mothers: Infanticide in England and New England, 1558–1803.* New York and London, 1981.

Johnson, Eric A. *Urbanization and Crime: Germany, 1871–1914.* Cambridge, U.K., and New York, 1995.

Johnson, Eric A., and Eric H. Monkkonen, eds. *The Civilization of Crime: Violence in Town and Country since the Middle Ages.* Urbana, Ill., 1996.

Küther, Carsten. *Räuber und Gaunerbanden in Deutschland.* Göttingen, Germany, 1976.

Muchembled, Robert. *La violence au village: Sociabilité et comportements populaires en Artois du XVe au XVIIe siècle.* Turnhout, Belgium, 1989.

Österberg, Eva, and Dag Lindström. *Crime and Social Control in Medieval and Early Modern Swedish Towns.* Uppsala, Sweden, 1988.

Roeck, Bernd. *Aussenseiter, Randgruppen, Minderheiten: Fremde im Deutschland der frühen Neuzeit.* Göttingen, Germany, 1993.

Rule, John, and Roger Wells. *Crime, Protest, and Popular Politics in Southern England, 1740–1850.* London, 1997.

Schulte, Regina. *The Village in Court: Arson, Infanticide, and Poaching in the Court Records of Upper Bavaria.* Cambridge, U.K., 1994.

Schwerhoff, Gerd. *Köln im Kreuzverhör: Kriminalität, Herrschaft, und Gesellschaft in einer frühneuzeitlichen Stadt.* Bonn and Berlin, 1991.

Sharpe, J. A. *Crime in Early Modern England, 1550–1750.* 2d ed. London and New York, 1984.

Spierenburg, Pieter. *The Prison Experience: Disciplinary Institutions and Their Inmates in Early Modern Europe.* New Brunswick, N.J., and London, 1991.

Spierenburg, Pieter. *The Spectacle of Suffering: Executions and the Evolution of Repression: From a Preindustrial Metropolis to the European Experience.* Cambridge, U.K., and New York, 1984.

Spierenburg, Pieter, ed. *Men and Violence: Gender, Honor, and Rituals in Modern Europe and America.* Columbus, Ohio, 1998.

Tobias, J. J. *Crime and Industrial Society in the Nineteenth Century.* London, 1967.

Ulbricht, Otto. *Kindsmord und Aufklärung in Deutschland.* Munich, 1990.

Wiltenburg, Joy. *Disorderly Women and Female Power in the Street Literature of Early Modern England and Germany.* Charlottesville, Va., 1992.

PROSTITUTION

Kathryn Norberg

The history of "the oldest profession" falls into four broad periods characterized by changes in the policing and organization of the sex trade: municipal regulation between 1300 and 1500, criminalization between 1500 and 1800, medical regulation between 1800 and 1890, and recriminalization from 1890 to 1975.

1300–1500: MUNICIPAL REGULATION

In the late Middle Ages, prostitution was tolerated, indeed encouraged by municipal elites throughout Europe. Prostitutes did not inhabit the margins of late medieval society; they were accepted members of the community with a special place in ritual life. In Germany, prostitutes were honored guests at weddings, and in Lyon they participated in municipal processions and festivals that defined civic space. Prostitutes were full members of medieval society because the city fathers considered them guarantors of domestic order. Like Saint Augustine (354–430), the fifteenth-century city fathers believed that prostitution was a lesser evil, an acceptable alternative to adultery or the rape of virgins. The brothel for these good Catholics provided an outlet for male sexual energy that might otherwise be directed at honest women. That most of the official prostitutes had compromised their virtue—or been raped by bands of young men—also soothed the burghers' conscience.

During the late Middle Ages and early Renaissance, officially sanctioned and regulated red light districts existed in most large European cities. In Florence, respectable citizens like the Medici owned the city's bordellos, and a special court known as the *onesta* moderated disputes between prostitutes and bordello owners. The situation in England was roughly similar. By the early fifteenth century port cities like Southampton and Sandwich had red light districts where prostitution flourished. In London prostitution was illegal save in the Bankside or Southwark neighborhood, where bordellos or "stewes" could be found as early as the thirteenth century. By 1500 the sex trade was the principal economic activity of this area, tolerated and regulated by the local authorities.

On the Continent, town governments actually owned and administered bordellos. Always pressed for ready cash, city governments usually auctioned off the right to run the bordello to an individual known variously as *Frauernwirt*, bordello padre, or abbess. Contracts between brothel managers and city governments can be found in the records of Strasbourg (1469), Munich (1433), Seville (1469), and Toulouse (1296). In return for a certain sum of money, the brothel manager had the right to charge the prostitutes for room and board and take as much of their earnings as he could. The city did oblige the brothel manager to observe certain regulations governing the hours and the clientele of the brothel. Most cities insisted that the municipal bordello be closed on religious feast days and that priests, Jews, and married men be banned at all times. The municipalities also fined prostitutes who lingered too long with a particular man so that clients did not become too attached to any woman.

In the streets next to the city brothel, a host of unofficial whores solicited in unlicensed drinking establishments. These unlicensed prostitutes tended to be younger, less experienced, and more expensive than the inmates of the official brothel. They were also a source of distress to the city fathers, who considered them illegal and uncontrollable. City governments in southern France, Seville, London, and Augsburg levied heavy fines on these women, whose numbers tended to proliferate as the sixteenth century approached.

1500–1829: CRIMINALIZATION

In the mid-sixteenth century, the medieval world of tolerated, municipally regulated prostitution came to an abrupt end. Criminalization replaced tolerance and city fathers closed the municipal brothels in Augsburg (1532), Basel (1534), and Frankfurt (1560). Spain followed suit somewhat later; Seville closed its bordello in 1621. Events were not so dramatic in Italy.

In a Brothel. Frontispiece by Crispin de Passe to *Miroir des plus belle courtisanes de ce temps (The Looking-glass of the fairest courtiers of these tymes)*, seventeenth century (NE 670 P2 MS. 1631, Cage, frontis.). BY PERMISSION OF THE FOLGER SHAKESPEARE LIBRARY, WASHINGTON, D.C.

Though they never officially closed the red light districts, authorities in Florence and Venice adopted a more stringent attitude toward prostitutes after 1511 and tried to suppress all manifestations of venal sex. Throughout Europe, authorities tried to eliminate clandestine prostitutes or at least limit where they could solicit. In France the 1560 ordinance of Orléans made owning and operating a bordello illegal. In Spain Philip IV officially banned brothels throughout his kingdom in 1623. By 1650 the municipal bordello, whether in France, Italy, or Germany, was a thing of the past.

Historians have been at pains to explain this change in attitude. Syphilis, which appeared in Europe in the spring of 1495, at first seemed to provide an answer. Europeans certainly understood how the disease was contracted and knew that prostitutes spread it. But most of the bordello closings occurred some thirty years after the worst syphilis epidemics, which occurred between 1495 and 1510. And in one case, Seville, a serious bout of venereal disease in 1568 led the city authorities to reopen, not abolish, the municipal bordello and its regulations.

What caused the closing of the official brothels? Religious change (not disease) appears to have been the single most important factor in changing attitudes toward prostitution. In Germany, Martin Luther

(1483–1546) condemned prostitution and criticized Saint Augustine's rationalization of mercenary sex. Luther and the other Protestant reformers believed that men were to be held to the same standard—chastity—as women and that the bordello, far from discouraging fornication, promoted the ruin of the young. Devout Catholics also railed against whores: in 1566 Pope Pius V threw all the courtesans out of Rome, and in 1556 the Venetian Republic made prostitution a crime. Moralists began to see in the whores a threat to honest women and the matrimonial order. In the Rhone valley, preachers in the 1480s condemned prostitution and with it the municipal bordello, which they regarded as a source of temptation and sin. Though it occurred later than elsewhere, a similar new morality led to the end of toleration in Spain. In Seville, Catholic reformers launched a campaign to reform prostitutes which led in 1620 to the closing of the municipal brothel.

Religious revival, whether in the form of the Protestant or Catholic Reformations, contributed to the criminalization of prostitution, but it did not cause it. Official bordellos were in trouble long before Martin Luther. In 1501 the city fathers of Frankfurt tried to auction off the management of the local brothel but they found no takers: the municipal house was no longer profitable. Too much competition had driven it out of business. The multiplication of clandestine prostitutes appears to have been the problem. In Spain, Italy, France, and Germany a rash of decrees banning clandestine prostitutes preceded the official brothel closings, indicating that new sexual attitudes and practices had made the public brothel obsolete even before religious reformers attacked it.

The proliferation of independent prostitutes indicates an important change in clients' taste: men no longer wanted to go to the public house and rub shoulders with a mixed, even dangerous crowd which was now made up of armed men—that is, soldiers. The large armies called into existence by the early modern state revolutionized prostitution and made it almost a branch of the military. Now hordes of prostitutes followed the armies that traversed Europe. No municipal regulation, not even military discipline, could control these women, who spread disease to the most powerful armies. In Strasbourg, Frankfurt, and Nürnberg, local authorities tried to disband the prostitutes who camped outside the city walls and prostituted themselves to soldiers in nearby forests. But they were powerless to rid the town of these unwanted visitors.

These women and their unruly clients made a mockery of Augustine's lesser evil: they did not guarantee the domestic order, they disrupted it. So too did another new kind of prostitute who posed an even more serious threat—the courtesan. In the late 1400s, preachers in Dijon, Venice, and Florence railed against a better sort of harlot, one who wore fine clothes and plied her trade secretly, a prostitute who seduced respectable men and distracted them from their domestic duties. This woman was called a courtesan, after the genteel women who accompanied the celibate clerics of Rome's papal court on their social rounds. A few of the Italian courtesans were women of letters, like the Venetian poetess Veronica Franco (1546–1591) or the Roman writer Tullia d'Aragona (1510–1556). These women offered more than sex, they offered eroticism—sex with an elegant and accomplished expert.

The courtesan, be she a Venetian poetess or a Parisian actress, enjoyed more independence and certainly more money than her camp follower or bordello sister. These privileged women probably benefited from the criminalization of prostitution, for they were independent entrepreneurs who escaped the brothel and its regulations. But not all early modern prostitutes were so lucky. The disadvantages produced by criminalization probably outweighed the advantages enjoyed by a minority. Criminalization made the prostitute vulnerable to third parties who profited from the prostitutes' need for secrecy and her fear of the police. Pimps, procuresses, touts, landlords, and blackmailers skimmed money off the prostitutes' earnings and diminished their autonomy.

Worse still were the police and other judicial authorities. By 1720 virtually all cities in Europe had adopted ordinances condemning prostitutes and subjecting them to harsh prison terms. In Paris the edict of 20 April 1684 was followed by a series of laws (1713, 1724, 1734, 1776, and 1778) that made prostitution punishable by incarceration in a syphilis hospital or prison for between three months and three years. To the east, Vienna and Prussia had stiffer penalties. In 1690 Frederick I of Prussia ordered all the bordellos closed and their inmates publicly flogged. Somewhat later, in 1750, Empress Maria Teresa established a Chastity Commission which also closed bordellos, arrested prostitutes, and sentenced them to labor as street sweepers.

Unlike its absolutist neighbors, the English Crown did not seek to repress prostitution. No English statutes made prostitution itself criminal. London constables could arrest streetwalkers on lesser charges like vagrancy or loitering, but most were disinclined to do so. In the first third of the eighteenth century, a series of private groups appeared to supplement police repression. Known collectively as the Societies for the Reform of Manners, these moral vigilantes waged open war against prostitution, homosexuality, and other forms of "riot" from 1690 to 1730. Though utterly without authority, members detained women and had them thrown in the Bridewell or a special prison for prostitutes where hard work was prescribed as an antidote to sin.

By 1730 the moral vigilantes had disappeared. Everywhere in Europe, police enforcement of antiprostitute statutes became lax and episodic. In major cities, certain districts—Covent Garden in London and the Palais-Royal in Paris—were set aside for prostitution, and whores congregated around public promenades, pleasure gardens, and theaters. The large numbers of streetwalkers and prostitutes testified to the lack of police enforcement. Nicolas Edme Restif de la Bretonne (1734–1806), a French writer, estimated that 20,000 women prostituted themselves in Paris, a city of some 600,000 souls. Restif's figures are almost certainly exaggerated, but it is clear that prostitutes were numerous because preindustrial women's work was particularly conducive to prostitution. Women who washed, mended linen, or sold food or secondhand clothes walked the streets, soliciting clients whether for honest or dishonest work. Once the woman had found a client, she was generally expected to bring the cleaned linen or food to his room, thereby facilitating sexual contact. A woman could prostitute

Punishment of Prostitutes. *Transport of Prostitutes to the Salpêtrière Prison* by Étienne Jeaurat (1699–1789). MUSÉE CARNAVALET, PARIS/©COLLECTION VIOLLET/THE BRIDGEMAN ART LIBRARY

herself without anybody, especially nosy neighbors, being the wiser. Full-time bordello inmates had a more difficult time hiding their occupation, but they could reenter the world of honest work with little or no trouble. Single women's work was casual and episodic, so it easily accommodated venal sex.

Only arrest labeled a woman as a prostitute, and arrest was becoming less and less common as a more tolerant attitude toward prostitution emerged. A decline in religiosity as well as a growing concern over venereal disease prompted this change. As early as 1724, Bernard de Mandeville (1670–1733) argued in *A Modest Defense of Public Stews* that prostitution was not criminal in and of itself. It was only dangerous when uncontrolled. Other, less well known authors called for the end to arbitrary penalties and the institution of regulation as a means of protecting families and promoting public order. Particularly prominent among these regulationists were physicians who regarded venereal disease as the greatest hazard of prostitution and proposed that some system of health checks be instituted.

Such publications proved prophetic. In 1792 Berlin instituted a system for regulating prostitutes which required police approval before a brothel could

be opened and compelled prostitutes to live in certain streets. Somewhat later, in 1796, the Paris Commune instructed its police officials to search out and register prostitutes. Registered prostitutes received a card, and in 1798 two physicians were given the task of examining Parisian whores. In 1802 a physician established a dispensary where prostitutes underwent compulsory examinations. Napoleon's prefects continued the struggle to contain and control prostitution. In Lyon, Nantes, Marseille, and other French cities, local officials undertook a census of prostitutes and bordellos. They also limited prostitution to a few preselected streets and required that all bordellos be registered— in other words, approved. At the fall of Napoleon, the foundations of a complete regulatory system existed.

1800–1890: MEDICAL REGULATION

In the nineteenth century, many European cities instituted an elaborate system of ordinances which permitted prostitution but limited and monitored it. These ordinances resembled Napoleon's measures: while there were variations, medical regulation was often referred to as "the French system." And as in

France, authorities claimed to be controlling syphilis. But the measures enacted also greatly increased the ability of the police to monitor working-class activity, sexual or political. The father and principal apologist of the regulatory system was the French social hygienist Alexandre Jean Baptiste Parent-Duchâtelet (1790–1836). In 1836 Parent-Duchâtelet published *Prostitution in Paris*, a two-volume study rife with statistics, tables, maps, and charts. *Prostitution in Paris* was the first "scientific" study of mercenary sex, for it used empirical evidence—principally Parent-Duchâtelet's own observations at the Parisian dispensary—to describe prostitution. Parent-Duchâtelet estimated that there were twelve thousand prostitutes in Paris, and he collected detailed data (including hair and eye color) on about one thousand.

For the first time we have a relatively accurate portrait of the prostitute. Parent-Duchâtelet found her to be between the ages of eighteen and twenty-four and a working woman engaged in traditional, as opposed to industrial, occupations (i.e., a seamstress or domestic). To his contemporaries' astonishment, she was usually a native Parisian (as opposed to a migrant) and almost never the fruit of an illegitimate union. Nor was she herself pregnant at the time she became a prostitute. The cherished scenario of the country girl seduced and abandoned in the city did not hold up to Parent-Duchâtelet's scrutiny; neither did the myths that prostitutes were infertile or possessed of biological abnormalities. Later in the nineteenth century, physicians would attribute prostitution to genetic deformities, but Parent-Duchâtelet gave social reasons for a woman's fall. "Lack of work and poverty," he wrote, "which is the inevitable consequence of low wages, are the unhappy source of prostitution."

Despite his scientific pretensions, Parent-Duchâtelet was no impartial observer. On the contrary, he was an ardent supporter of regulation, and his study argued for the imposition of mandatory health checks and an increase in police supervision. Like all regulationists, Parent-Duchâtelet believed that prostitutes had to be closely monitored and controlled, ostensibly in the interest of containing venereal disease.

The mandatory health check or pelvic examination was the linchpin of the regulationist system. When a prostitute went to the dispensary her name was inscribed upon a register and she was issued a card on which each subsequent visit was marked. This card constituted a license, which allowed her to prostitute herself. Failure to display the card when questioned by the police would lead to immediate imprisonment without trial or judicial recourse. Obviously,

regulation greatly increased the powers of the Parisian police. It is certainly not coincidental that nineteenth- and early twentieth-century French legislatures declined to approve—or even debate—regulation. For its entire existence, regulation was at best only semilegal; it was based on administrative decree alone, on the decision of the highest police officer, the prefect.

If the health check was the linchpin of regulation, then the brothel was its center. Proregulation physicians and policemen encouraged brothels because they facilitated police control. Madames enforced discipline and health checks, and the brothel walls assured that no prostitute escaped the all-seeing eye of the morals squad. If the brothel was transparent to the police, it was all but invisible to honest women and children. Municipal ordinance prescribed closed shutters and windows and permitted no distinct signs save the lone discreet red light. To ensure that these regulations were observed, the police both in Paris and the provinces bestowed licenses to run brothels only on certain individuals. Only women over twenty-five years of age could apply for a license, and they had to give proof that the owner of the building in question knew of its proposed use. Brothels could be located only in certain neighborhoods, had to be at least one hundred meters from public buildings, schools, and churches, and could be open only at certain times.

The bordello was the centerpiece of regulation, and it flourished in the home of regulation—France. In 1840 Paris had at least 230 licensed brothels. Provincial France too had "houses of tolerance," as official brothels were known. Montpellier, with a population of approximately 460,000, had twenty-four houses of tolerance, while Angers and Mans had fifteen and twenty-five, respectively. Usually these were small establishments with no more than seven prostitutes, excluding the auxiliary female personnel (maids and cooks), who also satisfied clients at times of high traffic, like market days or when new recruits were called up by the army. Outside France, the bordello was less popular. In 1881 there were only 1,119 brothels in the whole of Italy.

In the course of the nineteenth century, some kind of regulation was adopted by Italy (1860), Russia (1843), Prussia (1839), and Vienna. Officially, England did not follow suit. But between 1864 and 1886 the British War Office and Admiralty administered a series of ordinances that came very close to continental regulation. The Contagious Diseases Acts, as these ordinances became known, were meant to eliminate venereal disease by compulsory registration and medical exams, and the laws were enacted only in garrison towns and ports like Southampton and

Nineteenth-Century Brothel. *Reception Room in the Brothel on the Rue des Moulins,* painting (oil on cardboard) by Henri de Toulouse-Lautrec (1864–1901). MUSÉE TOULOUSE-LAUTREC, ALBI, FRANCE/ERICH LESSING/ART RESOURCE, NY

Plymouth. In these towns, a special police unit called the "water police" tracked down prostitutes and confined them in venereal disease prisons, known as lock hospitals.

The effects of regulation, whether in England or on the Continent, were highly detrimental to prostitutes, perhaps more detrimental than seventeenth- and eighteenth-century criminalization. To be sure, prostitutes could solicit if they had registered with the police and undergone the required health checks. But even registered, they also had to obey an array of ordinances which made it all but impossible for a woman to support herself through prostitution. In France and England prostitutes could not solicit in drinking establishments or near barracks. In Paris they could not occupy sidewalks or major thoroughfares except between seven and eleven o'clock in the evening. They could not stand near churches, schools, public buildings, or in public gardens. Prostitutes could not congregate in groups, speak in loud voices, or provide food or drink in their homes. In short, women could not solicit clients, which is tantamount to banning prostitution.

Far from removing the legal constraints on prostitutes, regulation only increased them. It subjected the prostitute to a more powerful, more invasive police force, thereby throwing her into the arms of pimps and other third parties. It also fixed her identity as a fallen woman by inscribing her name on a register. Regulation subjected prostitutes to consistent police harassment, to social stigma, and to economic hardship.

RECRIMINALIZATION:
1890 TO THE PRESENT

By 1880 the weaknesses of regulation caused many Europeans to turn against the system. Sometimes this movement—or rather movements, for there were many diverse opinions and groups—is called abolitionist because it opposed the existing prostitute statutes. However, it is more accurate to call its proponents antiregulationists, for they sought to reform, not abolish, laws against prostitution. None wanted to legalize or decriminalize prostitution. Most antiregulationists regarded prostitution as a terrible moral scourge and dire biological threat.

Of all the antiregulationists, the British militant Josephine Butler (1828–1906) was alone in manifesting real concern for individual prostitutes. Butler was a middle-class widow of deep religious sensibilities who considered the compulsory pelvic examinations imposed by the Contagious Diseases Acts (CDA) an affront to womanhood. In numerous public speeches, Butler pointed out that soldiers and sailors were not subject to the same invasive procedures, and she called for an end to the exams which she considered "instrumental rape." Through the Ladies' National Association, she mobilized middle-class women to fight against the CDA and aid prostitutes. This unprecedented alliance between middle-class and working-class women staged theatrical "rescues" of prostitutes and succeeded in galvanizing public opinion. In 1886 the CDA were rescinded, and many of Butler's crusaders turned their attention to women's suffrage.

Opposition to regulation did not end, Butler's success encouraged continental opponents of regulation. French abolitionists like Yves Guyot and Senator René Bérenger criticized not the excesses of the system but its inefficiencies. Of particular concern were the clandestine prostitutes, the large number of women who were never inscribed, never examined, and never monitored by the police. By 1890 they had come to represent more than half of the prostitutes in Paris, and they were thought to constitute a threat to the health and moral welfare of society.

The white slavery panic struck in the midst of this debate. In 1885 London journalist W. T. Stead (1849–1912) published an inflammatory account of child prostitution entitled "The Maiden Tribute to Modern Babylon" in the *Pall Mall Gazette*. Stead reported that lecherous old men regularly purchased children for five pounds on the streets of London. Stead's lurid accounts started the white slavery panic, which eventually spread from England to the Continent. In 1899 the first international conference on white slavery was convened in London and attended by the representatives of eleven European nations. Three years later sixteen countries sent envoys to the second international conference.

Historians once dismissed the white slavery panic as nothing but hysteria. The antitraffickers' rhetoric was extravagant—one French newspaper claimed that more girls had been killed by white slavers than by tuberculosis—but these zealots were reacting to real changes in the demand for and organization of prostitution. The great migrations of the late nineteenth and early twentieth centuries from Europe to the Americas created both a high demand for prostitutes and the networks to transport them from Europe to the New World. In Poland, for instance, Jewish vice networks grew as Jewish emigration increased. Once limited to Warsaw, Jewish pimps expanded their operations to embrace North and especially South America. In the 1910s many prostitutes in Buenos Aires were Jewish girls transported there by Jewish mafias operating in Poland and the Americas.

The great migrations also fed racism and with it biological explanations for prostitution. Friedrich Engels (1820–1895) did argue that prostitution was a product of private property, along with illegitimacy and other moral scourges. But socialists aside, most Europeans preferred the physiological fantasies of Caesare Lombroso (1835–1909) to the economic explanations of Engels or Parent-Duchâtelet. According to Lombroso and his followers, prostitutes were born, not made, and they possessed atavistic qualities like small heads, husky voices, or tattoos. To Lombroso, prostitutes were degenerates who threatened the biological integrity of the race by injecting hereditary syphilis into the population.

The early years of the twentieth century saw important advances in the diagnosis and treatment of venereal disease. But the Wasserman test and the arsenic-based "606" potion did not allay the fear of syphilis. Quite the contrary: anxiety over venereal disease became more widespread and intense during the interwar period. In France hereditary syphilis was blamed for (among other things) chronic French depopulation. Whether in France, Germany, or Britain, "degeneracy" was associated with syphilis, and prostitutes were subject to stricter measures of medical surveillance than ever before. In France the number of dispensaries where prostitutes were registered and examined multiplied: by 1940 there were over 2,000.

Other purely punitive measures joined these medical statutes. In 1885 the British Parliament passed the deceptively named Criminal Amendments Acts, which raised the age of consent and authorized the police to enter bordellos and arrest "seducers" (and prostitutes) at will. In France the law of 3 April 1903 made traffic in women punishable by three years of prison.

In many instances, special laws were enacted to "protect" minors. In England the Industrial Schools Amendment Act of 1880 authorized police search and seizure of underage prostitutes. In France the law of 11 April 1908 licensed similar police sweeps and provided special reformatories for the underage prostitutes. These statutes, like many others, targeted youth and probably reflected anxiety over the new freedom that life in the cities and the rise of service industries accorded young women.

Not just the young were experiencing a sexual revolution. During the 1890s, a new taste for seduction and eroticism manifested itself in the population at large and had a profound impact on prostitution. The demand for prostitutes changed: sexual need no longer brought the client to the prostitute. In most cities, workingmen had established their own homes and embraced a middle-class conjugal lifestyle. Henceforth, desire rather than need motivated the client, and he demanded more personal, more seductive forms of venal sex. The regulated house of tolerance, for example, tended to disappear. Beginning in the 1880s in Paris and 1900 in the provinces, official bordellos closed; by 1935 there were only twenty-seven official houses in Paris. Clients preferred the illusion of seduction to the regimentation of the bordello and the independent prostitute to the brothel inmate. Now men encountered prostitutes in new places, like the dance hall or the beer garden. Once contact was made, the client accompanied her to a new institution, the *maison de rendez-vous* or hotel that rented rooms by the hour. Gradually, the *maison de rendez-vous* completely eclipsed the bordello: in 1935 there were sixty-five recognized hotels in Paris and many more that had escaped police notice.

With the demise of the house of tolerance, prostitutes gained a measure of autonomy. Unlike brothel inmates, the independent prostitute was not enslaved by debt or forced to work long hours. But new forms of domination arose to replace the old. Stricter criminal statutes and police surveillance increased the need for secrecy and opened the door to parasitical third parties. In London, pimps first appeared in large numbers in the 1900s in the wake of anti–white slavery legislation. Isolated from the working class and marked as a "professional," the prostitute found herself at the mercy of criminal elements. In France and Italy hotel owners replaced bordello madames as the managers of prostitution and used their power to extract more work and longer hours from the prostitute. In some cities mafias and crime syndicates took control of prostitution and subjected prostitutes to a new, harsh work discipline.

Life was no better for the prostitute in the Soviet Union or the totalitarian states of Italy and Germany. In 1918 the Russian revolutionaries abolished the regulatory system which had prevailed in tsarist Russia and proclaimed that prostitution, an outgrowth of capitalism, no longer existed. Of course, women continued to sell sex, and they were subject to arrest under a series of ordinances prosecuting vagrants and antisocials. In the late 1920s, special workhouses or *propholactoria* were established where prostitutes were reeducated through forced labor.

In the fascist states, the approach was different in form if not in spirit. Mussolini reconfirmed Italy's tolerated brothels in 1923, 1931, and 1940. In Germany, the Nazis reinstated regulated brothels and made sure that strict racial and biological hygiene was observed within them. Throughout Europe, the militarization of society during World War II encouraged a brief, episodic return to regulation.

The years between 1945 and 1972 saw a recriminalization of prostitution that was both profound and paradoxical. In 1951 the United Nations adopted a resolution condemning the traffic in women and calling for an end to state regulation and criminalization of prostitution. Only five nations signed the resolution and most ignored it. In France, while one aspect of the old regulationist regime—the brothel— was abolished in 1945 by the so-called Marthe Richard law, another—compulsory registration—survived. A national health file was established, and any prostitute who failed to register was subject to arrest and imprisonment. Further, the law of 23 December 1958 recognized "passive solicitation" and made it a misdemeanor punishable by a steep fine. As in the past, French prostitutes were subject to police harassment and unpredictable official persecution.

In Italy the Merlin Law of 1956 abolished all forms of regulation, including registration, but prescribed jail terms for individuals convicted of "favoring" prostitution. While ostensibly directed against pimps, the law was used to harass prostitutes, who saw their husbands, boyfriends, and fellow prostitutes prosecuted under it.

In England the situation was no better. Unlike continental Europe, the United Kingdom had known neither true regulation nor even real criminalization: prostitution was not—and had never been—a criminal offense. This situation changed in the 1950s when the Wolfenden Committee recommended a set of new anti–sex trade laws. In 1956 the Sexual Offense Act prohibited brothel keeping and prescribed stiff penalties for those living off immoral earnings.

As in Italy, the antipimping law was turned against prostitutes themselves, and the notorious Street Offences Act of 1959 made the situation worse. According to this act, a woman could be convicted of soliciting on the word of a policeman alone and forced to pay a stiff fine. After two fines a woman was labeled a "prostitute" in all judicial documents for life, whether or not she continued to engage in sex work.

While prostitution was being recriminalized in France and England, a new approach was adopted in northern Europe, specifically in Holland and Germany. In Germany officially tolerated and regulated brothels called Eros Centers were established in Hamburg (1967) and subsequently in Bonn, Cologne, Stuttgart, and Munich. While these centers were supposed to eliminate third parties and curb violence, prostitutes declined to work in them because of the extreme regimentation and high room rental fees. In Holland a different, more laissez-faire approach emerged, with brothels and massage parlors being unofficially tolerated, at least in Amsterdam.

Amsterdam aside, the recriminalization of prostitution had a predictable consequence: prostitution went underground and became less visible. The telephone greatly facilitated this process, and today prostitution is all but invisible in most western European cities. Police surveillance and occasional harassment continues and is particularly harsh for those prostitutes left on the streets. These women constitute only 20 percent of the sex workers in most European cities, and yet they account for over 90 percent of the arrests. Even in the most lenient countries, fines and legal fees keep most prostitutes in debt and on the street. To protest these conditions, fifty prostitutes occupied the Saint-Nizier church in Lyon, France, in 1975. Soon prostitutes' groups arose in Grenoble, Montpellier, Toulouse, and finally Paris, leading to the creation of a national organization, the French Collective of Prostitutes. Not long thereafter, other prostitutes' rights groups emerged: in the United Kingdom, the English Collective of Prostitutes (1975); in Amsterdam, the Red Thread (1984); and in Berlin, HYDRA (1980), to name but a few. All of these groups are active today and campaign for the decriminalization of sex work in both national and international law. In 1985 the first International Congress of Whores convened in Amsterdam and addressed a range of issues—AIDS, police harassment, international traffic in women—concerning sex workers. Subsequent congresses have been held, signaling the advent of a new era in the history of prostitution: henceforth, prostitutes themselves will have a say in the organization and policing of the "oldest profession."

See also **Sexual Behavior and Sexual Morality; Illegitimacy and Concubinage; Sex, Law, and the State** *(volume 4)*.

BIBLIOGRAPHY

Bernstein, Laurie. *Sonia's Daughters: Prostitutes and Their Regulation in Imperial Russia.* Berkeley, Calif., 1995.

Bristow, Edward. *Prostitution and Prejudice: The Jewish Fight against White Slavery, 1880–1939.* Oxford, 1982.

Bullough, Vern, and Bonnie Bullough. *Women and Prostitution: A Social History.* Buffalo, N.Y., 1987.

Corbin, Alain. *Women for Hire: Prostitution and Sexuality in France after 1850.* Translated by Alan Sheridan. Cambridge, Mass., 1990.

Gibson, Mary. *Prostitution and the State in Italy, 1860–1915.* New Brunswick, N.J., 1986.

Harsin, Jill. *Policing Prostitution in Nineteenth-Century Paris.* Princeton, N.J., 1985.

Jenness, Valerie. *Making It Work: The Prostitute's Rights Movement in Perspective.* New York, 1993.

Karras, Ruth Mazo. *Common Women: Prostitution and Sexuality in Medieval England.* Oxford, 1996.

Otis, Leah Lydia. *Prostitution in Medieval Society.* Chicago, 1985.

Perry, Mary Elizabeth. *Gender and Disorder in Early Modern Seville.* Princeton, N.J., 1990.

Quétel, Claude. *A History of Syphilis.* Translated by Judith Braddock and Brian Pike. Baltimore, 1990.

Roper, Lyndal. "Discipline and Respectability: Prostitution and Reformation in Augsburg." *History Workshop* 19 (1985): 3–28.

Rossiaud, Jacques. *Medieval Prostitution.* Translated by Lydia G. Cochrane. New York, 1988.

Solé, Jacques. *L'age d'or de la prostitution: de 1870 à nos jours.* Paris, 1993.

Trexler, Richard C. "La prostitution florentine au XVe siècle: patronages et clientèles." *Annales: économies, sociétés, civilisations* 36 (1981): 983–1015.

Walkowitz, Judith R. *Prostitution and Victorian Society: Women, Class, and the State.* Cambridge, U.K., 1980.

WITCHCRAFT

J. A. Sharpe

Witchcraft is a subject that has attracted considerable scholarly attention as well as a lively popular interest, and around which a number of historical myths have gathered. Most of the scholarly work on this phenomenon has, understandably, centered on the era of mass persecutions, the so-called European witch craze, between about 1450 and 1750. Work on this period has produced an extensive and ever-expanding body of publications rich in varied, imaginative, and exciting interpretations. Yet beliefs in witchcraft, themselves part of a wider intellectual framework incorporating popular magic and what the modern observer would categorize as folklore, have been present in Europe throughout recorded history.

The terms "witchcraft" and "magic" have, of course, been used broadly and present considerable definitional problems. In 1937 the anthropologist E. E. Evans-Pritchard proposed a widely accepted set of definitions that attempts to distinguish clearly between witchcraft and magic. He argued, in effect, that witchcraft is normally thought of as an innate quality, probably inherited by the supposed witch, and is used primarily to inflict harm through the occult power of the witch's ill will. Magic, conversely, involves a number of techniques, and the ability to carry out these techniques is not inherited but rather acquired through learning.

It might be possible to sustain something like this distinction when dealing with witchcraft as a phenomenon in European history. Observers in 1600, for example, generally accepted a difference between the witch, normally female, illiterate, and lower class, and the magician, often learned, sometimes a member if the social elite, and nearly always male. Yet the village witch always existed in the intellectual context of a culture that enjoyed much wider beliefs in the magical, the occult, and the supernatural, and throughout the medieval and early modern periods terms that translate as witchcraft, sorcery, or magic tended to be used interchangeably. Witchcraft is, therefore, best understood as a broad range of beliefs and practices that flourished within a wider belief system that accepted the supernatural.

As noted, witchcraft attracts popular interest and has been surrounded by more than its fair share of historical myths. The problems resulting from this became increasingly marked in the twentieth century by the emergence of Wiccan and Pagan groups that adhered to witchcraft as an ancient, pre-Christian religion. While having no wish to offend people's religious sensibilities, one should point out that there is little evidence that what was described or persecuted as witchcraft in the medieval or early modern periods was an organized religion—though admittedly a number of contemporary theorists thought it was—and that the practices of Pagans and Wiccans have only tenuous connections with peasant beliefs of the fifteenth or sixteenth centuries. Modern witchcraft, despite its claims, seems to have little historical foundation.

The subject of witchcraft was also firmly lodged in the mentalities of learned writers in late medieval and early modern Europe, when it was referred to frequently in theological, medical, and scientific writing. Along with the peasant belief in witchcraft, demonological writers from the fifteenth century onward created a view of the subject that stressed the importance of the demonic pact, the witches' sabbat, and the notion that the witch was a member of an organized, heretical, satanic sect. Peasants had witchcraft, and members of the elite had natural magic, a set of occult ideas and practices that often attracted men of considerable intelligence and learning. The latter was closely connected to pursuits such as astrology and alchemy as well as to mathematics, astronomy, and science. Witchcraft existed in relation to a broad, rich, intellectual context.

FROM THE DARK AGES TO THE *MALLEUS MALEFICARUM*

Anthropologists have demonstrated that belief in witchcraft and associated phenomena was present in a wide range of societies and likely has been a part of the mental world of Europeans from the earliest times. As might be expected, however, evidence for early witch-craft beliefs and practices has to be drawn mainly from the works of Greek and, more important, Roman writers. The concept of *magia,* which seems to have corresponded roughly to medieval and early modern magic, was familiar in ancient Rome and compre-hended sorcery and witchcraft. Certainly by the end of the Roman period something like the witch image, so common in the sixteenth and seventeenth centu-ries, already existed. Consider the following descrip-tion given by the poet Lucan (A.D. 39–65) in his *Pharsalia* (book 6, lines 511–523):

> The gods of heaven, and the fact that she was still living, did not prevent her from hearing the silent converse of the dead, or from knowing the dwell-ing places of hell and the mysteries of subterranean Pluto. The witch's face is haggard and loathsome with age; her dreadful countenance, overlaid with a hellish pallor and weighed down by uncombed locks, is never seen in the clear sky; but if storms and black clouds take away the stars, she then comes forth from robbed tombs and tries to catch the night-time light-nings. Her tread blights the seeds of the fertile corn-field, and her breath poisons air that was previously innocuous.

The stereotype of the witch as the hag, the elderly, worn, and probably lower-class woman, clearly dates back to classical culture.

The problem of magic, witchcraft, sorcery, and the occult became somewhat more complex with the beginning of the era of the Christian conversions in about the fourth century. The realities of the situation meant that, despite the reservations of some Christian thinkers, the early church had to make a number of accommodations with the pagan religions it sought to supplant. Thus churches were built on or near the sites of pagan worship, saints' shrines were located in pagan holy places, and Christianity incorporated many aspects of the preexisting practices surrounding divi-nation, prophecy, and folk healing. The "magic of the medieval church" obviously helped make Christianity accessible and acceptable to the bulk of the popula-tion, although it never quite escaped the censure of religious purists. The learned held some practices un-warrantable despite an inherently ill-defined line be-tween the sacred and the profane. Partly as a result of this lack of definition, occasional charges of sorcery arose, and certain people, because of their actions or public opinion, were considered appropriate targets for accusations of witchcraft. Conversely, early law codes suggest that at least some rulers regarded accu-sations of witchcraft as ungodly and disruptive and consequently attempted to discourage them among their populations.

Certainly the religious observers upon whose writings much of our knowledge of early medieval Europe is founded were convinced that their world was full of magical practitioners, denounced variously as *praecantatores, sortilegos, karagios, aruspices, divinos, ariolos, magos, maleficos, inantantores, phitonocos,* or *ve-neficos.* (The terms defy precise or consistent transla-tion.) For these writers, however, the problem was still that occult practitioners offered a type of magic that competed with that of the church. They were diviners, fortune tellers, lot casters, and faith healers rather than malefic witches. The malefic existed, of course, but the tendency was to regard witchcraft and associated popular magical beliefs as a sign of ignorance and su-perstition rather than the presence of demonic influ-ences. Occasionally writings refer to witches being punished, like the tenth-century note of a woman proved guilty of witchcraft who was drowned "as is the custom with witches." But most stories about witchcraft end with a description of the clergy deploy-ing saints' relics or other holy items to defeat the witch's magic rather than with a description of execution.

This situation was to change during the fif-teenth century. The exact processes involved remain perhaps a little unclear, but three main factors seem to have been at work. First, there was a general theo-logical shift, perhaps as a by-product of the psycho-logical impact of the Black Death of the mid-four-teenth century, which emphasized the uncertainty of human life, the pervasiveness of sin, and the power and influence of the Devil. Second, in a series of treason-cum-sorcery cases among Europe's political elite, highly placed persons were found guilty of using sorcery and magic to harm monarchs and popes. Last, the persecution of heretics, which had flourished over the High Middle Ages, shifted its focus to include witches, now defined as a satanic sect. The witch was no longer the individual with occult powers that might occasionally be used to do harm but rather one of Satan's agents in the cosmic struggle between Good and Evil. The religious insisted on the importance of the pact between the witch and the Devil, and the development of ideas regarding the sabbat provided a collective image of witchcraft. The witch now flew to nocturnal meetings, where she met scores, hundreds, or even thousands of other witches, feasted on the flesh of newborn children, danced, drank, and en-gaged in orgiastic sexual intercourse, the whole pro-ceedings being presided over by the Devil.

By the late fifteenth century the witch myth was firmly established, and the witch, for the educated at least, was a willing tool of the Antichrist. Two changes had taken place. The developed witch stereotype was now generally that of a lower-class person, more than

Tool of Antichrist. Burning of witches in Baden, Switzerland. Woodcut, 1574.
ZENTRALBIBLIOTHEK ZÜRICH, SWITZERLAND

likely a female. In theory anybody could be a witch, but in practice it was peasant women who were most often accused. But contemporaries were aware that educated, relatively wellborn men also practiced magic. One of the contextual elements that allowed belief in witchcraft to flourish among Europe's elites was the involvement of some of their members and associates in magic, in attempts to contact the spirit world, in alchemy, in astrology, and in that broad neo-Platonic mode of thought that left ample room for the occult. The educated and the wellborn, of course, rarely incurred the wrath of officialdom for their magical or occult interests; peasant women were burned as witches by the thousands.

THE GREAT WITCH-HUNTS

Belief in witchcraft was firmly entrenched in late medieval Europe and was part of a wider system of thought that accepted the occult and magic as everyday realities. However, during the period following the Middle Ages, from about 1450 to about 1750, witchcraft enjoyed its highest profile as a historical phenomenon. That was the timespan of the persecution of witches, described by some historians as "the European witch craze" (Trevor-Roper, 1969). Because of deficiencies in the survival of records, it is impossible to determine how many people suffered legal prosecution as witches over those three hundred years. Certainly the figure of 9 million executed witches, once accepted in feminist and Wiccan circles, has been exploded. Scholarship of the 1980s and 1990s has suggested much lower figures, with perhaps 100,000 accused and 40,000 executed (Levack, 1995). What is also certain is that the period of the witch persecutions was the tragic outcome of a confluence of elite and popular concerns. This general conclusion is borne out by that handful of detailed scholarly local studies of the rise and fall of witchcraft persecution which have demonstrated what a complex and multifaceted phenomenon the craze was.

The crucial issue was the desire for a purer, more defined, and more rigorous Christianity, which lay at the root of the Reformation of the sixteenth century. In the two centuries preceding the Reformation, the struggle of the Catholic Church against heresy had continued, and during the fifteenth century the traditional village witch came to be identified as a member of a new, diabolical, heretical sect. At the same time that the inquisitors were beginning to try people for witchcraft, learned theologians in their libraries and studies were developing a new and more frightening image of the Devil. This formative phase of demonological theorizing was summed up in 1487 with the publication of the *Malleus maleficarum* (witches' hammer), written by two Dominicans, Johann Sprenger and Heinrich Kraemer. The importance of the *Malleus* has been overstated: it did not represent the ascendancy of a triumphant, hegemonic view of witchcraft but was rather a propaganda piece written to justify the actions of its authors in a set of controversial trials. One of its major objectives, in fact, was to convince sometimes reluctant secular authorities that they had a part to play in witch-hunting.

This last issue became less contentious as the sixteenth century progressed. The Reformation and the subsequent Catholic Counter-Reformation helped define Christian and hence anti-Christian beliefs and behavior more clearly. But these religious movements also had a political dimension: the secular concept of the good citizen was now inextricably enmeshed with the church's concept of the good Christian. At a crucial stage of state formation, many people in positions of influence thought they were attempting not only to bolster secular government but also to produce a "godly commonwealth." The witch became the enemy of the king and the magistrate as well as of the clergyman and the true Christian.

These long-familiar developments led to the once standard interpretation of the witch craze as concocted by bigoted, ignorant, power-crazed judges and clerics and foisted on the population to destroy pre-Christian beliefs. The subject was treated as an issue of intellectual rather than social history—until the early 1970s, when two British historians, Alan Macfarlane and Keith Thomas, developed a paradigm that put witchcraft accusations firmly in their social context. They shifted their focus of attention away from legal treatises and demonological tracts to court records and trial pamphlets on English witchcraft cases. Arguing that it was possible to write a history of witch-hunting "from below," they stressed that the phenomenon is explicable not just through the thoughts, policies, and actions of the powerful but also through the fears, strategies, and cultural horizons of the ordinary villager.

In particular Macfarlane's work, founded on a close examination of the unusually rich documentation for the English county of Essex, convincingly rooted witchcraft accusations in both village life and the broader socioeconomic changes of the sixteenth and seventeenth centuries. He noted that witchcraft accusations were normally brought by richer villagers against poorer ones. Probing more deeply, he discovered that a witchcraft accusation commonly was brought after a dispute between the accuser or members of his or her household and the accused over the denial of charity. The alleged witch, characteristically a poor and elderly woman, would come to the accuser's house and ask for money, food, drink, or perhaps the chance to work. Her request denied, the old woman would make off in an angry mood, possibly muttering threats. A little later an inexplicable illness or some other disaster would befall the refuser of charity, his family, or his farm animals. The earlier altercation, threats, or ambivalent phrases uttered by the supposed witch would be connected to the misfortune, especially if the woman requesting charity had already been suspected of witchcraft.

Macfarlane linked this model of witchcraft accusations after the refusal of charity to broader changes in the region during the period of accusations. In England, as in most of Europe, the sixteenth and seventeenth centuries were marked by steady population increase. This increase created tremendous pressure at the bottom of society, especially in that it created a large body of poor. Traditional forms of poor relief, in Macfarlane's model, were unable to cope with the extent of poverty, and it took time to put an effective poor law into operation. In the late sixteenth and early seventeenth centuries many substantial villagers were uncertain about how to deal with the poor, both in practical and in psychological terms. In harsh times the neighbor begging at the door was refused, but a lingering communal ethic made the refuser feel guilty. Under these circumstances, a witchcraft accusation was a method of transferring guilt: it was not the refuser of charity who was challenging community values but rather the perpetrator of malefic witchcraft. Macfarlane had learned from anthropology that witchcraft accusations ran along the fault lines in society, symbolizing redefinitions of community and the severing of social relationships. He connected the Essex cases to broad and familiar themes, such as the development of capitalist agriculture, the breakup of the traditional village community, and the rise of individualism.

Witch Hunter. Matthew Hopkins, witchfinder general, with his quarry. Engraving, seventeenth century. PRIVATE COLLECTION/THE BRIDGEMAN ART LIBRARY

Macfarlane's charity-refused model, although a consistent theme in accusations, has not proved universally applicable to early modern Europe. He and Thomas, however, did demonstrate convincingly that witchcraft can be studied in the context of peasant beliefs, which can no longer simply be dismissed as ignorant superstitions or ideas foisted on the peasantry by the elite. Rather, witchcraft on this level, however distant and alien to the modern observer, made sense and had a function for those involved in the phenomenon. In the 1970s historians' ideas about witchcraft trials were dominated by knowledge of the big crazes, which, for example, led to hundreds of burnings dur-

ing the early seventeenth century in the German territories of Ellwangen, Trier, Würzburg, and Bamberg. Further research demonstrated that the pattern Macfarlane established was far more common, and accusations were launched sporadically, normally against individuals or two or three supposed witches. Robin Briggs's work reveals that witchcraft accusations were an established feature of early modern Lorraine, for example, but they were located in the world of the peasant and in the petty disputes endemic to village life. Moreover, it became clear that over the whole of Europe the major peasant concern was with *maleficium,* the concrete harm supposedly perpetrated by witches, rather than the demonic pact or the witch's candidacy for membership in a diabolic heretical sect.

Another striking feature of accusations of witchcraft during the witch craze was that they were most frequently directed against women. A few regional case histories to the contrary, most court records containing witchcraft accusations demonstrate that the malefic witch was thought of as female. In Macfarlane's Essex sample, over 90 percent of the accused were women, and perhaps 80 percent of the accused in Europe as a whole were women. A number of differing interpretations attempt to explain the connection between women and witchcraft.

In the 1970s writers, most of them not academic historians, within the women's movement interpreted the gender imbalance in witchcraft accusations as one of the most overt and horrific outcomes of the male oppression of women. The acceptance of the estimate of 9 million executions made this manifestation of men's unpleasantness toward women seem all the more terrible. These writers did well to focus attention on and demonstrate the importance of an issue on which male historians had rarely commented, but few scholars of witchcraft history have regarded the inordinate accusations against women simply in terms of male oppression. Early modern Europe was a male-dominated society in which medical theory, science, and theology all agreed on the moral, intellectual, and physical inferiority of women, but it has proved difficult to establish exactly how this generalized intellectual context translated into individual witchcraft accusations.

Research has suggested a deeper set of issues. Pertinent questions are how frequently witchcraft accusations were launched between women, how often women acted as witnesses against women, and how often women participated in semiofficial actions against female witches, such as searching for the witch's mark. No political system, not even early modern patriarchy, works unless the majority of those it seeks to rule accept or at least acquiesce to it. Thus the involvement of women as accusers and prosecution witnesses in witchcraft cases might be further evidence of the dominance of male values. It seems more fruitful, however, to regard witchcraft as a phenomenon that operated to a large extent within the female sphere, in that world of female concerns over child rearing, the protection of domestic space, and the politics of reputations and local gossip that social and cultural historians of early modern Europe have been slowly reconstructing. A number of studies assert that accusations often revolved around the bewitchment, frequently to death, of children. Their mothers were

the accusers, and postmenopausal women were the accused. Psychohistorians have begun to explore this theme within the paradigm, familiar in psychoanalysis, of the malevolent mother. At the very least, examinations of popular attitudes toward menopause, rather than a consideration of generalized misogyny, are needed.

From court records and the published works of contemporary demonologists, moralists, and skeptics emerges a folklore of countermagic providing strategies for those who thought themselves bewitched to use against their alleged tormentors. On a village level witchcraft was about power. The accused witch was often an old woman who was unlikely to seek revenge through violence or litigation against those who had offended her, but she supposedly wreaked havoc on her adversaries through the deployment of occult forces. Her power could be counteracted by rival magic. Religious reformers argued that these countermeasures were without scriptural basis and hence were as ungodly as *maleficium,* but they had little impact on a population that desired more immediate and overt relief from witchcraft than the church's remedy, prayer. In hopes of alleviating the sufferings caused by witchcraft or transferring them to the witch, people scratched witches to draw blood from their faces, burned hair from their heads or thatch from their roofs, or made witch cakes from grain and the urine of the bewitched and burned them.

"Good witches" were crucial to this countermagic and an essential element in the broader culture of popular magic. The practitioners of popular magic, folk medicine, and divination, good witches were probably as common a feature of the period's witch beliefs as were the malefic witches who loom so much larger in the historical consciousness. Macfarlane and Thomas, in their studies of English witchcraft beliefs, gave due importance to those the English commonly called "cunning folk." Many contemporary writers observed that these folk were widespread and their services eagerly sought by the population at large. Cunning men and women offered medical services that were cheaper, probably less unpleasant, and possibly as effective as those available from the officially qualified physicians of the period. They could find stolen goods or identify the thieves who had taken them. They could tell fortunes and were consulted by young girls on the identities of their future husbands and by pregnant women regarding the sex of their unborn babies. They were the obvious counselors for victims of witchcraft, for they confirmed suspicions about who was behind the bewitching and recommended methods of combating the malefic witch and averting her witchcraft.

As might be expected, the equivalents of the English cunning men and women were to be found all over Europe. Research on Lorraine, for example, has demonstrated the importance of what were, literally, "witch doctors," specialists in treating witchcraft and identifying witches, who frequently played a key role in focusing and developing accusations. Some were itinerants, and even those who were not sometimes acquired reputations that spread over a radius of twenty miles. These *devins* or *devineresses* (soothsayers) did little more than confirm existing fears that an illness was supernatural and existing suspicions as to who was responsible for its occurrence. Much of the knowledge about them surfaces through records of formal prosecutions of witches, but their main objective was to keep their patients away from court action, which would undermine the good witches' position as the major source of relief and possibly attract the unwanted attention of officialdom. The activities of these Lorraine practitioners, like good witches everywhere in Europe, were illegal and reprehensible in the eyes of the church. The evidence in the Lorraine archives and elsewhere of the activities of *devins* and cunning folk constructs, in effect, a magical underworld.

The techniques used by the cunning folk and other practitioners varied widely. Mostly unlettered, they used charms and bastardized versions of Christian prayers. In England following the Reformation, for example, cunning folk apparently were fond of using doggerel fragments of the Latin prayers and creed of the old church, much to the distaste of the Protestant authorities. In Catholic areas like Lorraine, cunning folk often used prayer and holy water in their deliberations. All over Europe cunning folk used the sieve and shears, a practice in which the sieve, balanced on the points of a pair of shears, would move when questions were put to it. Another common technique involved primitive versions of the crystal balls popularly associated with fortune tellers. Other practitioners of folk magic employed more elaborate techniques, some of which point toward connections with the learned magic of the elite. By the mid-seventeenth century a reasonable proportion of cunning folk, in some regions at least, was literate, possibly signifying access to unusual and powerful knowledge in a period when illiteracy was the norm. Some had books, particularly of astrology, and used them when aiding their clients. No doubt the literate cunning man or woman had access to the almanacs and popular medical treatises of the period. As the frequent references to both cunning men and cunning women and *devins* and *devineresses* make clear, if malefic witches tended overwhelmingly to be female, good witches were of either sex, the implications of which deserve full exploration.

The cunning folk attracted particular odium from Protestant writers, locked as they were in the battle to inculcate right religion in the face of entrenched ignorance and superstition. The English Protestant theologian William Perkins (1558–1602) argued that, since good witches got their powers from the Devil as clearly as did the bad ones, they were equally deserving of death and were doubly reprehensible because they used devilish practices to convince the population that they were doing good. Nevertheless, good witches rarely received severe punishment. The secular authorities treated them lightly or subjected them to the generally weak penalties of the ecclesiastical courts. Yet the theologians' attitude brings into question officialdom's perception of witchcraft and why the witch-hunts declined.

The established tradition, in many ways correct, is that the Christian church, both before and after the Reformation, played a key role in creating the witch persecutions of early modern Europe. The church's revised view of the importance of the Devil, the perceived need for a more sharply defined Christianity, and the "acculturation" of the population at large, or at least some sections of it, to accept this official, more stringent Christianity were all of essential importance. Many societies have accepted that witches exist and that they are evil, but the European witch craze was a unique event that owed much to changes in official Christianity from about 1450 onward. Yet the church's role was not one of simple and unthinking repression. Some convinced and theologically orthodox Christians allotted witchcraft only a marginal importance. The key theological issue was the significance awarded to Divine Providence. Skeptical writers argued that many of the afflictions popularly attributed to witchcraft were, in fact, the product of the will of God, designed as a test for the faithful. This position was a little austere for the bulk of the population. People could take a witch to court or consult cunning folk about how best to deal with witchcraft, but such remedies were not available against the Almighty. A related position regarded the whole slate of witchcraft beliefs as the product of popular superstitions rather than of the influence of the Devil. Thus a conundrum arises. In some areas the processes of Christianization unleashed by the Reformation and the Counter-Reformation resulted in witch persecution, but in others they led to the attitude that witchcraft beliefs were a sign of popular ignorance, demanding the mild sanctions of the church courts and the education of the population rather than witch burnings.

While theologians and senior clerics developed a number of theoretical positions on witchcraft, judges and legal writers also demonstrated ambivalent attitudes toward the phenomenon. The legal codes of most if not all European states of the period included laws against witches, but witchcraft in many respects enjoyed a peculiar status as a criminal offense and was difficult to prove. To solve the problem some judges simply dropped the normal rules relating to evidence, especially to evidence and confessions elicited by torture, which frequently fueled the large witch-hunts. Other judges were more cautious. In England the high acquittal rate in witchcraft cases, the comparative lack of large-scale hunts, and the rarity of convictions after the 1650s owed much to the fact that assize courts, where most English witch cases were tried, were presided over by highly qualified and experienced judges appointed by the central government. In France, where those convicted of capital crimes had a right to appeal to the judges of the Parlement of Paris, most local convictions for witchcraft were quashed by the 1630s. In Scotland, Sir George Mackenzie, the lord advocate during much of the late seventeenth century, was extremely skeptical about witchcraft accusations and helped reduce the number of trials and convictions.

These signs of elite skepticism about witchcraft lead to that most complex of problems, the decline of the belief in witches and witchcraft. Some discussions of this development have centered around the marginalization of witchcraft beliefs by the scientific revolution of the seventeenth century. A new religious style stressing rational belief rather than extreme sensitivity to daily manifestations of Divine Providence was also of considerable significance. The importance of these factors is undeniable, yet seemingly the skepticism among the elite was caused as much by a cleavage between elite and popular culture as anything else. By about 1700 senior judges, senior ecclesiastics, senior bureaucrats, and learned and polite society in general were likely to deride witchcraft beliefs and witchcraft accusations as evidence of peasant ignorance and popular superstition, just as they might dismiss some manifestations of popular religion. To understand the end of the European witch craze requires an awareness of the social history of snobbery.

By 1750, except for a few isolated burnings, the persecutions had ended. In France, England, and much of Germany the executions had been reduced to a trickle by 1650. In the Dutch Republic, Spain, and Italy malefic witchcraft had never been a matter of much concern to the authorities. In some places, like Poland and Hungary, witch persecution came late, but even in these territories it had more or less collapsed by the mid-eighteenth century. The provincial elites, local clergy, petty noblemen, and urban patricians joined their social superiors in rejecting witchcraft beliefs, although this process was slower and less complete than might be imagined. Belief in witchcraft and magic had become the prerogative of the common people. Although such matters were rarely recorded in the late eighteenth century, the few extant reports of a good witch's activities, the occasional record of supposed malefic witches being assaulted or killed, the odd paper charm that survived, all suggest the resilience of what were by then subterranean supernatural beliefs.

THE SURVIVAL OF WITCH BELIEFS

For the elite the early eighteenth century marked the point at which, whatever their subsequent ideas about the occult, credence in the old style of witchcraft had waned dramatically. Among the lower orders, above all Europe's peasantry, the established beliefs in witchcraft, sorcery, and magic lived on, waiting to be rediscovered by nineteenth-century folklorists and country clergymen.

One of those clergyman, the Reverend J. C. Atkinson, recorded the existence of witchcraft beliefs and the pervasiveness of popular magic among nineteenth-century country dwellers. In 1841 Atkinson became vicar of Danby in North Yorkshire, a remote parish on the edge of the North York moors near the North Sea coast. England by that time regarded itself as a progressive, advanced society marked by science and industrialization. Atkinson, a southerner, was amazed to discover how widespread beliefs in witchcraft were. He wrote in 1891:

> I have no doubt at all of the very real and deep-seated existence of a belief in the actuality and the power of the witch. Nay, I make no doubts whatever that the witch herself, in multitudes of instances, believed in her own power quite as firmly as any of those who had learned to look upon her with a dread almost reminding one of the African dread of fetish. Fifty years ago the whole atmosphere of the folklore firmament in this district was so surcharged with the being and the works of the witch, that one seemed able to trace her presence and her activity in almost every nook and corner of the neighbourhood. (Atkinson, 1891, pp. 72–73)

Atkinson described beliefs in shape changing, concerns about *maleficium,* the widespread use of charms and amulets, and a general willingness to consult cunning folk.

Indications are strong that the situation Atkinson described probably prevailed in other rural areas of nineteenth-century England. Specific research demonstrates the persistence of witchcraft beliefs even in

The Survival of Witch Beliefs. *A Breton Sorceress,* painting (1872) by Robert Wylie (1839–1877). BRADFORD ART GALLERIES AND MUSEUMS, WEST YORKSHIRE, U.K./THE BRIDGEMAN ART LIBRARY

the urban lower classes, in London, for example, up to the mid-nineteenth century. Judith Devlin constructed an overview of France in the century and a quarter after the Revolution. Popular magic, quasi-magical manifestations of popular Christianity, and belief in the occult were still firmly entrenched. Christianity was still distorted by popular misconceptions, by a lively folklore surrounding saints and shrines, and by a refashioning of the fundamentals of the faith to meet the pragmatic devotional needs of the peasantry. Folk medicine, which depended on pagan rites, traditional techniques, miracles, and faith healing, still offered a viable alternative to "official" medicine. The popular mind, especially in rural areas, still accepted apparitions and prodigies and a world suffused with werewolves, monsters, fairies, elves, ghosts, and omens, and belief in demonic possession, astrology, and prophecy continued.

In this mental world, Atkinson's "folklore firmament," witchcraft enjoyed a central position. Devlin argued that witchcraft by this time was not a matter of explanatory and practical functions so much as an adaptable social vocabulary that allowed individuals to bring retrospective charges against those who they thought inflicted excessive or unnatural misfortunes on them. Countermagic, spells, charms, and good witches still helped against bad witches. But the basic functions of witchcraft in nineteenth-century France were, as had probably always been the case in peasant Europe, to reflect strained relationships in a backward, traditional society and to relieve and justify anxiety and anger. For people worried that they had fallen short of the ideals of their society, witchcraft transferred feelings of guilt or uncertainty onto others, who were accused as witches.

It might seem that developments in the early twentieth century finally rendered witchcraft beliefs redundant. How could such beliefs survive in a world marked by universal education, the triumph of science and technology, secularization, mass culture, and rapid communications? Over much of Europe witchcraft disappeared as a genuine traditional element in popular belief. Yet in the 1960s the French anthropologist Jeanne Favret-Saada, working in the Bocage region in western France, discovered persistent beliefs in malefic witches. Those who thought themselves bewitched sought help from "unwitchers," the equivalents of sixteenth-century cunning folk. Obviously witchcraft in the Bocage in the 1960s was not exactly the same as the witchcraft of the early modern period, but striking parallels appear, including concern about occult power and occult fields of force, apprehension over series of inexplicable misfortunes, feelings of helplessness in the face of bewitchment, and nervous confrontations and negotiations between witches and victims. Although most educated moderns would assume that the history of witchcraft ended three centuries ago, Favret-Saada's work leaves room for speculation as to what beliefs and practices have persisted in isolated parts of rural Europe.

Witchcraft has been the focus of considerable attention from specialist scholars, nonspecialist thinkers, and the general public. This attention has created a lively historiography that has postulated a variety of interpretations of the phenomenon, especially regarding the "burning times" in early modern Europe. Among these interpretations, social history methodologies have attempted to reconstruct what witchcraft and witchcraft accusations meant in the context of the village communities of late medieval and early modern Europe. Research in these periods, and that dealing with witchcraft in the nineteenth and twentieth centuries, has produced an unexpected possible conclusion. Often dismissed by historians as a marginal or even bizarre topic, witchcraft, defined as a set of beliefs that help people make sense of many aspects of their world, has been one of the most enduring components of popular mentality in European history.

See also other articles in this section.

BIBLIOGRAPHY

Atkinson, J. C. *Forty Years in a Moorland Parish: Reminiscences and Researches in Danby in Cleveland.* London, 1891.

Behringer, Wolfgang. *Witchcraft Persecutions in Bavaria: Popular Magic, Religious Zealotry, and Reason of State in Early Modern Europe.* Translated by J. C. Grayson and David Lederer. Cambridge, U.K., 1997.

Briggs, Robin. *Witches and Neighbours: The Social and Cultural Context of European Witchcraft.* London, 1996.

Cohn, Norman. *Europe's Inner Demons.* London, 1975.

Devlin, Judith. *The Superstitious Mind: French Peasants and the Supernatural in the Nineteenth Century.* New Haven, Conn., and London, 1987.

Evans-Pritchard, E. E. *Witchcraft, Oracles and Magic among the Azande.* Oxford, 1937.

Favret-Saada, Jeanne. *Deadly Words: Witchcraft in the Bocage.* Translated by Catherine Cullen. Cambridge, U.K., and New York, 1980.

Flint, Valerie I. J. *The Rise of Magic in Early Medieval Europe.* Princeton, N.J., 1991.

Levack, Brian P. *The Witch-hunt in Early Modern Europe.* London and New York, 1987, 1995.

Macfarlane, A. D. J. *Witchcraft in Tudor and Stuart England: A Regional and Comparative Study.* London, 1970.

Purkiss, Diane. *The Witch in History: Early Modern and Twentieth-Century Representations.* London and New York, 1996.

Roper, Lyndal. *Oedipus and the Devil: Witchcraft, Sexuality, and Religion in Early Modern Europe.* London, 1994.

Sharpe, James. *Instruments of Darkness: Witchcraft in Early Modern England.* London, 1996.

Thomas, Keith. *Religion and the Decline of Magic: Studies in Popular Beliefs in Sixteenth and Seventeenth Century England.* London, 1971.

Trevor-Roper, H. R. *The European Witch-Craze of the Sixteenth and Seventeenth Centuries, and Other Essays.* New York, 1969.

Willis, Deborah. *Malevolent Nurture: Witch-Hunting and Maternal Power in Early Modern England.* Ithaca, N.Y., and London, 1995.

BANDITRY

Paul Sant Cassia

As a type of predatory, acquisitive, and violent action by groups of men (sometimes including women), banditry has a long history dating from ancient Greece, Rome, and China. In central and eastern Europe and in the Balkans, it was found in the countryside, in specific conditions (such as following wars and massive dislocations) and in specific periods, especially in the late eighteenth and nineteenth centuries, when the modern nation-state was emerging. In Latin America it was part and parcel of an expanding frontier economy. Banditry tended to emerge in remote, difficult-to-control mountainous areas containing large numbers of semimobile and state-resistant pastoralists. Although there are examples of lone bandits, bandits tended to form into fluid bands, sometimes of up to twenty persons. Kinship, real or fictive, was an important component of their organization, and solidarity was reinforced through the institutions of blood brotherhood and adoption, as well as through feasting and other rituals. Banditry can be seen as a continuum from the camel raiding Bedouin, through the "noble bandits" of the nineteenth-century Greek Klephts, to contemporary armed autonomist groups (such as Chiapas in Mexico or Kurds in Turkey or Chechen fighters against Russian intervention in Chechnya) labeled as "bandits" by the state.

In Europe banditry assumed its most important forms in rural societies, particularly in Mediterranean regions and particularly as property relations changed in the eighteenth to nineteenth centuries. The following analysis focuses on this important category, where among other things causation has been carefully studied. But more informal kinds of banditry occurred in other settings. After wars, for example in the eighteenth century, veterans often roamed the country in predatory groups that some peasants regarded as bandits or brigands. Fears of banditry of this sort surfaced in 1789, during the French Revolution, and helped trigger rural risings. While banditry as an outcome of social instability has declined in most of Europe, thanks to firmer policing and changes in military recruitment and policies toward veterans, echoes persist, for example in the formation of criminal groups in the wake of the collapse of the Soviet Union in 1989.

SOURCES AND DEFINITIONS

More than most other social phenomena, the characterization of banditry depends upon how it is approached. Banditry can be seen as a legal category, a social category, and as a series of powerful stories and myths. Its meaning has changed across time and across disciplines. As a legal category, banditry is a pernicious form of crime that subverts the state's monopoly of legitimate violence. From the perspective of the modern nation-state, bandits (or brigands, a term more popular in the nineteenth century) are criminals who resist the civilizing power of the state through violence, brutality, extortion, theft, and protection rackets. Bandits are seen as beyond the pale of "civilized society," a symptom of the low level of development of the countryside, a problem impeding progress and thus meriting swift, equally brutal, suppression by the army or police, without much regard to the constitutional human rights the modern state claims to protect. Most of the historical sources on bandits are the words of army or police officers charged with ridding the countryside of such "sores" or "plagues" and are thus highly partial. From the perspective of the "bandit" himself, the situation may look different. To him, an escape to the mountains may be the only way of avoiding an unjust state summons or pursuing a private revenge. Other sources, such as ballads, popular accounts, and oral history—often bypassed by traditional historians engaged in depicting the history of the nation-state as the progress of civilization over barbarism—concentrated on bandits' roles as popular heroes.

Two pioneer historians who emphasized the social aspects of banditry were Franco Molfese and Eric Hobsbawm. In his celebrated book, *Bandits* (1969), Hobsbawm interpreted them as prepolitical rebels.

Social bandits were considered by their people as heroes, champions, and fighters for justice in a world that often denied them justice. Hobsbawm distinguished bandits from gangs drawn from the professional underworld and from communities for whom raiding was a normal way of life (such as the Bedouins). According to Hobsbawm, bandits were symptoms of major transformations in society, but they did not themselves transform it; they were activists, not ideologues, and after World War II they disappeared. Bandits were recruited from the most mobile segments of peasant society: young unmarried men, landless laborers, migrants, shepherds, ex-soldiers, and deserters. They took to the hills to right some personal wrong, becoming the noble robber. Although they were supported by the local community whose yearnings for a prepolitical just world they embodied, they were usually betrayed.

Hobsbawm's thesis has been criticized by Anton Blok and other anthropologists. Blok argued that there is more to brigandage than voicing popular unrest. By applying Norbert Elias's notion of power configurations to his historical anthropological research on Sicily, he suggested that Hobsbawm overemphasized class conflict and romanticized bandits. Rather than being champions of the poor, bandits often terrorized and oppressed them. Bandits prevented and suppressed peasant mobility by putting down collective peasant action through terror and by carving out avenues of individual social mobility that weakened collective action. Blok asserted that analysis must encompass the wider society within which bandits operated. Bandits required protection in order to survive; otherwise they were quickly killed by the landlords' retainers, the police, or the peasants. In Sicily, such support was forthcoming from mafiosi (local men of authority who often engaged in illegal activities and protection rackets) or local politicians. Blok formulated the "principle" that the more successful a bandit, the greater the protection he enjoyed.

BANDITRY IN
COMPARATIVE PERSPECTIVE

Where banditry has persisted, it can clearly be linked to the inability of the state to control the countryside. Although it would be simplistic to attribute the decline of banditry in the modern world to the state's increasing monopoly of violence, this is certainly important. Indeed, when used by state authorities, the pejorative "bandits" labels forms of violent resistance they cannot control except by equally brutal repression. The persistence or decline of banditry depends upon a complex interplay of variables, including the social structure and political ecology of a particular region; the nature and distribution of property and capital accumulation (whether landed or movable and precarious, such as livestock) and the means available to legitimate it; the presence or absence of trust and its relationship to the development of civil society; underdeveloped electoral processes, which may encourage strong-arm tactics; and the predominance of permanent insecurity rather than permanent misery at the grass roots, the former being more conducive to banditry. The political ideology of local elites and their relationship to the state is also important because bandits may either be co-opted by local elites as a means to resist the state (as occurred in Sicily in the immediate post–World War II period) or, reluctantly, by the state, as in nineteenth-century Greece, where they were used for irredentist adventures and to threaten the supporters of rival politicians. The state's policies toward landlordism, peasant cultivators, and pastoralists may also be a significant variable because they may favor one over the other, with radical implications for illegal practices. In certain situations peasants may have preferred the traditional depredations of pastoral bandits to the more extensive, sustained ones of the state, such as taxes, and in other situations the depredations of the potentates' henchmen may have been protected by powerful national interests.

In many societies, such as in southern Spain, Sicily, Greece, and the Balkans, banditry had a predominantly agro-pastoral base. In Sicily and Greece violent entrepreneurs from pastoral backgrounds managed to create new niches for themselves in the nation-state, especially when the new regime attempted to penetrate the countryside. In Sicily mafiosi were actively involved in the risorgimento (the nineteenth-century movement for Italian unification), backing the adherents of Giuseppe Garibaldi and managing to wrest effective control of landed estates from the absentee Sicilian aristocracy. They thus shifted their wealth into land, their pastoral backgrounds proving particularly useful both in co-opting bandits and in suppressing peasant unrest. In Greece banditry was intimately grounded in pastoralism and even had a seasonal cycle based on movements from the plains to the mountains. The age-old conflict between pastoralists and agriculturalists obliged the former to intimidate peasants, especially in the new Greek state, which radically reduced the amount of land available for pasturage and tried to encourage the expansion of the small peasant cultivator class. War increased dislocation and unrest in the countryside, further encouraging banditry.

For an analysis of banditry, it may be useful to steer a middle course, borrowing from the various perspectives that treat bandits as primitive social rebels (as Hobsbawm does), as individual opportunists, or as the co-opted henchmen of rural potentates (as Blok does). Often all these features coexist in particular examples of banditry, although one may be more dominant than the others.

Banditry in Europe traditionally appeared in areas where large-scale landholding coexisted with a relatively permanent intermediate strata of leaseholders or freeholders based upon family-sized plots, such as in Sicily, parts of Greece, and Cyprus. Sustained banditry required concealable, transportable wealth (cash, cash crops, animals, alcohol, narcotics) that left few traces. In the nineteenth-century Mediterranean, banditry was particularly strong where pastoralists occupied an intermediate position between small-scale cultivators and large-scale proprietors, as in northern Greece, or where overseers and sharecroppers occupied that position, as in rural Sicily, but also where pastoralism was prominent in its own right, as in Sardinia and Corsica.

There were basic differences between banditry in predominantly agricultural areas and in mountainous pastoral areas. In the latter, banditry appears to have been more resilient, especially where a combination of external factors militated against turning pastoralists into peasants. Banditry in agricultural contexts was usually more controllable and could be tamed more easily, especially when violent men from humble origins acquired secure property rights (usually through co-option or protection by elites) and thereby achieved legitimacy.

Banditry tended to appear less frequently in areas with large masses of rural proletarians, such as Puglia in southern Italy. In Puglia few legal or illegal opportunities were available for social mobility, and the social relations of production encouraged the emergence of collective solidarity and of anarcho-syndicalism (a doctrine advocating that workers seize control of the economy and government). Much the same appears to have happened in Andalusia, where absentee landlords were separated from a mass of largely landless laborers and where rural discontent increasingly took class forms.

A final important variable is the process of mythicizing at the local and national levels. In the Mediterranean and elsewhere the circulation of popular accounts of bandits was particularly significant, sometimes interacting in complex ways with the creation of the nation-state's history. Bandits were portrayed in texts as outsiders and hence dangerous, as residues from the past and hence ambiguous, or as insiders and hence admirable. They might move from the outside to the inside or vice versa. These portrayals affected how bandits were perceived and legitimated, even allowing them to legitimate themselves. In nineteenth-century Greece, ex-Klephts such as Theodoros Kolokotrónis used their memoirs to glorify themselves. Many bandit chiefs published pamphlets in their own defense claiming that, like all good Greeks, they were fighting the Turks, the Muslim outsiders who were the true brigands attempting to discredit the country. In the late nineteenth century Corsican bandits liked to present themselves as "Robin Hood" figures.

In reality bandits changed sides according to self-interest. Such definitions and redefinitions have created a vocabulary of justification, traces of which remained even at the end of the twentieth century. In Crete, for example, extensive livestock theft was legitimated orally by reference to highly selective, nationalist accounts of the "freedom-loving" Klephts of old mentioned in in schoolbooks. In Andalusia local communists turned nineteenth-century bandits into protorebels in the regional cause, symbols in their devolutionist struggles with Madrid. Stories about bandits are therefore an intrinsic part of the phenomenon.

POLITICAL DIMENSIONS OF BANDITRY

Throughout the Mediterranean, at least as far back as the eighteenth century, banditry has often been incorporated in nationalist and regional rhetoric. *Brigantaggio politico* had already emerged as a central feature of Corsican independence strategies against Genoa under Giacinto Paoli and Gian-Pietro Gaffori in the mid-eighteenth century. Political banditry often required outside support to be successful. This was the case in Corsica, southern Italy (Calabria), and Sicily in the early nineteenth century, when the British supported their "chivalrous brigand-allies" against the French. In postindependence Greece Klephtic heroes figured prominently in nationalist rhetoric. In Sicily the bandit Salvatore Giuliano's ambiguous notoriety in the post-1945 period, created partly through extensive press coverage, derived from his expression of regional Sicilian aspirations, despite the fact that he also massacred peasants. Like the contemporary "Bandit Queen" in India, Guiliano became the subject of novels and films.

The packaging of the myth of banditry in nationalist political rhetoric cannot be disregarded as unrelated to historical and anthropological analysis. Bandits were often romanticized after the fact by way of rhetoric and texts that circulated with a life of their own, giving the bandits a permanence and potency that transcended their localized domain and transitory nature. The ways in which bandits were portrayed in the modern nation-state and the ways such symbols were used to legitimate contemporary struggles are as significant as what the bandits actually did and represented. That is, it is an incontrovertible fact that bandits often terrorized peasants who appear to have voluntarily supported them; yet this fact does not exhaust or even address the issue of why and how banditry emerged, how it was sustained, or how bandit myths achieved such potency at both the local and national levels.

THE SIGNIFICANCE OF VIOLENCE

Traditional banditry has often been accompanied by extreme violence in both its expression and its repression. In banditry, as in feuding, from which it in part derives, personalized violence is crucial and finely graded; the intensity of violence, however distasteful to a modern sensibility, suggests a form of control. Violence is targeted specifically against persons and properties (usually animals) of persons, and displayed through stories. It functions as a warning and a deterrence against further acts of violence.

Terror and violence often had a personal element. Many bandits in Corsica, Sicily, Cypress, and elsewhere embarked on their careers through personal vendettas. A nineteenth-century observer noted that for the Corsicans the vendetta was a kind of religion. But betrayal to agents of the state was always a grave danger, unless the individual was protected by powerful interests. In Corsica, for example, many bandits were obliged to rely on the support of family and kin and thus soon found themselves further enmeshed in family feuds. They used their prepotency and violence to protect their kins' interests and thus ensure the support of family against betrayal to the state. The more protected an individual was, especially by powerful patrons, as in Sicily, the less he needed to use violence for the meanings it could convey and the more opportunities he had to employ ambiguity and courtesy—a point noted by many outside observers, although such courtesy must surely have been ironic. The more marginalized a bandit was, the more dependent he was on protection, the greater the risk of betrayal, and thus the greater the tendency for violence to appear "gratuitous"—that is, to signify itself.

As the genesis of banditry was personal, so too was its prosecution. In their typical form, most stories about bandits can be reduced to the following pattern: The triggering incident is a slight to personal or family honor by another family or individual of equal or superior status. A member of the slighted family, usually a young man, responds with violence, thereby breaking state law, and flees. Revenge in kind is threatened by the family who made the initial slight. The slighted family causes the death of the original offender. As both families resort to banditry, deeming their acts of illegal violence morally just, they become marginalized. The state attempts to capture the offenders and, if it is successful, executes them. Alternatively, the offenders are betrayed by other families, also resulting in their deaths.

A central way to express violence and damage one's opponent's interests was through the mutilation of both individuals and animals. As an exchange between individuals, banditry thus employed a specific set of finely graded messages involving violence to the body and property of the victim. Property, as a stand-in for its owner, was subjected to an excess of violence, such as the disembowelment of livestock, but not killed. The owner would thus be forced to complete the bitter destruction of his own herd. In other cases, such as in Corsica, mules' ears were cut off as a ritual death threat. Such actions served as a warning or an unambiguous omen of further action. Whereas smaller animals such as dogs were destroyed, larger ones such as sheep were grievously wounded, and the largest animals (bulls, mules, etc.) had marks left on them. The victim was therefore defined taxonomically.

Through the destruction of animals or other property of the offender, or even the killing of some other person, a surrogate victim is created. As René Girard noted in *Violence and the Sacred* (1988), by killing not the murderer himself but someone close to him, an act of perfect reciprocity is avoided and the necessity for further revenge is bypassed. The act resembles both a sacrifice—in that the victim of the second murder is not responsible for the first—and a legal punishment—in that the violent retribution can be seen as imposing an act of reparation on the offender.

After the selection and killing of the victim, whether the original offender or a surrogate, the body was often mutilated to underscore the significance of the act of revenge. The body had to be "prepared" retroactively—disassembled and then reassembled in a grotesque parody of the original body—to be offered back to the group who "made" it. This desecration of the body also defiled the bandit or perpetrator. Yet through that act the bandit embarked on his final transformation. He set himself up outside the community and thus as the ultimate sacrificial victim. The songs about the hardships of bandit life in Corsica, Greece, and elsewhere lament that becoming a bandit

Surviving a Bandit Attack. Votive painting by Stephan Praun, a German traveler, in thanksgiving for his surviving an attack by highwaymen on a journey to Italy, c. 1511. GERMANISCHES NATIONALMUSEUM, NÜRNBERG

was far from glorious. Most bandits in Corsica saw themselves as victims; they spoke about their "disgrace," "destiny," and "fate" (*poveru disgraziatu*). In Greece the notions of *atichos* (luckless) and *moira* (fate) were equally prevalent.

Thus it was not so much through their lives that bandits generated the sometimes powerful myth of nobility as through their deaths. Nor was it because they lived or died "nobly." It was rather that, by being betrayed and killed or publicly executed, they achieved sacrificial status. Either they became symbols of betrayal by more powerful vested interests, or the violence of their executions, and the disassembly of their bodies as public spectacle, demonstrated the irrepressible power of the state over the individual. When caught and juridically processed, their bodies became the subject of a publicly demonstrated spectacle of state power.

The bandit is thus not so much an expression of peasant reaction to oppression or a form of wish fulfillment as a transfiguration of peasant suffering, transformed from individual execution to the collective personification of sacrifice. The parallels between bandits and saints, and the linkage in the literature between bandits and monks, are not fortuitous, either in terms of the social conditions that gave rise to banditry or in terms of the iconography and models of suffering. Popular models of suffering were available in the lives and tortures of saints, and imprisoned bandits could become like saints, especially when they repented. Michel Foucault noted that the greater the spectacle of state punishment (and most glorifications of banditry by the peasantry date from the period immediately after the establishment of nation-states), the greater the risk that it would be rejected by the very people to whom such spectacles were addressed.

THE PROBLEM OF COMPLICITY

The extreme violence practiced by bandits against peasants in many contemporary accounts has been interpreted in two ways: as expressive or as instrumental. Hobsbawm tended to an expressive interpretation. He spoke of "pathological aberrations" and "ultra violence" as a manifestation of the "primitive" nature of bandits' rebellion, but he could not explain it adequately. Blok and others interpreted it in instrumental terms: violence ensures peasant submission. This interpretation is also problematic since violence reinforces the fragmentation of peasant collective consciousness but is not its direct cause.

It may be useful to distinguish between violence, as a performative act and a system of signs, and terror, as the effect of such actions on the wider social field within which bandits operate. Two famous Italian politicians, Luigi Franchetti and Sidney Sonnino, who conducted a wide-ranging investigation in Sicily in the late nineteenth century, noted that, unless one introduced the notion of complicity, it was difficult to understand why there was such widespread peasant submission to the activities of bandits. Peasant complicity was not always imposed through terror but could also be spontaneous and lucrative. Franchetti and Sonnino also noted a widespread admiration for bandits among the literati, who romanticized them, and paradoxically among landowners, the most likely to suffer from bandit depredations. Although fear and protection are critical components of bandit power, they are not a sufficient cause for bandits' sustained prepotency. A widespread and effective climate of fear would in any case be difficult to maintain if it were to be reduced to the potential violent actions of a few individuals, unless it were supported by a consent bandits received at the local level. Because they were embedded in local communities, bandits benefited from a grassroots solidarity against outsiders and state authority. Local codes of behavior such as *omertà* (Sicilian for "silence") obliged individuals to maintain a solidarity of silence and noncooperation with the authorities or risk extreme ostracism and revenge.

Consequently, it is difficult at the local level to distinguish those acts that can be called personal (such as a vendetta over a matter of honor) from those that can be labeled political (such as protecting the political interests of the elite). Clearly, bandits had an interest in encouraging the interpretation of their actions as personal and personalizing rather than political. Violence worked to encourage individuals to "mind their own business." Violent retribution was "justice," a private affair not to be reported to the state. Inevitably, state authorities viewed such violence as a sign of "barbarism" to be mercilessly extirpated, and as a moral weakness in the peasants who were duped by the bandits. Thus activities by bandits that had political implications (such as violence that kept the peasants cowed and docile) were often perceived as personal at the grass roots and hence of only limited concern, except to the participants.

Banditry employed a set of moral codes drawn and indistinguishable from kinship-based ideas of justice and retribution; hence a reaction against banditry was often impossible because it conflicted with the moral codes that regulated traditional society. As in many stateless societies, the distinction between the private and the public (that is, civil society) had limited significance. Banditry certainly possessed a cumulative political significance in suppressing peasant unrest, but the actions it employed were embedded in peasant morality. Thus peasant complicity might be either active or passive but equally significant in both cases. Passive complicity consisted of a series of unconnected individual acceptances of the status quo and served to conceal illegal violent acts.

Banditry employs a distinctive and extreme form of personal power and prepotency that requires constant reinforcement by means of a series of actions, such as selective generosity and magnanimity, as well as calculated arbitrariness. These practices contribute to the mythic value of the bandit or mafioso, which Diego Gambetta suggests is an essential precondition for the trust that mafiosi and others require to operate. Calculated arbitrariness in imposing one's will and extravagant generosity are two aspects of the same phenomenon. They personalize the mafioso's or bandit's power and prepotency, generate respect, and emphasize his inalienable symbolic capital. Stories that circulate about the bandit or mafioso often constitute an essential part of his power. That power can also be manifested in the paradoxical expressiveness of silence—the unspoken stories that say it all.

Banditry is therefore a phenomenon that is not only often refractory to the investigations of the outside observer but also concealed from the participants themselves. Stories about bandits should be treated as texts to be deconstructed. Caution must be exercised in reducing discernible sociological facts, such as the observation that a bandit successfully managed to evade capture for a long period, to single empiricist causes, such as powerful protection. Likewise, stories about bandits should not be treated as primary raw data on the bandits themselves or as simple expressions of hidden peasant aspirations, but rather as the result of a process of elaborated discourse (including textual discourse and reinterpretation) about power relations within society. These discourses are often metaphorically constructed, interpreted, and reinterpreted in various ways. Discourse on and about bandits in society indicates a great deal about that society and its power relations.

BANDITRY AND LITERATURE

Literary romanticization of bandits was pronounced during the formation of nation-states and was often coupled with the desire of the urban literati to discover sources of opposition (often to foreign rule) in the countryside. Guerrilla popular uprisings (casting "banditry" as an expression of the struggle for freedom) against outside despotism in Corsica in the mideighteenth century, and Greece in the early nineteenth, caught public imagination. In his *Contrat social* (social contract; 1762) the French philosopher Jean-Jacques Rousseau singled out the Corsicans in Europe as the one people fit to produce just laws. Rousseau's imagining of the Corsican way of life contains many of the germinal contradictory notions about bandits that developed in romanticism and have retained popular currency. He claimed that, whereas all Europe saw the Corsicans as a horde of bandits, he saw them as a free people capable of discipline. Similar views were initially entertained by Byron about the Greek Klephts.

The Rousseauesque utopia inverted traditional wisdoms and manufactured the bandit as the first modern primitive within the borders of Europe. Where there was no (state) law, Rousseau discerned justice; where the people were oppressed, Rousseau anticipated freedom; where the ancien régime recognized anarchic, bloodthirsty bandits, he discerned exemplary citizens capable of discipline. Bandits were natural men, outside time, but nevertheless potential lawmakers. Fully to realize themselves and the future, they had further to recover their bucolic pleasures and the simplicity and equality of the rustic life. Previously bandits were seen as "barbarians" with whom one could coexist, inhabiting the same time, and whose criminality was predictable but religiously condemnable. Now they were seen as living ancestors who inhabited a different time and who had to be tamed in the modern republic. Likewise, in the mid- to late nineteenth century, Klephts also figured prominently in Greek historiography, representing an often entirely fictional traditional opposition to Ottoman rule.

The myth of banditry may well, therefore, have a double function. In the hands of urban intellectuals it points to the bad old days before the establishment of the nation-state, when life and property were not secure. On the other hand it suggests that ordinary peasants or pastoralists, the source of national folklore and the social stratum from whom bandits were traditionally recruited, possessed the right ethnic sentiments in rejecting foreign authority, exploitation, and other abuses. That peasants were often misguided and ultimately shifted their loyalties only serves to demonstrate that they are incapable by nature of taking legitimate mass political action—unless, as Rousseau intimated, they are under the leadership of the more enlightened urban elites.

By the mid-nineteenth century the countryside of Europe's periphery became a theatrical topos where the vicarious fantasies and terrors of an emergent national literate bourgeoisie could be collectivized and enacted in literature. In Spain, Sicily, Greece, and Corsica (and, on the other side of the Atlantic, in

The Bandit Nonce Romanetti. The early-twentieth-century Corsican bandit Nonce Romanetti and his associates. ©HARLINGUE-VIOLLET

Latin America), bandits became important literary, as well as operatic and iconic, subjects. Novelists (such as Edmond About and Prosper Mérimée) traveled to remote places in Greece and Corsica, for example, to ground their texts in direct experience and observation. Local responses were mixed but increasingly hostile to such collective negative stereotypes.

Banditry in places like southern Italy and Sicily became the subject of numerous inquiries as well as massive army intervention. Between 1860 and 1870 more lives were lost during the Italian army's campaign in southern Italy against peasant brigandage than in the war of unification. From the perspective of the state, the Mafia and *brigantaggio* became part of the wider *questione meridionale* (the southern question): Why is the South backward, crime ridden, and state resistant? Brigandage moved from being a question of individual barbarism that the state had to extirpate by aggressive actions such as massive repression to one of collective measurement, documentation, education, and economic development.

Unsurprisingly, this view of the South aroused the ire of local intellectuals and politicians. As the Sicilian novelist Leonardo Sciascia (1921–1989) noted, an element of latent racism entered into the northern view of the South, and as soon as banditry and organized crime were posed as typically "Sicilian" phenomena emerging from its psychology and history, the Sicilian educated classes reacted by minimalizing the criminality. An earlier Sicilian novelist, Luigi Capuana (1839–1915), denied the Sicilianness of the Mafia and brigandage, claiming that, though the Mafia existed in Sicily, it was no different from criminality found elsewhere.

The mythology and rhetoric that surround banditry must be interpreted carefully. Following Hobsbawm, bandit myths are generic expressions of hidden grassroots aspirations; following Blok, these myths are largely irrelevant to banditry's political functions in the class war. The two interpretations are not necessarily opposed and indeed may coexist at different levels of analysis. Essentialist definitions are not helpful to understanding; yet because what passes as banditry cannot be analytically separated from wide areas of social life, its presentation in discourse is particularly significant. A full understanding takes into account not just the various ways in which strongmen were co-opted by the powerful but also how such men were portrayed by various strata of society.

Peasant idealization of bandits was also variable and a function of their subsequent political evolution. Bandits did not necessarily belong to the peasantry; they often belonged to those groups who sponsored or controlled the production of (often) literary symbols. In a number of places, however, bandits belonged to the peasantry through their presence in widely circulated chapbooks, which popularized and contemporized bandits.

380

CONCLUSION

Banditry is an aggressive form of illegality and of adventurist capital accumulation found in certain social contexts, especially those marked by insecurity and violence; in this sense it is a product of political economy. Neither solely a prepolitical form of protest nor a means of suppressing peasant unrest, it may have performed these functions among others. As a category of social behavior, banditry employs specific displays of violence to generate terror for personal ends. As a legalistic and political-social category, banditry is formed by the impact of the state on local communities, and its meanings have changed across time to reflect these changing relationships. From a statist perspective "banditry" can be labeled as a certain type of violent behavior, but it may not be viewed this way at the grass roots. It operates between the state-imposed system of law and social order on one hand and the local system of vengeance and grassroots conceptions of justice on the other. It is a specific form of arbitrary personal prepotency and agency with its own "aesthetic" and accompanying discourses, thriving on, and constituting itself through, a complex array of symbols. How authorities have responded to this form of prepotency (either through savage repression or co-option of strongmen) has itself influenced responses to banditry at the local level. The state is therefore complicit in the construction and interpretation of banditry.

Since the nineteenth century there have been two discourses on banditry, intimately tied with the nation-state and its imaginative geography. First, *bandites d'honneur,* heroes of the vendetta, exponents of personal honor on the periphery of society, are always presented on the horizon of the past, as traces of a nostalgic world that has been lost forever. The closer one gets to it, the more such positive features appear to recede. Conversely, there are "contemporary bandits" involved in protection rackets, common robberies, murder, and other crimes. An extreme form is contemporary political brigandage, which merges with political terrorism, blending political programs, covert violence, and protection rackets. "Genuine" banditry always seems to have existed in the past, never in the present. The modern state stereotypes regions within it as inhabiting a bygone era, thus rationalizing repression of legitimate regionalist, autonomist, and cultural aspirations by labeling them as banditry. If bandits are the backward, bloodthirsty, unthinking, "barbarians" the state (and army) portray them as, then it is the state's duty to suppress them in order to protect "civilized" values. So does banditry become a historiographical discourse about order, justice, and freedom.

See also the section **Rural Life** *(volume 2);* **Peasants and Rural Laborers** *and the section* **Social Protest** *(in this volume); and other articles in this section.*

BIBLIOGRAPHY

About, Edmond. *Le roi des montagnes.* Paris, 1861.

Blok, Anton. "The Peasant and the Brigand: Social Banditry Reconsidered." *Comparative Studies in Society and History* 14 (1972): 494–503.

Braudel, Fernand. *The Mediterranean and the Mediterranean World in the Age of Philip II.* 2 vols. Translated by Siân Reynolds. London, 1972.

Campbell, John. "The Greek Hero." In *Honour and Grace in Anthropology.* Edited by John G. Persistiany and Julian Pitt-Rivers. Cambridge, U.K., 1992. Pages 129–149.

Carrington, Dora. *Granite Island: A Portrait of Corsica.* London, 1971.

Davis, John, A. *Conflict and Control: Law and Order in Nineteenth-Century Italy.* Basingstoke, U.K., 1988.

Dickie, John. "A Word at War: The Italian Army and Brigandage, 1860–1870." *History Workshop* 33 (1992): 1–24.

Driessen, Henk. "The 'Noble Bandit' and the Bandits of the Nobles: Brigandage and Local Community in Nineteenth-Century Andalusia." *Archives européennes de Sociologie* 24 (1983): 96–114.

Fentress, James, and Chris Wickham. *Social Memory.* Oxford and Cambridge, Mass., 1992.

Foucault, Michel. *Discipline and Punish: The Birth of the Prison.* Translated by Alan Sheridan. New York, 1979.

Franchetti, Luigi, and Sidney Sonnino. *Inchiesta in Sicilia.* Florence, 1977.

Gallant, Thomas W. "Greek Bandits: Lone Wolves or a Family Affair?" *Journal of Modern Greek Studies* 6 (1988): 269–290.

Gambetta, Diego. "Fragments of an Economic Theory of the Mafia." *Archives européennes de Sociologie* 24 (1988): 127–145.

Hart, David. *Banditry in Islam: Case Studies from Morocco, Algeria, and the Pakistan North West Frontier.* Wisbech, U.K., 1987.

Herzfeld, Michael. *The Poetics of Manhood.* Princeton, N.J., 1985.

Hobsbawm, Eric. *Bandits.* 2d ed. Harmondsworth, U.K., 1985.

Koliopoulos, Johns. *Brigands with a Cause.* Oxford, 1987.

Molfese, Franco. "Il brigantaggio nel Mezzogiorno dopo l'Unità d'Italia." In *Archivio Storico per la Calabria e la Lucania* 42, Rome, 1975.

Moss, David. "Bandits and Boundaries in Sardinia." *Man* New Ser., 14 (1979): 477–496.

Sciascia, Leonardo. *Cruciverba.* Torino, Italy, 1983. See "Letteratura e Mafia," pp. 139–149.

Scott, James C. *Weapons of the Weak: Everyday Forms of Peasant Resistance.* New Haven, Conn., 1985.

Snowden, Frank M. *Violence and Great Estates in the South of Italy: Apulia, 1900–1922.* Cambridge, U.K., 1977.

Wilson, Stephen. *Feuding, Conflict, and Banditry in Nineteenth-Century Corsica.* Cambridge, U.K., 1988.

Zugasti, de, J. *El Bandolerismo Andaluz.* Madrid, 1934.

JUVENILE DELINQUENCY AND HOOLIGANISM

Kathleen Alaimo

Explicit in the term "juvenile delinquency" and implicit in the word "hooliganism" is a youthful connotation. Thus, their history is linked to the histories of children, childhood, youth, and adolescence. Historians have found that juvenile misbehavior and adult concerns about such misbehavior are recurrent themes in most sources about children and youth throughout history. Many investigations of juvenile delinquency highlight the significant dissonance associated with life-cycle transitions. This approach stresses the importance of examining juvenile delinquency in terms of the generalized norms established for youth in particular times and places.

In the overall project of socializing children, which was historically undertaken by family, church, employers, and schools, juvenile delinquency often appears as a direct challenge. However, it may represent both historically evolving adult expectations and the efforts of young people to find expression within variably constrained environments. In other words, juvenile misbehavior not only has a history marked by changes and continuities but also one linked to larger social, economic, political, and intellectual forces. Whether juvenile misbehavior is viewed as troublesome but tolerable, or acute and worthy of societal anxiety or attention, depends largely on historical context.

Social historians have focused on the changing constellation of youthful activities and behaviors identified as "delinquent" by different societies at various points in their history. Social history explores the processes by which definitions of juvenile delinquency have emerged and changed over time. In addition, social history has illuminated meaningful patterns of juvenile delinquency, tied to social, cultural, economic, and even political conditions of long historical moments. Social historians' interest in the everyday, lived experience and the lives of the seemingly voiceless has brought the study of juvenile delinquency and hooliganism into the arena of historical inquiry concerned with such matters as deviance, social control, classification, authority, resistance, life-stage transi-

tion, as well as socioeconomic dislocations and popular politics. This approach enriches the body of work that addresses the legal, reform, and policy aspects of juvenile delinquency. Of particular importance to social history is the nature of the link between juvenile delinquency (as a cluster of behaviors as well as an ever-changing concept) and processes of social and political change such as those associated with industrialization, urbanization, compulsory schooling, mass political mobilization, and the bureaucratization of the helping professions.

Several debates mark the current state of scholarship on juvenile delinquency and hooliganism in European social history. One that should be laid to rest is the vexing question, parallel to that asked about childhood and adolescence, of whether juvenile delinquency is a modern invention. Though the term itself may be of relatively recent origin, the reality behind the concept has long been present in European society. While some of the field's pioneers (mostly modern historians) variously declared the invention of juvenile delinquency in the early nineteenth, the mid-nineteenth, the late nineteenth, and the early twentieth century, the later work of medievalists and early modern historians argues for significant continuity in this area. Medieval Christian moralists, Renaissance city fathers, and Reformation theologians all spoke with a combination of trepidation and indignation about wild, disrespectful, disruptive youth. Still the approaches to juvenile delinquency and the institutional mechanisms used to respond to juvenile misbehavior differed in important ways between the early modern and modern periods. The debate about whether juvenile delinquency is a modern invention is best transformed into a series of investigations that seek to highlight the different manifestations and causes of juvenile misbehavior and the different meanings of and responses to those behaviors at various moments and places in history. Indeed, rather than debate whether juvenile delinquency is a modern invention, social historians should pursue lines of inquiry that illuminate the variable role of ruralism and urbanism in shaping conceptions of juvenile delinquency.

A second compelling issue in the social history of juvenile delinquency and hooliganism is the role of class. The overwhelming body of literature concerning juvenile delinquency and hooliganism targets children of the poor and working classes. This visibility is the result of two distinct but related approaches. One approach views the concept of juvenile delinquency as an expression of class conflict, both cultural and economic. Seeking stability, productivity, and order, the elites (comprising lawmakers, property owners, moralists, and social reformers) judge as deviant behaviors seen as commonplace or expedient in working-class cultures. Of particular significance here is the tendency of working-class youth, whether apprentices or street traders or unskilled laborers, to acquire some measure of independence through work and as a result to create peer group leisure activities that violate the norms of youthful dependency. Also important is the pressure on poor children to beg, pick pockets, or sleep on the streets when family support fails, especially in times of economic instability. In the industrial age the high incidence of property crimes committed by working-class youths may confirm the class character of juvenile crime, whether due to the experience of deprivation or the failure to internalize the values of private property. Another approach draws on the theoretical contributions of Michel Foucault, treating the construction of juvenile delinquency as an exercise of power through the use of classifications and models not only by the state (that is, public authority) but also by elite social groups. Foucault's insistence that power is fundamentally about access to knowledge and control of language has been particularly influential. The ability to classify certain behaviors and experiences, impose those classifications on others, and mete out discipline on the basis on those classifications is clearly an exercise in power relations. To some extent, then, the very coining of the term juvenile delinquency, apparently in the nineteenth century, emerges as part of a broad codification, surveillance, and control function.

Reflecting the emphasis of the primary sources, social historians have explored juvenile delinquency as a pattern of behavior among poor and working-class youth, albeit a pattern identified by the middling and upper classes of modern European society. A refreshing alternative is provided by historians of late medieval and early modern European youth who have found elite youth of Italian cities and French youth of the craft classes behaving in riotous and violent ways, creating fear among authorities. Contemporaries sought explanations in cultural traditions, espe-

cially in the role of the peer youth group, the fabric of the local community, expectations about the transition to adulthood, and the masculine ideals of the age.

Gender is a third issue confronting historians of juvenile delinquency and hooliganism. Until recently most work on juvenile delinquency focused on boys and young men. Public records reveal that male offenders were largely responsible for juvenile thefts, assaults, public disturbances, and vagrancy. Not surprisingly, female offenders appear primarily in the context of charges of prostitution (both forced and "voluntary") though occasionally they were linked to begging and petty theft. The historical tendency to see the girl problem as one of (im)morality and sexuality had a direct impact on the methods of correction and treatment proposed for wayward girls. Given the overwhelming domination of the juvenile delinquency landscape by boys, one is tempted to wonder if delinquency should be analyzed as a male problem. Pamela Cox has broadened the picture by examining the policing of girls in twentieth-century Britain that took place not at the center of the newly created juvenile justice system but rather in peripheral institutions such as rescue homes and venereal disease hospitals. Girls have also emerged from the shadows of crime and misdemeanors in recent studies focusing on nineteenth-century girl gangs in England.

The role of "age" as a category of analysis is an especially significant issue. Juvenile delinquency is a "status" phenomenon where behaviors sanctioned as juvenile delinquency result from the age of the offender; curfew violation and school truancy are two examples of status offenses. Moreover, many acts considered delinquent in young people, such as smoking or alcohol consumption, are acceptable adult behaviors. Juvenile delinquency and hooliganism are specifically associated with adolescence and youth, and thus shed light on the tension inherent in the shift from child to adult. The very idea of juvenile delinquency draws attention to the conflicts over authority between adults and those who are no longer children but not yet fully independent adults. The concept of juvenile delinquency implies a distinctive type of social deviance, and is linked to notions about the equally distinctive role and character of youth in society. In the nineteenth century sharpened concern over juvenile delinquency prompted a wide variety of intrusive efforts to deal with what contemporaries regarded as a problem of epidemic proportions. Juvenile delinquents found themselves subjected to intensive control and "protection" well into their teen years. This extended subordination of youth did not go unchallenged as young inmates in juvenile prisons and reform schools articulated their resistance to punishment and rehabilitation. By tapping the disciplinary files of such institutions as well as the reports of twentieth-century probation officers, social historians may give voice to the delinquents themselves.

THE PREMODERN AGE

During Europe's Middle Ages, though criminal responsibility was generally set at age fourteen, responses to youthful deviance appear flexible. An extended period of youth contributed to an adult willingness to tolerate, within certain parameters, youthful delinquency. Thus, first offenders and local youth received some consideration, and those who participated in communal demonstrations of moral judgment, the charivari, also could expect societal tolerance and even approval. Evidence of medieval penal practices that took account of the youthfulness of offenders exists, such as reduced sentences and even separate prisons (as in fourteenth-century Nürnberg), though the latter was not common. Swedish provincial laws suggested those who had attained the age of fifteen, the age of civil and therefore criminal responsibility, could not be held fully responsible for their actions if they still lived under the supervision of a household guardian, whether parent or master.

Youthful male sexual violence pervaded medieval urban communities. Cities in late medieval France and Italy tolerated rape, including gang rape. The aggressive sexual behavior of youths was driven by the desire to become "men" and resentment against a tightly regulated sexual economy. Municipal brothels, whose clients consisted largely of unmarried young men, channeled the otherwise aggressive and rowdy behavior of young males. Also, groups of armed youths posed as brigands in many medieval settings, and the participation of elite young men suggests links between aristocratic culture, war-play, chivalry, and youth violence. Street gangs engaged in turf wars disrupted medieval cities, as in the late fourteenth century when Florence witnessed a clash between rival gangs named Berta and Magroni that lasted nearly two months.

THE EARLY MODERN AGE

"Reasons of misrule," "guardians of disorder"—such expressions capture the spirit of juvenile misbehavior and convey the ritualized nature of youth culture in early modern Europe. The misrule of youth had its

Rowdy Children. *Children with Dwarves,* painting (1646) by Jan Miense Molenaer.
COLLECTION STEDELIJK VAN ABBEMUSEUM, EINHOVEN, NETHERLANDS

385

rationality and young people, particularly males, carefully guarded the disorder. The mischief of nocturnal outings, the challenge of youthful insult and assault, and the irreligious pranks of the young constituted habitual behaviors not unexpected by adults, which were often winked at, but sometimes taken seriously enough to be punished through the formal mechanisms of court.

Two particularly relevant circumstances of the age shaped youthful behaviors and adult responses. First, the overwhelming majority of young people lived within the parameters of household-based service. The adolescent years were spent away from the parental home; young people learned skills under the watchful eye of a master or mistress, integrated to some degree into their service family, and enjoyed the company of peers at community social gatherings and during free time. Second, the impact of the Protestant and Catholic Reformations reshaped attitudes toward and responses to youthful misbehavior as concerns about righteous living and social stability intensified.

Appreciating the challenges posed by an extended period of youth, situated between childhood and full adulthood, early modern European society accommodated youths' need to experiment with authority arrangements. The long passage to adulthood offered opportunities for tolerable disorder, such as carnival and other festivals, the charivari, and celebrations connected to familial and community events such as weddings. These occasions gave young people, especially boys, roles to play in coordinating and carrying out collective gaiety, playful folly, or community judgment. Songs, parades, floats, costumes, and the all-important mask became part of the ritual tumult that accompanied Mardi Gras or a demonstration against an unacceptable marriage. These events offered opportunities for disorder within a controlled setting, allowing young people to role-play the adult practices of making judgments and policing the community.

Though early modern European society created room for young people to run riot, express insult, and topple the traditional order within the parameters of rural and urban community life, it would be misleading to suggest that young people rarely crossed the line into disruptive and destructive behavior spurned by the community. Smashed lanterns, thefts from orchards, attacks on animals (the "great cat massacre" by Paris print-shop apprentices re-created by Robert Darnton is perhaps best known), fruits and vegetables flung at passersby, and street fights such as the "boys' wars" reported in Aachen in 1757 are part of a rich picture of rough, wild, disruptive behavior carried out on the streets of towns and villages in daylight and at night. German, French, and English sources reveal

wicked youth, drunk and cavorting amid bonfires and music, determined to commit some mischief before night's end. Though municipal edicts against nocturnal disorder existed, some cast with tones of intense emotion, the practice of municipal authorities was in fact relatively indulgent.

Judging such activities as youthful pranks that would come to an end with the arrival at adulthood, rather than criminal acts leading to a foreboding future, municipal authorities attended to such delinquency with certain, but not excessive, effort. In sixteenth-century German towns, little prisons or "cages" were built to provide short-term punishment for young people who had disturbed the peace or insulted the honor of a townsperson but who had not committed a serious crime. Apprentices in Rheinfelden swore an oath that they would not be noisy after the night bell rang. Even the ritual cherry wars, a distinctive type of fruit theft, provoked adult anger but not much in the form of repression. In London, despite an accumulated body of legal precedent that gave municipal authorities jurisdiction over apprentices, punishment was mild. Most problems with insubordination by apprentices were handled not in the Mayor's Court but at the level below in the Chamberlain's Court. The emphasis was on arbitration and the chamberlain acted less as judge and more as mediator. Rather than punish, which was within his authority, the chamberlain was more likely to reprimand and compel the disputants to reach a compromise outside of court. Many cases never made it beyond the chamberlain's clerk who also worked to mediate disputes between masters and apprentices. Still London did have two prisons, known as "Little-Ease" due to their low ceilings, for apprentices who had been referred by the chamberlain for stubborn indiscipline.

The Protestant and Catholic Reformation affected adult responses to juvenile delinquency. As children belonged to both God and society, the wicked and disobedient would be punished by both, that is in the afterlife and during the earthly life. Calvinist catechism was most explicit on this point, threatening everlasting pain as well as a miserable life. In seeking to close down a brothel, late-sixteenth-century church leaders in Basel expressed a zero-tolerance view: youth should never be forgiven, especially for sins of pleasure, but should be controlled through punishment. Municipal concern over disturbance of the nighttime peace intensified during the Reformation period, as did edicts seeking to control disruptive noises during religious services. Particular concern focused on alleged sexuality immorality. Preachers targeted such traditional courtship practices as dancing and playing

FIRST STAGE OF CRUELTY.

While various Scenes of sportive Woe
The Infant Race employ,
And tortur'd Victims bleeding shew
The Tyrant in the Boy.

Behold a Youth of gentler Heart,
To spare the Creature's pain,
O take, he cries—take all my Tart,
But Tears and Tart are vain.

Learn from this fair Example—You
Whom savage Sports delight,
How cruelty disgusts the view,
While Pity charms the sight.

Torturing Animals. "First Stage of Cruelty." Plate 1 from the series *The Four Stages of Cruelty* (1751) by William Hogarth (1697–1764). © THE BRITISH MUSEUM

pranks on girls to secure their attention, as well as popular nuptial rituals whereby young bachelors publicly taunted the newly married couple with a disruptive yodeling. As zealous ecclesiastics targeted youthful immorality, the young responded with hooliganish behavior, disrupting the services of preachers and staging nocturnal attacks on priests. Municipal authorities responded to pressure from churchmen with laws such as those in Württemberg that threatened escalating punishments for those caught repeatedly disturbing the peace.

In early modern Europe, disorderly youthful behaviors were generally either part of a repertoire of pranks intended to notify the adult world that play had rough edges or part of ritualized popular culture such as carnival and charivari that provided opportunities for controlled disorder by those who could still legitimately get away with such collective madness. In addition, male youth violence was expressed around issues of territoriality and sexual control of the local female population. Rural youth fraternities regularly engaged in brawls with outsiders who sought to court "their girls" and did not hesitate to turn the knife from a traditional tool into a weapon.

Paul Griffiths has persuasively argued that in early modern England youth constituted a "threatening subgroup" when their behavior challenged adult authority, particularly in the context of service. Citing numerous seventeenth-century sources, Griffiths finds English moralists fraught with anxiety about the dangers, mischief, and deviance of youth but at the same time hopeful that youth could be directed to make the right choices for the future. Griffiths questions the widely held view that youthful rituals of misrule were approved or at least tolerated by adult society, citing increasing complaints by residents and increasing arrests of young people engaged in festive rioting on May Day or Shrove Tuesday. At the center of his analysis is a more nuanced and textured reading of early modern youth culture, a reading that rejects the image of young people as strictly enclosed in the household and integrated into a mixed age social world through the practice of apprenticeship. Though most young people lived in service they were not completely shackled by this situation, but rather had some opportunities for autonomy within and outside the household. Rather than pranks or community-tolerated misrule, youthful disorder emerges as serious deviance intended to challenge adult authority. The insubordination of youth, especially in the context of service, appears then as a problem of socialization in the transition from childhood to adulthood, a problem rooted in the difficulty of reorganizing the balance between work and play and redefining the meaning of time. The seriousness of this problem is illustrated in the response of authorities, especially those of the urban areas where relatively large populations of young people existed. Though not literally labeled "juvenile delinquency," Griffiths identifies a "youth problem" in the discourse and practices of early modern English authorities.

Interpreted through a "politics of age" framework, the generally public punishments meted out to disobedient apprentices emerge as carefully planned efforts to visibly demonstrate the authority of the household, the master, and the community. When an early-seventeenth-century London fishmonger's apprentices wreaked havoc in the marketplace by throwing fish, swearing, attacking customers, and disrupting business, the fishmonger's court took action, arranging an "open" punishment for the apprentices. An audience of apprentices was gathered to witness the lecture and whipping administered to the wild boys. Griffiths also argues that anxiety about "masterless" young people resulted in the criminalization of independent youth who resisted service. Between 1623 and 1631, a young Jane Sellars was repeatedly detained, charged with vagrancy, whipped, and banished for failing to remain in service. From charges of idleness and vagrancy to charges of petty theft and ille-

gitimacy, Sellars was eventually designated a felon. The last mention of Jane Sellars is an order for execution recorded in December 1631. Griffiths argues that young people who were "at their own hand" or "out of service" constituted a threat to order and stability in early modern England because they placed themselves outside the institutions of socialization and control.

While early modern European society seems to have been comparatively tolerant of youthful mischief, evidence of severe punishment can be found. In Zurich, between 1500 and 1750, more than one hundred young people were executed for offenses including bestiality, sodomy, theft, arson and homicide. In an age when burning at the stake, being buried alive, and drowning were still common forms of execution for notably heinous crimes, young people were generally beheaded, a form of punishment considered more humane. Still the execution of a Hamburg boy, age eleven, for throwing a stone through the window of a Hansa official's house seems extreme. Moreover, the use of charitable institutions, such as orphanages, as settings for correctional measures suggests the need to look carefully at the ways in which early modern societies may have masked their treatment of juveniles whose behavior seemed to require punishment or reform. For example, Seville's eighteenth-century asylum for street waifs also served as a depot for delinquent children committed by family members or public authorities.

In general, however, early modern Europeans appear more willing than their descendants to accept youth as an age when natural and social inclinations required outlets for the expression of disorder. This tolerance extended primarily to boys, as girls were both formally and informally constrained from moving about freely outside the household, particularly at night. Indeed, the concerns of Protestant Reformers exacerbated the social restrictions on girls. Nonetheless, youthful deviance was not generally considered criminal and punishments, even those meted out by judicial or other supervising bodies, were moderate and generally symbolic. The most important concern seems to have been maintenance of order within the household world of service. Additionally, it should be noted that the greater mixing of younger and older youths not only meant broader alliances for mischief, such as the youth abbeys of early modern France, but also reduced the age-specific character of such mischief. Youth culture encompassed the teens and twenties and any associated deviance clearly had a broad age base. Thus the early-eighteenth-century Paris print-shop cat massacre comes down to us as the work of apprentices and journeymen, albeit led by the apprentices.

By the eighteenth century, nocturnal disturbances, especially in the cities, stood less chance of being overlooked. Concern with street safety resulted in the installation of lanterns and the deployment of police patrols. The goal of municipal order clashed with disruptive youth behaviors. Gangs of well-to-do young men, such as the Mohocks of London, troubled adult society with their random, belligerent, rakish behavior. Nor were rural environs immune to these concerns, as evidenced by the presence of eighteenth-century Irish "peasant societies" made up of young men who attacked enclosures. That these groups took names (Whiteboys, Oakboys) implies a degree of collective identity.

Shaped by local social and economic networks, generally more flexible and tolerant, certainly less bureaucratic and pessimistic, early modern European attitudes toward the varied expressions of youthful mischief and hooliganism began to change during the eighteenth century. The slide toward labeling such behaviors as "juvenile delinquency" and seeing in them signs of serious social danger, reflections of deep economic dislocation, and hints of a lifetime of criminality shaped much of the next century.

THE MODERN AGE

By the nineteenth century, an increasingly worried public viewed youthful misbehavior as deviant and even "criminal." Early modern reactions of toleration, mild rebuke, and moral exhortation had been rooted in the conviction that youthful disorder would be outgrown. In contrast, the nineteenth century witnessed the growth of differentiated, age-specific institutions intended to correct, punish, and reform delinquents over increasingly long periods of incarceration or surveillance. The conceptualization, codification, and bureaucratization of the "problem" of juvenile delinquency mark the modern experience of youthful hooliganism.

Social historians and others have mined the nineteenth century searching for patterns of delinquent behaviors, profiles of delinquent youths, sources of adult anxieties, and trends in approaches to juvenile corrections. Efforts to identify "turning points" in the evolution of a new, more anxious view of juvenile delinquency and attempts to assess the dual impact of urbanization and industrialization have figured prominently in many studies. Social historians have considered the role of the state, especially the judicial, police, and welfare functions. Legal thinking influenced by the ideology of childhood, the creation of professional municipal policing, and the expansion of publicly funded institutions designed to envelop the juvenile delinquent all abetted the social construction of juvenile delinquency. Social historians have not only scrutinized the cycles of cultural anxiety that contributed to revised definitions of juvenile delinquency but also examined the unfolding of the ideologies of childhood and adolescence during the nineteenth century.

Nineteenth-century crime statistics are difficult to use for arriving at solid conclusions regarding the incidence of youth crime, rates of change in youth crime, or the proportion of youth to adult crime. The science of statistics and the development of a state statistical bureaucracy varied across Europe. More importantly, as definitions of "juvenile" and "crime" changed over time, the statistics measured different phenomena. During the nineteenth century, new categories of offenses emerged especially in the area of juvenile behavior. In addition, the age-specificity of the statistics varies over time and from place to place. If various quantitative measures indicate an apparent increase in what nineteenth-century Europeans considered the "problem" of juvenile delinquency, then what does this reveal about the activities of youth, the anxieties of adults, the norms of society and the role of the state (including police, courts, prisons, and welfare institutions)?

The French political cartoonist, artist, and social critic Honoré Daumier captured adult anxieties about precocious urban childhood in an 1848 drawing for the newspaper Le Charivari. Amid the revolutionary atmosphere of Paris, Daumier's Paris Street Urchins in the Tuileries portrayed street children as participants in the overthrow of the monarchy. By the middle of the nineteenth century, Europe's middle classes appeared bewildered, unable to distinguish between deprived and depraved children. Urchins, street arabs, pickpockets, gamins, vagrants, orphans all seemed dangerous and endangered. Newspaper reports of accused children brought before Parisian courts during the July Monarchy juxtaposed natural innocence and unnatural precocity in an effort to navigate the murky terrain created by an evolving ideology of childhood and an increasing anxiety about the rising incidence of juvenile crime. By the middle decades of the nineteenth century, a "juvenile delinquent" may well have violated the criminal code but more likely violated a bourgeois standard of appropriate behavior, thereby committing an "offense" rather than a crime. As such offenses became increasingly codified and linked to penal corrections, the incidence of juvenile delinquency increased.

Industrial urbanization, the wage economy, migration, and increased illegitimacy contributed to making juvenile delinquency a social problem of

Deprived or Depraved? "The Dangerous Children" frighten an elderly couple. Plate 40 from the series *Alarms and Alarmists* by Honoré Daumier (1808–1879). CABINET DES ESTAMPES, BIBLIOTHÈQUE NATIONALE, PARIS

growing dimensions in the nineteenth century. As the percentage of young people in the European population rose, fears of precocious children and delinquent youth abounded. Moreover, as cities and towns attracted ever-larger populations of young workers and would-be workers, concerns about the decline of apprenticeships and the crafts and the concomitant rise of unskilled labor fueled fears of idle, and therefore unruly, youth. Wage-earning youth struck an independent and threatening image as potential gamblers and consumers of alcohol and tobacco. Industrial child labor exacerbated worries of stolen childhoods and rising immorality among children trapped in the vicious world of early factories. Not surprisingly, runaways and orphans constituted a large portion of those identified by authorities as "delinquents." In mid-nineteenth-century France, vagrancy and begging constituted over 50 percent of juvenile crime committed by boys. Girls were most often charged with prostitution and begging, the former being equivalent to a vagrancy charge for boys. In this context, homelessness and unemployment became "crimes" and the basis for commitment to a house of correction.

The bourgeois ideology of childhood shaped the nineteenth-century history of juvenile delinquency. It compelled a rethinking of the relationship between children and crime, raising questions about responsibility and discernment, punishment and rehabilitation. The notion spread that while children might not be fully responsible for their crimes, whether heinous or simply mischievous, they were surely a distinct population of offenders who required age-specific punishment and correction. Though children might be considered innocent of evil intent due to their age, adult observers could not help but conclude that children were more than capable of committing crimes and disturbances. The ideal of innocence clashed with the reality of vice; adults found the solution to this contradiction by creating distinct judicial and correctional methods tied to the youthfulness of offenders.

There is an important irony here. Innocence and inexperience emerged as the hallmarks of true childhood, and the delinquent child stood as either an unnatural aberration or a sympathetic victim of poverty or neglect or abuse in need of rescue. Relieving children of criminal responsibility for their mischief, adult authorities compromised the autonomy of young people. Removed from the adult criminal justice system, including its prisons, juvenile delinquents became a class apart, garnering so much special attention it could be smothering. Nineteenth-century contemporaries constructed the problem of juvenile delinquency, then proposed to reform, rescue, and protect "at-risk" children. The very uniqueness of children brought greater scrutiny, restriction, and confinement to those young people who seemed to confound the idealized image of the innocent and dependent child.

As early as the first two decades of the nineteenth century, English judges demonstrated a certain sympathy for child criminals. Between 1801 and 1836, 104 children received death sentences at the Old Bailey court though in fact none of these children was executed. An 1828 inquiry found that many judges were reluctant to bring children to trial because many crimes carried capital punishment sentences. The reform movement against capital punishment drew a good deal of its power from cases involving juveniles, no doubt influenced by the newly emerging ideology of childhood. The 1828 report also called for the development of a separate prison system for children. Three further developments occurred in England during the first half of the nineteenth century. First, many previously indictable crimes (that is, those tried by a jury) became subject to summary jurisdiction (that is, sentencing by a judge). Second, punishments meted out to child offenders became relatively less severe. Third, new types of crimes emerged as previously tolerated behaviors became defined as offenses. The interaction of these developments contributed to the "problem" of juvenile delinquency. In essence, more juveniles were punished more often, and for a wider range of mischief, but punishments were less severe. Still debated is the precise timing of this shift, with various historians pointing to the periods of 1790–1830, 1830s–1840s, or the 1850s. Peter King's analysis of English county court records demonstrates that in the early nineteenth century summary jurisdiction sharply increased the number of juveniles processed by the judicial system and sent into the correctional system. The relative absence of juveniles from the lists of indicted criminals, noticeable by the mid-1820s, is thus misleading when trying to identify the origins of the "problem" juvenile delinquency. By midcentury, in England, as elsewhere in western Europe, new institutions reserved exclusively for juvenile offenders dotted the landscape: Parkhurst Prison for boys in England, La Petite Roquette and Les Madelonettes in France.

Court records, police reports, and newspapers reveal the kinds of offences nineteenth-century juveniles committed. Crimes against property constitute a significant area of youthful mischief, especially in the case of boys. This includes pickpocketing, pilfering, vandalism, simple theft, and larceny. In Sweden in 1841, 93 percent of offenders under age fifteen had committed property offenses involving pickpocketing, theft, and burglary. Even for girls, theft accounted for all but one offense in this age group. By the latter decades of the nineteenth century, theft became the most common crime among boys, replacing vagrancy. In France, 4,718 of 5,800 youth cases judged in 1864 concerned simple thefts. Often these thefts involved goods of little value, reflecting perhaps the growth of consumer goods in European society. References to stealing handkerchiefs abound in the court testimony of young thieves in 1830s' London. Vagrancy, assault, premarital sex, and public disorder were other common juvenile crimes. In Sweden, the majority (fifty-one of seventy-five) of those charged with premarital sex in 1841 were female. As concern for public order intensified, bringing with it a great interest in cleaning up the urban environment, numerous public disturbance and curfew violations surfaced. Use of fireworks, "dangerous play," swearing in public, and loitering in groups (gangs) could all lead to detention of juveniles in the later decades of the nineteenth century.

Child thieves who worked the streets and alleys of major cities participated in an adult network of criminality that included those who fenced stolen goods and corrupt police who closed their eyes to the dishonesty of certain pawnbrokers and publicans in exchange for a part of the take. Such child offenders frequently emerge as victims of adult manipulation, including their neglectful or absent parents. As urban reform took hold, including the razing of congested alleys and winding streets in both London and Paris, the physical environment that had shielded young pickpockets gradually faded. The introduction of a more professional police presence in the second half of the nineteenth century also altered the environment in some municipalities. The creation of institutions designed to "protect" delinquent or at-risk juveniles added further to the changing world of juvenile criminality.

During the nineteenth century, the age for being conditionally responsible for criminal actions gradually increased, from fourteen to sixteen to eighteen years of age. Correctional methods evolved from imprisonment with adults and transportation to separate children's prisons, agricultural colonies, and houses of correction to schoollike reformatories and probationary surveillance by state guardians. Some of the earliest reform schools designed for juvenile delinquents were established in Belgium beginning in 1848, such as those at Ruysselede and Beernem. In general, punishment moved in the direction of distinguishing young offenders on the basis of age and developing methods considered age sensitive.

The nineteenth-century construction of juvenile delinquency harbored several contradictions, including the conflicting image of juvenile delinquents as threats to society and as victims of socioeconomic dislocations and/or family dysfunction. Though the two images coexisted through much of the nineteenth century, some historians have suggested that the delinquent-as-victim image came to predominate by the 1870s to 1880s. This shift coincided with major efforts on the part of states to implement programs designed to materially improve the lives of young people. Across Europe, though the timing varies from place to place, child labor laws and compulsory schooling laws converged toward the end of the century to produce a new lifestyle for children of the working classes. Concerns about child endangerment, both physical and moral, inspired laws regarding child protection. Many such laws targeted poor parents, not society, as the locus of neglect, cruelty, abandonment, and abuse. With this development, delinquent children were seen as victims of parental neglect or abuse, and therefore in need of being saved from such deplorable conditions. In many European countries, the fairly new prisons for children were replaced by youth reformation institutions, intended to be more like schools and less like prisons.

Nineteenth-century juvenile delinquency discourse and practice reveals the larger cultural trend toward discipline of juvenile nonconformity and independence. The growth of private and public agencies to carry out plans for punishment, correction, and reformation confirms this. Moreover, the quantitative evidence is unequivocal in demonstrating a pattern of increase in the number and percentage of young people caught in the web of institutions created to control, reprimand, and rehabilitate them. In the late 1820s, fewer than one hundred youths per year were sent to houses of correction in France, while that number jumped to close to three thousand per year in the early 1870s. In England, reformatory schools and industrial schools were created in 1854 and 1857 to handle convicted young offenders as well as those deemed in need of protection. Similar institutions appeared in Scotland and Ireland. In the decades after 1870 Prussia experienced a severe shortage of reformatory space as the number committed to such institutions skyrocketed. A fivefold increase in Prussian commitments to correctional education occurred between 1900 and 1914.

Had hooliganism spread so widely among European youth that it warranted these institutional responses? Had adult society become obsessed with the urge to "discipline and punish" the young? In the early modern period, most juvenile offenders were handled through the institutions of household and community; serious offenders were treated within the parameters of the adult system of criminal justice. And while adult complaints about youthful mischief abounded, there is little evidence of a profound sense of panic or crisis associated with juvenile behavior in the early modern period. By the nineteenth century, the elaborate efforts made to provide separate treatment for a seemingly vast and growing population of juvenile delinquents strongly suggests the emergence of a crisis surrounding the issue of youth behavior. Though the generous presumption of childhood innocence (at least as an ideal) lay at the heart of the formal provision of a separate system for juveniles, the result was to create a publicly recognized social problem of compelling intensity. This panic brought more and more juveniles under the vigilant eye of adult society. As European society developed age-sensitive institutions to treat the juvenile delinquent, reluctance to bring large numbers of young people before the civil authorities waned. This line of development culminated with legislation such as the Children's Act of 1908 in England and 1912 laws in France and Belgium creating special juvenile courts and auxiliary support institutions and personnel to aid in the prevention of juvenile delinquency.

Around 1900 heated cries about the crisis of juvenile delinquency rose again, perhaps reflecting the new standards of youth behavior associated with the evolving notion of adolescence and the emergence of a youth-oriented culture of leisure. Ironically, this new wave of anxiety coincided with a trend toward conformity in youth behavior as measured by the greater involvement of young people in structured, adult-run activities (for example, extended schooling and youth groups). One explanation for this wave of anxiety was the popularization of the psychology of adolescence which suggested that all young people were potentially troubled and troublesome. Though a class bias still placed poor and working-class youth at a disadvantage, the psychology of adolescence implied that the experience of puberty itself contained the seeds for rebellion, conflict, and misbehavior. Every adolescent was a potential delinquent in need of supervision and guidance. At the turn of the century, a pervasive wave of anxiety about the behavior of youth spread across Europe. Demographic and political developments heightened awareness of the quality and quantity of Europe's youth. In addition, the commercialization of leisure with the possibilities it offered young workers to define themselves through clothing, smoking, and dancing further contributed to that anxiety.

The model of adolescence popularized by social science experts, reformers, and bureaucrats promoted adult vigilance and youthful dependency. This model clashed with working-class experience and as a result these youths offered a point of resistance to the imposition of conformity. As the school-leaving age increased, the truancy of juveniles was often an assertion of independence and of a preference for work over school. Working-class memoirs and oral histories confirm that activities regarded as criminal and delinquent by police authorities appeared to working-class youths as so many examples of "larking about."

The street stood at the center of much young working-class social life where street-corner gambling, scuffles between neighboring gangs defending their territory, and girls, football, and petty theft all coexisted. In Vienna middle-class teachers and scout leaders claimed bands of wild working class youth (*Platten*) filled the streets. In Manchester working-class girls formed part of the scuttlers' world of "disorderly" conduct as weekend promenading transformed the streets into youth-dominated spaces. In Paris newspapers reported the rise of the apache, a sort of working-class version of a rake. In Russia juvenile crime *(bezprizorniki)* inspired fear in law-abiding residents of St. Petersburg who sensed that every juvenile delinquent was a potential hooligan bent on defying not only adults but also civilization itself. As hooligans, older male teens roamed St. Petersburg's streets, harassed pedestrians, shouted obscenities, carried brass knuckles, engaged in public drunkenness, threw rocks, invaded respectable neighborhoods, and projected a threatening image.

The years of World War I witnessed a sharp increase in the incidence of juvenile delinquency as European society experienced disruption in all facets of life. Soldiering fathers, working mothers, food shortages, and early release from school contributed to youth disorderliness. In Germany fears about unsupervised youths with money led military authorities to impose a savings program to limit their spending. In Hamburg officials even tried to regulate attendance at shows and smoking in public. In England juveniles under age sixteen charged with crimes increased during the war years from 37,500 to 51,000 per year.

The postwar period introduced some new direction in adult responses to juvenile delinquency. Although theories of adolescent development and the corollary of adult guidance were considered universal in application, working-class youths did not consistently attain the satisfactory outcomes signaled by conformity and dependence. Working-class girls seemed to defy "respectable" norms of behavior when it came to appearance and sexual habits. Confronting a decline in skilled jobs, resistant to continued schooling, trapped in "dead-end" jobs, sensitive to the pull of extreme political groups, and attracted by the freedom of the streets and its night life, working-class youths in the 1920s and 1930s posed a formidable challenge to those who sought a well-regulated, orderly youth experience. An army of professional youth workers, including mental health experts, developed strategies to identify and treat children and young people who challenged the model. By 1920 conventional explanations of juvenile delinquency focusing on deprivation and environment competed with the growing belief that delinquency had its roots in individual psychological dysfunction. By the mid-1920s Britain had borrowed the child guidance clinic innovation from the United States, as the therapeutic approach to juvenile delinquency spread throughout Europe. Weimar Germany adopted new legislation, including the National Juvenile Justice Act (1923) and the National Youth Welfare Act (1924), based on acceptance of a medicalized model of juvenile delinquency. Increasingly, heredity, environment, and personality were seen as interacting forces that could lead to mental and behavioral problems under certain circumstances of social instability. In England the Children and Young Persons Act of 1933 expressed the new effort by replacing discipline and punishment with discipline, welfare, and treatment. The old distinction between reform schools and industrial schools disappeared under a new rubric, "approved schools," intended to house delinquent, neglected, and at-risk youths. In Fascist Italy observation centers maintained a close surveillance of the youth population in an effort at delinquency prevention.

Juvenile delinquency statistics for the 1920s and 1930s confirm the continued centrality of property crime, especially petty theft. In 1928 Hamburg, fourteen- to sixteen-year-olds convicted of crimes were overwhelmingly convicted for property offences: 77 percent of boys convicted and 83 percent of girls convicted. Bicycle thefts were widespread while girls most often shoplifted from department stores or stole from their domestic employers. As the Depression set in, juvenile theft increased in many places. However, crimes against the state and public disorder committed by juveniles, usually males, increased too, especially in states where political tensions ran high. Thus in Hamburg juveniles accused of trespass, obstruction, and disturbance of the peace increased. Fears of cliques, wild hiking clubs of working-class adolescents, permeated Germany in the late 1920s. At the same time, panic over European cultural changes involving the popularity of dance, jazz ("Negro music"), cinema, and pulp fiction contributed to a perception of youthful immorality and led to legislation such as the 1926 German Law for the Protection of Minors against Smutty and Trashy Literature.

Trends set earlier in the century continued in the 1940s and 1950s. World War II ushered in an era of increased juvenile crime; explanations centered on the "broken homes" that resulted from the disruptions of war. Though most juvenile crime in the immediate postwar period seemed to be related to poverty and dislocation, some observers worried about the long-term moral impact of such "waywardness." In the later 1940s and 1950s, incidences of recorded juvenile delinquency were fueled by factors as diverse as youths' economic situation, over-surveillance of youth behavior, a widening psychological definition of delinquency, a treatment-oriented juvenile justice system, and the temptations of popular culture.

The optimism of the postwar period supported approaches to juvenile delinquency, real and imaged, that focused on social reconstruction. In Great Britain the Criminal Justice Act of 1948 proposed better ways to treat youth offenders, most notably by placing severe restrictions of the use of imprisonment, abolishing corporal punishment, and emphasizing the use of probation and residential training. The Federal Republic of Germany developed annual Youth Plans beginning in 1950 and attempted a thorough reform of its correctional practices, with an emphasis on voluntary commitments, family placements, protective supervision, and especially prevention of juvenile delinquency through youth activities and psychotherapy.

By the 1960s the emergence of an outspoken youth culture, defiant of adult authority and flaunting conventions of sexual morality, challenged the twentieth-century ideal of a conformist, regulated youth. This mostly bourgeois youth rebellion affirmed traditional working-class youth resistance to adult controls on autonomy. Music and fashion tended to bridge the chasm of class that had typically divided European youth. French working-class youth in the post-1960s tended to define themselves more in terms of their youthfulness and less in terms of class differentiation that had characterized pre-1960s gangs, promoting a vision of universal, natural youth. A wave of hooliganism *(teppismo)* swept Italy in the early 1960s involving vandalism of streetlights, "exhibitionist" fashion, street rowdiness, and car thefts. The work of teenage boys, these incidences of delinquency coincided with economic prosperity and point to the growing generation gap.

Ironically, 1960s youth turbulence seemed to confirm the idea of the fundamentally wild nature of adolescent development, especially in the area of sexuality. And in an environment of widespread material well-being and social services, factors such as poverty and family breakdown could no longer be held accountable for juvenile delinquency. With the therapeutic model in crisis, some advocated a return to a more tolerant approach to youthful misbehavior, reminiscent of the early modern world. Scandinavian studies found that to some extent juvenile crime as a stage of life phenomenon was "statistically normal." Social scientists advocated young people's right to self-identification. A nascent child's rights movement developed in Europe too. Applied to the issue of juvenile corrections, the idea that young people have rights has led to a reconsideration of all the measures associated with treating juvenile offenders as though the right to care and protection obviated the right to due process.

Modern European society has seemingly created a more rigid world for its youth, despite the disappearance of arranged marriages and the development of an independent youth culture. Formal schooling and organized leisure have increasingly come to shape young people's lives. At the same time, young Europeans have more pocket money than ever before and are more free to spend it as they wish. The paradoxes are relevant for understanding the evolution of juvenile delinquency and adult responses to it. Despite highly publicized but nonetheless rare instances of violent juvenile crime (child murderers also existed in previous centuries), hooliganism and juvenile delinquency remain very much tied to definitions orchestrated by adults. Laws imposing helmets on teenage Italian motorcyclists have been flouted by youths who say the helmets ruin their hairstyles and who resent adults making ageist laws. What counts as offense very much depends on demographics, cultural norms, institutional developments, political and economic environments, as well as the constantly tested hierarchy regulating adult-child relations. In contemporary Europe, discussions of hooliganism and juvenile delinquency often center on immigrant and minority youth on the one hand and right-wing youth on the other. Waywardness, disorderliness, and mischief appear as threads of continuity in the lives of European youth, while the social meaning of these behaviors reflect adult anxieties about the stability of family, community, and state.

See also **The European Marriage Pattern** *(volume 2);* **Street Life and City Space** *(volume 2);* **The Welfare State** *(volume 2);* **Youth and Adolescence** *(volume 4);* **Festivals** *(volume 5); and* **Policing Leisure** *(volume 5); and other articles in this section.*

BIBLIOGRAPHY

Bailey, Victor. *Delinquency and Citizenship: Reclaiming the Young Offender, 1914–1948.* Oxford and New York, 1987.

Cohen, Esther. "Youth and Deviancy in the Middle Ages." In *History of Juvenile Delinquency: A Collection of Essays on Crime Committed by Young Offenders, in History and in Selected Countries.* Edited by Albert G. Hess and Priscilla F. Clement. Aalen, Germany, 1990. Volume 1, pages 207–230.

Cox, Pamela. "On the Margins of Justice: Policing Girls in 20th Century Britain." Paper delivered at the conference "Becoming Delinquent: European Youth 1650–1950." Cambridge University, April 1999.

Crouzet-Pavan, Elisabeth. "A Flower of Evil: Young Men in Medieval Italy." In *A History of Young People in the West.* Vol. 1: *Ancient and Medieval Rites of Passage.* Edited by Giovanni Levi and Jean-Claude Schmitt. Cambridge, Mass., 1997. Pages 173–221.

Davies, Andrew. " 'These Viragos are no less cruel than the lads': Young Women, Gangs, and Violence in Late Victorian Manchester and Salford." *British Journal of Criminology* 39 (1999): 72–89.

Davies, Andrew. "Youth Gangs, Masculinity, and Violence in Late Victorian Manchester and Salford." *Journal of Social History* 32 (1998): 349–369.

Davis, Natalie Zemon "The Reasons of Misrule." In her *Society and Culture in Early Modern France.* Stanford, Calif., 1975. Pages 97–123.

Dickinson, Edward Ross. *The Politics of German Child Welfare from the Empire to the Federal Republic.* Cambridge, Mass., 1996.

Fishman, Sarah. "Juvenile Delinquency as a 'Condition': Social Science Constructions of the Child Criminal 1936–1946." In *Proceedings of Western Society for French History.* Edited by Barry Rothaus. Boulder, Colo., 1997.

Fuchs, Rachel G. "Juvenile Delinquency in Nineteenth-Century France." In *History of Juvenile Delinquency: A Collection of Essays on Crime Committed by Young Offenders, in History and in Selected Countries.* Edited by Albert G. Hess and Priscilla F. Clement. Aalen, Germany, 1990. Volume 1, pages 265–287.

Gillis, John R. *Youth and History: Tradition and Change in European Age Relations, 1770–Present.* New York, 1981.

Griffiths, Paul. *Youth and Authority: Formative Experiences in England, 1560–1640.* Oxford and New York, 1996.

Haine, W. Scott. "The Development of Leisure and the Transformation of Working Class Adolescence in Paris, 1830–1940." *Journal of Family History* 17 (1992): 451–470.

Harvey, Elizabeth. *Youth and the Welfare State in Weimar Germany.* Oxford and New York, 1993.

Hendrick, Harry. *Child Welfare: England, 1872–1969.* London, 1994.

Hess, Albert G., and Priscilla F. Clement, eds. *History of Juvenile Delinquency: A Collection of Essays on Crime Committed by Young Offenders, in History and in Selected Countries.* 2 vols. Aalen, Germany, 1990–1993.

Hess, Albert G. "Juvenile Crime in the Early Modern Age." In *History of Juvenile Delinquency: A Collection of Essays on Crime Committed by Young Offenders, in History and in Selected Countries.* Edited by Albert G. Hess and Priscilla F. Clement. Aalen, Germany, 1990. Volume 1, pages 231–244.

Hopkins, Eric. *Childhood Transformed: Working-Class Children in Nineteenth-Century England.* Manchester, U.K., 1994.

Humphries, Stephen. *Hooligans or Rebels? An Oral History of Working Class Childhood and Youth, 1889–1939.* Oxford, 1981.

Joutsen, Matti. "Treatment, Punishment, Control: Juvenile Delinquency in Scandinavia." In *History of Juvenile Delinquency: A Collection of Essays on Crime Committed by Young Offenders, in History and in Selected Countries.* Edited by Albert G. Hess and Priscilla F. Clement. Aalen, Germany, 1990. Volume 2, pages 599–623.

King, Peter. "The Rise of Juvenile Delinquency in England, 1780–1840: Changing Patterns of Perception and Prosecution." *Past and Present* 160 (1998): 116–167.

Lafont, Hubert. "Changing Sexual Behaviour in French Youth Gangs." In *Western Sexuality: Practice and Precept in Past and Present Times.* Edited by Philippe Ariès and André Béjin. Translated by Anthony Forster. Oxford, 1985. Pages 168–180. Translation of *Sexualités occidentales.*

Magarey, Susan. "The Invention of Juvenile Delinquency in Early Nineteenth-Century England." *Labour History* 34 (1978): 11–27.

May, Margaret. "Innocence and Experience: The Evolution of the Concept of Juvenile Delinquency in the Mid-Nineteenth Century." *Victorian Studies* 27 (1973): 6–29.

Mitterauer, Michael. *A History of Youth.* Translated by Graeme Dunphy. Oxford and Cambridge, Mass., 1992. Translation of *Sozialgeschichte der Jugend.*

Neuberger, Joan. *Hooliganism: Crime Culture and Power in St. Petersburg 1900–1914.* Berkeley, Calif., 1993.

Nilan, Cat. "Hapless Innocence and Precocious Perversity in the Courtroom Melodrama: Representations of the Child Criminal in a Paris Legal Journal, 1830–1848." *Journal of Family History* 22 (1997): 251–285.

Perrot, Michelle. "Delinquency and the Penitentiary System in Nineteenth Century France" In *Deviants and the Abandoned in French Society.* Edited by Robert Forster and Orest Ranum. Baltimore, 1978. Pages 213–245.

Peukert, Detlev. "The Lost Generation: Youth Unemployment at the End of the Weimar Republic." In *The German Unemployed: Experiences and Consequences of Mass Unemployment from the Weimar Republic to the Third Reich.* Edited by Richard J. Evans and Dick Geary. New York, 1987. Pages 172–193.

Piccone, Stella Simonetta. " 'Rebels without a Cause': Male Youth in Italy around 1960." *History Workshop Journal* 38 (1994): 157–178.

Rosenhaft, Eve. "Organising the 'Lumpenproletariat': Cliques and Communists in Berlin during the Weimar Republic." In *The German Working Class, 1888–1933: The Politics of Everyday Life.* Edited by Richard J. Evans. London and Totowa, N.J., 1982. Pages 174–219.

Rossiaud, Jacques. "Prostitution, Youth, and Society in the Towns of Southeastern France in the Fifteenth Century." In *Deviants and the Abandoned in France.* Edited by Robert Forster and Orest Ranum. Baltimore, 1978. Pages 1–46.

Roumajon, Yves. *Enfants perdus, enfants punis: Histoire de la jeunesse délinquante en France: Huit siècles de controverses.* Paris, 1989.

Sanders, Wiley B., ed. *Juvenile Offenders for a Thousand Years: Selected Readings from Anglo-Saxon Times to 1900.* Chapel Hill, N.C., 1970.

Schindler, Norbert. "Guardians of Disorder: Rituals of Youthful Culture at the Dawn of the Modern Age." In *A History of Young People in the West.* Vol. 1: *Ancient and Medieval Rites of Passage.* Edited by Giovanni Levi and Jean-Claude Schmitt. Cambridge, Mass., 1997. Pages 240–282.

Shore, Heather. " 'Cross Coves, Buzzers, and General Sorts of Prigs': Juvenile Crime and the Criminal Underworld in the Early Nineteenth Century." *British Journal of Criminology* 39 (1999): 10–24.

Springhall, John. *Coming of Age: Adolescence in Britain 1860–1960.* Dublin, 1986.

Tikoff, Valentina. "Orphan Asylums as 'Reformatories' in Old Regime Seville." Paper delivered at the conference "Becoming Delinquent: European Youth 1650–1950." Cambridge University, April 1999.

Wegs, J. Robert. *Growing Up Working Class: Continuity and Change among Viennese Youth, 1890–1938.* University Park, Pa., 1989.

Wegs, J. Robert. "Youth Delinquency and 'Crime': the Perception and the Reality." *Journal of Social History* 32 (1999): 603–621.

Weinberger, Barbara. "Policing Juveniles: Delinquency in Late Nineteenth and Early Twentieth Century Manchester." *Criminal Justice History: An International Annual* 14 (1993): 43–56.

POLICE

Haia Shpayer-Makov

Policing has taken many forms historically and has gone through radical transformations, making it difficult to offer a precise and universal definition of the term "police." This essay employs the term broadly to mean official organs entrusted with the enforcement of law and order and endowed with the right to use force for public ends.

Throughout most of history the police were only one, and not necessarily the prevalent, instrument of law enforcement. In the late Middle Ages and the Renaissance (1300–1600) a variety of institutions and individuals performed the functions of law and order maintenance that we now associate with the institutions called "police." Moreover, the authority to sanction violence in the name of law enforcement was not the monopoly of the rulers. Life in medieval Europe was highly localized, and this was reflected in the application of power and the control of crime as well. Political sovereignty was fragmented and local authority was largely independent of royal direction. Many cities authorized special patrols and watches to protect life and property and to bar strangers from entry, particularly at night. Manorial lords often imposed their will and/or defended their rights with their own private means of coercion. Some religious institutions, such as the Inquisition, deployed their own law enforcers to attain their sectional goals. The church, universities, guilds, and corporations had their own means of implementing administrative rulings. In the relatively unified kingdom of England, a more systematic policing structure emerged, based on local lords who were appointed by the Crown as justices of the peace, and on their subordinates, the constables, who helped them keep the peace and bring malefactors to justice. Service as a constable, though unpaid, was obligatory for adult men in the parish for one year by rotation or appointment.

In most places in Europe, however, a permanent coercive force was nonexistent, and the enforcement of laws, rules, and norms depended on the acceptance of their legitimacy by the local population. In general, sanctions and social pressure were sufficient to regulate internal affairs, and if not, the community often administered its own justice. Warnings, reprimands, and ostracism could compel conformity to rules. The local worthies (for example, the parish priest or the lord's agent) often acted as go-betweens to settle an injury, by agreement of both parties involved.

It is during the seventeenth century that the expansion and growing importance of the police in European society are first observable. This change did not signify any sort of break with the past. The emerging policing structure was rudimentary, and it functioned side by side with traditional patterns of law enforcement well into the modern period. The more intensive adoption of police organs, though, marked the beginning of a general trend, which in retrospect constituted one of the major societal developments of the modern era.

To be sure, no one system of policing was common throughout Europe at any one time, nor was this area unified by a similar chronology. The presence, character, functions, purposes, and authority of law enforcement agencies varied greatly not only between states but also from one region to the other and over time. Furthermore, the development of national policing systems proceeded at different speeds. Nonetheless, many parts of Europe experienced parallel developments with regard to their civil and criminal justice systems, and political bodies, whether local or central, private or public, took similar steps to enforce them.

European societies often looked to each other for models of policing, both positive and negative, to emulate or to discard. Whereas Russia, Prussia, Austria, and Italy were deeply influenced by the French mode of policing, in England opposition to police reform during the eighteenth and early nineteenth centuries, and the implementation of reform thereafter, were both guided by rejection of the French system, which was perceived as too authoritarian and intrusive for the British tradition of government. Later on in the nineteenth century police reformers on both sides of the Channel felt they had a lot to learn from

English Constabulary. Peelers or Bobbies, members of the police force established by Sir Robert Peel's Police Bill in the 1830s. MARY EVANS PICTURE LIBRARY

each other's systems. Once reorganized early in the nineteenth century, the English constabulary became a frame of reference for police forces all over the world. Conquest was also a factor in the import and transfer of ideas and practices from one part of Europe to another. French expansion under Napoleon resulted in the implementation of a centralized police system in some areas under subjugation. And policing arrangements in the European colonies were molded under the impact of European rule.

Thus, despite wide diversity, a pattern of policing evolved in Europe made up of different combinations of law-enforcing traditions and methods in each nation, but having a measure of uniformity. Processes of consolidation and convergence accelerated in the nineteenth century and by the early twentieth century were well established, resulting in a policing structure generally resembling that of today. Broadly similar in the various European states, the police became a fundamental component of the criminal justice system and a mainstay of all governments in Europe and, in light of the European influence, throughout the world.

EARLY MODELS OF POLICING

Clearly, the expansion of formal police forces at the dawn of the modern era was connected to broader social phenomena. Economic, social, cultural, and political forces, which comprised what we call the processes of modernization, made an indelible mark on police development. Nevertheless, it is widely accepted today that the expansion of the police in Europe cannot be explained apart from state formation during the late Middle Ages and early modern period,

although theorists interpret this relationship in varied ways. For example, marxist historians, while concurring that specialized police agencies developed in the context of the state, link the rise of police power more closely to the transition from a kin-based to a class-dominated society. Viewing class conflict as the driving force behind social change, and the emergence of private property at the end of the Middle Ages as the basis of class formation, marxists maintain that the need of the rising capitalist class to control the means of production accounted for the growth of police institutions. According to this interpretation, the state used its growing monopoly over violence and surveillance to support capital in its struggle to achieve and maintain a privileged position vis-à-vis labor. Indeed, both business and the state were concerned with preserving the socioeconomic order and thus often shared compatible and even overlapping objectives. Indubitably, the state commonly represented class interests, although it also had other goals that it strove to achieve and therefore cannot be seen solely as the servant of the capitalist class.

Viewed from the broader perspective of state building, the ability of emerging states to consolidate their power within clearly demarcated boundaries depended on their ability to impose uniform rule, coordinate internal control, and monopolize the use of force. Eroding or coopting the power of feudal lords and other independent political agents was thus essential for state builders. To attain these goals, sovereign states had to develop both their own sources of income and instruments of coercion. Invariably, the creation of standing armies accompanied the centralization of power. Aside from fighting wars to maintain the independence of the state, the army became the principal means of internal pacification in the early modern period (c. 1500–1800). Gradually sovereigns came to accept that they could not routinely achieve control and carry out law-enforcing functions without civil organs invested with punitive powers and loyal to the regime. The steadily growing role of the ruler as a legislator and source of ordinances made this requirement even more compelling.

In contrast to the army, a grid of police forces was not immediately established to meet the demands of consolidation. Initially, the state relied mainly on the army, judiciary, bureaucracy, and private entrepreneurs to collect taxes and gain control over its territories. Permanent, centrally directed police organs appeared only very slowly across the European landscape despite the absolutist character of most continental regimes in the early modern period. Not until the middle of the seventeenth century, with the accelerated growth of state bureaucracies, can we see the beginnings of a more resolute and methodical policy for the establishment of formal police institutions. The political scientist and police historian David Bayley has suggested that the centralization of law enforcement was likely to occur where attempts to consolidate state control were met by prolonged violent resistance. Three major European powers illustrate his point.

France, facing incessant attempts to stem the tide of state encroachment into local power bases, pioneered the notion of a centralized police structure which, though modified greatly over time, has persisted to the present. During the first half of the seventeenth century, royal officials were made responsible for administering justice, finances, and public order in provincial centers. However, a highly rebellious aristocracy and various instances of domestic disorder prompted Louis XIV (ruled 1643–1715) to reinforce royal power in 1667 by creating the specialized post of lieutenant of police for Paris under his direct control. This official and the policemen at his disposal were entrusted with a wide range of tasks. The considerable powers invested in the post, and close proximity to the king, made the head of police one of the most important officeholders in France. Additionally, as was customary in early modern Europe in the case of high offices, the upper echelons of the new Paris police held venal posts designed to meet the perpetual need of the monarch for revenues to finance his wars. Ever more intent on furthering central administrative control over the periphery at the expense of privileged individuals and bodies as well as on gaining revenue, Louis eventually nominated lieutenants of police and police commissioners in the principal cities and towns of France in 1699. A network of urban police administrations was thus created directly under the supervision of the police lieutenant in Paris, aimed at allowing the ruler closer surveillance over his kingdom. However, these venal posts were often purchased by a local count or bishop who took little notice of orders issues by the lieutenant in Paris, though he might have corresponded with the lieutenant and sent him information—if it suited the local official's interests. For all the efforts made by the French monarchs, policing in the provinces remained largely local.

Two other European powers, Prussia and England, support Bayley's argument from a negative perspective. Though no less absolutist, Prussian rulers allowed the Junkers (landed aristocrats) to exercise police functions in their own territories. The Junkers, having largely accepted the monarch's dominance and their own obligation to serve in his army and administration from the seventeenth century on, posed no threat to the growing concentration of power in the hands of the royal sovereign. Similarly, sporadic popular resistance to state activity was not perceived by the Prussian monarchs as threatening. With the unification of Germany in the early 1870s, each constituent state largely took charge of its own police matters, a situation that resumed in the post–World War II era in West Germany after the interlude of the Nazi period, when Adolf Hitler had established the Gestapo as a centralized police force. The relatively decentralized police structure in Prussia and later in Germany, however, did not prevent the rulers from using the police as a powerful political weapon or from maintaining strong control over policing in cities, towns, and counties. In England, where royalty had asserted control over its territories in the Middle Ages, considerably predating the consolidation of the modern continental state, the aristocracy was allowed to wield power locally as it presented no serious challenge to the unity of England. No centralized police system was created. English law enforcement continued to be based mainly on local justices of the peace and constables.

It is important to emphasize that even where the state took no systematic steps to set up centralized law enforcement, it nonetheless benefited from the spread of police control locally in the late seventeenth and eighteenth centuries. However unprofessional, unimpressive, and mostly socially inferior, local policemen exerted power through surveillance and represented legitimate authority. The element of sovereignty was implicit in the nature of their task and in their powers of prohibition and coercion. Moreover, certain locally controlled police, such as the constables in England, actually acted in the name of the monarch even if they were not under royal control. Thus, in an indirect way, wherever policing existed, it contributed to the general functioning of state institutions and the centralization of state power.

DUTIES OF THE POLICE IN THE EARLY MODERN PERIOD

Between the fifteenth and the eighteenth centuries the term "police" was understood altogether differently from today. It did not refer to personnel or to an institution but to the application of laws and ordinances. Coming into use during the fifteenth century in the German territories (in its German form *policey*), the word police (which derived from the Greek *polis,* meaning city-state) denoted the administration of domestic affairs generally. The tasks undertaken by organs associated with policing were thus far more extensive than in the twentieth century.

State security. An analysis of police activity in the early modern period reveals that only a small fraction of it concentrated on the detection or prevention of crime. As power in a given country became increasingly centered on the sovereign, and as the sovereign invested greater energy in securing the state against internal opposition, the relevance of the police as a political instrument grew steadily. As early as 1554, the Russian tsar Ivan the Terrible (ruled 1533–1584) set up the infamous *oprichniki,* a police force of six thousand uniformed men who, in addition to serving as his bodyguards, also supervised public places. Unbridled by any legal restrictions, this force used mass terror and torture to guard the sovereign and his regime against perceived threats from the aristocracy, the church, and the peasants. Members of the force were rewarded for their efforts by grants of land confiscated from their original owners. The *oprichniki* survived for only seven or eight years, though it set a pattern for successive Russian regimes for over four centuries. While the sixteenth century was not yet ripe for a permanent body of political policemen in Russia, various tsarist officials filled the task of forestalling subversion until, in 1697, as part of a broad centralization effort, tsar Peter the Great (ruled 1682–1725) established the Preobrazhensky Office to tighten his hold on the population. From then on, under different names and authorities, an almost uninterrupted chain of secret police organizations in Russia responded with varying degrees of repression to the slightest indication of discontent in the country, thereby undermining the development of a civil society distinct from the state.

Ivan the Terrible's Oprichnina. VISUAL COLLECTION

Besides disrupting or suppressing the activities of groups and individuals suspected of disloyalty, the organs charged with political policing engaged in amassing information on a multitude of subjects, a reflection of the broader strategy adopted by state makers of obtaining systematic knowledge as a way of enhancing state power and increasing revenue. Not satisfied with the employment of visible police forces, Louis XIV also resorted to extensive undercover police operations. This use of spies and informers was not unprecedented. Regimes everywhere had relied on such methods to protect themselves against real and imagined plots and conspiracies as well as any other opposition. Louis, however, was to excel in this respect. With the help of the lieutenants of the Paris police, he entrenched a nationwide system of surveillance while also utilizing the provincial police to maintain close control over dissidence. A century later, at the start of the French Revolution, this royal police force disintegrated, and attempts were made to establish locally elected forces in French cities. These efforts were short-lived, and successive regimes, whether headed by the Bourbons, revolutionary governments, the Directory, or the Bonapartes, continued (and under Napoleon even markedly extended) the tradition of utilizing both open and secret policing to strengthen central power. As with other aspects of French culture, this system was studied and in some cases adopted by rulers across the Continent.

The Habsburg monarchy was equally notorious in employing police officials to observe anyone who might be a potential enemy and to act vigorously upon this information. Having gained supreme royal power over the periphery somewhat later than France (in the mid-eighteenth century), Austria lagged behind in forming a systematic network of spies and informers. Still, Austrian monarchs, perceiving themselves as highly vulnerable, managed to outdo the French in the use they made of this potent tool. Greatly improving upon the existing mechanisms of social control, Emperor Joseph II (ruled 1765–1790) entrusted his agents with reporting on the activities and opinions of ordinary people as well as of the aristocracy, clergy, and such other institutions as charities and schools. In building this apparatus of surveillance, he was guided by Count Pergen, an innovator in police administration who, like General Aleksandr Benckendorff in early-nineteenth-century Russia and Joseph Fouché under the Directory, Napoleon I, and the restored Bourbon monarchy, was instrumental in helping monarchs organize and operate an extensive political-cum-police network. The French Revolution and its aftermath led to a tightening up of police operations almost everywhere in Europe. Haunted by fears of revolutionary ideas and French agents, Austria was galvanized into an incessant vigil over organizations and individuals who might fall prey to such ideas, over state officials to ensure their loyalty to the regime, and over possible spies.

Although governments also used various public servants of the Crown to look out for possible sources of sedition, it was the secret police who were most intensively involved. Generally better remunerated than ordinary policemen (when these were paid), secret agents were specially recompensed for their zeal in rounding up suspects or submitting incriminating reports. Countless innocent victims paid dearly for these efforts. The agents' intelligence gathering did not aim solely at overt activities but included reporting on opinions. Moreover, they also punished suspects. Their task was internal security, but these agents extended their operations abroad to keep track of travelers and to intimidate political refugees who flocked to other European cities as a result of repression at home, particularly during the nineteenth century. While the effectiveness of these operations is impossible to measure, clearly they did not manage to stop the spread of dissent and stem the tides of revolution in the late eighteenth and the nineteenth centuries, especially in those countries in which the police were all-powerful. They may, however, have prevented specific challenges to regimes, such as cases of potential assassinations.

Public order. Beyond the need to curb oppositional elements, routine order was also considered essential for social stability and state control. The notion that the sheer presence of police forces could deter lawbreaking and prevent acts of defiance was increasingly accepted in the eighteenth century by both national and local governments. European cities had long maintained official bodies acting in a police ca-

pacity, in addition to military garrisons, patrols, and watchmen, and now they were determined to expand policing arrangements in the locality. Reform of the administrative organs of state during the seventeenth and eighteenth centuries facilitated the evolution of more specialized and centralized systems of policing. The growing importance of cities as centers of both power and civil unrest impelled central authorities to concentrate on securing order and effective law enforcement in urban areas. As a result of both state and municipal efforts, cities had better-organized institutions of policing, while policing in the countryside was largely contingent upon local initiatives. Police administrators were nominated in some capitals. Paris led the way in 1667. St. Petersburg followed suit in 1718, Berlin in 1742, and Vienna in 1751. Directors of police were appointed in many other cities all over Europe during the course of the eighteenth century. London was the most prominent exception to this trend, although policing arrangements there underwent certain reforms in the eighteenth century. Significantly, the city teemed with petty crime and unruliness.

State security and public order were obviously interrelated, and therefore keeping the peace became an important factor in the widespread trend during the eighteenth century to restructure policing arrangements. Additionally, central and local rulers were impelled by the need to modernize their societies and provide solutions to mounting urban problems. A more prosperous and healthier population could also augment the resources of the state and its military capability. Local elites were also prompted by civic pride. While in Russia police regulations focused on the repressive and negative aspects of law enforcement, in French, German, Dutch, and Scandinavian towns police ordinances incorporated a plethora of constructive tasks, including essential municipal services such as street lighting, street cleaning, garbage collection, supervision of public hygiene, and monitoring the quality of the water supply. Depending on the institutional power structure in each locality, and in the absence of other officials to perform such jobs, police agents often became responsible for fire prevention, first aid, finding shelter for abandoned children, the provision of welfare and food supply, and the control of traffic. Sometimes policemen were assigned the task of reminding inhabitants to lock their doors. Whether in the interest of the state, the local authorities, or the common good, the police performed essentially noncoercive duties, which improved the quality of life in cities and towns. Eighteenth-century observers consistently commented on how safe, orderly, and hygienic Paris had become, certainly in comparison to London.

The maintenance of order in the countryside was also basic to state security. Particularly important was public safety on the roads and highways. Here, too, France proved prescient in organizing a patrol system responsible to the central authorities. The origins of the *maréchaussée,* a paramilitary body of mounted and foot constabulary tasked to look out for deserters and protect rural inhabitants from violence by soldiers, can be traced to the medieval period. In the sixteenth century the role of this body was expanded to include maintaining order, repressing highway robbery and smuggling, gathering information, and monitoring vagabonds and civil crime in the countryside, while at the same time its military character became more distinct. Performing both military and police duties, these ex-soldiers were fully armed and uniformed, lived in barracks, and operated in military conditions mostly under military authority. In the eighteenth century the *maréchaussée* was reorganized into a nationwide force with clearly defined tasks and a coordinated presence throughout the country. In 1791, at the height of police experimentation by the revolutionaries, it was restructured again, as the Gendarmerie Nationale, serving as a model for most European countries during the next few decades.

Policing economic activities and public morality.

State interests in early modern Europe went beyond the security of the regime and the preservation of order. No less important was the regulation of industry and commerce. Most European states pursued mercantilist policies aimed at augmenting national wealth and military power. In implementing such policies, national and local police officers in countries such as France, Prussia, and Austria intervened in various stages of the processes of production and trade by, for example, inspecting markets and fairs, supervising food prices, and checking the accuracy of weights and measures. In so doing, these officers penalized instances of usury and embezzlement and prevented monopolies and profiteering.

A key element in mercantilist strategies was to ensure the industriousness of the population. With demographic growth forcing surplus populations off the land, and the growing mobility of labor, governments and local authorities adopted policies of either criminalizing or domesticating transient labor and of setting paupers to work. The police played an active role in regulating the labor supply and inculcating the ethos of paternalism and hard work among the lower orders. Particularly targeted for police attention were masterless men and laborers who refused to work for low wages. The able-bodied unemployed were forced to work, runaway servants were apprehended, and insubordinate workers were punished. The aim was to reduce the number of indigents who became a burden on the community and to augment the supply of cheap labor. Even if these policies were implemented only sporadically and inconsistently, the police benefited both the state economy and the nascent capitalist class. Furthermore, acculturation of the surplus and marginal population was undertaken because this population was seen as a source of social instability. Subsequently, ordinances were issued and measures were taken all over Europe against beggars, vagrants, peddlers, gypsies, Jews, and/or casual workers.

The policing of economic activities was not carried out for material reasons alone. The police were also an important tool for regulating conduct and fostering conformity to accepted social norms. Fear of godlessness sometimes led to the enforcement of religious observance in Catholic and Protestant countries alike, with infractions of Sunday and holiday observance treated with particular harshness. This impulse to standardize moral behavior resulted in police attacks on various forms of popular culture and amusements throughout Europe. Feasts and festivals were often rigidly supervised, certain games prohibited, and theatrical performances censored. In some areas, dress was inspected and ostentation banned. Sexual misbehavior was also occasionally treated heavy-handedly by the police. In some places, mothers were punished for bearing children out of wedlock. It was also common for police to inspect lodging houses and regulate street prostitution. Police registration of local inhabitants and visiting foreigners enabled local and national authorities to gain information and monitor their movements.

LIMITATIONS OF
EARLY POLICING SYSTEMS

Clearly, policing in continental Europe in the early modern period implied growing penetration into the private lives of ordinary people. In comparison with today, however, such intervention was only intermittent and only partly the product of state regulation. The attempts to create strong states and achieve territorial consolidation by forming or expanding instruments of rule succeeded only partially. An array of bodies and offices fulfilling various, often overlapping, police and nonpolice functions continued to coexist in the different territorial entities, with little or no collaboration between them. Only some were part of the state bureaucracy, while others were controlled by local power holders or were privately employed. In fact, until the nineteenth century, no state had developed a full-scale nationwide police network. Small communities throughout Europe continued to rely on informal arrangements, and local lords still exercised both police and judicial powers. In eastern Europe, policemen were often the protégés of local dignitaries, who used them principally to execute their own private orders. All of this meant that large areas of Europe remained free of the presence of permanent forces of law and order, and the existing ones were unevenly distributed. Even as rulers enacted a growing number of laws and ordinances, they neither possessed adequate manpower nor allocated sufficient finances to implement them throughout entire territories. In times of disturbances they preferred to employ the military. This partial condition of law enforcement reflected the limited power of the absolute state. Paradoxically, in England, where constables were less intrusive and had a more limited range of duties, the policing system was relatively widespread and entrenched, though there, too, enforcement was patchy.

The sparse distribution of police agencies often impelled the community to rely on its own resources to pursue offenders. Local inhabitants in England were supposed to raise the hue and cry if they detected lawbreakers. The novelist Henry Fielding, who was a London magistrate in the mid-eighteenth century, along with his brother John, also a London magistrate, appealed to the general public and to pawnbrokers in particular to disclose any information they might have about stolen property, thieves, and their methods. In England and in many continental communities, redress for crime fell almost entirely on the victims. It was they who brought the crime to the attention of the authorities and they themselves were often responsible for capturing the offender, collecting evidence, finding witnesses, and bearing the costs of prosecution. The propertyless clearly had less access to the legal system, allowing a substantial number of culprits to be spared. The haphazard nature of law enforcement also gave rise to commercial enterprise. For example, the Thames Police of London (established in 1798) was initially funded by private insurance companies with a view to reducing theft from the London port and retrieving stolen property. The infliction of harsh punishments throughout Europe on selected offenders, often for the slightest deviation from the norms, was partly meant to serve as a deterrent to crime in the absence of systematic law enforcement.

THE EMERGENCE AND CONSOLIDATION OF THE MODERN POLICE

The modern police configuration took shape only gradually. During the course of the nineteenth cen-

tury, governments everywhere took steps to make policing routinized, pervasive, and constant, even though much of law enforcement was still locally controlled. Despite budgetary constraints, police forces were increasingly publicly funded and, initially in cities, uniformed foot patrols became the principal and largest component of the national policing structure. In 1829 two major cities in Europe—Paris and London—were provided with a system of uniformed police, followed in 1848 by Berlin, the first city in Germany to have a municipal police force. Provincial cities, towns, and villages soon acquired their own police as well. State-controlled gendarmeries appeared across almost the entire Continent, filling the vacuum in much of rural Europe where the law had been only sporadically enforced by official police forces. The authority of the gendarmeries sometimes extended to cities, as was the case in France and Prussia. The fact that most countries opted for a military style of force to police the countryside demonstrated the widespread impact of military models and culture on police development.

As a result of such initiatives, police forces grew in size and complexity, and the policeman became a familiar figure in almost every neighborhood. His uniformed presence was expected to be sufficiently threatening to deter would-be lawbreakers. Moreover, the policeman gradually became both a key agent for integrating people and territory and a visible symbol of the state's jurisdiction.

Evolving duties. The police labor force that emerged in the course of the nineteenth century was typically full-time, regularly paid, and subject to bureaucratic control. Work for the large proportion of policemen who composed the lower levels of the hierarchy was harsh, wearisome, and meagerly remunerated. However, the regularity of income and the various welfare benefits extended to policemen in many countries made the job attractive, especially for the unskilled and for displaced rural workers. For their part, decision makers in countries such as Britain generally preferred rural to industrial workers, since the latter were seen as less compliant and loyal. Police relationships with social groups from which they emanated form an important part of modern social history. Generally, police have reliably disciplined popular unrest when called upon to do so.

Police officers throughout Europe continued to discharge a mosaic of functions, retaining many of their old tasks. In addition to preventing and discovering unlawful activities and maintaining order and stability, the police still were expected to strengthen industrial discipline, control the indigent, and carry out various duties in the areas of public health and welfare. Supporting bourgeois standards, they policed deviations from moral norms and restrained popular pastimes. Some estimates suggest that a full half of police time in urban areas aimed at controlling popular leisure. In the same vein, police cleared public spaces of petty merchants, gamblers, and the drunk and disorderly even more vigorously than before. Traffic control and the prevention of juvenile delinquency became important police assignments toward the end of the nineteenth century. However, with the exception of the British force, the range of police tasks actually narrowed substantially during the course of the century. By the beginning of the twentieth century, for example, the police had largely abandoned the policing of the poor and the provision of a number of municipal services as other state administrators and agencies emerged to handle these functions. In contrast, while governments continued to employ armies throughout the nineteenth century to keep order in times of emergency, particularly during riots, civil disorder, and strikes, police reorganization allowed the gradual replacement of the army by the police, which during the twentieth century took predominant charge of maintaining internal public order, leaving the army as the principal guardian of external security.

Indeed, the general trend in the occupational world toward specialization and differentiation of tasks was reflected in efforts by police administrators throughout Europe to demarcate responsibilities more clearly and provide more specialized services. Separate departments were created for uniformed policing, detective work, political surveillance, and specialized tasks. These developments pointed to the growing professionalization of policing in Europe. A reflection of this trend was increasing attention to technical expertise. Toward the end of the nineteenth century police forces in Europe adopted the telegraph, telephone, fingerprinting, forensic science, photography, and other new technologies as indispensable tools for their work. Another modern notion was the application of uniform rules for the administration of the force. Entrants had to comply with a set of established selection criteria demanding not only physical stamina but also literacy skills, and the period of training that recruits underwent was progressively expanded. Whether as part of state or local government, the police were relatively ahead of private institutions in establishing standardized procedures, amassing systematic information, and compiling statistical records relating to various aspects of their work.

What also distinguished the new police was a growing tendency to follow due legal process or at least present a semblance of adherence to the rule of law. The spread of constitutional structures during the

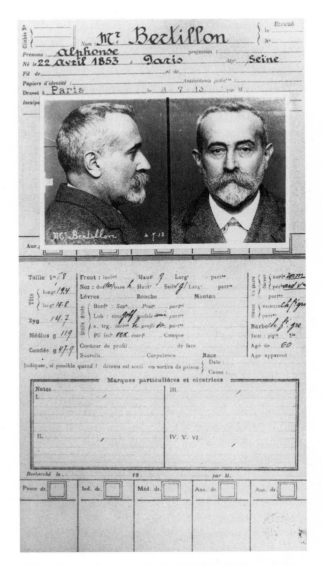

Police Technology. An official of the Paris Prefecture of Police in the late nineteenth century, Alphonse Bertillon (1853–1914) developed a system of identifying criminals called *anthropométrie* or *bertillonnage*. MUSÉE DE LA POLICE, PARIS/JEAN-LOUP CHARMET

nineteenth century meant that government in general was held more accountable, and heads of state were obliged to operate within the confines of the law. Among the most visible representatives of the state, the police, too, had to demonstrate that they were subordinate to the law. Although secret police departments often disregarded legal procedures, official rhetoric increasingly adopted the vocabulary of the Enlightenment. Sensitivity to public opinion became more evident during the latter part of the nineteenth century in such liberal societies as England, although even states which retained absolutist notions of government, like Germany, were forced to justify police activities.

Police and the public. In effect, state expansion only augmented the state's dependency on the cooperation of its citizens, whose loyalty now had to be won. Although the working classes were everywhere the primary target of both secret and open policing, their demands were also considered, especially after the revolutions of 1848. The more liberal the government, the more it stressed that the main objective of the police was not to serve the interests of the state or the privileged classes but to defend the individual and the community against unlawful intervention. Instructions to be cordial to the public pervaded the training of police constables in England. Clearly, surveillance and control needed to be less visible or explicit and more subtle, a tendency that coincided with the growing reluctance to use the might of the army to curb protest.

The policed population was never passive regarding police power. Hostility to police activity by the governed continued throughout the nineteenth century and beyond. By the beginning of the twentieth century, however, the presence of the police and their purposes had been accepted, if sometimes grudgingly, as a necessity. The appearance of police officers as major figures in European novels of the nineteenth century and the emergence of detective fiction at the end of the century illustrate the growing legitimacy and importance of police officials in modern society. As more people appealed to police for assistance even in private matters, the police in turn extended services relating to individual safety and everyday needs.

Historical accounts of the shift to full-time and systematic policing adduce a variety of factors. The weakening of the paternalistic face-to-face forms of control in rural areas, the rapid expansion of cities, and the growth of industrial capitalism, which required a disciplined labor force, created an underlying feeling that contemporary police arrangements were inadequate and inefficient. Incidents of collective violence and civil strife were commonly interpreted by the new bourgeoisie as symptoms of a social breakdown. Now in a better position than ever to influence state policies, this sector opposed any restraint on the expansion of the capitalist economy and any challenge to private property. Reports about rising crime rates and fears of the growing power of the industrial masses, the more organized nature of political protest, and the spread of socialist doctrines calling for the overthrow of the social order strengthened pressure to alter traditional policing arrangements. An organized and permanent police force was recommended as a

means of ensuring punishment. Democratization, the decline of overt public punishment, and the humanization of personal relations were also important in laying the groundwork for police reform. The restructuring of police forces was designed to improve control over cities, suppress new forms of crime, and supervise the lower social orders. The rise of new concepts of state management that stressed administrative efficiency and rationalization also shaped the new police.

English and continental police. Despite the convergence of varied national models into a generally discernible pattern of law enforcement during the nineteenth century, a broad dividing line was observable between the police in England and the police in the major continental powers such as France, Germany, and Italy. Early uncritical accounts of police development in England emphasized such a distinction by portraying the origins, aims, and practices of the English police as radically different from police histories elsewhere. Such observations mirrored the arguments of police reformers in nineteenth-century England who maintained that, unlike its continental counterparts, the constabulary system had arisen from the community and was therefore the custodian of traditional liberties and a servant of the people. Implicit in these arguments was the conviction that the mission of the English police was simply to protect the majority against a handful of violators of the law. Since the 1970s, police historians writing from the perspective of social history have challenged such interpretations and have shown that the difference between the police on the Continent and in England was more apparent than real. They have pointed to the fierce resistance that the new police encountered in all working-class areas and to their societal partiality. Various studies have focused on the role that the police played in suppressing demonstrations and popular forms of entertainment and in their biased and brutal interventions in industrial disputes. In these studies the new English police appear as an instrument of bourgeois reforms and interests. Research has also revealed that the English police were no less corrupt or corruptible than police forces across the Channel and that English policemen did not always adhere to the letter of the law.

Nonetheless, in some respects the English police may be contrasted with the majority of the continental powers. In much of mainland Europe the modern police emerged out of the politics of absolutism and matured against a background of uprisings and revolutions. The absence of such experiences informed the evolution of policing in England. The result was that

Police Intervention. Riot police and students, Boulevard St.-Michel, Paris, 18 June 1968.
©HULTON GETTY/LIAISON AGENCY

while continental police forces tended to pay greater attention to keeping rulers in power and less to the prevention of crime and protection of property, the emphasis in England was substantially different. Although British governments had used spies and informers to keep a sharp eye on agitators and assure internal peace, until the quite late establishment of the Special Branch (in 1884) to combat Irish and anarchist terrorism these agents had never been part of a permanent system, as was often the case on the other side of the Channel, and they had never been used as extensively. In fact, less occupied with state security, Britain was almost the only European power to extend asylum and shelter to the many political refugees fleeing persecution in Europe. Moreover, whereas a number of continental forces were responsible to central government, the English police continued to rely on a local system of policing, albeit against growing state intervention in police affairs as in other aspects of life. Of all the professional forces formed throughout England during the middle decades of the nineteenth century, only the Metropolitan Police of London were organized as a central body accountable to the Home Office. All other police, whether borough or county, were locally controlled.

In another context, all police forces in Europe bore some resemblance to military institutions, whether in the use of uniforms, rigid discipline, hierarchical structure, ritual, or violence. Yet countries with a strong military tradition, such as Germany, tended to follow military models more closely, while in England a widespread fear of military influence reduced the tendency to adopt military precepts in all parts of the British Isles, apart from Ireland. In German, French, and many other continental forces a military background was either a prerequisite or a preference for enrollment, and military weapons were commonly used, whereas many police administrators in England were reluctant to recruit ex-soldiers, firearms were deployed only under special circumstances, and a gendarmerie type of police was never created.

POLICING IN THE TWENTIETH CENTURY

Significantly, despite the reduction in police functions on the Continent and the legal constraints within which they increasingly operated, the police continued to grow and considerably strengthen their position and status during the twentieth century. They attained ultimate power after World War I in one-party states, whether fascist or communist, where they were unrestricted by law or tenets of public accountability. Totalitarian regimes, in particular, showed an obsessive reliance on both the secret and uniformed police to monitor the life of the people, ruthlessly suppress dissidence, and detain anyone considered an enemy of the regime. Some historians now claim that the numerical strength and intrusiveness of the police were greater in communist countries than in Nazi Germany and that state security institutions under the tsars were less coercive than under the Soviet regime. Studies have also shown that for all the terrorism perpetrated by the Gestapo and Soviet security forces, their efficiency depended to no small degree on collaboration and denunciations from the citizenry. Apparently, not only in nontotalitarian societies do the police need public cooperation.

By virtue of their wide dispersion, size, activities, and formal organization, the police everywhere served as vehicles of state expansion. Yet developments in Europe in the twentieth century highlight the complex relationship between the state and its law enforcement apparatus. While instances of police resistance to the rise of nondemocratic regimes have been recorded, police complicity was more prevalent. The same was true in areas under foreign occupation. Such responses indicate that the forces of law and order were not monolithic and not necessarily persistently loyal to the state they served, but followed their own inclinations. The tenuous support that the Weimar police (and army) extended to democratic Germany provides further proof of the ambiguous political role and attitude of some police forces.

Despite the cold war after World War II, the inhabitants of Western Europe on the whole enjoyed a growing liberalization of police practices. One manifestation of this was the gradual coopting of women to this male-dominated occupation. At the same time, police forces became more technically complex organizations. Cars and electronic equipment made it possible to offer quicker service, be more accessible to the public, and perfect the means of social control without seeming coercive. Communication devices also facilitated better supervision of subordinates by their officers. Indeed, by the end of the twentieth century the workings of the police had become much more controlled and subject to bureaucratic intervention. There was also a shift toward proactive techniques of law enforcement involving greater emphasis on surveillance by means of acquiring detailed knowledge of the population. Crime investigation has always taken up only a small proportion of the policeman's time (apart from detectives, of course). Now more than ever law enforcers—even patrol officers—engage in the processing of knowledge by writing reports, undertaking administrative duties, and collecting and sorting information. The use of computer technology for data storage, retrieval, and analysis has further enhanced the surveillance capacities of the police.

These intangible interventionist measures are currently causing grave concern in the liberal democracies of Europe. However, this is but one topic in the broader debate over the role of police in society, which includes such contentious issues as police accountability, selective enforcement, discriminatory policing of minority groups, and the question of officers' discretion. Beyond these concerns, the police figure prominently in public discourse, as reflected in the preoccupation of the mass media with the agencies of law enforcement. The interest in police and policing is no less extensive among academics of diverse disciplines. As part of the growing attention to crime and the criminal justice system among social historians during the 1970s, the police became a major field of scholarship. Since then, these historians have offered varied perspectives on how patterns of law enforcement were shaped by changing historical processes. Placing the police within a broad socioeconomic context, they emphasize the role the police play in mediating between centers of power and all areas of life. The police are seen as a social control mechanism, and their development is analyzed against wider strategies of power in society. The social history of the police thus affords insight into the machinery of government at various levels and its impact on ordinary people. A significant contribution relates to the ways that police have historically interacted with and reinforced social and cultural norms. Since the police have dealings not only with offenders but with the population at large, studies of the police facilitate a deeper understanding of collective mentalities and of the life of the nonprivileged sectors of society. Also instructive is the focus on the police as an independent agency with its own motivations and interests. During the 1990s scholarship shed light on the policeman as a worker and the ruling police elite as an employer. By combining high politics with history from below, social historians of the police have succeeded in broadening our horizons on the social dimensions of the past while at the same time enriching our appreciation of domestic politics.

See also **Street Life and City Space** *(volume 2);* **Absolutism** *(volume 2);* **The Reformation of Popular Culture** *(volume 5);* **Festivals** *(volume 5); and other articles in this section.*

BIBLIOGRAPHY

Axtmann, Roland. " 'Police' and the Formation of the Modern State. Legal and Ideological Assumptions on State Capacity in the Austrian Lands of the Habsburg Empire, 1500–1800." *German History* 10 (1992): 39–61.

Bayley, David H. *Patterns of Policing: A Comparative International Analysis.* New Brunswick, N.J., 1985.

Dandeker, Christopher. *Surveillance, Power, and Modernity: Bureaucracy and Discipline from 1700 to the Present Day.* Cambridge, Mass., 1990.

Dean, Mitchell. "A Genealogy of the Government of Poverty." *Economy and Society* 21 (August 1992): 215–251.

Diederiks, Herman. "Patterns of Criminality and Law Enforcement during the Ancien Regime: The Dutch Case." *Criminal Justice History* 1 (1980): 157–174.

Emerson, Donald E. *Metternich and the Political Police.* The Hague, Netherlands, 1968.

Emsley, Clive. *The English Police: A Political and Social History.* 2d ed. New York, 1996.

Emsley, Clive. *Gendarmes and the State in Nineteenth-Century Europe.* Oxford, 1999.

Emsley, Clive. *Policing and Its Context, 1750–1870.* New York, 1984.

Emsley, Clive, and Barbara Weinberger, eds. *Policing Western Europe: Politics, Professionalism, and Public Order, 1850–1940.* New York, 1991.

Ericson, Richard V., and Kevin D. Haggerty. *Policing the Risk Society.* Toronto, 1997.

Evans, Richard J. "In Pursuit of the Untertanengeist: Crime, Law, and Social Order in German History." In *Rethinking German History: Nineteenth-Century Germany and the Origins of the Third Reich.* London, 1987.

Fosdick, Raymond B. *European Police Systems.* Montclair, N.J., 1969.

Gellately, Robert. *The Gestapo and German Society: Enforcing Racial Policy, 1933–1945.* Oxford, 1990.

Giddens, Anthony. *The Nation-State and Violence.* Vol. 2 of *A Contemporary Critique of Historical Materialism.* Berkely, Calif., 1985.

Hingley, Ronald. *The Russian Secret Police: Muscovite, Imperial Russian, and Soviet Political Security Operations, 1565–1970.* London, 1970.

Johnson, Eric A. *Nazi Terror: The Gestapo, Jews, and Ordinary Germans.* New York, 1999.

Johnson, Eric A. *Urbanization and Crime: Germany 1871–1914.* Cambridge, U.K., 1995.

Knemeyer, Franz-Ludwig. "Polizei." *Economy and Society* 9 (May 1980): 172–196.

Levi, Michael, and Mike Maguire. "Crime and Policing in Europe." In *Social Europe.* Edited by Joe Bailey. 2d ed. London, 1998. Pages 177–202.

Lis, Catharina, and Hugo Soly. "Policing the Early Modern Proletariat, 1450–1850." In *Proletarianization and Family History.* Edited by David Levine. Orlando, Fla., 1984. Pages 163–228.

Radzinowicz, Leon. *A History of English Criminal Law and Its Administration from 1750.* 4 vols. London, 1956.

Raeff, Marc. *The Well-Ordered Police State: Social and Institutional Change through Law in the Germanies and Russia, 1600–1800.* New Haven, Conn., 1983.

Reiner, Robert, ed. *Policing.* 2 vols. Brookfield, Vt., 1996.

Spencer, Elaine Glovka. *Police and the Social Order in German Cities: The Düsseldorf District, 1848–1914.* DeKalb, Ill., 1992.

Stead, Philip John. *The Police of France.* New York, 1983.

Williams, Alan. *The Police of Paris, 1718–1789.* Baton Rouge, La., 1979.

PUNISHMENT

Abby M. Schrader

Penal practices as well as the theories behind them have varied considerably by region, the natures of the authorities involved in sentencing criminals, and the sociocultural contexts of their deployment. Moreover the practice of punishment has not always corresponded to the laws and philosophies that purportedly guided it. To further complicate matters, penalties have differed with regard to the social status, gender, and age of the convicted. Bearing in mind these distinctions, it is still possible to draw salient generalizations about punishment in Europe from the Renaissance through the twentieth century. This essay opens with a discussion of the general trajectories that characterized the evolution of European penal practices and proceeds to an analysis of how scholars have evaluated the political, social, and cultural significance of the practice and reform of legal punishment.

PENAL PRACTICES IN EARLY MODERN AND MODERN EUROPE

Generally early modern penalties targeted the criminal's body, whereas modern forms focused on the convict's soul. Both attempted to deter subjects or citizens from transgressing social and legal norms but in rather different manners. Early modern punishment strove to inculcate fear and set examples through public, corporal, and often cruel practices while simultaneously excluding criminals from society. In contrast, more modern penal systems tended to privatize punishment and confine criminals yet generalize disciplinary systems throughout society. Even as this pattern predominantly holds true, it is nonetheless necessary to note that penal practices overlapped and were used in combination with one another in both early modern and modern Europe. Moreover the transition from one form to another was neither simple nor without contradictions. Instead it was gradual, incomplete, and frequently contested. Corporal and capital punishments continued to exist alongside penal bondage and confinement, and penal innovations were subject

to challenges arising at the same time that authorities instituted the innovations.

To simplify this picture, this essay first discusses the various penalties meted out by judicial authorities, beginning with physical, public, and shaming forms of punishment. It then moves on to different types of penal bondage and institutions of confinement and an examination of extrainstitutional penal practices that developed during the late nineteenth and early twentieth centuries. Where appropriate, this essay notes how penal forms operated in combination with one another; how secular authorities drew on other idioms, such as ecclesiastical and military ones; and how certain penal forms came to displace other practices.

CORPORAL AND PUBLIC PUNISHMENTS

Early modern European courts meted out various corporal punishments. Flogging was the most prevalent form practiced. Whips or lashes consisting of leather thongs fastened to handles were common all across Europe, but some countries also developed specific devices. The metal-barbed knout constituted the harshest Russian penal instrument before 1845, and the English had the fearsome cat-o'-nine-tails, nine leather tails thirty-three inches long that were spiked with metal balls. The gauntlet, rows of soldiers armed with crops, was generally reserved for military offenders or those inhabiting militarized zones. Lighter corporal punishments, like the birch or rod, were used against less serious offenders or to "domestically" punish wives and children.

Like other forms of corporal and capital punishment, floggings were often public during the early modern era. However, once criticism of public punishment sharpened in the mid-eighteenth century, floggings increasingly transpired behind prison walls. For example, subsequent to 1820 floggings were privatized for male convicts in England. Nonetheless, floggings remained part of the penal language even

Corporal Punishment. Flogging in Russia. Nineteenth-century print. ©THE BRITISH MUSEUM, LONDON

once the prison gained hegemony in modern Europe. Flogging was used to punish convicts transported to French penal colonies through 1880, corporal punishment remained prevalent in German prisons through the late nineteenth century, and England finally abandoned the whip in 1967. The significance of flogging's publicity and its abolition is explored below.

In addition to floggings, early modern courts prescribed various forms of bodily mutilation. Putting out eyes, slitting nostrils, slicing cheeks, and amputating arms, ears, and tongues frequently accompanied whippings, the death sentence, transportation, or penal bondage. Courts generally sentenced criminals to the mutilation of body parts that symbolized the nature of the offense committed. In Germany executioners amputated a thief's hand and publicly displayed it to spectators to convey the message that the ruler would not tolerate theft. Similarly tongues were clipped in cases where criminals committed perjury, blasphemy, or other offenses involving speech. Often the ceremonies associated with mutilation emulated rituals of personal retaliation, which roughly followed the precept of "an eye for an eye" articulated by Judeo-Christian law. By appropriating these forms, early modern penal regimes suggested that public justice was supplanting private. These practices also demonstrate that early modern penal forms frequently retributed the transgression committed and were not tailored to individual criminals.

The most severe mutilation practices were in decline by the sixteenth century, yet bodily mutilation did not disappear from the lexicon of physical penalties in many places until the nineteenth century. The Dutch cut off some felons' thumbs until the early eighteenth century, Napoleon reinstituted the amputation of parricides' right hands in his 1810 penal code, and Russians continued to rend the nostrils of serious criminals until 1845.

Mutilation served other functions beyond the symbolic and retaliatory. Disfigurement also made it easier for authorities to identify recidivists and escaped convicts in an era when states lacked sufficient policing, and it served as a visual marker enabling honest societies to exclude offenders. Branding, another form of bodily marking, was similarly motivated. European states devised branding practices that at once underscored the ruler's sovereignty, denoted the nature of the crime, facilitated the identification of the criminals, and distinguished convicts from the rest of society.

During the early modern period, when state sovereignty was still questionable, brands identified offenders as subject to the monarch's will. Russian convicts bore the brand of the eagle associated with Peter the Great, and Netherlandish criminals were marked with the elector's coat of arms. A brand also identified the nature of the crime. French and Russian thieves were marked with a "V" for *voleur* (thief) and "VOR" for *vorovstvo* (theft), respectively. After 1650 the English burned the letters "AB" onto the foreheads of English adulterers and fornicators. Vagrants were a frequent target of authorities who, in the process of centralization, sought to clamp down on wanderers. The 1532 *Carolina*, the criminal code of the German emperor Charles V, authorized branding vagrants throughout the German states, while Russian ones were branded until 1863. Furthermore brands denoted the type of punishment to which the convict was sentenced. Criminals condemned to French galleys were branded with "GAL" (*galère*), and Russian hard laborers bore the scar "KAT" (*katorga*, exile at hard labor). Branding persisted well into the era of penal reform. In France considerable continuity existed between Old Regime branding rituals and those used after the French Revolution. Likewise the number and range of English offenses that compelled branding, first instituted by the Tudors, multiplied from the sixteenth century through the eighteenth century. Not until 1779 did England abandon branding. Branding as a form of punishment was abolished in Russia in 1845 but continued to be used as a police measure against vagrants and fugitive convicts for nearly another twenty years.

The third form of physical chastisement widely practiced in Europe from the fifteenth century through the nineteenth century was capital punishment. In the early modern era executions, like other penal forms targeting the body, symbolized royal power and were intended to safeguard society by prompting subjects to submit to the ruler's will. Early modern executions which took manifold forms, can be divided into those deemed honorable and relatively less painful, generally limited to beheading or death by sword, and those considered dishonorable, which involved painful, attenuated deaths. The latter included drowning, boiling in oil, burial alive, burning at the stake, breaking at the wheel, drawing and quartering, and hanging—the most enduring and prevalent form of dishonorable execution.

The most macabre forms of capital punishment annihilated every trace of the condemned. Until the late sixteenth century drowning and burial alive were frequently deployed against women who violated sexual or moral norms, and witches were burned at the stake during crazes that peaked in the era of the Reformation and Counter-Reformation. Drawing and quartering and breaking at the wheel were primarily used against men. The former was often reserved for regicides and traitors and was hardly ever employed after the sixteenth century, though the executions of Robert-François Damiens in 1757 and Yemelyan Ivanovich Pugachov in 1775 defy this rule. (Admittedly Pugachov was strangled before he was quartered.) In contrast, breaking at the wheel persisted into the nineteenth century as a penalty for robbery or wife murder because officials believed that its utterly terrifying nature was particularly deterrent. In spite of the endurance of these horrific penalties, the most gruesome forms of capital punishment were in decline by the late sixteenth century. This was largely due to the increased control that European authorities exerted over penal practices as well as the authorities' desire to ritualize punishment as a clear means of morally edifying witnesses.

A natural segue leads to the related concepts of dishonor and publicity. Across Europe scaffold ceremonies and stagings of punishment spectacles were as important as the contents of sentences. These rituals stigmatized the criminal and the society to which he or she belonged. Stripping and exposing the body, even when the criminal was subjected to less painful penalties such as the ducking stool, subjected the offender to disgrace and shame in the presence of witnesses and, in early modern Europe's corporatist societies, destroyed the perpetrator's civic identity, marking him or her as outcast.

The shame associated with flogging or execution was intensified by the executioner's touch. In the Germanies this contamination was so polluting that, if suspects survived torture and were acquitted, they were nonetheless exiled from their communities. Although executioners were central to the penal ritual, they were marginal figures who lived outside respectable communities and wore special clothes. In France and Germany executioners' children were excluded from honorable crafts and could marry only the children of other executioners. In the Baltics executioners also performed other disreputable jobs, like collecting night refuse and removing the dead. In Russia executioners were generally chosen from the ranks of convicts, and by the mid-nineteenth century executioners were so ignominious that criminals refused to volunteer for this role even though it would spare them the lash.

Because the executioner was considered a source of pollution by elites and popular society alike, members of those corporations bearing the greatest social status gradually were exempted from punishment involving the executioner's touch. Death by sword was reserved for nobles and "respected citizens" in France and Germany, and military courts in Germany and Russia replaced lashings with the gauntlet to preserve the dignity of officers and soldiers. By the nineteenth century even the gauntlet became incompatible with soldierly honor. Prussia and Russia abolished it in 1808 and 1863, respectively.

Thus the lower classes and outsiders, such as vagrants and Jews, felt the full force of the executioner's whip or the hangman's noose and were consequently subjected to the most defaming penalties. Even once the era of penal reform got underway in the late eighteenth century, the lower classes continued to be subject to corporal punishment. While Russian nobles were spared the lash and the knout beginning in 1785, peasants were flogged until 1904. Similarly the 1794 Prussian General Law Code began to replace lashings with imprisonment for elites but not for lower classes, and corporal punishment was not eliminated for most Germans until 1871. By the turn of the nineteenth century rulers differentiated between privileged and unprivileged members of their societies through, among other means, subjection to or exemption from floggings.

Like class, gender was a factor that mitigated the dishonor of public punishment. In France women were buried alive rather than hung prior to 1449 out of concern for modesty. This practice, which harkened back to ancient Rome, was also used in the Germanies

Dutch Gibbets. *The Gallows on the Outskirts of the Volewijk,* drawing (1664–1665) by Anthonie van Borssum. ©RIJKSMUSEUM, AMSTERDAM

and Russia in the early modern era. In England women were burned at the stake out of the same concern. Only female witches were drawn and quartered because they purportedly lacked feminine shame. When women were hung or lashed in France or Germany, their necks and faces were masked to protect their identities. Growing concern about baring the female torso contributed to the exemption of women from public whipping in England in 1817 and in Russia in 1863. While female exiles continued to be beaten in Russia for another thirty years, these floggings transpired privately after 1863. Across Europe crowds expressed especial affront at the sight of women's stripped, lashed, and hung bodies, and executioners were reluctant to administer beatings to female criminals. Thus while shame and dishonor were integral to the spectacle of public punishment, infamy had its limits, particularly when it threatened sexual mores and provoked erotic disorder.

Inculcating shame was only one object of scaffold rituals. They also conveyed sovereignty and allowed centralizing European states to symbolically monopolize control over violence. The ceremonies of public punishment frequently integrated ecclesiastical forms that implied the divine nature of secular justice. After the fifteenth century the Spanish monarchy employed the practices of the Inquisition, particularly the *auto da fé* (act of faith), to identify and prosecute deviance. Likewise seventeenth- and eighteenth-century German and Swiss rulers assimilated into the secular penal system religiously edifying forms of public punishment originally used by ecclesiastical courts. Public punishment often incorporated liturgical chants and funeral rites, and priests presided at the scaffold from England to Russia.

Authorities designed scaffold rituals to legitimate the capacity of the state to retribute crime. The appropriation of ecclesiastical practices constituted only one element of this enterprise. Rulers also encouraged popular participation in punishment because they required public validation of their supremacy. The presence of magistrates and soldiers with drawn swords, fearsome processions to the scaffold along the most populous routes, the enactment of punishment on the busiest squares on market days, and the ringing of bells and beating of drums were features common to penal rituals across early modern Europe. In many places authorities garbed convicts awaiting sentencing specially or mandated that they wear placards announcing their crimes. Formal clothes were also specified for the executioner and the officials presiding at the sentencing. These rituals underscored the majesty of the ruler and the consent of the gathered public to his or her sovereignty.

Yet public punishment's efficacy in expressing the ruler's legitimacy was dependent upon the correspondence between authorities' intentions and audiences' interpretations. Crowds were active agents in constructing the meaning of penal forms and as such were a necessary but potentially subversive component of the penal ceremony. Rulers were aware of this predicament. As they centralized their power, they began to regulate the scaffold more strictly to preclude the audience from interpreting these rites in ways that might sabotage their sovereignty.

While corporal and capital punishment originally transpired at the crime scene, from the seventeenth century through the nineteenth century, scaffolds occupied permanent locations. European officials also began to curtail the customary freedoms of the condemned. Seventeenth-century German rulers fearing it would provoke riots, repealed the Carolina's provision permitting criminals to curse their judges during the three-day interval between the proclamation of a death sentence and its execution. French authorities clamped down on the indulgences traditionally granted the condemned during the *nuit blanche* (last night) rituals. In a further effort to manage the penal spectacle, officials sought to repress the practice popular in France, Italy, Russia, the Germanies, and England wherein a man or woman condemned to public punishment would be pardoned if a virgin female or unmarried male, respectively, offered to marry the convict. Yet authorities were unable to prevent crowds from appealing for clemency on these grounds, even after they made it illegal in the eighteenth century.

Even earlier, in the mid-sixteenth century, Venetian officials attempted to abolish the centerpiece of the carnival festival because it challenged secular monopolization of penal rites. During the festival twelve pigs and a bull were chased ritually through the streets and penned up at the execution site in the square before the Palace of Doges. There blacksmiths garbed as executioners beheaded the animals in a parody of official justice. Although this ceremony transpired during a period of symbolic inversion—the days preceding lent—officials felt that it threatened their sovereignty, and their lack of success in repressing the practice clearly demonstrates the accuracy of their assessment. The parody pointed out the dangerous multivalent effects of the spectacle of punishment.

During the eighteenth century authorities became increasingly troubled by popular propensities to treat scaffold rituals as carnivalesque occasions. In England and on the Continent critics lamented that witnesses to floggings and executions behaved as if they were at a street theater. They took this as a sign of the masses' lack of civilization and tendency to trivialize death and bodily pain.

The same critics, however, simultaneously evinced a very different sort of anxiety. They feared that crowds might sabotage the scaffold by rioting. In England surgeons who removed the corpses of the executed for use in anatomy lessons were frequent targets of the crowd's ire. English authorities shifted their policies in 1749 and 1750, reserving bodies for friends and family, but this did little to quell popular discontent. The continued rioting that transpired along the Tyburn procession, the traditional route through London to the gallows, convinced officials to abolish the procession in 1783. Yet the removal of the scaffold to outside Newgate Prison failed to achieve the desired effect. Even once executions became rarer, crowds refused to grant uncomplicated consent to scaffold rituals, particularly when they perceived that the condemned was an ordinary member of their own society. Their celebration of convicts' heroism or martyrdom in broadsheets, ballads, and engravings continued to unsettle authorities, who eventually responded by abolishing public executions in England in 1868.

Similar riots transpired during the eighteenth century at scaffolds across Europe, taking place more regularly in France after the 1760s. In Germany crowds revolted at the sight of botched executions, a frequent occurrence. Although full-fledged execution riots were rare in the German states, scaffold punishments failed to convey the intended deterrent message, prompting Prussian officials to reform the laws governing public executions in 1805. As in England, they abolished scaffold processions and instead transported the condemned in closed carts. They also held back the crowd, encircling the punishment site with cavalry. Most importantly they authorized that executions be carried out only at dawn. Officials' fears about popular disturbances at the scaffold in the aftermath of the 1848 revolutions prompted all of the German states to move executions inside prison walls. Authorities further east noted that the Russian masses also absorbed mixed messages at the scaffold and attempted to contain the spectacle of punishment by eliminating the knout in 1845. When this failed to dissolve the specter of popular disturbance, Russian officials abolished public flogging altogether in 1863.

Social anxieties were not the only reasons that authorities restricted or abolished scaffold rituals. En-

Tyburn Procession. "The Idle 'Prentice Executed at Tyburn," engraving from the series *Industry and Idleness* (1747) by William Hogarth (1697–1764). ©THE BRITISH MUSEUM, LONDON

lightenment thought, the softening of morals associated with the civilizing process, and the rise of reformist evangelical movements combined to inculcate in elites a disdain for public and painful punishment. Nonetheless capital and corporal punishments were meted out against offenders, particularly those of the lower classes, into the twentieth century. While such penalties clearly were less acceptable and less prevalent throughout Europe by the mid-nineteenth century, the movement from physical punishments to confinement followed a complicated trajectory.

Many European countries repealed capital punishment in the nineteenth and twentieth centuries. Finland (1826), the Netherlands (1850), Belgium (1863), Norway (1875), Denmark (1892), and Sweden (1910) exemplify this trend. Yet abolition often proved impermanent. While Russia abolished the death penalty for all but political crimes in 1754, the autocracy sentenced thousands to summary executions after the 1905 Russian Revolution. Austria temporarily abolished capital punishment in 1786 but reinstated it after the French Revolution. Frequent reversals in policies regarding the death penalty characterized the situation in Germany well into the twentieth century. Although Maximilien de Robespierre vehemently decried executions, the French democratized and mechanized death in 1792 by introducing the guillotine, whose blade publicly lopped off offenders' heads until 1939. The English Parliament refused to revise the "Bloody Code" and between 1688 and 1820 increased four fold the number of offenses subject to capital statutes. While the monarch frequently exercised his merciful prerogative throughout that period, executions persisted in private through 1950. Thus, Britain practiced physical chastisements alongside penal forms.

BANISHMENT, PENAL BONDAGE, CONFINEMENT, AND DISCIPLINARY PRACTICES

In early modern Europe corporal punishment often was used in combination with fines and banishment. Generally monetary damages were imposed on elites, who were the only ones who could afford them. Until the eighteenth century primarily political dissidents of the upper class were subject to banishment, and rarely was an individual exiled from an entire country during this era. Prior to the rise of centralized states, troublemakers more often than not were barred from living in particular cities or small communities. Officials simply lacked the means of policing wider regions. As rulers consolidated their realms in the seventeenth and eighteenth centuries and the situation began to change, those who transgressed public order were banished from entire countries.

Penal bondage entailed several overlapping practices, such as galley and hulk labor, transportation, and imprisonment, and was more widely employed than banishment in early modern Europe. This punishment, which gradually developed from the sixteenth century through the nineteenth century, reflected the new values associated with the Reformation and the Counter-Reformation, including changing views of idleness and the desire to impose morality on wider social strata. It was additionally motivated by the new economic realities that expanding nation-states faced, particularly the need for regular militaries and the desire for colonies.

France, Spain, and Italy pioneered sentencing convicts to galleys. In the late fifteenth and early sixteenth centuries vagrants and beggars were consigned to this punishment alongside slaves. In 1530 the practice was extended to a wider range of minor and major offenders in Spain, and the trend persisted through the late sixteenth century, when galleys increased in both number and size. In seventeenth-century France galley labor became the primary penalty to which male convicts were sentenced.

The proliferation of galley sentences was largely attributable to naval expansion, and the abolition of the practice in Spain and France in 1748 resulted not from a change in penological methods or philosophies but from improved naval technologies. Galley sentences set the tone for hard labor patterns that emerged across Europe later in the early modern era. As Spanish colonialism advanced, more convicts were sentenced to work in mines and presidios. During the eighteenth century these work camps became full-fledged penal institutions that facilitated Bourbon economic development by mobilizing large work-forces at relatively minimal costs. The French galley system underwent a similar transformation. Once ships no longer required oarsmen, convicts were used on shore as hulk laborers.

Utilitarianism motivated transportation. England innovated this system, using it to colonize its possessions in North America and later in Australasia, endeavors that were fiscally beneficial but hotly challenged from penological and sociological standpoints. From 1718 to 1776 England transported 50,000 convicts to its New World possessions and sold many of them to private planters. The American War of Independence temporarily disrupted transportation, which resumed in 1780. At that time Australasia became the repository for over 180,000 English convicts, mostly property offenders and petty criminals. New South Wales, Van Diemen's Land (Tasmania), and Western Australia were all built on convict labor. While this system effectively expelled criminals from Britain, critics denounced it on contradictory grounds. Supervision was lax, the homesteads and profitable work in private enterprises available to convicts undermined penal objectives, and difficulties in transporting women prevented family economies from taking root in Australasia, contributing to the impression that Australia lacked civilization. Critics condemned

transportation as insufficiently dreadful yet simultaneously held that it sabotaged British efforts to attract voluntary settlers to the region. Whether in spite of or because of its profitability, British transportation was scaled back in 1838 and wholly dismantled in 1867.

Other European attempts to use transportation for state advantage were less successful than Britain's. From the seventeenth century through the nineteenth century Russia's efforts to settle Siberia produced dubious economic benefits and aggravated the marginal status of the borderland. Widespread criticism began in the mid-1840s, yet fiscal concerns, a lack of prisons, persistent desires to exploit Siberia, and the belief that some convicts could not be reintegrated into society impeded the substantive alteration of exile until the 1870s. Russians continued to banish large numbers of people to Siberia until the early twentieth century.

France also experimented with transportation, establishing a system just as Britain dismantled its own. A need for cheap colonial labor was one factor that led the French to begin transporting criminals to Guiana in 1852 and New Caledonia 1864, respectively. The French also sought to exclude "dangerous classes" from society in the aftermath of the 1848 revolution. Yet harsh conditions, morbidity rates that earned the colonies the epithet "bloodless guillotine," and inadequate discipline led the French to question the efficacy of transportation by the late nineteenth century. The system was curtailed in 1894 and abolished in 1947.

Operating under the same preconceptions the English held about women's capacity to civilize convicts, Russian and French authorities unsuccessfully attempted to import women to their penal colonies. The endeavors of all three countries failed dismally owing to a larger underlying tension. On the one hand authorities sought to exclude convicts from society and strip them of their civic identities, yet they simultaneously sent exiles a different message. By promoting marriages and homesteading exiles, they encouraged convicts to resume their normal lives in the colonies. On a material level this simply failed to achieve the desired effect. More fundamentally the paradox bankrupted transportation of its penological premise. The 1880 International Penal Congress questioned transportation's legitimacy and set the tone for its abandonment across Europe in subsequent decades.

Like banishment, confinement was motivated by the desire to exclude convicts from European society. Confinement began in Europe around 1600, when prisons gradually became institutions of forced labor. Early modern jails were places of detention for convicts awaiting sentencing and for debtors. The first workhouses confined the poor, elderly, and sick—not criminals. Whereas initially jail occupants remained idle, by the early sixteenth century workhouse inmates were submitted to labor regimens. By incarcerating vagrants in workhouses, Britons, Spaniards, Netherlanders, and French sought to crack down on idlers during the sixteenth-century economic crisis that swept across Europe. Labor appeared to have a redemptive quality, and the assumption was that work would turn beggars and the unemployed into productive subjects.

Beginning in 1596 the Dutch considered confinement in the Amsterdam *tuchthuis* (rasp-house or prison) a viable alternative to flogging and asserted that labor could correct criminality. Similar institutions were established across the Netherlands, and noncriminals were soon removed from the rasphouses to other specialized facilities. Although other countries emulated the Amsterdam *tuchthuis,* confinement for penal purposes remained rare outside of Holland. London's Bridewell (1555) was reserved for poor relief, and only in the late seventeenth century did English prisons become associated with the judicial system. Charity and the confinement of noncriminals predominated in German and Baltic prisons through the mid-eighteenth century. Families refused to deliver undesirable members to institutions associated with criminality. Only after 1650, when specialized workhouses were erected for offenders, did authorities in the Germanic regions begin to incarcerate criminals.

Early modern workhouses served multiple purposes and were with few exceptions marked by confused boundaries and an undisciplined disposition. They were less segregated from the outside world than their modern counterparts. In the sixteenth and seventeenth centuries the Royal Prison of Seville was a meeting ground where the underworld maintained strong ties with other city groups. Prison doors often remained unlocked, prostitutes came and went, and wardens and inmates intermingled. The eighteenth-century Newgate Prison operated similarly. Confinement also affected different social strata in distinct ways. Because inmates had to pay room and board, their access to financial resources determined whether they starved or lived lavishly. Newgate's guards rented out well-appointed apartments to the wealthy, while debtors shared squalid common rooms. The Dutch elite were generally exempted from labor and were confined separately from the poor.

Significantly the prison developed alongside other penal practices, and its ascendancy over these other forms was neither predetermined nor complete.

Corporal punishment continued to play an important role in disciplining offenders. Moreover imprisonment was often interchangeable with galley labor and transportation. If anything, the development of long-term incarceration, regimented labor practices, and increased tendency to close the prison to the public that became hallmarks of the penitentiary system lent the modern prison some of the mystique of other forms of penal bondage.

According to some historians, the contrasts between the early modern and the modern prison have been overdrawn. They suggest that the chaos of the eighteenth-century prison has been exaggerated and that the nineteenth-century prison was far from a "total institution." Nonetheless the penitentiary model that quickly influenced European developments did mark a transitional moment in penal history. While the early modern prison was not designed for long-term incarceration or rehabilitation of the convict, who generally lingered in it pending "real" punishment, by the early nineteenth century convicts were sentenced to lengthy confinement and subjected to routines aimed at encouraging their transformations. In addition, a movement developed to classify convicts according to crime, age, and sex. In stark contrast to early modern punishment, which focused on the offense, the nineteenth-century form penalized the offender by designing correctional tactics that accounted for his or her individual characteristics. Though this shift was marked by tensions, inconsistencies, and practical impediments, the alteration was momentous.

The new functions that specialists ascribed to punishment were both reflected in and fostered by the spatial organization of the penitentiaries founded across Europe during the nineteenth century. Early nineteenth-century reformers were enthralled with the architecture of North American prisons, particularly Philadelphia's. Like the blueprint of the panopticon produced by the English utilitarian Jeremy Bentham, radial prisons ensured constant supervision of inmates, whose cells were located along corridors branching off of a central inspection point. Advocates of this system asserted that spatial arrangements would allow them to reshape human nature. Confinement in austere, undecorated, and windowless cells seemingly compelled prisoners to contemplate their guilt and prevented them from consorting with one another in ways that might spread criminality. Inspired by such ideas, the British opened their first national prison at Millbank in 1816. While this prison was a costly failure, it set the tone for the much more successful Pentonville prison, founded in 1842. The Pennsylvania (or Philadelphia) system served as a model for Anglo-

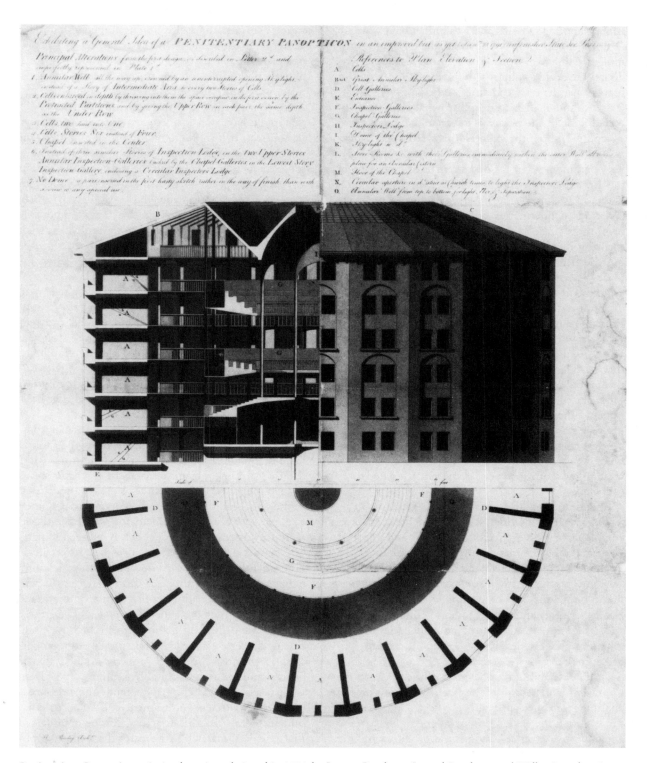

Penitentiary Panopticon. A circular prison designed in 1791 by Jeremy Bentham, Samuel Bentham, and Willey Reverley. A guard in the center can observe each prisoner's cell. BENTHAM PAPERS, LIBRARY, UNIVERSITY COLLEGE, LONDON

American developments and was influential elsewhere in Europe. For example, the Prussian penal code, promulgated the same year that Pentonville opened its doors, advocated solitary confinement and led to a spate of penitentiary construction beginning in 1844.

Although many European penal specialists invested faith in the power of separate confinement to discipline and reform inmates, this system posed great fiscal and architectural demands. Thus complete solitary confinement of prisoners remained rare, even in the heyday of the Pentonville model. Much more common was the Auburn System, whose more cost-conscious penitentiaries submitted inmates to silent communal work by day and solitary cellular confinement by night. Whereas the Philadelphia model required authorities to build new structures, the Auburn System permitted them to convert existing buildings into prisons. Embracing the Irish practice of gradual treatment, penal specialists in England, Prussia, France, Russia, and other countries instituted a system whereby convicts spent their first months in solitary confinement followed by communal living that was gradually increased for good behavior. While theoretically regenerating criminals and preparing them for eventual release, this approach also seemed more humane than complete solitary confinement. From the very start British, Prussian, and Russian penal reformers raised concerns that the total seclusion of inmates was excessively cruel and promoted insanity. Communal work and the stage system mitigated these problems.

Yet prison administrators faced difficulties in effecting even this modified system. Inadequate facilities and fiscal realities fostered overcrowding and impeded the categorization of offenders. Even in places like England and France, where the state devoted considerable resources to prison construction, convicts found numerous ways of evading separation, devising elaborate argots and other modes of communication, and homosexual subcultures flourished despite injunctions. Guard deficiencies compounded disciplinary problems.

The rehabilitative objectives of the penitentiary, however, mandated more than concern about proper confinement. Specialists also predicated the system's success upon the elaboration of labor regimens, moral and educative practices, and inspection. Work was the central organizing principle of life in the nineteenth-century carceral (prison). While this was nothing new, after all, prisoners had labored in the Amsterdam *tuchthuis* since the sixteenth century, work was more organized in the new penitentiaries, lending them at least theoretical similarity to the factories contemporaneously developing in Europe. Yet labor practices varied across Europe. Private entrepreneurs played a large role in the French penal system, which increased prisoners' productivity but detracted from the disciplinary philosophy of the prison. French entrepreneurs were more interested in maximizing profit and thus were unconcerned with teaching convicts skills that might have transformed them into useful citizens. In contrast, British penitentiaries often employed inmates at the treadmill ostensibly grinding corn but more frequently engaging in the unproductive task of grinding air. Although Russian reformers sought to introduce compulsory labor in the 1870s and 1880s, facilities were so overcrowded that it was impossible to allot adequate workshop space to implement their plans. Moreover penal administrators across Europe found it difficult to locate appropriate labor for convicts.

The paradoxes of the penitentiary system were also evident in moral regimes. Though prisons supposedly functioned as sites of educational and religious instruction, reformers failed to devise strategies for accomplishing these goals, and any developments in these directions remained uneven. Even where education existed, reformers found that this hardly impeded recidivism and ultimately perceived that literacy produced superior criminals.

That not all prisoners were men further complicated matters. It was difficult to fit women into a male-oriented disciplinary system. Reformers like the British nonconformist Elizabeth Fry, who spearheaded the foundation of women's prison associations in the 1810s, and penal specialists argued that women required special moral regimens that emphasized religion, the fostering of personal bonds between inmates and warders, and labor forms designed to inculcate domesticity. Gender-based modifications, which were embraced in many European countries after the second quarter of the nineteenth century, undermined much of the masculine penal complex. Even these changes were difficult to implement because pragmatic concerns impeded construction of gender-specific prisons, hiring of properly trained female guards, and location of suitably feminine labor. Even when authorities attempted to tailor the prison experience to women, punishment still failed to rehabilitate them. Authorities across Europe complained that female inmates posed greater disciplinary problems than male inmates and that incarceration seemingly bred deviance among women to an even greater extent than among men.

Penal reformers hoped that the inspection and nationalization of prisons would alleviate such problems. Britain established a national inspectorate in 1832, which resulted in the closure of many local prisons over subsequent decades and culminated in the nationalization of British prisons in 1876. Other European countries, such as Russia and Prussia, followed suit. While attempts to impose uniform disciplinary practices made prison regimes harsher, they nonetheless failed to enhance the rehabilitative potential of the penitentiary.

More than practical shortcomings frustrated the penitentiary's capacity to reform inmates. Rather, from its inception this system was undermined by a theoretical paradox. The twin goals of the nineteenth-century prison—rehabilitation and deterrence—worked at cross-purposes. By mid-century critics began to resolve this dilemma by separating criminals whom they sought to reform from hardened recidivists. The increased involvement of a whole range of specialists in penal reform; new scientific theories of criminality, including Cesare Lombroso's criminal anthropology and Social Darwinism; and greater public awareness of and fears about crime supported this medicalization of deviance. Experts argued that the prison failed to rehabilitate criminals because at least some offenders were incorrigible. Revising their penal philosophies, they used scientific practices to diagnose incurable criminals. Labeling this group degenerate, they advocated its incarceration in long-term facilities and applied to its members psychiatric treatment and eugenics principles then in vogue in Europe. They thus aimed to preclude members of this group from contaminating less serious criminals and reproducing deviance.

Taking cues from the principles that juvenile justice systems elaborated in the first half of the nineteenth century in Britain, France, and Germany, numerous countries established reformatories for corrigible convicts. These institutions, like the French agricultural colonies for youth, removed offenders from polluting urban environments into familial ones that inculcated domesticity, good health, and skills. Like their juvenile counterparts, these adult facilities came under considerable criticism in the years after World War I. Reformatories opened for inebriate women in Britain were judged excessively lenient, insufficiently rehabilitative, and exceedingly costly. The failure rate of such reformatories combined with the economizing demanded by the Great Depression led to their closure and replacement with more traditional penal confinement in some instances and cheaper, noncustodial arrangements in others.

Belgium first introduced the suspended sentence and probation in 1888. France (1891), Luxembourg (1892), Portugal (1893), Norway (1894), Italy (1904), Hungary (1908), Greece (1911), the Netherlands (1915), and Finland (1918) quickly followed suit, and much of eastern Europe emulated this model after World War I. Supervised parole, which remanded convicts into the custody of private patronage networks or police, developed simultaneously. First used experimentally on juveniles in the 1830s, parole was applied to adults in Portugal (1861), Saxony (1862), Germany (1871), and France (1885) and gained the approval of the 1910 International Prison Congress.

These noncustodial arrangements facilitated individualized sentencing and mainstreaming of former convicts, yet it is incorrect to equate them with deinstitutionalization. Rather, they amounted to the extension of the prison's disciplinary practices into society. By the turn of the twentieth century many states possessed the capacity to effectively regulate and supervise their populations and to inaugurate surveillance techniques, such as the French and Russian passports that clearly marked an individual's status as a criminal. In 1999, Britain introduced an electronic tagging system to monitor criminals granted early release from prisons.

The extension of disciplinary regimes into the community at large did not signify that prisons everywhere were dismantled or that convictions ceased to mount, even in countries committed to noncustodial penalties. As prison committals declined in countries like France, where the prison population halved between 1887 and 1956, they proliferated elsewhere. Even before the Nazis rose to power, the prison network in Germany expanded massively. Many socialist countries witnessed similar increases in convictions. After the 1950s western European prison populations swelled, and penal forms continued to coexist. Just as it is impossible to posit a unidirectional trajectory of development from corporal punishment to confinement, so is it problematic to suggest that the prison was replaced by noncustodial penal forms.

In summary, two distinct trends characterize the penal systems articulated in twentieth-century Europe. On the one hand, some countries sought to rehabilitate criminals and mainstream them into society. To these ends, diverse states such as those of Scandinavia, the Netherlands, France, and Italy introduced and refined non-institutional punishments such as furloughs, fines, community-based correctional systems, conditional release, and supervised parole. On the other hand, penal institutions simultaneously proliferated throughout Europe and prisons remained the preeminent form of punishment for criminals, and particularly for a more concentrated recidivist population. Even as public awareness of the brutality of Germany's and the Soviet Union's extermination and labor camps fueled a mounting social outcry against inhumane and cruel incarceration and led critics and statesmen to emphasize the importance of prisoners' rights and fair treatment within carceral facilities, the number of prisons and inmates increased markedly in Western and Eastern bloc countries alike. Moreover, in the late twentieth century authorities largely have rejected the notion that the prison might rehabilitate the convict, instead suggesting that the carceral constitutes an institution in which criminals are to be managed, identified, and set off from upstanding citizens.

EVALUATING PUNISHMENT: THEORY AND HISTORIOGRAPHY

Scholars have evaluated European penal practices and developments in varying ways. Some historians have perceived these changes through the rubric of humanitarianism and progress. Accepting as valid the arguments of eighteenth- and nineteenth-century penal reformers, historians such as Leon Radzinowicz (1948), J. R. S. Whiting (1975), and David D. Cooper (1974) asserted that the rise of the penitentiary was enlightened in its intentions and results because it supplanted barbaric corporal and capital punishments, others, like Bruce F. Adams (1996), who studied nineteenth-century Russian prison reform, modified this picture somewhat, suggesting that shortcomings in practice resulted from the problems of interpreting advanced Western theories in backward autocratic contexts. These positions mistake rhetoric for reality, overlook the continued use of corporal punishment after the rise of the penitentiary, assume that the regimens established in the prisons were humane, and generally fail to examine the larger power relations and authority structures in which the new prisons took shape.

The narrative has been substantially revised by other analysts. Revisionists, who fall into several camps, have asserted that it is essential to examine the wider context in which punishment was deployed. By and large they have privileged the social control aspects of penal change, arguing that reformers' enlightened rhetoric obscured more nefarious tendencies.

One group, which concentrated on punishment's economic effects, asserted that utilitarian aims impelled the replacement of executions and floggings with penal bondage and prisons. According to Marxists like Georg Rusche and Otto Kirchheimer (1939) and Dario Melossi and Massimo Pavarini (1981), the labor demands of nascent commercial capitalism led states to develop prisons that resembled factories. Empiricists demonstrated that penal labor bore little resemblance to factory work and instead was frequently far from productive, was traditionally organized, and existed in countries that evinced little capitalist development, rendering the Marxist argument suspect.

Other Marxists, such as Douglas Hay and Peter Linebaugh (1975), took a different approach. They contended that the sharpening class conflict constituted the ideological basis of criminal law and explains the continued commitment of the English Parliament to capital punishment even in the face of reformers' attacks on and popular riots against executions. Yet by belying that the lower classes benefited from and often championed the "Bloody Code," this position strips them of agency.

Still others of an orientation not necessarily Marxist insisted that, while the penitentiary's economic benefits were dubious, the context of capitalism's rise and state consolidation engendered and was facilitated by new penal modes that asserted greater discipline over criminals and noncriminals alike. Examining the power relations inherent in capitalism, Michael Ignatieff (1978) considered that the birth of the penitentiary constituted part of the process whereby government reformers, social critics, employers, and nonconformist evangelicals sought to locate new forms of social order that could manage the poor, given increased urbanization and the breakdown of traditional relations. In contrast to Ignatieff, Michel Foucault expressed no interest in the multiple discourses that informed penal transformations. Although ostensibly focused on penal practices, his influential *Discipline and Punish* (1979) is more concerned with the rise of modern disciplinary society. Tracing the late-eighteenth century movement away from executions that marked sovereign power in increasingly ambivalent spectacles of punishment, Foucault suggested that the nineteenth-century penitentiary was the site at which various discourses—penal, medical, and psychiatric—converged to form a carceral continuum. Operating in a manner similar to Bentham's panopticon, this institution at once imposed total supervision, individualized convicts by classifying them, and ensured the construction of permanent deviance that facilitated the reproduction of disciplinary practices and their eventual generalization throughout society, even as the process of punishment itself was increasingly privatized.

Both Ignatieff and Foucault take their arguments concerning social control too far. As Ignatieff (1981) noted, revisionists have predicated their positions on the misconceptions that the state monopolized penal regimes and was solely responsible for enforcing social order and that domination is the essence of all social relations. Foucault's portrayal of the carceral continuum is also marred by his attribution of agency to power, which in his account is totalizing. For Foucault disciplinary regimes are everywhere and unstoppable; any resistance ultimately reinforces and can never subvert discourses of domination.

Others have offered correctives to all these models. Some, like Pieter Spierenburg (1984; 1991), emphasized the gradual and overlapping nature of transformations from the scaffold to the prison. Extending Norbert Elias's argument concerning the civilizing process (1939), Spierenburg suggested that the amelioration of elite and popular morals, the increased visibility of and potential for managing marginal populations, and social pacification facilitated by urbanization and state building explain the demise of harsh bodily punishment and the rise of confinement.

According to Spierenburg's theory, during the sixteenth and early seventeenth centuries, feudal codes still held sway and, in the absence of well-developed and centralized state power and policing, individuals often took to arms and unquestionably accepted the violence that pervaded their societies. In contrast, from the late seventeenth century, as absolutist authorities began to monopolize the technologies of physical violence and began to pacify the societies that they governed, attitudes toward physical chastisements changed markedly. These sensibilities, which first developed among elites and only slowly spread to the masses, led to the privatization of corporal and capital punishment and helped fuel an ever widening critique of violent penal regimes.

Others emphasized that, more than humanitarianism or the civilizing process, social fears engendered penal change. Thomas Laqueur (1989), Arlette Farge (1993), and Abby M. Schrader (1997) modified Hay and Foucault's depictions of the scaffold spectacle, asserting that the crowd constituted the central actor and interpreter of executions. Authorities curtailed them because the effects of public executions became increasingly ambiguous and threatened state power. While V. A. C. Gatrell (1994) contended that the eighteenth-century crowd more frequently affirmed executions than negated them, he maintained that politicized spectators in the Victorian era forced the British government to abolish public hangings. That humanitarianism was never central to these abolition processes may explain the continued existence of corporal and capital punishment.

Historians like Patricia O'Brien (1982) suggested that social fears also motivated authorities to establish prisons. Concern about the political unrest of the dangerous classes led elites to replace executions with more generalized disciplinary practices, first articulated within prison walls and then generalized throughout society once states developed sufficient policing. Modifying Foucault's argument in important ways, O'Brien maintained that this process failed to strip convicts of agency. Inmates developed their own subcultures in dialogue with and resistance to penal discipline. Finally, disciplinary practices were never totalizing. Rather, disorder was as important as order in the penitentiary. Penal forms were continually combined, and at the same time that penal specialists articulated new disciplinary regimes, challenges arose to them. Likewise, Michelle Perrot (1980) and Lucia Zedner (1991) contended that modern "total institutions" were exceptional and can hardly be deemed successful.

Ultimately, as David Garland (1990) suggested, no single cause explains the development, reform, and abandonment of penal practices. All of these theorists articulated elements of truth. Humanitarian arguments were not merely empty rhetoric. Economic concerns certainly explain why particular labor regimes seemed attractive in certain contexts, and class conflict always pervaded but never predetermined social relationships. Likewise authorities were motivated to undertake reforms because of social fears but not exclusively for this reason. Resistance from below was neither wholly impotent nor completely powerful. Finally, disciplinary practices predominated but never completely controlled either the inmates' lives inside the prison or those of the free individuals outside it. As Foucault contended, punishment fulfilled a "complex social function" (*Discipline and Punish*, p. 23) in both early modern and modern Europe. History and historiography certainly confirm this impression.

See also other articles in this section.

BIBLIOGRAPHY

Adams, Bruce F. *The Politics of Punishment: Prison Reform in Russia, 1863–1917.* DeKalb, Ill., 1996.

Beccaria, Cesare. *On Crimes and Punishments, and Other Writings.* Edited by Richard Bellamy and translated by Richard Davies with Virginia Cox and Richard

Bellamy. Cambridge, U.K., and New York, 1995. Originally published in Italian in 1764 as *Dei delitti e delle pene*.

Bender, John. *Imagining the Penitentiary: Fiction and the Architecture of Mind in Eighteenth-century England*. Chicago, 1987.

Bentham, Jeremy. *The Panopticon Writings*. Edited by Miran Bozovic. London and New York, 1995. Originally published in French in 1791 as *Le panoptique*.

Cooper, David D. *The Lesson of the Scaffold: The Public Execution Controversy in Victorian England*. Athens, Ohio, 1974.

Dülmen, Richard van. *Theatre of Horror: Crime and Punishment in Early Modern Germany*. Translated by Elisabeth Neu. Cambridge, U.K., 1990. Translation of *Theatre des Schreckens*.

Elias, Norbert. *The Civilizing Process: The History of Manners*. Translated by Edmund Jephcott. Oxford and Cambridge, Mass., 1994. Originally published in German in 1939 as *Über den Prozess der Zivilisation*.

Evans, Richard J. *Rituals of Retribution: Capital Punishment in Germany, 1600–1987*. Oxford and New York, 1996.

Farge, Arlette. *Fragile Lives: Violence, Power, and Solidarity in Eighteenth-century Paris*. Translated by Carol Shelton. Cambridge, Mass., 1993. Translation of *Vie fragile*.

Finzsch, Norbert, and Robert Jütte, eds. *Institutions of Confinement: Hospitals, Asylums, and Prisons in Western Europe and North America, 1500–1950*. New York, 1996.

Foucault, Michel. *Discipline and Punish: The Birth of the Prison*. Translated by Alan Sheridan. New York, 1979. Originally published in French in 1975 as *Surveiller et punir: Naissance de la prison*.

Garland, David. *Punishment and Modern Society: A Study in Social Theory*. Chicago, 1990.

Gatrell, V. A. C. *The Hanging Tree: Execution and the English People, 1770–1868*. Oxford and New York, 1994.

Hay, Douglas, et al., eds. *Albion's Fatal Tree: Crime and Society in Eighteenth-century England*. New York, 1975.

Howard, John. *The State of the Prisons in England and Wales*. Warrington, U.K., 1777. Reprint, New York, 1923.

Ignatieff, Michael. *A Just Measure of Pain: The Penitentiary in the Industrial Revolution, 1750–1850*. New York, 1978.

Ignatieff, Michael. "State, Civil Society, and Total Institutions: A Critique of Recent Social Histories of Punishment." In *Crime and Justice: An Annual Review of Research*. Edited by Michael Tonry and Norval Morris. Vol. 3. Chicago, 1981. Pages 153–192.

Innes, Joanna. "Prisons for the Poor: English Bridewells, 1555–1800." In *Labour, Law, and Crime: An Historical Perspective*. Edited by Francis Snyder and Douglas Hay. London and New York, 1987. Pages 42–122.

Laqueur, Thomas. "Crowds, Carnival, and the State in English Executions, 1604–1868." In *The First Modern Society. Essays in English History in Honour of Lawrence Stone*. Edited by A. L. Beier, David Cannadine, and James M. Rosenheim. Cambridge, U.K., and New York, 1989. Pages 305–355.

Lincoln, W. Bruce. *The Conquest of a Continent: Siberia and the Russians*. New York, 1994.

McConville, Sean. *A History of English Prison Administration*. London and Boston, 1981–.

Melossi, Dario, and Massimo Pavarini. *The Prison and the Factory: The Origins of the Penitentiary System*. Translated by Glynis Cousin. London, 1981. Translation of *Carcere e fabbrica*.

Morris, Norval, and David J. Rothman, eds. *The Oxford History of the Prison: The Practice of Punishment in Western Society*. Oxford, 1998.

O'Brien, Patricia. *The Promise of Punishment: Prisons in Nineteenth-century France*. Princeton, N.J., 1982.

Perrot, Michelle, comp. *L'Impossible prison: Recherches sur le système pénitentiaire au XIXe siècle*. Paris, 1980.

Perry, Mary Elizabeth. *Crime and Society in Early Modern Seville*. Hanover, N.H., 1980.

Pike, Ruth. *Penal Servitude in Early Modern Spain*. Madison, Wis., 1983.

Radzinowicz, Leon, Sr. *A History of English Criminal Law and Its Administration from 1750*. Vol. 1: *The Movement for Reform, 1750–1833*. New York, 1948.

Rusche, Georg, and Otto Kirchheimer. *Punishment and Social Structure*. New York, 1939.

Schrader, Abby M. "Containing the Spectacle of Punishment: The Russian Autocracy and the Abolition of the Knout, 1817–1845." *Slavic Review* 56, no. 4 (1997): 613–644.

Spierenburg, Pieter. *The Prison Experience: Disciplinary Institutions and Their Inmates in Early Modern Europe*. New Brunswick, N.J., 1991.

Spierenburg, Pieter. *The Spectacle of Suffering. Executions and the Evolution of Repression: From a Preindustrial Metropolis to the European Experience*. Cambridge, U.K., and New York, 1984.

Whiting, J. R. S. *Prison Relief in Gloucestershire 1775–1820*. London, 1975.

Wright, Gordon. *Between the Guillotine and Liberty: Two Centuries of the Crime Problem in France*. New York, 1983.

Zedner, Lucia. *Women, Crime, and Custody in Victorian England*. Oxford and New York, 1991.

MADNESS AND ASYLUMS

Peter Bartlett

INTRODUCTION

It may be best at the outset to tame some demons which haunt the popular understanding of madness and asylums of the past. This popular view is of a history infused with horrors. The eighteenth century was a period where the insane were chained in cellars, left in the dark to rot. The nineteenth century moved the insane into stone fortresses, institutions growing over the course of the century to contain upward of a thousand lost souls, concealed for life behind gothic walls, out of sight and out of mind. These nineteenth-century lunatics, hollering in their isolated cells, were tamed and drugged into submission in the first half of the twentieth century. In this semi-conscious and dazed state they were left to rock back and forth, tied to their chairs for their own protection, until released at the end of the twentieth century to wander aimlessly in the public streets when the combined miserliness of governments and naïve optimism of civil-rights extremists resulted in the closure of medical facilities without development of adequate community alternatives. Over this tale lies the specter of the medical man: the quack in the eighteenth century; the distant, callous, and ineffectual administrator of the nineteenth; the chemical controller of the early twentieth, invested with unchecked legal powers; and later the wronged hero, able to provide solutions if only given the legal authority and financial resources to do so. And throughout lies the question of the condition of the patients themselves: were they really mad, or merely difficult; is mental illness really about medicine, or about social control?

Like many popular myths, this one is not without its bases in fact, but it by no means tells the whole story. Certainly, the close and damp quarters in which eighteenth-century lunatics were chained did exist, but as Roy Porter has shown, the eighteenth century could also be characterized by new and optimistic medical treatment. The nineteenth century certainly saw the exponential growth of institutional care of the insane, but it was not usually confinement for life:

roughly two-thirds of those admitted to English county asylums, for example, were released within two years. While contained in the asylum, the life of the patient might be regulated by a tight schedule, but relatively few patients were actually physically restrained for extended periods in padded cells or restrictive clothing. Nor was the schedule punitive. It might, for example, allow for a game of bowls on the lawn in the evening—quite a different image from the oppressive one offered in the popular myth. Certainly, the early twentieth century contained its share of drug treatments, but it also saw the rise of psychology and talking cures. And throughout the last four hundred years, institutional care has never replaced care by families and in the community more broadly. The perceived problems consequent on the release of persons with psychiatric difficulties at the end of the twentieth century are simply not new. Nor is the removal of people from psychiatric facilities into the community necessarily to be understood as a failure: while the perceived failures are visible, successes—and they are many—do not attract notice.

The perception at the end of the twentieth century is that the definition, care, and treatment of mental illness and those it affects are within the province of medicine. That is very much a late modern perspective. The colonization of madness by medicine has been a process spanning much of the last four hundred years, involving boundary disputes with law, politics, religion, and popular understanding. Even now, there are areas where the rout is not complete. In law, medical testimony will be relevant in determining insanity, but it is not necessarily conclusive; and among the public, studies continue to show that when confronted with a troubled person, the care of a friend or minister may be advised as often as a visit to a psychiatrist. The history of madness and the care of the insane is thus not necessarily simply a branch of the history of medicine.

The social and political influences on the development of understanding and care of the insane are complex. Psychiatry has been used for overtly po-

The Madhouse. Painting (1793) by Francisco de Goya y Lucientes (1746–1828). REAL ACADEMIA DE BELLAS ARTES DE SAN FERNANDO, MADRID/SCALA/ART RESOURCE, NY

litical purposes, as in the confinement of dissidents in pre-revolutionary France and the twentieth-century Soviet Union, but such overtly political cases have never formed a statistically large portion of psychiatric patients. Persons with psychiatric or developmental disabilities have been subject to extremist political programs, as for example in the policies of eugenics most extremely articulated in the practices of Nazi Germany. The temptation is to marginalize these policies as a function of the specific German régime, but the prevalence of eugenic thought in much of Europe and North America for much of the first half of the twentieth century suggests that a much more nuanced approach to the relations between medical science, political thought, and social history is necessary.

Certainly, there can be little doubt that psychiatry has been used as a method of social control. One social response to deviant behavior has often been to understand the individual as mad; but to label this "social control" places a particular critical edge to the analysis. Frequently, the people concerned posed real social problems. It is all very well to refer to the confinement of a violent and delusional person, for example, as social control; that does not mean it is necessarily a bad thing. At the same time, the articulation of madness itself can be understood as influenced by social, political, and philosophical factors. The doctors who developed diagnostic criteria lived in specific cultural climates, and were influenced by contemporary events and theories. Thus when we read in the

first part of the twentieth century of women's insanity being caused by "overambition," it seems difficult to divorce this from cultural attitudes toward women in the period.

There is of course a scientific story to be told, but other approaches are also important in the social history of madness and the care of the insane. Homosexuality provides a useful illustration here. Its history can be written from the perspective of the history of scientific medicine: there have been genetic, biochemical and psychological theories about its causes and incidence. That does not entirely explain the rise and fall of homosexuality as a mental disorder, however. Scientific inquiry into homosexuality did not cease when it ceased to be classified as a mental disorder, in the late twentieth century. The scientific investigation of homosexuality continues, suggesting the history of those inquiries has a life separate from the classification of diseases. It further seems that the science does not explain the chronology of medicalization as effectively as external factors. The placement of homosexuality in the medical model occurred in the late nineteenth century, when moral values of sexuality were being re-enforced. It is therefore not surprising that homosexual behavior was articulated in a framework of deviance. Similarly, its removal from medical taxonomy occurred during and after the sexual revolution of the 1960s and 1970s.

In the history of madness and the care of the insane, as in so much of social history, the history of

MOMENTS IN MADNESS: ASYLUMS IN TIME

1377: Prior of the Order of St. Mary of Bethlehem (later called "Bethlem") caring for insane.

1409: Valencia (Spain): Father Jofré opens an institution for the insane. By tradition, this is the first institution specifically designed for lunatics in continental Europe.

1656: Foundation of hôpital-général of Paris. French provincial counterparts follow in 1676. Not curative facilities, but place of early institutional care of the insane among others.

1690: John Locke publishes *An Essay concerning Human Understanding*. Places the ancient distinction between idiocy and lunacy on a philosophical ground. Idiocy is stated to be the inability to reason, and lunacy correct reasoning based on incorrect and deluded sensation.

1723: Tsar Peter the Great decrees that institutions for lunatics should be built. Decree not acted upon, apart from one 25-bed unit founded in 1776.

1751: Opening of St. Luke's Hospital (London), a charitable hospital for the care of the insane.

1764: Foundation of French dépôts de mendicité (workhouses). Another place of institutional care for the insane among others.

1796: Founding of the York Retreat, and the beginning of moral treatment in England.

1798: Establishment of the psychiatric service at Charité Hospital, Berlin, when the penitentiary where the insane had previously been held burned down.

1801: Publication of Philippe Pinel's *Traité médico-philosophique sur l'aliénation mental, ou la manie,* where moral treatment first discussed.

1805: Opening of the renovated asylum at Beyreuth, the first modern German institution for the insane.

1808: First English/Welsh County Asylums Act passed. Allows construction of asylums at public expense, for the accommodation of the insane poor.

1809: First major Russian mental hospital founded. Development of asylums in Russia slow. By 1910, only 438 psychiatrists in all tsarist domains.

1810 (approx): Monomania first identified by Esquirol.

1820s (early): General paralysis of the insane, a manifestation of neurosyphilis, identified by Antoine-Laurent Bayle

1828: English/Welsh Madhouses Act requires private madhouses to be licensed by justices of the peace. Creates inspectorate for London madhouses.

1834: English/Welsh Poor Law Amendment Act passed. Creates professional bureaucracy that allows for efficient development of county asylum system.

1838: Law of 30 June 1838 establishes national system of asylums in France.

1839: John Conolly becomes medical superintendent of the Hanwell Asylum (London). Beginning of the nonrestraint movement.

1844: Commencement of publication of the first German psychiatric journal, *Allgemeine Zeitshrift für Psychiatrie*

1845: New English/Welsh County Asylums Act makes the provision of county asylums mandatory, creating the legal structure of a national framework. Inspectorate, the Lunacy Commission, given a national mandate.

1850s: Identification of "circular insanity" (mania and depression) by Jean-Pierre Falret and Jules Baillarger. Renamed "manic depressive illness" by Emil Kraepelin in 1899.

1852: Foundation of the Société Médico-Psychologique, the association of French doctors specializing in mental medicine

1857: Rise of use of bromides as sedatives.

1877: Beginning of statutory scheme of boarding out, an early form of community care, in Scotland.

1860: Benedict-Augustin Morel publishes his taxonomy of mental disorders in *Traité des maladies mentales*. Insanity had long been thought to have hereditary characteristics, but Morel adds the theory of degeneration, that insanity gets worse in subsequent generations. In the twentieth century, when this argument intersects with genetic thought, the insane are perceived as a new sort of social danger.

1870s: Jean-Martin Charcot redefines and rejuvenates concept of hysteria

(continued on next page)

MOMENTS IN MADNESS: ASYLUMS IN TIME (continued)

1875: Robert Lawson of the West Riding Asylum (Yorkshire, England) begins using morphine as sedative and hypnotic for psychiatric patients.

1878: Benjamin Ball hired as first professor of mental medicine in France, at the University of Paris.

1885: General Medical Council (United Kingdom) introduces specialist course in psychological medicine. No one takes the examination in the first year.

1886: Viennese psychiatrist Richard von Krafft-Ebing publishes *Psychopathia Sexualis.* A variety of sexual behaviors enter the realm of psychiatric pathology.

1887: Establishment of the Dromokaition on Corfu, by private subscription, to replace the 1838 facility inherited from British occupation of the island. This is the only specialized Greek psychiatric facility until the foundation of a clinic at the University of Athens in 1904.

1889: Rimsky-Korsakov Institute founded; 1894, Kashenko completed, following public funding appeal. These are the first two significant psychiatric institutions in Moscow. The Bechterev, the prime psychiatric hospital in St. Petersburg, was not completed until 1908.

1893: Emil Kraepelin publishes taxonomy of mental disorders. To the traditional categories, he adds dementia praecox, later renamed schizophrenia, a category further developed in the eighth (1907) edition of his textbook.

1913: English/Welsh Mental Deficiency Act 1913 provides a framework for the institutionalization and community supervision of people considered "mental defectives." Parallel legislation introduced in Scotland the same year.

1920: Rise of prolonged sleep therapy, popularized by Jakob Klaesi (Zurich).

1921: Dispensaire system established in Union of Soviet Socialist Republics. Serves as administrative basis for the provision of good community care through the 1980s. By 1950s, handling only psychiatric cases. By 1957, 2,300 dispensaires contained in general health centers, and an additional 119 in free-standing centers.

1930: English/Welsh Mental Treatment Act 1930 allows voluntary admission to madhouses and asylums. Previously, all persons had been legally detained. Parallel legislation introduced in Scotland.

1933: First use of insulin coma therapy, Vienna.

1933: Rise of Nazis in Germany. During the Nazi regime, more than 100,000 persons with mental health difficulties or developmental disabilities were killed in an organized program of "euthanasia," in gas chambers located in psychiatric facilities.

1934: Ladislas von Meduna first induces convulsive shocks for treatment of psychiatric patients (Budapest).

1935: First lobotomy performed at the Santa Marta Hospital, Lisbon, by neurologist Egas Moniz.

1938: Ugo Cerletti (Rome) first uses electricity to induce convulsive shocks.

1943: Penicillin used in the treatment of neurosyphilis. General paralysis of the insane disappears quickly from asylums.

1949: Australian John Cade uses lithium on psychiatric patients. Introduced into Europe by Morgens Schou, a Danish psychiatrist, in 1952. Becomes treatment for mania.

1952: Chlorpromazine in use on psychiatric patients as treatment for schizophrenia.

1954: Inpatient psychiatric population peaks in England, at 148,000 (33.45 per 10,000 population). By 1981, inpatient rate drops to 15.5 per 10,000 population. By 1997–1998, inpatient beds total less than 46,000.

1955: Tricyclics used on psychiatric patients by Roland Kuhn (Switzerland). Becomes treatment for depression.

1959: English/Welsh Mental Health Act 1959. Major rewriting of legislation. Voluntary admissions become preferred, with confinement only to be a last resort.

1993: Homosexuality removed from International Classification of Disorders, the international standard of mental disorders coordinated by the World Health Organisation. It had been removed in the American DSM classification almost twenty years earlier.

the ideas cannot be conflated with the history of their application. Stated objectives and descriptions may well be open to challenge by modern empirical research. This has been most controversial when unfortunate and often unforeseen consequences are perceived to challenge the benevolent intentions of historical figures, but the past can equally be seen in a more sympathetic light than perceived by its contemporary commentators. Thus cure for nineteenth-century medical men was something near at hand, but still in the future. The perception that their asylums were full of chronic and incurable cases was their perception, not a twentieth-century gloss. As noted above, late-twentieth-century scholarship instead shows modest success at cure, if that is understood as release from the asylum and return to the community. Twentieth-century scholarship thus shows the nineteenth-century asylum to be more successful than it took itself to be.

The difficulty in confusing the history of ideas with the history of their application is illustrated by the confinement of women. The received history portrays the asylum as a place where women were subject to particular control at the hands of patriarchal ideology. Certainly, the history of psychiatry reflects broader social notions of women and their sexuality, which was portrayed as unbridled passion requiring restraint. Thus the French hydrotherapist Alfred Béni-Barde at the turn of the twentieth century claimed that "the hybrid neuropathy that has seized [hysterics] does not require calming. These female patients must be tamed. That is why cold water succeeds" (quoted in Shorter, p. 125). The social control implications are obvious, but such statements nonetheless do not translate simply into psychiatric practice. Thus for much of the nineteenth century, the large English county asylums admitted women only marginally out of their proportion to the population as a whole. The significant imbalance in an English context arises only in the twentieth century, when at least in theory the ideological marginalization of women was past its peak. This does not of course mean that the ideological history is irrelevant. It does mean that it reflects only one part of the puzzle of how the care of the insane actually worked in practice.

Several points may be drawn from this. First, it is simplistic to portray the history of madness, psychiatry, and the care of the insane as "good ideas gone wrong," and it is misleading to perceive the cast of characters in those histories as composed of heroes and villains. Such an approach diverts attention from the more interesting and detailed analysis of how that history developed. Second, while some scholars have approached the histories with particular emphases (on

Cold Water. A patient receives hydrotherapy. *Les Hydropathes: Deuxième traitement: Immersion, submersion et contorsion,* lithograph, late ninteenth century, by Charles Émile Jacque. NATIONAL LIBRARY OF MEDICINE, BETHESDA, MARYLAND

social control, or on the history of medical science, for example), and while such specific foci may enlighten some points, the histories of madness, psychiatry, and care are multifaceted. A unitary focus risks missing the richness of the tapestry. Third, as political and social factors influenced the development of the histories, they are to be understood not merely according to factors which span international boundaries, but also as a result of their local circumstances. It would be uncontroversial to suggest that the histories developed differently in the twentieth-century Soviet Union than in western Europe, but this can be understood as an extreme example of a general point: Europe is not one culture, and one must therefore think of European histories of madness.

All of this raises its share of difficulties. The history of madness and the care of the insane is not one history: it is a profusion of histories. Since the 1980s there has been an explosion in the academic study of these histories, but the scope for research is yet more vast. In many of the specific histories, research has only just started, and much remains to be done. Here, even more than in other fields, social history is a work in progress.

CARING FOR THE MENTALLY ILL

Until the creation of universal state-funded health services after World War II, and to a considerable degree beyond, care received by the mentally ill has been a function of the individual's financial means. In general up to the early nineteenth century, and often beyond, specialized care of the insane, whether provided by doctor, cleric, or lay person, would be provided only if the patient or his or her family could afford to pay, and the standard of care would depend on what the payer could afford. For the truly well off, such care might involve the complete avoidance of formal institutionalization and the provision instead of one or more paid carers. As insanity and developmental disabilities have long been viewed as a matter of shame, such carers might be formally appointed to other positions in the household, or presented as companion of the individual. In families with leisure, the care might further be left in the hands of relations, sometimes brought in for the purpose. While a doctor's services might form a part of the overall package, day-to-day carers would not be likely to be particularly medically trained.

Alternatively, the well-off might remove the insane person to a private establishment. Such private madhouses have a long history, but became considerably more common through the eighteenth century. They remained a chosen place of care for those with money throughout the nineteenth century, and can be seen to survive in private mental hospitals catering to an exclusive clientele. The private madhouse sector catered to all classes who could afford to pay for care. At the high end of the scale, such as the Ticehurst Asylum in England, patrons might be admitted with their personal servants, and the day was filled with recreation befitting the social standing of the inhabitants. These institutions would not necessarily be controlled by doctors. Instead, particularly prior to the mid-nineteenth century, they might be run by either clerics or laity. From the eighteenth century until roughly World War I, spas provided a variation on such private care, particularly for nervous disorders. While it is difficult to see that care for mental disorder has ever been fashionable, it is certainly true that care in an eighteenth- or nineteenth-century spa imported an air of exclusivity and privilege.

For those without such means, care was not nearly so plush. For families with some means, less expensive private madhouses might be an option for at least the short term. These were not the elegant establishments of the upper class. Sometimes, they might involve simply a family prepared to care for a small number of individuals to boost their own income, but increasingly, these madhouses became businesses in their own right. While not deliberately punitive, the economics of business made them much more Spartan than the establishments of the rich, with fewer attendants and more patients per room. By the mid-nineteenth century, these institutions sometimes contained hundreds of inmates and charged competitive rates, in an institutional environment usually overseen by a doctor.

Nonetheless, the realities in a world before disability insurance was that for the bulk of working people, the requirement to pay for care in such a madhouse might tax the family resources to the breaking point, particularly when the insane individual was the primary breadwinner. Such families frequently found themselves, like the respectable poor, trying to care for them at home. As long as the insane person was sufficiently placid and at least one responsible person was able to remain in the home to supervise, this might be an option. When this was not the case, poor relief, the old social safety net, might intervene to provide a small supplement to the family income, or to fund a carer for the individual in the home if possible. Particularly if the individual were violent the poor relief authorities might be prepared to pay for some form of incarceration. In the nineteenth century, this might be in any of a variety of places: a private madhouse, a jail or similar institution, a poorhouse or workhouse in countries where those existed, or in one of a small number of specialized places for the care of lunatics, generally run by religious establishments.

In the first half of the nineteenth century, the institutional ground shifted, and in much of Europe, specialized asylum care became available for the poor. These new institutions developed in parallel to existing private madhouse provision, although their scale eventually dwarfed such private provision. In England at the beginning of the nineteenth century, for example, only a few thousand insane poor were confined. By the end of the century, numbers had grown to close to 100,000. In German-speaking Europe there were 202 public asylums by 1891, and in France 108. In Germany itself, the number of insane persons confined rocketed from one in 5,300 in 1852 to one in 500 in 1911.

It is this explosion of care that has consumed much of the social historians' interests. It did occur in much of Europe, including the United Kingdom, the Netherlands, Switzerland, France, Italy, Sweden, and parts of Germany. It was by no means universal, however. Moscow did not acquire a significant lunatic asylum until the last decade of the nineteenth century, for example, and as late as 1900, two asylums sufficed for all of Portugal. While one of the first specialized facilities for the insane had opened in Spain in the fifteenth century, large-scale asylum-building did not occur there until the twentieth, and in Greece, the first three state-owned institutions were not founded until between 1912 and 1916.

For those nations where the move to institutional solutions did occur, the reasons for this explosion of care are a matter of hot scholarly debate. Andrew Scull places the rise of the asylum in the context of changing economic circumstances in the move toward capitalism. The move from cottage industries to factory work meant that fewer family members worked at home, and fewer could therefore combine work with the care of an insane family member. Further, the downward pressure on wages in the industrial economy made it more difficult to feed an unproductive member of the family. This argument has much to recommend it. Certainly, the case studies of patient records in nineteenth-century asylums would suggest that admissions occurred when a family could no longer cope with the insane person at home, or if the insane person had first been moved to a poor-law facility, when he or she became too unruly or violent to remain in that environment. The bulk of those admitted were either violent or suicidal. Individual admissions were the result of practical problems.

As Scull also points out, the period was one where institutional solutions were in fashion more broadly. Specific eighteenth-century progenitors of the asylum can be identified. In England, charitable medical institutions for the insane underwent a modest spurt of growth from 1751, when St. Luke's Hospital was founded. Eighteenth-century facilities are however notable for their diversity. France certainly had medical establishments for lunatics, the Salpêtrière and the Bîcetre in Paris being the most famous, and these like the eighteenth-century English charitable facilities can be seen as ancestors of the high Victorian asylum: institutions created on a hospital model, with a doctor in charge. At the same time, French eighteenth-century institutional care of lunatics also occurred outside medical settings, in hôpitaux-général, dépôts de mendicité, and religious institutions. Notwithstanding the name, the hôpitaux-général were not curative institutions, and not under medical control. They were instead institutions founded in the third quarter of the seventeenth century for the confinement and control of French riffraff generally, but including the disorderly insane. In 1764, the dépôts were created as workhouses for the poor, but they, too, quickly expanded to include the care of the insane poor. As in much of Roman Catholic Europe, the church also provided care. By 1789, the Chaitains, the Brothers of Saint-Jean-de-Dieu, were operating

seven institutions for the insane in France, and other religious orders also offered institutional care. These mixed models of care are reflected elsewhere in Europe. In Berlin, the insane were only moved to a hospital when their previous accommodation, the local penetentiary, burned down in 1798, and in Greece, the bulk of the insane seem to have been lodged in nonspecialized facilities for the poor well into the twentieth century. Even in England, where the asylum movement was strong, a quarter of the poor insane were lodged in poor-law workhouses throughout the nineteenth century.

The move to institutional solutions for social problems also occurs outside the realm of insanity. The growth of the asylum corresponds to the growth of the prison and the workhouse. The asylum may therefore be understood as reflecting a more general trend in the minds of policymakers. This is in turn consistent with the economic analysis. With the wealth flowing from industrialization, expensive institutions became an option in a way that was not previously possible in most of Europe. The broad policy move to institutional solutions may have affected the minds of the families involved as well. It may possibly have become more acceptable to send a family member to an institution as the period progressed.

The changing role of medical professionals also undoubtedly had its effect in the development of the asylum. The eighteenth century rejuvenated medical thinking, and by the beginning of the nineteenth century, doctors and others were, with a new enthusiasm, claiming that insanity could be cured. The new specialist band of alienists, as doctors specializing in mental disorders were then called, argued that the removal of the patient from family surroundings was essential for cure, and indeed that the asylum itself, as a place of order that would reorient the mad person back to their right self, had a curative effect. While such an approach was not the exclusive preserve of medical professionals, the image of the curative asylum enjoyed the support of the benevolent, but also the parsimonious, for while the asylum might be expensive in the short term, it promised the longer term removal of insane persons from poor rolls and their return to productive labour.

The movement toward institutional solutions must also be understood in the context of specific national histories: the rise of the asylum becomes possible when local infrastructures are sufficiently developed to make it a real possibility. Indeed, the administrative context of the asylum takes quite different forms depending on the nation involved. In the German states, for example, institutional provision appears to have been linked to universities. With roughly twenty universities, each vying for academic kudos, this was a viable possibility. In England, with Oxford and Cambridge the only universities prior to the opening of University College London in 1828, the university system would have been unable to support a network of asylums. Instead, the English poor law was reorganized in 1834 to include a professional cadre of administrators. While the foundation of the English county asylum system predates the so-called New Poor Law, it is only after 1834 that the asylum system, where admissions were administered by the poor-law authorities, begins to take hold and grow. In France, after a brief hiatus during the upheavals following the Revolution, the involvement of the church returned, and remained for much of the nineteenth century. Not merely did the Catholic Church own and operate its own asylums, it also provided the nursing staff for many of the state-owned facilities throughout the nineteenth century, marking the institutions with some degree of religious flavor and occasionally in ideological conflict with the medical officers. In Belgium, this system continued to the end of the twentieth century, with more than 80 percent of psychiatric institutions still administered by religious bodies.

The asylum regime. For much of the nineteenth century, the routine of daily life in the asylum was one of the prime curative features. Employment would be provided, appropriate to the social class and abilities of the individual. For the poor, this would usually involve needlework or laundry work for women and groundskeeping or farm work for men. Libraries were provided, stocked with morally uplifting literature. The food was not excessive, but a good diet was provided as essential to recovery. Asylums were built to ensure a healthy atmosphere for those confined in them, including proper ventilation for the summer and central heating for the winter. On many of these practical and measurable matters, the asylum offered a standard of living well superior to that of the poor insane person in the community. Unsurprisingly, at least some of those confined wanted to be there. At the same time, it was institutional living, controlled by staff and removed from the individual's family and community. Equally unsurprisingly, some inmates clearly did not wish to return to the asylum on their departure.

For much of the nineteenth century, the asylum's chief claim to cure rested in its regime. The bleedings, cuppings, and blisterings of the eighteenth century, treatments designed to restore to balance the bodily humors upon which early modern medicine was based, fell from fashion, although cold baths, emetics, diar-

rhetics, wine, and porter were slower to disappear from the landscape of treatment for mental disorder.

It was not until the last quarter of the century that new chemical treatments began to be used in asylums. The first set of these were sedatives: morphine, chloral hydrate, and bromides. Paris asylums alone were using over a thousand kilograms of potassium bromide per year by 1891 (Shorter, p. 200). For general paralysis of the insane (GPI), a psychiatric manifestation of neurosyphilis, fever treatments began around 1890, but were eventually superseded by treatments involving malarial injection about the end of World War I. These methods remained until the discovery of penicillin in 1943. The first half of the twentieth century saw its own additions to medical treatments in the form of coma therapy and shock therapies. As the name suggests, the object of coma therapy was artificially to place the patient in a coma, for periods occasionally up to two hours. Insulin was used to induce the coma, first in Austria by Manfred Sakel in 1933, who argued that coma therapy was a cure for schizophrenia. The procedure became particularly popular in Switzerland and the United Kingdom, although its efficacy was doubtful and its mortality rate significant. The object of shock therapies was to induce a convulsive seizure, which, largely by trial and error, was discovered to have therapeutic effects. The seizures were originally drug-induced, first in 1934 by the Budapest psychiatrist Ladislas von Meduna. In 1938, however, the Italian psychiatrist Ugo Cerletti discovered that the application of electricity to the brain produced a similar effect. Electroconvulsive therapy, or electroshock therapy was born, and within a few years became a very common treatment, particularly for depression. As with coma therapy, repeated treatments might be necessary to produce the desired effect.

The end of World War II marked a return to drug therapies. Chlorpromazine was first used as a treatment for schizophrenia in Val-de-Grâce military hospital in Paris in 1952, and within a year, it was in use throughout the French psychiatric system. Lithium was discovered as a treatment for mania by John Cade in Australia in 1949, and was first introduced into Europe three years later by Morgens Schou, a Danish psychiatrist. Tricyclic medications, so called because of their chemical structure, were first used on depressed patients by Roland Kuhn in Switzerland from 1955. All of these drugs became psychiatric staples, and for the first time, psychiatric drugs became big business. In 2000, psychiatric medications accounted for roughly one-quarter of the prescriptions in the United Kingdom National Health Service.

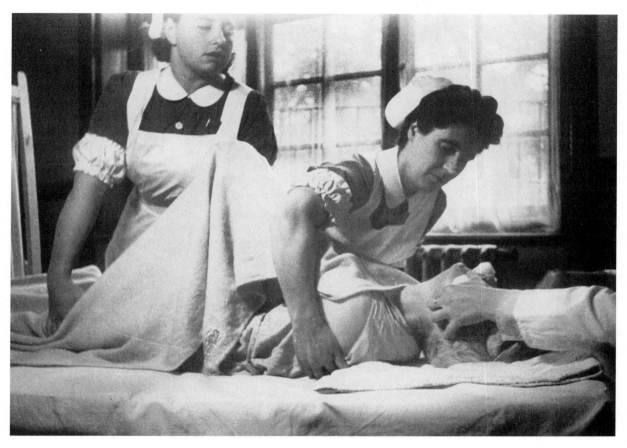

Shock Therapy. Nurses tending a patient receiving shock treatment at a mental hospital in England, 1946. ©HULTON GETTY/ LIAISON AGENCY

From asylums to community care. The postwar period saw a move from asylum-based care to community-based alternatives. English asylum accommodation peaked in 1954, with 148,000 beds. By 1997, there was less than one-third this number. The scholarly debate regarding this movement is as fractious as the debate regarding the growth of the asylum movement. Scull argues for an analysis based on economics and the sociology of the medical profession: after the war, money had become tighter and governments no longer wished to provide expensive institutional care; the psychiatric profession, its place of authority now secured, did not require the asylum as a visible symbol of its importance. Certainly, in the final decades of the twentieth century, when government policy throughout Europe tended to move to the right, the continuing trend to reduce the scale of inpatient psychiatric care can be seen as part of a larger political agenda, but that is more difficult to apply to the period after World War II, when governments

seemed more willing than ever to become involved in national systems of socialized medicine.

In part, the move can no doubt be understood as a result of new practicalities. While the nineteenth-century moral treatment required the curative regime of the asylum, and coma and shock therapies could be administered only in the closely supervised medical environment available in a psychiatric facility, the new drug therapies could be administered in outpatient clinics. Nonetheless, outpatient clinics did not begin with the introduction of these drugs. Jean-Martin Charcot had such a clinic in Paris as early as 1879, and they were common in German asylums by 1920. Care with families in the Belgian town of Gheel had originated in the eighteenth century, and continued through the nineteenth. From 1857, the Scots boarded out up to a quarter of their poor insane through a scheme given a formal legislative basis, and in 1860, more than half the Welsh poor insane were cared for outside institutions. These initiatives did not neces-

Charcot Lecturing. Jean-Martin Charcot (1825–1893) lectures on hysteria at the Salpêtrière Hospital in Paris. The patient is Blanche Wittmann, who is held by Joseph-François-Félix Babinski (1857–1932), who has hypnotized her. Sigmund Freud studied with Charcot in 1885 and 1886. Painting by André Brouillet (1857–1920). HÔPITAL NEUROLOGIQUE, LYON, FRANCE/ERICH LESSING/ART RESOURCE, NY

sarily diminish in the twentieth century. The English Mental Deficiency Acts were providing statutory community supervision for 43,850 people by 1939.

The new initiatives toward community alternatives can be seen as growing from older models. While care within the family is still often a very important element of these community alternatives, it is no longer a necessary component. Developing both from models of boarding out and from more sensitive social services and social housing policies responding to people who would never have been institutionalized in asylums in the past, governments now sponsor disability pensions for those who can live on their own or with their families, group homes for those who cannot, and day-care centers for both these groups. There are, of course, ironies to these "new" policies. The disability pensions have much in common with the older poor law relief provided under eighteenth- and nineteenth-century schemes. The group homes are frequently owned in the private sector, with care purchased from them by governments much as care might be purchased from private madhouses in the nineteenth century.

While modern drugs have created new possibilities for community care, the development of these programs from models predating the advent of the drugs suggest that the doctors as well as governments were in favor of blurring the lines between inpatient care and the community. Legal changes in English law are consistent with this view. Up until 1930, all persons admitted to county asylums and private madhouses were legally detained. The Mental Treatment Act 1930 introduced informal admission for the first time. In the Mental Health Act 1959, a preference toward such admissions became formal government policy. Moves were further made to integrate psychiatric populations with general hospital patients. By 1977, one-third of English psychiatric admissions were to psychiatric wards in these general hospitals, rather than to asylums for the insane alone. Italy went one step further, abolishing specialized psychiatric facilities in 1978 and treating all psychiatric patients either in the community or in general hospitals. Such moves can be seen as removing the high legal walls that, as much as their physical counterparts, had separated the psychiatric facility from the community.

In this context, the move to community care can be seen as a piece of a larger policy agenda. The complexity of these movements leads to conflicting results. Certainly, since the 1960s there has been a movement toward greater patient rights. Psychiatric patients sometimes enjoy much greater control over their treatments than before, although these rights often lag considerably behind North American systems.

There is also new regulation of clinical trials. The development of the drugs identified above occurred without approval of ethical committees, with remarkably little prior knowledge as to whether the treatment to be given was safe, and with no attention paid to the views of the patients who served as guinea pigs. In psychiatry as in the rest of medicine, considerable movement has occurred toward ensuring that experiments are safe and ethical. At the same time, the movement toward community care has brought with it calls for increased surveillance of people with mental health problems outside hospital, buttressed with enforced treatment regimes. If the values of the broader community have begun to enter the asylum, so controlling values of the asylum have also begun to enter the broader community.

MADNESS, CONTROL, AND MEDICINE

From the above history of the care of the insane, it will be clear that the medical colonization of madness cannot be seen as a foregone conclusion. Even today, the care of the insane can be seen as flowing from an uneasy tension involving doctors, the government, and the public, in which the insane themselves risk being lost in the shuffle: it is simplistic to say that medicine has somehow "triumphed." The history of those administering madness must, like the history of the care of the insane, be understood as infused with a variety of themes.

From politics to medicine. By the early nineteenth century, medical involvement was generally necessary prior to the admission of an individual to a lunatic asylum. This does not necessarily imply an acknowledged expertise in matters of insanity, however. France provides an example of how this involvement might be almost accidental. Prior to the Revolution of 1789, the insane had been confined under lettres de cachet, the Royal Prerogative of confinement without hearing or appeal, that had attained symbolic importance to the revolutionaries as an abuse of royal power. In one such abuse, some political dissidents, whose confinement would be particularly sensitive, were classified by the monarchy as insane, not merely criminal. The lettres de cachet could not be continued by the revolutionary government in their previous form, yet lunatics posed considerable practical problems if left without control. The solution was to take the confinement of lunatics out of the overtly political realm: doctors would decide whether a person was actually insane and requiring confinement. Thus this authority of doctors over confinement does not necessarily originate in an overwhelming case for expertise or

ability to cure, but rather in a matter of political expediency.

The movement of the medical profession to create a specialization in mental medicine was a somewhat haphazard affair, marked by contingency. Specialized training was usually limited. In France, courses in mental medicine were occasionally run as adjuncts to the main medical program, but it was not until 1878 that a professor of mental medicine was first hired at the University of Paris. Formal training was similarly sparse in the British Isles. Alexander Morison had instituted a course of lectures in 1823, John Conolly in 1842, and Thomas Laycock in the 1860s, but these courses were badly subscribed. Morison estimated that his course, over twenty years, attracted a total of little more than a hundred students. It was not until 1885 that a certificate course in psychological medicine was introduced by the General Medical Council, and no one applied for the first examination. Professional apprenticeship training did exist formally in the main psychiatric hospitals in France and informally as assistant medical superintendent positions began to appear in England in the second half of the century, but these produced relatively few experts to staff the growing number of facilities. While Jean-Étienne Esquirol by 1820 claimed the care of the insane to be a speciality within medicine, it was a speciality practiced by those trained as generalists.

And what of the disorders which were the subject of this apparent specialization? Here again, one can see a variety of themes in operation. Certainly, there are issues of control and professional interest. The doctors lived in their specific societies, however, and therefore the history of the disorders involves the history of philosophy and political contingency. There are also issues of the history of medical science, but here too the dividing line between science and philosophy and society is fluid.

The project of organizing insanity into categorical structures, and of identifying new forms of madness can be seen as an example of these intermingling themes. From antiquity, mental illness was understood as of two main sorts, melancholia and mania. The eighteenth century saw a revived interest in theorizing insanity, and, gradually, new categories of insanity were introduced and new theories of causation were articulated. The reasons are manifold. Certainly, there has throughout the period been an advantage to an individual's career in publishing texts detailing the nature and indications of insanity. Publication has always been a way to individual fame for the author. The publication of texts and taxonomies was also an exercise in professional development, however, for the placement of madness into an overtly medical frame emphasizes that it is the province of medicine. In this, the development of uniform systems of classification has a particular importance. Professionalism implies both expertise and objectivity. The development of a common language, uniformly applied by experts guided by ethical and professional principles, is an important part of this process. Disagreements between alienists were actively discouraged by the nascent nineteenth-century professional organizations, and remain controversial to this day.

Indeed, the history of classification in the late twentieth century reflects some of these concerns. Since 1949, International Classification of Diseases has included a section on mental disorders. The classificatory system contained therein and developed in ten-year amendments since that time can be seen as an attempt to introduce order and uniformity into diagnoses and categorization among psychiatrists internationally. The inclusion of mental disorders for the first time in 1949 in part reflects the foundation of the World Health Organization, which coordinates the compilation of the work. While the 1949 edition was considerably expanded overall, the inclusion of mental disorders can be seen as indicative of the increasing acceptance of psychiatric practice by general medicine—a process that had been a project of the alienists for a hundred years. This was arguably particularly important at this time. The abuses of psychiatry under the Nazi regime in Germany had come to light, and a reassertion of the professional nature of psychiatry can be understood as important in this period. Throughout the ongoing development of the ICD, consistency in application has been of particular importance. In the 1993 revision, consistency has been particularly important not merely among those using the ICD system, but also with those primarily in the United States and Canada, where the Diagnostic and Statistical Manual system is used instead of ICD. Prior to that time, there were marked divergences in diagnosis based on similar facts, with North Americans far more likely to diagnose schizophrenia than their European counterparts. Certainly, the desire for consistent categorizations and applications can be seen as scientifically important, but it is also difficult to deny that the prior divergences in practice caused considerable embarrassment to the medical professions concerned. The amendments are also thus in the professions' interests.

The creation of new categories of disorder can be seen as flowing in part from developments in medical science, and in part from social and professional interests. Some important disorders have existed in medical understanding and been developed for hundreds of years. Depression developed from melancho-

lia, a category that has existed since antiquity. The origins of psychotic disorders can be seen in the manias of history. Other disorders have come and gone, however. Monomania was identified by Esquirol in about 1810. It was understood as a single pathological obsession in an otherwise sane mind. By the late 1820s, it was a common disorder. Jan Goldstein notes that it accounted for 45 percent of admissions to the Charenton asylum in Paris between 1826 and 1833, and 23 percent of admissions to Montpellier asylum from 1826 to 1829. By 1870, it had all but vanished. Certainly, a scientific basis was articulated for the disorder, but Goldstein argues that it was also important in the turf war between doctors and lawyers as expertise in criminal insanity matters. Monomania allowed doctors to portray themselves as experts in court, by diagnosing a disorder not readily identifiable to laity. The political purpose was not restricted to self-interested professionalism. A finding of monomania allowed markedly increased flexibility in sentencing, in the context of an otherwise very strict Napoleonic Code. Monomania can thus be seen as lying at the intersection of doctors' political reformist views and professional advantage. When these background factors changed, the diagnosis become much less important, whatever its medico-scientific merits.

Other new diagnoses can be understood as broadening the market for psychiatric services. For much of the nineteenth century in France there was a glut of doctors. Goldstein argues that the rise in hysteria in the second half of the nineteenth century was in part the result of a need for mental specialists to find new markets for their services. Shorter makes a similar claim about the increasing number of neurotic disorders in the second half of the twentieth century. There are social control implications to these developments, as ever more people become involved in the psychiatric universe. At the same time the history of psychiatric administration over the twentieth century has increasingly focused on non-enforced treatment. If we see a rise in social control, it is increasingly social self-control.

The nineteenth century saw insanity as flowing from some combination of physical, moral, and environmental causes. A physical predisposition in the form of weak nerves, heredity, epilepsy, or a brain lesion, for example, was thought usual if not necessary for the onset of mental illness, but that would not usually suffice. While this might be the "predisposing" cause, an "exciting" cause was also necessary. The possibilities here were legion, including overindulgence in alcohol, an excess of religious devotion, bereavement, childbirth, use of drugs, ill-treatment by a spouse, the fear of poverty or unemployment, and

Pinel. Philippe Pinel in the courtyard of the Salpêtrière Hospital in Paris, as a woman patient is freed from her chains. NATIONAL LIBRARY OF MEDICINE, BETHESDA, MARYLAND

overwork. Certainly, there are social control implications to these categories, and the insane might be perceived in heavily moralistic terms. John Hadley, admitted to the Leicestershire and Rutland County Asylum in 1852, was said to possess "a large amount of animal cunning, low trickery, and all the paltry and petty devices of an abandoned character." Not all insanity was due to such moral failing, however. John Kettle, admitted to the same asylum three years earlier had been "remarkable for his steady, industrious and sober habits." His insanity was instead caused by the demise of his business. The doctors might even place the blame on broader social and environmental causes. Thus Elizabeth Spawton's insanity in 1851 was attributed to the "crowded and vitiated atmosphere" to which she was subjected in her many years employment as a factory hand. Economic factors such as those to which John Kettle was subjected and public health in factories were as much issues of social concern as the dissoluteness of the poor that formed the basis of John Hadley's characterization. In each case, the description of the inmate cannot be separated from broader social themes. The latter two cases do emphasize that while nineteenth-century alienism was about social control, it was also about creating broader understandings of how it was that social control became necessary.

Moral treatment. The ambiguities surrounding social control, and the mixture of themes in the de-

velopment of insanity, can also be seen in the creation and development of moral treatment. It was a philosophical advance that reconceptualized insanity to create the intellectual space for the development of this approach. In 1690, John Locke, himself a physician, recast the ancient distinction between idiocy and lunacy in a philosophic framework. While idiocy involved the inability to reason, lunatics could reason, but did so from incorrect and deluded sensations. The placement of insanity in the realm of sensation and unbridled passions was continued by Étienne Bonnet Condillac. The new emphasis on the ability of the insane person to reason provided the intellectual background for moral treatment at the beginning of the nineteenth century, treatment that was based on the patient's ability to correct his or her ways.

The foundation of moral treatment in France was based on political contingency. Philippe Pinel was a provincial doctor from Montpellier, who went to seek his fortune in Paris in 1778. There he was effectively shut out of the medical establishment until the revolution. The system of medical accreditation then in effect meant that his Montpellier qualification had no validity in Paris, and it was only with the revolution that Pinel was able to come to prominence. At that time, he was politically well placed to do so: he had become a partisan of the revolution and in 1790 obtained municipal office in Paris, where several of his friends were in positions of considerable influence. In 1793 he was appointed to the medical directorship of

441

the Bicêtre, and two years later he was transferred to the Salpêtrière. While there, he developed his system of moral treatment, which he published first in 1801. This system marked a move from the physical treatments of the eighteenth century to a system where the alienist interacted instead with the personality of the patient. Hope and encouragement were offered, and deluded ideas directly challenged, by an alienist whose authority was re-enforced through physical and moral means of control. These were not techniques derived from medical theory, but instead from Pinel's observation of his own lay orderlies at the Bicêtre, although Pinel did place the techniques in a scientific context.

Independently but contemporaneously, a similar approach was being taken by William Tuke at the York Retreat, founded in 1796. The Retreat, however, was founded in direct reaction to medical control and its abuses at the charitable York Asylum. Based on a Quaker ethos of dignity, piety, and charity, the Retreat treated its patients as members of a family under the guidance of the superintendent. As with Pinel's version, an attempt was made to connect with the patient at his or her level of understanding, and to build on that. Suitable employment was provided, both to occupy the insane in a reasonably pleasant way, and to prepare them for a return to the community.

Moral treatment was influential across Europe, but particularly in England, where coopted and somewhat modified to emphasize the absence of physical restraints and pervasive surveillance by asylum personnel, it became the basis of the curative asylum of the mid-nineteenth century. Again, there is an issue as to how much this is to be understood as a medical development. The traditional version of history is that the nonrestraint system in England was popularized by John Conolly, the medical superintendent at the Hanwell Asylum from 1839. While certainly the medical specialists adopted it as their own in the middle years of the nineteenth century, Akihito Suzuki has suggested that Conolly himself was not instrumental in the introduction of the approach, which was instead developed by the justices of the peace who formed the administrative board of the asylum.

Much has been made of the shift in emphasis implied by this approach, from control of the body to control of the mind, of the self. Michel Foucault characterizes this as a new technology of power, that where the old treatments had controlled the body of the insane person, the new treatments were a battle to control the individual's mind or self. There is a strong case to be made for this view, in that the object of moral therapy was self-control, in the hope that the individual might reintegrate as a productive member of society. In the twenty-first century, this remains the object of mental health policy. Those who choose not to take their medication, those who choose madness, and as a result who choose not to fit in are characterized as immoral. Certainly, there is a significant social control element, but the ethics of this element is difficult to gauge. Integration is, after all, the object of many of those who have been involved in the psychiatric system. Does this mean that social control is the mutual aim of the carers and the insane person, in which case is it control at all? Or does it instead mean that the social control has worked, and that the controlling view has been truly internalized?

See also **Health and Disease** *(volume 2); and other articles in this section.*

BIBLIOGRAPHY

Bartlett, Peter. *The Poor Law of Lunacy: The Administration of Pauper Lunatics in Mid-Nineteenth-Century England.* London, 1999.

Bartlett, Peter, and David Wright, eds. *Outside the Walls of the Asylum: The History of Care in the Community 1750–2000.* London, 1999.

Bynum, William F., Roy Porter, and Michael Shepherd, eds. *The Anatomy of Madness: Essays in the History of Psychiatry.* 3 vols. London, 1985–1988.

Castel, Robert. *The Regulation of Madness: The Origins of Incarceration in France.* Translated by W. D. Halls. Cambridge, U.K., 1988.

Digby, Anne. *Madness, Morality and Medicine: A Study of the York Retreat, 1796–1914.* Cambridge, U.K., 1985.

Foucault, Michel. *Madness and Civilization: A History of Insanity in the Age of Reason.* Translated by Richard Howard. Reprint New York, 1973.

Goldstein, Jan. *Console and Classify: The French Psychiatric Profession in the Nineteenth Century.* Cambridge, U.K., 1987.

History of Psychiatry. A scholarly journal devoted to the history of psychiatry, containing both scholarship relating to the social history of psychiatry and the history of psychiatry as a medical science. Much of the research concerns European psychiatry.

Medical History. A good journal that includes both social and scientific histories of medicine, including a good selection of articles on the history of psychiatry.

Porter, Roy. *Mind-Forg'd Manacles: A History of Madness in England from the Restoration to the Regency.* London, 1987.

Scull, Andrew. *Decarceration: Community Treatment and the Deviant—A Radical View.* 2d ed. Englewood Cliffs, N.J., and Oxford, 1984.

Scull, Andrew. *The Most Solitary of Afflictions: Madness and Society in Britain, 1700–1900.* New Haven, Conn., 1993.

Shorter, Edward. *A History of Psychiatry: From the Era of the Asylum to the Age of Prozac.* New York, 1997.

Showalter, Elaine. *The Female Malady: Women, Madness and English Culture, 1830–1980.* London, 1985.

Social History of Medicine. A scholarly journal devoted to the social history of medicine, with a good selection of articles on the social history of European psychiatry.

Suzuki, Akihito. "The Politics and Ideology of Non-Restraint: The Case of the Hanwell Asylum." *Medical History* 39 (1995): 1.

Section 13

SOCIAL PROBLEMS
AND SOCIAL REFORM

CHARITY AND POOR RELIEF:
THE EARLY MODERN PERIOD

Brian Pullan

In the teachings of the Christian churches, charity was a religious emotion, a divine fire that destroyed the love of self to make room for the love of God and neighbors. Closely related to charity or *caritas* was mercy or *misericordia*. According to the vision of the Last Judgment in chapter 25 of the Gospel of St. Matthew, salvation depended absolutely on willingness to be merciful to the poor, as if each one were Christ himself. A good Christian would strive at once to imitate Christ and to find him in deprived and afflicted people and in wanderers, pilgrims, galley slaves, and the inmates of jails.

"I must be a suitor unto you in our good Master Christ's cause," wrote the bishop of London to the king's secretary in 1552. "I beseech you be good to him. The matter is, Sir, alas, he hath lain too long abroad (as you do know) without lodging, in the streets of London, both hungry, naked, and cold. Now, thanks be to Almighty God, the citizens are willing to refresh him, and to give him both meat, drink, clothing and firing."

Whereas charity could flourish between equals, mercy denoted transactions between the strong and the weak, the rich and the poor, even the living and the dead. "Charity and mercy are distinct virtues," pronounced the Jesuit Jerome Drexel (1581–1638), for many years a preacher at the court of the elector of Bavaria. "Friendship and charity are given or received by equals, but mercy excels in that it looks to and supports a lesser person. Charity embraces human beings for their goodness, mercy for their wretchedness, for merciful people are like God to those whom they assist."

In practice mercy and charity were seldom so clearly distinguished from each other, and associations devoted to mercy and to charity were equally concerned with the relief of the poor. Six works of mercy were commended in the Gospel, but the tradition of the Catholic Church had added a seventh, the burial of the dead. To balance those works of "corporal" mercy, which were performed toward the body, Catholic catechisms listed an equal number of others done

for the benefit of the soul. The seven works of "spiritual" mercy included offering prayers and masses for souls suffering in purgatory; teaching Christian doctrine to children and ignorant adults; rescuing public sinners, including common prostitutes, whose way of life exposed them to damnation; and converting unbelievers, among them Jews and Muslims.

Through its links with corporal and spiritual mercy, charity became associated with poor relief, education, and campaigns for moral improvement. But legal definitions of charity, as in Tudor England, also included public-spirited attempts to better the lives of communities by providing or maintaining amenities. Indeed the preamble to an English statute of 1597, which remained in force until 1888 and established an official list of proper charitable uses, referred not only to various forms of poor relief but also to "repair of bridges, ports, havens, causeways, churches, sea banks and highways."

Poor relief, however, was not inspired solely by the religious motives of charity and mercy, and some relief was financed by rates and taxes rather than by voluntary contributions. Worldly, practical, and humane reasons lay behind attempts to relieve poverty. Conspicuous among them was the fear of public disorder. Riots erupted if the poor were made desperate by shortages of bread or if the government of a state or city failed in its fundamental duty of guaranteeing supplies of food and frustrating the maneuvers of speculators who attempted to amass quantities of grain and profit from soaring prices. Another prominent reason was the fear of disease, especially the notorious plague that might invade a community if vagrants were allowed to wander freely from infected to healthy areas. Third was the desire to protect the economy against heavy losses of population through epidemic or famine, since few governments doubted that a large population containing a high proportion of skilled workers made for a strong and prosperous state. Last was the need to tide the labor force over spells of slack trade or seasonal unemployment. Most of the poor laws passed from the sixteenth century onward contained provisions for set-

The Works of Mercy. "Feeding the Hungry," from *The Acts of Mercy,* glazed terra-cotta relief by Giovanni della Robbia (1469–1529) on the Ospedale del Ceppo, Pistoia, Italy. OSPEDALE DEL CEPPO, PISTOIA, ITALY/ALINARI/ART RESOURCE, N.Y.

ting the able-bodied poor to work. These measures were influenced by religious disapproval of idleness (which was regarded as sinful as well as antisocial), and perhaps even more by the desire of merchant capitalists to secure cheap, disciplined labor to perform simple tasks, such as spinning wool, winding silk, beating hemp, or rasping dyewood, as in the London Bridewell established in the 1550s or the Amsterdam workhouse opened in the 1590s.

Some people devoted their leisure to charitable activities not, perhaps, from purely religious motives but because they saw them as a path to prestige and the control of patronage. Since acts of charity were highly esteemed, positions on the boards of management of hospitals or other concerns conferred status and bore witness to a person's probity. Sometimes, as in early modern Venice and eighteenth-century Turin, these positions compensated certain social groups (in Venice the citizens, in Turin the court aristocracy and the merchants) for their exclusion from power in the state. Other times, as in sixteenth-century Bologna, control over charities consolidated the power and authority of the senatorial families who dominated the city.

In other instances, as in Amsterdam, the task of running an orphanage, hospital, or house of correction served as an apprenticeship for members of the political elite before they entered the senate. A statue or bust in the hall of a hospital or a commemorative tablet in a church reciting a benefactor's good deeds conferred a kind of immortality in almost any country. The practice of benevolence was described in the English *Gentleman's Magazine* in August 1732 as "the most lasting, valuable and exquisite Pleasure."

METHODS OF POOR RELIEF

Poor relief schemes generally included harsh measures intended to correct the rebellious poor who refused to work, seemingly in contradiction to conventional notions of Christian charity, though they could be represented as a form of tough love. In the early eighteenth century Lodovico Antonio Muratori (1672–1750), a scholar, parish priest, and archivist to the duke of Modena, argued in a controversial treatise that punitive measures should be regarded as acts of charity toward the body politic if not toward the individual. "If we show little indulgence towards defective members," he wrote, "this becomes charity towards the whole body." To deny alms to a wastrel could be an act of charity, since such a refusal might spur him or her into leading a better life.

Between the sixteenth and the eighteenth centuries societies waged a war on begging and vagrancy rather than a war on poverty. In its broadest sense poverty was the condition of being compelled to labor in order to live and having no savings or independent income in reserve if prevented from working. It was accepted as part of the natural or providential order, in which the rich and the poor were complementary, each supporting the other. The benevolent almsgiver needed the prayers of the poor in return for his or her acts of charity. Sometimes poverty was seen as a vital spur to industry on the assumption that, unless driven by the fear of starvation, most people would not choose to work. Charity was a conservative force designed to palliate poverty but not to uproot it by a radical redistribution of wealth. It was intended to preserve the existing social order, and people often showed a special tenderness to distressed gentlefolk and respectable people who had fallen on hard times and were ashamed to beg.

Most early modern societies, however, tried to promote one kind of change by transforming the idle poor into the industrious poor and by equipping solitary and unprotected young people to take their proper places in society and the family. This involved apprenticing orphaned boys and abandoned children to useful trades and placing girls in domestic service and eventually providing them with dowries that would enable them to marry respectable husbands.

At least from the twelfth century ecclesiastical lawyers authorized almsgivers to discriminate between the worthy and the undeserving poor both on economic and on moral grounds and to favor those who were in greater need and those who were better behaved. By the sixteenth century organized private charities and public relief schemes were clearly endeavoring to concentrate their resources on the genuinely needy. This group included not only the widows and orphans whom every ruler traditionally vowed to protect, not only the aged and feebleminded, but also working families burdened with large numbers of dependent children or plunged into destitution by the prolonged sickness or disablement of the principal wage earner. Instead of waiting for the poor to present themselves at the charity's headquarters, officers visited homes and systematically compiled censuses. About 1603 the officers of San Girolamo della Carità, a religious society devoted to poor relief that expected to cover one-third of the districts in Rome, were instructed by their society to take account of "female children of any age and males up to the twelfth year" and to exclude from relief all families with fewer than three children and parents in good health.

Concern for the respectable, hardworking poor, for victims of circumstance who patiently accepted their misfortunes, and for the young and the aged was balanced by harshness toward drunkards, gamblers, idlers, and the tricksters who bulked large in the literature of almost every European country. By the late seventeenth century parts of France and Italy exhibited an ambition to carry out what Michel Foucault has called a "great internment" of beggars, lunatics, and social undesirables in general hospitals. Here they would be separated from the public and subjected to a quasi-monastic regime based on regular work, sexual abstinence, and compulsory piety. But few if any societies actually possessed the resources to carry out such a far-reaching measure, and beggars' hospitals were often restricted to women, children, and invalids.

ADMINISTRATION OF POOR RELIEF

Charity and poor relief were administered partly by the Christian churches, partly by voluntary organizations, partly by the foundations of individual philanthropists, partly by the town, village, or parish, and partly by the state. Public authorities tended to intervene drastically only in emergencies, but many cities in continental Europe established public health offices and food commissions charged with taking preventive measures against plague and famine. Both church and state claimed the right to supervise charities and inspect their accounts. The Catholic bishops insisted on performing this task after the Council of Trent empowered them to do so in the 1560s. Calvinist churches appointed deacons with a special responsibility for collecting and dispensing alms to the poor. In Catholic societies much of the work was in the hands of the lay officers of religious fraternities, hospitals, or other foundations who were subject to clerical advice and surveillance but enjoyed a certain degree of autonomy.

It is arguable whether or not the theological differences of Catholics and Protestants gave rise to distinctive approaches to the problem of poverty. Catholics insisted on the crucial role of good works, which included acts of mercy and a great many other pious deeds, in accumulating the religious merit vital to salvation. They often contended that the highest aim of all acts of mercy and charity ought to be the salvation of souls, those of the receivers as well as the givers of charity. Protestants held that good works were but the fruits and signs of salvation through the merits of Christ alone and through belief in his sacrificial death. They saw poor relief as a means to creating an orderly and God-fearing society, a truly Christian commonwealth.

Catholics and Protestants also defined the objects of charity rather differently. Catholics gave to members of religious communities who had renounced all worldly goods and made themselves poor, to pilgrims traveling to sacred places, and to souls suffering in purgatory, on whose behalf they celebrated masses. Sometimes several hundred masses were offered for the sake of a single soul, and special funds were set up to finance them. For Protestants only the involuntary living poor, who had neither chosen poverty nor descended into poverty out of dissolute behavior, could be proper objects of charity. Apparently Protestants were better able to concentrate on the needs of society rather than the needs of souls insofar as the two could be separated, for sins such as fornication and incest could be countered by improving degrading social conditions.

However, it seems certain that from the 1520s onward both Catholic and Protestant cities in western Europe attempted to adopt poor relief schemes on broadly similar lines, seeking to centralize or coordinate the dispensation of charity, to suppress or control begging, and to provide work for everyone capable of doing it. Such schemes may have originated in Lutheran Saxony, but they proved broadly acceptable to

Dispensers of Charity. *The Regentesses of the Old Men's Almshouse, Haarlem,* painting (1664) by Frans Hals (c. 1582–1666). FRANS HALS MUSEUM, HAARLEM, THE NETHERLANDS/THE BRIDGEMAN ART LIBRARY

many Catholic communities in Flanders, France, Italy, and Spain. In Flanders and Spain representatives of the begging friars, the traditional champions of the poor who saw their own interests threatened by the bans on begging, vigorously opposed the poor laws, arguing that they would deprive the poor of a fundamental human right to ask for alms as they chose and to travel freely from the more barren to the more prosperous parts of a country. But the University of Paris approved the principles behind the poor law scheme of Catholic Ypres in 1531, and the misgivings of the mendicant orders were not shared by all the Catholic clergy or by Catholic magistrates.

Similarities should not be exaggerated, for Catholics continued to favor organizations of which reformed communities disapproved. To take an obvious example, brotherhoods and sisterhoods devoted to pursuing their own salvation by good works continued to flourish and multiply in Catholic societies until the mid-eighteenth century. Elsewhere they were swiftly abolished at the Reformation, and their absence cleared the way for the parishes, their traditional though not invariable rivals.

In 1523 an ordinance written by the reformer Martin Luther for the small town of Leisnig in Saxony conceded that, if voluntary charity and endowments proved unequal to the task of sustaining the local poor, the authorities would be entitled to levy a compulsory contribution from the more prosperous members of the community. However, most communities in continental Europe clung to the belief that giving to the poor ought to follow from personal choice rather than legal coercion. Only in England did the parish authorities regularly levy poor rates, which parliamentary statutes had empowered them to impose since 1572. Although only about one-third of English parishes were accustomed to using their statutory powers in 1660, the practice had by 1700 become almost universal. On the other hand, in many communities outside England the moral pressures to give were intense enough to constitute a "charitable imperative," with only slight differences between a voluntary subscription and an obligatory payment or between a religious undertaking and a civic duty.

By virtue of parliamentary legislation and its local enforcement, England developed something close to a national system of poor relief, although the practice of levying rates did not eliminate the need for private action. In continental Europe most towns and cities made their own arrangements, which depended on large institutions located in cities that often served the surrounding districts as well. Such foundations were supported by bequests, gifts, and the proceeds of collections taken on the streets or through poor boxes in churches. Occasionally the state or town government or a benevolent ruler supported a particular charity by allocating to it the proceeds of certain indirect taxes or judicial fines.

To generalize is difficult, but it is reasonable to suggest that in any particular city the institutional arrangements consisted of a combination of some though not necessarily all of the following elements: religious brotherhoods and sisterhoods or voluntary societies whose concerns included poor relief, visiting and nursing the sick, or moral improvement, or all of these things; hospitals or hospices, which could be both poorhouses and places for medical care; workhouses and houses of correction; institutions for the care of rphans, lost or abandoned children, and girls thought to be in moral danger; houses for reformed prostitutes or otherwise dishonored women; public pawn banks designed to lend money freely or at nominal rates of interest against pledges to customers who could prove need; free schools intended chiefly to teach the elements of Christian doctrine; medical care provided by publicly salaried physicians, surgeons, and apothecaries and by nurses, who were often themselves poor people; and public granaries and food stores.

Some attempts were made to simplify these complicated structures. In many cities of northern Italy, France, and Spain magistrates and ecclesiastical authorities endeavored, from the mid-fifteenth century onward, to consolidate small hospitals into larger and better-supervised organizations. In the 1520s the newly Protestant towns of Germany led the way by a few years in establishing "common chests" or central almonries to control all relief paid to people who remained in their homes. Similar institutions soon followed in the Low Countries and in France.

Not all forms of organized charity were directed primarily toward city dwellers. For instance, the *Monti Frumentari* or grain banks of Italy lent seed corn or food for consumption to farmers and hoped to recover their loans at harvesttime. The charity workshops of eighteenth-century France benefited smallholders and agricultural laborers during the months when seasonal unemployment was most severe. Despite their name, they were to pay wages rather than dispense alms, chiefly for road building and textile work. Rural Finland, perhaps in response to the famines of the 1690s, developed a system whereby peasant households were divided into groups known as *rote*. Each group was charged with looking after one of the parish poor, who might either lodge with one particular household or move at intervals between one household and another in the group.

Beyond all institutional charity lay innumerable personal transactions and informal neighborly acts. They have left no documentary traces but must have been crucial to the subsistence of the poor. Survival may have depended as much on the neighborly charity of the poor toward each other as on the merciful condescension of the rich and the sometimes grudging agreement of prosperous folks to pay the poor rate levied on social superiors.

See also other articles in this section.

BIBLIOGRAPHY

Cavallo, Sandra. *Charity and Power in Early Modern Italy: Benefactors and Their Motives in Turin, 1541–1789.* Cambridge, U.K., 1995.

Cohen, Sherrill. *The Evolution of Women's Asylums since 1500: From Refuges for Ex-Prostitutes to Shelters for Battered Women.* New York, 1992.

Critchlow, Donald T., and Charles H. Parker, eds. *With Us Always: A History of Private Charity and Public Welfare.* Lanham, Md., 1998. Includes essays on the early modern Dutch Republic, France, and Italy.

Dauton, Martin, ed. *Charity, Self-Interest, and Welfare in the English Past.* New York, 1996. Includes essays on Europe.

Foucault, Michel. *Folie et déraison: Histoire de la folie à l'âge classique.* Paris, 1961. Abridged English translation *Madness and Civilization: A History of Insanity in the Age of Reason.* Translated by Richard Howard. New York, 1965. Includes discussions of the French general hospitals and of Foucault's theory concerning the "great internment" of the poor.

Grell, Ole Peter, and Andrew Cunningham, eds. *Health Care and Poor Relief in Protestant Europe, 1500–1700.* London and New York, 1997.

Grell, Ole Peter, and Andrew Cunningham, with Jon Arrizabalaga, eds. *Health Care and Poor Relief in Counter-Reformation Europe*. London, 1999.

Hufton, Olwen H. *The Poor of Eighteenth-Century France 1750–1789*. Oxford, 1974.

Jones, Colin. *The Charitable Imperative: Hospitals and Nursing in Ancien Régime and Revolutionary France*. London and New York, 1989.

Lindberg, Carter. "There Should Be No Beggars among Christians: Karlstadt, Luther, and the Origins of Protestant Poor Relief." *Church History* 46 (1977): 313–334.

Lis, Catharina, and Hugo Soly. *Poverty and Capitalism in Pre-industrial Europe*. Atlantic Highlands, N.J., 1979.

Muratori, Lodovico Antonio. *Trattato della carità cristiana e altri scritti sulla carità*. Edited by Piero G. Nonis. Rome, 1961.

Pullan, Brian. *Poverty and Charity: Europe, Italy, Venice, 1400–1700*. Aldershot, U.K., 1994. Reprints of essays published over the last thirty years.

Riis, Thomas, ed. *Aspects of Poverty in Early Modern Europe*. Vol. 1. Alphen aan den Rijn, Brussels, Stuttgart, and Florence, 1981. Vol. 2. Odense, 1986. Vol. 3. Odense, 1990. Essays on poverty, charity, and poor relief in many parts of western Europe, including the Scandinavian countries.

Slack, Paul. *Poverty and Policy in Tudor and Stuart England*. London, 1988.

Van Leeuwen, Marco H. D. "Logic of Charity: Poor Relief in Preindustrial Europe." *Journal of Interdisciplinary History* 24 (Spring 1994): 589–613.

CHARITY AND POOR RELIEF:
THE MODERN PERIOD

Timothy B. Smith

In the late twentieth century, massive national welfare states consumed up to 40 percent of the gross national product (GNP) in several western European nations. Charities performed vital services, but they were shadows of their former selves. Their total spending paled in comparison to state social welfare spending. The accident of charity has been replaced by the guarantee of social insurance. Cradle-to-grave welfare states, providing insurance against illness, disability, unemployment, and above all old age poverty, shelter Europeans from life's major risks.

The welfare state is young. In Europe prior to the 1920s charity and poor relief predominated over social insurance. These were by definition concerned with providing the minimum necessary for survival. Charities often were as concerned with providing moral and religious guidance as they were with providing financial assistance. The welfare state is concerned with ensuring a basic level of material comfort and in Europe generally does not mix morals with money.

State-provided social welfare matched private charity in strength in the 1920s in France and Britain. In Germany this occurred a little earlier, and in other European nations, such as Italy, it was a little later. But everywhere charity was the bedrock of poor relief throughout the nineteenth century. London had over seven hundred charities in the 1880s, and Paris had several hundred. Spending by charities overshadowed spending by public authorities. In Lyon, France, private charities spent over 18 million francs in 1906, whereas public social welfare cost only 1.34 million francs. Giving and receiving private charity was a crucial part of the urban experience in nineteenth-century Europe, figuring at the center of civic life, where the state did not. In Russia the almost complete absence of public assistance in the early nineteenth century meant that mutual aid within estates and private charity were indispensable. Charity flourished even in places notorious for their poorly developed civil society and their tiny middle class, such as Russia.

As late as 1900 most European states extracted only 3 percent of the GNP through taxes. By the end of the twentieth century that figure averaged 45 to 50 percent. The states did not have enough public money to redistribute before the 1930s to 1950s. Private charity and local poor relief helped keep the European social order intact but little else. It set its sights low and promised even less. Ultimately, as Western Europe moved toward an open, prosperous, and egalitarian society in the 1950s, private charity diminished. Although it still flourished in Britain and to a lesser extent in some continental countries, charity was displaced entirely by the welfare state in many nations. In Germany and Scandinavia the state so dominated the social service scene that it squeezed charity to the margins of civil society.

Until the 1960s charity was by definition an asymmetrical exchange between unequal partners. Presuming that social inequality, while possibly regrettable, was nevertheless inevitable, it has dealt with the symptoms rather than the roots of poverty. Throughout history charity has been what Enlightenment critics like Paul-Henri-Dietrich d'Holbach called an "accidental virtue." Charity might be well established in one city but weak or nonexistent in another. Critics on the left, especially in France and Germany, charged that charity was necessarily antidemocratic. Charity and the poor law tended to stigmatize recipients, so many British politicians, among them Aneurin Bevan, worked to create the universal welfare programs of the 1940s. Considerations of dignity thus combined with the inadequacy of private charity to spur the establishment of state-sponsored welfare.

THE PREDOMINANCE OF PRIVATE CHARITY IN NINETEENTH-CENTURY EUROPE

Although they date from much earlier in European history, charity and poor relief in the nineteenth century exhibited some special features. First, churches, the traditional providers of charity, came under recurrent attack by secular reformers. Where the churches

Charity by a Religious Institution. A friar distributes food, Rome, 1809. Engraving by Pinelli. ©BETTMANN/CORBIS

weakened, as in France, serious questions arose regarding the institutional base of charity. Even there, however, churches remained fundamental to the charitable effort. Second, industrialization and urbanization made poverty more visible. Population increases also had an effect, for example, enlarging the number of abandoned children. Third, middle-class beliefs challenged the validity of charity. Strict economic liberals urged that charity harmed the recipient, making him or her dependent rather than self-sufficient. Many cities tried to ban begging because it contradicted a proper work ethic. Similar beliefs lay behind efforts in England to tighten poor law provisions and to force recipients into unpleasant workhouses. Benevolent institutions attempted to distinguish the worthy poor, who simply could not work because of illness or old age, from the lazy, who should be prodded into the active labor force. Charity continued nevertheless, but on less secure cultural foundations.

Regional differences were important. Orthodox Christianity had always heavily emphasized charity, and in countries like Russia that emphasis continued unchanged. Some have argued that the emphasis on charity there delayed political measures to aid the poor. The debate over religion as the basis for charity in France was not replicated in England, where concerns about charity's demoralizing effects were more prominent.

Outside of England and parts of Germany, where the poor law was tax-financed and a major annual expense, publicly funded social assistance, even at the local level, was relatively undeveloped. In the vast majority of French, Spanish, and Italian towns and villages, private charities and the church provided the lion's share of poor relief throughout the nineteenth century. In many towns publicly funded assistance simply was not available. In many French departments, the ninety county-sized administrative units that make up the country, lay charities did not exist in 1900. But charity was heavily concentrated in the wealthier regions of France and Europe, and was almost nonexistent in some of the poor, remote areas. Between 1800 and 1845, six of ninety French departments, Seine, Rhône, Nord, Seine-et-Oise, Haute-Garonne, and Bouches-du-Rhône, received one-quarter of all charitable bequests. In western and central France the church was still heavily involved in charitable activity, to the point of monopolizing it. Typical was the city of Angers, which in 1890 had sixty charities, all private and Catholic. The Seine department was home to no less than 3,227 charitable institutions in 1897. At the end of the century Lyon had at least 245 private charities, and when multiple branches are included the figure is over 1,000.

In France and other parts of Europe the Catholic Church expanded its charitable activities in the nineteenth century. From the 1830s, for example, the Société de St.-Vincent-de-Paul (Society of Saint Vincent de Paul) spread its roots across Europe and North America. By 1860 it had over 1,500 chapters and

100,000 members in France alone. Religious orders, particularly the female ones, multiplied at an incredible rate in the 1820s and 1830s. In Lyon, the first to be officially reconstituted in 1825 were the Ursulines, the Carmelites, and the Soeurs de Saint-Joseph et Saint-Charles (Sisters of St. Joseph and St. Charles). The Jesuit Congrégation des Messieurs (Brotherhood of Gentlemen) was one of the most active male orders on the charitable scene. With the support of the church, these orders devoted their energies to teaching the catechism to the working classes and to charitable works. Dozens of providences for orphans and young children, such as the Providence de Saint-Bruno and the Providence de Saint-Pierre, were established between 1815 and 1825. In the early stages of industrialization, the church's charities were crucial to coping with social problems.

Until the 1890s the church generally took a fatalistic view toward poverty, reminding workers that the poor would always be here. Church and bourgeois politicians alike viewed religion as the last rampart between civilization and proletarian barbarians, yet the church was generally opposed to official state social reform. It devoted its energies to supporting voluntary charity, whether directly, through the parish system, or indirectly, through lay but religiously inspired institutions, such as the *Association catholique de la jeunesse française*, (Catholic association of French youths) which had sixty thousand members by 1905.

Despite its shortcomings, private charity kept the social world from falling apart, especially in France, Italy, and Spain, which had no poor law. Even in areas where public assistance was unusually well developed, such as the Pas-de-Calais department in northern France, 73 percent of the families of agricultural laborers in 1913 received some form of charity. In Saint-Chamond, France, 60 percent of the population of one parish, 2,200 of 3,600 inhabitants, received assistance in 1844. In times of trouble private citizens organized ad hoc charities.

THE INTERRELATIONSHIPS OF WORK AND CHARITY

The predominance of private charity in nineteenth-century Europe shaped relations between employers and workers. Employers wrote letters recommending admission of their laid-off workers to charity, poor relief, or the local hospice. Local elites pulled strings for "their" protected poor, usually the poor of their *quartier* or neighborhood. Those who donated to hospitals and charities had a say in who received assistance. Political clout helped too. One family might

control all the major relief institutions in a small town of France. In some small villages, like Sommieres in Gard southern France, one person ran both the hospital and the welfare bureau for twenty years. Clearly in such a setting a bad reputation would immediately disqualify a person from relief. In many small, remote towns during the first half of the nineteenth century, the *bureau de bienfaisance* (poor relief bureau) was merely a revived *maison de charité* (house of charity) of the Ancien Régime, run by the same people, usually the Sisters of Charity. Many were in fact located next to convents, such as in Châtillon-sur-Seine.

Charities determined the so-called "poverty line" on a daily and individual basis. A reputation for unusual generosity earned Charles Neyrand, a nineteenth-century French industrialist, the nickname of "father of the poor." Charity and work could become inseparable in small cities, where the same people provided or denied both. "The provision of aid by local notables and wealthy bourgeois defined the nature of their relations with workers almost as much as wages did" (Accampo, 1989, p. 147). The leaders in smaller cities and towns "alternate[d] roles of benefactor and [boss]" and assured that charity was a face-to-face affair. The degree of power a person gained over another through the provision of charity was viewed in the twentieth century as antidemocratic and a violation of citizenship rights.

The downside to this state of affairs was an erosion of families' self-sufficiency. Charity, after all, was needed due to insufficient wages and unstable jobs. For every *centime* (cent) gained, some small degree of self-sufficiency and self-respect was lost. Many workers could live with this bargain, but others found it a bitter pill to swallow. England's great tradition of workers' self-help or mutualism, as revealed in the proliferation of its tens of thousands of friendly societies, was also based to a certain extent on fierce pride of independence from charity. Seeking charity admitted a lack of self-sufficiency. The hallmark of respectability was independence.

CHARITABLE GIVING AND IDENTITY: CLASS, GENDER, COMMUNITY

Charity formed a significant component of local elites' self-conception. The religious view of charity was by definition a localized, parish-based one. Charity solidified the loyalty of the populace and often tolerated no outside state interference, that is, no outside authority that might compete with local elites for the sympathies of the poor. The hand that gave liked to remind recipients of just who had given. "Charity," wrote the philosopher Victor Cousin during the debates on the right to assistance in 1848, "knows no rule, no limit; it surpasses all obligations. Its beauty is precisely in its liberty" (Smith, 1997). The existence of charity justified a certain degree of inequality.

In poor regions, such as the hinterland of Toulouse, France, southern Italy, southern Spain, and much of the Massif Central, that relied on sharecropping and were largely unaffected by economic change, poverty was pervasive. Rural notables capitalized on this poverty by distributing charity to cement the loyalty of the peasants. In much of western France traditional noble-peasant patronage relationships survived until the mid-nineteenth century. In some parts of western France, châteaus were still the principal source of poor relief as late as the 1880s. At that time the key source of relief in small rural communes in Aube, Doubs, Meurthe-et-Moselle, Corsica, Savoie, Ardèche, Hautes-Alpes, and several other deparments was private alms. Seasonal migration and door-to-door soliciting of alms was a way of life for many French in 1900. In some areas, like Brittany and Aveyron, hospitality for vagrants was still a widespread custom, provided for the most part out of fear, as late as 1900. This type of charitable activity was not unique to France. In parts of southern Italy and Spain, traditional patron-client relations, in the context of highly inegalitarian and agriculturally backward societies, were fixed with the seal of charity. It was a small price to pay for the elites, who owned up to 95 percent of the wealth and almost all the land in these regions.

Charity in nineteenth-century Europe was practiced out of civic pride. It brought prestige to the city, as in eighteenth-century Hamburg, and those who administered it acquired considerable social and political capital. The same was true if not more true in smaller cities and in medium-sized towns, where the hospital might be the largest and most imposing building other than the church or the city hall. Baron de Verna, president of the Lyon hospital board, noted in 1828 that for some families serving the poor was their raison d'être. "As in the time of our fathers," de Verna said, "municipal honors [and offices] almost always become the recompense for he who has devoted himself *au service des pauvres*" (to the service of the poor).

Local charities and hospitals were powerful sources of elite identity. A seat on the board at the famous hospitals in Berlin or Vienna was a plum position. London's high society ran the city's voluntary hospitals. In France hospitals from Aix-en-Provence to Montpellier to Lyon to Beaune figured at the core of provincial identities. The burghers of Amsterdam, immortalized by artists for centuries, commonly struck

poses as civic leaders and as philanthropists. In English cities like Manchester, elite men built substantial public reputations by serving on charity boards. The rich and the respectable vied with each other in good works, and no noblewoman was without "her" poor. Indeed the wives of nobles and the bourgeois often framed their entire social lives around the practice of charity.

Membership on hospital boards or on the administrative boards of longstanding charities came with privileges. Early in the nineteenth century, in Lyon for example, it was a badge of social preeminence and also "the required passage to arrive at the high magistrature." Those who accepted the call to service had come, to use their words, to "ennoble themselves" through administering "the sublime work of charity, the most noble of virtues." In 1900 the Abbé Vachet observed that the call to office retained the same prestige: "The title of hospital administrator is, in Lyon, a veritable title of nobility, it is the highest rank a man can strive for." Henri Boissieu sounded the same note in 1902: "The hospital administrators are today what they were in 1600: notables. The title 'hospital administrator' remains a consecration of notability."

Charity grew in tandem with the rise of the middle class. In Lyon, France, for example, the wealth of the middle class increased over fourfold between the 1840s and the 1860s. The number of charities doubled during this period, the fastest rate of growth in the city's history to that date. At best this was a sign that the middling ranks were more compassionate towards the poor. At worst, it was a sign that they were laundering their new riches and cleansing their consciences through charitable works. Charities across Europe relied on the largely unpaid charitable forces in most large cities: including bourgeois women who served as administrators and visited the poor, Sisters of Charity who staffed hospitals and refuges for the elderly, middle-class men of the merchant class who organized charity concerts to support the workforce of their troubled industry.

In their function as *dames de charité* (ladies of charity), middle-class French women maintained important links to the public sphere, and they played no small role in upholding it. Women, usually married, middle-aged women and especially *dames religieuses* (nuns) were indispensable in running the system. In 1841 and 1874 the directors of Lyon's welfare bureau admitted that it was powerless without women: "To each his mission: the members of the *bureau de bienfaisance* [relief committee] can administer and supervise very well; but absorbed with their family duties and business affairs, they cannot visit and assist the needy as well as the sisters, who have devoted their entire lives to this saintly task." Indeed in 1893, twenty thousand women worked on a full-time, paid basis in philanthropic institutions in Britain. In addition 500,000 women worked full-time without pay in charities. After domestic service, philanthropy was the primary occupier of women's time. Perhaps 1 million women and children attended mothers' meetings each week. By the late nineteenth century several of Britain's most important philanthropists and social reformers were women such as Octavia Hill, Beatrice Webb, Helen Bosanquet, Josephine Butler, and Clara Collet.

Bonnie Smith wrote of the women of the Nord department, near the French border with Belgium who visited neighbors in distress and held monthly "days" (*journées*) on which the poor could come knocking to receive money, clothing, or food. As Smith showed, female charity was geared toward needy mothers and their children, providing day care centers, crèches, and maternal aid societies. Male charity favored unemployed male workers, housing cooperative societies, and retirement or accident insurance through mutual aid societies.

When national social welfare legislation was in the works, some elites were reminded what they might lose. Throughout the century opponents of public assistance argued that legal charity or publicly financed social assistance would deprive the philanthropist of this opportunity. F. M. L. Naville warned in his influential treatise, *De la charité légale:*

> in making this duty [private charity] a legal obligation . . . [a national poor tax] imposes upon the individual, by force, sacrifices which, when they are made voluntarily, are a source of the most sweet and noble pleasures. [The tax] threatens his wish that he may have a happy future beyond the grave. Whereas he hopes to acquire the approval of God and forgiveness for his faults by practising charity, it [legal charity] interposes itself between him and the supreme judge, and deprives him of this source of hope and consolation.

Many French and other Europeans believed that the charitable impulse must remain just that, an impulse, and not a legally mandated responsibility. As the guidebook used by relief administrators and volunteers in Paris, *Manuel des Commissaires et dames de charité de Paris* (1830) reveals: "charity . . . is the calling of the well-to-do. Charity is tender and affectionate; [but] it examines before its acts; it surveilles . . . it attaches to its relief consolations, advice and even paternal reprimands. . . . It allows [the giver] to become rich in good works."

One of the century's most influential works on the social question, the Baron de Gérando's *Le visiteur du pauvre* (1832), went through several editions during the 1830s and found a space in the libraries of most of France's charities. A veritable bible for philanthropists and welfare bureau administrators, this pocket-size, 480-page book speaks to the European elite's desire to be actively involved in the lives of the poor. Gérando toed a familiar line on the sublime virtues of personal charity, its healing effects on class relations, and its ability to rejuvenate society. The key to understanding the social question, he argued, was to picture society as a family that includes those who owe care and protection, as a father owes his children, and those who owe others their obedience and gratitude, as children owe their parents.

The Hospitaliers-Veilleurs of Lyon, like countless other Catholic charities in nineteenth-century Europe, were quite frank about their intentions. The charity's director instructed the volunteers in 1897: "As well as tending to your patients' corporal needs, you will seek to save their souls, to develop within them religious sentiments and practice, to prepare them for a saintly death, and, in that, to work for your own sanctification." The secretary of the Société de Patronage des Jeunes Filles (Society of Protection of Girls) reminded her colleagues, "Your reward is the sweet certainty of knowing that you are working for your own eternal happiness." As with so many others who engaged in the charitable exchange, these administrators were as concerned about their own futures as those of their charges.

LOCALISM AND VOLUNTARISM: THE GUIDING PRINCIPLES OF NINETEENTH-CENTURY CHARITABLE ACTIVITY

The essentially local and voluntary nature of most poor relief and charitable activity distinguish it from modern welfare states. In most Western countries in the twentieth century, social solidarity was a national sentiment. The well-off of Paris or Berlin generally accept the idea that the poor of Provence or Bavaria are just as worthy of government assistance as the poor of their own cities. But prior to the twentieth century many elites' sense of social solidarity stopped at the parish or city boundary, and outside of Germany no welfare state to speak of existed. Prior to the 1880s, when Germany pioneered the welfare state, private charity and local poor relief systems were the norm across Europe. In addition outside of England, where the poor law provided in theory a legal right to assistance, few Europeans had a right to assistance before the twentieth century.

When notables died, their wills often included bequests to the poor of their particular parish or street.

Well into the nineteenth century it was common for notables to have permanent patron-client relations with the local poor. The parish remained the moral anchor of the notables, and only the parish poor were owed charity.

The *pauvres honteux,* or shame-faced, locally known poor, were assisted. In several French and German towns, the locally known "humble" poor were even granted a regular spot in annual processions. Thus marginals were often fully integrated, symbolically as well as materially, into society. Charity was a civic event, a unifying force, a way to bring the local community together to affirm reciprocal bonds. In processions, parades, and even in the annual Lord Mayor's Day parade in London in the 1880s, the common people were reminded of the beneficence of the rich.

But, in the end, the poor generally had no right to make a claim. In an age of limited resources, elites drew the line to ward off excessive claims with moral and religious litmus tests and residency requirements. One of the primary functions of the Lyon hospital administrative board, which met every week, was to determine which of the *vieillard* (elderly indigent) applications to accept. It helped to have friends in high places or at least to live near a rich or influential member of the community. In 1840, to pick a random year, three of the first four names on the *vieillard* admission list had social connections. Marguerite Plailly had been sponsored by the widow of a former accountant at the Hôpital de la Charité (Charity Hospital); Jeanne Binet was recommended by the family of Marguerite Berthon-Fromental, who had bequeathed over 200,000 francs to the Hospices Civils a few years earlier; and Jean-François Gautier was sponsored by the Comte de Bussy.

Traditional charity involved an entirely different set of authority relations from those of the 1920s or later. No universally valid, impartial criteria determined who would or would not receive aid. Charity, assistance, medical care—all forms of philanthropic activity—were grounded in inegalitarian social relations between the donor and the recipient. Gaining admission to the hospitals for the local poor was a sign of the persistence of local notables' social power, which they frequently exercised in both life and death. Bequests often contained clauses spelling out what type of person would be eligible for assistance.

Significantly, the men and women who administered and dispensed public assistance went to great lengths to determine the merit of each individual case. To understand why this was so requires a conscious leap in the historical imagination to a time when the indigent had no legal claim to relief, when the needy had to prove their moral and religious worthiness, when no clear idea of what constituted "poverty" or "need" existed, and when no rigid conception of a "poverty line" had developed. Since no clear criteria for establishing need existed, many needy were refused assistance for no good reason or for political or religious reasons. As a result poor relief systems in the nineteenth century were often quite arbitrary.

However, some guidebooks were published. In his influential 1847 pamphlet *Du paupérisme en France,* François Marbeau defined the worthy poor: "The good indigent is honest, respectful, appreciative, and resigned. . . . [He] is grateful for the services we provide to him, and he is always ready to devote himself to his benefactors. . . . He is humble: he suffers with patience the ills he cannot avoid. Resignation [is] the virtue of the poor" (*Marbeau,* 1847, pp. 25–26). This pocket-size guide to public policy, like the Baron de Gérando's *Le visiteur du pauvre,* served as a sort of policy bible.

The French, of course, had no monopoly on this sort of face-to-face approach to the charitable vocation. The famous German "Elberfeld system," named for the town, became a model for Europe late in the century. It was ostensibly a rigorous, "scientific" approach to charity with thorough screening processes. It relied on the existence of a vibrant voluntary sector and required elites with time on their hands. By the late twentieth century the upper middle class generally worked and had little time for charity.

The Elberfeld system suggests that Europe's elite was still confident in its ability to cope with the social question with rudimentary local poor relief systems and purely private, personalized, and local charities. At least this was their wish. Significantly, many European charities emphasized the re-creation of the family in their works. This is important because the family was the dominant paradigm of the age. It was only natural that the civic elite should turn to its most familiar and trusted institutions, family and church, to help keep the social fabric intact. The state was not trusted by most people. It was distant yet intrusive, a threat to local liberties and pretensions. A sense that private and local interests were powerless to solve the social question had not yet emerged, and most Europeans were not yet ready to jettison the two sturdy pillars of society, family and church, and turn to the state to solve the social question. This would require an intellectual breakthrough, the likes of which do not occur overnight. It happened only in the 1880s to the 1920s, depending on the nation. Private charity was given six or seven decades to prove its capacities to cope with the urban social question that emerged, in the eyes of elites, in the 1830s.

CHARITY, MORALITY, AND SOCIAL CONTROL

Debates over the poor law provided part of the context for English charity. Originally established in 1601 to deal with growing poverty associated with a more commercial economy, the poor laws provided meager aid, mostly in kind, to the poor and unemployed. Poor law reform in 1834 instituted more middle-class or liberal principles—greater encouragement to work, less local variance, and lower taxes. Greater centralization was combined with lower funding and more rigorous tests for applicants. Able-bodied people were supposed to be forced to work, and unpleasant workhouses sheltered those who received aid. Workers attacked the system—in fact, a critique of the poor law was one components of the Chartist movement—but it survived until the twentieth century.

At the same time Great Britain was home to the world's most developed charitable sector in the nineteenth century. Religious pluralism begat philanthropic and educational pluralism. The annual revenues of the more than seven hundred charities in London were greater than the entire budgets of several small European states in the 1890s. Charitable giving was an ingrained part of British middle-class households. One study in the 1890s calculated that on average middle-class households spent a larger share of their income on charity than on any other item in their budget except food. A survey of artisans and working-class families in the same decade revealed similar results. Half of them made weekly donations to charity, and a quarter also gave to a church. This invisible welfare state, the charity of the poor toward the poor, was crucial to the survival of working-class families. As Ellen Ross demonstrated, in late nineteenth century working-class London, women's informal support networks kept people going when the going got tough. This of intraclass charity was ubiquitous but left fewer traces in the historical record than official, elite-sponsored charity.

It is common to portray charitable activity as a means of social control. The middle class used charity as an entry point into the lives of the poor. Ladies visited working-class mothers and peddled their "domestic imperialism" with one hand while giving with the other. Historians such as Gareth Stedman Jones have portrayed charity as a bourgeois ploy to placate the poor. Others, such as Jane Lewis and Ross have emphasized the moral gaze of middle-class female visitors and school attendance officers.

It is too easy to dismiss this historical school as overly hostile toward the middle class. Much commends this school of thought, and it of course applies to the rest of Europe. Philanthropic societies, usually with some sort of religious inspiration, bombarded the poor with advice. They lectured the poor, demanded to see proof of good morals, and asked intrusive questions. This was done at British Sunday schools, charity schools across Europe, day care centers (*salles d'asile* in France), apprentice schools affiliated with the poor law in Britain, hospitals, mutual aid societies, reading societies, and *cercles* (clubs) in France.

The multitude of charitable organizations operating in the nineteenth century boggles the mind. In addition to those just listed orphanages; old age refuges; agricultural colonies for young wayward youth; Magdelan asylums for prostitutes; and charities for the deaf, the blind, the deaf-mute, to teach marriage, and to construct working-class homes functioned. Religious minorities, such as Jews and Protestants in France, and foreigners, such as the Swiss in Lyon, ran reading societies, workers' garden societies, and charities.

The wealth of charitable institutions, many of which peddled morality, attests to charity's central role in society. But charity was instrusive. The conservative historian Gertrude Himmelfarb wrote, "The Victorians, taking values seriously, also took seriously the need for social sanctions that would stigmatize and censure violations of those values" (Himmelfarb, 1994, p. 142). It was only natural that they would demand adherence to some sort of moral code while they dispensed their charity.

Every cause had its champion, and every denomination had its cause. Evangelicalism was a call to action on almost every conceivable public issue, including the abolition of slavery, child labor, child prostitution, child poverty, the prevention of cruelty to animals and children, and of course the suppression of vice. For the British, humanitarianism became a sort of surrogate religion during the nineteenth century. As Webb noted in 1884, "social questions are the vital questions of today: they take the place of religion". Most nineteenth-century charities, whether British, French, German, lay, church, or officially secular, aimed at the moral improvement of the poor. As Himmelfarb argued, the late-twentieth-century language of morality, when applied to social issues, is usually assumed to be the language of conservatives. The nineteenth century was obsessed with the issue of "character" and "respectability." Charity shared the obsessions of responsibility, restraint, decency, decorum, industriousness, foresight, religiosity, and temperance. In the nineteenth century charity asked questions and preached solutions before it dispensed relief.

Despite what many people would regard as an outdated concern with mixing morals and money, by

Nineteenth-Century Charity. Soup kitchen operated by Quakers for the unemployed in Manchester. Woodcut from *Illustrated London News,* 22 November 1862. THE ILLUSTRATED LONDON NEWS PICTURE LIBRARY

1900 European philanthropy was in fact moving with the times. Charities and social policy organizations, such as the Charity Organisation Society and the Office Central des Oeuvres de Bienfaisance (Central Office of Institutions of Charity), were becoming national in scope, bureaucratic, and professionalized, although both attempted to rationalize and limit charity. In Britain the Salvation Army had 100,000 members in 1906. In addition the Church Army, Dr. Barnardo's, the Jewish Board of Guardians, the Catholic Federation, and the Society of St. Vincent de Paul were formidable actors on the national political scene, advocating causes as well as dispensing relief. Some leaders of charities tried to defend their turf against the growing powers of the national state. Others, especially those run by female advocates of maternal and child welfare, used their charitable mission as a vehicle to advance the national welfare state.

THE WITHERING OF CHARITY, THE GROWTH OF THE STATE

By the late nineteenth century in many countries the veneer of self-help and laissez-faire was wearing thin. Charities abounded, but poverty persisted. In 1899 in London, for instance, charities spent over 6 million pounds, more than the budgets of some small European countries and more than the French national public assistance budget. Despite this, as Charles Booth's social survey *Life and Labour of the People of London* (1885–1905) demonstrated, some 30 percent of Londoners were, by his widely accepted calculations, poor.

State assistance expanded because it had to. The second industrial revolution, associated with heavy industry, steel, shipbuilding, and metalworks, began in the 1870s. The insufficient capacity of the older collective forces, such as localized charity and the church, to bear the consequences of these new economic forces and to cope with urban ghettos and cyclical, industrywide depressions required greater state intervention. New industrial suburbs sprouted in England, France, and Germany, and the church could not keep up. The old parish system of charity began to break down. Germany began the process of building a welfare state in the 1880s, and France, Britain, and Scandinavia followed in the 1890s and 1900s.

Between the two world wars cities across Europe, from London to Paris to Vienna, constructed miniwelfare states. Private charity was finally eclipsed, at least in a few large cities. Cities across Europe raised their taxes but also delivered more goods to their residents between the wars. The most famous example of this is Vienna, where a socialist municipal council created the world's most advanced miniwelfare state during the 1920s. As municipal social services expanded, charity was displaced, but not erased, from the civic landscape.

England experienced a fivefold increase in central state expenditures on social welfare services between 1918 and 1938. In 1918, 2.4 percent of the GNP was spent on the social services, and by 1938, 11.3 percent of the GNP was devoted to them. By the 1930s between 40 and 50 percent of British working-class families received some form of government contribution to their income. By the mid-1930s public welfare spending amounted to at least ten times the sum spent by private charity in Great Britain. In Germany the state provided more social services. Social welfare was now conceived as a sort of civic right and the antithesis of private charity dispensed by the bourgeoisie on their terms.

Everywhere in Europe the old spirit of noblesse oblige and the institutions that grew out of it were ill equipped to deal with the social problems born of total war. By the end of World War I inflation had taken its toll on charity and hospital endowments, and

Employment Exchange. An unemployed miner receives his benefits and a railway voucher—to transport him and his family to a cottage homestead in Reading—at an employment exchange office in Durham, England, February 1939. HULTON GETTY PICTURE LIBRARY

Volunteer Medics. Members of the Arciconfraternita della Misericordia, Florence, aid a patient, July 1969. The confraternity, which traces its origins to the early thirteenth century, is devoted to the transport of the sick. TED SPEIGEL/©CORBIS

in the 1920s the balance finally tipped toward public funding. As new medical technologies sent expenses on an upward spiral, small charitable hospitals, largely funded by small private bequests, could not keep up. The state had to step in. Traditional charity simply could not cope with higher medical costs or the generally higher public expectations after the war.

Between 1920 and 1940, as the state grew in strength, wealth, and influence, the financial backbone of private, local charity withered away. In France by 1944 hospitals' endowments provided only 7 percent of their revenues, down from 12 percent in 1932. Annual donations distinct from a long-term endowment, accounted for between 1.2 and 2.4 percent of revenues in the 1930s, but they were down to 0.8 percent in the 1940s.

After World War II the shift from traditional charitable medicine to state-sponsored or provided medicine was dramatic. In France, for example, by the 1950s most hospitals received over 90 percent and in some cases 98 percent of their revenues from *frais de séjour* (patient-day expenses), which were reimbursed by public authorities and by the social security system. In Britain the process was even more direct. Voluntary, that is, private or charitable, hospitals simply

were taken over by the new National Health Service funded by general taxation.

As Europe became prosperous and as expectations of the state increased, the accident of charity was replaced or, as historians such as Lewis would argue, complemented by the guarantee of social security. As Europeans reformulated the idea of citizenship to include all men, regardless of birth or property, and as of 1918 all women, they moved away from the old moral strictures that guided charitable efforts in the past. As of 1918 receipt of poor law assistance in Britain no longer disqualified a person from voting rights and full citizenship rights. The right to social welfare was enshrined in the new German constitution of 1919. Privately operated charity seemed at odds with an expanding notion of citizenship rights. Private charity was crushed under the Bolsheviks, who argued that the socialist state had no need of bourgeois charity.

In Western Europe charity was quietly surpassed by state insurance. Citizenship rights came to mean a constant set of rights available to all on equal terms in all parts of any given country. Charity guaranteed none of this. Above all charity was tainted by its association with inegalitarian values. Charity discriminated and implied inequality among the classes. Charity did not disappear overnight, certainly not in Britain, where at least 110,000 charitable trusts existed in 1950. But it was overshadowed by the state's expanding services. Charity survived and in some nations, Britain in particular, retained its long-standing, quasi-public status, helping to pick up the slack when state resources were squeezed. Nevertheless, the old spirit of voluntary charity, of noblesse oblige or of moralizing toward the poor, is in most places extinct.

"I do not like mixing up moralities and mathematics," claimed a young Winston Churchill in 1909. As Europe moved away from charity and toward social insurance, it effected a divorce between morality and social policy that came to define the essence of the European welfare state. In many ways modern European welfare states became the very negation of nineteenth-century charity. Perhaps this is charity's greatest legacy.

See also **The Welfare State** *(volume 2); and other articles in this section.*

BIBLIOGRAPHY

Accampo, Elinor. *Industrialization, Family Life, and Class Relations: Saint Chamond, 1815–1914.* Berkeley, Calif., 1989. Good chapter on charity and rich-poor relations.

Andrew, Donna T. *Philanthropy and Police: London Charity in the Eighteenth Century.* Princeton, N.J., 1989. A local history on the earlier period.

Barry, Jonathan, and Colin Jones, eds. *Medicine and Charity before the Welfare State.* London, 1991. Several important essays.

Beaudoin, Steven. "'Without Belonging to the Public Sphere': Charities, the State, and Civil Society in Third Republic Bordeaux." *Journal of Social History* 31 (Spring 1998): 671–699. An important article that attempts to revise the revisionists.

Bremner, Robert H. *Giving: Charity and Philanthropy in History.* New Brunswick, N.J., 1994.

Brenton, Maria. *The Voluntary Sector in British Social Services.* London, 1985. Discusses how important charity is in the United Kingdom.

CEDIAS Musée social et al. *Le social aux prises avec l'histoire. Vol. 3: La question sociale.* Paris, 1991. A special journal edition of *Vie sociale* and other collaborators with short essays on French and Belgian philanthropy.

Duprat, Catherine. *Le temps des philanthropes.* 2 vols. Paris, 1993. Massive.

Engels, Friedrich. *The Condition of the Working Class in England.* Harmondsworth, U.K., 1987. First published in 1844. Contains a classic indictment of British charity.

Fraser, Derek. *The Evolution of the British Welfare State.* 2d ed. Basingstoke, U.K., 1984. Good chapter on self-help ideology and voluntary charity.

Fuchs, Rachel Ginnis. *Poor and Pregnant in Paris: Strategies for Survival in the Nineteenth-Century.* New Brunswick, N.J., 1992.

Gibson, Ralph. *A Social History of French Catholicism, 1789–1914.* New York, 1989.

Guillaume, Pierre. and André Gueslin, eds. *De la charité mediévale à la sécurité sociale.* Paris, 1997.

Himmelfarb, Gertrude. *The De-Moralization of Society: From Victorian Virtues to Modern Values.* New York, 1995.

Himmelfarb, Gertrude. *The Idea of Poverty.* London, 1985.

Himmelfarb, Gertrude. *Poverty and Compassion: The Moral Imagination of the Late Victorians.* New York, 1991. A lament for the good old days of charity and morality.

Jones, Colin. *Charity and Bienfaisance: The Treatment of the Poor in the Montpellier Region, 1740–1815.* Cambridge, U.K., 1982. An important study that sets the stage for the nineteenth century.

Kidd, Alan J. *State, Society, and the Poor in Nineteenth-Century England.* Basingstoke, U.K., 1999. Useful for students, with a good chapter on private charity.

Koven, Seth, and Sonya Michel, eds. *Mothers of a New World: Maternalist Politics and the Origins of Welfare States.* New York, 1993.

Lees, Lynn Hollen. *The Solidarities of Strangers: The English Poor Laws and the People, 1700–1948.* New York, 1998. Possibly the best book on poor relief.

Lewis, Jane. *The Voluntary Sector, the State, and Social Work in Britain: The Charity Organisation Society/Family Welfare Association since 1869.* Aldershot, U.K., 1995. One of many important studies in this field by Lewis.

Lindemann, Mary. *Patriots and Paupers: Hamburg, 1712–1830.* New York, 1990.

Lindenmeyr, Adele. *Poverty Is Not a Vice: Charity, Society, and the State in Imperial Russia.* Princeton, N.J., 1996.

Luddy, Maria. *Women and Philanthropy in Nineteenth-Century Ireland.* Cambridge, U.K., 1995.

Lynch, Katherine A. *Family, Class, and Ideology in Early Industrial France: Social Policy and the Working-Class Family, 1825–1848.* Madison, Wis., 1988.

Mandler, Peter, ed. *The Uses of Charity: The Poor on Relief in the Nineteenth-Century Metropolis.* Philadelphia, 1990. Several good essays.

McCants, Anne E. C. *Civic Charity in a Golden Age: Orphan Care in Early Modern Amsterdam.* Urbana, Ill., 1997. A remarkable study.

Michel, Sonya, and Seth Koven. "Womanly Duties: Maternalist Politics and the Origins of Welfare States in France, Germany, Great Britain, and the United States, 1880–1920." *American Historical Review* 95, no. 4 (October 1990): 1076–1108. A wide-ranging article.

Mooney, Gerry. "'Remoralizing' the Poor?: Gender, Class, and Philanthropy in Victorian Britain." In *Forming Nation, Framing Welfare.* Edited by Gail Lewis. London, 1998. Pages 49–91.

Norberg, Kathryn. *Rich and Poor in Grenoble, 1600–1814.* Berkeley, Calif., 1985.

Owen, David Edward. *English Philanthropy, 1660–1960.* Cambridge, Mass., 1964. A landmark study.

Pansu, Henri. "L'analyse de la fortune et des livres de comptes de ménage: L'exemple d'un grand bourgeois lyonnais de la fin du XIXè siècle." *Bulletin du Centre d'Histoire économique et sociale de la région lyonnaise* 3 (October 1973).

Penslar, Derek J. "The Origins of Modern Jewish Philanthropy." In *Philanthropy in the World's Traditions.* Edited by Warren F. Ilchman, Stanley N. Katz, and Edward L. Queen II. Bloomington, Ind., 1998. Pages 197–214. An addition to the series "Philanthropic Studies."

Petit, Jean-Guy, and Yannick Marec, eds. *Le social dans la ville en France et en Europe (1750–1914).* Paris, 1996. Important but dense essays.

Price, Roger. *A Social History of Nineteenth-Century France.* London, 1987. Several good sections on charity and rich-poor relations.

Prochaska, F. K. *Royal Bounty: The Making of a Welfare Monarchy.* New Haven, Conn., 1995.

Prochaska, F. K. *Women and Philanthropy in Nineteenth-Century England.* Oxford, 1980. A rich, detailed study full of fascinating anecdotes.

Prochaska, Frank. "Philanthropy." In *The Cambridge Social History of Modern Britain.* Edited by F. M. L. Thompson. Cambridge, U.K., 1990. Pages 357–393. An important, opinionated, synthetic essay.

Ross, Ellen. *Love and Toil: Motherhood in Outcast London, 1870–1918.* New York, 1993.

Seeley, Paul. "Catholics and Apprentices: An Example of Men's Philanthropy in Late Ninteenth-Century France." *Journal of Social History* 25 (1992): 531–545.

Shapely, Peter. "Charity, Status, and Leadership: Charitable Image and the Manchester Man." *Journal of Social History* 32 (Fall 1998): 157–177.

Smith, Bonnie G. *Ladies of the Leisure Class: The Bourgeoises of Northern France in the Nineteenth Century.* Princeton, N.J., 1981.

Smith, Timothy B. "The Ideology of Charity, the Image of the English Poor Law, and Debates over the Right to Assistance in France, 1830–1905." *Historical Journal* 40, no. 4 (December 1997): 997–1032.

Smith, Timothy B., "The Plight of the Able Bodied Poor and the Unemployed in Urban France, 1880–1914." *European History Quarterly* 30, no. 2 (April 2000): 147–84. How charities and poor relief systems tended to neglect the able-bodied.

Smith, Timothy B., "Republicans, Catholics, and Social Reform: Lyon, 1870–1920." *French History* 12, no. 3 (September 1998): 246–275. How politics and charity intertwined.

Stedman Jones, Gareth. *Outcast London: A Study in the Relationship between Classes in Victorian Society.* Harmondsworth, U.K., 1984. The social control theory of charity.

Ullman, Claire F. *The Welfare State's Other Crisis: Explaining the New Partnership between Nonprofit Organizations and the State in France.* Bloomington, Ind., 1998. An attempt to rescue the French voluntary sector from obscurity.

Van Leeuwen, Marco H. D. "Logic of Charity: Poor Relief in Preindustrial Europe." *Journal of Interdisciplinary History* 24 (Spring 1994): 589–613. A sweeping, synthetic article.

Vernier, Olivier. *D'espoir et d'espérance: L'assistance privée dans les Alpes-Maritimes au XIXè siècle, 1814–1914.* Nice, France, 1993. Nice pictures.

Vincent, David. *Poor Citizens: The State and the Poor in Twentieth-Century Britain.* London, 1991. A lament for the days of mutual aid, the charity of the poor toward the poor, before the intrusive middle-class welfare state.

Weissbach, Lee Shai. "*Oeuvre Industrielle, Oeuvre Morale: The Sociétés de patronage of Nineteenth-Century France.*" French Historical Studies 25 (Spring, 1987): 99–120.

SOCIAL WELFARE AND INSURANCE

Young-sun Hong

The welfare state is one of those essentially contested concepts that haunt all narratives of modern society, and, as a result, even the most basic account assumes a prior interpretation of its origin, nature, and significance. Its genealogy has often been traced to the first organized measures, both public and private, to deal with the masterless, migrant poor who emerged as a distinct social group at the end of the Middle Ages as a result of the breakdown of manorial community, parish, and extended household. However, the use of the term "welfare" to describe all such efforts to meet the needs of society's weakest members over the past six hundred years inflates the concept beyond all usefulness and obscures the novelty of modern welfare systems which have developed since the 1880s and the important changes they brought about in the relationships between state, market, individual, and the family.

THE CONCEPT OF WELFARE

The origin of both the "social question" and the modern systems of poor relief, welfare, social insurance, and social security which have developed in response to it can be traced to the rise of the market society, the commodification of labor, and the increasing dependence of individual well-being on the ability to secure the necessities of life through the labor market alone. The social question has been defined, on the one hand, by the complex relationship between work and character (for example, individual responsibility, industry, and foresight) and, on the other, by concerns about the corrosive impact on family, community, and national solidarity of the growing economic insecurity of wage labor, an experience which was itself the obverse of the expansion in the economic freedom of the individual associated with the coming of the market. Welfare may be understood as an attempt (by either the state or voluntary associations) to alter the distribution of wealth and opportunity that would result from the unrestricted play of market forces in order

to achieve a greater degree of equality (of outcome or opportunity); strengthen the solidarity of the community (which can be seen either as intrinsically valuable in itself or as a political necessity in an age of intensified national competition); discharge a moral obligation to protect children, the family, the sick, the elderly, and the unemployed; increase the economic and/or demographic strength of the nation by insuring the fullest development of its human capital; or any number of other goals.

The development of the welfare state and its systems of social welfare, social insurance, and social security is significant for the social history of the modern West in a number of ways. These programs affect the standard of living and quality of life of a large section of the population both directly through the monetary assistance and services they provide and indirectly through their impact on the dynamics of the labor market. They redistribute both income and opportunity, and they strengthen the bonds of social solidarity upon which the legitimacy of the nation-state ultimately depends. However, this Whiggish perspective must be counterbalanced by an awareness that the provision of welfare benefits and services is never a socially neutral act. For example, there are many different ways of providing benefits to the unemployed, the sick, the elderly, or single mothers, and the specific strategies adopted to meet the perceived needs of these groups are often of greater significance than the level of benefits itself. Consequently, the various regimes of social service provision define the concrete meaning of the rights of the individual and, through this, the meaning of citizenship, the nature of the state, and the structure of individual subjectivity and experience. The most important and creative studies of welfare and the welfare state in recent years have been comparative studies of the differences between welfare systems, the heretofore hidden ways in which these systems have created and reproduced social inequalities and gender roles, the cultural assumptions underlying these systems, and the political processes that have determined their contours.

Veterans' Home. *Chelsea Pensioners Reading the Waterloo Despatch,* painting (1822) by Sir David Wilkie (1785–1841). Chelsea Royal Hospital was founded by King Charles II in 1681 for retired soldiers; the hospital opened in 1692. Wilkie's painting shows the pensioners receiving the news of the Duke of Wellington's victory over Napoleon at the Battle of Waterloo in June 1815. The hospital, designed by Christopher Wren, is visible through the trees at the left. APSLEY HOUSE, THE WELLINGTON MUSEUM, LONDON/THE BRIDGEMAN ART LIBRARY

FROM POOR RELIEF TO WELFARE

The emergence of welfare can only be understood against the horizon of—and as a reaction to—the specific forms of assistance for the poor and the laboring classes established in the nineteenth century. Up to the late nineteenth century, many members of both Christian and secular social reform circles, especially in western Europe, regarded indigence as prima facie evidence of individual moral failing, which manifested itself in sloth, improvidence, various forms of vice and deviance, and ultimately in the material and moral distress of the needy. On the basis of this individualist, voluntarist conception of poverty, two antithetical yet complementary systems for providing for the needs of the poor were established across the middle decades of the nineteenth century in Europe and the United States. While the deterrent, disciplinary public poor relief system provided the most minimal assistance under harsh and socially stigmatizing conditions in order to insure that assistance in no way undermined individual responsibility, industry, and foresight, an extensive network of voluntary charity provided supplementary aid to the deserving poor whose need was not considered to be the result of individual moral failings. In England, these policies were institutionalized by the Poor Law Amendment Act of 1834 and the formation in 1869 of the Charity Organisation Society. In Germany the model was established in 1853 by the reform of municipal poor relief in the town of Elberfeld. In France, by contrast, the Catholic Church and its associated voluntary organizations continued to be the primary provider of assistance to the needy, and France was the only west-European country without a statutory municipal assistance program until the 1890s. These programs were designed to satisfy the universally recognized moral obligation to aid the needy, but to do so in a way that would not further demoralize those persons whose indigence was already regarded as a sign of their weakness of character or impair the efficient functioning of the labor market.

Beginning in the 1880s and 1890s, this individualist conception of indigence was gradually displaced by a new social perspective on poverty, which regarded poverty less as the result of individual moral failing than as the result of social factors that lay outside the control of the individual: the unequal distribution of income; the impact of business cycles on employment levels; dangerous working conditions; unsanitary living conditions; the susceptibility of the laboring classes to the existential uncertainties of accident, old age, and illness; the financial burdens of large families (especially when coupled with the death or disability of the family breadwinner); and the inability of working-class women to shoulder the multiple burdens of work and family. This social perspective on poverty reflected the changing living and working conditions created by continued urbanization, massive migration, and the second industrial revolution. However, the resulting social dislocation acquired its immediate political resonance due to the rise of socialism among the skilled, organized factory working classes, the concern among the propertied classes that the working-class milieux were breeding moral disorder and weakening the health and physical constitution of the nation and race, and the sense that these developments were negatively impacting the unity of the nation at the very moment when economic, political, and military competition between the industrial nations of Europe and the world was reaching an unprecedented intensity.

On both sides of the Atlantic, the rise of Progressivism—with its logic of social solidarity and its concern for national efficiency—reflected the fact that industrialization and urbanization had fundamentally altered the social foundations of the prevailing individualist understanding of poverty and the minimalist, deterrent approach to charity and poor relief to which this conception had given rise. Public poor relief and voluntary charity had operated on the assumption that the public provision of services and monetary assistance—before the individual had exhausted all available resources and was faced with imminent indigence—would place a premium on sloth and improvidence and thereby fatally demoralize the working classes. The Progressives insisted that benefits to both the nation and the individual of positive public measures to prevent these new kinds of systemic poverty far outweighed the potential dangers to individual morality. Similarly, the Progressive willingness to use public power to intervene directly in social and economic relations in order to compensate for the deleterious social consequences of impersonal social forces went beyond the limits on state intervention imposed by nineteenth-century legal and social thought. A new conception (based on Progressive commitment to social solidarity and national efficiency) of social citizenship and the development of new strategies for dealing with the social question

marked the birth of the modern notion of welfare and the new form of political organization that came to be known as the interventionist, social, or welfare state.

For social reformers, the many dimensions of the social problem condensed around two distinct complexes: the working-class family and the question of social reproduction on the one hand, and, on the other, the worker question and the need to combat the socialist temptation among the predominantly male, organized working classes. The development of separate social programs designed to meet the needs of each of these groups led to the crystallization of the classic two-track structure of the twentieth-century welfare state: preventive, therapeutic social welfare programs to address the perceived crisis of social reproduction and social insurance to reduce the economic and social insecurity of workers who formed the backbone of the socialist movement.

PREVENTIVE SOCIAL WELFARE PROGRAMS

Beginning in the 1880s, voluntary organizations and municipal governments across Europe began to create an increasingly dense network of social assistance programs that were designed to extend the social rights of the urban poor by compensating for the impersonal, structural risks of working-class life. The most serious source of existential insecurity for the working classes was the lack of work. Initially, social reformers advocated rural labor colonies to discipline casual laborers, habitual malingerers, and vagrants, who were particularly prone to drink, panhandling, and petty criminality. However, the impact of projects for disciplinary social engineering for these marginal groups was limited, and in the 1880s and 1890s the "discovery" of unemployment as a systemic social problem for the solid members of the working classes pointed to the need for new departures. Labor exchanges represented an important attempt to reduce un(der)employment and the indigence of casual labor by rendering the national labor market more transparent and efficient. Also, beginning in the mid-1880s, many cities began to rely on public works projects to relieve the need of the working classes during economic downturns. Though these efforts to relieve the poor through labor exchanges and public works programs did reflect a change in spirit, their potential was limited to managing need rather than preventing it.

The first unemployment benefits were those provided on a voluntary basis by workers' friendly societies (often with subsidies provided by middle-class reformers) and by unions. The first attempt to move from such voluntary assistance to genuine insurance was taken in 1894 when the Swiss canton of Saint Gall instituted a compulsory insurance scheme, which soon faltered due to inadequate financing. The decision by the Belgian city of Ghent in 1901 to provide municipal subsidies to existing union unemployment insurance plans was more successful due to its sounder actuarial foundation. The Ghent system was emulated across much of Europe over the following decade, and the better understanding of the possibilities and the limits of such schemes powered the learning process that ultimately made possible the establishment of national unemployment insurance programs. However, the political sensitivity of support for the unemployed insured that progress in this field would be laborious and ultimately quite limited, and most countries did not take the decisive step toward unemployment insurance until after World War I.

This same period saw the proliferation of preventive, social hygiene programs to combat chronic, contagious diseases, such as tuberculosis, social problems that stemmed from poor living and working conditions, and infant mortality and related maternal health problems. The cornerstone of these programs were the maternal and infant welfare centers, which were established in many cities to couple the medical observation of newborns with the dissemination of hygienic advice to mothers. Because bottle-feeding and related digestive tract infections were the leading cause of infant mortality, these centers generally maintained close relations with municipal and/or voluntary programs that offered premiums—paid upon visits to these centers—to encourage needy mothers to nurse their children or that made sterilized milk available either free or at reduced prices to those women who could not or would not nurse their children. By 1914, many European countries had passed labor laws requiring that pregnant women not work during the weeks immediately preceding their expected due date or for a specified period after the birth of their child. However, because this legislation did not provide adequate replacement for the wages lost during this period of enforced abstention from work, expectant and nursing mothers often had no choice but to turn to municipal public assistance. This intrinsic limitation of maternal welfare programs gave rise to a broad movement on both sides of the Atlantic for the creation of mothers' pension and child benefit programs. However, these efforts generally did not bear fruit until the late 1930s and later.

Around the beginning of the twentieth century, social reformers in many European countries began to call for the establishment of school lunch and health inspection programs, which they argued were necessary for the realization of the goals of public schooling. The provision of both school lunches and school medical inspections proved to be surprisingly controversial precisely because it represented an especially clear example of the state taking over the direct provision of services that had previously been the responsibility of the family alone.

The conflict between the principles of deterrence and prevention was one of the major fault lines in the politics of welfare reform. The debate over public guardianship for children, reform schooling, juvenile justice reforms, and the entire panoply of programs aimed at abandoned, endangered, and delinquent youth raised with particular sharpness the question of the implications of preventive, therapeutic social programs for the rights of their ostensible beneficiaries. Although these measures were justified in the name of the national interest in preventing criminality and insuring the proper education of future citizens and workers, they were so controversial because they entailed the extension of state power into the sphere of family and parental authority. The necessity of intervening in the lives of endangered children *before* they had committed a punishable offense clearly contradicted the principles of liberal jurisprudence. The ensuing debate over the logic of prevention gave birth to a new social conception of law and to a new notion of social citizenship, in which the rights to work, health, and education were extended to the individual but coupled in an uneasy manner with positive obligation of the recipients to engage in socially useful work, actively maintain their health, insure the adequate socialization of their children, and, more generally, discharge those social obligations whose fulfillment was the primary purpose for extending these rights in the first place. However, Jacques Donzelot and Detlev Peukert have argued that, far from bringing about a real extension in the social rights of the individual, the efforts of these programs—and by extension, all preventive, therapeutic social programs—to rationalize juvenile behavior in accordance with the norms of middle-class society actually entangled the individual in a close-meshed network of surveillance and tutelage, which ultimately absorbed and negated, rather than extended, the sphere of individual freedoms.

Reformers also searched for ways to provide for specific groups of the worthy poor that would be more adequate to their real needs and entail none of the social stigma or political disabilities associated with poor relief and charity. One example is the movement for public pensions for the elderly and also for working-class mothers. A first step toward the development of pensions for the elderly was taken in 1891, when

Denmark approved a plan to provide nondisqualifying monetary aid to those worthy, elderly poor who had previously led upright lives (those who had not depended on poor relief). This movement was given additional momentum by the establishment of a non-contributory old-age pension plan in New Zealand—a member of the British Commonwealth—in 1898. France (1905) and Britain (1908) both adopted non-contributory, but means-tested old-age pensions (though in 1925 the British program was reformed in the direction of a contributory system). Sweden went even further, establishing the world's first universal, non-contributory old-age pension program in 1913. The Germans, on the other hand, were reluctant to follow this trend and instead opted to meet the needs of the elderly through an old-age and invalidity insurance program. However, due to the low level of benefits and limited coverage, the Germans still had to rely on poor relief and covert subsidies from other social insurance programs to support the worthy elderly.

The emergence of welfare measures in the late nineteenth century has generated a considerable comparative historiography dealing with such issues as the greater commitment to voluntary insurance schemes on the part of the French, versus the more systematic German approach. At the beginning of the twenty-first century this debate also focused on the differing degrees to which various welfare programs emphasized women as welfare recipients and on the emergence of aid to families as an area of particular concern. Finally, social historians continue to grapple with the issue of the impact of welfare measures in welfare's early period: What kinds of welfare measures had an effect, given the limitations in coverage—the focus on urban workers, for instance—and the range of benefits offered? Certainly, early welfare initiatives did not stem the growth of socialism and trade unions, though they did sway many socialists toward a reformist rather than a revolutionary approach.

SOCIAL WELFARE PROGRAMS IN INTERWAR EUROPE

World War I led to the exponential growth of welfare programs that, until the war, had still faced stiff opposition from the proponents of deterrence. Social programs played a vital role in solidifying the home front by counteracting the disruptive social consequences of total war and promising a greater degree of social citizenship to the working classes. After 1918 the growth of welfare programs continued to accelerate in response to the expanded public commitment of many states—often inscribed in their new constitutions—to the social welfare of their citizens, and the 1920s was a period of unprecedented intensity for major social legislation in both western and eastern Europe. However, the expansion of state social intervention was not an unmixed blessing, for the very act of identifying one social group as deserving of special public solicitude invariably created a sense of discrimination by those groups who were not included. As a result, expanded state social intervention in the interwar years tended to divide the polity as much as unify it, especially when this intervention was accompanied by the struggle for scarce resources and competition between social service providers to shape the norms informing such activity. The later 1920s witnessed a retreat from the optimism that had characterized welfare reforms over the previous decades, and this trend was reinforced by the severe financial retrenchment in the welfare sector during the Great Depression.

One of the more interesting issues in the history of social welfare in the interwar years is the role of welfare in Nazi Germany. Toward the end of the twentieth century, social welfare in Nazi Germany received intense scholarly scrutiny because it has become increasingly clear that social and welfare policies to benefit productive and racially valuable members of the national community cannot be separated from policies designed to segregate and ultimately annihilate those persons whose poverty and social deviance were regarded as evidence of their racial inferiority. Despite the undeniable continuities in welfare theory and practice across the 1933 divide, scholars continue to debate the modernity of Nazi racial policies and the legitimacy of regarding them as a variant of the modern "welfare" state.

THE DEVELOPMENT OF SOCIAL INSURANCE

In contrast to welfare programs for those who stood outside the labor process or were only partially integrated into it, social insurance was designed primarily to protect the organized, largely male working classes and through them also protect their families against the threat of destitution due to the risks of accident, old age, sickness, and unemployment. The predication of benefits on prior contributions limited the applicability of this strategy of social security to better-paid and regularly employed workers, primarily men employed in the skilled trades. The willingness of the propertied classes to accept the idea of a legal right to benefits depended above all on the adoption of the principle that such a right would strengthen, rather than diminish, the incentive to individual thrift and

Nazi Welfare Office. Interior of the central office of the Public Welfare Office of the National Socialist Party, Berlin, during a visit by the Duke of Windsor, 1937. HULTON GETTY PICTURE LIBRARY/LIAISON AGENCY

foresight, as Winston Churchill (1874–1965) insisted with regard to the British unemployment insurance system. As François Ewald has argued, it was the adoption of the technology of insurance that made it possible to transcend the rigid individualism that had dominated nineteenth-century thought in the name of a more social, solidarist worldview.

Under the chancellorship of Otto von Bismarck (1815–1898), Germany took the lead in establishing workers' insurance programs against sickness (1883), work accidents (1884), and old age and invalidity (1889). The introduction of this legislation represented a two-pronged attempt to forestall the further radicalization of the working classes. Bismarck hoped that state subsidies to the insurance funds would gain the allegiance of the workers by demonstrating the paternalistic concern of the state for their well-being and that the very existence of such insurance programs would reduce the number of instances in which these workers would be forced to turn to deterrent, discriminatory municipal poor relief. These insurance programs, and those established in other states over the following decades, were constructed on the foundation laid earlier by friendly societies, unions, and other, often semipublic insurance funds. The novelty

of German social insurance legislation lay in the combination of compulsory membership and the decision to insure the actuarial soundness of the programs by initially restricting them to those skilled trades that were politically most sensitive but economically most insurable because of their relatively high wages and steady employment patterns. Although employers were required to contribute to sickness and disability insurance (and bear the entire cost of accident insurance), the redistributive impact of these programs was limited. Workers paid for their benefits in the form of contributions, and the propertied classes benefited from tax reductions loosely tied to anticipated reductions in poor relief costs. The funds were administered by workers and employers (the "social partners") on a parity basis. However, Bismarck's policies failed to stem the rise of Social Democracy in Germany, and in fact, the social insurance funds quickly became administrative strongholds of German Social Democracy.

Informed by the German experience but inspired by the transatlantic Progressive spirit that Daniel Rodgers describes in *Atlantic Crossings,* national insurance programs against accident, sickness and disability, and old age were established (either on a compulsory basis or through state subsidies to voluntary programs) in almost every European country by the 1930s, with most of the remaining gaps being closed immediately after World War II. (See table 1.) During these years, the existing social insurance systems were expanded to cover additional risks and include new social groups—white collar workers, self-employed and farmers, dependent family members (in health insurance, for example), and survivors (in pension insurance). By 1939, almost every west European state had introduced insurance programs that were designed to provide minimal income as security against the major causes of economic insecurity.

Unemployment insurance was usually the most controversial because it entailed the most radical break with liberal political economy. In contrast to the actuarial predictability of accident, sickness, and old age, business cycles—and therefore employment levels—were far more volatile. Moreover, insurance against unemployment was a classic example of moral hazard. And lastly, no system capable of insuring against the high levels of structural unemployment and the extraordinary economic problems of the Great Depression would have been financially feasible in any case. In 1911, Britain established the first compulsory nationwide unemployment insurance program. Although contributions by workers and employers provided the lion's share of the financial means, the state agreed to subsidize the program (though these subsidies were justified less in terms of their redistributive impact than as compensation for anticipated reduction in poor relief costs). The system was linked in an integral manner to the labor exchanges to reduce frictional unemployment and test willingness to work. The incentive to work was to be maintained by waiting periods and limits on the duration of benefits. The British example was followed by a number of other countries after World War I. However, the Great Depression forced all of these countries to retreat from a rigorously constructed system of insurance to various mixtures of unemployment insurance, assistance provided without means testing, and means-tested outdoor relief—the notorious "dole."

FROM SOCIAL INSURANCE TO SOCIAL SECURITY

The immediate postwar period brought a new wave of social legislation in many European countries. The most influential document of this period was the report prepared for the British government by the economist William Beveridge (1879–1963) in 1942. The Beveridge Report proposed the creation of a national minimum benefit to guarantee freedom from want for all citizens. It also laid out the rationale for legislation on family allowance, old-age pensions, and a national health service, and it was conceptually linked to the postwar commitment by Britain and other states to full employment and Keynesian economic policies (counter-cyclical deficit spending intended to maintain a high level of aggregate demand, in contrast to older economic orthodoxies which espoused the importance of balanced budgets). The Beveridge plan had such an extraordinary resonance across the Western world because its underlying commitment to social justice appeared to hold the key to rejuvenating democratic political systems that had failed in so many respects during the 1930s. Historians have disagreed over whether this postwar wave of social reform was made possible by the expanded influence of the working classes or by Conservative acquiescence to the social programs they had fought tooth and claw before the war. In fact, Social Democratic support for social insurance marked a sharp departure from their previous insistence that such insurance was intrinsically reactionary because it failed to correct the fundamental problem of working-class distress: exploitation that deprived the worker of the full fruits of his or her labor. There was also a similar political moderation on the right, and after 1945 Tory paternalism and the Christian Democratic idea of a social market economy came together with an increasingly deradicalized socialist movement on the common ground of the welfare state. Peter Baldwin has convincingly argued that the universalist, egalitarian social insurance schemes developed in the Scandinavian states and, in part, in the Beveridge system were based not on the weakening of prewar class antagonisms and the acceptance of redistributive social insurance programs, but rather on the incorporation of the middle classes into the welfare system in ways that allowed them to benefit from the socialization of risk while limiting the redistributive burden imposed upon them.

As with every other major welfare program, the movement for family and child allowances had developed in an ad hoc, experimental manner before World War I, but the idea achieved widespread acceptance only from the 1930s. France (1913) was the first country to establish a nationwide system of family allowances, though most U.S. states established similar programs between 1911 and 1919. During the 1930s, Sweden established child allowance and maternity benefit programs, financed through general revenues. Family allowances were regularized as part of the broad expansion of social services in every country after 1945.

By the postwar period at the very latest, most of the states of Western Europe had developed a fairly

TABLE 1
CORE SOCIAL INSURANCE LAWS IN WESTERN EUROPE

Country	Industrial accident insurance		Sickness insurance		Pension insurance		Unemployment insurance	
	Employers' liability	*Compulsory*	*Subsidized voluntary*	*Compulsory*	*Subsidized voluntary*	*Compulsory*	*Subsidized voluntary*	*Compulsory*
Austria		1887		1888		1906 (employees) 1927 (workers)		1920
Belgium	1903		1894	1944	1900	1924	1907	1944
Denmark	1898	1916	1892	1933 (semi-compulsory)		1891 (national pensions) 1922 (national pensions rev.) 1933 (invalid/old age insur.)	1907	
Finland		1895 1917		1963		1937	1917	
France	1898	1946		1930		1910 1930		1914 (unempl. assistance) 1959 (collective labor agreements) 1967
Germany		1884		1883		1889		1927
Italy		1898	1886	1928 (collective labor agreements) 1943	1898	1919		1919
Netherlands		1901 1921		1913 1929		1913	1916	1949
Norway		1894		1909		1936	1906	1938
Sweden	1901	1916	1891 1910			1913	1934	

Country	Industrial accident insurance		Sickness insurance		Pension insurance		Unemployment insurance	
	Employers' liability	Compulsory	Subsidized voluntary	Compulsory	Subsidized voluntary	Compulsory	Subsidized voluntary	Compulsory
Switzerland		1911	1911			1946	1924	
United Kingdom	1906	1946		1911 1946		1908 (national pensions) 1925		1911 1920

Flora, Peter, and Arnold J. Heidenheimer, eds. "The Historical Core and Changing Boundaries of the Welfare State." In *The Development of Welfare States in Europe and America*. New Brunswick, N.J., 1981. Page 59.

similar network of social insurance programs. Together, social services and social insurance provided a minimal degree of economic security and insured the needy at a minimal level necessary for them to be considered full-fledged members of the national community. A shift in the development of the welfare state came between the mid-1950s and the early 1970s. During this period, social insurance was extended from workers to the middle classes and the goal of these programs shifted from minimalist income replacement and the equalization of the most egregious class differences of industrial society to the active promotion of the highest quality of life for all citizens in order to give more substance to the idea of social citizenship. To achieve this goal, income maintenance programs became nearly universal, and their benefit levels were constantly improved. Pensions were reformed (Germany, 1957) so that benefits for present retirees reflected real increases in productivity and income, rather than past contributions; this permitted retirees to participate in the postwar economic boom and maintain their relative standard of living, rather than simply satisfy their basic needs. Unemployment benefit systems became less restrictive, and benefits became more generous. Child allowances became increasingly universalistic and were gradually uncoupled from need. The compensation for actual loss of income was increasingly supplanted by preventive measures to forestall the risk through health services, occupational training and rehabilitation, and education, while the scope and quality of all of these services—especially medical care and education—expanded steadily. In England, the victory of prevention over compensation was symbolized by the replacement of contributory national health *insurance* with a universal, tax-based national health *service* in 1948. All of these factors contributed to the constantly increasing rate of growth in social spending from the late 1950s through the 1970s. During the postwar decades, the creation of a more comprehensive, more universalist, more solidarist system of social services devoted to the prevention of need and the active promotion of higher standards of living and quality of life all came together to form that new system of welfare known as social security.

WELFARE STATE REGIMES IN POSTWAR EUROPE

To affirm the existence of broad trends is not to say that all welfare states and systems are the same. The act of choosing between the various means available for meeting a perceived need always reflects an understanding of the nature of the problem as determined by previous policy precedents, political and cultural traditions, economic and social trends, prevailing perceptions of gender roles, state administrative capacities, and the prevailing balance of political forces. These differences were largely ignored in the first generation of comparative research on the welfare state, which regarded aggregate public social spending as the key to understanding the development of the welfare state.

The most influential comparative analysis of the different forms of the postwar welfare state is the typology of welfare state regimes developed by Gøsta Esping-Andersen in *The Three Worlds of Welfare Capitalism* (1990). This ideal typology is based on the manner and extent to which welfare systems emancipate the individual by de-commodifying labor, the patterns of income redistribution and social stratification created by these programs, and the relationship between the state, the market, and the family implied by these programs.

Religious Welfare Organization. Salvation Army members distribute food to indigent women during the Christmas season, Paris, 29 December 1931. ©BETTMAN/CORBIS

The liberal or residual welfare state is based on a dual system. For the majority, individual welfare is to a large degree determined by the play of market forces. For those persons who cannot satisfy their basic needs through the labor market, minimal transfer payments (such as the American Social Security system) and limited entitlements and means-tested public assistance are provided. Such programs do little to reduce social inequalities. The United States, Canada, and Australia are the archetypal examples of this type of welfare regime.

In contrast, in conservative, corporatist welfare states the state plays a much larger role in promoting social security. However, the purpose of this state intervention is not to promote equality, but rather to insure social security in a way which will preserve existing status and income differentials between occupational groups. This type of welfare regime is often described as a "pillared" system because separate health care, retirement, and so on exist for each major occupational group. Benefits are of necessity related most directly to earnings and contributions (rather than citizenship or need), and they are usually determined as a percentage of earnings. Premiums are paid by both employers and employees, and the management of such programs is generally devolved onto the social partners on a parity basis. Occupational benefits are supplemented by means-tested public assistance for those outside the labor force. Family members are generally covered through the breadwinner, rather than each individual member being eligible for benefits in his or her own right by virtue of his or her status as a citizen. The religious, socially conservative nature of this regime type is reflected first in its commitment to the preservation of traditional family structures and discouragement of female labor-force participation, and second in its insistence that public social service providers intervene in a subsidiary manner only if voluntary or confessional agencies are unable or unwilling to provide necessary services to the family or individual. This corporate regime has developed most fully in Germany, which has a strong statist tradition, and in Austria, France, Italy, and the Benelux countries, whose welfare systems have been deeply influenced by social Catholicism.

The third welfare state regime, which is identified most closely with Scandinavian—especially Swedish—Social Democracy, is characterized by the fusion of a high degree of universalism and an equally high degree of de-commodification. Its primary policy goal is less to compensate for the loss of income than to promote a higher standard of living and a more fulfilling way of life for all citizens. This was necessary in order to give substance to the idea of social citizenship and meet the political challenge of capturing the support of the new middle classes for such a solidaristic system. In this Scandinavian system, all occupational and social groups enjoy identical rights and participate in a single universal system, though benefits are graduated according to actual earnings. This system was built on the foundation of the proto-Keynesian ideas developed by Swedish Social Democracy in the 1930s. In addition, by providing grants directly to children and assuming direct responsibility for caring for children, the elderly, and the disabled, the Scandinavian welfare system diverges from the male breadwinner model to a greater extent than in most other states by meeting the needs of these persons in a way that makes it possible for women to choose between work and household.

Not all countries fit neatly into this classificatory schema. From the end of World War II until 1979, Britain was a hybrid mixture of the universalism most closely identified with the Social Democratic model and the low level of benefits (which is the correlate of financing through general tax revenues) characteristic of the liberal, residual model. However, the precise balance of this mixture shifted in the liberal direction under the prime ministers Margaret Thatcher and John Major. Also, some people have suggested that the states of southern Europe, including Spain, Portugal, Greece, and Italy, constitute a fourth regime. In these states, welfare services are provided primarily by church, family, and voluntary organizations, rather than the state, and the systems are marked by fragmented coverage and uneven distribution among occupational groups.

SOCIAL WELFARE IN COMMUNIST EUROPE

The mirror image of the dynamic Swedish model was to be found in the Soviet Union and other communist states of postwar Eastern Europe. Under communist rule the right to work was constitutionally guaranteed, and the integral connection between economic and social policy that was forged in postwar Western Europe by Keynesian fiscal policy was made in communist systems by centralized state planning for industrial production and full employment. The model of forced industrialization and agricultural collectivization that was implemented in the Soviet Union by Stalin and, later, the communist parties of Central and Eastern Europe, did bring about a rapid increase in productivity and income in these relatively backward regions during the first decades of communist rule. This spurt in economic development made possible

real improvements in virtually every area of social security in comparison to the precommunist era.

From the 1930s, social services in the Soviet Union were linked to the performance of that productive labor which was deemed essential to the construction of socialism, and a substantial proportion of social services in the Soviet Union and its East European empire were provided through the workplace, including housing, health care, child care, leisure and cultural activities, and vacation facilities. These services were not fringe benefits, but a necessary complement to wages that were set at an artificially low level in accordance with the dictates of central economic planning. In theory at least they obviated the need for any separate welfare programs except for those persons who were never fully integrated into the labor process. In addition, these communist states also promoted public welfare through substantial state subsidies of basic consumer goods and services, such as food, housing, transportation, energy, and health care.

However, these initial developments were impressive only in relation to the low level of previous social programs in these regions. The institutionalization in the 1950s and 1960s of an industrial model based on abundant unskilled labor, outdated technology, and productivity that stagnated at a low level could not sustain the long-term improvements in social security beyond the level reached during the initial spurt. The welfare systems of communist Europe also suffered from a number of structural problems. The ambitious commitment of these states to the welfare of their citizens led in practice to the extensive growth of a social service system that was so inefficient and so systematically starved of resources that it was often incapable of providing an even minimal level of basic services to all. Housing shortages, the frequent absence of basic medical equipment in polyclinics, and low pension rates were the most egregious examples of this dysfunctionality. The ensuing shortages created the opportunity for corruption and the temptation to allocate scarce social services on the basis of bribery, nepotism, and/or patronage. In the paternalistic "welfare dictatorships" of communist Europe, everything was done by the party state for the people, who were systematically excluded from the formulation of welfare policies and who had no legally enforceable right to challenge the decisions of the state. The right to social services was limited to individual conformity to the system, creating a vast potential to instrumentalize control over scarce social services for political ends—to reward those groups loyal to the regime and to punish opponents. Despite the state's commitment to the prevention of need, the development of the welfare system was subordinated to the imperatives of production. This, together with the limited scope for public opposition, led the governments of the Soviet Union and Eastern Europe systematically to injure the health of their populations "by requiring work in health-damaging environments, by polluting the earth and atmosphere, and by presiding over a social system that indirectly encouraged alcoholism, unhealthy diet and suicide" (Deacon, p. 3). The negative impact of these trends was even more severe because of the ideological insistence that these societies had already attained a level of development at which the class tensions and contradictions of bourgeois society had been overcome. This view prevented communist policy makers from recognizing the new social, economic, and cultural problems created by the postwar transformation of these societies and developing social policies to meet the challenges posed by these developments.

The combination of political alienation and the inability to redeem those social promises on which communist regimes based their claim to the superiority of their system were major factors in the eventual collapse of communism. In the late-twentieth-century period of transition toward parliamentary democracy and capitalism (at least in most former communist countries), state policy makers faced a sharp dilemma. The legitimacy of these new states rests to no small degree on their promise that capitalism will finally make good on those welfarist promises made by the communists. Yet it is difficult to resolve the contradiction between the fiscal constraints imposed by market-oriented reforms and the pressing need for social services to buffer the consequences of inflation and unemployment. Postcommunist governments have begun to turn their attention to social policy, and the politics of social policy in these states will be shaped by a variety of factors: macroeconomic conditions, institutional legacies from the communist period, precommunist social policy traditions, the ideological orientation of the governing parties, and the structure of the political system within which they operate. However, it is still too early to predict with any accuracy how the welfare systems in these states will evolve in the twenty-first century.

WOMEN, GENDER, AND THE WELFARE STATE

Family policies have been explicitly based on assumptions concerning gender roles. The specific social rights established by welfare programs depend upon whether the beneficiary is regarded primarily as a worker or a citizen, a man or a woman, a father or a mother, the family breadwinner, the family caregiver, the guardian of domesticity, or as the mother of a new generation.

European feminists initially advocated mothers' pensions and family allowances because they hoped that such programs would expand the rights and choices available to women as citizens, regardless of their marital status, and enhance their independence either by recognizing the social value of unremunerated domestic labor and compensating them for it or by freeing them to pursue work outside the household. However, the family policies of most European welfare states have been based fairly explicitly on the ideal of the male breadwinner and stay-at-home housewife. The primary aims of family allowances have been the elimination of children's poverty and/or the promotion of state population policy, not the provision of an alternative to the male breadwinner model. In contrast, the maternity and family policies of the Scandinavian countries have gone the furthest toward extending the rights of women as citizens, rather than in their capacity as mothers.

Esping-Andersen has been criticized by feminist historians, who argue that essential aspects of women's experience within the welfare state are systematically obscured by his gender-blind analysis of work and welfare. More specifically, they point out that, given prevailing patterns in the sexual division of labor, the de-commodification of women's labor has generally led to the restriction of women to the domestic sphere where, secondly, they become primary yet unremunerated providers of welfare services to others. This reflects the fact that most welfare programs were originally designed to reinforce the family wage system and, therefore, had a distinctly paternalist character. Consequently, while de-commodification of labor has been regarded as an important indicator of emancipation for men, these critics argue that for women de-commodification has not led to greater economic independence or enhanced the social citizenship rights available to them outside of marriage.

In the 1990s, feminist historians made important steps toward a fuller incorporation of gender as an independent analytic dimension in accounts of the welfare state. Ann Orloff has, for example, suggested that any adequate description of welfare systems must take into account the extent to which they promote women's access to paid labor and establish those rights necessary for them to maintain an autonomous household independent of their roles as wives and mothers. Other writers have argued that the analysis of gender and the welfare state must focus on "caring regimes," which determine the ways in which the family influences the structure of the labor market by means of the unpaid provision of welfare by women rather than analyzing the relationship between paid and unpaid labor.

CRISIS, RETRENCHMENT, AND NEW DEPARTURES SINCE THE 1970s

The post-1945 consolidation of the welfare state in Western Europe led to steadily accelerating growth in social spending. By the mid-1970s total social spending amounted to between one-fourth and one-third of the gross national product in most western welfare states, and it substantially exceeded this latter proportion in some countries. In the 1970s, this accelerating growth came to an abrupt halt. It appeared that the growth of the welfare state had reached its limits though it was not clear whether this was due to external fiscal constraints or whether the internal forces which had propelled this growth had been exhausted. Conservatives argued that the welfare state had become "ungovernable" because the responsiveness of democratic government to popular political pressures was leading to unsustainable levels of public social spending. Neo-marxists, on the other hand, attributed the looming crisis to the heightening contradiction between the need for ever-greater social spending (to reconcile the laboring classes to the continued existence of capitalism and/or socialize the costs of the reproduction of labor which would otherwise have to be borne by capital alone) and the requirements of the accumulation of capital.

The economic crisis of the 1970s led to substantial cuts in social spending in almost every country. These retrenchment measures did not lead to the abandonment of the basic features of the existing welfare regime in any country. Retrenchment strategies included such measures as increasing contributions and tightening the connection between benefits and contributions in Bismarckian-type welfare systems; restricting eligibility through greater use of income- and means-testing in flat-rate, Beveridgean systems; increasing co-payments; combining reductions in basic benefits with greater use of means-tested supplements to target expenditure on those who need it most; and changing complex formulas in order to alter conditions and costs of retirement programs.

In Britain and the United States, the Thatcher and Reagan administrations used the economic crisis as a springboard for a broad ideological attack on the welfare state consensus that had prevailed in both countries since the 1940s. However, despite their initial hopes, the Thatcher administration was able to make only incremental changes rather than effect a root-and-branch reform of social service provision. For example, the 1986 Social Security Act in Britain did not bring about the wholesale transfer of pension provison from the state to the private sector, but rather implemented several measures designed to make pri-

Local Welfare Office. Elderly people collect their pensions at the post office in Nelson, Lancashire, 1954. ©HULTON-DEUTCH COLLECTION/CORBIS

vate pensions more appealing while at the same time making it easier to opt out of the public pension system. The effect of this legislation was to shift the British welfare system toward the liberal, residual model. The plan put forth by the French prime minister Alain Juppé in 1995 was based on an eclectic mixture of policy principles. On the one hand, he proposed transforming the corporatist organization of the national health insurance system into a universalist public health system along the lines of the British model. On the other hand, the increased reliance on means-testing to target family allowances moved in the opposite direction from that universalism which he was trying to establish in the health care system.

Three important socioeconomic forces have been driving European welfare reform since the 1980s. First, the aging of the population and the emergence of new family structures and patterns of labor market participation are creating new needs and altering the patterns of work, family, and gender upon which Western welfare states have rested. In addition, the aging of the population is leading to higher expenditures for pensions and health care, and these fiscal pressures are further intensified by the corresponding reduction in the ratio of active workers to the retired population.

Second, the political economy of the postwar welfare state in Western Europe was altered by the emergence of a new industrial regime, which was based on a more flexible organization of production through electronically controlled machines operated by increasingly highly skilled and highly paid workers, dependence on continuously accelerating technological innovation, and new forms of corporate structure to manage these processes. From 1945 through the 1980s, the state linked the interests of organized capital and labor in a program of full employment and social welfare. Changes in the organization of production have distinct implications for the Keynesian welfare system.

This reorganization of production cannot be separated from a third major force: economic globalization and the increasing integration of the European nation-states into the European Union. The enforced harmonization of social policies is an essential element of the logic of European integration, and the necessary changes put pressure on those national compromises concerning wages and social spending which had been the foundation of the Keynesian welfare state. By making the boundaries of the national economic and social space more porous and subject to the disruptive effects of international economic competition, globalization increases the demand for social programs to cushion the population against these disruptions at the same time that the pressures of international competition are diminishing the capacity of the state and industry to pay for these programs. The disjunction between the global scale of production and the national provision of welfare has even been pulling at the solidarist glue that has held the European welfare systems together for the past half-century.

See also **The World Wars and the Depression; Since World War II** *(volume 1);* **The Life Cycle; The Welfare State; Communism** *(volume 2);* **The Family and the State; Motherhood; Widows and Widowers; The Elderly** *(volume 4);* **Working Classes; Labor History: Strikes and Unions; Socialism** *(in this volume); and other articles in this section.*

BIBLIOGRAPHY

Alber, Jens. *Vom Armenhaus zum Wohlfahrtsstaat: Analysen zur Entwicklung der Sozialversicherung in Westeuropa.* Frankfurt and New York, 1982. An influential version of the logic of industrialization approach to the welfare state.

Amin, Ash, ed. *Post-Fordism: A Reader.* Oxford and Cambridge, Mass., 1994.

Baldwin, Peter. *The Politics of Social Solidarity: Class Bases of the European Welfare State, 1875–1975.* Cambridge, U.K., and New York, 1990. An influential, critical reinterpretation of the class account of the growth of the welfare state.

Bock, Gisela, and Pat Thane, eds. *Maternity and Gender Policies: Women and the Rise of the European Welfare States, 1880–1950.* London and New York, 1991.

Bonoli, Giuliano. *The Politics of Pension Reform: Institutions and Policy Change in Western Europe.* Cambridge, U.K., 2000.

Bradshaw, J., J. Ditch, H. Holmes, and P. Witeford. "A Comparative Study of Child Support in Fifteen Countries," *Journal of European Social Policy* 5:3 (1993): 175–197. Constructs a typology of welfare state regimes from the perspective of the provision of child benefits.

Briggs, Asa. "The Welfare State in Historical Perspective." In *The Collected Essays of Asa Briggs.* Volume 2. Champaign-Urbana, Ill. 1985. Pages 177–211. Originally appeared in the *European Journal of Sociology* 2 (1961).

Canning, Kathleen. *Languages of Labor and Gender: Female Factory Work in Germany, 1850–1914.* Ithaca, N.Y., 1996. The most ambitious attempt to redefine the social question as a question of gender and family rather than class.

Childs, Marquis William. *Sweden, the Middle Way.* Rev. ed. New Haven, Conn., 1947.

Deacon, Bob, ed. *The New Eastern Europe: Social Policy Past, Present, and Future.* London, 1992.

Dingwall, Robert, and Anna Kwak, eds. *Social Change, Social Policy, and Social Work in the New Europe.* Hants, U.K., and Brookfield, Vt., 1998.

Donzelot, Jacques. *The Policing of Families*. Translated by Robert Hurley. New York, 1979.

Eghigian, Greg. *Making Security Social: Disability, Insurance, and the Birth of the Social Entitlement State in Germany*. Ann Arbor, Mich., 2000.

Esping-Andersen, Gøsta. *The Three Worlds of Welfare Capitalism*. Princeton, N.J., 1990. The most influential typology of welfare state regimes based on the comparative study of pensions and labor market policies.

Esping-Andersen, Gøsta, ed. *Welfare States in Transition: National Adaptations in Global Economies*. London, 1996.

Ewald, François. *L'État Providence*. Paris, 1986. A difficult but pathbreaking Foucauldian interpretation of how social insurance and the technology of risk made possible the transition from a liberal, individualist approach to poverty to a social, solidarist one.

Ferrara, M. "The 'Southern Model' of Welfare in Social Europe." *Journal of European Social Policy* 6:1 (1996): 17–37.

Flora, Peter, ed. *Growth to Limits: The Western European Welfare States since World War II*. 4 vols. Berlin and New York, 1986–1988. Volume 4 contains exhaustive detail on the history and structure of the different programs in the various states covered by the book.

Flora, Peter, et al. *State, Economy, and Society in Western Europe, 1815–1975: A Data Handbook in Two Volumes*. Volume 1: *The Growth of Mass Democracies and Welfare States*. Frankfurt, 1983.

Flora, Peter, and Arnold J. Heidenheimer, eds. *The Development of Welfare States in Europe and America*. New Brunswick, N.J., 1981. The most influential version of the logic of industrialization interpretation of the welfare state.

Garland, David. *Punishment and Welfare: A History of Penal Strategies*. Brookfield, Vt., 1985. Excellent account of the variety of social-scientific discourses brought to bear on the problem of poverty and deviance in conjunction with the development of a social perspective on poverty.

Gordon, Linda, ed. *Women, the State, and Welfare*. Madison, Wis., 1990.

Götting, Ulrike. "Destruction, Adjustment, and Innovation: Social Policy Transformation in Eastern and Central Europe." *Journal of European Social Policy* 4:3 (1994): 181–200.

Heclo, Hugh. *Modern Social Politics in Britain and Sweden: From Relief to Income Maintenance*. New Haven, Conn., 1974.

Hong, Young-sun. *Welfare, Modernity, and the Weimar State, 1919–1933*. Princeton, N.J., 1998.

Jones, Catherine, ed. *New Perspectives on the Welfare State in Europe*. London and New York, 1993.

Köhler, Peter A., and Hans F. Zacher, eds. *The Evolution of Social Insurance, 1881–1981: Studies of Germany, France, Great Britain, Australia, and Switzerland*. London, 1982.

Kornai, János, et al., eds. *Reforming the State: Fiscal and Welfare Reform in Post-Socialist Countries*. Cambridge, U.K., 2001.

Koven, Seth, and Sonya Michel, eds. *Mothers of a New World: Maternalist Politics and the Origins of Welfare States*. New York, 1993.

Lewis, Jane. "Gender and the Development of Welfare Regimes." *Journal of European Social Policy* 2 (1992): 159–173. Develops a typology of welfare regimes based on an analysis of the welfare effects of paid and unpaid labor.

Lewis, Jane. "Gender and Welfare Regimes: Further Thoughts." *Social Politics* 4:2 (Summer 1997): 160–177, and the responses on 177–207. An influential argument for the incorporation of gender as an independent analytic category in the interpretation of the welfare state.

Lewis, Jane, ed. *Women and Social Policies in Europe: Work, Family, and the State.* Brookfield, Vt., 1993.

O'Connor, Julia, and Gregg Olsen, eds. *Power Resources Theory and the Welfare State: A Critical Approach: Essays Collected in Honor of Walter Korpi.* Toronto, 1998.

Offe, Claus. *Contradictions of the Welfare State.* London, 1984.

Orloff, Ann Shola. "Gender and the Social Rights of Citizenship: The Comparative Analysis of Gender Relations and Welfare States." *American Sociological Review* 58 (1993): 303–328. An important analysis of the limitations of gender-blind interpretations of welfare state regimes.

Palier, Bruno, ed. *Comparing Social Welfare Systems in Europe.* [France] Mission Recherche et Experimentation, Ministère des Affaires sociales. 3 vols. to date [1996–]. The most recent major comparative survey of welfare programs and practices across Europe.

Pedersen, Susan. *Family, Dependence, and the Origins of the Welfare State: Britain and France, 1914–1945.* Cambridge, U.K., and New York, 1993.

Peukert, Detlev. *Grenzen der Sozialdisziplinierung: Aufstieg und Krise der deutschen Jugendfürsorge, 1878–1932.* Cologne, Germany, 1986.

Pierson, Paul. *Dismantling the Welfare State? Reagan, Thatcher, and the Politics of Retrenchment.* Cambridge, U.K., and New York, 1994.

Rhodes, Martin. "Globalization and West European Welfare States: A Critical Review of Recent Debates." *Journal of European Social Policy* 6:4 (1996): 305–327.

Ritter, Gerhard Albert. *Social Welfare in Germany and Britain: Origins and Development.* Translated by Kim Traynor. New York, 1986.

Rodgers, Daniel T. *Atlantic Crossings: Social Politics in a Progressive Age.* Cambridge, Mass., 1998.

Rosanvallon, Pierre. *The New Social Question: Rethinking the Welfare State.* Translated by Barbara Harshav. Princeton, N.J., 2000.

Sainsbury, Diane, ed. *Gender and Welfare State Regimes.* Oxford and New York, 1999.

Sainsbury, Diane, ed. *Gendering Welfare States.* London, 1994.

Shalev, Michael. "The Social Democratic Model and Beyond: Two 'Generations' of Comparative Research on the Welfare State." *Comparative Social Research* 6 (1983): 315–351. An important critique of the logic of industrialization and class interpretations of the welfare state.

Thane, Pat. *Old Age in English History: Past Experiences, Present Issues.* Oxford, 2000.

ALCOHOL AND TEMPERANCE

George Snow

Alcohol has played an important role in human society since the accidental discovery of the effects of ethyl alcohol—the product of the natural fermentation of honey or fruit. The agricultural development and domestication of grape stock—viticulture—resulted in wines that were considered to have, in addition to other qualities, salutary medicinal benefits. The agricultural revolution that led to the production of wines also led to the manufacture and consumption of beer—a beverage relying on the fermentation of large amounts of starchy grain.

ALCOHOL IN EARLY SOCIETY

Wines and beers of varying strengths and description became the primary beverages among European populations confronted with unpotable drinking water, since the antiseptic power of alcohol, along with the natural acidity of wine and beer, killed many pathogens in the questionable water. In addition to these salutary properties, wine especially acquired a reputation as a means of settling the stomach, as a prophylactic in the prevention of colds, and as an antiseptic in the cleansing of wounds. Consumption of alcoholic beverages also temporarily altered behavior—elating and gladdening some, enhancing the feeling of physical strength of others, promoting camaraderie and fellowship for many more, and lowering personal and social inhibitions for all. These attributes of alcohol led churches throughout Europe to inveigh against its excessive consumption—that is, drunkenness (*ivrognerie, Trunksucht, p'ianstvo,* and *borrachera* in French, German, Russian, and Spanish, respectively)—from the Middle Ages on. All of this was in spite of the fact that wine was central in the celebration of the Eucharist and that in European climates conducive to viticulture, the church frequently operated the biggest and best vineyards at a considerable profit.

By the Renaissance the process of distillation to produce spirits—a process invented earlier by the Arabs—had gradually spread first to Italy and then to northern Europe, reaching the extreme north and northeast—Scandinavia and Muscovy—by the mid-fifteenth century. The powerful spirituous beverages aquavit and vodka—names that derive from the word "water" in Scandinavian languages and Russian, respectively—resulted from a process that used a boiling water–alcohol mixture to derive a condensation with a higher alcohol content than that of the starting liquid. Distilled alcoholic beverages could pretend neither to nourishment nor to low alcohol content—but they became widely popular in some areas of Europe (for example, Russia), where they replaced wine and beer as the preferred beverages in daily life and in the celebration of church holidays and ceremonial occasions, such as births, christenings and baptisms, marriages, deaths, and wakes. Distilled beverages did not carry the sacral associations of wine, which remained the chief potable of Catholic countries, such as France, Italy, Spain, and Portugal. But the increasing availability and strength of distilled alcoholic beverages in the post-Reformation period produced seemingly higher levels of drunkenness and the accompanying official concerns.

The predominantly rural and agrarian nature of most early modern European societies did not make a social problem of alcohol consumption—whether in the form of beer, wine, or distilled spirits. In the agricultural way of life the sense of time, the ebb and flow of seasonal activity, the compulsion to work, and the consumption of intoxicants were all of a kind of "natural" process. That is, the line between work and life was blurred, permitting a greater intermingling of labor and social intercourse in which drinking played an important role and did not seriously inhibit the performance of tasks central to agricultural production. Then, too, in eastern Europe, and particularly in Russia, a drink of vodka was both a ceremonial and an official confirmation of an agreement or a bargain in rural villages, and village work parties were frequently paid on this basis, a natural consequence of undermonetized economies. Consequently, criticism of alcohol consumption remained muted and was only

Distilling Alcohol. Engraving by Joannes Galle after Jan van der Straat (Joannes Stradano; 1523–1605). BIBLIOTHÈQUE NATIONALE, PARIS/GIRAUDON/ART RESOURCE, N.Y.

expressed when consumption reached excessive levels. Many homilies were, therefore, directed against the practice of drinking to get drunk.

Other subterranean rumblings against excessive alcohol consumption during this period came from moralists disturbed by the spread of distilled spirits—with the matter betraying national animosities: the French accused the Italians of introducing distilling techniques learned from the Arabs, the Germans accused the French of the same thing, and the English claimed that their soldiers had been introduced to gin drinking in Holland during the wars of the sixteenth century. Behind all of these concerns was the fact that strong liquor was being drunk everywhere in Europe by the eve of the Enlightenment, and virtually every country, using the same basic techniques and custom-built still, had begun to fashion its own indigenous beverage: Scotch among the Scots, *Branntwein* and schnapps among the Germans; and arrack and raki, made with rice from the Far East, in the western Mediterranean.

Economics of alcohol. As consumption of alcohol in its various forms became more widespread and popular in the sixteenth and seventeenth centuries, European governments saw its manufacture, distribution, and sale as potential sources of revenue—both direct and indirect. Consequently, the English Parliament required licenses of alehouses (1552), Boris Godunov's Muscovite government (1598–1605) taxed the sale of vodka by the *kabaki* (taverns), and the French King Louis XIV (1638–1715) taxed the sale of eaux-de-vie sold by cabarets at the same level as wine. An inestimably valuable source of indirect taxation that served a redistributive function, the direct or indirect sale of alcoholic beverages by the state legitimated their consumption in some quarters. In many cases, this association made bars and taverns a focus of attention for both tax inspectors and, later, temperance reformers. In some other cases, for example in Russia, it made the government itself the target of temperance critics.

Alcohol consumption as a moral issue. Although it was recognized that alcoholic beverages differed in strength, there was little widespread perception of their heavy consumption as either a medical or a social problem. Indeed, alcohol consumption was for a long while seen as a moral problem. In England the respectability of places for the retail sale of some alcoholic beverages increased during the Restoration. A similar lack of concern existed in France during this period, while in Russia the redistributive nature of alcohol sales was institutionalized: the *kabaki* became a state monopoly, a status recognized by the *Ulozhenie* (legal code) of 1649.

By the eighteenth century, however, leading elements in England, the Germanies, and France had begun to express concern about alcohol abuse—although for different reasons and on different bases. The concern reflected in William Hogarth's engravings and in Wesleyan religious sensibilities in England and the growing medical awareness of alcohol's debilitating effects in the Germanies were directed against distilled alcoholic beverages. Beer and wine continued to be viewed as "natural" and therefore less harmful than the products of distillation. This distinction remained a basic feature of much temperance thought to the beginning of the twentieth century. Because

Concern about Alcohol Abuse. *Gin Lane,* engraving (1750) by William Hogarth (1697–1764). BURSTEIN COLLECTION/©CORBIS

wine was for a long time the main alcoholic beverage consumed by Frenchmen, concern with alcohol abuse was slow to develop in France. But by the end of the eighteenth and the beginning of the nineteenth century and with the increased appearance of distilled alcoholic beverages, French and German physicians were coming to see the excessive consumption of alcohol as a public-health problem.

Alcohol consumption as a health issue. The concern about alcohol consumption as a public-health problem was first expressed in early-nineteenth-century England when the term "delirium tremens" was used by the physician Thomas Sutton to describe the violent restlessness, hallucinations, and other phenomena associated with prolonged alcohol abuse. During this same period physicians of diverse nationality published studies of the effects of alcohol abuse on the liver. Not a few of them posited that such abuse was a form of disease, a contention that led to the emergence of the disease model that later played so important a role in European temperance movements and eventually replaced the moral paradigm. Associated with this model was the assumption that it was a degenerative disease not only for the drinker but for his or her progeny as well—an assumption that played a significant role in late-nineteenth-century racial degeneration theories and in some temperance literature. Knowledge about the effects of alcohol on the human body was, in any event, scattered and fragmentary, varying from country to country.

This situation was remedied by the synthesizing work of the great Swedish physiologist and researcher Magnus Huss (1807–1890). Huss's contribution to the emerging concern about alcohol abuse and the myriad physical problems associated with it was the product of his extensive familiarity with international literature on the subject plus his own wide travels and personal observations, as a physician in Swedish hospitals, of the ravages of drink among the poor. All of these elements came together in his great work *Alcoholismus chronicus* (1849), originally written in his native Swedish and translated three years later into German. Huss's neologism "alcoholism" not only was succinct but followed common scientific usage in applying the suffix "-ism" when describing a disease. He systematically classified the physiological and psychological changes attributable to excessive, long-term alcohol consumption, as described by the English physician Wilfred Batten Lewis Trotter and clinicians like the German Fuchs and the American Benjamin Rush. Rush had been among the first to describe chronic drunkenness as a disease, and one that was implicated in other diseases—including epilepsy.

Huss's work provided an international framework for analysis and diagnosis: the enemy now had a name and a symptomatology—tools that were invaluable to temperance proponents throughout Europe, despite Huss's own focus on the harmfulness of distilled alcoholic beverages and his acceptance of the naturalness of fermented ones. Huss's work also supported the general apprehension that the consequences of alcohol abuse led ineluctably to race degeneration. Such theories of alcohol-created degeneration later found their fullest expression in the mid-century clinical works of the Frenchmen Bénédict Morel and Valentin Magnan—theories that influenced Émile Zola's widely read Rougon-Macquart novels and later influenced middle-class intellectuals and reformers devoted to the temperance cause.

THE SOCIAL CONTEXT FOR CONCERNS ABOUT ALCOHOL ABUSE

The rise of medical concern about alcohol abuse was contemporaneous, or nearly so, with two major social phenomena. One was the great industrial upsurge during this period, which drew a large labor force to rapidly developing towns and cities to work in mills, foundries, and factories. Attendant on the growth of this urban labor force was a middle- and upper-class apprehension about these laborers' proclivity for strong drink. This proclivity and the working classes' relative poverty, substandard living conditions, and high levels of violence and crime constituted a witches' brew that alternately frightened and appalled polite, middle-class society from England to Russia. Although the members of society reacting to excessive alcohol consumption among the working classes were largely merchants; professionals, such as physicians, lawyers, teachers; and clergy—what has been described as civil society—and people from the privileged classes, small artisans and even industrial workers themselves also reacted to alcoholism, often associating abstinence from strong drink with self-improvement. Factory, mill, and foundry owners were also concerned about workers' proclivity to abuse alcohol, especially because agrarian patterns of alcohol use imported into the more rigid time and production constraints of industrial capitalism resulted in damaged machinery, delayed production, and general financial loss.

European intellectuals and political leaders viewed the alcohol issue in a broader social and political context. Friedrich Engels posited a direct relationship between industrial capitalism and alcoholism, attributing workers' drinking problems to the physical demands of their working conditions and the pollution of their environment by industry—in short, he argued that alcoholism was merely an epiphenomenon and that capitalism was the real culprit. Karl Marx was more than a little hostile to temperance both as a concept and as a movement. For him places such as English gin shops epitomized the essence of capitalist economic relations and were rightly the only Sunday pleasures of the people. Hence, he dismissed "economists, philanthropists, humanitarians, improvers of the condition of the working class, organizers of charity, members of societies for the prevention of cruelty to animals, *temperance fanatics,* and hole-and-corner reformers of every kind" as coteries of the bourgeoisie. Similarly, the German Social Democratic leader Karl Kautsky emphasized the importance of the tavern as a gathering place for workers to discuss politics and as a center for German workers' social network, while the Russian I. G. Pryzhov in *Istoriia kabakov v Rossii* (A history of taverns in Russia) claimed the same function for his country's drinking places. Yet Marx also decried drunkenness, along with prostitution and usury, as "the interest charged by the bourgeois against the vices of ruined capitalism." Little wonder, then, that European socialists were split into two camps over the issue: those who agreed with Kautsky, and those who followed the Belgian socialist Émile Vandervelde, who preached total abstinence as a means by which the worker could escape an unjust and exploitative system. Militant Social Democrats during Russia's prewar revolutionary period continued this latter tradition, viewing total abstinence from the coils of "the green serpent" of alcohol abuse as a form of the spartan self-denial and discipline demanded of the revolutionary vanguard.

The second social phenomenon contemporaneous with and, to some extent, intimately connected with increased medical concern was the emergence of a civil society in various European states. Developing models of the formation of middle-class attitudes, sensibilities, and awareness, modern social historians see the activity of this civil society as extending along a continuum from promotion of private-property rights and the rule of law, to movements for professionalization, to the development of a public sphere independent of the state. In short, this society constituted a network of voluntary associations that served as a major means by which the bourgeoisie attempted not only to set the tone in the material and cultural spheres but increasingly to influence public policy on a host of issues. These issues included public health, education, and penology. A civil society further implies a critical mass of educated individuals, professional societies, and cultural organizations, all of which established intermediate identities between the family

and the state. This was, then, the promotion of activity for the public good rather than for private gain, the practical and purposive activity of citizens rather than subjects.

EARLY TEMPERANCE EFFORTS

The earliest recorded temperance group in Europe was established in Sweden in 1818 as a result of the efforts of the Lutheran clergy. This temperance effort was directed against the consumption of schnapps and continued to condone the moderate consumption of wine and beer. Only later in the century did the concept of temperance divide along lines advocating moderate consumption or total abstinence, or teetotalism. This division came to characterize virtually every European temperance movement save one—the German—before World War I. The Lutheran clergy was also responsible for the earliest temperance efforts in the Russian Empire—in the Baltic provinces in the 1830s.

In England and Russia organizations less formal than the government took the lead in fostering temperance. In England parliamentary legislation attempted to combat alcohol abuse by introducing laws that would permit the freer licensing of drink shops (which, proponents believed, would end the monopolistic practices that promoted excessive alcohol consumption). Such legislative efforts were grounded in the belief that government regulation of drinking places fostered adulteration, high prices, smuggling, and drunkenness. Ending monopolies and introducing free licensing would, advocates believed, end these evils as well as eliminate the artificial attractions of drink that stemmed from government favor. The Beer Act, which capped a decade devoted to this kind of approach, thus extended the free-market principle to the sale of drink, with the anticipation that the lower price of beer under this new system would encourage Englishmen to drink it instead of gin. It was thus yet another variation of the "pure" alcoholic beverage versus distilled alcoholic beverage debate.

In Russia the same reasoning lay behind the growing criticism of the government's exploitation of the vodka tax farm (*otkup*). However, the Russian government was caught in a dilemma: it opposed efforts by the Lutheran clergy in the Baltic provinces, but at the same time its officials were concerned about increased levels of alcohol consumption—especially of the non-taxed homemade vodka *(samogon)* sold in unlicensed speakeasies *(korchmy)*. The government addressed the issue not only of abuse but of the illicit sale and consequent adulteration of vodka by studying the related issues in a series of commissions. Unlike the English, however, these bodies suggested greater official regulation of the drink trade by controlling, among other things, its location near schools and public buildings, restricting the size of licensed *kabaki,* and increasing the price of vodka to make it less affordable to the masses. France, in contradistinction to England and Russia, increased the number of officials overseeing the cafés.

MORE FORMALIZED TEMPERANCE EFFORTS

True temperance movements—that is, voluntary organizations formed by essentially private members of society—began in England and Germany only in the 1830s and 1840s, in France in the 1870s, and in Russia in the late 1880s and 1890s.

While not the first to organize temperance groups, England witnessed the most rapid development of quite diverse organizations—many of which inspired efforts in other countries. Independent societies were among the first of these groups, followed by national organizations—the National Temperance Society in 1842 (later the National Temperance League) and the British Association for the Promotion of Temperance in 1835 (later the British Temperance League). In England these organizations advocated teetotalism—a position not popular in other European states. Over the decades other groups were formed: workers' associations, fraternal temperance orders—including the Order of Good Templars (an import from the United States)—denominational temperance societies, and women's temperance associations. England also had specialized societies for, among others, soldiers and sailors—two groups that had historically been given alcoholic beverages to reward them for performance in the field or to warm and fortify them, out of a belief in alcohol's restorative and reinvigorating properties.

The English temperance model greatly influenced the development of temperance groups in Russia in the 1890s. Norman Kerr's *Inebriety: Its Etiology, Pathology, Treatment, and Jurisprudence* (1888) was one of the earliest treatises on the subject of temperance to be translated into Russian, although the works of German and French scientists and clinicians were ultimately the most widely circulated. There were significant differences of course. While there had been antialcohol protests in rural Russia in the period 1859–1861, they were directed less toward moderation or total abstinence than toward the high cost and low quality of vodka sold by tavern keepers under the *otkup.* Some of this protest was clearly anti-Semitic—

directed against Jewish tavern keepers and illicit drink sellers more often than against gentile ones.

The transition from the tax farm to an excise system in the 1880s helped stimulate a true temperance consciousness among Russian public-health physicians, lawyers, and other professionals. While on the surface directed against the new system for increasing drinking and alcohol abuse among the urban working class, much of the sentiment against the excise originated with officials and intellectuals who found introducing entrepreneurship into the drink trade an unwanted form of competition. Clerical involvement was restricted until the late 1880s due to Orthodox Church officials' disapproval of temperance efforts. With the introduction of the state vodka monopoly in 1894, however, temperance in Russia was officially recognized and significantly boosted, and the number of groups championing the cause grew exponentially. This included state-sponsored organizations—the Guardianships of Popular Sobriety.

The efforts of all these groups in Russia were similar in tone and form to those in England: basic literacy, education, skill training, entertainment, libraries, reading rooms, encouragement of tea consumption as an alternative to alcohol, and, above all, propaganda on the debilitating economic, physical, and mental consequences of alcohol consumption. The Russian movement also became fully committed to the disease model of alcoholism and advocated creating specialized institutions for the treatment instead of punishment of alcoholics. Like English and French groups, Russian temperance organizations published journals, newspapers, and pamphlets devoted to educating people on the harm of alcohol consumption. Unlike in England, church temperance organizations were held at arm's length by others in the movement, and legislative support for temperance became possible only with the third state Duma after 1907.

Germany experienced many of the same tensions as England and Russia. The early German temperance movement (1830s and 1840s) insisted on the moderate consumption of beer and wine and the avoidance of distilled liquors. But teetotalism made little headway. The German movement was characterized by the same religious and moralistic features as denominational temperance activity in England and as some local parish activity in Russia. As in England and Russia, these early groups required adherents to take a vow renouncing spirits. However, German temperance underwent a sea change after mid-century and by the mid-1880s had come, in the form of the German Association for the Prevention of Alcohol Abuse (DMVG), to emphasize a more scientific approach. This included devoting attention to the medi-

Temperance Crusaders. "Singing Hymns against Drunkenness," drawing by Émile Bayard, nineteenth century. ©BETTMANN/CORBIS

cal and treatment aspects of alcoholism and lobbying the state for changes in German licensing laws as well as for laws that would permit the legal, institutional treatment of alcohol abusers. Because of the central importance that German socialists gave to beer halls as social and political gathering places for workers, the DMVG stressed moderation only. The Good Templars did not, therefore, enjoy a warm response among German socialists.

France represents the final example of temperance in a major European state. As with most European societies, drinking in general—and the consumption of wine in particular—had traditionally been seen as a source of refreshment as well as a symbol of a bond. Hence a drink was often a means of sealing a business agreement. However, as early as the eighteenth century, the cabarets were seen as contributing to heightened levels of drunkenness and as places for idlers. As in Germany, distinctions were made between more "natural" alcoholic beverages and the stronger, physically more harmful eaux-de-vie. Added to this mix was the perception, so ably expressed by Honoré de Balzac, that the cafés selling alcoholic beverages were, in and of themselves, "parliaments of the people." Thus, following the revolutionary era, both republican and imperial French governments so feared this aspect of drinking places that they established special arms of the law to watch over them in the countryside, villages, and small towns.

As in other European countries, the increasing concern of the bourgeoisie, public-health officials, and the medical profession with alcoholism among urban workers was notable in France. Moreover, in France as elsewhere in Europe, industrialized distillation made for a deadly combination of large quantities and low prices. Thus in France, too, consumption levels increased markedly in the course of the nineteenth century. Wine was increasingly replaced by beer and cognac and, in the final quarter of the century, by the deadly absinthe. Yet for all this, not until 1872 was the first voluntary temperance organization—the Association contre l'Abus des Boissons Alcooliques—formed in France.

In the last decades of the nineteenth century French temperance groups—although few in number and small in membership compared with England—sponsored legislative efforts to control alcohol production and decrease alcoholism. The French groups, while consciously avoiding a teetotal position, sponsored the same family-oriented activities and entertainments as the British and, similar to the Russian movement, were anxious about worker housing as a causal nexus for alcohol abuse. Worker temperance organizations also enjoyed some popularity in France, indeed to a much greater extent than in Russia because in France a nationwide worker organization—the Federation of Anti-Alcohol Workers (FOA)—was formed in 1911, whereas in Russia the tsarist govern-

Absinthe. A woman carrying her child passes two men drinking absinthe. *Mother,* painting (1899) by Jules Adler (1865–1952). ©ARS, NY/Giraudon/Art Resource, NY

ment's restrictive policies in the years before World War I precluded formation of such a group.

Aside from the major nations of Europe, only Sweden attempted and, to some extent, succeeded in combating both the liquor traffic in general and the rising levels of alcohol abuse in particular through the Gothenburg System of 1865. This system involved creating limited-dividend corporations for the manufacture and sale of drink and local monopolies for the retail sale of brandies; in addition, there was a rationing of the population, and on-premise consumption of alcoholic beverages was prohibited except in eating places. Only Russia's vodka monopoly attempted to achieve some of these effects—for example, by attempting to make the state vodka shops monopolies for the sale of drink by the bottle for off-

premises consumption but allowing its consumption by the glass in first-class restaurants, some taverns, and the dining rooms of railway stations. Sweden's far-reaching efforts were not replicated in most European states, however. The Gothenburg System's major shortcoming was its inability to control the importation of spirits and the sale of beer and wine. Not until 1919 did Sweden reform the system further by attempting to eliminate private profit from every branch of the manufacture and sale of alcohol.

INTERNATIONAL TEMPERANCE EFFORTS

What pulled all of these disparate national temperance efforts together was the International Congress against

Alcoholism held in various European capitals from the 1880s up to the eve of World War I. These gatherings—increasingly teetotal in spirit and content—addressed the burning issues of the movement: alcoholism as disease; the nature, scope, and desirability of institutional centers exclusively for the treatment of alcoholism; and the regimens to be followed in such centers, including the increasingly popular use of hypnotism as a therapeutic measure. These assemblies also addressed issues such as the relation between alcohol abuse and public-health problems and social issues. Tuberculosis and epilepsy were among the myriad ailments associated directly or indirectly with alcohol abuse. Moreover, social issues such as wage levels, housing conditions, crime, and the workplace environment—including conditions in factories—also preoccupied the delegates to these gatherings.

Still, by the eve of World War I, for all these efforts, anomalies persisted. In France, for example, the continued popularity and productivity of home-made alcoholic beverages—the *bouilleurs de cru*—and in Russia the troublesome problems of home manufacture and illicit sale of home-manufactured alcoholic beverages—particularly vodka—remained unsolved. Both countries also failed to rally women to their temperance causes. In other European countries and in the United States, women were seen as the natural allies of temperance—because they had not yet acquired the bad habit of drinking and because patriarchal views held that they were either made of nobler stuff than men or less influenced by alcohol due to physical or mental inferiority. Despite the evidence from the United States and England, temperance groups in France and Russia failed to attract large numbers of women and had only a handful of women temperance leaders.

The outbreak of World War I was seen as an occasion to make a new, alcohol-free beginning. But very little action was taken to restrict access to alcoholic beverages. Except, that is, in Russia, where the tsarist government temporarily prohibited the sale of alcoholic beverages during mobilization (to avoid the drunken excesses witnessed during the Russo-Japanese War of 1904–1905, when alcohol was readily available to newly mobilized troops) and then totally prohibited the manufacture and sale of alcoholic beverages for the duration of the war. There were even intimations that this policy would be made "perpetual."

TEMPERANCE AFTER WORLD WAR I

The Russian experiment was not successful, and home brewing, cases of alcohol poisoning, and liquor riots soon appeared. Antialcohol and temperance propaganda was largely ignored and, hence, unsuccessful in both France and England as well. With the war's end, in the 1920s the state became increasingly involved in the matter of alcoholism and temperance, an approach that prevailed for the remainder of the century.

In Russia the October Revolution initially carried a promise of reform in the alcohol problems of the previous centuries by a group philosophically opposed to alcoholism on the basis of marxist theory. Not only was abstention viewed as "heroic" by many worker-Bolsheviks, but the Communist Party took the position that alcohol abuse had been an epiphenomenon of the deep-seated contradictions of capitalism. Declaring war on alcoholism as a social disease, with V. I. Lenin labeling it a plague of the petite bourgeoisie, the new Communist state announced that the proletariat would root it out through the propagation of the "Communist ideal." Thus, sweeping measures were enacted to combat and eliminate drinking: distillers were shut down; inebriates were declared subject to arrest and prosecution; the death penalty was prescribed for members of the Red Army who abused alcohol; "narcological dispensaries" were organized to treat alcoholics; and prison terms of at least ten years were mandated for the illegal manufacture of alcoholic beverages—especially *samogon*. The new government also began publishing a monthly temperance journal, *Trezvost' i kul'tura* (Sobriety and culture), to spearhead the drive for sobriety and to promote demonstrations in favor of it and the formation of temperance societies. Yet these efforts were more Potemkin villages, and the societies were never independent or effective. The narcological dispensaries in Moscow reported an increasing annual turnover of patients, leading one early Soviet alcohol researcher to calculate an alcoholism rate of thirty per one thousand population for the city and more than one million chronic alcoholics in the nation.

In the 1930s fiscal imperatives led Joseph Stalin to increase production of alcohol and to control its sale—a classic redistributive method of the tsarist period. Yet the ranks of heavy drinkers did not increase during this decade despite the stresses of urbanization, industrialization, repression, and fear. Rather, alcohol consumption—and, one must assume, alcoholism—slowed both because the standard of living could not accommodate the regular purchase of alcoholic beverages and because the loss of their agricultural products slowed the peasants' production of *samogon*. There was, too, the additional fear that "decadent behavior" such as heavy drinking could lead to incarceration or worse. The other side of the coin, however, was Stalin's wartime return to the practice of issuing a daily

TABLE 1
PER CAPITA CONSUMPTION OF SPIRITS (IN LITERS)
FOR SELECT EUROPEAN STATES, 1899–1905

	1899	1900	1901	1902	1903	1904	1905
Denmark	10.4	9.8	9.8	9.8	9.5	9.2	9.2
Finland			(Calculated as part of the Russian Empire)				
France	6.6	6.7	5.0	4.6	5.1	5.7	5.2
Germany	6.3	6.3	6.2	6.1	5.8	5.8	5.4
Sweden	6.2	6.3	6.3	5.8	5.4	5.1	5.2
United Kingdom	4.1	4.2	4.1	3.9	3.8	3.6	3.4
Norway	2.4	2.4	2.4	2.4	2.5	2.5	2.2
Russia	3.8	3.7	3.5	3.5	3.8	3.6	—*

* Data unavailable

The Encyclopaedia Britannica: A Dictionary of Arts, Sciences, Literature, and General Information. 11th ed. Vol. 26 (1911), p. 81.

ration of vodka to soldiers. But with war's end, alcohol consumption and attendant alcoholism rose in Soviet society in the 1950s, 1960s, and 1970s. One scholar of the phenomenon calculated that in the Russian Federation alone, 11.3 percent of the population aged fifteen and older were alcoholics. The data for this period produced by Western scholars were largely inferential, however, since the Soviet Union continued to regard such figures as tantamount to state secrets.

With the antialcohol campaign launched initially by Yuri Andropov and continued by Mikhail Gorbachev in the 1980s, Western scholars saw the first real public discussion of alcoholism and temperance in the Soviet Union since the 1920s. Multifaceted in its conception and calling for the creation of a state temperance society, the campaign claimed by late in the decade significant decreases in alcoholism and its associated problems. Beneath the surface, however, the manufacture of *samogon* had soared, and to avoid the state's strictures on hours of sale and quantity of bottles allowed for per capita purchase, the public had turned to strong, often poisonous substitutes, such as antifreeze and shoe polish. Consequently, this great state temperance campaign died with a whimper not too long before the collapse of the state that sponsored it.

France experienced many of the same problems as the other European nations after World War I. During the war alcohol consumption declined, but fol-

lowing the restoration of peace, production and consumption rose markedly, as did alcoholism. Indeed, the few antialcohol barriers raised during the war were removed, government intervention was discouraged, and rates of consumption and alcoholism rose steadily into the late 1930s. Temperance simply was neither popular nor economically desirable. Then, too, American Prohibition smacked too much of puritanical moralism to many Frenchmen. Only the Family Code of 1939 and its creation of the Haute Comité sur la Population represented any effort to restrict alcohol consumption.

Real declines in alcoholism in France were made possible only by World War II, which, with defeat and occupation by the Germans, ended the laissez-faire policies with respect to alcohol production and consumption. What the Vichy government started was continued in the post–World War II period by the Fourth and Fifth Republics—that is, extensive state involvement in antialcoholism and temperance. In this, it is much like—albeit more effective than—the Soviet example. Unlike the Soviet Union, however, there was a revival and extension of legitimate private antialcohol groups. The state also became convinced, through the research of Sully Ledermann, that the greater the level of alcohol consumption in a society, the greater the amount of alcohol-related harm. With the Fourth and Fifth Republics' assumption of responsibility for medical care and rational economic

TABLE 2
PER CAPITA CONSUMPTION OF ALCOHOL OF ALL VARIETIES
(IN LITERS PER CAPITA OF 100 PERCENT ALCOHOL)
FOR SELECT EUROPEAN STATES, 1990–1996

	1990	*1993*	*1994*	*1995*	*1996*
Denmark	9.8	9.9	10.0	10.1	10.3
Finland	7.8	6.8	6.6	6.4	6.3
France	12.6	12.3	11.8	11.9	12.1
Germany	11.7*	11.8	11.5	11.2	10.8
Sweden	5.8	6.0	6.1	5.7	5.2
United Kingdom	7.6	7.1	7.3	7.0	7.2
Norway	4.1	3.8	3.8	3.9	4.0
Russia	–	5.5	5.3	5.2	5.2

* Figures for the Federal Republic only
The International Order of Good Templars

planning, then, the state increasingly viewed alcoholism as a disease with both societal and economic consequences for which the state had responsibility. This approach was perfectly consonant with the social philosophy of the so-called welfare state of other European countries after 1945. Consequently, a series of enactments provided impetus for a state antialcohol campaign mandating treatment, compulsory blood tests for criminals to measure blood alcohol levels, and measures against drunk driving—many of which remained in effect in the 1990s.

Like the Soviet Union and France, Scandinavian countries involved the state in antialcohol efforts. Finland, for example, repealed prohibition in the early 1930s but established ALKO to control the production of and trade in alcoholic beverages. ALKO was also charged with operating retail stores for spirits, wine, long drinks (spirits mixed with soft drinks), and strong beer. Unlike the unrealistic U.S. goal of total prohibition, Finland, like Sweden, Denmark, and Norway, strove from 1918 to the 1990s to reduce the detrimental effects of alcohol use by steering consumption and habits in a "healthy" direction—a goal reminiscent of both the prerevolutionary tsarist alcohol policy and the Gothenburg System. Finnish municipalities, like those in Sweden, are obliged to provide services for people with substance-abuse and related problems. Moreover, many hospitals in Fin-

land have detoxification units operating as part of the national health-care system. Sweden began dealing with detoxification in the late 1940s by creating outpatient clinics for alcoholics. Both states legislated close interaction between nongovernmental organizations, municipal governments, and essentially private treatment centers in the struggle with alcoholism, with Sweden providing such services under the auspices of its Social Services Act of 1982. Sweden and Finland, like Denmark and Norway, have introduced strict limitations on alcohol advertising as part of an ongoing preventive approach.

The German flirtation with antialcoholism and temperance in the years after World War I displayed the same ambivalence as in the period before 1914. High levels of consumption and abuse characterized the Weimar years. The Great Depression had the same flattening effect on alcohol consumption and alcoholism in Germany as it did elsewhere in Europe. Further, there was no "official" antialcohol posture adopted in the period 1933–1945, despite Hitler's well-known abstemiousness—that is, with the exception of those German physicians who, mirroring the early racial degeneration temperance approaches of the nineteenth century, saw alcohol abuse as a factor undermining Aryan racial purity. The division of Germany into the German Democratic Republic and the Federal Republic of Germany from 1945 to 1990 makes generalization difficult, but alcohol consumption was the most widespread chronic disorder even after reunification. Nonetheless, several provinces set up mass-media campaigns focusing on sobriety in specific situations. But of all the European nations, Germany remained behind in both governmental and private temperance efforts at the end of the twentieth century.

Britain experimented with prohibition early in World War I, when David Lloyd George was chancellor of the exchequer, but ultimately settled for the creation of the Liquor Control Board—which closed pubs in the mornings, afternoons, and early at night, a practice that survived in attenuated form until the 1990s. Scotland, however, did introduce local option even before the outbreak of war in 1914. Despite this, a broad array of church-based and secular temperance organizations remained active into the 1920s, their efforts aided by the inevitable drop in consumption during the Great Depression. Only after 1945 and the achievement of a parliamentary majority by the Labor Party, with its wide-ranging program of welfare and public-health services, did alcoholism and measures for its treatment or eradication become concerns of the state—again, an approach perfectly consonant with other European states of the time.

Recovery from the devastation of World War II and growing prosperity in Britain produced increased levels of alcohol consumption—which approximately doubled between 1950 and 1980. This troubling phenomenon and its attendant problems sparked the creation or reorganization of government departments charged with administering health issues as well as the creation of a new organization called Alcohol Concern. Alcohol education issues were mandated to be handled through an independent body (Action on Alcohol Abuse, or AAA) under the aegis of the Royal Colleges of Medicine. (The AAA was discontinued after 1989 due to insufficient funding.) A series of acts in the 1970s and 1980s required, among other things,

mandatory licenses for shops and beverage distributors; established legal age limits for consumption; and restricted the hours for sale of alcoholic beverages. In 1990 the Portman Group, an association of alcohol manufacturers, established a "Proof of Age" card to encourage compliance with the legal age limits for the purchase of alcoholic beverages. As with other countries in the European Union, severe penalties for driving under the influence of alcohol were introduced in 1967 and 1981 (the Road Safety Act and the Transport Act, respectively). And finally, as with other European states, under the rubric of prevention a detailed set of guidelines regulated the advertising of alcoholic beverages on radio, television, and in various print and advertising media.

Although international temperance and anti-alcohol conventions were held after 1945, they had far less importance than before 1914. Uniformity of action by the European states on this issue came only in 1990 with the formation of EUROCARE-Advocacy for the Prevention of Alcohol Related Harm in Europe, an alliance of voluntary and nongovernmental organizations concerned about the impact of the European Union on alcohol policy in member states. EUROCARE maintains a Web site detailing alcohol statistics for nations in the European Union. [For statistics of alcohol consumption, see tables 1 and 2.]

With the World Health Organization's recommendations for reduction of alcohol production in various states and the European Union's insistence that potential members adopt equitable alcohol taxation policies, many of the aspects of alcohol consumption, abuse, and temperance that had been the concern of European civil society from the eighteenth through the early twentieth century appeared well on the way to standardization through state or national and even supranational efforts at the dawn of the twenty-first century.

BIBLIOGRAPHY

Books

Barr, Andrew. *Drink.* London and New York, 1995.

Barrows, Susanna, and Robin Room, eds. *Drinking: Behavior and Belief in Modern History.* Berkeley, Calif., 1991.

Chevalier, Louis. *Laboring Classes and Dangerous Classes in Paris during the First Half of the Nineteenth Century.* New York, 1973.

Christian, David. *Living Water: Vodka and Russian Society on the Eve of Emancipation.* Oxford, 1990.

Clark, Peter. *The English Alehouse: A Social History, 1200–1830.* London and New York, 1983.

Deichman, E. I. *Alkogolizm i bor'ba s nim.* Moscow and Leningrad, 1929.

Dion, Roger. *Histoire de la vigne et du vin en France des origines au XIXe siècle.* Paris, 1959.

Gordon, Ernest. *The Anti-alcohol Movement in Europe.* New York, 1913.

Haine, W. Scott. *The World of the Paris Café: Sociability among the French Working Class, 1789–1914.* Baltimore, 1996.

Harrison, Brian. *Drink and the Victorians: The Temperance Question in England, 1815–1872.* Pittsburgh, 1971.

Hayler, Guy. *Prohibition Advance in All Lands: A Study of the World-Wide Character of the Drink Question.* London, 1913.

Kassow, Samuel D., James L. West, and Edith W. Clowes. *Between Tsar and People: Educated Society and the Quest for Public Identity in Late Imperial Russia.* Princeton, N.J., 1991.

Prestwich, Patricia. *Drink and the Politics of Social Reform: Antialcoholism in France since 1870.* Palo Alto, Calif., 1988.

Pryzhov, I. G. *Istoriia kabakov v Rossii v sviazi istoriei russkogo naroda* (A history of taverns in Russia in connection with the history of the Russian people). St. Petersburg, 1868.

Shiman, Lilian Lewis. *Crusade against Drink in Victorian England.* New York, 1988.

Smith, R. E. F., and David Christian. *Bread and Salt: A Social and EconomicHistory of Food and Drink in Russia.* New York, 1984.

Sournia, Jean-Charles. *A History of Alcoholism.* Oxford, 1990.

Spode, Hasso. *Die Macht der Trunkenheit: Kultur- und Sozialgeschichte des Alkohols in Deutschland.* Opladen, Germany, 1993.

Articles

Bynum, W. F. "Alcoholism and Degeneration in 19th Century European Medicine and Psychiatry." *British Journal of Addiction* 79, no. 1 (1984): 59–70.

Hutchinson, John. "Medicine, Morality, and Social Policy in Imperial Russia: The Early Years of the Alcohol Commission." *Social History* 7, no. 14 (1974): 201–225.

Hutchinson, John. "Science, Politics, and the Alcohol Problem in Post-1905 Russia." *Slavonic and East European Review* 58, no. 2 (April 1990): 232–254.

Marrus, Michael R. "Social Drinking in the Belle Époque." *Journal of Social History* 7, no. 2 (1974): 115–141.

McCandless, Peter. " 'Curses of Civilization': Insanity and Drunkenness in Victorian Britain." *British Journal of Addiction* 79, no. 1 (1984): 49–58.

Phillips, Laura L. "Message in a Bottle: Working-Class Culture and the Struggle for Revolutionary Legitimacy, 1900–1929." *Russian Review* 56, no. 1 (1997): 25–43.

Roberts, James S. "Drink and Industrial Work Discipline in 19th Century Germany." *Journal of Social History* 15 (1981): 25–38.

Roberts, James S. "Drink and the Labor Movement: The Schnapps Boycott of 1909." In *The German Working Class, 1888–1933: The Politics of Everyday Life.* Edited by Richard J. Evans. London, 1982.

Snow, George E. "Alcoholism in the Russian Military: The Public Sphere and the Temperance Discourse, 1883–1917." *Jahrbücher für Geschichte Osteuropas* 45, no. 3 (1997): 417–431.

Snow, George E. "Change and Continuity: Alcohol and Alcoholism in Russia and the Soviet Union. A Review Essay." *Social History of Alcohol Review* 17 (1988): 7–15.

Snow, George E. "Perceptions of the Link between Alcoholism and Crime in Pre-revolutionary Russia." *Criminal Justice History* 8 (1987): 37–51.

Vallee, Bert L. "Alcohol in the Western World." *Scientific American,* June 1998, 80–85.

ORPHANS AND FOUNDLINGS

David L. Ransel

Historical research on orphans and foundlings dates to the mid-nineteenth century when large studies of municipal and regional institutions to care for them appeared. Prominent examples include Andrea Buffini's study of the Milan foundling hospital (1844) and Franz Hügel's wide-ranging report on the Austrian empire and many other parts of Europe (1863). Impressive works on national care programs for unwanted children followed in subsequent decades. Léon Lallemand surveyed the history of abandoned children in France in 1885. M. D. van Puteren did the same for Russia and also drew instructive comparisons with other parts of Europe in 1908. The authors of these and similar studies on other municipalities, regions, and countries were not professional historians, and their purpose was not so much to write history as to influence contemporary debates about the moral and practical consequences of government-assisted care of illegitimate or unwanted children. They did nevertheless compile a wealth of historical material that late-twentieth-century social historians used as a point of departure for their studies.

This new historiography of child welfare began in the 1970s with works by Olwen Hufton and Natalie Zemon Davis on the development of public services in early modern times and has continued in a series of studies on social and institutional responses to child abandonment, including the works of John Boswell on antiquity and the Middle Ages; Claude Delasselle, Rachel Fuchs, and Janet Potash on France; Richard Trexler, Philip Gavitt, David Kertzer, Volker Hunecke, and many others on Italy; Joan Sherwood on Spain; and David Ransel on Russia. Interest in this topic was stimulated initially by the French "Annales school" and its attention to demography and the processes of everyday living. The political protests of the 1960s in the United States and France intensified historians' interest in the lives of the common people and the poor. The rise of movements for women's rights and an unprecedented entry of women into the historical profession in the 1970s fueled research into the primary spheres of female activity: family, work,

childbearing, and child rearing. The study of abandoned and orphaned children offered a good vantage point from which to examine issues related to women and the family, such as survival strategies of the poor, the productive and reproductive roles of women, the value of children, the growth of municipal and state institutions for assisting women and families, administrative and policing strategies, the classification and ordering of modern urban life, and industrial production.

John Boswell's study of child abandonment from late antiquity to the Renaissance introduced the novel idea that the disposal of unwanted children in city squares, garbage dumps, and dung heaps was a mechanism for redistributing human resources and balancing out a disorderly reproductive process. Some families produced more children than they needed and by abandoning them either contributed children to others who had too few or delivered them into the hands of slavers and jobbers who could recoup the cost of rearing the children in their later use or sale. Despite Boswell's impressive command of sources, his work received criticism for its transparent moral and political aims and his failure to consider conflicting evidence. One of Boswell's aims was to convince readers that the conventional family models based upon blood or marital relations were recent impositions and not the typical family arrangement known to Western history. Another was to argue that before governments and private charities stepped in with modern technologies of categorization and exclusion such as foundling homes and orphanages, people quite naturally and logically redistributed children among themselves and that they did so with virtually no damage to the children. This libertarian notion, that in the absence of intervention by government and welfare institutions social problems are worked out to the advantage of all concerned, failed to take into account the very high toll in infant life that such an informal mechanism inevitably entailed. Indeed, Boswell contended that most of the abandoned children of antiquity survived, a conclusion that flies in the face of all that has been learned since about infant survival under such conditions. It is difficult, however, to deny Boswell's point that the institutional care of modern times, especially the foundling care programs of the eighteenth and nineteenth centuries, were likewise accompanied by an excessive infant and childhood mortality.

ABANDONMENT AND INFANTICIDE

In antiquity the decision about whether to spare the lives of children was left to the family or, more accurately, to the father. At first this power was absolute and enduring, but gradually legal restrictions narrowed its scope until a decision to dispose of a child was permitted only in the case of newborns. Not until the end of the fourth century was infanticide outlawed by the Christian church, but the practice scarcely came to end just because a law was passed. Although the church brought about this protection for children, it may initially have shown some tolerance for abandonment and infanticide so long as these acts were not an excuse for unlicensed sexual pleasure. The early church fathers distinguished between infanticide as a way of avoiding the consequences of one's lust, and infanticide for economic reasons. Penitentials proposed much lighter penalties for infanticide committed by a poor woman than for the same act committed by a wealthy woman. This stance was common in the West until at least the eleventh century.

Along with some tolerance of infanticide to keep population in line with economic resources, there may also have been some acceptance of nonmarital sexual activity in the early centuries of Christianity. But this changed in the eleventh century after the Council of Rome in 1074. The church began to stress the importance of confining sexual indulgence to marriage, an emphasis that was strengthened toward the end of the Middle Ages and carried forward even more vigorously by the Reformation. While bastards and the women who bore them were widely tolerated in the Middle Ages, after the Reformation the position of the unwed mother became increasingly isolated and precarious. She faced social ostracism and the prospect of having to turn to prostitution or other unsavory means of staying alive if she did not rid herself of her baby before its existence became known. It is impossible to say if abandonment and infanticide increased, but they became different. If they had earlier occurred with some degree of understanding from the community, they now became a desperate means of escaping communal censure. These acts became personal rather than social, and they arose from and

contributed to the mounting misogyny of Christian Europe as the Roman and Protestant churches campaigned ever more vigorously against social deviance, especially as personified in the most exposed and vulnerable women.

By the sixteenth century, states joined the churches in the crusade against extramarital intercourse and its products, the illegitimate child and infanticide. In several countries, unmarried servant women were regularly inspected to see if they had breast milk. The presence of milk in the breasts justified, according to article 36 of the Constitutio Criminalis Carolina, introduced in the Holy Roman Empire under Charles V in 1532, the application of torture to discover the cause. The even more draconian article 131 introduced a presumption of guilt for murder in cases in which an unmarried woman was alone at the time of birth, hid the baby, and the child was later found dead. This rule was subsequently written into French law in 1556 and confirmed as late as 1708. Presumption of guilt based on similar or slightly modified conditions, usually involving failure to register an extramarital pregnancy, subsequently found its way into the codes and practices of many other countries, including England in 1624, Sweden in 1627, Württemberg in 1658, Denmark in 1683, Scotland in 1690, and Bavaria as late as 1751. Punishment was harsh and usually included painful or prolonged death (being cast upon a fire or buried alive). A misogynous regime in Russia brought equally ferocious punishment, even if there matters never went so far as to fix in law a presumption of guilt for an unwed mother whose child had died.

THE FIRST FOUNDLING HOMES

While the church had led the way in campaigning against illegitimacy and infanticide, it was also the first institution to come to the aid of unmarried women and innocents. The religious orders of the Italian cities began establishing foundling homes as early as the thirteenth century, with the opening in Rome of the San Spirito hospital in 1212. (Some sources date the first such home to 787 in Milan, but little is known about this effort.) The stimulus for creating the San Spirito refuge was said to be the scandal of women throwing babies into the Tiber River. Similar hospitals soon appeared in other Italian cities. In Florence during the late thirteenth and early fourteenth centuries two hospitals, the Santa Maria da San Gallo and the Santa Maria della Scala, took in unwanted children. These multipurpose institutions also accepted poor people needing medical assistance. In time, strain on the limited resources of the hospitals led to differentiation and specialization. In the mid-fifteenth century, the city fathers collaborated with the silk guild to establish an institution dedicated to the care of foundlings, the great Ospedale degli Innocenti.

By this time, Florentines considered the work of these hospitals essential to the character and stability of their community. Failure to aid exposed and abandoned children would not only undermine their society by reducing its population, but would also erode the myths of solidarity that bound the community together in its earthly life and linked it to the heavenly city. Thus, children left to die were not considered only as a sanitation problem but as amputated limbs of the communal body and unbaptized souls lost to God. Efforts to save the children were valued as a means of drawing the community together, and the rescued children played an important role in the salvation of the community because of the blessings that their prayers were thought to bring to the city.

During the late Middle Ages and the Renaissance the Italians worked out an approach to foundling care that relied on large institutions supported by a combination of religious, corporate, and municipal resources. Usually the infants brought to the institution were screened and sent out to wet nurses in the town or more often the surrounding countryside. Eventually the survivors returned for education at the institution, and finally were assigned to apprenticeship, military service, menial labor, or marriage. This approach, known as the Latin or Catholic system, moved across the Alps into France and Austria, where in the sixteenth century humanist writers stressed the need for organized relief and other public welfare measures to curb increasing problems of urban disorder. Begging and vagrancy were their major concerns, but humanist values also promoted a new solicitude for poor children. For the smallest and most helpless, the abandoned and exposed babies, many towns provided foundling homes on the Italian model. For poor or unsupervised children who had survived early childhood, towns established institutions for their care and training in line with the humanist belief in education as an instrument for making good citizens.

France offers the best example of the development of the Latin system north of the Alps. A multipurpose hospital, the Grand Hôtel-Dieu de Notre-Dame-de-Pitié in Lyon was taking in children as early as the beginning of the sixteenth century. Marseille and Paris may have provided such assistance earlier still. By 1536 the state began to play a role. Francis I opened a hospital in Paris designed exclusively for the care of foundlings and named it the Hospice des

The Turning Cradle. The *rota* (modern Italian *ruota*, wheel) was a revolving cradle built into the outer wall of the Ospedale degli Innocenti (foundling hospital) in Florence. Parents could abandon their child anonymously by placing it in the cradle, which would then be turned by a member of the Ospedale staff, bringing the infant inside the building. Installed in 1660, the *rota* was removed in 1875. Engraving, nineteenth century. ©BETTMANN/CORBIS

Enfants-Dieu. An important contributor to this work in the next century was the clergyman Vincent, later St. Vincent de Paul, who devoted much of his life to caring for abandoned children. With the help of the Dames de la Charité (Ladies of Charity), he opened the Hôpital des Enfants Trouvés in Paris in the 1630s. Within a few decades this institution was having difficulty managing its growing population of foundlings, difficulties that arose even before the great explosion of illegitimacy and child abandonment in the eighteenth century.

THE EIGHTEENTH CENTURY

By early in the eighteenth century, the sight of infant corpses lying in ditches, on garbage heaps, and in sewer drains was familiar throughout Europe. Sewers, being less visible, were evidently the most frequent points of deposit. After a fire that devastated Rennes, France, in 1721, workers rebuilding the city opened the sewers and found the skeletons of over eighty babies. Even in the 1690s the slaughter had been disturbing enough that the crown ordered municipalities to use their local Hôtel-Dieu as a receiving point for abandoned children. But many localities were not able to shoulder the cost of caring for foundlings, and when the burden on local institutions became too heavy, they discouraged admissions. People responded by bringing their unwanted children to the Paris hospital, often over long distances, because the Paris home had support from the crown and accepted nearly everyone. By the mid-eighteenth century, a brisk trade had sprung up between the provinces and the capital, as people paid carters to convey babies to the Paris foundling home. Some local welfare facilities even organized their own expeditions to deliver abandoned children to the Paris institution.

During the eighteenth century, public opinion was swinging away from the punitive approach to the unwed mother. Concerned with population growth, enlightenment writers fostered a new understanding of her plight and encouraged a revolt against the ferocious penalties that had been visited upon her. In the sentimental literature of the age, unwed mothers were portrayed as victims as often as were their children. The public was persuaded that both the children and the mothers had a better chance of surviving if the mothers could anonymously dispose of their babies, and a consensus formed in favor of an open admissions policy like that of the central Paris foundling home. This policy was usually symbolized by the turning cradle, a device that allowed a woman to deposit her baby unseen at the door of the home by rotating a cradle that pivoted between the outside and the inside of the building. First used in Italian foundling homes, the device spread to other Roman Catholic and even some eastern Orthodox lands by the late eighteenth and early nineteenth centuries.

For much of Europe the use of the turning cradle was limited to the time of the Enlightenment revolt against persecution of unwed mothers. It was most often found and remained longest in strongly Catholic lands, with their strict norms against premarital sex and opposition to paternity searches in cases of illegitimacy. Conservative Catholic authorities defended the turning cradle as much for its role in protecting the honor and sanctity of the family as for preventing desperate women from killing their infants. By concealing the identity of unwed mothers, the device shielded families from scandal and from the property claims of illegitimate offspring. Communal solidarity required protection of family interests in places where the family formed the essential building block of society. The country in which families most effectively dominated social and political life, the kingdom of Sicily, was also the quintessential home of the turning cradle. By law, every town in the kingdom had to erect a foundling home with this device and keep it open day and night. The turning cradle was common in other Mediterranean lands and their dependencies. Spain and Portugal supported homes

with the devices throughout their metropolitan provinces and also exported them to their American colonies. To the east, the turning cradle appeared in Orthodox lands of the Balkans and was instituted in Russia by Catherine the Great as early as 1764 and maintained right into the 1890s, later than in any other country.

Something different happened in the north and northwestern parts of Europe. During the Renaissance, foundling homes on the Italian model had reached as far north as many of the German cities, but they did not endure there. The retreat of the sponsoring Roman Catholic institutions after the Reformation partly explains this. Although some writers believe that the Protestant emphasis on personal rather than communal responsibility was also a major factor, this emphasis may only have reinforced a preexisting family system and moral climate. Even in Catholic principalities of Germany, cities soon turned away from large central foundling hospitals and sought to lay the cost of support for illegitimate children on the parents. In contrast to Latin Europe, paternity searches were legal in the north, and families were expected to maintain control over their members and not look to the community to care for the products of misbehavior.

Later, responding to the humanitarian revolt of the eighteenth century and the new sympathy for unwed mothers, some northern cities erected large foundling hospitals and allowed anonymous admission. In Denmark, for example, such an institution was established in the middle of the eighteenth century when a turning cradle was attached to the Copenhagen workhouse. Institutions in London and Stockholm provided the same opportunity. But, as had happened farther south, this open admissions policy soon generated a deluge of children, including the importation of unwanted infants from outlying areas, and in the case of Denmark, even from a foreign country, Sweden, across the sound. In 1774 the Danes replaced the turning cradle with a system requiring unwed mothers to rear their own children, if necessary with financial assistance from the community. England and Sweden soon turned away from large centralized foundling operations for the same reasons. So, once again, as in the Renaissance, this type of institution proved short-lived in the north. England, the Nordic countries, and much of Germany henceforth provided homes and training only for true orphans or other children for whom no one could be found to take responsibility. Homes of this type were supported either by municipal governments or civic and religious organizations such as the Free Masons and Pietists. Orphans were usually brought up to about age eight

In an Orphanage. *The Orphans,* painting (1879) by George Adolphus Storey (1834–1919). FORBES MAGAZINE COLLECTION, NEW YORK/THE BRIDGEMAN ART LIBRARY

and then turned over to masters as apprentices or servants.

In the north, the structure of financing the care of unwanted children and the values that underlay this structure differed from those in the Catholic Mediterranean lands and in Russia. In England and the continental Protestant countries, the cost of foundling care was borne directly by the community or its immediate representatives and was not cushioned by large private endowments, self-generated revenues from associated enterprises, or church and central government subsidies. Accordingly, in Protestant lands, ratepayers or their representatives imposed limits on the amount of money available for this service and forced tighter admissions policies. Underlying this approach to public welfare were the strength in Protestant countries of corporate bodies other than the family and no doubt, too, the emphasis on personal rather than community responsibility. The disclosure of illegitimacy and the assignment of responsibility for it were lesser threats to community solidarity in these lands than were its concealment and the laying of its cost upon the public. Since the Reformation, the temporal powers had taken a greater role in enforcing social norms, and the family, which was less crucial to maintaining social discipline than was the case in the south, required less protection from the disorderly behavior of its members.

THE NINETEENTH CENTURY

Between the wholly Catholic lands to the south and the Protestant-dominated polities to the north stood France and Belgium, whose experience revealed an ambivalence about the application of the two prevailing systems of foundling care. The turning cradle came late to these lands and then briefly swept all other systems aside. Before the nineteenth century, foundling care was a local matter, and the large area encompassed by Belgium and France subsumed a variety of value systems and corresponding diversity of responses to child abandonment. Methods in Flanders and Brittany resembled those in Protestant lands. In Flanders, the parish alone bore responsibility for abandoned infants or illegitimate children whom parents could not support; in Brittany, a subdivision similar to the parish, *the générale des habitants,* played the same role. Unlike other jurisdictions in France and Belgium, these two permitted, even demanded, paternity suits so that the father could be made to support his illegitimate child and relieve the parish of the burden.

Morals in Brittany were severe and illegitimacy low. But, by the same token, nearly all unwed mothers sought to escape shame by abandoning their infants. In the factory areas of northeastern France, illegitimacy was judged less harshly, its incidence was higher

501

than in Brittany, and a smaller proportion of women abandoned their children. There people were more likely to condemn an unwed mother for abandoning her child than for keeping it, especially after the initiation of aid for unwed mothers in the middle of the nineteenth century. This attitude contrasted sharply with the moral climate of southern France, which in its concern for family honor and solidarity was more like that in the neighboring Mediterranean lands. Despite these varied value systems, both the adoption of the turning cradle early in the nineteenth century and its removal after 1840 occurred as a single process throughout France and Belgium, an example of the universalizing effects of the French Revolution. In 1811, in order to fulfill the promise of the Revolution to care for all illegitimate children, the national government ordered foundling shelters everywhere to use the turning cradle. But it soon became clear that this decision complicated rather than facilitated the goal of caring for illegitimate children, since the system of anonymous admissions led to the deposit not just of illegitimate children but also a burgeoning number of legitimate children and soon exhausted the resources intended for the care of the illegitimate. Moreover, many abuses were discovered. Married women would contrive to abandon their babies to the foundling hospital and then receive back their own children as nurslings. For this wet nursing and fosterage of their own children they obtained a regular subsidy and eventually a pension. Although the authorities tried to counter this fraud by transporting children deposited in one province to another for nursing and fosterage, this solution simply led to a skyrocketing death rate among the children. The French soon declared the system of blind admissions a failure, and by midcentury the turning cradle was rapidly being phased out and replaced by a system that identified and excluded legitimate children and provided financial assistance to needy unwed mothers to rear their own children.

Although Catholic conservative opinion continued to argue for the turning cradle on the grounds that its abolition would increase infanticide, cause scandal in the family and community, and entrust the rearing of children to women of demonstrated immorality, the move away from institutional care and toward a modern welfare system of individual subsidies proceeded apace. The Belgians adopted the French reform within a few years and returned to the methods in use earlier in Flanders. Others soon followed. Spain began to phase out anonymous admissions in the 1850s, and Portugal did so between 1867 and 1871. In Italy, the birthplace of the turning cradle, the process began about the same time, and by 1878 only one-third of the Italian homes continued to operate with the devices.

In Russia the change did not come until the 1890s, a tardiness associated with the peculiar history of the Russian imperial foundling homes. Catherine the Great, a German princess by birth, and her education adviser, Ivan Betskoi, a man who had spent many years in western Europe, established these institutions, which in time became the largest in all of Europe. The Russian foundling homes were consciously designed on the most progressive Western models and constituted another aspect of the country's rapid, self-conscious westernization in the eighteenth century. Founded at the height of the humanitarian revolt against the persecution of unwed mothers, they enjoyed the most liberal admissions policy on the continent. Children were accepted at all hours with no questions asked. At first, admissions were even artificially stimulated by advertisement of the homes. The reasons for this liberality were two. First, Catherine and Betskoi hoped not merely to save illegitimate children but also to build from them an educated urban artisan and service class, "a third rank of people," as they said, a social estate that Russia then lacked. Second, the homes, constructed on a lavish scale in the heart of the Moscow and St. Petersburg, were intended to serve as symbols of tsarist solicitude for the common people.

Not surprisingly, the homes were soon swamped with unwanted infants. At their peak in the mid-nineteenth century, admissions at the Moscow home alone surpassed seventeen thousand children a year. The hope of building an urban estate from these children quickly faded, because even the much smaller numbers entering the facility in the late eighteenth century could not be kept alive in urban institutions and had to be turned over to wet nurses in the countryside for care and feeding. Local fosterage saved some children, but even so mortality rates ran as high as 85 percent. When the English reformer Thomas Malthus visited Russia in 1789 in connection with a survey of foundling hospitals throughout Europe, he assessed the mortality at the Russian homes and quickly punctured the rosy public image of this tsarist philanthropy. He remarked dryly that "if a person wished to check population, and were not solicitous about the means, he could not propose a more effectual measure, than the establishment of a sufficient number of foundling hospitals [like these], unlimited in their reception of children" (quoted in Ransel, p. 58). The symbolic importance of the Russian homes as the most visible and well-financed tsarist charity nevertheless remained and caused difficulties for reform. Modifications in the admissions policy were introduced now and again, in particular at the time of the great reforms of the 1860s and 1870s, but fundamental reform did not take place until 1892, and the homes continued to operate right up to the Bolshevik revolution.

PUBLIC STANDARDS FOR PERSONAL DECISIONS

The arguments for reform of the open admissions policies in southern Europe, France, and Russia were based on an understanding of the rapidly changing social terrain of the countries in which the turning cradle was used. Critics acknowledged that in the past the family had been the key to social discipline and needed protection from property claims and from the implied loss of control that illegitimacy signaled. The turning cradle had afforded the required secrecy. But, the critics continued, the family had changed, individuals had become less dependent on the family and less loyal to it. In these circumstances, the turning cradle acted more as an assault on the family than a protection, since it permitted married couples to turn their children into wards of the state. As for unwed mothers, it was far better, contended opponents of the turning cradle, to oblige them to declare themselves so that they could benefit from the financial assistance, professional guidance, and encouragement that would persuade them to keep their children. In these arguments one sees the emergence of a central idea of modern social-work intervention: the imposition of public standards on personal decisions about the size and character of families. It led directly to what Jacques Donzelot called the "policing of families," for if subsidies were to be furnished to women who were not only poor but also regarded as immoral, then the same program would have to be extended to other more deserving women such as widows with children, mothers of large families, and working mothers. In short, according to Donzelot, the reform of foundling policy planted the seed of the modern family allowance and the state surveillance that accompanied it.

The advent of the welfare state, government subsidies, and fosterage of unwanted children ended the era of the large-scale institutionalization of unwanted children in western and central Europe. In the twentieth century, children's homes continued to operate in most large cities, providing care for children who could not be placed with families and helping to manage periodic surges in the orphan population that resulted from war and other calamities. The Armenian massacres of 1915 spawned tens of thousands of orphans, who were placed in homes in Russian Armenia

Orphans in Bucharest, Romania, 1990. REUTERS/MIKE FISHER/ARCHIVE PHOTOS

and Greece. The number of children orphaned and abandoned during the Spanish civil war reportedly ran to ninety thousand. World War II is thought to have produced a staggering thirteen million abandoned and orphaned children. As many as a half million were artificially manufactured by a Nazi policy of kidnapping children from occupied countries and Germanizing them so that they could be turned into loyal instruments of state policy (the Lebensborn program).

In Eastern Europe the socialist regimes established in Russia in 1917 and elsewhere after World War II introduced welfare measures to protect mothers and children. Even so, on occasion, the number of abandoned and runaway children reached catastrophic proportions, as in Soviet Russia following the civil war and famine of the early 1920s. Estimates of the number of "unsupervised children" in Russia in those days range between four and seven million. This crisis was scarcely brought under control when a new wave of orphans appeared in the wake of the brutal campaign to collectivize agriculture and the devastating famine that followed in the early 1930s. World War II produced another generation of orphaned children in Russia, and in the late twentieth century, as a result of the political and economic collapse of the Soviet Union, the numbers again mounted into the hundreds of thousands. Romania, where abortion and contraception were banned under the dictatorship of Nicolae Ceauşescu (ruled 1974–1989), maintained a large and miserably cared for orphan population that became an unfortunate legacy for the regimes that followed. The Balkan wars of the 1990s produced a new stream of East European refugees, including a substantial new orphan population.

In sum, the very different approaches to child abandonment that characterized the southern and northern regions of Europe from the Reformation to the end of the nineteenth century ultimately resolved themselves in a welfare system that provided subsidies to mothers to care for their own children or, in the case of true orphans, opportunities for fosterage, adoption, and, in infrequent cases, institutional care. Russia and some other countries of eastern Europe, despite public commitments to provide full welfare services and protection for mothers and children, failed to deliver on these promises for a number of reasons: lack of sufficient prosperity to support such services, choices to invest in heavy industry and military goods rather than social services, and periodic political and economic crises.

See also **Childrearing and Childhood; Concubinage and Illegitimacy** *(in this volume); and other articles in this section.*

BIBLIOGRAPHY

Books

Ball, Alan M. *And Now My Soul Is Hardened: Abandoned Children in Soviet Russia, 1918–1930.* Berkeley, Calif., 1994.

Boswell, John. *The Kindness of Strangers: The Abandonment of Children in Western Europe from Late Antiquity to the Renaissance.* New York, 1988.

Buffini, P. Andrea. *Ragionamenti storici economico-statistici e morali intorno all'ospizio dei trovatelli in Milano.* Parts 1 and 2. Milan, 1844–1845.

Donzelot, Jacques. *The Policing of Families.* Translated by Robert Hurley. New York, 1979.

Fuchs, Rachel. *Abandoned Children: Foundlings and Child Welfare in Nineteenth-Century France.* Albany, N.Y., 1984.

Gavitt, Philip. *Charity and Children in Renaissance Florence: The Ospedale degli Innocenti, 1410–1536.* Ann Arbor, Mich., 1990.

Hufton, Olwen. *The Poor of Eighteenth-Century France, 1750–1789.* Oxford, 1974.

Hügel, Franz Seraph. *Die Findelhäuser und das Findelwesen Europa's: ihre Geschichte, Gesetzgebung, Verwaltung, Statistik, und Reform.* Vienna, 1863.

Hunecke, Volker. *Die Findelkinder von Mailand: Kindesaussetzung und aussetzende Eltern vom 17. Bis zum 19. Jahrhundert.* Stuttgart, Germany, 1987.

Lallemand, Léon. *Histoire des enfants abandonnés et délaissés.* Paris, 1885.

Nichols, Reginald H., and Francis A. Wray. *History of the Foundling Hospital.* London, 1935.

Puteren, M. D. van. *Istoricheskii obzor prizreniia vnebrachnykh detei i podkidyshei i nastoiashchee polozhenie etogo dela v Rossii i drugikh stranakh* (A historical survey of the care of illegitimate and abandoned children and the current status of such care in Russia and other countries). St. Petersburg, Russia, 1908.

Ransel, David L. *Mothers of Misery: Child Abandonment in Russia.* Princeton, N.J., 1988.

Sherwood, Joan. *Poverty in Eighteenth-century Spain: The Women and Children of the Inclusa.* Toronto, 1988.

Utterström, Gustaf. *Fattig och föräldralös i Stockholm på 1600- och 1700-talen.* (The poor and parentless in Stockholm during the seventeenth and eighteenth centuries) Umeå, Sweden, 1978.

Werner, Oscar Helmuth. *The Unmarried Mother in German Literature, with Special Reference to the Period 1770–1800.* New York, 1917.

Edited Collections

Enfance abandonnée et société en Europe XIVe–XXe siècle. Rome, 1991. A collection of forty-six articles, mainly in Italian and French, on all regions of Europe where foundling institutions operated.

Mayer-Koy, Josef, ed. *Neudeutsche Findelhäuser.* Munich, 1920. Collection of writings and materials on infanticide and foundling homes. Though edited by a person wishing to establish foundling homes in Bavaria, it includes materials representing other points of view.

Dissertation

Potash, Janet Ruth. "The Foundling Problem in France, 1800–1869: Child Abandonment in Lille and Lyon." Ph.D. Dissertation, Yale University, 1979.

Journal Articles

Delasselle, Claude. "Les enfants abandonnés à Paris au XVIIIe siècle." *Annales: économies, sociétés, civilisations* 30 (1975):187–217.

Kertzer, David I. "Gender Ideology and Infant Abandonment in Nineteenth-Century Italy." *Journal of Interdisciplinary History* 22 (1991):1–25.

Kertzer, David I., Heather Koball, and Michael J. White. "Growing Up as an Abandoned Child in Nineteenth-Century Italy." *The History of the Family: An International Quarterly* 2 (1997):211–228.

Tilly, Louise, Rachel G. Fuchs, David I. Kertzer, and David L. Ransel. "Child Abandonment in European History: A Symposium." *Journal of Family History* 17 (1992):1–23.

Trexler, Richard. "Foundlings of Florence, 1395–1455." *History of Childhood Quarterly* 1 (1973):259–284.

DEVELOPMENTAL AND PHYSICAL DISABILITIES: THE "BLIND," "DEAF AND DUMB," AND "IDIOT"

David Wright

Physically and developmentally disabled individuals occupied the fringe of modern social history. They represented to contemporaries the margins of society, and have been treated by historians accordingly. Individuals with disabilities come into view only to illuminate the pious endeavors of clerics, the revolutionary experiments of medical men, the unselfish generosity of philanthropists, or the pioneering work of educational theorists. Too often, individuals with disabilities are cast as grateful recipients of alms or helpless victims of the historical drama of industrialization—important not for the social reality that they experienced but rather for the advances that "civilised" society has achieved.

PERSPECTIVES ON DISABILITY

The recent emergence of disability studies in academic circles has helped to promote a gradual, if slow, appreciation of disability as a legitimate area of inquiry. Yet despite recent interest, huge gaps in our knowledge remain. Historians are too often faced with the stock character of the medieval "blind beggar," the ubiquitous "village idiot," or the lamentable "deaf and dumb" child. To compensate, some disability researchers overemphasize the great "self-emancipators" who achieved success "despite their disability" or, like John Milton, *during* their disablement. Little is known of the great mass of individuals who did not conform to these unrepresentative portraits, individuals who carried out quotidian lives in their local communities.

We also know relatively little about the demography of disability in past time. On the one hand, some researchers suggest that, lacking the intervention of modern medical techniques, disability in the early modern period would have been more common than it is today. Developmental disability (through neonatal complications or lead poisoning) and physical disability (such as smallpox-induced blindness) could have contributed to an overabundance of disability in previous centuries. On the other hand, the bare sub-

sistence level at which most people existed might have meant that the life expectancy of those with disabilities was significantly lower than that of the general population. Child abandonment, or even infanticide, of disabled offspring should not be discounted. This may have depressed the numbers of disabled people in past time. Lastly, there may well have been epochs in which certain types of physical disability would have been particularly relevant, such as during and immediately after the great European wars of the nineteenth and twentieth centuries.

The importance disability gained in popular and elite cultures has also ebbed and flowed over the last four centuries. The ideas of the Enlightenment—with its emphasis on the improvability of humankind—directed sustained attention on the moral and ontological status of disabilities. Disabled children in particular became the subject of novel experiments in education, as new medical and philosophical belief systems interacted and informed each other. The disabled become the objects of experimentation and segregation, important as the antithesis of the self-sufficient, educated, physically perfect modern citizen. Disabilities therefore should not be seen as a constant in either an epidemiological or conceptual sense, but as heavily dependent during certain epochs on transformations in society, culture, the economy, and medical science.

Histories of disability place great emphasis on the "backwardness" of premodern attitudes to the "blind," the "deaf and dumb," and the "idiot." However, it is not clear the degree to which poor agricultural communities would have considered, say, deafness as something that, by its very nature, isolated afflicted individuals from their social surroundings. By contrast, the dramatic transformation of European society during the modern era—from local economies dependent primarily upon small-scale agricultural production and local kinship ties to a more impersonal wage-driven industrial society of factories and urbanization—must have boded ill for those who, by the new definition of efficiency, could not compete as effectively as the newly defined "able-bodied." Certain social and economic changes may thus have made certain conditions more "disabling" than they had previously been. Thus, portraying the history of disability as a great upward march from ignorant superstition and social isolation to enlightened scientific medicine and integration is wholly inadequate. The history of disability must be approached with a consideration of the ambiguities of human actions and social change.

This article will summarize the social history of disability in modern Europe. It will draw upon recent historiography to explore the transformation of social welfare, the educational revolution regarding children with disabilities, the medicalization of disability, and the emergence of disability rights. It will look in particular at three disabilities as defined by contemporary society, namely the "blind," the "deaf and dumb," and the "idiot." Contemporary terminology will be used in order to bear witness to popular methods of describing disability in past time. Language tells us a great deal about the understanding of disability. Rather than trying to erase these terms from collective historical memory, we should address the issues they raise and seek to understand why we no longer consider them acceptable in a current context.

DISABILITY AND THE EARLY MODERN STATE

States in early modern Europe have a long history of regulating the property of, and providing relief to, individuals who were incapable of governing their own affairs due to a permanent disability of mind or body. European statutes regarding "idiots"—those defined as having permanent mental infirmity to the extent that they could not govern their own affairs—date back to the thirteenth century, providing ward status for such individuals and setting out the means by which their property would be managed. "Idiots" were recognized as separate and distinct from "lunatics," individuals who had temporarily lost their reason but could still have lucid intervals. This simple distinction between idiots and lunatics reappears repeatedly in legislation governing mental disorder throughout the early modern period and continues in current usage in the differentiation between the developmentally disabled and the mentally ill.

As European states began to organize social relief during the early modern period, other categories of disability and dependency began to appear on the registers of churches, parishes, and towns. Under the Elizabethan Poor Laws, for instance, parishes in England and Wales were responsible for providing relief

to their destitute poor, regardless of the cause. The terms "blind" and "deaf and dumb" were widely used by magistrates and overseers of the poor adjudicating on cases of families petitioning for relief in the seventeenth and eighteenth centuries. Overseers of the poor and local magistrates in the England were experienced, if not enthusiastic, in dealing with cases of disability and adopted local solutions to resolve situations in which family and kin care had broken down. In such situations of household crisis, some parishes paid allowances to families to continue caring for dependent relatives within the home; others hired nonrelated individuals to care for disabled individuals in other households, a system known as "boarding-out." In countries across Europe, Catholic orders took on many of the responsibilities that had been subsumed by civil parishes in Protestant regions. Clergy considered ministering to the disabled as a sign of Christian piety; parables from the Bible describing Jesus tending to the "lame," the "blind," and the "deaf and dumb" provided moral guidance to those who dedicated themselves to the church. Indeed, many churches ran "hospitals" with a changing, and poorly defined, clientele of the sick, the aged, and the disabled.

Religious denominations in Spain experimented with the first organized system of teaching the "deaf and dumb" to communicate. A sixteenth-century Benedictine monk named Pedro Ponce de León adapted for use with the deaf his monastery's system of communicating by signs and gestures. He did this because the deaf were being prevented from joining the priesthood because of an inability to speak. Such restrictions of religious and civil rights of those with disabilities were widespread within Europe at this time. Thus the new techniques championed by Ponce de León and others became important to the propertied and clerical classes. It is probably accurate to say, however, that apart from the aristocracy, local informal traditions of nonverbal communication persisted alongside new techniques formalized by individuals such as Ponce de León. Fragmentary evidence of travel diaries in early modern Europe, for example, describe encounters with "deaf-mutes" who functioned perfectly well within their communities.

Over the course of the eighteenth century, more secularized institutions were increasingly complementing religious provision. In France, the power and wealth of the monarchy enabled successive sovereigns to establish large medical institutions for their disabled and sick poor, such as the Salpêtrière and Bicêtre hospitals in Paris. Creating hospitals for the sick poor was both a means of signifying the wealth of nation-states and a vehicle for engendering popular sympathy for the benevolent dictatorship of autocrats. In response to the growing commercialization of society, there was also an emerging for-profit sector in the eighteenth century, where lay and medical proprietors operated small homes for disabled members of the prospering middle classes, although the extent of the private sector caring seems to have differed dramatically between regions. The impact of the Enlightenment, however, and the growing wealth of most western European countries provided the basis for emerging charities and educational institutions dedicated to teaching and training the disabled.

EDUCATION AND SPECIAL INSTITUTIONS

The second half of the eighteenth century witnessed an explosion of interest in the teaching of disabled children. Jacob Rodriquez Pereire, a Portuguese teacher who emigrated to France, refined techniques for teaching "deaf-mutes" to speak. He gained notoriety teaching children of the French nobility, launching the audist tradition of instruction (placing emphasis on lipreading and the spoken word). In 1760 Louis XV subsidized the establishment of a school for "deaf-mutes," the Institution Nationale des Sourds-Muets (National Institution for Deaf-Mutes) in Paris. In 1776 the French Abbé de L'Épée published a book on the instruction of "deaf-mutes" by "methodological signs," the other dominant tradition of communication now known as signing, or sign language, which he had used at another famous Parisian school, the Institut National de Jeunes Sourds (National Institution for Deaf Youth). Schools for "deaf-mutes" were also opened in Germany and Scotland in the 1760s and the 1770s as the ideas of the Enlightenment spread throughout the educated elite of Europe. Much competition subsequently arose over the presumed advantages and disadvantages of the two competing systems of deaf communication.

Experimentation was also taking place in the education of the "blind." Valentin Haüy opened the Institution Nationale des Jeunes Aveugles (National Institution for Blind Youth) in Paris in 1784. He pioneered the use of embossed print and promoted the education of blind children, as outlined in his *Essai sur l'education des aveugles.* Encouraged by Diderot's famous *Lettres sur les aveugles à l'usage de ceux qui voient* (Letter on the blind for the use of those who see; 1749), Haüy refined the practice of reading embossed characters, each representing individual letters. After the Revolution, Haüy migrated eastward, establishing a school in Berlin before settling in Russia. Simultaneously, similarly minded groups, some in-

spired by the French example, others emerging independently, established schools for the blind, in Liverpool (1791), Vienna (1804), Berlin (1806), Milan (1807), Holland (1808), Prague (1808), Stockholm (1808), St. Petersburg (1809), and Zurich (1809), Copenhagen (1811), Denmark (1811), Aberdeen (1812), Dublin (1816), and Barcelona (1820).

At approximately the same time, Francesco Lana-Terzi's *Prodromo,* an Italian treatise delineating symbols of lines and dots representing letters of the alphabet, was published in French. Lana's treatise suggested that the characters could be embossed for blind students, a system that was eventually adopted and refined by the French army as a means of reading coded messages in the dark. An officer, Charles Barbier, sent his system to the French National Institution for Deaf-Mutes for use in teaching. One young adult student, Louis Braille, refined the system of embossed dots into simple two-by-three matrices. It was only one of many different systems in use, but its flexibility and simplicity quickly ensured that the Braille method would succeed as the most important system of reading, being endorsed as the approved European method by the end of the nineteenth century.

The establishment of state or philanthropic institutions for the "blind" and the "deaf and dumb" provided an impetus for the creation of a professional medical discourse on the treatment and training of the developmentally disabled. Shortly before Haüy escaped revolutionary France, Jean-Marc-Gaspard Itard, a physician at the Institution Nationale des Sourds-Muets, commenced educational experiments on hearing acquisition and speech formation. As a young physician, he had been brought a mute boy, captured running wild in the woods. Philippe Pinel, the famous psychiatrist who had "unchained" the lunatics at the Salpêtrière Hospital, declared the boy an "incurable idiot." Itard, we are informed, rejected the pessimism of Pinel and sought to "elevate the boy from savagery to civilization." Although Itard largely failed in his endeavor to render Victor (as the boy was sometimes called) "civilized," he did manage to teach him to identify letters and interpret simple words.

The philosophical and social implications of Itard's experiment, published in *De l'éducation d'un homme sauvage* (Paris, 1801), were widely circulated by the French Academy of Science and influenced similar experimentation in the large French hospitals, particularly by a handful of French physicians associated with the Salpêtrière and Bicêtre hospitals. In 1837 Edouard Séguin, a student of Itard, experimented with the training of idiot children using "physiological" and "psychological" methods. At the Hospice des Incurables and at the Bicêtre he claimed

The Braille Method. A student at Henshaw's Institute for the Blind at Old Trafford, Lancashire, England, learns to use a Stainsby frame to write braille, 1954. ©HULTON-DEUTSCH COLLECTION/CORBIS

that he achieved success in training "idiot children" to speak, write, and count. In 1841 he published the first of several treatises on the treatment and education of "idiots," most of which were eventually translated into English and German. The mantra that the "idiot could be educated" reverberated across the European medical and philosophical communities.

The apparent success of Itard and Séguin influenced a young Swiss medical student, Jacob Guggenbühl, who had become interested in "cretins." Frustrated by the lack of educational initiatives for their education and treatment, Guggenbühl persuaded the Swiss Association for the Advancement of Science to fund a demographic study of the prevalence of cretinism in his own country. His numerical findings, combined with his enthusiasm for the French school of training and education, sufficiently impressed the Swiss Association that they agreed to subsidize the construction of a small retreat. Guggenbühl built this institution on the side of Abendberg Mountain, in the miasmatic belief that the "odors" and bad air of the Swiss swamps were part of the reason for the high rate of Swiss cretinism. Thus by the 1830s French and Swiss physicians challenged the "irreversability" and "ineducability" of idiocy and associated forms of developmental disability.

Despite the attention being paid to the training of "idiots," "deaf-mutes," and the "blind" at national institutions, local authorities across Europe were not rushing to establish residential schools at taxpayers' expense. Rather, the concern for public order which had been heightened by urbanization and migration prompted the construction of local institutions for "lunatics" throughout the nineteenth century. Medical superintendents of public asylums were overwhelmed by admissions of individuals with a wide range of physical and mental disabilities. A significant minority of admissions to these new mental hospitals were "idiots" and the "deaf and dumb." The pressure of numbers in state asylums, combined with the growing awareness of educational efforts with the disabled, gradually persuaded charitable organizations and civic institutions to establish specialist hospitals for the "blind" and "deaf and dumb," and asylums for idiots across Europe throughout the latter half of the nineteenth century. Institutionalization, however, was not a foregone conclusion, as class, gender, household structure, occupational background, and geographical location dictated the type of accommodation and support those with disability might receive outside the home.

The construction of teaching and residential institutions for disabled individuals provided subjects for the generation of new medical discourses on the etiology and pathophysiology of developmental and physical disability and led to the advent of new inventions for better diagnosis. Hermann Ludwig Ferdinand von Helmholtz invented the ophthalmoscope in 1850, providing more accurate means of observing and measuring pathological processes of the eye. Thereafter followed the invention of the retinoscope, the slit lamp, and other diagnostic tools for eye examination. The utilization of anesthesia and antisepsis in the mid-Victorian period paved the way for later corrective ear and eye operations, such as cataract surgery. Specialist "eye" and "ear, nose, and throat" hospitals were created in the latter half of the nineteenth century as physicians and scientists incorporated rapidly advancing knowledge in cell biology, physiology, anatomy, and bacteriology. Medical specialization also occurred in the area of psychological medicine, as asylum superintendents proposed increasingly detailed lists of mental ages and psychiatric classifications. As medical ideas gained prominence in most western European societies, a new biologically based discourse of disability crept into popular discussion and social policy in the last decades of the nineteenth and first decades of the twentieth centuries; this would pro-

Jacob Guggenbühl. NATIONAL LIBRARY OF MEDICINE

foundly change attitudes to, and the conditions and treatment of, those with disabilities.

RACIAL HYGIENE

Although the establishment of institutions for the disabled was precipitated and encouraged by great intellectual optimism, this sanguine outlook had changed by the end of the nineteenth century. Several factors account for a new popular and professional belief in the relationship between disability and what was then known as "degenerationism." First, urban middle classes in many European countries were beginning to fear an allegedly uncontrollable and physically stunted lumpen proletariat. Second, there was a growing awareness of hereditarian influence in the pathogenesis of diseases, and many commentators felt that mental backwardness and physical disability resulted from a degenerative "taint" passed down through families. With the proliferation of Darwin's views on natural selection, medical treatises and social commentaries increasingly incorporated hereditarianism into their medical explanations of disease etiologies. Societies were conceptualized as competing with each other for survival, what is now known as "social darwinism." Third, national government statistics seemed to suggest a dramatic increase in the numbers of disabled individuals, those deemed the least "fit" of society, while alerting the public to the decline in fertility of the "successful" members of the new middle class. Alarmist commentators suggested that such a differential fertility rate between the "worst" and the "fittest" of society would inevitably lead to social or "race" degeneration. The ideology that formed the basis for the national eugenics movements of the early twentieth century was thus based upon a revolution in intellectual thought, a transformation in the medical understanding of disease, the growing confidence of doctors to become involved in public policy, and the heightened tensions of arms races between industrialized countries.

The advent of national elementary education in Western countries in the last three decades of the nineteenth century also contributed to the heightened fear of the multiplication of individuals with physical and developmental disabilities. Children who had previously been outside the public view were brought into state classrooms and soon caused problems for school officials. Although the Scottish Education Act of 1872 made provision for the education of blind along with seeing children in public schools, teachers in most other European countries complained that children with disabilities disrupted the proper envi-

Alfred Binet. NATIONAL LIBRARY OF MEDICINE

ronment for teaching, and education authorities soon agreed to erect separate day or residential schools for the training of children whose disabilities were considered incompatible with regular teaching. Hence local elementary state schools for the "blind," "deaf," and developmentally disabled arose at the turn of the twentieth century and dominated education provision for "handicapped" children for the next eighty years.

Decisions over who were "mentally deficient" and who were not, prompted educators to debate the boundaries between the mentally "normal" and the mentally "subnormal." Charged with a desire for more "accurate" and quantitative measurement of social phenomena, medical practitioners sought measures to quantify "mental subnormality." The most famous of these were devised by the French lawyer Theodore Simon and his psychiatrist student Alfred Binet, whose names were given to the first standardized mental test developed at the Sorbonne between 1900 and 1905. The Simon-Binet test was supplanted in 1915 by the intelligence quotient (IQ), a mathematical score ranked on a normal distribution curve. The IQ test purported to give medical doctors and educationalists a finer instrument for discriminating between and among populations of children. From then onward, vague social categories, such as "idiot,"

"imbecile," "moron," "feebleminded," and "backward" were associated with numerical equivalents and increased scientific legitimacy.

Armed with new and apparently more accurate measurements of intelligence, with social surveys purporting to show the link between hereditary mental disability and crime, and with the fear over the differential fertility rate, eugenics movements emerged within intellectual circles in most European countries during the first three decades of the twentieth century. Borrowing their name from Francis Galton's term for "well-born," eugenicists actively encouraged the state to promote what they termed "racial hygiene" through selective breeding. Although national movements took on different characteristics, the common elements were a belief in the hereditarian nature of disability, the close association of mental disability with other social evils, and the belief that the disabled were "breeding" at a rate outstripping more "fit" elements of society. Public policy became centered on the needs of society to segregate and control the "feebleminded" and other disabled individuals. Moreover, campaigns began in many countries to forcibly sterilize disabled women who were thought to be "at risk" of breeding further "degenerates" and to restrict the fertility of disabled individuals who were thought to be likely to pass on their disability to future generations.

In Nazi Germany, the confluence of eugenics, a highly racialized polity, and the heightened extremism of war-torn Europe led first to segregation and later to the sterilization and, ultimately, the murder of thousands of disabled individuals. The 1933 Sterilization Act attempted to advance the cause of racial hygiene by instituting the mandatory sterilization of all people with disabilities linked to heredity, including deafness, "mental deficiency," and blindness. The execution of "mentally deficient," physically disabled, and elderly individuals in hospitals constituted the first, and sometimes forgotten, wave in the Nazi "Final Solution." Although precise figures are difficult to determine, well over a hundred thousand developmentally and physically disabled children and adults were executed by firing squad or gassed in the concentration camps in Germany and Poland between 1940 and 1945. Rather than seeing the extermination of the disabled as a horrific but unique act, it is more sensible to see it as the most extreme consequence of a new professional and popular collectivist discourse on disability that was shared across Western society.

POSTWAR DEVELOPMENTS

Despite the experience of the Holocaust, many of the interwar policies of segregation and sterilization continued in European countries for decades after the end of the war. Institutions for the "mentally deficient" grew to enormous proportions in the 1950s and 1960s, housing many patients from early childhood until death. Many European countries, particularly the Scandinavian nations, continued to have policies of "voluntary" sterilization and "euthanasia," whereby parents could take their handicapped children to undergo surgery, or where disabled children were not giving life-sustaining treatment due to their disability. The emergence of prenatal screening techniques, such as amniocentesis, permitted family practitioners and obstetricians to counsel parents to terminate pregnancies in the cases of fetuses with genetic abnormalities, such as Down's syndrome. These decisions made about selective procreation, which might have decreased the overall number of those children born with severe disabilities, were counterbalanced by medical and public-health changes that led to increasing life expectancy of those born with disabilities and, by the 1980s, to the survival of significantly premature babies who have developed severe mental and physical disabilities later in life.

Meanwhile residential schools continued to evolve throughout the period 1945 to 1970 into separate communities distinct from and independent of society. Starting from the very beginning of the twentieth

century, schools for the "blind" and schools for the "deaf" built additional "sheltered workshops" where the pupils (many of them adults) could work at trades and offset the costs to their families and to the state. A widely accepted public discourse prevailed whereby separate institutions, most often residential, were considered better for the disabled individual and better for the family. Disability became a condition requiring removal from general society into specialized institutions.

This dominant attitude was challenged during the 1960s, when civil-rights movements in North America and Europe addressed the status of social groups marginalized by gender, race, language, or disability. Wolf Wolfensberger, among others, articulated a set of policies, broadly known as the ideology of "normalization," which sought to place the disabled in a "culturally normative" set of social roles and experiences. The focus of his critique was a set of residential facilities and educational policies that sought to segregate the disabled from society, ostensibly for their own benefit. Normalization, by contrast, sought to eliminate special schools and residential facilities and reintegrate the disabled into society. The last three decades of the twentieth century were dominated by the debate over "streaming" versus "destreaming." Gradually many large, long-stay institutions for the

Schools for the Deaf. A student at the Maud Maxfield School for the Deaf, Sheffield, England, is taught to speak, 1950s. ©HULTON-DEUTSCH COLLECTION/CORBIS

"mentally retarded," for the "blind," and for the "deaf" have been closed, or dramatically reduced in size, and replaced by integration in "normal" schools and by accommodation in smaller group homes.

The language used to describe certain types of disability has also changed dramatically. Advocacy groups have argued that older terms such as "the mentally deficient," "the blind," and "deaf and dumb" (and their continental linguistic equivalents) stigmatize the individual concerned and influence negatively the social options open to them. Many groups advocate placing people first, hence *people* with disabilities, *people* with developmental handicaps. Others have gone further by arguing for the absence of any disability descriptor and for emphasizing the plurality of abilities which all individuals share. This view has been particularly pronounced in the field of hearing impairment, where some researchers challenge the conceptual framework of deafness as a disability, preferring to see people with hearing and speech impairment as communicating in a visual rather than auditory world. The debate over the role of language in the labeling of individuals and in their possible stigmatization continues to rage throughout society and government.

Just as the language describing disability has changed, so too has the composition of that group of individuals seen or labeled as disabled. The demographic revolution in European countries over the last two centuries, from young societies under siege from infectious diseases to older societies suffering from chronic ailments, has altered the stereotypes of disability. Impairments of hearing, sight, and cognitive functioning are becoming more and more common among an increasingly numerous population of the elderly. In the public mind, a disabled person is more and more likely to be old, rather than the disabled child typical of Enlightenment discourse. Moreover, disability is no longer viewed as an either/or proposition (someone is either blind or not). Advocacy groups emphasize that disability constitutes a spectrum of impairment.

Most recently, disability rights groups have called for access (on all levels) to social programs and activities, with some success. The physical infrastructure of society has been gradually transformed by wheelchair ramps, braille lettering on elevators, and a thousand other minor but important alterations making government and leisure services accessible to those who previously could not use them. Such changes have been hard-won. Advocacy groups have taken their campaign for disability rights to legal as well as political remedies. The European Court, with its own declaration of rights to which all European Union nations are bound, has acted as a vehicle against overt and subtle discrimination against people with disabilities.

CONCLUSIONS

The social history of people with disabilities has thus been one of profound ambiguities and contradictions, of real and Pyrrhic victories. Nor has the experience been uniform across different types of disability. Economic changes in European countries toward an "information-based society" pose fewest problems for the hearing impaired and more for the visually impaired. Recent closures of long-stay residential institutions for individuals with hearing or visual impairment have proved successful—less so for the severely developmentally disabled. The emergence in the last two decades of the twentieth century of a culture of extended work hours, a renewed emphasis on individual responsibility and self-sufficiency, and the fragmentation of the nuclear household has left many developmentally disabled individuals alone in the community and as devalued by society as ever. Accommodating the needs and aspirations of people with disabilities in the postinstitutional era remains one of the most demanding challenges facing modern European societies.

See also Section 17, **Body and Mind** *(volume 4); and other articles in this section.*

BIBLIOGRAPHY

Covey, Herbert C. *Social Perceptions of People with Disabilities in History.* Springfield, Ill., 1998.

Fischer, Renate, and Harlan Lane, eds. *Looking Back: A Reader on the History of Deaf Communities and Their Sign Language.* Hamburg, Germany, and Washington, D.C., 1993.

Lowenfeld, Bertold. *The Changing Status of the Blind: From Segregation to Integration.* Springfield, Ill., 1975.

Scheerenberger, R. C. *A History of Mental Retardation.* Baltimore, 1983.

Van Cleve, John Vickery, ed. *Deaf History Unveiled: Interpretations from the New Scholarship.* Washington, D.C., 1993.

Wright, David, and Anne Digby, eds. *From Idiocy to Mental Deficiency: Historical Perspectives on People with Learning Disabilities.* London, 1996.

PUBLIC HEALTH

Dorothy Porter

The health of populations helps to reveal transformations in social and economic conditions and highlights the changing relationships between the state and civil society. At one time the history of public health was written by public health professionals who wrote administrative histories of preventive health services and of the control of epidemic diseases. This historiographical tradition often traced a chronology of events from ancient to contemporary times, identifying the development of public health as a progressive achievement representing a triumph of rational knowledge over superstitious ignorance. In the late twentieth century, however, the history of public health was investigated by social historians, who explored the cultural significance of epidemics, the impact of disease upon demographic structure and economic change, and the role that protecting population health has played in state formation. Social histories of public health have also revealed the political and ideological conflicts created by collective actions aimed at improving the health of populations. This essay will examine the impact of such actions upon the changing social, political, and cultural relations of European societies from late medieval times, when Europe experienced one of its most devastating pandemics, the Black Death.

THE PLAGUE AND EPIDEMIC CONTROL

As the historian Paul Slack has pointed out, epidemics share many characteristics with other natural catastrophes like earthquakes and tidal waves. But the responses provoked by each vary widely. While all natural catastrophes disrupt social order, they attack the basis of social cohesion in different ways. Epidemic diseases not only cause widespread mortality that affects economic production and the defense capacities of societies, they also impose social stigma and alienation upon individual victims. The enduring metaphor of the social death of medieval leprosy sufferers, who were ordered to be segregated from the rest of

society by the Third Lateran Council in 1179, continued to haunt the world of the infectious and chronically sick. Collective actions taken to limit the impact of epidemics therefore risk heightening social tension as much as they manage it.

The disease that eliminated up to a third of Europe's population in the fourteenth century, commonly referred to as the Black Death, is much disputed by contemporary historians. The traditional view that the Black Death was an epidemic of bubonic plague does not fit easily with the pattern and rapidity of the spread of the disease between 1348 and 1353 or some of the contemporary accounts of victims' symptoms. Some historians have therefore attributed the epidemic to other rapid killers such as anthrax. Whatever the organic origin of the disease, the Black Death affected European societies dramatically. Not only did it thin out social and political elites, it also devastated the agricultural laboring population, creating opportunities for social and economic mobility that severely weakened an already fracturing feudal system based upon rigid hierarchies and tied labor. Epidemic visitations of plague continued over the next three hundred years. New civil administrative structures to deal with plague were created in Renaissance and early modern Italian city-states that became models for public health administration throughout Europe.

The Black Death stimulated the first application of what became the favored method of epidemic control by early modern states, quarantine. Venice first closed its port to all suspected vessels for thirty days in March 1348. The period was extended to forty days, and quarantine was eventually adopted by all European port authorities to prevent the importation of numerous infectious diseases. Political authorities also adapted the system to isolate inland communities by enforcing military cordon sanitaires to prevent diseased travelers and goods from entering cities or fleeing from them. In premodern times, the most rational response to an infectious disease like plague was to flee an infected location, and this was resorted to by many who had the resources to do so. Political authorities anxious to maintain existing ruling structures tried to limit the hemorrhage of both the powerful and the productive classes. Reduction of ruling elites could create opportunities for social rebellion, especially as epidemics stimulated panic. Thus, from the time of the Black Death, Italian city-states set up special health boards to institute measures to control the spread of the disease by controlling the movements of both sick and healthy populations.

As outbreaks of plague continued after 1348, civil policing to suppress panic and disquiet grew incrementally throughout Europe during the Renaissance and the early modern period. Local civil authorities sometimes taxed those wishing to flee and posted guards to protect the property of the absent. Elaborate regulations were developed in order to control the behavior of the urban poor, whose swelling numbers were viewed as an increasing risk to social stability. The poor and the socially deviant were perceived as the prime victims and bearers of plague. Political authorities in Italian city-states recognized that economic deprivation, social deviance, and plague were a potentially volatile cocktail. Health regulations targeted the movements of the morally outcast, such as prostitutes, "ruffians," and beggars, as well as the plague-sick poor. Measures were also taken to separate the sick from the healthy through the establishment of isolation hospitals, often outside city walls. While health authorities justified their actions as necessary steps to prevent the spread of plague, their primary goal was maintaining social stability by controlling the mobility of the anarchic, unpredictable underclass. For similar reasons, the English central state in the sixteenth and seventeenth centuries reproduced many Italian plague controls. Here house arrest and isolation of victims' families were adopted in order to keep people in their place at moments of crisis in the same way as the Elizabethan Poor Law enforced local settlement when communities faced periods of economic failure and shortage. The English plague regulations, however, stimulated violent opposition and thereby contributed to increasing disorder.

Plague controls brought civil authorities into conflict with the interests of other ruling elites. Quarantine greatly interfered with trade and was vigorously resisted by merchants and their laborers, who were both adversely affected. Such tensions increased throughout the early modern period. By the seventeenth century the power and prestige of many Italian city health boards grew to the point where they were able to challenge the authority of the church. Festivals, religious assemblies, processions, and other public gatherings were often banned in epidemic times despite the strong opposition of the clergy. Health authorities justified their actions on the basis of experience. For the church, plague was the result of divine wrath that could be assuaged only by penance and observance. For health officials the divine origin was less significant than the miasmas that spread the disease along with the anarchy that it threatened to provoke.

SYPHILIS AND STIGMATIZATION

If plague prevention instituted new levels of political intervention into civil life, epidemic syphilis in the fifteenth and sixteenth centuries highlighted the consequences of stigmatization for disease sufferers. In the Renaissance and early modern world fears of social disorder were matched by the dread of the moral corruption that could result from disease. In the late fifteenth century the disease that came to be identified as *morbus gallicus* (French disease) was believed to be a new contagion. Numerous contemporary observers wrote accounts of a new epidemic pox appearing in Italy in 1495 following Charles VIII's campaign against the Spaniards for control of Naples. His army, which consisted largely of mercenaries from Belgium, Germany, southern France, Italy, and Spain, was believed to have spread the disease as it disbanded and soldiers returned to their homelands. Within a decade of the first outbreak noted at Fornovo, epidemic syphilis had spread throughout Europe. The stigma of syphilis is reflected in the way that national cultures frequently identified it as the disease of their enemy, but it was most commonly referred to as *morbus gallicus.*

The *morbus gallicus* was recognized to be spread venereally. Christian ideology accounted for it as divine retribution for licentiousness, but contemporaries such as Joseph Grunpeck also attributed it to astrological sources. From the sixteenth century the American origin of the disease was the source of much controversy and remains so even today. Isolation of sufferers was attempted by some authorities, the syphilitic being subjected to stigmatization similar to lepers in medieval times. Stricter controls were instituted against beggars and vagrants in France, where old leper houses were converted into accommodations for "incorrigible paupers." The hôtel-Dieu (city hospital) overflowed with émigré pox victims in the 1520s, who were provided with money to return home. In France inspection and stricter regulation of prostitutes was established from 1500. In Edinburgh in 1497 the city council required patients sick of the "gradgor" to be removed to the island of Inch until they were completely cured. Anyone resisting the

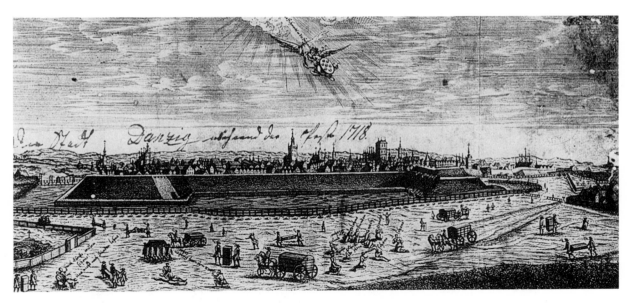

Bringing Out the Dead. View of Danzig showing people praying and removing victims of the plague, 1718. NATIONAL LIBRARY OF MEDICINE, BETHESDA, MARYLAND

regulations faced the penalty of complete exile and the branding iron.

Changing attitudes toward sexual practices were already evident in Renaissance societies. The late medieval tradition of the steam bath, which had been part of a cult of pleasure rather than an instrument of cleanliness or hygiene, began to decline in the sixteenth century. Many famous hotels offering the steam bath as a main attraction disappeared throughout Europe. The custom of visiting the steam bath to conduct a discrete liaison or simply to enjoy free and easy frolicking among naked men and women also began to decline. The pleasure dome of the steam bath became a target of the guardians of public morals, but their decline coincided with the rise of epidemic syphilis. The epidemic significantly affected changing attitudes toward libertine pleasure, adding caution to the justification for new codes of moral discipline. The aims of public authorities to control syphilitic contagion were assisted by broader changes in cultural beliefs and social behavior regarding the pursuit of pleasure. What may not have been successfully achieved through coercive public policy was perhaps accomplished through new moral ideologies.

THE SOCIAL SCIENCE OF HEALTH IN THE EARLY MODERN PERIOD

As plague retreated from Europe from the late seventeenth century, geographical exploration, urban development, and imperial expansion created new disease patterns in the eighteenth and nineteenth centuries. Epidemic diseases of isolated communities became endemic in urban environments. By the eighteenth century shock invasions were replaced by rising levels of endemic infections and chronic sickness that occasionally became epidemic, such as malaria, smallpox, and gout. The absence of catastrophic disasters meant that emergency disease control was no longer a priority. Instead, the age of the Enlightenment became a period in which a new interest in the social scientific analysis of the health of populations developed. The eighteenth century also witnessed innovations in sanitation and immunization, and late Enlightenment thought made new connections between social improvement and environmental reform. By the nineteenth century the Enlightenment study of political arithmetic and human longevity evolved into the statistical enumeration of human misery and the social physics of human improvement. The Enlightenment pursuit of happiness through a felicific calculus translated into a social science of amelioration (investigations undertaken by voluntary researchers and social reformers into the social conditions of economic depravation and destitution that were aimed at informing social policies of improvement) in the nineteenth century that was inherently bound to the improvement of population health. ("Political arithmetic" is the term used by the seventeenth-century English man of letters William Petty to describe his quantitative analysis of what he called the political anatomy of Ireland; Petty believed that the quantita-

Immunization. Free vaccination at Paris, 1890, photogravure by J. Scalbert. In the courtyard
an attendant extracts the cowpox virus from a cow. NATIONAL LIBRARY OF MEDICINE,
BETHESDA, MARYLAND

tive analysis of the strength of the state—including
the analysis of the health of the population, levels of
production and "market research" into the sale of individual commodities—should become a general form
of enquiry called political arithmetic. "Social physics"
is the term given by the early nineteenth-century Belgian astronomer Lambert Adolphe Jacques Quételet
to the quantitative analysis of social conditions, including the health of the population, using the statistical concept of the normal frequency distribution.
"Felicific calculus" is the term given by the late eigh-
teenth- and early nineteenth-century English political
philosopher Jeremy Bentham to the analysis of the
greatest happiness of the greatest number as the
founding principle on which to base utilitarian philosophy of government.)

The relationship between the health and wealth
of nations was extensively explored in political, economic, and social theory in the eighteenth century.
The development of what the French ideologue Con-
dorcet called "social mathematics" was highly significant in the development of the relationship between
the emergent modern state and the health of its subjects. Various methods of counting the subjects of the
state and measuring its size and strength in terms of
their number and their health were introduced in the

early modern period. These practices were supported
by the political philosophy of mercantilism, which
viewed the monarch's subjects as his paternalistic
property and equated the entire well-being of society
as coterminous with the well-being of the state as embodied by the sovereign. The political bookkeeping
that enabled the state to measure its strength in terms
of the size of its healthy population guided its administrative goals and objectives.

These were the early foundations of "vital statistics" and epidemiology that, by the nineteenth century,
became a prerequisite for systematic disease prevention.
Lambert Adolphe Jacques Quételet (1796–1874), a
Belgian astronomer who devised the theory of the
normal frequency distribution curve, took up the
quantitative analysis of social physics in the early nineteenth century. A generation younger than Condor-
cet, Quételet believed that social physics could provide the basis of the scientific management of society.

In France in the early nineteenth century, the
application of social physics did not lead to social reform. Instead, it created a new academic inquiry into
the conditions that determine health and disease, an
inquiry that founded the nineteenth-century European science of hygiene. An ex-army surgeon, Louis
René Villermé, who was a friend of Quételet, trans-

lated social physics into elaborate studies of the differential mortality of the rich and poor and the health conditions of the proletariat and their average expectation of life. However, these studies did not stimulate political action. Villermé warned against the involvement of the state in health reform and suggested instead that the remoralization of the poor would eliminate epidemic disease and premature mortality.

In Britain the "geography of health" was examined as part of the discovery of the social conditions of the poor. Statistics was embraced as a tool for measuring social inequality by early Victorian reform movements. Statistical studies of health and the social determinants of disease were set up in response to the shocking effects of the cholera epidemics of the 1830s and 1840s, and subsequently Victorian epidemiology sought to eliminate the spread of disease by destroying the environment that bred it.

HEALTH AND THE MODERN STATE

The early modern state linked the investigation of population health to political strength through a mercantilist philosophy. This philosophy also inspired Enlightenment public health promotion through methods of "medical police" developed in Prussia and Sweden and explored theoretically, above all, by the Austrian court physician Johan Peter Frank. Public health featured prominently in the rhetoric of revolutionary democracy at the end of the eighteenth century, both in the newly established American republic and in the declarations of the revolutionary governments in France. The French revolutionaries declared health, like work, to be a right of man, making it an obligation of the social contract between the modern democratic state and its citizens. By the middle of the nineteenth century, the British state had translated this principle into a civil right, in which all possessed equal rights under the law to protection from epidemic disease. In 1848 French and German revolutionaries identified the key to improved population health to be the establishment of "state medicine." In France Jules Guérin, in the *Gazette médicale de Paris*, and in Prussia Rudolf Virchow, in his reports on typhus in Upper Silesia, both suggested that democratic freedom, universal education, and social amelioration would prevent epidemic diseases. In France and Prussia supporters of social medicine urged the medical profession to take on a political role and become attorneys to the poor and statesmen in disguise.

The political role of preventive medicine within the modern state became an urgent material as well as an ideological issue as exponential rises in epidemic and endemic infections among urbanized populations accompanied the process of industrialization in European societies. The diseases of industrial, urbanized civilization were those transmitted relentlessly among overcrowded populations living in appalling insanitary slums with totally inadequate refuse and sewage removal, drainage, and little or no access to uncontaminated water. Typhus, typhoid, amoebic diarrhea, tuberculosis, diphtheria, and, despite the introduction of smallpox vaccination throughout Europe, smallpox continued to haunt industrialized as well as agricultural populations. But perhaps the disease that conjures up the classic image of industrial society under siege from contagion is cholera. Asiatic cholera followed troop movements out of India through eastern, central, and western Europe between 1830 and 1832 and became the first of several pandemic invasions. Overall, cholera killed far fewer than endemic fevers, but the social psychological effect of the suddenness of its invasion and the speed and manner in which it killed was dramatic. Cholera highlighted the tenuous social stability of the class structures of European societies. Conspiracy theories were rife among the European proletariat and peasantry. Rioters in Russia attacked nobles and officials because they believed that the water was being poisoned as part of a Malthusian effort to reduce surplus population. The homes of noblemen and the offices of health authorities were ransacked throughout Prussia, and officials were murdered in Paris. In Britain Bristol's poor rioted in protest against the removal of the sick to isolation wards, believing that this was a means of providing the medical profession with bodies to anatomize.

Cholera coincided with crisis in nineteenth-century Europe, but often conditions were made ripe for its spread by social upheaval. Cholera was spread by social dislocation—the mobility of population created by the expansion of trade in the nineteenth century, which brought rural populations into the cities—and subsequently exacerbated it. This pattern of social dislocation and epidemic spread is equally demonstrated for another acute infection characteristic of the times, typhus. Typhus has a long history of being associated with war and famine, frequently flourishing in military encampments and jails, but it became almost endemic among some urban populations during the nineteenth century.

Sanitary reform developed at different rates in European states throughout the nineteenth century. By the end of the century most major European cities had sewage and drainage infrastructures and improved water supplies. Most northern European states established various types of local and, in some cases, central government health authorities who monitored health

Measures against Cholera. *Cholerapräservativmannes,* a man taking precautions against cholera. Engraving, 1832. CULVER PICTURES

conditions and administered a wide range of public health regulations. Some city administrations, such as the Paris Health Council, became models for national governments. Other cities avoided the costs of public health imperatives as long as possible. When cholera attacked Hamburg in 1892, long after it had retreated elsewhere in Europe, the city-state paid a political price for neglecting to filter its water systems by being taken over by Prussian administration. Incremental environmental sanitary reform throughout Europe in the nineteenth century slowly reduced the effects of lethal infections. While historians and historical demographers continue to dispute the determinants of population growth, increased protection from the environmental hazards of industrial urbanization continue to figure prominently in assessments of mortality decline by the turn of the twentieth century. Historical epidemiologists still consider the reduction of infant amoebic diarrhea through cleaner, filtered water supplies to have played a significant role in that decline.

Providing for the health of communities, however, could lead the modern state to sacrifice the civil liberties of individuals. Movements developed in mid-nineteenth century Britain, France, and Germany opposing compulsory smallpox vaccination as tyranny rather than salvation. Acts passed by the British state establishing the compulsory inspection of prostitutes in garrison towns in the 1860s were opposed on similar political grounds. In the 1870s and 1880s the campaign to repeal the Contagious Diseases Acts in Brit-

ain interpreted the enforcement of health as a gross violation of civil liberties by a centralized power exercising a form of medical despotism and a double moral standard. By the end of the century, however, the Notification of Infectious Disease Acts in Britain interned those sick of a listed infection in an isolation hospital until they either recovered or not, but they provoked no libertarian opposition or alarm.

The civil disorder stimulated by state action during the cholera epidemics throughout Europe in the early nineteenth century was not repeated at the end of the century as modern democratic states made more and more interventions into the socioeconomic and biological lives of citizens. In industrialized and modernizing European states, a new political ethos of collectivism encouraged the development of compulsory social insurance schemes to protect workers from injury, sickness, unemployment, and old age. Population health policies began to incorporate medical services to vulnerable groups, including mothers, infants, school children, and the mentally retarded. In the twentieth century, obtaining population health was no longer limited to the prevention of disease but began to include public provision to cover the costs of medical services along with new strategies for encouraging individuals to adopt healthy lifestyles.

HEALTH CARE SYSTEMS IN THE TWENTIETH CENTURY

The twentieth century witnessed the incremental growth of comprehensive, state-funded public health and medical services throughout Europe. In the interwar years a preliminary model welfare state with integrated health and medical services developed in Weimar Germany. Between 1919 and 1933 the Weimar Republic viewed the economy as an organism that could be managed by the state, which would redistribute wealth through welfare benefits. Weimar welfare facilitated the socialization of health and prioritized the goals of the social hygiene movement, focusing on the prevention of chronic disease, the health of mothers and children, and the treatment of psychiatric disorders.

The development of health services under Weimar was motivated by organisist, collectivist social ideology that included beliefs in regenerationist biology. Eugenic ideals about the need to plan population development were compatible with ideals of collective responsibility for welfare in numerous other European contexts during the same period. Demographic and eugenic concerns led to new directions in health and social policy in Scandinavia, Britain, and France. On

Measures against Polio. First injections of polio vaccine, Hendon clinic, England, 6 May 1956. ©HULTON GETTY/LIAISON AGENCY

the one hand, prioritizing the health of mothers, infants, and children and encouraging large families was legitimated as protecting the health of future generations and ensuring demographic balance. Pronatalism was promoted in Sweden and France following World War I. In Scandinavia, Belgium, France, and Germany various forms of family allowance were developed to ease the economic burdens of parenthood. On the other hand, preventing the reproduction of the eugenically "unfit" through restrictive marriage laws, the segregation of the mentally retarded and mentally ill, and the voluntary or compulsory sterilization of various social groups was aimed at reducing the potential for biological and racial decline.

Positive and negative eugenics in Europe before World War II was one expression of the increasingly influential ideology of social planning. The corporate management of capitalist economies based upon the ideas of John Maynard Keynes gained legitimacy in European states as the failures of unregulated markets threatened the survival of industrial capitalism. A comprehensive, integrated system of health and medical services for workers and their dependents was one of the linchpins of the vision of the welfare state outlined by the British liberal intellectual William Beveridge, whose 1942 report influenced the development of health and social security policies throughout Europe following the war.

According to the social policy theorist Gosta Esping-Andersen, three "worlds" of welfare emerged after World War II that relied on more or less bureaucratically administered state funding, voluntary and compulsory insurance, and market mechanisms. A significant division developed between the generous insurance-based social security systems that operated in parts of continental Europe and the lower level of insurance plus tax-funded, means-tested state benefits that operated in Britain. Further divisions occurred between universal statutory insurance-based systems constructed in Europe and the private insurance plus means-tested welfare provision that operated in the United States.

Within these broad frameworks different rates of welfare expansion continued for the first three decades following 1945, until international economic crises in the 1970s ended what has been eulogized as a "golden era" of political consensus, economic growth, rising living standards, and social justice. While the viability of the welfare state was increasingly challenged in the 1980s, comprehensive health coverage has been the most politically resilient of its features. In the 1980s New Right assaults on what it viewed as the culture of dependency produced by "nanny states" sought only to reform rather than remove state-funded health care systems. The continued popularity of state-funded health care perhaps ema-

Norwegian Anti-Smoking Poster. MINISTRY OF HEALTH, NORWAY/NATIONAL LIBRARY OF MEDICINE, BETHESDA, MARYLAND

nated from the fact that, as the left wing British economist Julian Le Grand pointed out in 1982, the middle classes benefited from them most.

HEALTH CARE AND INDIVIDUAL BEHAVIOR

While the public provision of health care continued to be politically popular in the 1990s, fears concerning the demographic structures of twenty-first-century postindustrial societies support a culture of personal health responsibility that had been promoted by the state and commercialized by the marketplace throughout the twentieth century. As state medicine throughout Europe became involved in the provision of personal services, new emphasis was placed upon individual prevention through the development of healthy lifestyles. In the interwar years new perspectives on preventive medicine were developed in the Soviet Union, Germany, Belgium, and Britain that attempted to make clinical medicine a social practice through the interdisciplinary amalgamation of medi-

cine and social science. Following World War II social medicine focused upon prevention through public education about health hazards to the individual. A precedent was set in the health education campaign aimed at reducing lung cancer through the prevention of cigarette smoking.

The antismoking campaign in Europe exemplified the new message of the clinical model of social medicine: the key to the social management of chronic illnesses—such as lung cancer—was individual prevention, fostered by raising health consciousness and promoting self-health care. While antismoking has achieved a degree of success in Europe, it has had much greater influence in North American societies. However, the model of prevention through individual education gathered momentum in the wake of the antismoking campaign. Subsequent postwar campaigns offered lifestyle methods for preventing heart disease, various forms of cancer, liver disease, digestive disorders, venereal disease, and obesity.

In 1981 T. Hirayama published the results of a study that demonstrated that nonsmoking wives of heavy smokers had a higher risk of contracting lung cancer than did the wives of nonsmokers. The campaign to prevent "passive smoking" subsequently took on the character of a nineteenth-century campaign to prevent infectious disease. Like all such public health campaigns, the collective benefit of state action penalized and stigmatized a specific social group, whose members were represented as social pariahs and failures and moral inferiors.

The mixed messages involved in the prevention of tobacco consumption have been fully represented in the campaigns against a new lethal infectious virus appearing in the early 1980s, human immunodeficiency virus (HIV), which leads to a fatal syndrome commonly referred to as AIDS. The emergence of a new killer infection in the early 1980s reawakened all the public health concerns associated with an earlier era. AIDS was initially compared to dramatic historical invasions of the past such as plague and cholera. The initial impact of AIDS upon popular, political, and expert perceptions raised familiar issues regarding the right of the state to police and regulate the spread of infection through surveillance, notification, screening, and quarantine. Those who favored authoritarian intervention called for the institution of compulsory testing, identity cards for people who were HIV-positive, and their isolation. Most of these goals were not taken up by national policymakers, but the question of identity cards came close to realization in some local contexts, such as Bavaria.

By the late 1980s its transmission through needle-sharing among impoverished intravenous drug users meant that AIDS was spread more and more by poverty and social despair rather than unprotected sexual intercourse. The length of time between contracting the HIV virus, the onset of the AIDS syndrome, and the death of the sufferer lengthened as more effective therapeutic treatment slowed the physiological progress of the disease. Thus by the 1990s AIDS began to be perceived as a chronic disease among minority high-risk groups rather than an epidemic infection. AIDS victims have suffered legal and social discrimination in the popular mind and by official agencies. The implication of bodily and spiritual corruption has persisted as a powerful contemporary trope.

A new social contract of health has been promoted in public health campaigns from antismoking to AIDS prevention. It is a contract based upon a model of prevention that utilized medical and social scientific analysis to maximize health chances by encouraging individuals to change their lifestyles. However, the state and its public health agencies have not had a monopoly on the promotion of health through lifestyle management. Health promotion through lifestyle education has also been successfully commercialized.

Since the eighteenth century "self-health" has been successfully commercialized through the publication of advice manuals and the promotion of dietary aids and exercise regimens by various entrepreneurs. In the nineteenth and early twentieth centuries health reformers promoted physical culture cults such as calisthenics, eurythmics, vegetarianism, and mastication techniques. Such traditions continued in the advertising campaigns for mass-produced foods such as cereals as health aids and in a commercialized exercise culture. In the early twentieth century the value of exercise for healthy living was commercialized by American entrepreneurs such as Eugene Sandow, Bernarr Macfadden, and Charles Atlas, who established their own brands of competitive bodybuilding and physical culture systems. In the United States and in Europe, the interwar years witnessed the symbolic association of the healthy body with racial health and national supremacy.

Following World War II bodybuilding expanded as a commercialized competitive sport and, along with the increased popularity of spectator sports as a leisure pastime, spawned a new fitness industry. The fitness and beauty industries in the late twentieth century became hugely successful international markets involving the sale of sportswear, health foods and dietary aids, commercial health and gymnasium clubs, health and beauty holiday resorts, fitness training, and plastic surgery. Slimming alone has become a large market

industry. The message of the commercialized health industry mirrors that promoted by the state: health is an individual responsibility that has to be worked for through individual effort and paid for from individual pockets. By the early 1990s the healthy body became a symbol of social and economic success and the diseased became associated with social failure and dysfunction. As liberal democratic societies within and beyond Europe retreated from the public funding of health and social welfare, both the state and the marketplace sought to blame ill health on individual irresponsibility and ignorance.

Although the contract of health between the social democratic state and its citizens is thus being reconfigured, at the beginning of the twenty-first century there are, nevertheless, signs that the structural causes of ill health are not being entirely overlooked. As the gap between the affluent and the impoverished widens in postindustrial societies throughout Europe, the relationship between poverty and ill health has again become a focus of state concern. Mortality differentials and rising levels of the traditional diseases of poverty, such as tuberculosis, have re-created an awareness of the impact of inequality on levels of health. Poor people die earlier because their health is compromised by low incomes, unemployment, poor housing, and social exclusion. Population health is compromised in areas with poor social facilities and where people are intimidated by high levels of crime and disorder. The poor and industrial workers are also often exposed to greater risks from environmental pollution and occupational hazards.

The impact of inequality upon health is beginning to be taken into account by social democratic policymakers in Europe. In Britain, for example, New Labour health ministers acknowledge that in tackling the root causes of avoidable illness, "in recent times the emphasis has been on trying to get people to live healthy lives" (Dobson and Jowell, *Our Healthier Nation,* p. 2). The New Labour government suggests, however, that they want to try an approach with "far more attention and Government action concentrated on the things which damage people's health which are beyond the control of the individual" (*Our Healthier Nation,* p. 2). The consequences of the absence or shrinkage of welfare states in industrial societies throughout the world also impacts upon European thought regarding the restructuring of networks of social security that help to ensure population health. Population health within and beyond Europe, however, continues to be an ongoing negotiation between civil society and the state. The outcome of that negotiation depends, as it has always done, upon the political will of both.

See also **Health and Disease** *(volume 2);* **Urbanization** *(volume 2);* **The Welfare State** *(volume 2);* **Doctors and Medicine** *(volume 4); and other articles in this section.*

BIBLIOGRAPHY

Carmichael, Anne G. *Plague and the Poor in Renaisance Florence.* Cambridge, U.K., 1986.

Cipolla, Carlo M. *Fighting the Plague in Seventeenth-Century Italy.* Madison, Wis., 1981.

Coleman, William. *Death Is a Social Disease.* Madison, Wis., 1982.

Crosby, Alfred, W. *Ecological Imperialism: The Biological Expansion of Europe. 900– 1900.* London, 1986.

Dobson, Frank, and Tessa Jowell. *Our Healthier Nation: A Contract for Health.* London, 1998.

Esping-Andersen, Gosta. *The Three Worlds of Welfare Capitalism.* Princeton, N.J., 1990.

Esping-Andersen, Gosta, ed. *Welfare States in Transition: National Adaptations in Global Economies.* London, 1996.

Evans, Richard J. *Death In Hamburg. Society and Politics in the Cholera Years, 1830– 1910.* Oxford, 1987.

Fee, Elizabeth, and Daniel M. Fox, eds. *AIDS: The Making of a Chronic Disease.* Berkeley, Calif., 1992.

Flora, Peter, ed. *Growth to Limits: The Western European Welfare States Since World War II.* Berlin, 1986.

Fox, Christopher, Roy Porter, and Alan Wokler, eds. *Inventing Human Science: Eighteenth-Century Domains.* Berkeley, Calif., 1995.

Gilman, Sander I. *Sexuality: An Illustrated History.* New York, 1989.

Hacking, Ian. *The Taming of Chance.* Cambridge, U.K., 1990.

Hardy, Anne. *The Epidemic Streets: Infectious Disease and the Rise of Preventive Medicine, 1856–1900.* Oxford, 1993.

Hardy, Anne. "Urban Famine or Urban Crisis? Typhus in the Victorian City." *Medical History* 32 (1988): 401–425.

Johannisson, Karin. "The People's Health: Public Health Policies in Sweden." In *The History of Public Health and the Modern State.* Edited by Dorothy Porter. Amsterdam and Atlanta, 1994. Pages 165–182.

Porter, Dorothy. *Health, Civilization, and the State: A History of Public Health from Ancient to Modern Times.* London, 1999.

Quetel, Claude. *History of Syphilis.* Translated by Judith Braddock and Brian Pike. London, 1990.

Slack, Paul. *The Impact of Plague in Tudor and Stuart England.* London, 1985.

Twigg, Graham. *The Black Death: A Biological Reappraisal.* London, 1984.

Vigarello, Georges. *Concepts of Cleanliness: Changing Attitudes in France since the Middle Ages.* Translated by Jean Birrell. Cambridge, 1988.

Weindling, Paul. "Eugenics and the Welfare State during the Weimar Republic." In *The State and Social Change in Germany, 1880–1980.* Edited by W. R. Lee and Eve Rosenhaft. Munich, 1990. Pages 131–160.

ISBN 0-684-80579-0